CW01064267

The Christian's Only Comfort in Life and Death

The Christian's Only Comfort in Life and Death

An Exposition of the Heidelberg Catechism

Volume 2: Lord's Days 27–52

by
Theodorus VanderGroe

Translated by Bartel Elshout
Edited by Joel R. Beeke

REFORMATION HERITAGE BOOKS and
DUTCH REFORMED TRANSLATION SOCIETY
Grand Rapids, Michigan

Reformation Heritage Books
2965 Leonard St. NE
Grand Rapids, MI 49525
616-977-0889 / Fax 616-285-3246
orders@heritagebooks.org
www.heritagebooks.org

Printed in the United States of America
16 17 18 19 20 21/10 9 8 7 6 5 4 3 2 1

ISBN 978-1-60178-498-8

For additional Reformed literature, request a free book list from Reformation Heritage Books at the above regular or e-mail address.

Contents

The Doctrine of Holy Baptism Defended

The like figure whereunto even baptism doth also now save us (not the putting away of the filth of the flesh, but the answer of a good conscience toward God,) by the resurrection of Jesus Christ.

—1 PETER 3:21

Question 72: Is then the external baptism with water the washing away of sin itself?

Answer: Not at all; for the blood of Jesus Christ only, and the Holy Ghost cleanse us from all sin.

Question 73: Why then doth the Holy Ghost call baptism "the washing of regeneration," and the "washing away of sins"?

Answer: God speaks thus not without great cause, to wit, not only thereby to teach us that as the filth of the body is purged away by water, so our sins are removed by the blood and Spirit of Jesus Christ; but especially that by this divine pledge and sign He may assure us that we are spiritually cleansed from our sins as really as we are externally washed with water.

Question 74: Are infants also to be baptized?

Answer: Yes, for since they, as well as the adult, are included in the covenant and church of God; and since redemption from sin by the blood of Christ, and the Holy Ghost, the author of faith, is promised to them no less than to the adult; they must therefore by baptism, as a sign of the covenant, be also admitted into the Christian church; and be distinguished from the children of unbelievers as was done in the old covenant or testament by circumcision, instead of which baptism is instituted in the new covenant.

Nehemiah 4:17 records the peculiar event that the Jews engaged in while rebuilding the broken-down walls of Jerusalem upon their return from Babel to their own land. They encountered great opposition from their hostile neighbors, and therefore the laborers, in order to turn away the enemies who assaulted them, "every one with one of his hands wrought in the work, and with the other hand held a weapon."

We may also assert this regarding the godly authors of the Heidelberg Catechism. Having emerged from the spiritual Babel of anti-Christian popery, and engaging by way of this Catechism in rebuilding the broken-down walls of "the truth which is after godliness" (Titus 1:1), they had, on one hand, to build up the fortress of true doctrine and, on the other, to defend and safeguard it against its enemies.

We observe this in their treatment of the doctrine of holy baptism, for no sooner did they articulate and affirm this doctrine in the previous Lord's Day than, so to speak, they were compelled in this Lord's Day to uphold and protect it with the other hand against hostile assaults by all who err in this regard and contradict it. We will now address this matter in some detail. May the Lord by His grace and Spirit enable us so to do, and may He bless His Word to our souls. Amen.

The instructor deals in the following order:

1. with the efficacy of the sacrament of holy baptism, thereby countering the teaching of Roman Catholicism and, to some extent, also that of our Lutheran brethren (Questions 72 and 73); and

2. with the necessity of baptizing young children, thereby countering the teaching of the Mennonites or Anabaptists (Question 74).

Regarding the efficacy of holy baptism, the instructor asks his pupil, "Is then the external baptism with water the washing away of sin itself?" (Question 72). The brief formulation of this question articulates the difference between us and Roman Catholicism and Lutheranism with regard to holy baptism, and we will therefore first address this in some detail.

In conformity to the Holy Scriptures, we teach that holy baptism is but an external sacrament, a sign and seal of the covenant of grace. The Lord Jesus prescribed and instituted this sacrament in His church so that, by the power of His Holy Spirit, there would be signified and sealed to the hearts of His believing people that by faith they truly have fellowship with Him, as well as with His blood and Spirit—and that they are truly cleansed from their sins and the pollution of their souls unto their salvation and eternal redemption. We addressed all of this extensively in the previous Lord's Day.

There we observed that external water baptism is rendered efficacious only by the grace of the Holy Spirit, who thereby powerfully assures and reassures all true believers of their being partakers of the Lord Jesus, and thus of their justification and sanctification in Him, doing so to comfort them, strengthen their faith, and fortify their godly walk.

The Papists counter this doctrine in an utterly brazen, unspiritual, and carnal manner, teaching that external water baptism as it is administered to the children of believers has the inherent efficacy actually to wash away completely man's innate original sin, thereby infusing in all who are baptized a holiness and righteousness that is internally efficacious. This enables them to live a holy life from that point forward and to obey God's law perfectly. This would even equip them to serve God more fully and comprehensively than God prescribes or requires in His law. Therefore, they deem the efficacy of external water baptism to be such that it not only washes away all of a man's sins, but also that it completely transforms, regenerates, sanctifies, and renews a man according to God's image so that his holiness and perfection are that of Adam before the fall.

What a dreadful and wicked doctrine this is, for thereby the only foundation of salvation is utterly overturned! As is usually the case, several other abominable errors issue forth from this major error. These are:

1. that all unbaptized children cannot be saved to all eternity, for they have not been cleansed from their sins by way of baptism, and therefore, at death, they are consigned to a special place in close proximity to hell, which they call the *portal of unbaptized children*; and

2. that persons other than ministers, and even women, may administer the sacrament of baptism in the event of an emergency to prevent the damnation of such children.

Our Lutheran brethren also entertain a unique notion, for their error regarding the doctrine of the Lord's Supper parallels their error regarding the doctrine of holy baptism by their carnal perception concerning the nature and efficacy of the holy sacraments. They do not concur with the Papists that baptism has the universal and inherent efficacy to renew and transform all men and to wash away their sins. However, they posit that external water baptism is the vehicle that encompasses the rudiments of the grace of faith, regeneration, and the forgiveness of sins. They posit that this grace, as to its seed and foundational principle, is in actuality applied and communicated to all who are chosen unto eternal life, and therefore all the elect who are baptized externally thereby receive the seed of God's grace in their hearts. This, however, remains (as they say) concealed in them until the germination of this seed, which then culminates in the breaking forth and increasing of the acts of faith and repentance.

We have thus set before you the true nature of the differences between us and the Papists and Lutherans regarding the sacrament of holy baptism. Though the Papists and Lutherans differ greatly from one another, they nevertheless have in common that they ascribe more to external water baptism than merely the signifying and sealing efficacy of the Holy Spirit's grace to the hearts of true believers in regard to their fellowship with the Lord Jesus, His blood, and His Spirit unto their justification, sanctification, and deliverance from their sins.

From the Holy Scriptures, we will now affirm our sentiments in greater detail, while at the same time briefly refuting these other notions, following as much as possible in the footsteps of the instructor, who customarily addresses matters briefly, transparently, and succinctly. First, he defends our doctrine in Question 72, and then he defends it in Question 73 against opposing parties.

Regarding the first, he affirms this doctrine negatively and then positively, which is a very good and suitable order for defending the truth.

He first refutes the teaching of the Papists that external water baptism is the equivalent of the washing away of sins, and he does likewise with the teaching of the Lutherans, who posit that baptism is the means whereby grace in its seminal form is in actuality infused into the elect. The instructor's refutation is not only founded upon and rooted in God's Word, but is also consistent with the nature of the matter itself. Let me simply affirm this by stating that if it is true that external water baptism washes away sin and thus sanctifies and renews a man, or if it is a means whereby the seed of that grace is infused into the elect, it must necessarily follow that a person can have neither faith, regeneration, nor the forgiveness of sins prior to being baptized. Now neither Papists nor Lutherans can or will contradict this logical conclusion.

However, we will prove from God's Word that when adults are to be baptized, they must first believe in the Lord Jesus, repent of their sins, and thereby have received the forgiveness of their sins. Baptism must then subsequently signify and seal for their comfort and the strengthening of their faith this benefit of God's grace. We affirm this doctrine by the following passages:

In Romans 4:11, Paul testifies regarding Abraham that "he received the sign of circumcision, a seal of the righteousness of the faith which he had yet being uncircumcised." Abraham already believed in God and, by that faith, he was already converted and his sins had already been forgiven prior to his being circumcised. His circumcision was to him a sign and seal of having been justified before God by faith. Subsequently, we will demonstrate that whatever is true with respect to circumcision is true also concerning baptism.

In Acts 2:38, Peter admonished the Jews upon the day of Pentecost, saying, "Repent, and be baptized every one of you in the name of Jesus Christ for the remission of sins." Peter admonished the Jews that they must repent prior to being baptized so that their baptism would be to them a sign and seal of the forgiveness of their sins.

In Acts 8:37, Philip replied to the eunuch when he desired to be baptized, "If thou believest with all thine heart, thou mayest." It is very clear that the eunuch had first truly to believe in the Lord Jesus with his heart, and thus be converted and have received the forgiveness of sins, before he would be permitted to receive the sacrament of baptism.

In Matthew 28:19, we have Christ's institution and command to baptize, commissioning His apostles and disciples first to teach the nations and then to baptize "them in the name of the Father, and of the Son, and of the Holy Ghost." Why is it necessary that such instruction first should be given other than to be the means whereby people first become believing followers and disciples of the Lord Jesus—the latter being implied in the original Greek word translated as "to teach"?

The foregoing proves clearly that when adults are to be baptized, faith, the forgiveness of sins, and the grace of regeneration and renewal must be present prior to their baptism. By baptism these glorious benefits must then inwardly be signified and sealed to them to their comfort and the strengthening of their faith.

Regarding little children who cannot manifest externally that they possess such grace, being yet incapable of affirming their faith in word and deed, we must view them in their believing parents as being true believers and as true partakers of God's covenant until, by their conduct, they make manifest the contrary to us.

It thus follows that external water baptism in no wise possesses any efficacy to wash away sin or to transform and convert man internally. It is also not the means whereby the seed or principle of this grace is infused in the elect, for whatever ought to be found in a man prior to baptism can by no means be communicated to him by baptism. Peter therefore teaches emphatically in our text that external water baptism can neither save nor redeem the elect. This can be achieved only by an entirely different type of baptism—an internal and spiritual baptism of the heart by the blood and Spirit of Christ. Read Peter's words carefully, for he says that "the like figure whereunto even baptism doth also now save us." By means of what baptism? Peter continues, "Not the putting away of the filth of the flesh"; that is, not by way of external water baptism, which cleanses the body of its filth, but rather, "the answer of a good conscience toward God" (1 Peter 3:21). The apostle, thus speaking of the internal baptism of the soul by the blood and Spirit of Christ, emphatically teaches, and our instructor correctly affirms, that external water baptism contributes nothing to our redemption or to the washing away of our sins. Furthermore, the instructor goes a step further in showing the absurdity of this sentiment, saying that "the blood of Jesus Christ only, and the Holy Ghost cleanse us from all sin." There is no need to articulate and affirm this truth any further, for we did so extensively in the previous Lord's Day, having expounded for you the internal and spiritual mysteries of holy baptism. Suffice it to say in accordance with the Holy Scriptures only that there is no way whereby sin can be washed away but by means of the precious blood and Spirit of the Lord Jesus. Only the blood and Spirit of Christ possess the efficacy and power to justify and purify us from our sins, which by no means can be achieved by external water baptism.

The instructor continues to defend this doctrine in Question 73 in response to objections raised by its opponents, asking, "Why then doth the Holy Ghost call baptism 'the washing of regeneration,' and the 'washing away of sins'?" As they desire to prove the validity of their views, Papists and Lutherans do so primarily by referring to three passages of the Holy Scriptures in which external water baptism is referred to as "the washing of regeneration" and the forgiveness or washing away of sins. In Titus 3:5, Paul declares that "according to his mercy he saved us, by the washing of regeneration, and renewing of the Holy Ghost." In Acts 2:38, Peter exhorts the Jews, saying, "Repent, and be baptized every one of you in the name of Jesus Christ for the remission of sins." And in Acts 22:16,

Paul testifies that Ananias said to him, "Arise, and be baptized, and wash away thy sins."

By way of these three passages, the Papists and Lutherans want to endorse their notion regarding the efficacy of external water baptism. However, their reasoning is without substance, for they expound these three passages in an entirely erroneous manner.

Regarding Titus 3:5, Paul is not at all referring to external water baptism when he speaks of "the washing of regeneration, and renewing of the Holy Ghost" as being the means whereby God saves believers. Rather, he is referring to Christ, who, together with His grace, Spirit, merits, and benefits, becomes to all believers "the washing of regeneration, and renewing of the Holy Ghost." Zechariah therefore sets Him before us as "a fountain opened to the house of David and to the inhabitants of Jerusalem for sin and for uncleanness" (Zech. 13:1). Paul affirms this by placing "the washing of regeneration, and renewing of the Holy Ghost" in contrast to the works of man's own righteousness. The Holy Scriptures always place Christ, as well as His grace and merits, in contradistinction to the works and righteousness of man.

Regarding Acts 2:38, Peter is by no means instructing the Jews that the pardon of their sins will in any way accrue to them by the efficacy and instrumentality of external water baptism. The very opposite proves to be what Peter has in mind, for he exhorts them uprightly to repent, prior to being baptized, so that they may secure from God the gracious pardon of their sins only for Christ's sake. To that end, they had to submit themselves to baptism *for* the forgiveness of their sins; that is, as a holy sign and seal thereof.

This is also true regarding Acts 22:16, where Ananias says to Paul, "Arise, and be baptized, and wash away thy sins." Ananias did not teach that external water baptism would wash away Paul's sins, for prior to being baptized, Paul already had been converted to the Lord Jesus and his eyes already had been opened. His sins had therefore already been washed away prior to his baptism. This is very evident upon comparing Paul's own account in Acts 22 with that which is recorded in Acts 9. However, upon his conversion, Paul also had to be baptized in accordance with Christ's command as a sign and seal of having received from God the gracious washing away of his sins prior to his baptism. This is the essence of what Ananias wished to communicate.

The instructor expounds these passages in a similar fashion, saying, "God speaks thus not without great cause, to-wit, not only thereby to teach us, that as the filth of the body is purged away by water, so our sins are removed by the blood and Spirit of Jesus Christ." He who understands the true essence and nature of the holy sacraments knows that there is a most intimate and essential relationship between the external signs and seals and the internal, spiritual essence of that which is being signified and sealed; he who receives the one by true faith always receives the other as well.

God therefore commonly unites the external and internal aspects in His Word as though they were one and the same, doing so to comfort His believing people and to strengthen them increasingly by means of the sacraments. This also occurs in baptism, for the forgiveness or washing away of sins is most intimately connected to the external administration of baptism—as if they were one and the same matter. Thereby the hearts of true believers are all the more efficaciously persuaded that God's gracious pardon of their sins is as steadfast, certain, and incontrovertible as is their reception of the external administration of the sacrament of baptism. This is the point the instructor is trying to make.

However, when these holy and spiritual mysteries are incorrectly assessed and understood, these matters are confused by attributing to the external sign and seal that which pertains only to the internal matter that is being signified and sealed. If such erroneous sentiments have been imbibed from one's youth and have been deeply embedded in one's mind, they are very difficult to be dissuaded. Therefore, how blessed are they who have been taught by the Lord Himself the truth as it is in Jesus! But there is yet another great error regarding holy baptism that must also be refuted.

Having thus far purified the doctrine of baptism from the errors of Roman Catholicism and Lutheranism, we must likewise briefly seek to expose the heretical doctrine of the Mennonites or Anabaptists. This error differs completely from the ones we have already addressed. The instructor formulates this briefly by asking in Question 74, "Are infants also to be baptized?" The essence of the controversy is this: the Mennonites teach that one neither may nor must baptize anyone other than adults who have come to the years of discretion and are thus capable of making a credible profession of their faith. Therefore, they teach that young or small children should by no means be baptized, for they are neither capable of confessing their faith nor can know whether they are true believers.

We counter by positing, on the basis of God's Word, that all children of believing parents may and must be baptized, and that their baptism may therefore by no means be postponed until they can make a profession of their faith. Please note that we are not teaching that one may and must baptize all children indiscriminately, such as the children of Jews, heathens, and Muslims. Rather, only the children of *believing parents* are to be baptized; that is, when one or both parents are believing partakers of the Lord's covenant, whether they do so in sincerity and in truth or whether this be feigned and merely external.

Since the internal and infallible judgment regarding one's spiritual state can be rendered only by an omniscient God, we can proceed here only by observing one's public confession and visible walk. As to the external ministry of the gospel and the administration of the Christian ordinances, all who confess publicly the Christian faith, confessing their sins and their condemnable and impotent state, testifying that they believe in the name of Christ alone, and whose walk within the Christian church is blameless, are to be viewed by virtue of their public confession as true Christians and believing partakers of the Lord's covenant. In so doing, we leave the judgment regarding their internal state entirely to the Lord and refrain from intruding into that which is the prerogative of God, who has reserved the judicial judgment of both good and evil men to Himself. It is contrary to His will in this sense that one would make himself equal with God. Nevertheless, we must not be remiss in exhorting such external professors most earnestly to be upright and in confronting them with the dreadful wrath of God toward all pretenders and hypocrites.

The argument in support of the foregoing is that we are neither omniscient nor capable of rendering an infallible judgment. It is therefore the Lord's will that we would focus only upon that which can be observed externally to be in conformity with His Word, and leave that which is hidden from us to His judgment.

However, this by no means removes the explicit responsibility of examining, counseling, and guiding the souls of all true Christians. Ministers in particular must be most diligent to instruct all men concerning their inner state by what they observe and hear externally, and then to instruct, admonish, and direct them judiciously in conformity to God's Word. This, however, is an entirely different matter, and in this regard we must distinguish specifically between addressing a man's spiritual state and the ecclesiastical administration of the ordinances that have been instituted by Christ. Nevertheless, it needs to be asserted that ministers of the gospel are obligated to oversee this faithfully and carefully so that these ordinances are not desecrated. However, in so doing, we are not to act merely on our subjective assessment of one's spiritual state by the light that the Lord has granted. Rather, we are to judge men by their external profession, religious practices, and walk, for we otherwise will open the door to endless difficulties and harmful confusion. This, in turn, would lead to the disruption and destabilization of the external state and economy of the church.

Please note therefore that children of believing parents are those children whose parents, or one of their parents, have made a public profession of their faith and are living blameless lives in the Christian church, leaving their inner state to be judged by the Lord. When such children are presented for baptism, we are to view them in their believing parents, and thus as believers and true partakers of God's covenant. The promise of future covenant blessings is consequently theirs according to the declaration of God's Word as recorded in Acts 2:39. This does not mean, however, that all children of believing parents (or they who are deemed to be such) are truly believing children who are elect unto salvation and internally and spiritually belong to God's covenant. This is by no means the case, for the Holy Scriptures and experience teach that this is true for only a small number of children. The truth of the matter is that we cannot know with certainty regarding a single child what his internal state is or shall be; whether the Lord has already begun a work of grace in him or shall do so in the future; or whether he shall never be the recipient of grace. This is known to God the Lord alone, and we are therefore not to focus on the spiritual state of the children as such; that is, what they presently either are or are not, or shall yet be in terms of the gracious work of God's Spirit in them. We must therefore leave this alone as a matter hidden to us and known only to the Lord—unless it pleases the Lord to reveal something of it to godly parents.

Instead, we are to focus exclusively upon those gracious promises of God that He has made universally not only to us but also to our children, namely, that He, moved by infinite and sovereign grace, is pleased also to enter into covenant with them from their youth and even from the moment of their birth, when as yet they know neither good nor evil. With spiritual eyes, we are to consider in what manner the Lord God, according to His great mercy, has been pleased to enter into covenant with us sinners, and how He has also been pleased to include therein our small children. Considering this great mercy of the Lord our God, as well as the adorable way of His sovereign grace, we must not reject in unbelief the Lord's precious promises that He is as willing to encompass our young children in His covenant as He is willing to do for us. Rather, with heartfelt humility and gratitude, we must embrace these sure promises of God also in regard to our small children and apply them believingly to them and to their spiritual state. Consequently, by God's gracious way and promises, we must by faith deem and acknowledge our children to be true partakers of the Lord's covenant, as adopted children, and even as being holy in Christ Jesus. In so doing, we are to lean solely and exclusively upon the fact that the Lord has promised this in His covenant, and it shall therefore most certainly be true.

Upon this foundation we must baptize all children of believing parents as partakers of God's covenant, and we are to deem and acknowledge them as such until, in growing up, they manifest the contrary in their conduct. We may not deal with this any differently.

This is the essence of the controversy we have with the Mennonites, who teach that young children of believing parents (that is, of those who are esteemed as such) neither may nor must be baptized. The instructor, however, powerfully proves the contrary to be true, specifically giving us six proofs that we shall briefly expound for you.

The instructor proves that young children of believing parents must necessarily be baptized because:

1. "They, as well as the adult, are included in the covenant of God." It is a transparent truth that God, in His covenant of grace, has embraced both young children and adults to be partakers of His covenant in order to save and redeem them in Christ. If it were not for this truth, there would be not a single child dying in infancy that could be saved, for outside of God's covenant, there is no salvation for anyone. This is clearly taught in the Holy Scriptures, for God established His covenant of grace with Abraham and his seed after him (Gen. 17:7–10). All the children that came forth from Abraham's loins, however young they may have been, were to be reckoned as belonging to this seed. This was confirmed by the fact that, by virtue of God's covenant, they had to be circumcised on the eighth day.

However, God has established the identical covenant as truly with His believing people in the New Testament as He established it in the Old, and therefore we need to perceive and acknowledge that the covenant God made with Abraham is the same covenant that He made with him as being the father of all believers. The Lord elevated His servant Abraham to this lofty and glorious state, for all true believers, from the beginning until the end of time and unto the ends of the earth, are Abraham's seed and children (Gal. 3:9, 29). According to God's way and precept, they must deem Abraham to be their spiritual father, who by faith and in obedience to God has gone before them—especially when he stood ready to sacrifice his son Isaac.

In the New Testament, however, God makes the same covenant with Abraham's children—a covenant that is, in essence, identical to the one He made with our father Abraham. The nature of the covenant that God established with him was such that it also pleased Him to include his small children and his entire seed in it. Consequently, the Lord God still deals with all believing children of Abraham in this manner. Paul therefore testifies that the children of believers are holy (1 Cor. 7:14), for from the moment of their birth, they already are included in God's covenant. This inclusion is not by virtue of their personal acquiescence, for as infants, they are not yet capable thereof, unless at their birth God immediately and in a special manner regenerates and sanctifies them. However, the latter He does only rarely.

Young children are in God's covenant solely by the acquiescence of their parents on their behalf, irrespective of whether the parents did this in truth or hypocritically. This, however, does not affect the state and situation regarding children. Later, when the children reach maturity and God powerfully converts them, they personally acquiesce in God's covenant, thereby affirming the acquiescence of their parents on their behalf before God in their youth. Such is the manner in which children of believers are immediately in God's covenant upon birth, and consequently, they are holy.

Therefore, whereas young children are as truly in God's covenant as are adults, and since elect children who die in their infancy are saved only by that covenant, it is self-evident that holy baptism, as a sign and seal of God's covenant, is to be administered to them as much as to adults.

2. "They, as well as the adult, are included in the church of God." God also counts the little children as belonging to His congregation and His kingdom. Christ therefore laid His hands upon them, blessed them, and said, "Suffer little children, and forbid them not, to come unto me: for of such is the kingdom of heaven" (Matt. 19:14). When God expressed His will that His congregation here on earth come together and be sanctified, He not only commanded the adults to be gathered together, but also "the children, and those that suck the breasts" (Joel 2:16). Therefore, take note that the Lord our God is completely consistent within Himself, for He is true and upright in all His ways, and one will never find the least contradiction in them. Since God also makes this covenant with our little children, promising to do so in His Word, if He were nevertheless neither to incorporate them into His congregation nor truly deem them to be members of the body of His Son, He would then be guilty of contradicting Himself. However, the Lord also deems our children as belonging to

His congregation and includes them as true members in His kingdom. When He commands His people, saying, "Sanctify the congregation," He commands them to sanctify their children as well as themselves, commanding them to use all available means for their renewal and sanctification so that also their children will be a holy people unto the Lord.

Since our young children belong to God's congregation and to His kingdom, and since they are as much her true members and subjects as are the adults, the sign and seal of incorporation into the congregation pertains as much to them as to the adults. Baptism is this sign and seal whereby we are externally incorporated into the congregation.

3. "Redemption from sin by the blood of Christ, and the Holy Ghost, the author of faith, is promised to them no less than to the adult." Since, as we have observed, the young children of believers are in God's covenant by virtue of the acquiescence of their parents, they have therefore also a claim upon all the blessings, promises, and benefits of that covenant—being Christ, as well as His merits, grace, and Spirit—unto their justification, sanctification, redemption, and salvation. As we already have indicated, "for of such is the kingdom of heaven" (Matt. 19:14), and the promise of the covenant is unto them (Acts 2:39); that is, all the promises of the holy gospel that God makes to adults and believers in His covenant, promising them faith, justification, sanctification, and eternal life through Christ.

In short, all the grace and salvation God promises to adult believers, He promises equally to their children, and He is a faithful God to them as much as He is to us. This does not mean that these promises and benefits of God's covenant already have their effect and are already theirs when they are baptized. Rather, God has promised these benefits to elect children in His covenant, promising that they shall truly and continually possess them when they truly believe and repent. Holy baptism is therefore also administered to them to signify and seal their future possession of the promises and benefits of God's covenant, for the holy sacraments are administered to signify and seal to believers both future and present benefits and promises of God's covenant. A perfect state of salvation and glory in Christ is promised by the Lord to all His believing people, and this is sealed to them by means of the sacraments. Though they do not yet possess these benefits, the sacraments seal to them in the name of the Lord that these benefits shall be theirs in the future.

4. "They must therefore by baptism, as a sign of the covenant, be also admitted into the Christian church; and be distinguished from the children

of unbelievers." This speaks for itself and needs no further proof, for already we have proven that the young children of the congregation are in covenant with God, belong to His congregation, and have a claim upon Christ and the promise of the covenant. They must therefore necessarily be incorporated as such into the Christian church and be visibly and tangibly separated from and distinguished from the children of unbelievers. This can be accomplished only by baptism as the sign and seal of the covenant. It is contrary to God's will that children of believers, even externally, be equal to and be intermixed with children of unbelievers, for by virtue of His covenant, they are *holy* children, whereas the others are *unholy*. However, what shall distinguish our children, when they are small and in their infancy, from the children of unbelievers other than holy baptism, whereby the Lord externally seals the children of believers with the seal of His covenant? It is as if He proclaims with a loud voice to the entire world: "I declare and publicly make known that these children are *holy*, and that I have entered into covenant with them, and that it is My desire to deliver them from their sins by justifying and sanctifying them through the blood and Spirit of My Son. I therefore command all who will have oversight over them and interact with them to consider them as being My children and to teach them 'the ordinances of [My] justice' (Isa. 58:2), so that they would fear Me as their God."

5. Thus it "was done under the old covenant or testament by circumcision, instead of which baptism is instituted in the new covenant." Under the Old Testament, God commanded that the young children of believers be circumcised upon the eighth day after their birth, and this was a sign and seal of their being partakers of God's covenant of grace and of its spiritual benefits and promises. Paul teaches that baptism in the New Testament was instituted and ordained in the place of circumcision (Col. 2:11–12). It is therefore self-evident that baptism must be administered to the small children of believers as a sign and seal of God's covenant as much as was previously done with circumcision.

6. It is very probable that during the time of the apostles, they also baptized small children. We also wish to add this proof, although this has not been expressly recorded. But indeed, we do read that entire households were baptized simultaneously, such as the households of the jailor, Lydia, and Stephanus.

By way of the foregoing, we conclude that it is a certain and incontrovertible truth that not only may one freely administer holy baptism to the small children of believers, but we must also, at their baptism, deem and consider them to be true partakers of God's covenant.[1]

Before we conclude, however, we wish to add the following for the instruction of our readers:

First, regarding the efficacy and effect of external water baptism toward the souls of baptized children, no one ought by any means to think that this external baptism yields any change or improvement in their hearts or communicates to them any measure of grace that they did not already have. Beloved, baptism leaves children as they are, for it has no more than a signifying and sealing efficacy. Baptism signifies and seals to elect children the promises and precious benefits of God's covenant, such as regeneration, faith, repentance, and the washing away of sin. These infants, upon being baptized, either in actuality or in principle, already possess these benefits of the covenant in a concealed manner, or they shall receive them in the future by virtue of God's eternal election. For it can be, though it happens very rarely, that a child of believing parents, at the moment he or she is baptized, truly possesses grace, as well as the rudiments of regeneration, faith, and functional sanctification—albeit that it cannot yet be affirmed by tangible evidence.

The Holy Scriptures afford us examples of such children, who from birth were graciously wrought upon by the Lord and thus were also sanctified. If

---

1. Jonathan Neil Gerstner is helpful in pointing out that three views were held by Reformation and Dutch Further Reformation writers with regard to how covenant children should be viewed with regard to their holiness as expressed by Paul in 1 Corinthians 7:14. Some adhered to an "internal holiness" view, i.e., that the holiness Paul refers to means that children are to be regarded as true, inward partakers of God's covenant, so that covenant parents are encouraged to believe that the seed of regeneration is planted within them from infancy and that they are to be viewed as saved. Others held to an "external holiness" view, i.e., that the holiness Paul refers to means that covenant children are to be regarded as externally holy. They are set apart from the world covenantally for God and His service, but need to be told that they must repent and believe the gospel and its promises personally for themselves as they grow into the years of discretion. This view teaches that parents ought not to view their children as already regenerate, but ought to view their children "in a special sphere in which they were most likely to be regenerated through the means of grace" as they grow in years. A third view can be called "seminal holiness" in which covenant children, as Gerstner writes, "are not yet internally holy in the full sense, nor are they totally devoid of internal holiness. God has planted in the elect (generally assumed to be the majority without clear Scriptural warrant) the seed of regeneration, usually in the womb. If the child died, one had every reason to believe that God would honor that seed and he would be saved. As he grew up, the seed would only germinate into regeneration through the preaching of the Word." Gerstner, *The Thousand Generation Covenant: Dutch Reformed Covenant Theology and Group Identity in Colonial South Africa*, 1652–1814 (Leiden: E. J. Brill, 1991), 5–10.

such is the case, then for such children, their baptism is a sign and seal of these benefits of God's covenant; that is, insofar as they either already possess them in actuality, in principle, and in conformity to the measure of their inner receptivity, or shall yet receive them in the future.

However, with the majority of elect children, this is very different, which is evident as they grow up. The majority of them are utterly void of all grace at the moment of their baptism, and by virtue of sin, they are subject to God's wrath, curse, and condemnation. At that moment, they possess nothing other than the fact that from God's side, they are known by Him as His children, whom He has eternally chosen unto salvation and whom He has given to His Son to be redeemed by Him. At the appointed time, He will therefore also most assuredly call, sanctify, and regenerate them, and by faith unite them to Christ. When the sacrament of baptism is administered to these children, it serves only to signify and seal to them these future blessings and benefits of salvation that they shall most certainly receive from God at His appointed time.

Behold, this is how we are to understand the baptism of infants, and not otherwise.

Second, let us now consider those infants of believers who are baptized and yet are not chosen by God unto eternal life. Instead, they are reprobates and will therefore always continue to live in sin and will despise and reject God's covenant to the very end, being unwilling to believe in the Lord Jesus and to repent of their sins. The sacrament of baptism was indeed administered to them externally. However, since they are not comprehended in God's covenant, no signifying and sealing efficacy issued forth from their baptism, and for them it has not been a sacrament; that is, it has not been a sign and seal of the covenant. It is therefore a matter of utmost importance for everyone, upon having arrived at the years of discretion, to engage in serious self-examination whether one is truly in God's covenant and whether one's baptism is to him truly a sign and seal of the covenant. A man's salvation and eternal redemption hinge on this, and everyone can know this by God's grace from his unfeigned faith and his genuine conversion.

Third, in conclusion, we must address the question asked of the parents at the administration of the sacrament of baptism, namely, whether they acknowledge that their children "are sanctified in Christ, and therefore, as members of his Church ought to be baptized." We need to note here that this question is not a general question pertaining to all children who are baptized externally. It also does not pertain to the specific children who are being presented for baptism, but rather, it is a question that pertains to *our* children in general; that is, the children of us as believers, who are in God's covenant, who in the future will be called efficaciously by Him, and to whom the promises of God therefore belong. It is regarding these children that we are being asked whether we believe and acknowledge that they, as true partakers of God's covenant, "are sanctified in Christ," and as such must receive the sacrament of holy baptism. No one is able to deny this without having to contradict God's truth and God's Word.

As to our child or children whom we present at baptism, we can know neither specifically nor with certainty whether they are truly in God's covenant. However, believing and godly parents must, according to God's promises, nevertheless view and esteem their children to be true partakers of God's covenant, and as such they are to consecrate them unto the Lord in baptism, beseeching Him fervently that He would bestow His grace and His Spirit upon their children. They must also raise them as true partakers of God's covenant and avail themselves of all the means subservient to their repentance and faith. The Lord will surely require this from their hands, and if their children die in early youth, either prior to or subsequent to their baptism, they must consider them as saved by virtue of having been born in God's covenant.

These are the matters that we were called upon to set before you as a further exposition and affirmation of the doctrine of holy baptism. We humbly ask the Lord for His divine blessing upon the Word that has been spoken and expounded. Amen.

The Sacrament of the Lord's Supper

And as they were eating, Jesus took bread, and blessed it, and brake it, and gave it to the disciples, and said, Take, eat; this is my body. And he took the cup, and gave thanks, and gave it to them, saying, Drink ye all of it; for this is my blood of the new testament, which is shed for many for the remission of sins.
— MATTHEW 26:26–28

Question 75: How art thou admonished and assured in the Lord's Supper that thou art a partaker of that one sacrifice of Christ, accomplished on the cross, and of all His benefits?

Answer: Thus: that Christ has commanded me and all believers to eat of this broken bread and to drink of this cup in remembrance of Him, adding these promises: first, that His body was offered and broken on the cross for me, and His blood shed for me, as certainly as I see with my eyes the bread of the Lord broken for me and the cup communicated to me; and further, that He feeds and nourishes my soul to everlasting life, with His crucified body and shed blood, as assuredly as I receive from the hands of the minister, and taste with my mouth the bread and cup of the Lord, as certain signs of the body and blood of Christ.

Question 76: What is it then to eat the crucified body, and drink the shed blood of Christ?

Answer: It is not only to embrace with a believing heart all the sufferings and death of Christ, and thereby to obtain the pardon of sin and life eternal; but also, besides that, to become more and more united to His sacred body, by the Holy Ghost, who dwells both in Christ and in us; so that we, though Christ is in heaven and we on earth, are notwithstanding "flesh of His flesh, and bone of His bone"; and that we live, and are governed forever by one spirit, as members of the same body are by one soul.

Question 77: Where has Christ promised that He will as certainly feed and nour-ish believers with His body and blood, as they eat of this broken bread, and drink of this cup?

Answer: In the institution of the supper, which is thus expressed: "The Lord Jesus the same night in which He was betrayed took bread: and when He had given thanks, He brake it, and said: Take, eat, this is My body, which is broken for you; this do in remembrance of Me. After the same manner also He took the cup, when He had supped, saying: this cup is the new testament in My blood; this do ye, as often as ye drink it, in remembrance of Me. For, as often as ye eat this bread, and drink this cup, ye do show the Lord's death till He come."

This promise is repeated by the holy apostle Paul, where he says: "The cup of blessing which we bless, is it not the communion of the blood of Christ? The bread which we break, is it not the communion of the body of Christ? For we, being many, are one bread and one body; for we are all partakers of that one bread."

———————————

It was customary in former days, as is also the practice among us, that the bridegroom, upon entering into the marriage union with his bride, would give her a wedding ring or some other valuable object. This she would receive as a pledge of the sincere love and faithfulness of and union with her bridegroom. A bride would therefore highly value and esteem such a pledge or wedding ring, and would not readily permit anyone to take it from her. She would preserve it as a precious symbol and pledge of the sincere love and faithfulness of her bridegroom, testifying thereby also that she was permanently united to him, and therefore also was obligated from her side to be unwavering in cleaving to and loving him.

This is analogous to the spiritual and precious marriage union between Christ and His believing bride or people. This beloved and blessed savior con-descended to enter into a holy and spiritual marriage bond with His poor and needy people by giving Himself to them as a bridegroom, head, and husband, and taking them to be His bride and wife. He thereby betrothed them, through faith, eternally to Himself. Having been willing to condescend to such depths, the savior, Jesus, has given His believing bride, so to speak, a precious and invaluable wedding ring. He did so that she would thereby receive and esteem it as a pledge of His most tender love for and immutable faithfulness toward her, and that eternally they would most intimately be bound and united to each other. The Lord Jesus did this so that, by faith, His bride and wife would cleave all the more steadfastly to Him.

His holy supper is the Savior's wedding ring, for during the last night of His life, He ordained and instituted this supper for all His believing people here upon earth, to their comfort and the strengthening of their faith. With the instructor, we will now proceed to expound for you the doctrine of the Lord's Supper.

In the two previous Lord's Days, the instructor addressed the sacrament of holy baptism. He now proceeds in similar fashion in three Lord's Days to address the sacrament of the Lord's Supper. In this Lord's Day, he will expound for us, in conformity with the Holy Scriptures, the true character and nature of this sacrament. In the two Lord's Days hereafter, he will further defend and affirm this doctrine by countering the heretical views of those who do not belong to our church.

This is again a very weighty subject, and therefore it is of the greatest importance for us to have a correct and spiritual understanding of this matter. May the Lord therefore lift up the light of His countenance upon us, and may His people see light in His light.

With God's gracious blessing and assistance, we will endeavor to open this up for you as transparently and simply as possible, and as much as possible we will follow in the footsteps of the instructor:

1. We will expound for you the true character and nature of the sacrament of the Lord's Supper.
2. We will address the external decorum with which this sacrament is to be administered in the Christian congregation in conformity with the institution of Christ and His command.

Regarding the true character and nature of this sacrament, we shall say a few words:

1. of its name; and
2. of the sacrament itself.

Regarding its name, this sacrament is denominated as *the Lord's Supper*. Paul refers to it as such, saying, "When ye come together therefore into one place, this is not to eat the Lord's Supper" (1 Cor. 11:20), for it was instituted by the Lord Jesus during the last night or evening of His life. For this, He used the format of an external meal, thereby depicting His grace and His internal and spiritual union with His believing people.

It is expressly referred to as the *holy supper* or *Lord's Supper*, for it was instituted and ordained with a holy objective and exclusively for true saints (i.e., holy ones), and thus for believers only. It must therefore be distinguished from common meals, and it is to be used by Christians in a holy, believing, and spiritual manner as a holy sacrament, or sign and seal of the covenant of grace.

However, in addition to this sacrament being denominated as the holy or the Lord's Supper, this sacrament is also set before us in the Holy Scriptures by various other names, such as the Table of the Lord, the breaking of bread, and the communion of the body and blood of Christ. The rationale for these names is derived either from the external signs or seals or from the internal mystery of this holy sacrament.

From the names of this sacrament, we will now proceed to consider the matter itself. As is true of the sacrament of holy baptism, three specific matters are also to be noted and expounded by us concerning the holy supper:

First, there is an externally visible sign and seal, suitable and appropriate to display and to seal inwardly the Lord Jesus with all of His grace and benefits to the souls of believers.

Second, there is an internal, invisible, and spiritual matter that is signified and sealed to believers by this external sign and seal.

Third, the Word of God reveals to us that such a sacrament has been divinely instituted and appointed.

We will consider these three matters in greater detail. Regarding the external sign and seal of the Lord's Supper, it is simply the eating of the broken bread and the drinking of the wine as poured forth into the cup. Thus, the external sign and seal of the sacrament of the Lord's Supper depict for us a well-prepared meal consisting of both food and drink suitable to feed and to sustain our bodies. Consequently, two specific elements are to be considered in regard to this external sign and seal, namely, bread and wine.

1. Regarding the bread, it should simply be the common bread we are daily accustomed to eating for the sustenance of our bodies. By no means should we follow the Papists and Lutherans, who use wafers that are expressly baked for the celebration of the holy supper of the Lord. This practice deviates from the express and instituted command of the Lord Jesus Christ, as well as from that which the holy apostles instituted and decreed. It also contradicts the character and nature of the matter itself, for the use of bread is designed to signify and seal for us how the Lord Jesus, with His grace and merits and by His Word and Spirit, is efficacious to the nourishing, satisfying, and sustaining of our souls.

This disqualifies the use of wafers, for they are not suitable to the nourishing of our bodies. We must therefore use only common daily bread that is readily available, and thus proceed with simplicity, as did the Savior when He instituted and appointed His supper in that night, for He used no other bread but the bread on the table that He and His apostles had eaten.

2. Wine is the other element that belongs to the external sign and seal of the Lord's Supper, and we are to proceed here with the same simplicity as with the bread, that is, to avail ourselves of common wine without limiting ourselves to a certain type or brand. Were we to do so, we would again deviate from what the Savior instituted, for when He administered His supper, He simply used the wine at hand on the table.

These two elements, that is, the bread and the wine, must be combined and be used and partaken of by all believing communicants at the Table of the Lord. Both the wine and the bread (and not merely the bread) are to be given to everyone at the table. The Papists teach the latter only, thereby denying to the laity the cup of wine and only permitting the priest to drink from it. They give only the wafer to the laity. This is the logical outcome of their vile heresy that the wine of the Lord's Supper is transformed into the actual and physical blood of Christ. They are fearful that some of the blood of Christ could be spilled or that a drop of that blood could remain lodged either in the mouth or the beard of a communicant. To prevent any blood being wasted, these deluded people have judged it best that the cup of wine be withheld from the laity, giving to them at the Lord's Supper only the appearance of bread by way of a baked wafer.

This is truly a most vile violation and transgression of Christ's command, for He gave to His believing people both bread and wine as the signs and seals of His grace. You might ask, "How is the popish Antichrist able to justify such an abominable perversion?" He does so by way of a public act of ungodliness whereby he opposes and exalts "himself above all that is called God, or that is worshipped" (2 Thess. 2:4). The Papists have decreed and formulated this perversion in the acts of the Council of Constance, where everyone still can read the following: "Albeit that Christ and the apostles have instituted the Lord's Supper as such (that is, by using the two elements of bread and wine), and albeit that the early Christians have always observed the Lord's Supper as such, this illustrious synod or ecclesiastical assembly has for good reason approved and stipulated that the common laity shall not be permitted to receive the cup."

Such is their argument in support of their popes being wiser than and having authority that exceeds that of Christ, the apostles, and the early Christians.

The Romish harlot could not have branded herself with a more abominable mark than this. Nothing is clearer and more certain and true than that the bread and wine must be conjoined in the Lord's Supper as a singular sign and seal. They are to be given to all true believers, who are to partake of them by a true faith, so that both Christ, as well as His benefits and graces, may thereby be inwardly signified and sealed to their hearts, and thereby they might be comforted and have their faith strengthened. The Lord Jesus has instituted the Lord's Supper as such, and we are to observe it and partake of it accordingly.

The foregoing affirms that the external sign and seal of the holy supper, as instituted by the Lord, consists solely in the eating of the broken bread and the drinking of the wine as it has been poured forth into the cup. This is not merely an observance of these external elements, but in doing so, there is an actual partaking of them with the mouth of one's physical body by eating and drinking.

Having considered the external and visible signs and seals of the Lord's Supper, we now proceed to consider the internal signification and sealing of the essence of this supper. This is a great, holy, and spiritual mystery, and no one can be saved without a true knowledge of it. May the Lord by His Spirit Himself lead us into this truth and give us to speak with transparency and simplicity. May He be pleased to bless our instruction to the souls of many as we engage therein, fully following our instructor as we expound his words.

He asks, "How art thou admonished and assured in the Lord's Supper, that thou art a partaker of that one sacrifice of Christ, accomplished on the cross, and of all His benefits?" to which the pupil replies, saying, "Christ has commanded me and all believers to eat of this broken bread and to drink of this cup in remembrance of Him, adding these promises: first, that His body was offered and broken on the cross for me, and His blood shed for me, as certainly as I see with my eyes the bread of the Lord broken for me and the cup communicated to me."

Beloved, you need to know, and may the Lord Himself teach you, that the matter being internally signified and sealed in the Lord's Supper is but the true spiritual union and communion of all true believers with the Lord Jesus and with His crucified body and blood. True believers are nourished and refreshed internally unto eternal life with the spiritual food and drink of His body and blood. All God's children, while utterly forsaking all that is of themselves and whatever may be found under the sun, have surrendered themselves to God in Christ as poor and needy sinners. By faith, they are all truly and spiritually united to the Lord Jesus, as well as to His grace and benefits, for Christ dwells in their hearts by faith (Eph. 3:17). With all His merits and precious benefits, He gives Himself to them in the same manner as a husband who obligates himself to give himself and all his goods to his wife, to whom he is united by the bond of marriage. Christ sacrificed Himself on the cross and died for all His believing people. For them, He permitted His body to be broken and His blood to be shed, so that thereby He would deliver them from their sins and from eternal death, reconcile them unto God, sanctify and renew them, and give them eternal life. In fact, it is the Lord Jesus who gives them His broken body and His shed blood, and who transforms it for them into spiritual food and drink unto eternal life. By way of His precious body and blood, He desires to refresh, strengthen, comfort, and satisfy their barren, contrite, and troubled souls, and to unite them most intimately with Himself. Therefore, He says in John 6:54–55: "Whoso eateth my flesh, and drinketh my blood, hath eternal life; and I will raise him up at the last day. For my flesh is meat indeed, and my blood is drink indeed." From this sole fountain proceeds all the salvation of believers. By faith, they fully cleave to the Lord Jesus, trusting in and relying upon Him alone, and thus in and upon His broken body and shed blood. The more they embrace this by the Spirit of faith, and the more they appropriate the Lord Jesus and His broken body and shed blood—putting all their hope and confidence therein while completely looking away from themselves and abandoning all that is of self and of the creature—the more blessedness they receive and the more true spiritual life issues forth in their souls from Christ, who is the fountain of their life. They increasingly are grafted into Him and enter more deeply into blessed communion with Him, for God's children derive all their salvation and blessedness from the Lord Jesus.

Therefore, the more their faith grows and increases, the more intimate their union and communion is with Christ, their head. They increasingly have their joy in Christ, who is the origin and fountain of their entire salvation, and the Scriptures therefore testify, "For by grace are ye saved through faith" (Eph. 2:8a). The Lord's Supper thus has as its purpose to foster and to increase this faith of God's children, so that thereby their true fellowship with the Lord Jesus and with His broken body and shed blood is affirmed, and they are inwardly assured thereof. And so it follows that the purpose of the Lord's Supper is to strengthen and comfort believers inwardly by way of the body and blood of Christ, and to cause them to be increasingly and spiritually united with them.

This is what the instructor teaches, positing that Christ, in the Lord's Supper, promises two matters to all His believing people, assuring them:

1. that as truly as they witness the bread being broken and as truly as they may partake of the cup, so sure it is that His body on the cross has been offered and broken for them and that His blood has been shed for them to their deliverance and eternal salvation; and

2. that as truly as they eat the bread and drink the wine, and are nourished and strengthened according to the body, so true it is that Christ also nourishes and refreshes their souls unto eternal life with His broken body and shed blood, causing them to eat His flesh and to drink His blood spiritually, so that they are nourished, strengthened, and satisfied according to the inner man.

Behold, these are the two matters that Christ promises to His believing people, and by His Holy Spirit He inwardly assures them thereof by sealing the matter to their hearts.

However, the instructor is not satisfied with a mere external and verbal affirmation of this truth, for in Question 76 he proceeds to expound in more detail what is the divine and spiritual mystery of the Lord's Supper. There he explains more explicitly what is actually meant by eating the crucified body of Christ and drinking His shed blood spiritually, for he asks, "What is it then to eat the crucified body, and drink the shed blood of Christ?" The pupil then responds, "It is not only to embrace with a believing heart all the sufferings and death of Christ, and thereby to obtain the pardon of sin and life eternal; but also, besides that, to become more and more united to His sacred body, by the Holy Ghost, who dwells both in Christ and in us; so that we, though Christ is in heaven and we on earth, are notwithstanding 'flesh of His flesh, and bone of His bone'; and that we live, and are governed forever by one spirit, as members of the same body are by one soul."

In no wise can the natural man either understand or even begin to comprehend this. This can be known and experienced only by God's people. As the instructor proceeds to expound for us what it means to eat Christ's crucified body and to drink His shed blood spiritually, he posits that this consists of two matters, the first of which is the believing reception of Christ and all that pertains to His passion and death by a true and sincere faith. The second is the spiritual and internal union of our hearts with Christ as it necessarily proceeds from faith and as it steadily increases and progresses in proportion to its vitality and exercise.

We will now expound these two matters for the congregation.

To eat and drink Christ's crucified body and His shed blood consists first and foremost in a believing and heartfelt reception of Christ and all that pertains to His passion and death. By this believing reception, believers have and obtain the pardon of sin and eternal life.

It is a known truth that the genuine faith that unites us with Christ and saves us is frequently presented to us in the Holy Scriptures as a *receiving* of Christ and of all His benefits, grace, and merits. In John 1:12 we read, "But as many as received him, to them gave he power to become the sons of God, even to them that believe on his name," and in Colossians 2:6, we read, "As ye have therefore received Christ Jesus the Lord, so walk ye in him." This *reception* presupposes that Christ willingly offers Himself to us poor sinners with all that is His, and that He truly gives Himself to us, for "a man can receive nothing, except it be given him from heaven" (John 3:27). There must therefore necessarily be a gift or bestowal by Christ to our souls, and without it we would be incapable of receiving Him. Many neither receive Christ nor sincerely believe in Him, for they can neither perceive that Christ is given to them nor have an absolute need for Him. Nevertheless, Christ gives Himself most generously to us poor sinners, and He desires of us that we would wholeheartedly embrace and receive Him unto our eternal salvation.

There are as many convincing evidences and proofs of this as there are promises regarding His offer and presentation of these benefits in the holy gospel. Since, however, our hearts are by nature completely hardened and unbelieving, and since our minds are entirely blind and ignorant, we need a mighty work of the Holy Spirit and a powerful and convicting proclamation of the holy gospel to incline our hearts toward Christ and to persuade us, by faith, to embrace and receive both Him and all that pertains to His passion and death. The Savior affirms this by saying, "No man can come to me, except the Father which hath sent me draw him" (John 6:44).

In order that we would wholeheartedly and in all simplicity receive Christ in response to the revelation of Himself, we must necessarily, by the powerful operation of the Holy Spirit, be wrought upon so that we have a lively sense and realization regarding the completely lost, wretched, and helpless condition in which we find ourselves because of sin. We must first fully surrender, and from our side, we must utterly despair of securing salvation and redemption by our own efforts. We must see that we are subject to the curse and wrath of God. We must recognize that the danger of eternal death and condemnation is therefore inescapable, and that we are incapable of contributing even the very least to our salvation. Only then can we be led to a pure, heartfelt, believing, and unconditional receiving of both Christ and all that pertains to His passion and death. Only then shall we be ready to be saved by Him purely by grace alone; that is, according to His own way as our mediator, surety, and redeemer.

People may speak of receiving Christ and all that pertains to His passion and death, claiming that they believe in Him. However, as long as they have not truly seen themselves as utterly hell-worthy and lost, and cannot speak of this by way of personal experience, their faith is purely imaginary, and all their sweet love for the Lord Jesus is merely a glossed-over illusion from which they will awake with great fear when they come to themselves.

To receive Christ sincerely and all that pertains to His passion and death, we must be inwardly persuaded in our hearts by the power of the Holy Spirit and by means of the doctrine of the gospel of how absolutely necessary Christ is for us, as well as of His complete suitability and all-sufficiency to deliver us, poor sinners, by His passion and death from all our sins, and also from eternal death and condemnation. We must thus be inwardly persuaded that we need Christ for our justification, our sanctification, our reconciliation with God, and our being made partakers of eternal salvation. We must also be persuaded of Christ's favorable disposition and of His good will toward us in particular; that is, how He offers Himself to us unto our salvation; how friendly His invitation is and how He calls us unto Himself; how He is willing to do all this purely out of free and sovereign grace; how He came into the world to save poor sinners; how He suffered and died for us; how freely we may come to Him no matter how wretched, condemned, and hell-worthy we are; and that He shall neither reject nor cast us out.

Until we, by the powerful working of the Holy Spirit, are persuaded of this in our hearts with a measure of clarity and conviction, so that we wholeheartedly endorse the doctrine of the holy gospel, we by no means receive Christ and all that pertains to His passion and death, nor do we embrace Him by a true faith as our redeemer and savior. We have no sincere desire to be united with Christ in the way that He has ordained.

Finally, another constituent component of receiving the Lord Jesus Christ and all that pertains to His passion and death is that, by the power of the Holy Spirit, we must utterly look away from self and all that pertains to us and radically cease to put any trust either in ourselves or any other creature. As poor and impotent sinners, we must turn fully to the Lord Jesus, surrendering ourselves fully to Him with soul and body in order to "be found in him, not having

[our] own righteousness, which is of the law, but that which is through the faith of Christ, the righteousness which is of God by faith" (Phil. 3:9). Therefore, whoever truly and fully turns away from self, and in so doing surrenders himself fully to Christ by a true faith, receives Him with all that pertains to His passion and death, and entrusts himself fully to Christ in order to be graciously saved and redeemed by Him.

The instructor then posits that all who have done so in truth and uprightness by the power of the Holy Spirit are in Christ. By His passion and death, they are the recipients of the pardon of sin and eternal life, for by faith we receive true fellowship with the Lord Jesus, as well as with all His merits and benefits. His holy passion and death, and all His fullness and righteousness, then become our portion, and in our hearts we are inwardly clothed with that righteousness. God now views us as being united to His Son, Christ, and for His sake, He eternally pardons both our original and actual sins. It is as though we never either had or had committed any sins and as if all the righteousness of God's law and the obedience to it, as was secured by Christ on our behalf, had been secured by ourselves. Psalm 32:1–2 then applies to us: "Blessed is he whose transgression is forgiven, whose sin is covered. Blessed is the man unto whom the Lord imputeth not iniquity."

Furthermore, in and through His Son, Christ, and by grace, God then also grants us eternal life, for by His Holy Spirit, Christ then makes His abode in our hearts. He raises us from being dead in sins, He regenerates, renews, and inwardly sanctifies us, and in so doing, He becomes to us "a quickening spirit" (1 Cor. 15:45). We therefore read in John 3:36, "He that believeth on the Son hath everlasting life." To eat and drink Christ's broken body and shed blood consists in this believing reception of Christ and all that pertains to His passion and death, and the Lord's Supper signifies and seals this to all true believers.

This becomes all the more evident when we briefly consider the similarities between physical eating and drinking and the believing reception of Christ.

He who physically eats and drinks:

1. Perceives within himself that he is empty and in need of some nourishment, and he then partakes of food and drink to satisfy his need. Likewise, he who by a true faith receives Christ and all that pertains to His passion and death inwardly perceives himself also to be utterly destitute of all righteousness, peace, comfort, and salvation. Neither he himself nor anything that proceeds from the creature is by any means capable of sustaining spiritual life. This he finds to be true, for in himself he perceives his wretched spiritual deficiency and

his sins, as well as the absence of God and of all salvation. His blindness, naked-ness, and impotence greatly oppress him and render him utterly perplexed, and therefore he no longer can bear to consider anything that is of himself.

2. Has a desire after food and drink, and hungers and thirsts for it. A true believer does likewise in the spiritual realm when he fully receives Christ and all that pertains to His passion and death. Such a soul has a heartfelt desire to become a partaker of and to delight in Christ and all His merits and benefits. He hungers and thirsts after Christ, as well as after His precious grace, fullness, and righteousness. He has an inward longing in his heart after Christ and after peace with God through Him. Just as a man who is physically hungry and thirsty cannot live without being nourished by food and drink, likewise such a soul cannot live without Christ and without desires to have Him in response to His own offer, in His own way, and entirely as He is, for He is to them precious and "altogether lovely" (Song 5:16) in all that He is.

3. Also receives and enjoys his food and drink. Likewise, he who by a true faith receives Christ and all that pertains to His passion and death inwardly in his heart receives and enjoys Him with all His saving benefits. He fully appro-priates Christ and all that pertains to Him, and esteems Him to be his Christ, his redeemer, and his savior, trusting in and leaning upon Him alone. With his entire heart, he trusts in Him, and through Him, receives peace with God, the forgiveness of sins, sanctification by the Spirit, and all comfort, joy, and salva-tion—even more than he could possibly have desired.

4. Is nourished, refreshed, filled, and satisfied with this food and drink in such a manner whereby he ceases to be hungry and thirsty or to suffer any lack. Likewise, he who, by a true faith, receives Christ and all that pertains to His passion and death is also nourished, refreshed, and inwardly satisfied in his heart with this spiritual food and drink. Immediately thereupon all that he lacks spiritually in his soul is completely addressed and fulfilled by Christ, for a true believer finds everything in *Him* to overflowing—that is, all that he needs unto his salvation for both time and eternity. He can say with David, "The LORD is my shepherd; I shall not want" (Ps. 23:1). This is also the thrust of what Jesus is communicating when He says, "I am the bread of life: he that cometh to me shall never hunger; and he that believeth on me shall never thirst" (John 6:35).

5. Does this not only once, but repeatedly. Time and again, a new need causes new hunger and thirst. This is also true in the spiritual realm. He who receives Christ and all that pertains to His passion and death does so not just once, for he repeatedly sins, and therefore he is repeatedly needy and undone.

Consequently, he is continually in need of Christ, and by renewal he is in need of embracing and receiving Him. By a true faith, he repeatedly takes refuge to Him alone, so that he may continually receive grace for grace out of His fullness (John 1:16). Christ is the nourishment that must be used continually and daily by God's children to remedy all that they lack spiritually in their souls. Continually they must practice, "As ye have therefore received Christ Jesus the Lord, so walk ye in him" (Col. 2:6). They must continually "live by the faith of the Son of God, who loved [them], and gave himself for [them]" (Gal. 2:20), for "the just shall live by his faith" (Hab. 2:4).

6. Is most intimately united with the food and drink he may enjoy. He even becomes one with it, for his food and drink are absorbed by his body. Again, this is also true in the spiritual realm. He who by a true faith receives Christ and all that pertains to His passion and death is thereby united to Him as intimately as the body is united to the soul.

The instructor proceeds to define the second aspect of spiritually eating and drinking the flesh and blood of Christ, saying that it consists in becoming "more and more united to His sacred body, by the Holy Ghost, who dwells both in Christ and in us; so that we, though Christ is in heaven and we on earth, are notwithstanding 'flesh of His flesh, and bone of His bone.'" It belongs to the essential nature of true saving faith that the hearts of believers are increasingly united to the Lord Jesus by the operation of the Holy Spirit. By faith, believers find so much sweetness, salvation, and all-sufficiency in Christ and His grace that they can tolerate no separation from or estrangement between Him and their souls. Rather, they desire to be increasingly united to Him in the Spirit, and therefore they earnestly supplicate for and crave this, saying with the bride, "O that thou wert as my brother…when I should find thee without, I would kiss thee" (Song 8:1). The Spirit of faith draws the heart increasingly to Jesus and causes her to "count all things but loss for the excellency of the knowledge of Christ Jesus my Lord" (Phil. 3:8).

From His side, the Lord Jesus also seeks to unite Himself all the more intimately with His believing people. He yearns and labors to conquer and possess their hearts more and more, and to fill them with His heavenly Spirit and grace. Therefore, by the Spirit of faith and His continual influence and powerful operation, Christ and the believing soul interact with one another and do not let go one of the other. Rather, they mutually strive to achieve a more intimate, heartfelt, upright, and spiritual union with one another, and they become as one plant, or as one head and one body.

Christ expresses this in John 6:56, saying, "He that eateth my flesh, and drinketh my blood, dwelleth in me, and I in him." This is not contradicted by the fact that Christ is in heaven above and that His people dwell here below upon earth, for Christ is actively present in the hearts of His people by His Word and Spirit, by which He lives, dwells, and works in them. He governs and directs them, and continually stirs up, sustains, and strengthens their faith so that they thereby follow and cleave to the Lord Jesus in all things and are one spirit with Him (1 Cor. 6:17). They are even "members of his body, of his flesh, and of his bones" (Eph. 5:30). Since this union between true believers and Christ is continual and eternal, already here on earth Christ gives "them eternal life; and they shall never perish, neither shall any man pluck them out of [His] hand" (John 10:27–28).

Such is the manner in which all true believers eat and drink the crucified body and shed blood of the Lord Jesus. Thereby they are internally united unto Him in the Spirit, resulting in their being nourished, strengthened, and satisfied unto eternal life.

Such is the most glorious and spiritual mystery of the Lord's Supper, and the Holy Spirit instructs and stirs them up accordingly by means of this sacrament. In so doing, He affirms and assures them in their hearts of this great and precious salvation in a most comforting and delightful manner:

1. By the broken bread and the poured-out wine that believers behold with their eyes, it is spiritually signified and sealed to them that Christ's precious body has also been broken on the cross for their sins, and that His precious blood has also been shed for them. In the Lord Jesus, they are therefore fully cleansed from all their sins, and they are sanctified and justified (1 Cor. 6:11).

2. By the eating and drinking of the bread and wine, the Holy Spirit signifies and seals to believers that the body and blood of Christ have also been broken and shed for them; that also for them, this has become spiritual food and drink unto eternal life; that, by faith, He is truly received and enjoyed by them; that their souls are inwardly united with Him; and that, by His body and blood, they are refreshed, nourished, strengthened, and satisfied. Consequently, the cup of the Lord's Supper sacramentally becomes to all believers "the communion of the blood of Christ" and the bread "the communion of the body of Christ" (1 Cor. 10:16).

We have hereby sufficiently expounded and opened up for you the internal and spiritual mystery of the Lord's Supper. May it please the Lord further to open this up for you by His Holy Spirit, so that you might know these things spiritually and experientially unto your salvation.

This precious sacrament of the Lord's Supper is by no means a human ordinance, for it would then be utterly useless, vain, and inefficient. We would neither be able nor permitted to observe it obediently, but as He has done with the sacrament of holy baptism, Christ Jesus Himself, as the Lord and head of His congregation, has also ordained and instituted this sacrament for all true believers. He has given a clear description of its institution in His Word, and the instructor will now briefly mention something of this in Question 77, where he tells us that the Lord Jesus instituted the Lord's Supper for four specific reasons. He did so:

1. To assure His believing people in their hearts of their being partakers of Him, as well as of His grace, love, and faithfulness toward them, so that thereby they would be comforted and their faith strengthened.

2. That it would yield a vivid proof and affirmation of their mutual relationship and friendship, whereby they mutually embrace one another in tender love and are most intimately and spiritually united to one another. Just as good friends occasionally have a meal together, whereby their mutual friendship is enlivened, stimulated, and affirmed, likewise the Lord Jesus, in the Lord's Supper, prepares a love meal for His believing people and inwardly delights or overcomes them with His precious flesh and blood. He comes to His believing people with His love, grace, and Spirit. They open their hearts to Him, and He thus sups with them and they with Him (Rev. 3:10). The love, friendship, and relationship between Christ and His believing people, which from their side would otherwise be greatly diminished and weakened, are by renewal enlivened, stimulated, and affirmed. This greatly benefits believers, who must derive all their strength, life, and salvation from this friendship and relationship with the Lord Jesus.

3. That His believing people would exercise very intimate and mutual fellowship with one another in the Spirit, thereby most intimately and mutually uniting themselves as members of the same body in a most tender love, being so bound together that they "have been all made to drink into one Spirit" (1 Cor. 12:13).

4. That His believing people would observe this supper in remembrance of Him. Although He is physically absent from them, He is spiritually most intimately united to them and dwells in their hearts, and so they thereby "shew the Lord's death till he come" (1 Cor. 11:26). Nothing is so subservient to the

enlivening of faith and the stirring up of love as is the spiritual beholding and showing forth of Christ's death, atoning sacrifice, and second coming.

Finally, both the external administration of the Lord's Supper as well as the rituals to be observed in it are to be done in great simplicity and according to the letter of Christ's ordinance or institution:

First, it must be administered by a minister who has been lawfully called and ordained by the church, for at the Lord's Supper, he is called to represent the person of Christ.

Second, there must be communicants who receive and enjoy this sacrament. They must be true believers, lest they eat and drink judgment to themselves. We have always and most earnestly instructed the congregation accordingly whenever the Lord's Supper has been administered among us.

Third, these believing communicants must be seated at a table with their minister—just as Christ and His apostles were seated at a table.

Fourth, the external rituals to be performed are as follows: as Christ did, so must the minister take, bless, and break the bread before the eyes of the communicants, and as he distributes it to them, he must exhort them to eat it as being Christ's body. Thereafter, he must also take and bless the wine-filled cup and pass it to the communicants, exhorting them that they should all drink of it as being the blood of the New Testament. In turn, the communicants must, as did the apostles, receive the bread and wine out of the hand of the minister, and then eat and drink with a true faith, thereby showing forth the Lord's death till He comes.

Fifth, the Lord's Supper must be administered wherever the congregation commonly gathers for public worship.

Sixth, the time and frequency of the Lord's Supper are not stipulated in God's Word. Its only general stipulation is that it must be administered *frequently*.

May the Lord be pleased to bless this exposition and graciously accompany it with the ministry of His Holy Spirit. We must therefore solemnly call upon His holy name with true faith and confidence. May everyone therefore, by the grace of the Lord, stir up and prepare himself to that end. Amen.

The Doctrine of the Lord's Supper Defended

Wherefore, my dearly beloved, flee from idolatry. I speak as to wise men; judge ye what I say. The cup of blessing which we bless, is it not the communion of the blood of Christ? The bread which we break, is it not the communion of the body of Christ?
—1 CORINTHIANS 10:14–16

Question 78: Do then the bread and wine become the very body and blood of Christ?

Answer: Not at all: but as the water in baptism is not changed into the blood of Christ, neither is the washing away of sin itself, being only the sign and confirmation thereof appointed of God; so the bread in the Lord's supper is not changed into the very body of Christ; though agreeably to the nature and properties of sacraments, it is called the body of Christ Jesus.

Question 79: Why then doth Christ call the bread His body, and the cup His blood, or the new covenant in His blood; and Paul the "communion of the body and blood of Christ"?

Answer: Christ speaks thus, not without great reason, namely, not only thereby to teach us, that as bread and wine support this temporal life, so His crucified body and shed blood are the true meat and drink, whereby our souls are fed to eternal life; but more especially by these visible signs and pledges to assure us, that we are as really partakers of His true body and blood (by the operation of the Holy Ghost) as we receive by the mouths of our bodies these holy signs in remembrance of Him; and that all His sufferings and obedience are as certainly ours, as if we had in our own persons suffered and made satisfaction for our sins to God.

Second Thessalonians 2:11 is a remarkable prophecy of the apostle Paul. Speaking of the coming of the Antichrist into the world (who is none other than the pope of Rome and his followers), he prophesies that "for this cause God shall send them strong delusion, that they should believe a lie." The judgment that God will impose upon men will be grievous and dreadful, for in the preceding verse the apostle testifies that "they received not the love of the truth, that they might be saved."

Truly, nothing provokes God the Lord to anger more than the despising, maligning, and rejection of His truth, which He causes to be proclaimed and ceaselessly has caused to be preached to the children of men. When men refuse to acknowledge and embrace this truth in love unto their eternal salvation, the Lord generally hardens, darkens, and sears their hearts, causing pernicious and soul-damning errors to emerge among them, by which they are completely drawn away from the truth. Then, as by a mighty stream, they are swept away into a sea of error and deceit, in which they will eternally drown and perish in a most dreadful manner.

As Paul thus prophesied, God has executed such a judgment in a most extraordinary manner upon the Papists. When the Antichrist, the son of perdition, came into the world, and men "received not the love of the truth, that they might be saved…God…sent them strong delusion, that they should believe a lie." The Antichrist introduced the most grievous errors and deceptions into the church, whereby the doctrine of salvation was completely corrupted and perverted. All those whom God, in His just judgment, gave over to their own selves believed these errors and deceptions unto their eternal perdition.

This still occurs in the world, for the same errors and deceptions foisted upon it by the son of perdition, the Antichrist, are still flourishing in the midst of Roman Catholicism. They are even deeply rooted in the hearts of all unconverted and natural men, irrespective of what their religious persuasion may be. In Roman Catholicism, however, these errors and deceptions are fully enthroned, and the effect of this delusion is, by God's just judgment, so great and all-encompassing that her members cannot but believe the lie.

In former Lord's Days, we have seen clear evidence of this in regard to the doctrine of the justification of the sinner before God, as well as in regard to the doctrine of holy baptism. Presently, we again encounter such deception, and again it will be proven no less powerfully to be the case whereas that same deception is found in their teaching of the doctrine of the Lord's Supper—a doctrine that Roman Catholicism, by way of insidious deception, has so dreadfully obscured and corrupted. Therefore, with the instructor, we will expound this matter for you in this Lord's Day.

After having so clearly expounded the doctrine of the Lord's Supper in harmony with God's Word in the previous Lord's Day, the instructor now proceeds to defend and affirm this doctrine against the pernicious and abominable doctrine of the Papists, a matter of urgent necessity, for recent converts from Roman Catholicism need to be further built up and affirmed in the doctrine "which is after godliness" (Titus 1:1). We will follow in the instructor's footsteps by endeavoring to address these matters in such a fashion that we will not spend all of our time, as so many commonly do, in the disputation of these errors, but that our exposition will yield instruction to our edification, the exercise of our faith, and the practice of godliness.

The instructor now proceeds in his exposition:

1. In Question 78, he articulates the essential difference between our doctrine and that of Roman Catholicism, and in so doing, he affirms the doctrine of the Lord's Supper.

2. In Question 79, he defends this doctrine further by countering the objections of Roman Catholicism.

Before we proceed, let me affirm that whereas the instructor addresses here only the doctrine of the Lord's Supper in contrast to that of Roman Catholicism, we also have doctrinal differences with our Lutheran brethren. We will therefore first address the issue we have with Roman Catholicism, and afterwards we will briefly defend the true doctrine of the Lord's Supper against the Lutherans.

As we follow the instructor, we will address:

1. the true nature of our differences with Roman Catholicism; and

2. the objections of Roman Catholicism against our doctrine.

The instructor begins by asking, "Do then the bread and wine become the very body and blood of Christ?" By this question, the instructor articulates the very essence of our dispute with Roman Catholics. In summary, their view regarding the Lord's Supper consists in this: they posit that upon the very moment the priest utters the words "for this is my body," the substance of both the bread and the wine is immediately and essentially transformed into the true substance of the actual body and blood of Jesus Christ as He hung on the cross. The bread is therefore no longer bread and the wine is no longer wine, but they have been fully transformed into the actual body and blood of Christ, and thus Roman Catholics teach that the communicants then literally eat His body and the priest literally drinks His blood with their physical mouths, and by so doing, they claim they are physically united to His true body and blood.

They denominate this transaction as *transubstantiation*; that is, the transformation of substance whereby the essence of the bread and wine is miraculously transformed into the actual and true body and blood of the Lord Jesus.

This is the pernicious and wicked doctrine of Roman Catholicism regarding the Lord's Supper and regarding the manner in which believers are thereby united with Christ. Satan himself could not have articulated this in a more despicable, carnal, or abominable manner unto the perdition of souls.

Roman Catholicism must be viewed by us as being entirely carnal, and its adherents as entirely carnal men who are void of the Spirit, and therefore it should not surprise us at all that their entire religion is carnally minded (Rom. 8:5–7). Therefore, they are utterly void of spiritual light, and they dwell in an abyss of dreadful darkness. How vile and carnal is their doctrine regarding the sacrament of holy baptism, as we have recently exposed it to be, when they suggest that the external water of baptism washes away sin and fully transforms, renews, converts, and sanctifies men! This is equally true for their doctrine regarding the sacrament of the Lord's Supper, for its foundational principle is nothing but the carnality of natural men who do not understand the things of the Spirit of God. Therefore, they cannot possibly understand them to all eternity, "because they are spiritually discerned" (1 Cor. 2:14).

Recently, we considered how great a spiritual mystery the Lord's Supper encompasses. By the grace of the Holy Spirit, it clearly depicts to believers and powerfully assures them inwardly in their souls:

1. that by faith, they are truly and spiritually united with the Lord Jesus and with His crucified body and shed blood unto their justification and the cleansing of their sins; and

2. that by means of the body and blood of Jesus Christ, their souls are inwardly, spiritually, and truly nourished and refreshed unto eternal life.

This is, however, a great, holy, and divine mystery that can be known in one's soul and, in some measure, be rightly understood only by way of true spiritual experience. Since the natural man in himself is nothing but darkness and flesh, he can have only a carnal conception or notion regarding this spiritual eating and drinking of the body and blood of Christ with the mouth of true faith. We read of this regarding the Jews of Capernaum, who were entirely unregenerate, natural, and carnal men, and thus were void of light, the Spirit, and life. When they heard the Lord Jesus speak regarding the eating of His flesh and the drinking of His blood, and that without such eating and drinking one would be and remain dead in himself and thus void of any true spiritual life, they understood neither the matter nor the doctrine He was addressing. He spoke of a spiritual mystery, but they understood it only in an entirely carnal manner and according to their natural comprehension. To them, it was as if the Savior taught that one must physically eat and drink His body and blood with one's physical mouth. They became greatly offended by what He had said, and therefore exclaimed, "How can this man give us his flesh to eat?" (John 6:52). From that moment forward, many turned away from Jesus and left Him, for they did not understand His doctrine.

Such is also true for the Papists, for their vile sentiments proceed from the same principle; that is, from the carnality and darkness of their minds. We will now briefly and more explicitly refute their sentiments and demonstrate to you how utterly absurd they are.

As we have observed, they teach that in the Lord's Supper, the physical substance of bread and wine is fully removed and is replaced by Christ's literal and true body and blood—that same body and blood to which Mary gave birth and which was also slain by being nailed to the wooden cross. This alleged transformation of the bread and wine is such, however, that the external characteristics and qualities of both remain unchanged, such as size, aroma, taste, and color. However, the Papists believe that in the Lord's Supper, they are not eating bread, but rather, that they are eating the true body of Christ, and that the priest drinks the actual and true blood of Christ. What an abominable doctrine this truly is!

The instructor refutes it plainly and clearly by comparing the sacrament of the Lord's Supper with that of holy baptism as he responds to the question "Do then the bread and wine become the very body and blood of Christ?" by saying, "Not at all: but as the water in baptism is not changed into the blood of Christ, neither is the washing away of sin itself, being only the sign and confirmation thereof appointed of God; so the bread in the Lord's supper is not changed into the very body of Christ; though agreeably to the nature and properties of sacraments, it is called the body of Christ Jesus."

Both baptism and the Lord's Supper are sacraments of the covenant of grace and are identical in nature, efficacy, and rank. They differ only in focus and in the manner whereby they are administered. Therefore, as to the essence of the matter, whatever transpires with the one must also transpire with the other, for otherwise, they would then be two sacraments that are entirely distinct as to their essence and nature, which neither is nor can be true. Two things transpire when the sacrament of baptism is administered. The instructor posits:

1. that the external element of water, and thus the external sign and seal, by no means is in any way transformed into the blood of Christ; instead, as even the Papists believe, it remains what it is: water; and

2. that the external sign and seal of baptism—that is, the water—by no means is the washing away of sin itself, the water being only the sign and confirmation thereof appointed of God. Its only function is to signify and seal inwardly to the hearts of believers, by the power of the Holy Spirit, the blood of Christ and the washing away of sins, so that thereby they may be comforted and have their faith strengthened. Along with the instructor, we incontrovertibly proved this from God's Word when we recently dealt with the sacrament of holy baptism. This is the true essence and nature of the sacrament of holy baptism.

However, it is equally true for the sacrament of the Lord's Supper, for its essence and nature do not differ from the sacrament of holy baptism:

First, the visible elements of bread and wine, constituting the external sign and seal, are by no means transformed into the true body and blood of Christ. They remain unchanged, even as the water remains unchanged in baptism. Could the visible elements in the Lord's Supper be changed, it would be an entirely different and more efficacious sacrament than baptism. And this can neither be shown nor proven from God's Word.

Second, just as the water of baptism serves only to signify and seal to believers the blood of Christ and the washing away of sins thereby, so likewise the bread and wine serve only to signify and seal to believers the true body and blood of Christ, and how thereby believers are spiritually united to Him and how their souls are inwardly nourished and refreshed unto eternal life. Again, were it otherwise, the sacrament of the Lord's Supper would be of an entirely different essence and nature from that of baptism.

The instructor thus refutes this Roman Catholic doctrine, the doctrine of transubstantiation, by doing a parallel comparison of the two sacraments, holy baptism and the Lord's Supper.

We shall now briefly add some additional reasons in support of this:

First, it is very evident from the Holy Scriptures that the bread and the wine of the Lord's Supper are by no means changed into the true body and blood of Christ, for Scripture is clear that it is merely plain bread at the Lord's Supper that one eats with his physical mouth, and it is merely wine that one drinks from the cup. Paul speaks accordingly in 1 Corinthians 11:26, 28, saying, "For as often as ye eat this bread, and drink this cup, ye do shew the Lord's death till he come.… But let a man examine himself, and so let him eat of that bread, and drink of that cup." Throughout Scripture, the Lord's Supper is spoken of in such terms.

Second, that the bread and wine remain unchanged in the Lord's Supper is also evident from the institution of the Lord's Supper by Christ, for there we observe not the slightest suggestion that the bread and wine in any way change into the body and blood of Christ. On the contrary, it is evident from the words of the Savior that after the consecration—meaning, the utterance of the five words, "for this is my blood"—not the least change occurred and the wine remained wine. Furthermore, Christ subsequently referred to it expressly as the "fruit of the vine," saying, "I will not drink henceforth of this fruit of the vine" (Matt. 26:29).

Moreover, if bread and wine had truly been transformed at the occasion of Christ's administration of the Lord's Supper, they should have been transformed into Christ's *broken* body and *shed* blood, for He uttered these words, "This is my body, which is broken for you" (1 Cor. 11:24). And regarding the wine and the cup, we read, "This cup is the new testament in my blood: this do ye, as oft as ye drink it" (1 Cor. 11:25). However, this could not have transpired in the literal sense of the word, for at that moment, Christ's body had not yet been broken or His blood shed. These were matters that still had to transpire.

Third, the fallacy and error of the Papists is also evident when considering the objective of the institution of the Lord's Supper. Its objective is that it be observed in remembrance of Christ, doing so to show forth His death until He comes (Luke 22:19; 1 Cor. 11:26). If it were true that the bread and wine are transformed into the true body and blood of Christ, Christ Himself would then physically be present, and the Lord's Supper could then not be administered in remembrance of Him, for one cannot remember a person who is present, but one who is absent.

Fourth, that there is not the least transformation of the bread and wine into Christ's true body and blood at the Lord's Supper is also very evident from the fact that the Holy Scriptures teach that Christ, in His human nature, is no longer physically here on earth, but only in heaven, and that He will remain there until the Day of Judgment (John 16:28; 17:11; Acts 3:21). Christ therefore exhorts us most earnestly, saying, "If any man shall say unto you, Lo, here is Christ, or there; believe it not.... Wherefore if they shall say unto you, Behold, he is in the desert; go not forth: behold, he is in the secret chambers; believe it not" (Matt. 24:23–26). Therefore, when the Papists now claim that He resides in their sacramental structures, "believe it not."

Finally, this abominable doctrine of Romish transubstantiation completely contradicts the most important articles of the old and universal Apostles' Creed. It also runs counter to the natural reason with which God has endowed the souls of all mankind in creation and according to which they shall once be judged. Furthermore, it fully contradicts the nature of the natural senses of the human body. This doctrine therefore consists of the most abominable and grievous absurdities imaginable, so that even Jews, Gentiles, and Muslims abhor it.

Having affirmed the true doctrine of the Lord's Supper over against the grievous error of Roman Catholicism, he now proceeds to dismantle their preeminent argumentation by which they seek to affirm their doctrine from God's Word.

They base their doctrine entirely upon the institutional formula of the Lord's Supper, and the instructor addresses this by asking in Question 79, "Why then doth Christ call the bread His body, and the cup His blood, or the new covenant in His blood; and Paul the 'communion of the body and blood of Christ'?"

We know that when the Savior instituted His holy supper, He spoke of the external signs and seals figuratively and sacramentally, saying of the bread, "For this is my body," and of the wine or cup, "This is my blood of the new testament, which is shed for many for the remission of sins" (Matt. 26:26–28). When Paul speaks of the bread and wine, he says: "The cup of blessing which we bless, is it not the communion of the blood of Christ? The bread which we break, is it not the communion of the body of Christ?" (1 Cor. 10:16).

Since Papists lack the Spirit of discernment, they interpret this in a literal and carnal manner. Thus, they establish their error entirely upon that foundation, and we have already observed that they do likewise with the sacrament of baptism.

As to the passage in which the apostle Paul posits that the bread and the wine, or the cup of the Lord's Supper, are the communion of the body and blood of Christ, it yields not the least proof in support of the heretical view of the Papists. Paul is by no means speaking of any physical fellowship between believers and the body and blood of Christ, as the Papists do regarding what transpires at the Lord's Supper. Paul rather speaks of the internal and spiritual fellowship believers have by faith with the body and blood of Christ as it is signified and sealed by the bread and by the wine.

This becomes all the more evident when we consider that he contrasts the fellowship that believers have with the body and blood of Christ with the ungodly fellowship with devils that comes about by eating what has been sacrificed unto idols. When eating the substance of such a sacrifice, one would not eat the devil himself, but rather, by eating such food, one would enter into fellowship with the devil in a mysterious manner. Likewise, by eating the bread and drinking the wine, one does not eat the body and blood of Christ. And yet, by the act of eating and drinking at the Lord's Table in true faith, one enters into spiritual fellowship with Christ's body and blood. It is such inward and spiritual fellowship that Paul has also in mind here.

Regarding Christ's words at the institution of the Lord's Supper that the bread is His body and the wine (or the cup) His blood, nothing is so obvious and certain than that these words are to be understood in a figurative sense; that is, in a sacramental sense. Christ expressed thereby only that the bread and wine of the Lord's Supper depict and exemplify His body and His blood to believers, powerfully assuring them of their inward communion with Him.

Although we could abundantly affirm this, we are satisfied to focus only on the exposition of our instructor, for he says, "Christ speaks thus not without great reason, namely, not only thereby to teach us that as bread and wine support this temporal life, so His crucified body and shed blood are the true meat and drink whereby our souls are fed to eternal life."

The words of the Savior must therefore be understood in the sense they are here expounded by the instructor. By the visible signs of bread and wine in the Lord's Supper, and by the eating and drinking thereof, He wishes to depict in the clearest possible manner to His believing people (thereby assuring their hearts in a most efficacious manner), what their inward fellowship is with His broken body and shed blood unto their justification, their sanctification, their full deliverance from sin, and their eternal salvation. He furthermore wishes to communicate to them that by His broken body and shed blood, which serve as internal food and drink to their souls, they are internally nourished and refreshed unto eternal life.

To assure them all the more efficaciously of this great grace and salvation, the Savior refers to the bread as His own body and to the wine or the cup as His own blood. His objective in so doing is that believers would not separate these two matters, but rather, by faith, they would simultaneously with the bread embrace and receive the body of Christ and with the wine the blood of Christ, so that, by the sacrament of the Lord's Supper, their faith would be more established and strengthened, and they, by the Spirit, would thereby exercise true and essential communion with Christ.

For this reason alone, Christ refers to the bread as His body and to the wine as His blood, and therefore it does not signify in any way that the bread is being transformed into His body and the wine into His blood. Such teaching as this doctrine of transubstantiation will be utterly erroneous and deceitful to all eternity, as it utterly unravels all that pertains to spiritual life and salvation, and will forever cause men to remain carnal and sold under sin.

We hereby judge to have sufficiently refuted from God's Word this abominable and wretched doctrine of the Papists, and we will now leave it to the discretion of a merciful God to reveal His truth at His time and in His manner to all His people by His Word and by His Spirit, and thereby sanctify them in the truth and make them free from sin.

It now remains to say a few words regarding the erroneous view of our Lutheran brethren regarding the Lord's Supper. Beloved, the Lutherans fail to have a clear grasp regarding the essence and nature of the holy sacraments, as they fail to understand to what end and purpose the Lord Jesus ordained them. They are of the opinion that there is more to the sacraments than the simplicity of the signifying and sealing efficacy that issues forth from the grace of the Holy Spirit. We have already observed how erroneous their view of the sacrament of baptism is. They are no less in error regarding their view of the sacrament of the Lord's Supper, teaching that Christ is then physically present in, with, and under the bread and the wine, albeit in a manner that is entirely invisible and intangible. They have designated this as the doctrine of *consubstantiation*; that is, there is a manner in which the body and blood of Christ coexist in a real sense with the bread and the wine in the Lord's Supper.

The argument that undergirds their doctrine is their erroneous view regarding the omnipresence of the body of Christ subsequent to His ascension. If, subsequent to His ascension, Christ's body were indeed omnipresent, as is His divine nature, it would be self-evident that Christ would also be physically present at the Lord's Supper. However, with the instructor in Lord's Day 18 (which addresses the Savior's ascension), we have already clearly and forthrightly refuted this doctrine of the physical omnipresence of Christ while here on earth or subsequent to His ascension. We then showed from the Holy Scriptures that such a doctrine is utterly absurd, and that Christ, as to His body, now resides only in heaven and shall remain there until the Day of Judgment. Thereby the entire foundation for the Lutheran notion of consubstantiation is dismantled, and their erroneous view regarding the Lord's Supper is necessarily rendered null and void.

In conclusion, I now wish to speak a brief word of instruction and exhortation to my readers. It would be a matter of great bliss if the true doctrine regarding the Lord's Supper, such as is taught biblically in the Reformed Church in accordance with God's Word, were to be known and understood by all in a genuinely spiritual fashion. Of what avail will it be when our doctrine, which is according to godliness, is taught fully and purely among us if we nevertheless do not truly understand it or if our understanding of it is entirely erroneous due to our darkened, carnal, and unregenerate understanding?

I know, however, how grievous and lamentable the situation is among us, how fearfully ignorant and ill-informed our people are regarding the true doctrine of the Lord's Supper, and how they refuse to be instructed regarding it. If only you would be willing to hear us, as you, according to God's command, are obligated to do! By God's grace, I would then endeavor to lead you to a proper view and to the acknowledgment of the profound ignorance of yourself and of most others, as well as of your grievous abuse of the Lord's Supper. May this cause you to be truly humbled and to seek light and grace from the Lord to the healing of your soul. May you therefore avail yourself, in all seriousness, of all means to your conversion and instruction that the Lord still so graciously offers and grants to you.

The Lord has revealed to me two matters regarding this, doing so in order that I, in turn, would publicly make this known to others by placing this light upon the candlestick:

1. By far the majority among us who partake of the Lord's Supper do so in an entirely blind and erroneous manner without having proper knowledge or understanding regarding the doctrine of the Lord's Supper. Just ask the great majority of members both here and in other localities how, in the Lord's Supper, the body and blood of Christ are eaten and drunk by them in a spiritual

manner, and thus with the mouth of true faith—and also how this external supper exercises an internal efficacy in them, thereby comforting and strengthening their hearts. Consider what the people know of this, and you will observe that they know absolutely nothing.

And yet, everything is at stake here! He who is entirely ignorant of this, and he who lacks a spiritual and experiential understanding of this, misuses the Lord's Supper and renders himself exceedingly guilty of the body and blood of the Lord. Oh, that the Holy Spirit would impress this upon the hearts of our people so that it would produce inward contrition and humiliation!

2. The Lord has also led me to see that however sound their confession of the true doctrine of the Lord's Supper may be, by far the majority among us partake of the Lord's Supper in a manner that, as to the root of the matter, differs little from the manner in which Roman Catholics partake thereof.

Dear friends, let me briefly demonstrate this to be so, and may you all give heed to my words. The Papists partake of the Lord's Supper in an entirely carnal manner. Their eating and drinking is merely external and with their physical mouths. They have no knowledge of a spiritual eating and drinking of Christ's body and blood with the mouth of true faith. However, this is also true for the majority among us, who merely eat and drink the bread and the wine externally with their physical mouths and are as ignorant of the spiritual eating and drinking of Christ's body and blood as are the Papists.

Furthermore, the Papists partake of the Lord's Supper as a good work, believing they will thereby be saved, and the same is true for the majority of our Reformed people. Many of you partake of the Lord's Supper by placing a great deal of confidence in your external profession of faith, believing that this renders you to be good and pious people who will surely be saved. Such thinking is prevalent and deeply embedded in the recesses of the hearts of men. Many are of the opinion that by partaking of the Lord's Supper, they have performed a good deed, and they are hopeful that God will thereupon be gracious to them, albeit that our Reformed doctrine, with which they are more or less acquainted intellectually, would not permit one to confess publicly such a notion.

Finally, partaking of the Lord's Supper does not render Roman Catholics any more holy or godly, for they remain the same carnal and unholy men and continue to live in their sins. However, anyone to whom the Lord has granted a measure of light can perceive that this is equally true for the majority of our Reformed, who but confess the truth with their lips. Irrespective of how frequently they partake of the Lord's Supper, they become neither a stitch better nor holier. They rather continue to be the same sinful and unrepentant persons, who become increasingly hardened and brazen in their sinful practices. There is no other explanation for this than that they partake of the Lord's Supper only externally, doing so as an external duty, the performance of which is void of faith and without a wholehearted repentance toward God.

Dear reader, may you be convicted of this by the compassionate grace of God, so that you may be exposed as to who you are and be persuaded of your grievous and wretched state outside of God and Christ. Oh, that the Lord would open your eyes and cause you to see that you still live in sin, are void of faith, and are the object of God's wrath! Oh, that you would see that your partaking of the Lord's Supper will help you as little as your external confession of the Reformed faith, and that it will add to the severity of your condemnation if you remain unrepentant and continue to live in your sins!

Oh, that inwardly you would be humbled and become contrite before the Lord regarding your sins and your miseries! If then you no longer can find within yourself either any comfort or anything to rely upon, there would be a true need for the Lord Jesus to be your surety and mediator, who would cause you to be reconciled with God and deliver you from your sins.

May you find rest for your soul only in knowing for yourself what it truly is to be united to Him by faith and thereby be made a suitable and legitimate partaker of the Lord's Supper. May the Lord grant this to you by the grace of His Holy Spirit and according to His good pleasure. Amen.

The Popish Mass and the Character of a
True Partaker of the Lord's Supper

Behold Israel after the flesh: are not they which eat of the sacrifices partakers of the altar? What say I then? that the idol is any thing, or that which is offered in sacrifice to idols is any thing? But I say, that the things which the Gentiles sacrifice, they sacrifice to devils, and not to God: and I would not that ye should have fellowship with devils. Ye cannot drink the cup of the Lord, and the cup of devils: ye cannot be partakers of the Lord's table, and of the table of devils

1 CORINTHIANS 10:18–21

Question 80: What difference is there between the Lord's supper and the popish mass?

Answer: The Lord's supper testifies to us that we have a full pardon of all sin by the only sacrifice of Jesus Christ, which He Himself has once accomplished on the cross; and, that we by the Holy Ghost are ingrafted into Christ, who, according to His human nature is now not on earth, but in heaven, at the right hand of God His Father, and will there be worshipped by us—but the mass teaches that the living and dead have not the pardon of sins through the sufferings of Christ, unless Christ is also daily offered for them by the priests; and further, that Christ is bodily under the form of bread and wine, and therefore is to be worshipped in them; so that the mass, at bottom, is nothing else than a denial of the one sacrifice and sufferings of Jesus Christ, and an accursed idolatry.

Question 81: For whom is the Lord's supper instituted?

Answer: For those who are truly sorrowful for their sins, and yet trust that these are forgiven them for the sake of Christ; and that their remaining infirmities are covered by His passion and death; and who also earnestly desire to have their faith more and more strengthened, and their lives more holy; but hypocrites, and such as turn not to God with sincere hearts, eat and drink judgment to themselves.

Question 82: Are they also to be admitted to this supper, who, by confession and life, declare themselves unbelieving and ungodly?

Answer: No; for by this, the covenant of God would be profaned and His wrath kindled against the whole congregation; therefore it is the duty of the Christian church, according to the appointment of Christ and His apostles, to exclude such persons by the keys of the kingdom of heaven till they show amendment of life.

Religious errors resemble the waves of the sea, for one wave successively causes another to emerge and to roll onward. Likewise, one error causes another to emerge, and these errors mutually stimulate and powerfully sustain one another. Once a person departs from the pathway of sound truth, he does not merely espouse one error. Rather, having begun to err, he increasingly errs and necessarily imbibes one error after another until, at last, he fully dispenses with the truth and is under the complete control of deceitfulness and error.

We have clear illustrations of this with Roman Catholicism and the errors that it espouses regarding the doctrine of the Lord's Supper. As we observed in the previous Lord's Day, these were initiated by the dreadful and abominable heresy that the bread and wine at the Lord's Supper are essentially transformed into the true body and blood of Christ. This, in turn, generated another heresy, which is no less wicked and abominable; namely, the so-called sacrifice of the Mass. This heresy has spawned yet another multitude of vile heresies whereby all the truths of God's Holy Word are rendered fully null and void. We will presently consider these matters in greater detail. Oh, that the Lord would shed forth His light upon us and lead us into His truth!

In this Lord's Day, the instructor addresses three matters. He teaches:

1. of what the popish Mass consists (Question 80);

2. what the requisite disposition or character must be of all true partakers of the Lord's Supper, for whom the Lord Jesus instituted this holy sacrament (Question 81); and

3. who must be barred from the sacrament as being unworthy of it (Question 82).

Since the latter of these are particularly applicable to us, we will focus primarily on them, and therefore be brief in our consideration of the popish Mass.

We will achieve this:

1. by expounding to some extent of what the popish Mass consists so that you may understand what is at stake here; and

2. by considering how the instructor refutes the popish Mass as he demonstrates that it is heretical and absurd.

Roman Catholicism derived the name *Mass* for its administration of the Lord's Supper from the Latin word *missa*. This, in turn, was derived from the erroneous and misguided practice of the early Christians in antiquity, for when the Lord's Supper was administered after the sermon, all who were not members were dismissed from the sanctuary. One of the deacons would publicly exclaim, "*Ite missa est*"; that is, "You must depart" or "You are being sent away."

These early Christians had neither authority nor power to act in this manner, for God's Word nowhere teaches that all who are not members of the congregation are to be dismissed from the sanctuary when the Lord's Supper is to be administered. On the contrary, it is better and more appropriate that they would remain in the sanctuary and witness the administration of the Lord's Supper with the hope that it would please the Lord to bless it unto their hearts. Therefore, we wish publicly to admonish all who are not yet professing members among us that they would not absent themselves from church when the Lord's Supper is to be administered—or, as some have done, leave the sanctuary when this is about to take place. Instead, they should remain in the sanctuary until the entire worship service has been concluded.

If all who are not professing members had to depart from the sanctuary when the sacrament of the Lord's Supper is to be administered, they also would have to depart when the sacrament of holy baptism is to be administered, for the one is no more a sign and seal of the covenant than is the other. Therefore, such departing is nothing other than a public despising of the holy sacraments and of public worship, and it cannot but follow that at His time, the Lord will punish such conduct.

All of this has culminated in the papal practice of assigning the name *Mass* or *missa* to the Lord's Supper. There is, however, neither the least support for this designation in the Word of God nor any support for the matter itself.

To explain in what the popish Mass actually consists, we shall set before you the words by which the Papists described and presented their doctrine at the Council of Trent: "The Sacrifice of the Mass is propitiatory both for the living and the dead. And forasmuch as, in this divine sacrifice which is celebrated in the mass, that same Christ is contained and immolated in an unbloody manner, who once offered Himself in a bloody manner on the altar of the cross; the holy Synod teaches, that this sacrifice is truly propitiatory and that by means thereof this is effected, that we obtain mercy" (22nd Session, Doctrine on the Sacrifice of the Mass, Chapter II).

This is the Roman Catholic Church's own description and representation of their doctrine. We recently observed how they posit in the Lord's Supper that the bread and wine are transformed into the true body and blood of Christ. Thereupon, it must be sacrificed by the hands of the priest (or the papal minister of the Mass) unto God to make atonement for the sins of both the living and the dead. Christians must therefore render religious worship unto this sacrifice. Anyone who has some knowledge and understanding regarding these matters will readily understand that this doctrine of the popish Mass rests entirely upon the foundation of transubstantiation, for Roman Catholics posit that in the Mass, they are sacrificing the body and blood of Christ as they issue forth from the bread and wine by way of transubstantiation.

In the previous Lord's Day, however, we used God's Word clearly and forcefully to refute the vile and ungodly doctrine of transubstantiation. Having completely dismantled it, the popish Mass has consequently been completely discredited. We could rest our case here without any further refutation of this heresy, but since the instructor proceeds explicitly with the refutation of the Mass, we shall briefly follow him.

Let me preface this by contributing something to this refutation apart from what the instructor has to say. As we have heard, Roman Catholics describe the Mass as being a real and true sacrifice, a sacrifice analogous to the Old Testament sacrifices. They describe the Mass as a sacrifice of the true body and blood of Christ, represented by the bread and wine—their sacrifice being made unto God by the hand of the priest unto the remission of the sins of the living and the dead, as well as unto the receipt of other graces and benefits from God.

If, however, the popish Mass is to be a true and real atoning sacrifice, it must necessarily contain all the components of a true and real atoning sacrifice. These components are six in number:

1. The sacrifice must be performed by lawful and true priests.

2. There must be a physical altar upon which this sacrifice is made.

3. There must be visible and tangible matter that is to be sacrificed.

4. This tangible substance must be visibly consumed upon the altar.

5. Real blood must be shed at the performance of such an atoning sacrifice.

6. In such a sacrifice, a gift must be dedicated unto God that man cannot in any way appropriate unto himself.

All of these must be true at the performance of all true and real atoning sacrifices. Roman Catholics are not able to point to a single atoning sacrifice in the Bible where these components are not all to be found. If, therefore, their Mass is to be a sacrifice in the true sense of the word, as they claim it to be, then these six components must be found in it.

We will now demonstrate to them that not a single one of these components is to be found in their Mass. Their fabrication will therefore of necessity implode.

First, there is no genuine and legitimate priest who executes the sacrifice of their Mass. Though they refer to their popish ministers as such, they are by no means either legitimate or genuine priests, for they have neither been called nor appointed to this office by way of a divine ordinance. In the New Testament, God abolished the entire physical priesthood. He prohibits anyone from functioning as such, for the former priesthood was merely a ministry of shadows that anticipated the ministry of Christ and His believing people. Therefore, in the New Testament, we read of no other priesthood than one that is both internal and spiritual.

Second, there is no actual and genuine altar upon which the Papists sacrifice their Mass, for the altar upon which they perform this sacrifice is as unlawful as the priest who is performing it. Again, in the New Testament, God abolished and prohibited the priesthood and the use of all physical altars. Paul clearly teaches this, saying regarding all true believers that "we have an altar [that is, Christ Jesus], whereof they have no right to eat which serve the tabernacle" (Heb. 13:10).

Third, the popish Mass does not consist of a visible and tangible sacrifice, but rather, is both invisible and intangible. The Papists claim indeed that they are sacrificing the body and blood of Christ under the appearance of bread and wine. Since, however, the body and blood of Christ are concealed by the appearance of bread and wine and are completely obscured thereby, they can neither be seen nor touched.

Fourth, in the popish Mass, there is no consumption of the sacrifice upon the altar, for the Papists themselves claim that only the external appearance of the bread and wine are consumed. Instead, they maintain that the body and blood of Christ, being the true and essential components of the sacrifice, remain in an unaltered state and are repeatedly sacrificed afresh.

Fifth, there is also no shedding of any blood in the popish Mass, for the Papists refer to it as an *unbloody* sacrifice. However, how can the Mass then be a true atoning sacrifice unto the remission of sin, considering that Paul teaches so plainly that "without shedding of blood is no remission" (Heb. 9:22b)?

Finally, nothing is either given or consecrated to the Lord in the popish Mass, for that which is sacrificed by the priest is completely consumed by him, and thus there is nothing that remains for the Lord.

Such are the six essential matters that constitute an atoning sacrifice according to the Holy Scriptures. None of them are to be found in the popish Mass, and it is therefore a reasonable conclusion that the Mass is by no means a true and genuine atoning sacrifice. Rather, it is a vile fabrication of Roman Catholicism for which there is not the least support in the Word of God, which is to be the sole foundation of all our doctrines.

Furthermore, the instructor now proceeds to refute the popish Mass by showing how it completely contradicts the true doctrine of the Lord's Supper as articulated in the Holy Scriptures. He therefore asks, "What difference is there between the Lord's supper and the popish mass?"

In his answer, the instructor gives three arguments for the obvious contradiction between the Lord's Supper and the popish Mass. He then concludes that the popish Mass is both heretical and abominable.

According to the instructor, the obvious contradiction between the Lord's Supper and the popish Mass consists in this: God's Word teaches that "the Lord's supper testifies to us, that we have a full pardon of all sin by the only sacrifice of Jesus Christ, which He Himself has once accomplished on the cross." We clearly and effectively demonstrated this in Lord's Day 23, when we dealt with the doctrine of the justification of the elect and believing sinner as being "of mere grace" and only on the basis of the merits of Christ.

We will now affirm this truth merely by way of a few passages from God's Word. In Ephesians 1:7, Paul testifies of Christ that believers have in Him "redemption through his blood, the forgiveness of sins." In 1 John 1:7, we read that "the blood of Jesus Christ his Son cleanseth us from all sin."

This truth is taught most clearly and effectively by Paul in Hebrews 9 and 10. There he demonstrates succinctly how the Lord Jesus once died and was sacrificed for all the sins of His believing people, saying that "by one offering he hath perfected for ever them that are sanctified" (Heb. 10:14). After this service, everyone ought to read these two chapters for themselves.

This truth is clearly taught in the Lord's Supper, for both the bread and wine signify and seal to believers their true and internal union with the Lord Jesus, and that His body was broken for them upon the cross and that His blood was shed on their behalf unto the complete remission of all their sins. This we addressed when we dealt with the doctrine of the Lord's Supper.

Now consider, according to the instructor, what is taught in the popish Mass, namely, "that the living and dead have not the pardon of sins through the sufferings of Christ, unless Christ is also daily offered for them by the priests." Such teaching flatly contradicts what the Holy Scriptures teach regarding the doctrine of the Lord's Supper.

The instructor then proceeds to present a second argument whereby the popish Mass is obviously contradictory to the doctrine of the Lord's Supper. He supports with Scripture the fact that the Lord's Supper teaches that believers "by the Holy Ghost are ingrafted into Christ, who, according to His human nature is now not on earth, but in heaven, at the right hand of God His Father, and will there be worshipped by us." Believers inwardly become partakers of His true body and blood. This we showed you from the Word of God when we expounded the doctrine of the Lord's Supper, having demonstrated how believers, by a spiritual eating and drinking of Christ's true body and blood with the mouth of true faith, are increasingly and inwardly united to the Lord Jesus and His holy body and blood, so that they become flesh of His flesh and bone of His bone.

The instructor then posits that the popish Mass is entirely in error by saying that "Christ is bodily under the form of bread and wine, and therefore is to be worshipped in them," teaching that believers physically eat Christ and, by such eating, are literally and physically united to Him. This obviously contradicts what the Holy Scriptures teach regarding the Lord's Supper.

The Lord's Supper reaffirms the truth of God's Word that Christ "according to His human nature is now not on earth, but in heaven, at the right hand of God His Father, and will there be worshipped by us." We extensively proved and addressed this truth in Lord's Days 18 and 19, when we expounded the doctrine of the Savior's ascension and His session at God's right hand. That this truth is also taught in the Lord's Supper has become evident as we have recently expounded this doctrine.

Again, the popish Mass teaches the very opposite, saying that "Christ is bodily under the form of bread and wine, and therefore is to be worshipped in them." All of this affirms clearly that the popish Mass teaches an entirely different doctrine from what God's Word teaches regarding the Lord's Supper.

The instructor therefore draws the following conclusion: "The mass, at bottom, is nothing else than a denial of the one sacrifice and sufferings of Jesus Christ, and an accursed idolatry." This is most certainly true, for by positing that the Mass is a daily sacrifice that must be performed for the sins of the living and the dead, one dishonors and denies publicly the one and only atoning sacrifice the Lord Jesus accomplished on the cross, implying that this sacrifice is neither sufficient nor capable for the removal of sin.

Furthermore, the instructor argues that the popish Mass "is at bottom… nothing else than…an accursed idolatry," for one worships the bread and the wine as one would worship God, thereby putting his trust in them.

Having expounded the doctrine of the Lord's Supper, and having further affirmed it over against the vile heresies of Roman Catholicism, the instructor now proceeds to consider who, according to the Holy Scriptures, may or may not partake of the Lord's Supper.

Regarding the first, the instructor asks in Question 81, "For whom is the Lord's supper instituted?" This is a most essential question, and it is a matter of utmost importance that we have a proper knowledge of this, for to the extent that people do not understand the mystery of the Lord's Supper due to their ignorance and foolhardiness, they likewise do not understand for whom the Lord's Supper has truly been instituted. Many therefore partake unworthily of the Lord's Supper, making themselves guilty of the body and blood of the Lord Jesus Christ. Oh, that men would receive grace from the Lord to consider this matter duly and that, with God's help, they would truly examine themselves!

The Lord instituted His supper only for His believing people; none but sincere believers, who are united to the Lord Jesus and are partakers of His body and blood, are invited to partake of it. For everyone's instruction and exhortation, it is therefore stated clearly in the Form for the Administration of the Lord's Supper that Christ "hath ordained [it] only for the faithful"; that is, only for those who believe in Him with true hearts and sincerely embrace Him and His grace, surrendering themselves to Him for justification, sanctification, complete redemption, putting all their trust in Him alone. They, and they alone, have a right to partake of the Lord's Supper.

In order that, by the grace of the Holy Spirit, everyone would rightly examine himself whether he be in the faith, the instructor sets before us three matters that must be found in us if we shall and rightly may partake of the Lord's Supper to the comfort and strengthening of our souls. We shall address them briefly.

According to the instructor, the first requisite that must be found in all true partakers of the Lord's Supper is that they "are truly sorrowful[1] for their sins."[2] This is as much as to say that by the convicting grace of the Lord's Holy Spirit, they must inwardly have a right knowledge of their sins and miseries; of their wickedness; of the innate as well as actual and abominable corruption of their souls; of their hell-worthiness; of their being subject to God's just curse and wrath; of their being subject and in bondage to Satan; and of their utter impotency within themselves to facilitate their salvation or redemption even in the least.

Furthermore, inwardly, and thus within their hearts, they must be truly humbled regarding their sins and miseries. They must be humbled and contrite before the Lord, and they must therefore loathe themselves that they

---

1. The Dutch rendering of this phrase is, "Voor degenen, die zichzelven vanwege hun zonden *mishagen*"; that is, they who *loathe* themselves because of their sins. The phrase "loathing themselves" is derived from Ezekiel 36:31, the text that is referenced by VanderGroe in his footnote below. This also explains his subsequent and repeated reference to this loathing of one's self.

2. VanderGroe adds this footnote: With this simple expression "truly sorrowful for their sins," the instructor articulates the entire doctrine of true contrition as it is also expressed in Ezekiel 36:31. This being sorrowful for sins consists of four matters:
1. the knowledge of sin as to its:
   a. origin, or in regard to original sin;
   b. pervasive corruption, or in regard to actual sin;
   c. incurred guilt as having been committed against an infinite, holy, majestic, and just God; and
   d. punishment, being eternal death;
2. the sorrow over sin, and being oppressed and troubled by God's wrath toward sin;
3. being ashamed of one's sins, and a loathing of one's self—both to be observed in the publican; and
4. the humbling of one's self before God, which is properly included in the Form for the Lord's Supper.
The means whereby this true knowledge of sin is acquired are the following:
   (1) God's law;
   (2) God's Spirit and His illuminating, convicting ministry.

are such vile, abominable, unclean, and despicable sinners, who in their perverse wickedness have thus sinned against the Lord and are inclined to sin
against Him in thoughts, words, and deeds. They must inwardly be sincerely
sorrowful and contrite regarding this, and they must have a heartfelt sorrow
after God.

Such an inward loathing of ourselves proceeds from a true knowledge
of our sins and miseries. We then no longer find anything good within ourselves, but we view ourselves as utterly polluted and abominable sinners who
are supremely guilty and condemned before the holy and righteous God. This
prompts us to look away from ourselves entirely as being utterly wicked, abominable, and impotent, and to put all our trust in Christ and His grace, and thus
seek our comfort and help outside of ourselves.

Such was the experience of Ephraim, who cried out, "Surely after that I was
turned, I repented; and after that I was instructed, I smote upon my thigh: I was
ashamed, yea, even confounded, because I did bear the reproach of my youth"
(Jer. 31:19).

Such loathing of oneself, such deep shame and humbling of oneself before
the Lord because of one's sins is to be found in all true believers—albeit not
always to the same extent and in the same measure. This is in proportion to
the light and grace one receives from the Lord, for the Lord promises this to
His people as being a benefit of His covenant with them, saying, "Then shall ye
remember your own evil ways, and your doings that were not good, and shall
lothe yourselves in your own sight for your iniquities and for your abominations" (Ezek. 36:31).

This is then the first requisite that must be found in us: we must be sorrowful for our sins and loathe ourselves because of them. Therefore, he who has
no true knowledge of his sins and does not truly humble himself before the
Lord in tender contrition, who still is thinking that something good is yet to be
found in him and is still able to find some comfort and delight within himself,
should by no means partake of the Lord's Supper.

The instructor then proceeds to address a second requisite that is no less
essential for all true partakers of the Lord's Supper: they "yet trust that these
sins are forgiven them for the sake of Christ; and that their remaining infirmities are covered by His passion and death." The loathing of oneself because of
one's sins is not alone sufficient. By no means! By the grace of the Holy Spirit,
this must be accompanied by a true and upright faith, whereby we, laboring
and heavy laden due to our sins and miseries, cannot find any help or comfort

within ourselves, and therefore cast the eyes of our souls upon the Lord Jesus as He is offered and presented of God in the gospel as our surety, mediator, head, and king. We then acknowledge Him to be fully able, all-sufficient, and willing to deliver us, purely out of free and sovereign grace, from all our sins; to reconcile us unto God; to sanctify and convert us; and, in our forsaking of all that is of ourselves, turn fully to Him, so that we are desirous to be most intimately united to Him and to be found in Him alone. In so doing, we take hold of Him and His strength and righteousness by a true faith unto our justification and sanctification, trusting in Him alone and in His fullness and grace for the forgiveness of our sins to obtain eternal salvation freely through Him alone.

Such a taking refuge by faith to the Lord Jesus with our sins and miseries, and such a casting of ourselves upon Him and His all-sufficiency and free grace in order to be saved, is the second requisite that must be found in a truly believing partaker of the Lord's Supper. If such a trusting in Christ and His grace is not truly found in someone, because he is still resting for his salvation in or upon something other than Christ, such a person may not partake of the holy supper of the Lord. If, however, he nevertheless does so, he will make himself guilty of the body and blood of the Lord by his unbelieving frame and the despising of Christ and His grace—even if he does so in blind ignorance.

However, they who, by the power of the Holy Spirit and with an upright faith, turn to the Lord Jesus as poor lost sinners, and in Him to God's free grace, certainly have this confidence of faith in their hearts and put into practice that of which the instructor here speaks: "that these [their sins] are forgiven them for the sake of Christ." This is the great promise of the gospel, for "to him give all the prophets witness, that through his name whosoever believeth in him shall receive remission of sins" (Acts 10:43). To claim that one desires the Lord Jesus and wholeheartedly believes in Him, and yet have no confidence that in Him "we have redemption through his blood, the forgiveness of sins, according to the riches of his grace" (Eph. 1:7), is to have only a treacherous and counterfeit faith, for he who truly believes in Christ with his heart receives Him and all His benefits in response to the promise of the holy gospel. He embraces Him as an all-sufficient, complete, and willing savior, and he appropriates Christ's righteousness and all His merits. Upon the basis of God's gracious promises, believers wholeheartedly trust "that these [their sins] are forgiven [them] for the sake of Christ."

If someone neither believes nor trusts in this, he neither acknowledges nor receives Christ as a complete and all-sufficient savior, but rejects Him and His promises in unbelief. Therefore, that which the instructor here sets before us is nothing more than the essential nature, character, and activity of true saving faith.

Nevertheless, it is also certain that this true faith and confidence regarding the forgiveness of sins is often very weak and deficient in God's children, and it is accompanied by many carnal doubts and satanic assaults. By the power of the Holy Spirit, however, they must always resist these doubts and assaults in order to prevail, seeking to have their faith progressively strengthened.

Wherever and whenever this confidence is truly and genuinely found in a person, however weak and feeble his faith may be, that person may and must freely approach the Lord's Table. The only requisite is that he be upright in his intentions and that he desire to have and to receive Jesus Christ entirely and solely as his savior, king, and redeemer, while forsaking all that is outside of Him.

The instructor then proceeds with a third requisite, which must be found in all true partakers of the Lord's Supper. It consists in that they "also earnestly desire to have their faith more and more strengthened, and their lives more holy." Thus, there must be in us a sincere inclination and a true heartfelt desire increasingly to deny ourselves and increasingly to surrender ourselves to the Lord Jesus, and by faith be increasingly united to Him. By His grace, we should also increasingly forsake all sin, and increase in true holiness and godliness before God and men.

It is evident from the nature of the matter itself that this desire must be truly found in us if we are rightly to partake of the Lord's Supper, for the Lord ultimately ordained and instituted this hallowed supper so that all true believers would thereby be strengthened in their faith by the grace of the Holy Spirit, and thereby increasingly progress and advance in true holiness and godliness. If the Lord's Supper is truly to achieve this objective in us, there must then necessarily be a heartfelt desire and longing that our faith be thus strengthened and our life thus sanctified.

This longing and desire is to be found in the hearts of all true believers. By the renewing work of the Holy Spirit, it is to be found at the very core of their hearts, for:

1. Where true faith resides in one's soul, that person can live only by and out of faith, thereby obtaining from the Lord the fullness of his salvation and

redemption. Consequently, such a person considers this to be a matter of great importance, wishing to do so within the context of this faith, with the desire that his faith be strengthened and increased. Nothing grieves him more than that his faith is so fragile, weak, and deficient. This, in turn, generates in the soul those earnest and sincere desires to have one's faith increasingly strengthened by all available means and by the Lord's grace. From this proceeds a great deal of prayer, striving, and persistent wrestling for the strengthening of one's faith, beseeching the Lord that He would help their unbelief. It necessarily follows that a true believer, particularly one whose faith is weak, has at the bottom of his heart an upright desire, stimulated continually by the Lord Himself, that his faith be increasingly strengthened by the grace of the Holy Spirit.

2. By the grace of the Holy Spirit, there is in the true believer also an inward and upright desire to improve his walk of life. By virtue of his gracious and inward renewal, a true believer, however weak he may be in faith, hates and abhors nothing more than sin. When he truly considers himself, he finds himself beset from all sides with very many sins and sinful deficiencies. By the inward illumination of the Holy Spirit, he perceives that his entire life is stained with sin, and that in him, that is, in his flesh, dwelleth no good thing (Rom. 7:18). It cannot but be that this grieves and perplexes him greatly, and causes him to humble himself before the Lord. This generates within him a heartfelt desire and longing, as he yearns that he might be delivered from his sins and that he would live a better, more holy and godly life in his walk before God and men.

A true believer, by the Holy Spirit's renewing ministry, has an intense desire and yearning for holiness according to the inner man. It would constitute his supreme blessedness if he could but be fully delivered from all sin and, with a perfect heart, walk according to all the Lord's commandments. His desire is that he would not yield to a single sin, however insignificant or trivial it may seem. It is his desire to be perfectly holy, as He who has called him is perfectly holy (1 Peter 1:16).

When such a sincere desire for the strengthening of faith and for the improvement of one's life is not to be found in truth, such a person ought not partake of the Lord's Supper, for he will otherwise only aggravate his judgment and condemnation.

Beloved, we have thus given you a simple description of what must necessarily be found in a true partaker of the Lord's Supper. When by the grace of the Holy Spirit, these things are truly found in a person, he may and must partake of the Lord's Supper, and with all the joy and freedom of our hearts, we permit such a person to approach the Lord's Table. It matters not whether he has previously been a member,[3] whether he is young or old,[4] whether he knows much or little, or whether he can read. We do not even consider these things if, by the grace of the Holy Spirit, he but possesses these three matters in truth as they have been set before us in all simplicity by the instructor. This alone is sufficient for the partaking of the Lord's Supper.

However, where these three matters are not found in truth in any person, he neither can nor may in any wise partake of the Lord's Supper—even if he has been a member of the church for many years, is very knowledgeable regarding the specific truths of God's Word, is a man highly esteemed by the world, is an office-bearer in the church, and his life outwardly proves to be very virtuous. If these three matters are not found in him, he may by no means partake of the Lord's Supper. The instructor therefore adds the following: "But hypocrites, and such as turn not to God with sincere hearts, eat and drink judgment to themselves."

By referring to "such as turn not to God with sincere hearts," the instructor is speaking indiscriminately of all unbelieving and unconverted men and women—be it that they live in public sin and are ungodly, are moral and reputable citizens, are ignorant or very knowledgeable, or whatever else may or may not be the case with them. If they lack even one of these three requisites, and thus do not truly loathe themselves due to their sins, or do not uprightly and by faith trust in Christ and His grace, or do not have a heartfelt desire for the strengthening of their faith and the betterment of their lives according to God's Word, the instructor testifies here, without any respect of persons, that, in accordance with Paul's explicit testimony in 1 Corinthians 11:29, they "eat and drink judgment to themselves."

By partaking of the Lord's Supper, all such persons aggravate their judgment and condemnation, and they make themselves guilty of the Lord's holy body and blood because they do not sincerely believe and repent of their sins.

---

3. VanderGroe is not saying here that church membership via public confession of faith is an indifferent matter, but he is stressing the necessity of personal, saving faith. One can be a church member and lack saving faith. As for those who have saving faith but lack as yet professing church membership, some Dutch Further Reformation divines allowed such people to attend the Lord's Supper once and then encouraged them to become a confessing church member as soon as possible.

4. VanderGroe here is not sanctioning paedo-communion, but is referring to younger and older believers who are of age to discern the Spirit's saving work within them.

Such persons, therefore, without any respect of person and as much as possible, must be barred from the Lord's Supper.

The instructor also addresses this by asking, "Are they also to be admitted to this supper, who, by confession and life, declare themselves unbelieving and ungodly?" Please consider that in accordance with God's Word, the instructor indiscriminately bars from the Lord's Table all "who, by confession and life, declare themselves unbelieving and ungodly." This refers to all of whom it becomes public knowledge and it can be demonstrated clearly by their verbal confession, as well as by their walk, that they do not truly believe in the Lord Jesus Christ. And thus, before God and the world, they do not live godly lives in conformity to the standard of Christianity.

We are referring to all offensive sinners, to all vain and worldly people; to all unrepentant sinners; to all who are ignorant; to all who teach false doctrine; to all who are accustomed to despise God's Word and public worship, and who neglect the assembling of themselves together; to all who are accustomed willfully to desecrate the Lord's Day by unnecessary labor or vain entertainment; to all who despise and spurn the ministers of the gospel; and to all who refuse to submit themselves obediently to the Christian ordinances of the church. In a word, we are referring to all who demonstrate by their talk or walk that they do not truly believe in God and neither serve nor fear Him uprightly. The instructor testifies here indiscriminately of them all that no such person may be permitted to partake of the Lord's Supper, for then "the covenant of God would be profaned, and His wrath kindled against the whole congregation."

There is no sin that provokes God more to wrath than the public defilement and desecration of His covenant by unbelievers and the ungodly—and also when this is permitted to take place without any restraint. God's wrath is then kindled against the entire congregation. This proved to be true in the congregation of Corinth, which was severely chastised by the Lord for having admitted unbelievers and offensive sinners freely to the fellowship of the Lord's Supper (1 Cor. 11:30).

"Therefore it is the duty of the Christian church, according to the appointment of Christ and His apostles, to exclude such persons, by the keys of the kingdom of heaven, till they show amendment of life." The ministers and elders of the congregation must, with utmost zeal and commitment, bar from the Lord's Supper all unbelieving and unconverted men, as well as all offensive sinners, to the end that their souls may be void of offense and God's covenant be not desecrated. In the next Lord's Day, the instructor will teach us how this is to be accomplished.

May the Lord bestow His gracious blessing upon these expositions about the Lord's Supper to the glory of His holy name and to the salvation of our souls. Amen.

The Keys of the Kingdom of Heaven
and Christian Discipline

And I will give unto thee the keys of the kingdom of heaven: and whatsoever thou shalt bind on earth shall be bound in heaven: and whatsoever thou shalt loose on earth shall be loosed in heaven.

—MATTHEW 16:19

Question 83: What are the keys of the kingdom of heaven?

Answer: The preaching of the holy gospel, and Christian discipline, or excommunication out of the Christian church; by these two, the kingdom of heaven is opened to believers and shut against unbelievers.

Question 84: How is the kingdom of heaven opened and shut by the preaching of the holy gospel?

Answer: Thus: when according to the command of Christ it is declared and publicly testified to all and every believer, that, whenever they receive the promise of the gospel by a true faith, all their sins are really forgiven them of God, for the sake of Christ's merits; and on the contrary, when it is declared and testified to all unbelievers, and such as do not sincerely repent, that they stand exposed to the wrath of God and eternal condemnation, so long as they are unconverted; according to which testimony of the gospel, God will judge them both in this and in the life to come.

Question 85: How is the kingdom of heaven shut and opened by Christian discipline?

Answer: Thus: when according to the command of Christ, those, who under the name of Christians, maintain doctrines or practices inconsistent therewith, and will not, after having been often brotherly admonished, renounce their errors and wicked course of life, are complained of to the church, or to those who are thereunto appointed by the church; and if they despise their admonition, are by them forbidden the use of the sacraments; whereby they are excluded from the Christian church and by God Himself from the kingdom of Christ; and when they promise and show real amendment, are again received as members of Christ and His church.

The preeminent basis for all human societies and civil relationships is a well-ordered government to which everyone's actions and activities are subjected, having beneficial laws according to which the good are rewarded and the wicked and disobedient are punished. Given the corrupt state of the world, it would be absolutely impossible that a beneficent society of men could exist without such means.

This is also true for the external church or congregation of Christ, consisting of those who profess the Christian faith outwardly and are gathered into a body and congregation by the preaching of the gospel, as well as by the administration of the sacraments. Such a church or visible congregation can by no means exist without sound government, beneficial laws, and the orderly administration of discipline.

Since most professing members are unregenerate and carnal men who confess Christianity only outwardly, and since they are yet completely in Satan's bondage, they are prone to the commission of grievous sins and improprieties both as to their confession and their walk. They break forth into such misconduct to a greater or lesser degree, and thereby disgrace the gospel and the name of Christ. Even true believers, due to the weakness and perverseness of their flesh, occasionally fall into grievous and offensive sins.

If such a church is therefore to remain steadfast in regard to sound doctrine and godliness, and if everything is to be conducted in good order, there must be not only essential and beneficial laws for everyone, but also a benevolent government that is authorized and empowered to comfort the good and to pronounce peace upon them, and to punish the wicked and the unfaithful, so that by God's grace and in this way, they may be led to repentance, faith, and improvement of life.

Christ has ordained and instituted such laws, governments, and discipline in His church here upon earth. We will now consider this in more detail. In the previous Lord's Day, the instructor taught that upon the command of Christ and His apostles, it is the duty of the Christian church to bar from the Lord's Supper, by means of the keys of the kingdom of heaven, all who manifest themselves as being unbelieving and ungodly by their confession or walk. In connection herewith, he proceeds in Lord's Day 31 to deal more specifically with these keys of the kingdom of heaven, consisting of the sound discipline and order of the church. With the help of the Lord, we shall follow suit.

As is his custom, the instructor addresses these matters in a very appropriate and efficient manner, expounding for us:

1. what we are to understand by the phrase *the keys of the kingdom of heaven* (Question 83); and
2. the lawful use of these keys according to Christ's command and ordinance (Questions 84 and 85).

Regarding the exposition of the keys of the kingdom of heaven, we must consider:

1. the terminology; and
2. the matter itself, as communicated to us by way of this terminology.

Regarding the terminology, you already have heard, from the reading of our text, how Christ speaks of the good discipline, order, and government of His church. When He commanded His apostles accordingly, promising that He would empower them subsequent to His departure, He spoke to them of this by using the terminology *the keys of the kingdom of heaven*. By the kingdom of heaven, we are to understand the very essence of that glorious and blessed state of grace in which God, in Christ and by the Holy Spirit, has dominion over the soul—a state in which men fully and inwardly submit themselves as subjects to the triune God as their lawful king and Lord, doing so by forsaking all that is of themselves and of all that is of the dominion of Satan and the world.

All men are by nature in the kingdom of the devil and consequently reject God's government and fully serve themselves, the world, and sin. The reprobate will eternally live in this kingdom of Satan, a kingdom of darkness, and do so with delight, pleasure, and relish, without ever having any interest in God and His kingdom. For the elect, there comes a moment, however, when they depart from Satan's kingdom in the way of faith and repentance, and they then willingly submit to the power of Christ and enter through Him into the kingdom of God. Through Christ, they are reconciled with God, and by the renewing ministry of the Holy Spirit, they subject themselves unto Him and are thereby fully at His disposal. Initially, this occurs at the time of regeneration and conversion, and this continues to be so by the progressive and sanctifying ministry of the Holy Spirit, until at last they do so perfectly upon the glorification of both soul and body.

In His Word, the Lord Jesus exhorts that we seek first this kingdom of God, saying, "But seek ye first the kingdom of God, and his righteousness, and all these things shall be added unto you" (Matt. 6:33); that is, diligently endeavor in all things first to be God's subjects and to forsake the kingdom of Satan, and then all other things of which you have need will necessarily be provided for you. This is the kingdom of God that one can neither see nor enter "except a man be born of water and of the Spirit" (John 3:3–5). It is indeed for the coming of this kingdom that Christ commands us to pray daily (Matt. 6:10).

This kingdom of God has existed from the very foundation of the world. However, in the New Testament and subsequent to Christ's death on the cross, God has established and expanded it among men in a most glorious manner by completely abolishing the Old Testament ministry of shadows. He now desires nothing but that His subjects serve Him in the Spirit and in the obedience of faith. John the Baptist had this in view when he proclaimed, "Repent ye: for the kingdom of heaven is at hand" (Matt. 3:2).

This kingdom of God is here denominated as the kingdom of heaven, because it is not an earthly, but a spiritual and heavenly kingdom. We shall expound in more detail that the king, His subjects, His laws, and His possessions are all spiritual and heavenly in nature. How blessed they all are who may be subjects of this kingdom of heaven and who, by God, have been drawn out of the dominion of darkness and translated into His kingdom!

To this kingdom of God, this kingdom of heaven, Christ ascribes the keys He promises to give to His apostles, saying, "I will give unto thee the keys of the kingdom of heaven." In connection with this, we need to understand that God's kingdom, consisting of believers who truly are elect, called, and sanctified, and who serve and obey God in Christ and by the Holy Spirit, is compared in the Holy Scriptures to a city surrounded by walls with gates that are opened and closed (Rev. 11:2). It is also compared to a house that is opened and closed by means of a door (1 Tim. 3:15).

In the same manner as a city or a house has keys whereby its gates and doors are either opened or closed, admitting those who are good and denying entry to those who work wickedness, God's spiritual kingdom likewise has keys by which it is opened unto the good, that is, unto His righteous people, so that they may thereby enter in, whereas it is closed unto the wicked, who are thereby denied entry. He who is the lawful proprietor of these keys is able therewith to open and shut God's kingdom. In essence, these keys consist in the power to open the kingdom of heaven to some, enabling its true subjects to enter in freely (and, in actuality, they also do enter in), whereas it is shut to others so that they by no means shall enter in, but are denied entry and shut out by virtue of being disobedient rebels.

These keys of God's kingdom can be one's lawful possession in a twofold manner, and they differ substantially from one another. One has possession of them in an absolute and supreme sense, whereas all others possess them in a subordinate and ministerial manner. No one but Christ possesses the keys of God's kingdom in an absolute and supreme sense. He is the sovereign Lord and King of the kingdom of heaven, and therefore He alone has the power either to open or to close it unto whomsoever He wills. Consequently, Christ is expressly denominated as "he that hath the key of David, he that openeth, and no man shutteth; and shutteth, and no man openeth" (Rev. 3:7).

He who thus desires to be a subject of the living God and who desires to enter into the kingdom of heaven must first of all turn to Christ Jesus and beseech of Him that, by the keys of His Word and Spirit, He would be pleased to open the kingdom of God for him and to bring him into it, thereby delivering him from the kingdom of Satan and the world.

Second, the keys of the kingdom of heaven are also held in possession in a subordinate and ministerial manner by the ambassadors and servants of Christ, who, here on earth, are appointed by Him to oversee the government of His kingdom and, according to His command, to open it unto the good and to close it unto the wicked. This is analogous to rulers and kings who give to their servants the keys of their cities, their gardens, and their residences, authorizing them, in conformity with their commission, to open and to shut them. This ministerial use of the keys of the kingdom of heaven is the actual subject of our consideration.

The instructor proceeds by inquiring of these keys, "What are the keys of the kingdom of heaven" by which the kingdom of God here upon earth is opened to the good and shut to the wicked by Christ's servants? He responds, "The preaching of the holy gospel, and Christian discipline, or excommunication out of the Christian church; by these two, the kingdom of heaven is opened to believers, and shut against unbelievers."

You will observe that the keys of the kingdom of heaven are two in number:

The first key is the *proclamation or preaching of the holy gospel*. We addressed this in Lord's Day 25, when we expounded how the Holy Spirit works and strengthens the faith of God's children by the preaching of the holy gospel. We then demonstrated to you that in its essence, the proclamation of the holy gospel consists of the precious presentation and revelation of the counsel of God's gracious redemption in Christ Jesus. We have shown how God not only was pleased, but that He also purposed completely within Himself, to justify, sanctify, redeem, and save an ungodly, hell-worthy, accursed, and impotent sinner, doing so without there being any worthiness, strength, merit, or wisdom on the part of the sinner, and thus freely and purely by sovereign grace alone in and through the crucified mediator, Christ Jesus, His Son.

We have also shown how, to that end, He caused all the fullness of light, righteousness, and strength to dwell in Christ for the poor, blind, and naked sinner, offering Him freely and graciously in all His fullness, as well as His all-sufficiency, to the hell-worthy sinner, promising to all sinners that through Him they may receive the pardon of their sins and eternal life.

All that remains for the sinner to do is to be well pleased with this counsel of God's gracious redemption in Christ Jesus, and, while forsaking himself and all things, to receive willingly and with a heartfelt delight out of God's hand this offered surety and mediator with all of His fullness and all-sufficiency. He then completely rests and trusts in Him for the entire work of His redemption and salvation without contributing or desiring to contribute anything thereto, but only acknowledging God to be faithful and true regarding what He has testified of His Son that the life of the world is in Him.

Beloved, this is the proclamation of the holy gospel, and it is one of the two keys whereby the kingdom of heaven is opened and shut.

The instructor then posits that *Christian discipline* is the second key, saying that this key is that of "Christian discipline, or excommunication out of the Christian church." The essence of Christian discipline is the exercise of ecclesiastical discipline to maintain good order in the church and to bring to repentance all offensive sinners and disobedient members of the congregation according to Christ's command.

Christian discipline has always been exercised by the church, and this must necessarily be so, in order that the congregation of the Lord may thereby be cleansed from sins and offenses, but also that everyone would be fearful of such offenses and be self-disciplined to such an extent that, at least outwardly, they would live blamelessly before the world. Such discipline constitutes the second key of the kingdom of God. The instructor will subsequently demonstrate that by means of these two keys, the kingdom of heaven is opened to believers and shut to unbelievers.

However, we must first briefly consider to whom the Lord Jesus has given and entrusted these keys of the kingdom of heaven. They have His authority and His command to open the kingdom of heaven unto the good and to shut it unto the wicked with these keys. Since the Savior now physically resides in heaven and normally works through means, it is essential that He has servants here upon earth by whom He can govern and build up His congregation. To achieve this, "He gave some, apostles; and some, prophets; and some, evangelists; and some, pastors and teachers; for the perfecting of the saints, for the work of the ministry, for the edifying of the body of Christ" (Eph. 4:11–12).

Initially, Christ gave the keys of the kingdom of heaven to Peter and the other apostles, who were appointed to be the overseers of His congregation on His behalf. This is confirmed by our text, in which He says to them, "And I will give unto thee the keys of the kingdom of heaven." Subsequent to the death of the apostles, Christ gave these keys to those pastors and teachers whom He appointed to be overseers of His congregation in the place of the apostles, and today this is also true for all who, by a lawful calling, have been appointed by Christ wherever His church or congregation gathers.

The pastors, teachers, and overseers of the congregation have received the keys of the kingdom of heaven from the Lord Jesus so that, in His Name, they would use them to direct and govern the congregations entrusted to their care.

Regarding this, it should be noted:

First, that the oversight and use of the keys of the kingdom of heaven is a purely spiritual administration from which the secular authorities are entirely excluded, considering that Christ said His kingdom is not of this world.

Second, that the pastors and teachers, in their ministry and in their use of the keys of the kingdom of heaven, must act in full conformity to Christ's command, and they may not in the least use their authority arbitrarily or in partiality, for if they act contrary to Christ's command, even in the very least, the congregation neither may nor must by any means obey them; and

Third, the office of the civil government toward the church consists in this:

1. to establish the church in the land and to eradicate all false religions and heresies;

2. to stipulate and formulate, from and according to the Holy Scriptures in the lawful ecclesiastical assemblies of the church, what the canons of doctrine and discipline should be for the

church, doing so with the counsel, assistance, and acquiescence of the servants of the church;

3. to see to it that the servants of the church faithfully discharge their respective offices according to these canons of doctrine and discipline;

4. to use its political power in the service of the church by effectively protecting it against all interference regarding the discharge of their respective offices; and

5. to use all available means to sustain public worship and the ministry of the church's office-bearers.

Let us now proceed, briefly considering in what the use of the keys of God's kingdom consists and in what manner the pastors and teachers, in Christ's name, open and shut the kingdom of God here on earth. The instructor expounds this with utmost clarity in regard to each key.

Regarding the first key, the preaching of the holy gospel, the instructor asks in Question 84, "How is the kingdom of heaven opened and shut by the preaching of the holy gospel?" to which he answers, "Thus: when according to the command of Christ it is declared and publicly testified to all and every believer, that, whenever they receive the promise of the gospel by a true faith, all their sins are truly forgiven them of God for the sake of Christ's merits; and on the contrary, when it is declared and testified to all unbelievers, and such as do not sincerely repent, that they stand exposed to the wrath of God and eternal condemnation, so long as they are unconverted; according to which testimony of the gospel, God will judge them both in this and in the life to come."

Here the instructor teaches:

1. how the kingdom of heaven is opened when the pastors and teachers proclaim the holy gospel; and

2. how, in the proclamation of the gospel, they shut the kingdom of heaven.

As to the first, the kingdom of God is opened by the preaching of the holy gospel "when according to the command of Christ it is declared and publicly testified to all and every believer, that, whenever they receive the promise of the gospel by a true faith, all their sins are truly forgiven them of God for the sake of Christ's merits."

The matter itself is plain and simple. The gospel in its essence is the proclamation of the promises of God, in which God causes the forgiveness of sins and eternal life in Christ to be proclaimed and freely offered to all perplexed sinners who yearn for salvation, inviting them to embrace and receive this offered salvation and grace accordingly by a true and upright faith.

The apostles, according to Christ's command, proclaimed the gospel of pure grace to both Jews and Gentiles in this manner, promising, in the name of the Lord, to all and every believer, the forgiveness of sins through Christ. Peter thus preached to the Jews on the day of Pentecost, saying, "Repent, and be baptized every one of you in the name of Jesus Christ for the remission of sins" (Acts 2:38). Paul thus preached to the Jews in their synagogue at Antioch of Pisidia, saying, "Be it known unto you therefore, men and brethren, that through this man is preached unto you the forgiveness of sins: and by him all that believe are justified from all things" (Acts 13:38–39).

In like fashion, this precious gospel of God's grace in Christ is still preached wherever the Lord causes His gospel to be preached, for it is an eternal and immutable gospel. Presently, God causes His Son, Jesus Christ, to be presented to all sinners as an able and all-sufficient surety, mediator, and redeemer, promising them through Him, freely and purely by grace, the forgiveness of sins and eternal salvation.

If, however, a needy sinner is to become a true partaker of Christ Jesus and of the forgiveness of sins, and thus of salvation through Him, the Holy Spirit must work in him a true and upright faith, whereby, looking away from and forsaking all that is of self, he takes complete refuge to the promises of the gospel, receiving with a true heart Christ Jesus as He is set before him by the Father as a complete surety and mediator. In so doing, the sinner embraces the gracious benefits of the forgiveness of sins and eternal life through Christ, fully resting for his salvation and redemption in this divinely ordained way.

If, by the grace of the Holy Spirit, someone truly engages himself as such, he truly and immediately receives of God, through Christ and by grace, the complete forgiveness of all his sins. Thereby he becomes a child and subject of God, and will be received as an heir of eternal life.

However, as often as he subsequently falls into new sins by virtue of weakness (as takes place frequently every day), and in so doing again becomes guilty and hell-worthy before God, when, laden with his guilt and sin, he again takes refuge to the promises of the gospel and embraces them with a true faith, so often does such a person receive by renewal from God in Christ a gracious acquittal and pardon of all his sins.

God causes this truth to be repeatedly proclaimed to all believers by the pastors and teachers of the congregation. This is the commission of the ministers of the gospel, and Christ commands them, as His ambassadors and in His name, that they must ceaselessly comfort His people, proclaiming these glad tidings to all true believers, that "whenever they receive the promise of the gospel by a true faith, all their sins are truly forgiven them of God for the sake of Christ's merits."

As with a key, the kingdom of heaven is opened to all true believers, and it is publicly proclaimed to them on Christ's behalf that they are God's true children and subjects, that God is eternally reconciled with them, that they may acknowledge Him to be their merciful king and gracious Father in Christ, that they may expect all good things from Him for the sake of Christ, and that they will eternally be partakers of all the benefits of God's kingdom.

Such is the way in which the kingdom of God is opened to all and every believer by the preaching and proclamation of the holy gospel.

The same key by which the kingdom of heaven is opened is also the key that fully shuts it to unrepentant and unbelieving sinners. The instructor therefore proceeds by saying, "On the contrary, when it is declared and testified to all unbelievers, and such as do not sincerely repent, that they stand exposed to the wrath of God and eternal condemnation, so long as they are unconverted: according to which testimony of the gospel, God will judge them both in this and in the life to come."

"Unbelievers, and such as do not sincerely repent" refers to all who refuse to embrace the promises of the gospel with a true faith, and who, in response to the proposition of the gospel, do not sincerely desire to be justified and sanctified of all their sins by grace and in Christ's blood. They do not want to forsake all and fully surrender themselves to Christ—however sound they may pretend their confession to be and however attractive their demeanor of godliness may appear to be. Such would rather remain unconverted and would rather continue in their sins while flattering themselves with a false and vain hope that they shall be saved by Christ as much as others. To such an unbelieving and unrepentant people, whatever their state or condition may be and irrespective of whether they are young or old, Christ commissions His servants publicly to declare in His Name "that they stand exposed to the wrath of God, and eternal condemnation, so long as they are unconverted."

Such is the language of the Holy Scriptures, for we read in John 3:36, "He that believeth on the Son hath everlasting life: and he that believeth not the Son shall not see life; but the wrath of God abideth on him." In John 3:5, we read, "Verily, verily, I say unto thee, Except a man be born of water and of the Spirit, he cannot enter into the kingdom of God."

Therefore, ministers may not preach in any other way to unbelievers and the unrepentant, no matter how angry and bitter their hearers may become in response to their preaching, no matter whether the unbelieving and unrepentant intensely hate, revile, and slander them, and no matter if they will be greatly persecuted and oppressed by them or killed by them. Ministers may therefore not alter their preaching in the least, but they must continue steadfastly in the might and power of the Lord, and publicly proclaim and declare in the name of God "that [unbelievers and the unrepentant] stand exposed to the wrath of God, and eternal condemnation, so long as they are unconverted." They must proclaim to them that they will most certainly be sent away into hell and will not be saved to all eternity as long as they do not repent, for Christ Himself testifies, "He that believeth not the Son shall not see life; but the wrath of God abideth on him" (John 3:36).

Paul testifies to all men who impenitently continue to live in their sins, saying, "After thy hardness and impenitent heart treasurest up unto thyself wrath against the day of wrath and revelation of the righteous judgment of God" (Rom. 2:5). If sinners persist in being unrepentant and unbelieving, ministers must faithfully continue to pronounce upon them God's curse, God's wrath, and eternal condemnation, and they are not to desist even if people are not willing to listen to their preaching. Such was the experience of their Lord and master, who, with the exception of a few, was forsaken by all because of the hardness of their hearts and their intolerance of His doctrine (John 6).

When ministers preach this way, the kingdom of heaven is shut to all who are unrepentant and unbelieving, for, according to Christ's command, it is declared to them that because of their unbelief and their failure to repent, "they stand exposed to the wrath of God and eternal condemnation." Salvation shall eternally be denied them as long as they remain in this state, and it is proclaimed to them that they have no part in the kingdom of Christ. They do not belong to it, for the dogs and "all that defileth" shall be without (Rev. 21:27; 22:15).

So that no one in any way would despise or lightly esteem the preaching of God's servants and ambassadors, the instructor adds, "according to which testimony of the gospel, God will judge them, both in this, and in the life to come." Even as the ministers are preaching here according to Christ's command, so it shall truly be and transpire, for they are not preaching in their own names, but only in the name of God and Christ. Since they are His servants and ambassadors, God Himself is preaching through them, and their preaching to both believers and unbelievers is completely in accordance with truth, and everyone is to esteem and receive it as such.

Christ said to His apostles, and in them to all His servants and ministers, "And I will give unto thee the keys of the kingdom of heaven: and whatsoever thou shalt bind on earth shall be bound in heaven: and whatsoever thou shalt loose on earth shall be loosed in heaven" (Matt. 16:19). In John 20:23, Christ says to His apostles, and thus to all ministers of the gospel, "Whose soever sins ye remit, they are remitted unto them; and whose soever sins ye retain, they are retained" (John 20:23). Paul testified emphatically that "God shall judge the secrets of men by Jesus Christ according to my gospel" (Rom. 2:16)—the gospel he had everywhere preached.

Oh, that everyone would truly believe this truth! How much more the preaching of ministers would be taken to heart, for God shall judge in conformity to what they have preached upon Christ's command!

We have thus seen how, by the use of the first key of the preaching of the holy gospel, the kingdom of God, upon Christ's command, is opened to all true believers and shut to all who neither repent nor believe.

It now remains for us to expound for you the second key, that is, Christian discipline. The instructor therefore asks in Question 85, "How is the kingdom of heaven shut and opened by Christian discipline?" He responds, "Thus: when according to the command of Christ, those, who under the name of Christians, maintain doctrines or practices inconsistent therewith, and will not, after having been often brotherly admonished, renounce their errors and wicked course of life, are complained of to the church or to those who are thereunto appointed by the church; and if they despise their admonition, are by them forbidden the use of the sacraments; whereby they are excluded from the Christian church and by God Himself from the kingdom of Christ."

By the instructor's answer, you will observe that the essence of Christian discipline is someone's complete excommunication from the Christian congregation of which he formerly was an external member. Christian discipline fully cuts off a person from the congregation as being one who is a useless, corrupt, and harmful member. Consequently, he no longer remains a member of the Christian congregation, but is excluded from her fellowship. Upon your arrival at home after the service, you ought to read the form for excommunication, and you will receive further instruction regarding the nature of Christian discipline.

The instructor posits that according to the command of Christ, this key of Christian discipline must be used toward all "who under the name of Christians, maintain doctrines or practices inconsistent therewith." He is referring to those who either teach a false or heretical doctrine that strongly contradicts the doctrine of Christ, or who live a life of offensive sin and ungodliness that contradicts the nature and essence of true Christianity. Generally such persons profess the name of Christ outwardly and reside within the Christian congregation. According to the instructor, all who manifest the foregoing sins in their lives must first be frequently admonished to repent, and they are to conduct themselves in both life and doctrine in a manner worthy of being called a Christian.

If they refuse to give heed to these frequent admonitions, and instead stubbornly persevere in being unchristian either in doctrine or in life, they must be brought to the attention of the congregation, that is, to the attention of her elders, and they too must first earnestly rebuke them and urge them to repentance.

If they also give no heed to them, and instead impenitently persist either in adhering to their evil doctrine or in living offensively, then the elders must forbid them the use of the sacraments, and so, by barring them for a season, they may ascertain whether by this means they might be brought to repentance.

If this also proves fruitless, then such as stubbornly persevere in their sins must, by the exercise of Christian discipline, be fully excommunicated from the Christian congregation. They are then no longer either to be considered as members of Christ or to be viewed as Christians, but they are to be viewed by us as heathens and publicans.

All of this must transpire according to the command of Christ as we find it expressed in Matthew 18:15–18, as well as according to the testimony of the holy apostle Paul (1 Cor. 5:11; 2 Thess. 3:14–15; Titus 3:10).

They who are excommunicated from the Christian congregation by her elders, must, according to the instructor, be viewed as having been excluded from the kingdom of Christ by God Himself, and in that state they can in no wise be saved.

Such, then, is the manner in which the kingdom of God is shut to sinners by using the key of Christian discipline, and such exclusion must continue until such sinners, according to the instructor, "promise and show real amendment," for they then can be "again received as members of Christ and of His church." This takes place when the excommunication is reversed of those who, by a true faith and repentance toward the Lord, fully distance themselves from the error of their way. Then, by renewal, they are received into the bosom of the congregation and readmitted to the holy sacraments. Thereby the kingdom of heaven, which had before been shut to them, is then again opened for them.

Beloved, we have set before you, according to God's Word, the true doctrine regarding the keys of the kingdom of heaven. Oh, how everyone ought to be greatly concerned and exercised whether he is a true subject of the kingdom of heaven! Only in that kingdom is eternal salvation to be found, and outside thereof is nothing but eternal misery and perdition. Whoever still is outside of this kingdom:

- is still a rebellious and disobedient enemy of God;
- is still subject to God's wrath;
- is still in the kingdom of Satan; and
- has nothing to look forward to but eternal perdition.

On the contrary, he who is in this kingdom:

- lives in a relationship of peace and friendship with God;
- serves and obeys God;
- fully forsakes the service of Satan and of sin;
- already enjoys the firstfruits of salvation; and
- may most certainly look forward to eternal salvation.

Therefore, all who are not yet in the kingdom of God must examine themselves most earnestly. We are referring to those:

- who do not yet know God and still dwell in darkness;
- who do not yet believe in the Lord Jesus with a true heart and who have not yet fully submitted themselves in obedience to His scepter;
- who neither have fully forsaken the kingdom of Satan and the world nor do battle against it;
- who are not yet born again, and who have not yet repented of their sins and turned unto God;

- for whom their salvation is not yet found solely in serving and obeying Christ in purity of heart, but who serve sin and the world;
- who despise the preaching of the holy gospel, whether they neglect to hear it or, though they faithfully hear it, neither receive, believe, nor obey it;
- who despise Christian or ecclesiastical discipline, do not fear it, and, when subjected to it, do not repent; and
- who do not obey their ministers and elders, and have no regard for their admonitions.

Oh, that all such would:

- know their wretched state,
- become truly perplexed and contrite,
- have a true yearning and desire to become true subjects of the kingdom of God, and
- take refuge entirely to Jesus, who alone can transform them into such a people and is "He that hath the key of David, he that openeth, and no man shutteth; and shutteth, and no man openeth" (Rev. 3:7)!

It is our desire that the Lord would graciously bless our exposition to that end, and that He would so strengthen His subjects, working in them by His Spirit, that they would walk worthy of the gospel and of the name "Christian" whereby the followers of Christ are called.

May the Lord keep from His congregation all sin and offensive conduct, and may He increasingly clothe His people with the adornment of true godliness and holiness, to the end that they would always manifest themselves as a rod of His planting and as a work of His hands, so that He would be glorified. Amen—so be it by the grace of our God and savior Christ Jesus.

The Necessity of Good Works

The great God and our Saviour Jesus Christ; who gave himself for us, that he might redeem us from all iniquity, and purify unto himself a peculiar people, zealous of good works.

—TITUS 2:13b–14

Question 86: Since then we are delivered from our misery, merely of grace, through Christ, without any merit of ours, why must we still do good works?

Answer: Because Christ, having redeemed and delivered us by His blood, also renews us by His Holy Spirit after His own image; that so we may testify, by the whole of our conduct, our gratitude to God for His blessings, and that He may be praised by us; also, that every one may be assured in himself of his faith by the fruits thereof; and that, by our godly conversation others may be gained to Christ.

Question 87: Cannot they then be saved, who, continuing in their wicked and ungrateful lives, are not converted to God?

Answer: By no means; for the Holy Scripture declares that no unchaste person, idolator, adulterer, thief, covetous man, drunkard, slanderer, robber, or any such like, shall inherit the kingdom of God.

In the words of the text, the apostle Paul sets before his son Titus not only Christ's eternal love and grace on behalf of His people by giving and sacrificing Himself for them, but also the glorious and precious purpose for which He did so, namely, "that he might redeem us from all iniquity, and purify unto himself a peculiar people, zealous of good works." With the entire world, Christ's believing people were by nature sold under sin, utterly hostile toward God, haters of all godliness, and dead in trespasses and sins. However, the great savior,

Christ Jesus, came into the world to give Himself for His elect and believing people, doing so not only to deliver them from God's curse and wrath, as well as from eternal damnation, but also to deliver them from sin itself and all unrighteousness, sanctifying and renewing them by His Spirit so that they would be a peculiar people unto Him, zealous of good works.

Nothing is further from the truth than to suggest that they who have been delivered by Christ and are under grace still live in some measure in sin and serve unrighteousness, for by virtue of the redemption in Christ Jesus, they must fully and eternally depart from all unrighteousness. Henceforth, they must walk in newness of life, worthy of the gospel of Christ and of the holy and heavenly calling with which they have been called. No less can a good tree bring forth evil fruits than a redeemed believer would be able to continue to live in sin and have fellowship with sinners. This is by no means possible, for upon his soul being united to the Lord Jesus, he became a new creature. Therefore, he cannot possibly do anything other than live a new and godly life, and bring forth fruits worthy of repentance by the power of Christ and His Holy Spirit.

In this Lord's Day, the instructor addresses this truth in greater detail, proceeding with the third segment of his instruction. In the first and second segments of his Catechism, he expounded, in a very transparent, simple, and straightforward manner, the entire work of the redemption of elect believers by the Lord Jesus. In the third and final segment, he proceeds to explain the great purpose and necessary consequence of this glorious redemption by Jesus Christ, that is, the sanctification and renewal of all His believing people according to His image, whereby He purifies "unto himself a peculiar people, zealous of good works."

The instructor will proceed to address this great and weighty matter of sanctification in an excellent and most suitable manner. In this and subsequent Lord's Days, he will expound:

1. The requisite and essential obligation of all redeemed believers who have been graciously delivered by Christ from their sins and miseries. Being His property, believers are obliged, with soul and body, fully to live to His honor and glory. They are therefore to depart from all iniquity and to abound in good works and in all fruits of righteousness, to the praise and glory of God through Jesus Christ.

2. The absolute necessity of sanctification, and, upon having done so, the instructor will expound in Lord's Day 33 the way or means

whereby all redeemed believers are rendered capable of such holiness or newness of life, namely, by a true conversion of the heart that Christ works in them by His Holy Spirit. As a result, they mortify the old man of sin in all its motions and lusts, and "put on the new man, which after God is created in righteousness and true holiness" (Eph. 4:24). By such a conversion, they become fully desirous to walk in newness of life and to do all good works, doing so in a manner worthy of their calling and redemption as it is in Christ Jesus.

3. The good works of redeemed and converted believers, which they wholeheartedly desire to do and whereby they serve and glorify God through Christ.

4. How all good works must fully conform to what is prescribed in God's holy law. The instructor will therefore proceed to address God's holy law in Lord's Days 34 through 44. He will expound the ten distinct commandments as being the prescriptive rule of true holiness. Christ redeems and renews all His believing people unto such holiness by His blood and Holy Spirit. Since, however, God's children, and thus all redeemed and converted believers, cannot accomplish anything as to the practice of their sanctification apart from the power and immediate efficacy of the Lord's grace, they must repeatedly pray to God in Christ's name in order to secure all their power and grace from Him in Christ.

5. The duty of prayer in eight successive Lord's Days, thereby concluding his Catechism.

This is the good and delightful way in which the instructor will expound for us the glorious doctrine of a Christian's sanctification. We will again follow in his steps, being desirous that the Lord would graciously bless our preaching.

Presently we shall consider in greater detail the sacred obligation of all true believers, as a redeemed people and as the recipients of the Lord's grace, to live before Him in true holiness and godliness by the habitual doing of good works. The instructor will:

1. explain and expound this sacred obligation in Question 86; and

2. further affirm this in Question 87 by demonstrating that no one can possibly be saved apart from living a holy life and doing good works.

Regarding the first, the instructor asks, "Since then we are delivered from our misery, merely of grace, through Christ, without any merit of ours, why must we still do good works?" He is speaking here of God's people, concerning whom he has demonstrated how, apart from any of their own works or merits, and thus purely by grace, they have been eternally delivered from the misery to which they have subjected themselves by their sins. With them in mind, he asks whether, in light of such a gracious deliverance in and through the Lord Jesus, they are still obligated to do good works and to live before the Lord in all holiness and godliness.

In Lord's Day 24, we considered how all natural men, all who are hostile to the truth regarding this true doctrine unto salvation, claim that such a doctrine will necessarily breed ungodly and careless men. We teach according to God's Word that the elect are saved by grace alone and are freely justified by God through the redemption that is in Christ Jesus. This is the ground upon which they either are accepted by God or rejected, and He does so without any of their own works being even remotely considered, whether they are good or evil. The natural man, with his darkened and works-oriented understanding, can come only to the conclusion that such a doctrine must necessarily result in casting aside the good works of men as well as all virtue and godliness, thereby opening the door widely for everyone to be ungodly and careless.

Given that, in the redemption and justification of elect sinners, God will in no wise receive any of man's good or evil works into consideration, redemption and justification being freely gracious in and through Christ, it appears that it is a matter of indifference whether men live godly and do good works. Consequently, it gives the appearance that one has not the least obligation or duty to live a holy and godly life. Such is the assessment of a natural, darkened, and unspiritual person, who is incapable of any other assessment regarding the doctrine that is unto godliness, "for they are foolishness unto him: neither can he know them, because they are spiritually discerned" (1 Cor. 2:14).

All natural and unregenerate men function entirely within the context of the covenant of works, and regardless of what their religious mindset may be, their singular objective is to be justified before God by their own merits and by the works of the law. Therefore, if they hear any mention made of a covenant that is purely and freely gracious in and through the crucified surety and mediator Christ Jesus, or if they are directed to anything other than this covenant of grace and to this mediator, being called upon to lay aside and fully to forsake all their own strength and righteousness, and admonished from the

Holy Scriptures that they are to believe alone in Him who justifies the ungodly because they are unable to accomplish anything themselves—I say, the moment this occurs, these people are of the opinion that such a faith will render them careless, whereby sin will then necessarily have dominion over them.

Natural men have always thus judged the doctrine of salvation by grace alone. In Romans 3, we read how the Jews accordingly slandered the doctrine of the apostle Paul. However, in Lord's Day 24, the instructor plainly refuted this carnal and erroneous prejudice, pointing out that the soul's union with the Lord Jesus by faith is the fountain from which true thankfulness or sanctification necessarily and principally issues forth.

At this occasion, however, the instructor gives reasons why this must necessarily be so, explaining that although we are delivered from our misery without any of our own merits, and thus by grace and through Christ alone, we must nevertheless do good works "because Christ, having redeemed and delivered us by His blood, also renews us by His Holy Spirit, after His own image."

The instructor here sets before us three specific reasons regarding the necessity of good works for a redeemed Christian, viewing these works:

1. as they pertain to God;
2. as they pertain to ourselves; and
3. as they pertain to our neighbor.

Regarding the first, all who are graciously redeemed by Christ and believe in Him with a true heart, according to the instructor, must necessarily live holy and godly lives and do all kinds of good works, "because Christ, having redeemed and delivered us by His blood, also renews us by His Holy Spirit, after His own image."

The instructor here sets before us two very precious and glorious benefits that Christ bestows upon His believing people, and he then deduces their sanctification from this as a necessary consequence.

The first of these two benefits is that Christ has "redeemed and delivered us by His blood." Elect believers, along with all men, wallow by nature in a bottomless pool of wretchedness, misery, and perdition, being enemies of God, children of wrath, and slaves of sin, hell, and Satan. In and of themselves, they will never be able to reconcile themselves with God, nor will they be able to deliver themselves from His curse and wrath or from the power of sin and the devil. Therefore, left to themselves, they will eternally and utterly perish. However, here the Lord Jesus comes to the fore as their all-sufficient surety and mediator, who was given and appointed by the Father eternally to deliver all His elect from their sins and wretched misery. To that end, taking their place as surety, He took all their sins and debts upon Himself, suffering and dying on their behalf on the cross, and, by so doing, bore the curse and punishment of their iniquities in His flesh, and, by a perfect obedience, fully performed all that the law required.

By the price of His precious blood and perfect obedience, the Lord Jesus purchased His elect and believing people from His Father, and consequently received them as His property. By this purchase and redemption, there comes a moment in time when He lays hold of His elect as His property and, in very deed, works in them by His Spirit. He unites them to Himself, and by the faith that He works in their hearts by His Word and Spirit, He grafts them into Himself. He reconciles them personally with God and justifies them from all their sins by clothing and adorning them with His righteousness. He calls them out of the world and out of the kingdom of Satan. He translates them into His kingdom and regenerates, sanctifies, and converts them.

This is the manner in which the Lord Jesus delivers His elect and believing people, or, to use the language of the instructor, "having redeemed and delivered [them] by His blood." This is taught throughout the Holy Scriptures, for Paul testifies in Acts 20:28 that Christ has purchased His church "with His own blood," and in 1 Peter 1:18–19, the apostle writes that believers "were not redeemed with corruptible things, as silver and gold, from [their] vain conversation received by tradition from [their] fathers; but with the precious blood of Christ, as of a lamb without blemish and without spot."

To what end has Christ thus redeemed His elect and believing people with His blood and delivered them from their wretched misery? Is it that they would be fully absolved from all obligations to be obedient to God's law, and henceforth to live according to their sinful lusts and desires? By no means, for then they would turn "the grace of our God into lasciviousness" (Jude 4), and Christ would then fully be "the minister of sin" (Gal. 2:17). These two thoughts would be the most abominable and extreme ungodliness that could be imagined in the life of a truly gracious person, and therefore it is absolutely impossible that such could be true.

On the contrary, the true purpose for which Christ redeemed His believing people and purchased them with His blood was to make them free from sin; that is, that He "might redeem us from all iniquity, and purify unto himself a peculiar people, zealous of good works." When believers are thus redeemed by Christ and purchased with His blood, they fully become the property of God and Christ, both body and soul, so that they cleave to, serve, and glorify only Him. The apostle admonishes and teaches accordingly, saying, "For ye are bought with a price: therefore glorify God in your body, and in your spirit, which are God's" (1 Cor. 6:20).

It is self-evident that I must be fully subject to Him whose complete property I am. I must therefore fully serve and obey Him, and in all things He must have me at His disposal. Given that believers are fully and eternally the property of God and Christ through the redemption that is in Christ Jesus, they must necessarily fully and eternally surrender themselves to God and to Christ Jesus, their king and redeemer, to serve and obey Him. With all that is within them, they must then be wholly inclined and prepared to do so without desiring to hold back even the very least from the Lord. Paul, in Romans 11, having set before the Lord's people their glorious redemption through Christ, therefore admonishes the Lord's people in Romans 12:1, "I beseech you therefore, brethren, by the mercies of God, that ye present your bodies a living sacrifice, holy, acceptable unto God, which is your reasonable service."

Please read Romans 6, in which Paul specifically and emphatically endeavors to set before us the necessity of the believer's sanctification by virtue of his redemption through Jesus Christ. Is there any true believer who would view himself as the purchased possession of God and Christ who would not be inclined and willing in his heart to surrender himself fully and eternally to the Lord's service, laboring "that, whether present or absent, we may be accepted of him" (2 Cor. 5:9)? Who among them would not desire fully and eternally to sacrifice even a thousand souls and bodies unto the Lord and for His service, thereby demonstrating that they are "the branch of [His] planting, the work of [His] hands, that [He] may be glorified"? (Isa. 60:21).

Indeed, all who are delivered by Christ from sin and eternal death neither know nor desire any other salvation than being the property of the triune God, that with their entire soul and body they might be subject to Him, and that they "might walk worthy of the Lord unto all pleasing, being fruitful in every good work, and increasing in the knowledge of God" (Col. 1:10). This clearly proves the necessity of the sanctification and godly walk of the Christian, for Christ has "redeemed and delivered us by His blood."

The instructor now proceeds to demonstrate in greater detail that a redeemed believer must live a holy life in all kinds of good works by stating that Christ, having redeemed and delivered them by His blood, "also renews us by His Holy Spirit, after His own image, that so we may testify, by the whole of our conduct, our gratitude to God for His blessings, and that He may be praised by us."

It is certain that Christ will also engage Himself to sanctify by His Spirit all His believing people for whose sins He suffered and whom He reconciled with God, for of God He has been made unto them "wisdom, and righteousness, and sanctification, and redemption" (1 Cor. 1:30). No sooner does He unite them to Himself by faith than He grants them His Holy Spirit, and by that Spirit He makes His abode in their hearts. Consequently, He renews, sanctifies, and converts them completely in principle, so that believers are truly transformed after Christ's image in true righteousness and holiness. This truth is clearly taught throughout the Scriptures.

It is therefore an incontrovertible distinctive of true faith that the Lord Jesus lives and dwells in the hearts of His believing people and is formed within them. Thereupon, believers become entirely new creatures in Christ, and they receive the mind of Christ. This glorious transformation, renewal, and conversion of believers will be addressed in greater detail in the next Lord's Day.

It should be noted here only that from this inward and spiritual renewal and transformation after Christ's image, it must necessarily follow that believers must live before the Lord in all good works, and that they no longer should walk according to the flesh, but in the Spirit. According to the instructor, Christ renews believers according to His image "that so we may testify, by the whole of our conduct, our gratitude to God for His blessings, and that He may be praised by us."

The true gratitude that redeemed believers are obligated to demonstrate to the Lord for the precious benefits of His grace ultimately consists in being in Christ, and that with soul and body, they must fully sacrifice themselves to Him. They are thus to devote themselves to His praise and service, so that they might live to His honor by forsaking themselves and the world. The Lord therefore testifies regarding His redeemed and believing people, "This people have I formed for myself; they shall shew forth my praise" (Isa. 43:21). Peter instructs and admonishes believers, saying, "But ye are a chosen generation, a royal priesthood, an holy nation, a peculiar people; that ye should shew forth the praises of him who hath called you out of darkness into his marvelous light" (1 Peter 2:9).

In order that believers should be both willing and able to do this, Christ renews them by His Spirit according to His image, and they consequently become "his workmanship, created in Christ Jesus unto good works, which God hath before ordained that we should walk in them" (Eph. 2:10). Having thus been renewed by Christ after His image by His Holy Spirit, true believers have become enemies of all sin, and, according to their renewed and gracious inner self, they cannot even sin any longer to all eternity, for this life originates in God. We read in 1 John 3:9 that "whosoever is born of God doth not commit sin; for his seed remaineth in him: and he cannot sin, because he is born of God." With Paul, they accordingly "delight in the law of God after the inward man" (Rom. 7:22). They have no other desire or inclination but perfectly and eternally to serve and glorify a triune God.

This again affirms, in the clearest possible manner, how absolutely essential it is for believers, upon being delivered by Christ from their misery, to abound in all good works, for "if we live in the Spirit, let us also walk in the Spirit" (Gal. 5:25).

The instructor proceeds to present another reason why all true believers, being redeemed by Christ, must necessarily and in all aspects live lives of good works, namely, "that every one may be assured in himself of his faith by the fruits thereof." The greatest and most essential matter every man must pursue in this life is to be united to God in Christ by a true faith, and thereupon to arrive at a certain and steadfast assurance of his gracious state and the sincerity of his faith. Without such knowledge, it is absolutely impossible that we can live in true peace and comfort. It is indeed true that the unregenerate men of this world have generally little or no concern about these matters, and they pacify themselves with a false, imaginary, and vain hope, being of the opinion, according to their corrupt judgment, that it is very simple to secure salvation. They are quickly satisfied that they are living pious and virtuous lives, and they continue to live peacefully in their sins although eternal perdition is at their very doorstep.

However, God's people are of an entirely different mindset, for they often are greatly concerned about the great matter of their salvation. They often struggle with many concerns, fears, and doubts, for they understand the great weightiness of their salvation and how few are saved. They have also been taught how untrustworthy and deceitful their hearts are, and they also know how much false and deceitful counterfeit faith there is in the world. They know how far a temporal believer can progress and yet nevertheless perish with the common gifts and operations of the Holy Spirit.

It can also be that they walk in much darkness, and have but little knowledge with many besetting sins that greatly estrange them from the Lord. Nevertheless, they are upright within, they desire truth in their inward parts, and they are fearful of all self-deceit. All these matters cause God's children at times to be very troubled, for it pleases the Lord, for wise and adorable reasons, as yet not to give them a great measure of comforting assurance regarding their state of grace. Nevertheless, it is the Lord's will that His children would seek by faith to attain to such assurance and not be satisfied until the Spirit witnesses with their spirits that they are children of God, for such assurance and affirmation of their state of grace is of great benefit to their faith and sanctification.

To that end, the Lord has revealed in His Word sure and reliable marks whereby His children, by the grace of the Holy Spirit, can be convinced and assured regarding the uprightness of their faith and of their inner state of grace. Among these marks, sanctification and fruitfulness in all good works are among the most prominent and excellent, for sanctification is an essential and inseparable fruit of faith. As there can be no true sanctification without faith, there can be no true faith apart from sanctification. Faith and sanctification always coexist as a mother and daughter dwell together, and whoever separates the two entirely unravels all salvation, and this proceeds from the devil rather than from God.

The Savior taught this truth clearly, saying, "A good tree cannot bring forth evil fruit, neither can a corrupt tree bring forth good fruit" (Matt. 7:18). A tree cannot be known in any other way except by its fruits. The Holy Scriptures therefore frequently set before us good works and sanctification as the true marks by which one is to be examined. The apostle James, addressing those who pretended to have true faith in Christ and yet did not have the works or fruits of faith, says of them: "Even so faith, if it hath not works, is dead, being alone. Yea, a man may say, Thou hast faith, and I have works: shew me thy faith without thy works, and I will shew thee my faith by my works" (James 2:17–18). He presses this matter so far that he posits that one is justified by his works—not as the meritorious cause of justification, for only Christ's perfect righteousness is its meriting cause, but rather, as the essential evidence of our faith and its righteousness. Therefore, a faith without works is dead, and we neither can be justified nor saved by a dead faith. The apostle John also teaches this: "And hereby we do know that we know him, if we keep his commandments. He that saith, I know him, and keepeth not his commandments, is a liar, and the truth is not in him" (1 John 2:3–4).

Therefore one not only must be assured of his faith by the fruits, but must also ascertain his state of grace by his good works and a godly life. This foundation of good works is a matter of utmost significance for a redeemed and believing Christian, and no one readily attains to a comforting assurance of his personal state of grace apart from a careful, tender, and godly life.

The instructor then adds a third and final reason why a believing Christian must do good works and live a holy and godly life: "that, by our godly conversation others may be gained to Christ." Every true Christian readily admits and acknowledges that it is the bounden duty of a converted person to do his utmost, by God's grace, to lead others to repentance and to win them for the cause of Christ. The Holy Scriptures clearly exhort the Lord's people that this is their obligation, for the Savior said to Peter, "When thou art converted, strengthen thy brethren" (Luke 22:32). The apostle James admonishes believers accordingly, saying, "Brethren, if any of you do err from the truth, and one convert him; let him know, that he which converteth the sinner from the error of his way shall save a soul from death, and shall hide a multitude of sins" (James 5:19–20).

This is an established truth; in proportion to the grace given him, every believer must be engaged in the edification, winning, and salvation of his neighbor who either is still unconverted or who is backslidden in regard to godliness. All who know what constitutes the redemption and eternal salvation of never-dying souls and are committed to the extension of the kingdom of Jesus will readily believe this.

What are the best means whereby a Christian can win his neighbor? This can indeed be accomplished by instruction and admonition, but it is especially achieved by an upright and godly walk. It is a common adage among us that admonitions arouse men, but exemplary conduct attracts them. With the Lord's blessing, nothing is more suitable for the edification and conversion of others than a holy, godly, and exemplary life. This has far greater effects upon the hearts of others than all words and admonitions combined.

When unconverted sinners behold the unfeigned and tender godliness of the godly, observing their zeal, love, moderation, heavenly-mindedness, humility, meekness, discretion, and other Christian virtues, contingent upon the Lord's blessing, it greatly impresses upon their hearts not only the majesty and holiness of God, but also that He is worthy of being known, loved, and feared. This most effectively convicts them of their sinful and unholy lives, and, by the grace of God, brings them to conversion, so that they say to God's people, "We will go with you: for we have heard that God is with you" (Zech. 8:23).

Paul therefore testifies to the Corinthians, "Your zeal hath provoked very many" (2 Cor. 9:2b). Likewise, the Savior admonishes His believing people, "Let your light so shine before men, that they may see your good works, and glorify your Father which is in heaven" (Matt. 5:16). In a similar vein, Peter admonishes believers, saying, "Having your conversation honest among the Gentiles: that, whereas they speak against you as evildoers, they may by your good works, which they shall behold, glorify God in the day of visitation" (1 Peter 2:12).

This is all the more essential, considering that others are greatly offended by the sins and failures of God's children, thereby hindering them from entering into the kingdom of God. When a Christian at times regresses into living an offensive and careless life, he can tear down much more than others are able to build up by their godly lives. Oh, that all who are Christ's would fully crucify the flesh and the lusts thereof, and that among the truly godly, none would intermingle with anyone other than they who live truly godly lives and no longer desire to be conformed to this world. The world, to its own detriment and perdition, would then not stumble over the deficiencies of the godly as so frequently takes place today.

The foregoing has therefore demonstrated clearly how essential it is for a redeemed Christian to live a life and pursue a walk that consists in the doing of good works.

Upon having expounded this truth, the instructor affirms it by positing the opposite in Question 87, namely, that no one can be saved apart from a holy life and the doing of good works. "Cannot they then be saved, who, continuing in their wicked and ungrateful lives, are not converted to God?" To this question, the instructor responds, "By no means; for the Holy Scriptures declare that no unchaste person, idolator, adulterer, thief, covetous man, drunkard, slanderer, robber, or any such like, shall inherit the kingdom of God."

The Holy Scriptures teach clearly and abundantly that neither unconverted nor unholy men who continue to live in their sins and refuse to break with them can either be saved or enter into Christ's kingdom. His kingdom is a holy kingdom in which one serves God in newness of life and utterly hates all sin, whether great or small. Therefore, if someone continues to serve sin and refuses to repent toward God with all his heart, he is most certainly lost, and he will perish and die in his sins. He neither has any part in Christ nor in His salvation. As we have already observed, Christ delivers His people from their sins and cleanses them from all unrighteousness so that they might serve the living God.

This is a further affirmation that true sanctification and being fruitful in good works are most absolutely essential for all true believers, they being graciously delivered by Christ from their misery apart from their own strength or merits. In the following Lord's Day, the instructor will proceed to consider the glorious benefit of conversion whereby, in principle, Christ Himself equips believers to pursue true holiness of life by resurrecting them from being dead in sin—a state to which they are all fully subject by nature.

Beloved, by these proposed and expounded grounds, the necessity of true sanctification of a redeemed believer has been lawfully deduced from the Holy Scriptures. How blessed therefore they are who have received a sincere desire after true holiness and no longer find the least delight in the service of sin; who have no other desire but that they might fully live unto the Lord, the triune God, desiring to be fully and eternally delivered from all sin! With Paul, our wish and prayer for such people is: "And the very God of peace sanctify you wholly; and I pray God your whole spirit and soul and body be preserved blameless unto the coming of our Lord Jesus Christ. Faithful is he that calleth you, who also will do it" (1 Thess. 5:23). Amen.

The True Conversion of Man

The Lord is not slack concerning his promise, as some men count slackness; but is longsuffering to us-ward, not willing that any should perish, but that all should come to repentance.

—2 PETER 3:9

Question 88: Of how many parts doth the true conversion of man consist?

Answer: Of two parts: of the mortification of the old, and the quickening of the new man.

Question 89: What is the mortification of the old man?

Answer: It is a sincere sorrow of heart that we have provoked God by our sins, and more and more to hate and flee from them.

Question 90: What is the quickening of the new man?

Answer: It is a sincere joy of heart in God, through Christ, and with love and delight to live according to the will of God in all good works.

Question 91: But what are good works?

Answer: Only those which proceed from a true faith, are performed according to the law of God, and to His glory; and not such as are founded on our imaginations, or the institutions of men.

In the previous Lord's Day, the instructor addressed the necessity of sanctification and the doing of good works by all true believers, meaning believers who have been delivered by Christ from their misery purely by grace and without any strength or merits of their own being taken into consideration. He addressed how this redeemed people, with both body and soul, must henceforth live in all true holiness and godliness before the Lord. In this Lord's Day, he proceeds to expound for us how, in principle, the Lord enables His people to live accordingly by means of a true conversion of heart whereby they "put off concerning the former conversation the old man, which is corrupt according to the deceitful lusts.... And...put on the new man, which after God is created in righteousness and true holiness" (Eph. 4:22, 24). With the instructor, we will now proceed to consider this blessed and glorious benefit of conversion. May the Lord sustain us by His Holy Spirit, and may He bless our preaching.

The instructor addresses two matters in this Lord's Day:

1. He expounds for us the true conversion of elect and believing sinners (Questions 88–90).
2. He describes and explains the nature and essence of those good works that proceed from conversion (Question 91).

The instructor observes the following order in regard to the conversion of a sinner:

1. He delineates for us in Question 88 what are the essential components of conversion.
2. He expounds in greater detail the two components of conversion in Questions 89 and 90.

Regarding the first, we must address the meaning of the word *conversion*, after which we will address the matter itself.

The benefit of God's grace, as it is addressed here, is set before us by the term conversion. On the one hand, the thrust and essential meaning of the word conversion is a turning away from and forsaking of something, while on the other hand, it is a turning to something of one's choosing that one affectionately receives and embraces. This word is therefore very suitable to express the great inner change and renewal of man that is wrought within as a result of this inner transformation. When an elect sinner repents, he wholeheartedly turns away from the service and slavery of sin to which, by nature, he is subject in both body and soul, and he sincerely turns to God, to His holy service, and to His communion, seeking and taking hold thereof entirely in Christ.

In His Word, the Holy Spirit customarily describes the conversion of the sinner in a variety of ways. He commonly refers to it as "returning"—that is, a turning to God from whom all men have departed through sin—as "being contrite," or as "becoming wise again." All of these are descriptive of conversion, for the repenting sinner indeed returns unto God. He is truly contrite, and inwardly he is grieved and sorrowful regarding his sins and having lived apart from the Lord. He again becomes wise and turns away from his former foolishness and imprudence.

Regarding the sinner's conversion or his return unto God, the instructor first gives a general description when he posits that conversion consists "of the mortification of the old, and the quickening of the new man."

To understand this correctly, you need to know that when God's Word refers to the *old man* and the *new man*, it refers to the twofold state of God's children: their natural state and their regenerate or renewed state of grace. The Holy Scriptures also commonly refer to these as *flesh and spirit*. To differentiate correctly between these two states of God's children is a matter that requires considerable discernment—the sanctified discernment the saints have as a result of being anointed by the Father.

When God's Word speaks of the *old man*, it is to be understood as referring to the natural state into which believers and all men are born. Until their regeneration and conversion, they continue wholly in this state, and subsequent to their conversion and being united to Christ, their old man always cleaves to them, even unto death.

What is the *old man*; that is, what does this natural state of man consist of? It consists of radical ungodliness, of being utterly estranged from God, and it has dominion over the entire man in both body and soul. It proceeds from Adam's transgression, by which the entire human race fully departed from God, the consequence being that mankind no longer knows, loves, serves, or glorifies God in even the least degree. The old man is therefore this ungodly creature whose "carnal mind is enmity against God: for it is not subject to the law of God, neither indeed can be" (Rom. 8:7). It is nothing but darkness and the "bond of iniquity" (Acts 8:23), a being utterly void of God, and a "being alienated from the life of God through the ignorance that is in them, because of the blindness of their heart" (Eph. 4:18). During that period of life, we were entirely "without Christ, being aliens from the commonwealth of Israel, and strangers from the covenants of promise, having no hope, and without God in the world" (Eph. 2:12). The old man is therefore an accursed creature that is fully subjected to the curse and wrath of God and is condemned by Him to eternal death and perdition. The fact that the Holy Scriptures designate this natural state of ungodliness and alienation from God as the old *man* is due to this innate ungodliness having complete dominion over the entire man in both soul and body, so that the intellect, the judgment, the will, the affections, the members, the senses, and whatever else constitutes man have fully departed from God and manifest absolute hatred and enmity toward Him. The old man is thus in bondage to sin and to vanity.

Another reason why this ungodliness is designated as the old man is primarily due to man being born in this state. The old man is therefore his old and innate nature. By the renewing work of the Holy Spirit in Christ Jesus, this old man increasingly must be hedged in, disappear, and vanish—until, upon the death of the body, it shall fully and eternally perish and be annihilated.

In contradistinction to this old man, there is in God's children the *new man*, consisting of a spiritual and new creation. This new man, begotten of God in Christ and by the Holy Spirit, lives in all true believers from the moment when, by faith in the Lord Jesus, believers are internally united to Christ and embrace Him unto justification and sanctification. At that moment, they become partakers of the triune God Himself, as well as of His light, love, grace, and image, and they are internally united to Him. Their nature is principally transformed and renewed according to God's image, and, with Christ, they are resurrected from the dead and made alive, receiving within them "the law of the Spirit of life in Christ Jesus," which "hath made [them] free from the law of sin and death" (Rom. 8:2). They begin to know, love, serve, and glorify God in Christ and by the Holy Spirit. This proceeds from the inward principle of spirit and life that God has created within them by faith and regeneration. This new nature is therefore designated as "the new man, which after God is created in righteousness and true holiness" (Eph. 4:24).

This new creation in God's children is, in all things, the exact opposite of their old man and is designated as the new *man* because it encompasses the entire man. Therefore, the intellect, the judgment, the will, the affections, the members, the senses, and whatever else constitutes a man have principally been transformed and sanctified unto the service of the triune God. It is called the *new* man because this grace has been newly wrought in the believer by the Spirit of the Lord, and, as such, he is increasingly wrought upon as one who previously had none of this, for "if any man be in Christ, he is a new creature: old things are passed away; behold, all things are become new" (2 Cor. 5:17).

We have thus set before you in what the old and new man essentially consist. The instructor teaches regarding the old and the new man that true conversion consists of the mortification of the old and the quickening of the new man.

One of the components of conversion is the *mortification of the old man*, which the Holy Scriptures also designate as a "casting off" (Rom. 13:12), the crucifying of the old man (Rom. 6:6), the "destruction of the flesh" (1 Cor. 5:5). As to the essence of the matter, this is nothing but a dismantling and destruction of this old man of sin and the innate ungodliness within us. All who are converted by God begin to cease and desist in their enmity toward Him, and they part with their former ungodliness and unrighteousness. I have said that they *begin* to do this, for no one should think that when God's children are regenerated and converted by the Spirit of the Lord, their old man of sin, that is, their sinful flesh, completely dies and is so utterly annihilated that nothing of it remains. This is by no means so, for this old man of sin remains alive in God's children as long as they dwell here upon this earth. To their great sorrow and grief, the old man always cleaves to them, and they will not be fully delivered from the body of this death until their death.

In conversion, the old man is mortified in principle and by grace is subdued and broken to such an extent that it never is able, to all eternity, to have complete and unopposed dominion over believers as prior to their conversion, when they were in bondage to sin and uncleanness. However, from the time of their conversion and forward, the old man or the flesh is mortified in them. It then gradually and incrementally dies, and increasingly it is subdued by the Spirit as to its internal motions and lusts, until the old man, with the body of this death, is completely and eternally annihilated. This is the first component of conversion.

According to the instructor, the other component of conversion is the "quickening of the new man." The Holy Scriptures also refer to this as the putting on of the new man (Eph. 4:24). This occurs when believers are inwardly united to Christ and when the principle of true spiritual life is established and activated within them—when, from being dead in sin, they are raised unto a new life and enter into the knowledge, service, and fellowship of God in Christ by the Holy Spirit. This is taught abundantly throughout the Holy Scriptures. Though this new man, when initially quickened in believers at conversion, is complete from the outset in all of its constituent parts, it is by no means complete as to degree, for in their initial conversion, believers receive a very small beginning of life and of grace, and it is as tender and weak as is the newly born child. However, having been created for eternity and unto perfection, this new creation, by the immediate infusion of grace and the operation of the Holy Spirit in Christ, gradually increases "till we all come in the unity of the faith, and of the knowledge of the Son of God, unto a perfect man, unto the measure of the stature of the fulness of Christ" (Eph. 4:13). In proportion to the daily decline and mortification of the old man, this new creation in God's children increases and arises in Christ Jesus their head until, at last, at the death of the body, it will be eternally perfect.

The conversion of man therefore consists of our old man of sin being mortified within us and a new and spiritual man being quickened in us by virtue of our union with Christ. When this occurs, we are truly converted and depart from our former ungodliness. With body and soul, we then return to the triune God in the way of His covenant and submit to Him, our lawful king and Lord, to serve and glorify Him, and to find all our salvation for time and eternity in Him.

The instructor is not satisfied with addressing this subject merely in general terms, for he proceeds to expound briefly of what these two components of conversion consist, and we will follow him and do likewise. To have more insight into the character and nature of true conversion, the instructor explains here what constitutes 1) the mortification of the old man, and 2) the quickening of the new man.

Regarding the first, the instructor teaches that the essence of the mortification of the old man is "a sincere sorrow of heart that we have provoked God by our sins, and more and more to hate and flee from them." When the Lord Jesus converts His elect people, He illuminates their darkened understanding and, by His Word and Spirit, opens their blind eyes. He causes them to see how greatly and dreadfully they have sinned against the Lord their God and have fully forsaken Him and His holy service. They view this in light of the fact that they should have rendered Him all love, filial fear, and obedience with soul and body; that they should have glorified only Him, their creator and king, in all things; and that all their salvation consists solely in serving Him and having communion with Him.

They now perceive how dreadfully and grievously they have dishonored the Lord by breaking His yoke and willfully casting it from their necks, and instead have served Satan, the world, and themselves without ever inquiring of and seeking after the Lord. This is all clearly uncovered to the elect in their conversion. They see clearly and vividly how they have dishonored God the Lord and provoked Him to wrath by fully cleaving to and serving such as are no gods. They acknowledge that God is supremely holy and just, and therefore must punish the sinner temporally and eternally. They acknowledge that the Lord's wrath toward them is justified and that God would be just were He to cast such vile sinners as they are into hell eternally, being unwilling to bestow the least measure of grace upon them. They view themselves as being utterly guilty, hell-worthy, abominable, and despicable, and by no means are they able to find within themselves the least measure of goodness or virtue. It cannot be otherwise, for they confess their ungodliness and that they have eternally forfeited the right to live—that is, in and of themselves, they have no standing before God by virtue of His infinite majesty, holiness, and justice. All this greatly grieves them and causes them inwardly to be sorrowful, perplexed, and ashamed before the Lord in the deepest recesses of their souls. They are truly sorrowful and troubled about their sins and the fact that they have forsaken the Lord. They therefore abhor themselves. They are as Ephraim, who cried out regarding himself, "Surely after that I was turned, I repented; and after that I was instructed, I smote upon my thigh: I was ashamed, yea, even confounded, because I did bear the reproach of my youth" (Jer. 31:19).

One may verbally speak of these things, but it cannot be truly expressed in words how intense and tender is the sorrow that God's children generally experience in their conversion—this heartfelt sorrow, deep shame, grievous perplexity and contrition of soul, inward brokenness and humiliation before the Lord, and humble longing and groaning to be reconciled with God in Christ. This can be known only by the true and inward experience of the heart. How blessed they are who can speak of this by such knowledge, and in whose hearts has been verified all that the Holy Spirit abundantly testifies regarding these matters in His Word!

Does the mortification of the old man consist only in God's children having such heartfelt sorrow and contrition because they have provoked God by their sins? No! According to the instructor, they "more and more…hate and flee from them." The apostle Paul describes this when he writes, "For godly sorrow worketh repentance to salvation not to be repented of" (2 Cor. 7:10).

Another preeminent aspect of conversion is that God's children depart from all ungodliness. They truly hate all iniquity and therefore fully part with it in their inner man. In their hearts, they abhor it and no longer are either able or willing to have even the least fellowship with such iniquity.

It cannot be otherwise. He who has learned to see his sins as a most dreadful and abominable evil that utterly alienates him from God, as dreadful and evil because God is utterly dishonored and provoked, now sees his sins and is greatly grieved, contrite, and humbled in light of them, and therefore cannot but utterly hate sin as sin and exceedingly abhor it. Believers are admonished accordingly in Psalm 97:10, "Ye that love the LORD, hate evil." Such persons cannot have the least fellowship with any measure of sin—with all that deviates from God's holy law even in the least degree. Instead, they wholeheartedly hate and abhor sin, for God is thereby dishonored, despised, desecrated, and provoked.

By virtue of such innermost and righteous hatred against sin, such persons endeavor, by the grace of God in Christ Jesus, to part with all sin—not only sinful deeds and practices, but also their sinful nature and the least inclination they detect within themselves toward sin. They declare themselves to be enemies of all that opposes God and His holy law, and they desire to distance themselves utterly from sin, "hating even the garment spotted by the flesh" (Jude 23).

Such is the manner whereby a converted Christian, by the Spirit, is tender before the Lord in Christ Jesus, and all his wrestling and striving against sin proceed entirely from this disposition. This increases daily according to the measure of his grace, and does not cease until he is fully and eternally delivered from his sinful flesh, after which he is fully in subjection unto God.

According to the instructor, this constitutes the essence of the mortification of the old man. The old man, or our sinful flesh, is dying when we perceive within ourselves such a heartfelt sorrow over our sins, whereby we dishonor and provoke God. We therefore utterly hate and flee from sin and all that in the least degree is related with it. This increasingly manifests itself in us by the grace of the Holy Spirit. Hereby the old man of sin within us, so to speak, is mortally wounded, and thereby is so stripped of its efficacy that never to all eternity will it have any dominion over him. Instead, by the increase of God's grace within, and by virtue of its initial mortification, the old man increasingly becomes weaker and more feeble, until at last he is fully and eternally mortified—that is, when the life of Jesus and of His Spirit shall be fully manifested in His children.

We have thus considered the first component of conversion, namely, the mortification of the old man, as well as what constitutes this mortification. We must yet briefly address the other component of conversion, namely, *the quickening of the new man.* According to the instructor, this consists in "a sincere joy of heart in God, through Christ, and with love and delight to live according to the will of God in all good works."

May the Lord teach you this experientially by His Spirit, that when an elect sinner is inwardly renewed and converted, he goes to God in and through

Christ and has true communion with Him by faith. No sooner does he perceive himself utterly to have departed from God through sin, to be subject to His righteous curse and wrath as one who is utterly impotent, poor, blind, and naked, than he at once completely desists from seeking life within himself. He exclaims that he is utterly ungodly and worthy of death, that it is all beyond hope for him, and that he cannot contribute anything whatsoever to his salvation, but that he must eternally perish, since God is infinitely holy and just, before whom he, as an ungodly one, cannot stand even for one moment.

To such an impotent, helpless, and truly perplexed sinner, God, by means of His Word and Spirit, and in accord with the content of the gospel, sets before him the counsel of His grace. He spiritually reveals to his mind the mediator, Christ Jesus, His Son, in His suitability, fullness, all-sufficiency, and sweet willingness. God does so with such clarity and with such discerning light proceeding from His Spirit that the heart of the sinner is thereby powerfully inclined toward the Lord Jesus and His free and sovereign grace. By the powerful ministry of the Spirit, the sinner completely and fully turns away from himself and turns unto the Lord Jesus and His fullness, taking hold of Him and His offered strength and righteousness as proposed in the gospel (Isa. 27:5). By faith, he does so purely and sincerely, and he fully and unconditionally surrenders himself, upon the basis of free and sovereign grace, to the Lord Jesus unto justification and sanctification. He is fully inclined and prepared by faith and by grace to expect his entire salvation and redemption from God in Christ.

By faith, the sinner does not merely cleave to Christ. In and through Him, he goes unto God, who reveals Himself to him in Christ. He confesses his sins unto God, acknowledging his hell-worthiness and impotence. The sinner comes before God with the all-sufficient righteousness of the mediator Jesus, beseeching of Him that He would receive him for the sake of that righteousness and not impute his sins to him. He experiences that God is entirely well pleased with this and that He graciously and for Christ's sake pardons all his sins fully and eternally. God therefore is no longer angry with him, but in and through His Son, Christ Jesus, He is fully reconciled to him. Thereupon such a sinner receives and enjoys from God such a measure of love, grace, and benevolence, and so much fills his soul from God through Christ that he cannot express in words the eternal love and sovereign mercy of God in Christ regarding him, who is such a vile, hell-worthy, and ungodly sinner. This greatly exceeds all that he could have imagined, and it greatly transcends the capacity of his amazement and adoration that God would be reconciled to an ungodly sinner in such a way, and eternally unite and turn him to Himself. Such a sinner will never be able to magnify, praise, and exalt God in the measure whereof He is worthy. Although he had a thousand mouths and tongues, he would infinitely come short in doing this, for he cannot rightly express to other men in what measure his heart is now filled with the sweetest love, peace, comfort, and joy in God. All of his joy, delight, confidence, and desire is now only in God through Christ, "whom having not seen, [he loves], in whom, though now [he sees] him not, yet believing, [he rejoices] with joy unspeakable and full of glory" (1 Peter 1:8).

This is the blessed joy and peace of a sinner who in God through Christ is the recipient of grace and reconciliation. The Holy Scriptures speak of this joy and peace in such sweet and glorious terms, but this remains utterly hidden from flesh and blood. It is a joy that increasingly leads the sinner away from all that is of self and from all that is not to be found in the Lord Jesus, but increasingly unites him with God in Christ. This joy that the soul now finds in God through Christ constitutes the internal and spiritual life of the soul, and this begets the new man in the soul that is now truly born of God.

According to the instructor, this sincere and spiritual "joy of heart in God, through Christ" is inseparably connected to the desire "with love and delight to live according to the will of God in all good works." This joy in God is a true, spiritual, and holy joy, for the soul who thus rejoices and delights herself in God through Christ fully loves God and His holy attributes, and she has no desire but to be fully subject to Christ in both soul and body. Such a soul is also desirous that never again will she sin against Him, but that in all things she might do His good and holy will. This alone becomes her intent and desire. She now finds all her salvation in continually walking "worthy of the Lord unto all pleasing, being fruitful in every good work, and increasing in the knowledge of God" (Col. 1:10). This walking "worthy of the Lord unto all pleasing" is now chosen by the soul to be her best portion, and she thereby fully bids an eternal farewell to the service of sin, having but one desire—"to live according to the will of God in all good works."

Such a person now belongs to Jesus's own, willing people, whom He has purified "unto himself [as] a peculiar people, zealous of good works" (Titus 2:14). If time permitted, with the Lord's help, I would expound this in greater detail, for the *quickening of the new man* consists in this "sincere joy of heart in God, through Christ, and with love and delight to live according to the will of God in all good works."

If someone has experience of what we have set before you, a new man and a new creature have been quickened within him, and internally he has been transformed and renewed according to God's image in true righteousness and in holiness.

Thus, we have briefly expounded for you in what the "the mortification of the old, and the quickening of the new man" consists, and this constitutes the true conversion of man. He who experiences these two matters within himself turns from sin unto God. He forsakes his natural ungodliness and returns unto the service of the triune God and His communion, from which he had utterly departed through sin.

How supremely blessed are such people who have been converted unto God in truth! No one should entertain the thought that such a conversion proceeds from man himself—as if man could be converted unto God by his own power, suitability, and ability. Beloved, man cannot convert himself. Man is intimately and inseparably intertwined with his sins, and he can do no otherwise but utterly hate God and His holy service. Conversion is and remains the duty of man, and God will punish the unconverted with eternal condemnation because they would not turn unto Him. Nevertheless, conversion is and remains the Lord's work as to its outset, continuation, and completion. For all His elect, Christ is the Alpha and Omega, the beginning and the end. "Him hath God exalted with his right hand to be a Prince and a Saviour, for to give repentance to Israel, and forgiveness of sins" (Acts 5:31).

Having explained and expounded the conversion of a sinner, the instructor proceeds to consider those *good* works that all truly converted men are now desirous to do and so to walk in accord therewith. In Question 91, the instructor will explain what good works are and what the constituent elements of such good works are. Since, however, this is a matter of great importance and of far-reaching ramifications, we will expound this more particularly in a subsequent Lord's Day. It is the wish and prayer of our soul that the Lord would be pleased graciously to bless our exposition to the initial conversion of dead sinners and to the further renewal and conversion of His people and children. Amen. So be it for the Lord's sake!

Concerning Good Works

*For we are his workmanship, created in Christ Jesus unto good works,
which God hath before ordained that we should walk in them.*
—EPHESIANS 2:10

Question 91: But what are good works?

Answer: Only those which proceed from a true faith, are performed according
to the law of God, and to His glory; and not such as are founded on our imaginations or the institutions of men.

Regarding the four creatures shown to the prophet Ezekiel in a vision, it is
noteworthy to read that they had wings and that "they had the hands of a man
under their wings on their four sides" (Ezek. 1:8). It is not our intent either to
investigate nor further to expound the mysteries that the Lord here communicated to the prophet Ezekiel by way of this vision regarding the four creatures.
It is the common opinion of Bible expositors that these four creatures are sym-
bolic representations of the holy angels. However, we will let this rest.

We wish to note here only that the Word of the Lord is exceedingly broad
as to its dimensions and common applications. All matters that are addressed
in the Scriptures can be to our instruction and comfort by accommodation or
application without in the least altering or distorting the actual meaning of a
given passage of Scripture. "All scripture is given by inspiration of God, and is
profitable for doctrine, for reproof, for correction, for instruction in righteousness: that the man of God may be perfect, thoroughly furnished unto all good
works" (2 Tim. 3:16–17).

Therefore, not only may we, but rather, we must make a proper personal
application of all matters to be found in the Scriptures and use it to our profit.
According to this rule, by accommodation, we may consider the four creatures

seen by Ezekiel in a vision as metaphorical likenesses or representations of all true believers.

First, just as these creatures had wings, all true believers have spiritual wings, namely, their faith, for thereby they fly upward to heaven. Thereby they draw near with their hearts unto God in heaven, leaving behind this lowly earth and all of its vanity. Oh, what precious wings they are! He who is not equipped with such wings of faith will never succeed in disengaging his heart and affections from this earth and soaring upward to heaven. This is unique to true believers only, and the Holy Spirit therefore testifies in Isaiah 40:31, saying: "But they that wait upon the LORD shall renew their strength; they shall mount up with wings as eagles. They shall run, and not be weary; and they shall walk, and not faint."

Second, those creatures in Ezekiel's vision not only had wings, but they also had the likeness of human hands underneath them. Likewise, true believers have not only the wings of faith by which they soar heavenward, but they also have hands with which they must continually labor and perform all the good works that have been commanded them of God in His law. These two matters are most intimately intertwined in all true Christians. They have not only the wings of faith, whereby they continually soar heavenward, but they have also the hands wherewith they are diligently to labor in performing all the duties that pertain to true holiness and true godliness. As the hands were conjoined to the wings, so must *faith* always be conjoined to *good works*. Those creatures could neither fly with their wings apart from the engagement of the hands nor work with their hands apart from flying with their wings. Likewise, a true Christian can neither believe without working nor work without believing, for faith without works is dead, and works are dead apart from faith.

Finally, the hands of Ezekiel's creatures were positioned in such a manner that they were *under* the wings. Thus, when the creatures were not flying and their wings were hanging down upon their hands, the wings would prevent the hands from being engaged in labor. They always had first to lift up their wings in flight, which gave room for their hands to be engaged in labor, and the same holds true in the lives of all true believers. Their hands are also situated beneath their wings, and when they permit their wings of faith to hang down motionlessly without engaging them in flight, they also are unable to labor with their hands in the diligent performance of all manner of such good works—works that they are commanded by the Lord to perform. If they are to use their hands freely and to be spiritually enabled and equipped to obey God's commandments and to do good works, they must first always lift up the wings of their faith. Thereby they fly upward, for all good works must issue forth not only from faith, but also from the spiritual strength one draws forth continually from the Lord Jesus by believing in Him. When in the aforementioned text (Isa. 40:31) it is testified regarding all true believers that "they shall mount up with wings as eagles," it is immediately added that "they shall run, and not be weary; and they shall walk, and not faint." The one activity signifies their faith and the other their active engagement; that is, their true godliness issuing forth from the vitality and lively exercise of their faith.

In the three previous questions of this Lord's Day, the instructor delineated for us in what the true conversion of man consists. We have seen how, by the Holy Spirit, this great benefit of God's free and sovereign grace powerfully and inwardly renews and transforms all elect and believing sinners. As a result, they turn their backs upon the wretched service of the world and of sin, and surrender themselves with a heartfelt willingness to Christ their savior, and so they engage themselves in the blessed service of this triune God, that they might belong only to Him and live only unto Him.

Thereupon, the instructor proceeds to give a description of the *good works* of believers in Question 91 of this Lord's Day. Having been converted and inwardly renewed by the Holy Spirit, believers must daily endeavor to do good works. Now, by virtue of being in the Lord Jesus, the hearts and persons of believers having been completely renewed and transformed by the power of the Holy Spirit that has been bestowed upon them by God, there must necessarily be a transformation of their works. Just as, prior to their conversion, they could do only sinful and evil works, likewise, having been regenerated and converted, they must now also walk in all good works, for "a good tree cannot bring forth evil fruit, neither can a corrupt tree bring forth good fruit" (Matt. 7:18). Also here, the words of Matthew 12:33 are applicable: "Either make the tree good, and his fruit good; or else make the tree corrupt, and his fruit corrupt: for the tree is known by his fruit."

Much hinges on our correct understanding of the essential nature of good works, and it is therefore a matter of the highest importance to understand the principle from which they proceed in converted believers; that is, according to which rule and unto what end. I am convinced that there are but very few who, in some measure, have a correct understanding regarding this. Due to a lack of the spiritual and experiential light of faith, many Christians are very much in the dark regarding this, and only by such light is one able to distinguish between clean and unclean, and between good works and evil works.

If only we were so blessed that we not only indeed performed good works, but also that we more actively lived and walked in accord therewith, we would also have a better understanding of what good works are. Daily and earnestly, we would then supplicate at the gate of heaven for divine grace, whereby we would be equipped to practice and to exercise good works. But sadly, regarding this great matter, we are deficient both in knowledge and in practice. And yet, the doing of good works constitutes the very essence of Christianity. Christianity does not consist in *talking*, but it consists in *doing*. It is easy to speak, and everyone is more than ready to do so. However, it is the doing that is the essence of the matter. The measure of a person's Christianity is determined by what he does and by his works—nothing more than that. "The kingdom of God is not in word, but in power" (1 Cor. 4:20).

What a sad spectacle it is when we regard present-day Christianity! In gatherings and in coffee bars, people talk so much whereby they render themselves almost deaf and dumb—and yet, nothing whatsoever is being done. I must say, for it is bound upon my heart, that we presently live in evil and grievous times. I hear the Lord loudly calling me, saying: "Put them in mind…to be ready to [do] every good work…. This is a faithful saying, and these things I will that thou affirm constantly, that they which have believed in God might be careful to maintain good works" (Titus 3:1, 8).

It is certain that, with God's blessing, we shall be able to salvage the ship of Christianity only if, without delay, we discontinue our useless conversations and immediately cast deeply into the ground two anchors, namely, faith and good works, thus using our wings and hands simultaneously. We will now proceed to consider good works in more detail. May the Lord be pleased graciously to bless our exposition.

As we proceed, we will closely follow the instructor, for he provides a very good, precious, and clear description of good works. One could not ask for any better or for an alternative description. The instructor asks, "But what are good works?" to which he replies, "Only those which proceed from a true faith, are performed according to the law of God, and to His glory; and not such as are founded on our imaginations or the institutions of men."

We will consider:

   1. the term *good works*; and

   2. the matter itself.

Good works are thus the subject matter that is to be addressed, and generally speaking, we understand them as referring to the holy and active deeds that converted Christians perform by the grace and influence of the Holy Spirit. With both soul and body, they engage in them in conformity to God's law, their aim in the performance of them being that all might be to God's glory, to the benefit and edification of their neighbor, and to the advancement of their own salvation in Christ Jesus their Lord.

These holy deeds and activities of converted Christians are here designated as good works. They are generally referred to as such in the Word of the Lord— a matter that is sufficiently known by each. What matters, however, is whether we truly comprehend the reasons and the grounds for such a designation.

The good and holy deeds of Christians, that is, their godly actions, are referred to as good works for two reasons:

First, a Christian performs and executes them by the grace of the Holy Spirit. They are the actual deeds or works that the Christian himself engages in as the secondary, rational, and independent cause. We need to understand this correctly. All the good a believing Christian does by virtue of the immediate influence of the grace and power of the Holy Spirit, he does with his natural and sanctified faculties. He has received them from God respectively at his first and at his new birth, and the Lord always sustains and strengthens them in him by a secret and efficacious influence. These actions are therefore all the Christian's own personal deeds and activities. If he performs a good work, it is in that sense his own act or work, and if he commits an evil deed, it is also his own act or work. As a holy and just judge, God shall once judge them both, for the Scriptures declare that "God shall bring every work into judgment, with every secret thing, whether it be good, or whether it be evil" (Prov. 12:14).

It is not profitable and necessary to engage in philosophical hairsplitting by focusing on distinctions and subtleties. We should simply believe that it is incontrovertibly true that whatever a Christian does, whether it be good or evil, he does himself. God's holy sentence will thus most certainly be pronounced upon one's deeds and works, and God will reward good works and punish evil works. If anyone wishes to argue with you about this, merely respond by saying: "I will not argue about this. I simply believe it." It is true what is expressed in this Latin adage, *Contra principia negantes non est disputandem*; that is, we must not dispute with those who either deny or argue the transparent and simple principles of a given truth. The godly deeds and activities of Christians are therefore referred to as "works," for they themselves perform them by the immediate grace and influence of the Holy Spirit, who continually and efficaciously works all good things for and in them. The holy apostle Paul teaches this, saying: "Work out your own salvation with fear and trembling. For it is God which worketh in you both to will and to do of his good pleasure" (Phil. 2:12–13).

Second, the doing and the execution of these good works and activities always require a serious commitment of labor, diligence, strength, and zeal in light of the great resistance and sluggishness of our evil and sinful flesh. In this life, the latter always greatly cleaves to God's people, and it exceedingly hinders them in the exercise of godliness. With Paul, they must therefore always complain, "I find then a law, that, when I would do good, evil is present with me" (Rom. 7:21). Consider the many temptations to which God's children are subjected by an evil world and by Satan, and by which they are greatly impeded in the way of godliness. It is to his grief and sorrow that each Christian experiences this more than enough every day.

A Christian must therefore labor ceaselessly, by the Holy Spirit's grace, to engage in his duty and to live in all true godliness before the Lord. Every good deed is consequently a work—something that requires exertion, strength, zeal, and diligence. Throughout the Holy Scriptures, believers are therefore earnestly exhorted and admonished to labor, to strive, to be diligent, to seek, to do violence.[1] This could be affirmed from God's Word by a multitude of texts.

These are the two reasons why the godly deeds of believers, and thus their holy activities, are designated as works. However, they are not only called works, but *good* works—not to be understood as if the godly works and activities in which believers engage, by the grace of the Holy Spirit, are already in this life completely good, holy, and perfect without being in any way stained by sin and corruption, for the best works of a Christian in this life are always very imperfect and stained with sin. On this side of eternity, God's children always consist of a mixture of flesh and spirit, of the old man and the new man, and thus of the two contrary principles of good and evil. A believer always lives and works by these two principles within him. With the mind, he serves the law of God and always does that which is good, and with the flesh, he serves the law of sin and always does that which is evil (Rom. 7:26). This continues until his death.

Consequently, all the deeds and works in which God's children engage with soul and body are a mixture of good and evil, and all their activities are partially

---

1. The expression "to do violence" is an obvious reference to Matthew 11:12: "And from the days of John the Baptist until now the kingdom of heaven suffereth violence, and the violent take it by force."

good and partially evil. Proportionate to the influence of the new man upon a given deed, so much goodness there is in this deed, and proportionate to the influence of the flesh, so much sin and evil there is in a given deed.

If, by the heavenly grace of faith, the spiritual man is rendered strong and lively, there then is more goodness and spirituality in the work that the Christian performs. If, however, in the absence of heavenly grace, the spiritual man is more sluggish, weaker, and feebler, then there is proportionally less goodness in his work. Therefore, in the very best works of God's children, there is always found a great deal of deficiency and sinfulness, causing them always to loathe themselves—even with regard to their very best works. Consequently, they by no means succeed in finding rest for their souls in their performances, but always by a true faith, they must go outside of themselves and take refuge in the perfect righteousness of our Lord Jesus Christ, continually taking hold of Him for reconciliation and sanctification, and putting their trust in Him alone. In Lord's Day 44, the instructor will address this matter in greater detail.

Why then does the Lord call the works of His children good works, given the fact that they nevertheless are imperfect? He designates them as good works according to His pleasure by the small measure of goodness that, by His Spirit, He has caused to come forth from them, rather than designate them according to the evil that is found in their works by their sinful flesh. If the Lord were to designate our works according to what proceeds from within us, He would have to designate them as evil and wicked works rather than good works. However, He is pleased to designate our works as good by virtue of what we contribute by His grace, rather than by what proceeds from us. Therefore, the Lord refers to them as good works rather than evil works, for He does not disqualify His own grace. In the performance of all our good works, this should then lead us to exclaim with a humble and self-effacing heart, "Not unto us, O LORD, not unto us, but unto thy name give glory, for thy mercy, and for thy truth's sake" (Ps.115:1). Here we would also say with Paul, "Yet not I, but the grace of God which was with me" (1 Cor. 15:10b).

Christians, consider therefore that our works are designated as good works because God delights to magnify His own work within us, and we magnify His name when we immediately return the honor that is due unto Him. This is the primary and most significant reason for this designation, and it is of utmost importance for us that we grasp it.

Let us also consider some reasons of lesser importance as to why the Lord designates our godly deeds as good works. He designates them as good works:

1. Because thereby He distinguishes them from the works of sinners and the unconverted, whose works, in the Holy Scriptures, are generally referred to as wicked works, evil works, carnal works, and the unfruitful works of darkness. In so doing, the Lord holds His fan in His hand, whereby He separates the chaff from the wheat. He does not paint our godly works with the same brush as the works of the ungodly. Rather, He very carefully wishes to distinguish one from the other.

2. Because they proceed through the influence and grace of the Holy Spirit. They thus come forth out of the good ground of a believing and sanctified heart that is upright before the Lord, that is, a heart that He has washed and cleansed from sin by His Spirit. Since the Lord Himself has made the soil and foundation of the heart good and has caused it to bring forth fruit, He therefore also designates the fruit as good.

3. To remind and assure us that for the sake of the merits of His Son, Jesus Christ, He graciously pardons all that is evil and sinful, and is always yet to be found, even in our very best works. Furthermore, He never holds us accountable for our sinful deficiencies concerning which we grieve so wholeheartedly. In His love, the Lord therefore makes no mention regarding all that is evil and deficient even in our very best works, but refers to them only as *good works*.

4. Because thereby He expresses pleasure and great delight in our godliness. As much as He hates evil, so much does He greatly delight in the good that His children may do, for it is all the fruit of the work of His good Spirit, who leads them "into the land of uprightness" (Ps. 143:10). Paul wishes to express this when he prays that the Lord would make believers "perfect in every good work to do his will, working in [them] that which is well-pleasing in his sight, through Jesus Christ" (Heb. 13:21).

5. Because nothing but good will issue forth from them, for, as we will soon hear, they all aim for the praise and glory of the Lord. They are also subservient to the edification and conversion of their neighbors, and therefore, as the instructor taught in Lord's Day 32, "by our godly conversation, others may be gained to Christ." We ourselves also will find therein and thereby a great measure of heavenly sweetness, comfort, peace, and joy, for "it is joy to the just to do judgment" (Prov. 21:15), and "godliness with contentment is great gain" (1 Tim. 6:6).

We shall now proceed to consider in some detail the true nature and character of good works. The instructor asks, "What are good works?" This is a weighty and essential question, for only few actually know what good works are. Many designate as good works activities in which no trace of true godliness is to be found. There are many works that appear to be good, but which are no more than cosmetic apples of Sodom that externally appear to be beautiful, but within are grievously corrupt. Nothing deceives people more than when such works are viewed as good works. Men think that they already have secured a good supply of them in their lives, whereas they have absolutely none. How grieved and distraught many will be in the Day of Judgment when Christ will find not a single good work among all their works!

Oh, that this would cause us to listen in all earnestness so that we might know what good works truly are! The instructor gives a correct description of good works, saying that only they are good works "which proceed from a true faith, are performed according to the law of God, and to His glory."

Take careful note of how the instructor prefaces all he says with the word *only*, for this must be strongly emphasized. It teaches us that there are no good works other than those here identified by the instructor. All that is mentioned here by him must truly be found in our works, for our works are otherwise suspect. We need to give heed to this, for this is the true touchstone whereby everyone can daily examine all of his works to see whether they are good or evil. Therefore, the instructor gives a description of:

1. what good works are; and
2. what are not good works.

According to the instructor, all good works are characterized by three special and essential characteristics, without which they cannot be considered as good and godly works. They must be performed by us:

- by a true faith;
- according to God's law; and
- to God's glory.

The first of these points us to true faith as being the origin, the second gives the prescribed rule for them, and the third sets before us the objective or focal point of all good works. We will now proceed with a brief exposition of each of the three.

The first essential requirement of all good works is that they must be performed by us as proceeding from a true faith. This communicates two matters to us, namely, that all good works must be performed by us upon the foundation of a true faith and by means of the true exercise of faith. We must understand these two matters well.

If we are to perform any good and godly work that will be pleasing to the Lord, it must be performed by us as truly proceeding from faith; that is, from a truly believing heart that God has purified from sin by faith (Acts 15:9). Before all things, we must possess the true saving faith that the Holy Spirit has wrought in us, whereby we have been truly and internally united with the Lord Jesus, and whereby we have been adopted as God's reconciled children, having been truly justified and sanctified in respect to our sins. If such is not the case, we shall never be able to perform any good or holy work that is pleasing unto the Lord. As long as our hearts are still absolutely governed by unbelief and we are thus without God and without Christ, our persons and all that pertains to us will appear before God as being utterly ungodly, abominable, loathsome, accursed, and incompatible.

Only true, upright faith is the means whereby our persons and our works are rendered good, for we are then viewed as being in union with Christ and in a reconciled state with God. Therefore, before God is able to approve of any of our works and before we are able to engage in any work that shall be good, we must necessarily be the recipients of true faith in our hearts by the powerful operation of the Holy Spirit. True faith renders us spiritually alive before God in Christ Jesus, for "he that believeth on the Son hath everlasting life: and he that believeth not the Son shall not see life; but the wrath of God abideth on him" (John 3:36).

If we still lack this faith, we are still spiritually dead, and as little as a dead person can perform any work, so little shall we also who are in that state be able to perform any good works. The Scriptures therefore teach that "without faith it is impossible to please [God]" (Heb. 11:6a), and that "whatsoever is not of faith is sin" (Rom. 14:23b). Without faith, we cannot please God as to our persons, and much less can we therefore please Him by way of our works, for God must obviously first receive our persons favorably before our works are acceptable to Him. Therefore, it is written, "And the LORD had respect unto Abel and to his offering" (Gen. 4:4). Do you not see that the Lord first received Abel's person favorably in light of him being a true believer, and thereafter he had respect unto his work or sacrifice that he performed by faith? It is therefore self-evident that we must first have a *good* faith before we can do a *good* work. It is abundantly clear that all men who are not united to the Lord Jesus by true saving faith cannot do anything other than sin. They may be as near to true Christianity as possible, and their confession, religion, sincerity, and zeal may externally be so attractive that in many things outwardly they surpass such as are truly godly. Nevertheless, they do no good works, and nothing that is good proceeds from them. The Lord takes no pleasure whatsoever in anything they do. A sincere and heartfelt sigh of one of His children is more pleasing to Him than all the religious works of such as are without Christ and are void of faith.

Oh, that by God's grace this would make a true impression upon the hearts of the many in Christianity who, irrespective of all they think to have, are yet void of a good and true faith, and secretly in their hearts rest upon their external duties, religious exercises, frames, virtues, and activities. Oh, that the Lord would give them eye-salve to see that they are putting all their trust solely in an amalgamation of splendid sins! How dreadfully they will prove to have been deceived when they will finally open their eyes in eternity! It is God's work, however, to convince them of this. It is thus evident that all good works must be performed by us as proceeding from the fountain of a true faith.

The other matter is that all our good works must be performed by a true exercise of faith. To state it briefly, this faith, as to its very essence, consists of the lively and spiritual activity of faith in our hearts, whereby we, in the power of the Holy Spirit, have a steadfast and personal confidence that all that God has revealed in His Word is absolutely truthful, and specifically, that all that the holy gospel reveals as truth is absolutely true.

In and of ourselves, we are utterly sinful, unclean, accursed, impotent, and incapable of doing any good. We also believe, however, that the Lord Jesus Christ has once died on the cross for our sins and has accomplished all things for us. We believe furthermore that God has graciously bestowed His perfect righteousness upon us, and, for His own name's sake, eternally and fully has forgiven us all our sins and our sinful nature. Moreover, He has adopted us as His reconciled children, so that, by free and sovereign grace, we have in Christ everything we need for every aspect of our full salvation.

When we believe this in our hearts with a lively and steadfast faith, when we actively engage ourselves to be assured of this grace of God in Christ, rely upon it with our hearts, and rest sweetly in it, thus entrusting ourselves truly and fully with all our sins and sinful deficiencies to Christ as our all-sufficient savior—and therefore upon God's eternal love and sovereign grace in Him— that, and that alone, is the pure and true exercise of faith. Whatever opposes this, by whatever attractive name it may be called, is pure unbelief.

It is by such true, lively, and active exercises of faith that we bring Christ, along with His Spirit and His grace, into our hearts, and in so doing, we simultaneously draw all the strength and vitality of our spiritual life from Christ, our living head, unto the mortification of our sins and evil lusts, and unto the diligent and zealous performance of good works. Our faith unites and keeps us united to Christ as our stem, root, and vine. Our entire life is to be found in Christ, according to the immutable testimony of the holy gospel (1 John 5:11).

Therefore, when we believe, we "live by the faith of the Son of God, who loved [us], and gave himself for [us]" (Gal. 2:20). If this is how we live, we do good works, for we then are alive unto God by willingly serving and obeying His Son, doing His will with delight and in a most painstaking and spiritual way.

When we believe in Christ, we also abide in Christ and remain actively united to Him. And what does Christ say regarding this? Or have we already forgotten to keep His Word? Christ says, "He that abideth in me, and I in him, the same bringeth forth much fruit: for without me ye can do nothing" (John 15:5). This means that we do all our good works by faith; and thus, as we have seen, when we continue to rely with our hearts upon Christ and upon God's grace in such a lively and steadfast manner, we soar heavenward with our wings, and our hands are engaged. We stand securely in our heavenly steadfastness and strength, for we then have taken "the shield of faith" (Eph. 6:16). We are able to fight manfully against sin and against all our enemies, for we give preeminence to Christ, our great captain. He strengthens us with all might, so that we are "strong in the Lord, and in the power of his might" (Eph. 6:10).

To summarize all this (for whoever enters into this truth sinks away into a bottomless depth, as "corn shall make the young men cheerful, and new wine the maids" [Zech. 9:17]), we are then able to "do all things through Christ which strengtheneth [us]" (Phil. 4:13).

Oh, beloved, believing is everything! It is the focal point and soul of all spiritual life. If we have faith, we have good works, for true faith always "worketh by love" (Gal. 5:6). Believing Christians are always active Christians. A windmill is always churning in proportion to the blowing of the wind, and so a Christian is working for the Lord in proportion to the wind of faith blowing in his heart.

Such faith as we have described is not always and equally exercised in all of God's people, for "God hath dealt to every man the measure of faith" (Rom. 12:3). All God's children are therefore not always equally engaged in doing good works, but everyone is engaged in proportion to the inner exercise of his faith—and thus, whether strong or weak, or be it much or little, "for as the man is, so is his strength" (Judg. 8:21). There are weak believers and there are strong believers, and a perfect believer is yet to be born. Weak believers generally stir up a great amount of noise but accomplish very little. Stronger believers are generally quieter and accomplish much more. They are much more fruitful in all good works.

Why is it that in our time, Christianity has regretfully become so dead in regard to the doing of good works? The answer is not only that many presume to be Christians who have but a dead faith, but also that there is so little pure and spiritual faith found even among true Christians. Oh, we have lost *the* faith—the old Christian apostolic faith, which is the fountain of all good works and the door into heaven. This most holy faith is so far gone that, for quite some time already, we have begun to engage ourselves to make do with something less in its place. We can give it beautiful names, but we should not expect anything else from this but a Laodicean church, which Christ soon will spew out of His mouth. Sadly, with great strides we are moving into that direction. Oh, that the Lord would give us eye-salve!

From the foregoing, it is now evident how all good works can be performed only by true faith. We have dwelt so long upon this doctrine because it constitutes the entire soul of Christianity, and therefore we never are able sufficiently to speak of and admonish one another regarding it.

The instructor states, as the second requisite for all good works, that they must be performed *according to God's law*. This matter is sufficiently clear in the doctrine itself. All distinctions between that which morally is either good or evil have their origin in the specifications of God's law. This law is an expression of God's essential and immutable holiness, and our goodness and holiness must necessarily be most painstakingly conformed to and aligned with it, and, so to speak, be molded by it. The law of God is like a straight line in which there is not a single curvature. Therefore, all of our deeds and activities, both in soul and body, must strictly conform to this law and strictly adhere to it without any deviation. Only then will they be good and proper. However, whatever deviates in the least degree from this law, or merely approximates it, must at once be viewed as sinful, wrong, and evil. The Lord has therefore said, "To the law and to the testimony: if they speak not according to this word, it is because there is no light in them" (Isa. 8:20).

During His sojourn here on earth, the Savior taught clearly and transparently that our godliness must by no means consist of a splendid confession, but rather, of a determined practice of the entire law of God with both soul and body. In Matthew 7:21, He proclaimed, "Not every one that saith unto me,

Lord, Lord, shall enter into the kingdom of heaven; but he that doeth the will of my Father which is in heaven." This is consistent with what Paul teaches, saying, "And as many as walk according to this rule, peace be on them" (Gal. 6:16).

God the Lord has clearly revealed His law to us in His Word, and with the finger of His Holy Spirit, He wrote it upon the tables of the hearts of all believers, so that they all would "delight in the law of God after the inward man" (Rom. 7:22). Therefore, whenever they steadfastly cleave to and follow the Lord Jesus with their hearts and by faith, they also have a steadfast love for God's law in their inward man. Believers remain focused on that law and have deep respect and esteem for it, always meditating upon it day and night. They always consult with it, endeavoring in all their actions not only to conform themselves to the law of the Lord as painstakingly as possible, so that they may do willingly all that the Lord commands them to do, but also refrain from doing all that He forbids. There is not one single commandment that is too difficult and too grievous. On the contrary, it is their delight to observe and obey the entire law of God with both soul and body, doing so as painstakingly as possible. They cry out with David: "Thou hast commanded us to keep thy precepts diligently. O that my ways were directed to keep thy statutes! Then shall I not be ashamed, when I have respect unto all thy commandments" (Ps. 119:4–6). This proves sufficiently how all good works must issue forth from faith and be done in conformity to the law of God.

The instructor then proceeds to set before us the third requisite regarding all good works, namely, that they must be done to *God's honor.* This means that in all we do or refrain from doing, we must always have the unadulterated honor and service of the triune God in view. This is to be bound upon our hearts, and in all of our works we are to endeavor steadfastly, and as much as possible, only to serve and praise God in all our actions, doing so without having any other motive in mind. Our works can never be considered good if the unadulterated praise and honor of God is not the chief and only end that we are pursuing.

It ought not to surprise us that this is so, for within the context of the covenant of grace, all true believers serve this God who is supremely majestic and glorious, "for of him, and through him, and to him, are all things: to whom be glory for ever" (Rom. 11:36), for "the LORD hath made all things for himself: yea, even the wicked for the day of evil" (Prov. 16:4). He knows of no other praise and honor but His own, and He has formed His people for no purpose but that they should show forth His praises (Isa. 43:21), "the praises of him who hath called [them] out of darkness into his marvellous light" (1 Peter 2:9).

All true believers must therefore necessarily answer to this lofty and divine purpose, for they are vessels of honor (Rom. 9:21). This is the ultimate fruit of the redemption accomplished by Jesus Christ, our savior, for He glorified His Father on earth (John 17:4). Consequently, all the works of believers, if they are to be genuinely good and proper, must necessarily, fully, and solely have God's honor as their focus. In all that they do, believers must utterly forsake themselves and all creatures, and in Christ Jesus, they must live and work solely for the glory of God.

Consider the earnest exhortation of the holy apostle Paul, when he writes, "For ye are bought with a price: therefore glorify God in your body, and in your spirit, which are God's" (1 Cor. 6:20). Consider also when he writes, "Whether therefore ye eat, or drink, or whatsoever ye do, do all to the glory of God" (1 Cor. 10:31).

If the previous two requisites are found within us, it cannot possibly be otherwise. If we sincerely endeavor to engage in our work by faith and according to the law of God, we always do it to God's glory as well. Faith teaches us not only utterly to forsake ourselves and all that is not of God, but also to consecrate ourselves fully to the triune God as "a living sacrifice, holy, acceptable unto God, which is your reasonable service" (Rom. 12:1).

We have thus considered the third requisite of a good work and have determined in what the doctrine of good works consists. These three matters or characteristics must necessarily be found in them, for God will not consider anything other than we have considered to be good works. All our works are ungodly and sinful, and we neither engage in them with a pure motive and according to a perfect rule, nor aim for the lofty goal that has been set before us. The instructor now desires to instruct us regarding the latter.

He proceeds by fully rejecting all other works done by men, denouncing them as being evil and wicked works, saying that they are "such as are founded on our imaginations, or the institutions of men." In general terms, the instructor is here referring to all the counterfeit works of men; that is, all external observation of duties and religious activities, all presumed virtues practiced by men and proceeding from their own natural inclinations and exercised by their own carnal strength. Such works are performed void of a true faith in the Lord Jesus, void of a heartfelt love to obey God's law in a most spiritual manner, and void of a sincere determination only to praise and honor the triune God.

All such counterfeit good works proceed from the fountain of man's own darkened and carnal understanding, and the instructor refers to them as being "founded on our imaginations." These human imaginations are utterly hostile to God and are radically opposed to the only way in which God is pleased to save and redeem poor sinners in His Son, Jesus Christ. Therefore, all such counterfeit works of men have as their sole objective, be it to a greater or lesser degree, to establish one's own righteousness before God, however sophisticated and attractive the manner may be in which men bring them forth (for "the heart is deceitful above all things, and desperately wicked: who can know it?" [Jer. 17:9]). Thereby men seek to absolve themselves from their need for Christ's perfect and holy righteousness, abandoning the covenant of grace in favor of the covenant of works.

However beautiful and adorned such human works may be, they are in truth nothing but deficient works, evil works, and unfruitful works of darkness. The very best of them are but splendid sins, vain spider webs, ashes that nourish a deceitful heart, wicked reeds upon which one cannot lean, "broken cisterns, that can hold no water" (Jer. 2:13), sparks from a fire that one himself has kindled (Isa. 50:11), but which shall consume him eternally. The very best of them are works that ultimately will be consumed and burned. God does not give such works the least of any consideration, and He turns away His eyes from them. He abhors them, saying of them, "But in vain they do worship me, teaching for doctrines the commandments of men" (Matt. 15:9). Furthermore: "When ye come to appear before me, who hath required this at your hand, to tread my courts? Bring no more vain oblations; incense is an abomination unto me; the new moons and sabbaths, the calling of assemblies, I cannot away with; it is iniquity, even the solemn meeting" (Isa. 1:12–13). If only we would truly hear and understand this word of the Lord!

Herewith, we conclude our exposition of this matter—if ever it can be sufficiently expounded. It has become evident what are good works and what are evil works. Never were we afforded a better or more suitable opportunity for application, exhortation, conviction, and admonition in regard to the converted as well as the unconverted. And yet, as I conclude, I see a grievous thing, for with the prophet Ezekiel I see a valley full of dead bones, and if the Lord were to ask me, "Son of man, can these bones live?" I would respond to Him, "O Lord GOD, thou knowest" (Ezek. 37:3).

May the Lord bless this word. Amen.

General Introduction to God's Law

Open thou mine eyes, that I may behold wondrous things out of thy law.
—PSALM 119:18

A noteworthy history is recorded for us in Exodus 15:23–25. There we read the account of the children of Israel arriving at Marah in their journey through the wilderness. Being very thirsty, they found there an abundance of water. However, the water was very bitter, the people could not drink of it, and a murmuring arose among them. But the Lord was gracious to the people and delivered them in their need and perplexity. He directed Moses to a piece of wood, and upon God's command, Moses cast it into the bitter water of Marah. The wood immediately transformed the bitter water into water that was sweet and delightful. All its bitterness was removed, and the children of Israel were able to drink with delight. They were greatly refreshed by it. The Lord intended to teach the people of Israel a spiritual lesson by means of this unique and wondrous event, thus directing their attention to heavenly matters by earthly matters. The Lord dealt with His people in such a gracious and paternal manner so that, by all suitable ways and means, He could instruct them regarding matters pertaining to salvation.

The purpose of this unique event was to set before them a clear mirror or illustration as to how the precious cross of Christ, on which He would hang and whereby He would be put to death, would have divine efficacy to take whatever has become bitter through sin and again make it sweet and delightful for that poor, believing soul who takes hold of the cross of Christ and casts it into his own bitter water. This would enable him again to drink the bitterest water with great delight, for the cross of Christ would fully remove all bitterness. Whatever then would come into contact with it would be rendered completely sweet and delightful.

For sinful man, there is no more bitter water than the holy and perfect law of God. In Paradise, the law for Adam was a very lovely and delightful drink. He could not drink enough of that heavenly nectar in his perfect and holy state. All the beautiful rivers of the garden of Eden were unable to delight him as much as did the precious law of the Lord. However, the moment Adam sinned by willfully transgressing God's law, he also began to drink iniquity like water. Consequently, for him and all his sinful descendants, the law was transformed into very bitter water that they no longer could drink. For a sinner, the law now brings forth nothing but curse and wrath, and no flesh can be saved or justified by it.

However, the most high God, in His infinite mercy, has also devised a means for a poor, contrite, and believing sinner to transform the water of the law, having been made so bitter by our willful transgression, into water that is most sweet and delightful. He has done so by means of the precious cross of our savior, Jesus Christ. The moment a poor sinner who truly is sorrowful and contrite regarding his sins takes hold of the cross of the Lord Jesus, casting it into the bitter water of the law as an ungodly and impotent sinner who, by the law, is eternally accursed and condemned by God to the punishment of hell, and, completely looking away from himself, takes refuge solely to the cross of the Lord Jesus so that thereby alone he may obtain his entire salvation from God and by grace, the bitter water of the law becomes entirely sweet, lovely, and delightful for him. The Lord Jesus then removes the entire curse of the law and delivers His believing people from the guilt of their sins. For them, He obtains reconciliation with God and also secures His favor. He inwardly sanctifies and renews their hearts by His Holy Spirit so that the law becomes their utmost desire and delight, and they become desirous to render obedience to it in love, as well as to order their walk and conversation accordingly.

The cross of Christ again thus renders the law sweet and delightful to our souls, so that we will never be able to satisfy ourselves as much as we would desire. These are the matters that we will now consider in greater detail.

In the previous Lord's Day, the instructor addressed the conversion of man. In principle, man is thereby sanctified and enabled, as one of the redeemed people of the Lord, to live before Him in true gratitude and to walk with body and soul upon the pathway of true godliness. In the same Lord's Day, he also dealt with the good and godly works of converted souls—works that proceed from a true faith, are according to God's law, and are done to the glory of God. He then proceeded to address God's law in particular as being the only rule and perfect standard to which all our deeds, both inwardly and outwardly, must always be conformed if they are to be good and pleasing to the Lord. During the next eleven Lord's Days, the instructor will address this by expounding the entire law of God briefly and succinctly, setting before us all the good that the Lord commands us to do and all the evil and sinful deeds that He prohibits.

However, if we are to have a good understanding of the entire exposition of the instructor by the illuminating grace of the Spirit of the Lord, it is absolutely essential that we be first instructed regarding the true nature and essence of the law of the Lord as our rule of life.

All members of Christendom, whether within or outside of the church, with the exception of some heretics who are called Antinomians (that is, they who oppose the law), readily confess and admit that the law of the Lord is the perfect rule and standard for our lives, and that we are obliged to keep every component of it and to obey it with soul and body. As such, this is a good confession that is beyond reproach. However, most people generally do not understand very well how the law of God is to be kept by us purely by the grace of our Lord Jesus Christ, as well as by the heavenly power of His Holy Spirit—that is, in conformity to the new covenant of the gospel, in which all believers are united to God in Christ. This is indeed the great mystery of godliness that but few among us are given to understand by the Spirit of the Lord. All natural and unregenerate men are utterly blind and in the dark regarding this, for "the natural man receiveth not the things of the Spirit of God: for they are foolishness unto him: neither can he know them, because they are spiritually discerned" (1 Cor. 2:14). They are ignorant of the holiness, perfection, and spirituality of God's law, and they therefore are also ignorant of their spiritual impotence and their condemnable and lost state due to sin. They do not yearn earnestly to be united with Christ by a true faith, so that, by virtue of His precious atoning blood and by grace, they might be delivered by Him from the curse of the law and from their sins.

Instead, they bypass all the aforementioned, although they may confess and acquiesce in these matters intellectually. They endeavor only in some measure outwardly to obey and fulfill the law of God as a law of the covenant of works, attempting to do so by their own natural strength and apart from Christ. By obeying the law in this manner, they believe that God will grant them salvation, and thus they seek by their own works to be justified either partially or fully before Him.

This is the erroneous pathway that all unconverted and unregenerate men wholeheartedly pursue—a way that will lead to the wretched perdition of so many thousands in our churches. It is therefore of the utmost importance, prior to embarking upon the exposition of the law of the Lord, that with the instructor, we first consider in greater detail the actual occasion when the law was given and how we are to keep this law of the Lord as a holy rule or standard for our walk and conversation in the gracious covenant of grace—a covenant into which we have been incorporated by a true and genuine faith in the Lord Jesus, "who of God is made unto us wisdom, and righteousness, and sanctification, and redemption" (1 Cor. 1:30).

Oh, that the Lord would be pleased to bless this sermon and that, with David, we would all fervently beseech Him, "Open thou mine eyes, that I may behold wondrous things out of thy law" (Ps. 119:18). Therefore, at the present time, we shall not proceed with the exposition of our Catechism, but we will address the matter of the law of the Lord in general terms only. We will do so by:

1. setting before you a few specific matters that need to be correctly understood if we are to have a correct and proper understanding of God's law; and

2. showing in greater detail the purpose for which the Lord gave His law to a sinful people such as we all are, and how we, in true faith and by the power and grace of the Lord Jesus, are to observe and obey this law as a rule of life in the gospel covenant of grace. However, in so doing, we will not engage with anyone in polemical dispute about this. With Paul, we say, "If any man seem to be contentious, we have no such custom, neither the churches of God" (1 Cor. 11:16). Let those who wish to debate this subject do so, but we have no desire for it. We have learned that God's truth is pure and transparent if our eyes are but pure and transparent. The truth functions like the light of the sun. When the truth is set before us transparently and in all simplicity, it radiates its own inherent light, and thus we need not be concerned, for it clears up all obscurity and controversy posited by men who claim to be wise.

Regarding the first, we will focus on five specific matters regarding the law of the Lord:

1. its origin,
2. its spirituality,
3. its perfection,
4. its immutability, and
5. its holiness and righteousness.

We must have a thorough knowledge of all these matters if, in some measure, we are to have a good and correct understanding regarding the law of the Lord. It is our intent to limit ourselves to these five matters only and to consider all other matters in subsequent sermons.

The subject of our consideration is the law of God, and by this term, we are simply to understand all that the Lord God has comprehensively prescribed unto us, the children of men, in His Holy Word as a rule for our conduct in both soul and body. More specifically, we are to understand hereby the *law of the Ten Words or Commandments* as they were communicated through the ministry of Moses and as they were engraved on two tables of stone by God Himself. This law of the Ten Commandments is preeminently designated as the law of God, for it comprehends in summary form the essential content and foundation of all that the most high God has either prescribed or forbidden to men throughout His entire Word. This all converges in these Ten Commandments, and the law of the Ten Commandments therefore functions as the stem and root from which issue forth all specific duties of our reasonable worship (cf. Rom. 12:1)—just as small or larger branches issue forth from a tree. The law of the Ten Commandments is therefore specifically and preeminently designated as the *law of God.*

This law is not of human origin. Its origin is purely from heaven and divine. God Himself, the Lord of hosts, has given this law to us, the children of men, to be a rule or standard for our lives, having revealed it verbally from heaven in the form in which it is presently read by us. It is therefore written at the very beginning, "And God spake all these words, saying…" (Ex. 20:1). The reason for this is self-evident, for God is the supreme creator and sustainer of heaven and earth, as well as of all creatures that are to be found therein. Out of nothing, He created them all, and He sustains and governs them immediately by His omnipotent hand. This great and most glorious God is therefore the supreme Lord and king of all the children of men. He is King of kings and Lord of lords, who "giveth to all life, and breath, and all things" (Acts 17:25b).

All men must therefore fully and perfectly serve and obey God as their supreme king and sovereign Lord, doing so with soul and body and with all their strength. They must exist and live entirely for Him, continually glorify Him alone, and be ready to serve Him, for "The LORD hath made all things for himself" (Prov. 16:4).

Aside from this indiscriminate, permanent, natural, and complete dependence of all men upon God as His creatures, there is another dependent relationship with God that does not pertain to all men. Rather, this pertains only to true believers, whom God, by His sovereign grace, delivers from sin and the power of the devil through His Son, Christ Jesus, and whom He, by His Holy Spirit, re-creates after His image. In the covenant of grace, they have wholeheartedly surrendered themselves to this triune God to be His eternal property with soul and body, and to live fully and solely for Him alone and according to His will and command. Since God the Lord is thus the natural, supreme, and sovereign king of all men by creation and providence, and since He is also specifically Lord and king of all believers by their gracious redemption in Christ Jesus, God must necessarily give His law to all men in general and particularly to His elect people. He must reveal and make known this law to them as the established rule or precept according to which He must be ceaselessly served and feared, and painstakingly obeyed with body and soul—just as an earthly sovereign or king gives laws to his subjects according to which they are to live. Therefore, we read in Isaiah 33:22 that "the LORD is our judge, the LORD is our lawgiver, the LORD is our king."

The Lord God has therefore acted accordingly, for as Paul teaches in Romans 2:14–15, upon creating man, He immediately impressed His holy and perfect law upon his heart, so that man, in spite of sin, has not fully lost this permanent imprint of God's law. Nevertheless, by no means has the Lord left it at that, for subsequently, He has more fully, and in a variety of ways, revealed His holy law to man. The most extraordinary and solemn revelation of the law of God was given to the children of Israel in the wilderness at Mount Sinai, when the Lord established His covenant with them—a covenant He already had established with their fathers long before. It then pleased the Lord to reveal His holy law in an extraordinary manner from heaven and to inscripturate it in ten distinct words or commandments, thereby clearly and succinctly stipulating in summary form in what man's obedient service would consist.

This is the holy and perfect law of God that the children of Israel initially received from God the Lord Himself in a most glorious manner through the ministry of Moses. From that time forward, this law has always had a place in this world, and it will continue to be a steadfast and precise rule for the lives and conversations of all men as it pertains inwardly to the heart and outwardly to the body. This law is therefore entirely of divine origin. God gives it to man, and He and none other is the one who speaks and commands in this law.

As to the content of the law of the Lord, it is also most spiritual. That is to say, this law pertains not only to man's body and all its related physical activity, but also to man's spirit or heart, and all his inner thoughts, motions, desires, and stirrings. Paul clearly teaches this, saying, "For we know that the law is spiritual: but I am carnal, sold under sin" (Rom. 7:14). Oh, if only we would understand this rightly! Man consists of two components, namely, soul and body, and with both he must serve, love, and obey God as His creator and Lord—and by no means is the Lord satisfied when we merely obey Him outwardly with our bodies. On the contrary, He requires of us that we primarily obey and fear Him inwardly with our souls and with all the powers, motions, and activities of our hearts. The soul is the noblest part of man, and therefore it is especially the soul that must be offered up unto God in the way of service and obedience. The Lord speaks accordingly, saying, "My son, give me thine heart, and let thine eyes observe my ways" (Prov. 23:26); that is, "Serve, fear, and love Me with your heart and with all its internal propensities and activities." "Let thine heart retain my words: keep my commandments, and live" (Prov. 4:4).

God has therefore given this law of the Ten Commandments to obligate both the soul of man, in all of its inner motions, and the body, in all of its outward deeds, to strict obedience. However, no one understands this correctly except they who are truly regenerated and converted; that is, they whose understandings have been inwardly illuminated by the Lord through His Holy Spirit. Unconverted natural men generally are of the opinion that all is well if they outwardly observe the letter of God's law and outwardly conform their actions and deeds accordingly. They do not concern themselves with whether their souls are inwardly inclined toward an upright love for and obedience of the law. Their entire walk "is like a silly dove without heart" (Hos. 7:11). Such was the young man's behavior as is recorded in the Gospels. When the Savior held before him the commandments of the law, he boldly responded, "All these things have I kept from my youth up: what lack I yet?" (Matt. 19:20). He considered only his outward deeds and walk, but he had no knowledge of his heart and had never observed that it was filled with evil and hostility toward God's law. During the Savior's sojourn, the Pharisees and scribes were likeminded. They obeyed the law outwardly and conformed their lives and walk accordingly. However, they transgressed the law inwardly, within their hearts, and had no concern about it. Christ therefore said to them: "Woe unto you, scribes and Pharisees, hypocrites! for ye make clean the outside of the cup and of the platter, but within they are full of extortion and excess. Thou blind Pharisee, cleanse first that which is within the cup and platter, that the outside of them may be clean also. Woe unto you, scribes and Pharisees, hypocrites! for ye are like unto whited sepulchres, which indeed appear beautiful outward, but are within full of dead men's bones, and of all uncleanness" (Matt. 23:25–27).

The law of God is, however, of an entirely different nature, for by no means is it sufficient that our outward life conforms to the law. Our hearts must also conform inwardly to the law in all things. All our thoughts, considerations, desires, and inclinations must fully conform to this law. Consider, for instance, the Lord's prohibition in His law, "Thou shalt not steal." It is by no means acceptable that we refrain outwardly from all manner of theft and dishonesty, for the law's positive meaning is that we may not have the least inward desire or inclination toward any theft or dishonesty. Otherwise we immediately transgress God's law in our hearts and will be subjected to its curse. Again the Savior teaches, "Ye have heard that it was said by them of old time, Thou shalt not commit adultery: but I say unto you, That whosoever looketh on a woman to lust after her hath committed adultery with her already in his heart" (Matt. 5:27–28).

Here we observe that the least emerging desire or lust of the heart against any commandment of God, though one does his utmost not to break forth in the deed itself, is an immediate and grievous transgression of the heart against God's law, and therefore a condemnable and an accursed sin whereby man provokes God to wrath. As a willful transgressor of the law, he deserves to be punished eternally, for his heart is not subject to God's law in true obedience. Though we may not commit any sinful deeds, we are nevertheless sinning against God with our hearts, and that alone is sufficient reason to be cast eternally into hell with both soul and body. All unregenerate men fail to understand that this is the source and fountain of all their misery and wretchedness, and from this lack of understanding issues forth man's vain notion of being virtuous, as well as all the pride and carelessness that so greatly dominate him. Consequently, unregenerate men are incapable of rightly perceiving their sin and wickedness, as well as their accursed and impotent condition, and therefore they neither humble themselves in truth before God nor yearn for Christ unto the justification and sanctification of their souls.

Such was also true for the apostle Paul in his unregenerate and unconverted state, for he was ignorant of the pure holiness and spirituality of the law. He thought it sufficient and acceptable if he only refrained from evil and sinful deeds, and diligently conformed and adapted his outward conduct to God's law.

How this all changed when God converted him and, by His Spirit, inwardly opened the blind eyes of his understanding and gave to him a clear view of the power and spirituality of the law! Paul then recognized that the least desire or emerging lust within the heart of man against any of God's commandments is a vile violation or transgression of the law of the Lord—a transgression that renders man worthy of eternal damnation. Listen to his own confession when he says, "Nay, I had not known sin, but by the law: for I had not known lust, except the law had said, Thou shalt not covet" (Rom. 7:7).

Thus we observe Paul, in his unregenerate state, as having said and heard much about sin, but he had never truly known nor understood what sin actually was, for he "had not known sin." Only when God acquainted him with the spirituality of the law did Paul become acquainted with sin. Only then did he become, in his own eyes, as vile, ungodly, unclean, and condemnable as he formerly had appeared good and virtuous to himself.

There is nothing more important for a man to know than this spirituality of the law of God. Without a correct knowledge of this spirituality, no one can either be saved or fear God in truth. This is "the secret of the LORD [that] is with them that fear him" (Ps. 25:14). Nevertheless, this spirituality of the law must be unceasingly preached and made known to the people, so that, by the grace of God, they might attain to a true knowledge of their sins and be made ready for the Spirit of the gospel. This concludes our consideration of the origin and spirituality of the law of God.

We will now proceed to consider the third matter, the *perfection* of God's law. David, the man after God's own heart, speaks of this: "The law of the LORD is perfect, converting the soul" (Ps. 19:8) and "I have seen an end of all perfection: but thy commandment is exceeding broad" (Ps. 119:96). The apostle James therefore calls the law of God "the perfect law of liberty" (James 1:25; 2:12).

As this is stated generally regarding the entire law of God and set before us throughout the entire Word of God in its broadness, it is also specifically and certainly true regarding the law of the Ten Commandments, for, as we already have seen, this law is the root and foundation of all God's commandments. Every commandment or prohibition in the entire Word of God is either rooted in or derives its principle from the law of the Ten Commandments. All admonitions and duties set before us in the Holy Scriptures by way of either precepts or prohibitions are but so many further explanations and expositions of the law of the Ten Commandments. They are all shoots and branches proceeding from the same tree. This law therefore is a complete and perfect rule or precept for our lives and conversation—both inwardly and outwardly—prescribing for us a complete and perfect obedience and religious practice. He who succeeds in keeping God's law both in body and soul is a perfect man, "thoroughly furnished unto all good works" (2 Tim. 3:17). More is not necessary than to be as perfectly holy and godly as Adam was prior to the fall. All that is required is a correct observance of the law of the Ten Commandments. He who is capable of doing this without the least stumble, neglect, evil desire, or lust, and is able to do so consistently from his birth until his death, will not be damned, but will most surely inherit eternal life. Therefore, when the rich young ruler asked the Savior, "Good Master, what good thing shall I do, that I may have eternal life?" He responded to him, saying, "Why callest thou me good? there is none good but one, that is, God: but if thou wilt enter into life, keep the commandments" (Matt. 19:16–17). He then held before him a portion of the law of the Ten Commandments.

If the rich young ruler simply had been able to keep this law of the Ten Commandments, he would have been saved and have inherited eternal life. He would then have had a perfect obedience, and he would have been completely perfect and without any sin.

It is therefore an absurd and ungodly sentiment of the Papists, Socinians, and Arminians, who insist that the law of the Ten Commandments was not perfect and that the Old Testament required neither perfect worship nor obedience. They posit that only in the New Testament was it perfected by Christ, by reason of His addition of several unique and new commandments, and by expansion of the parameters of some older commandments. However, these parties are not worthy of a rebuttal, for they have no understanding whatsoever of the law of God, and they are utterly bereft of all spiritual and salvific light. Therefore, they neither are capable of understanding the spirituality and the infinite perfection of the law of God, nor willing to understand it. The moment they would have a correct understanding regarding this matter, all their erroneous doctrines regarding the way of salvation would collapse at once, and nothing would remain for them but to proceed at once, in conformity to our Reformed faith and in full reliance upon free grace, to seek all of their salvation in the Lord Jesus. However, because of their wretched blindness, they reject and grievously slander this doctrine and cast it away as being not according to godliness.

It is therefore certain that the law of the Ten Commandments is of pure and divine origin and is entirely spiritual, and therefore it is also completely perfect.

God has given it to us to be a perfect rule or precept for our lives, which "if a man do, he shall even live in them" (Ezek. 20:11).

The fourth truth that must rightly be known and believed is the *eternal immutability* of this law of the Lord. As to its essence and expressed content, this law issues forth from God's essential and supremely perfect holiness. Therefore, whatever is therein commanded or prohibited fully presupposes the natural relationship all men have as dependent creatures with God, their sovereign Lord and most exalted creator. The law was therefore immediately impressed upon Adam's heart at creation, and, from that time forward, has remained unchanged as the perfect standard of conduct for the inward and outward aspects of our entire human existence. As impossible as it is for God, who gave this law, to change, so to all eternity, this law can never be altered whatsoever. Even in heaven, and thus throughout a blessed eternity, this law will remain in force without the least alteration, and the salvation of the inhabitants of heaven shall consist in the perfect obedience and observance of this law. In fact, on the great day of the final and general judgment, this law of the Ten Commandments will be positioned at the right hand of Christ, the supreme judge of the living and the dead. Just as this law is publicly and orally read each Lord's Day in our churches, likewise shall that same law be read orally by Christ Himself before the ears of the entire world population; both the good and the evil, shall then be judged according to this law. All who have kept it by the grace of our Lord and savior Jesus Christ shall live and enter into eternal joy, but they who have not kept the law shall be damned and be subjected to eternal grief and sorrow. This confirms how steadfast and immutable this holy law of God is, and how it shall endure throughout all eternity.

The heavens and the earth, as to their physical essence, are a very steadfast and well-grounded edifice. However, one would sooner observe that this great and steadfast edifice would vanish than that you would witness a single letter of God's law rendered null and void. Therefore, when our Savior, at a given occasion, wished to impress the necessity of sanctification upon His believing people, He said to His disciples, and thereby taught them: "Think not that I am come to destroy the law, or the prophets: I am not come to destroy, but to fulfil. For verily I say unto you, Till heaven and earth pass, one jot or one tittle shall in no wise pass from the law, till all be fulfilled" (Matt. 5:17–18).

This was also the reason that the Lord initially gave His law to Israel in writing. He did not communicate it orally or have it recorded in a book, as occurred with other divine revelations, but He recorded this law Himself with His own finger upon two tables of stone. Never before or after did God do anything like this, and thereby He clearly wanted to teach the world the eternal steadfastness and immutability of the essential contents of the commandments of His holy law. It is certain that in this law of the Lord, some peripheral and unique formulations were added to its external text that pertained only to the unique status of the people of Israel, to whom this law was initially and most solemnly given. Consider, for instance, what is written at the beginning of the law, namely, that the Lord had led them out of Egypt and out of the house of bondage, as well as the promise annexed to the fifth commandment, "that thy days may be long upon the land which the LORD thy God giveth thee" (Ex. 20:12). At that particular moment, it only pertained to the land of Canaan, which the Lord gave to the children of Israel by virtue of the covenant He had made with their fathers. These and such incidental circumstances and phrase-ologies of the law pertained specifically, in an external sense, to the people of Israel, and in that sense, we may view them as mutable. However, this by no means pertains to the essential contents of the law, but they are mere incidental events and circumstances that, though they may change, nevertheless do not yield the least change in the law itself.

The law consists of ten specific commandments, and all have a specific meaning. These Ten Commandments constitute the essence of the law, and their formulation is such that, as to their essence, they express an eternal morality and immutability. Therefore, he who would teach or judge otherwise violates the law of God and demolishes God's most holy precepts. Such will be subjected to the grievous judgment that Christ threatened to execute upon them, saying, "Whosoever therefore shall break one of these least command-ments, and shall teach men so, he shall be called the least in the kingdom of heaven: but whosoever shall do and teach them, the same shall be called great in the kingdom of heaven" (Matt. 5:19). This sufficiently affirms the eternal steadfastness and immutability of the law.

We need to address one more matter that is also of very great import and must be correctly understood by us, namely, the *holiness* of God's law and our perpetual obligation, issuing forth from it, to obey it with soul and body in absolute perfection if we are to be saved and enjoy God's favor eternally. The apostle Paul speaks of this, saying, "Wherefore the law is holy, and the com-mandment holy, and just, and good" (Rom. 7:12). Peter also speaks of "the holy commandment [being] delivered unto them" (2 Peter 2:21b). This holiness and righteousness of the law consists essentially in that it completely issues forth from God's most holy being and essence, and therefore it is a transcript or manifestation of the immutable holiness that resides in God Himself. Consequently, He fully delights in His divine glory and attributes, and He infinitely hates all that militates against it. It therefore necessarily follows that there never can be any other holiness, righteousness, or goodness than that which consists in the perfect obedience and observance of this law of God. Consequently, whatever in the very least deviates from it or opposes it is a grievous act against God's holiness. It is an act of disobedience toward the most high God. It is dishonoring to His illustrious majesty, but also an expression of wicked enmity toward Him, and the Lord can no less fail to hate and punish this than He can fail to love and promote Himself and His own attributes.

It is therefore most evident that since God's law is both holy and righteous, it must be obeyed and observed by us and by all men with superlative perfection and without the least deviation or transgression, lest the penalty of eternal death and condemnation be executed upon us. God teaches this regarding all men most clearly in His Word, saying, "Cursed is every one that continueth not in all things which are written in the book of the law to do them" (Gal. 3:10). Previously, the Lord said the same thing in the Old Testament, saying to the people of Israel, "Cursed be he that confirmeth not all the words of this law to do them, and all the people shall say, Amen" (Deut. 27:26). This express sentence of God is so intimately linked to the law that the law cannot exist without it. He who reads the law divorced from this divine sentence and declaration does not know what he is reading, for the law cannot be understood unless we correctly understand this sentence, namely, that every transgressor of this law, however insignificant his transgression may appear to be, will truly be accursed of God. That curse and penalty will therefore as certainly be imposed by God's own hand as it is certain that God has pronounced this curse upon the transgressor.

We must give heed to this, and we may not mock when God threatens, for we have to do with a God who is both holy and true. "God is not a man, that he should lie; neither the son of man, that he should repent: hath he said, and shall he not do it? or hath he spoken, and shall he not make it good?" (Num. 23:19).

We must therefore establish with certainty and designate it as the foundational truth of our entire faith that, with soul and body, we must keep the law of God in all of its constituent parts with absolute perfection, doing so consistently throughout our entire lives from our birth until our death. The moment we deviate or stumble even in the least, we will immediately be accursed of God the Lord, and we will be condemned to the eternal punishment and condemnation of hell.

Before all things, we must first believe this, and this must be the starting point of our faith in God's truth, for he who does not wholeheartedly and sincerely believe this also does not believe a single divine truth. Such a person shall therefore eternally be damned as an unbeliever (cf. Mark 16:16).

We must not come forward with the coverings of shame of which the unregenerate men of the world generally avail themselves to cover up their guilt and ungodliness, saying: "No one can serve God perfectly; we are doing as much as we can according to our deficient ability. We are therefore hopeful that God will forgive the rest." Friends, God by no means shall do so, for this is, alas, the direct path upon which multitudes of our Reformed people are traveling to hell. If our precious souls are to be saved, then we must, as we have already shown, first believe and affirm what our absolute obligation and commitment toward God's law must be.

If someone were to ask: "What shall then become of man? Have not all men transgressed God's law, and is it not so that we are therefore no longer capable of keeping it perfectly? What counsel do you then have for us?" we respond with this counsel: by God's grace and before anything else, we shall first reflect upon our transgression of God's holy law. We shall most certainly appropriate the dreadful curse of the law and believe with our hearts that, by our sins, we have all been subjected to the curse of the law. The Scriptures teach this, saying, "For as many as are of the works of the law are under the curse" (Gal. 3:10). We will then fully view ourselves as accursed sinners and, without any hesitation, deem ourselves to be wretched scoundrels who are truly condemned by God to eternal punishment and condemnation in hell. We shall be so fully focused on this until we perceive that our hearts, by the Spirit of conviction, have thereby become deeply troubled, grievously wounded, perplexed, and contrite—until our eyes have become a fountain of tears. We will then proceed to sign our death sentence and say: "God is holy and righteous, but we are ungodly, wicked, and abominable. Woe be unto us that we have sinned in such a measure and that we so dreadfully have provoked God to wrath." We will say, "I acknowledge my transgressions: and my sin is ever before me" (Ps. 51:3).

Do you now wish to know how we shall then proceed? Just as criminals who have been condemned by a worldly judge, we will, with them, weep and lament bitterly, and we will grieve deeply about our wretched condition. Before

God and men, we shall be ashamed of our wickedness, and we will acknowledge that our condition is now utterly hopeless and desperate, and that we know of nothing whatsoever that we can contribute unto our salvation. By the grace and operation of the Holy Spirit, who is the Spirit of faith, we will assume the position of the publican in the gospel, and we will appear before the most high God of heaven in a most humble and contrite disposition, and cry out to Him from afar and with downcast eyes, "Oh God, be merciful to me a sinner!" (Luke 18:13). As ungodly, accursed, and impotent sinners, we will then come to Christ Jesus, and by the Word of the holy gospel, we will allow ourselves to be fully persuaded of His absolute indispensability, His complete suitableness, His all-sufficiency, and His genuine willingness. By the hand of true faith, we will then take hold of Him as our all-sufficient surety, redeemer, and savior, and we will fully surrender ourselves to Him for our salvation. By His death on the cross and by grace, He shall then deliver us from all our sins and from the curse of the law, and convert and enable us, by His Holy Spirit, genuinely to obey the entire law of God.

By the grace of the Lord Jesus, this law will then be used toward us with three great objectives in view. It will serve as a mirror whereby I may know my sins. It will serve as a schoolmaster to drive us out of ourselves unto Christ. And it will serve as a rule for our lives, so that we may keep it with a regenerate and believing heart. These are the three objectives God has in view in giving His holy law to a sinful people such as we are.

May the Lord bless the word that we have expounded for you. Amen.

The Preamble of the Law (1)

And God spake all these words, saying....
—EXODUS 20:1

We can never meditate with sufficient gravity on the Word of the Lord recorded in Isaiah 66:2b: "But to this man will I look, even to him that is poor and of a contrite spirit, and trembleth at my word." Many people today discuss what constitutes a Christian and true Christianity, as well as what is necessary to be a good Christian and to have a well-founded hope upon heaven and salvation. We need neither to dig very deeply for this nor to initiate an extensive search for it. This passage from Isaiah at once teaches us who the true Christian is—a man who truly fears God. He is a man who "is poor and of a contrite spirit" and trembles at God's Word. The Lord promises that only upon such does He look with the eye of His favor, His grace, His love, and His mercy. Such ones He acknowledges to be His people and children. As a gracious Father, He communes with them, and by His Spirit, He inwardly reveals Himself as such to their hearts. If one earnestly desires to know whether he truly is a child of God, it is here displayed before your very eyes. Let such a person attentively, calmly, and sincerely ask himself two things in the majestic presence of God:

1. Considering my own insignificance, sinfulness, hell-worthiness, utter misery, and impotence, am I truly one who is "of a contrite spirit," who seeks all my comfort, redemption, and salvation entirely outside of myself in the free grace and satisfaction of Jesus Christ? Do I trust in Him alone with my heart without finding anything in myself and without seeking of myself to contribute even the least?

2. Do I within my heart and in a holy and humble manner truly tremble at God's Word, having such deep reverence and esteem for the Word as being God's Word? Is it my heartfelt desire to embrace this Word not only, and most

certainly, to believe it, but also, with soul and body and all my strength, to order my conversation in full accord with the Word of the living God, the supreme creator and king of heaven and earth? Let me illustrate: if there is a gracious promise, such a person heartily comforts himself with this promise and fully relies upon it. If there is a precept to be observed or any commandment of the Lord to be obeyed, without delay and with body and soul, he fully obeys it, and should there be an admonition or a threat, he is troubled, grieved, and distressed by it.

Behold, if someone, by grace, truly finds within himself these two things, he may most assuredly believe that he is a converted person, that he fears God with his heart, and that the Lord, as a gracious Father, looks upon him as His beloved child. If, however, these two matters are not truly to be found in him, it is but a vain effort for such a person to look for evidence that he is a Christian, for he is most certainly still in an unconverted and most wretched state. Whatever he may think of himself is but the deceit of his treacherous heart and a devilish delusion.

Beloved friends, though, by the grace of God, I am a minister in the church of Christ, I do not want you to think of me as a Christian if you cannot in some measure observe in me with some clarity that in my entire life and doctrine I am one who is "poor and of a contrite spirit" and that I have learned to tremble at God's Word—though I must confess with sorrow that I have but a very small measure of these matters.

On the other hand, do not require of me that I would deem you to be a truly godly and converted Christian if I cannot in some measure detect and with some clarity observe these two matters in you, namely, that God, by the grace of His Spirit, has truly made you to be "poor and of a contrite spirit" and that He has taught you to tremble at His Word.

I wish to address more specifically this latter matter, namely, this heartfelt trembling at God's Word, in the most comprehensive sense of the word as being the soul and innermost marrow of true godliness. This is an unconditional trembling at *all of God's Word,* and thus of everything that God communicates in His Holy Word in any way or form to us, the children of men. It is the great and preeminent sign of all who have a truly godly heart that the moment any of God's words enter their ears and their hearts, they immediately detect deeply within their hearts a lively principle of holy fear, reverence, respect, and awe for that Word of God. By the grace of the Holy Spirit, this, in turn, brings forth in them the exercises of faith, hope, love, and obedience. The more one finds this continually within himself, the more holy and godly a person he will be, and the more pious and the more edifying and godly his outward walk shall be, as well as all the words and works that proceed from him.

This truth is the immovable pillar and mainstay of Christianity. Therefore, if one wishes to find a Christianity in which such a true fear of God and its outward evidences are lacking, then he must turn to the devil, for he will educate him regarding such a counterfeit Christianity.

However, beloved, this is not what God teaches in His Word, for whoever desires to be saved must before all things tremble at His Word, and particularly, he must especially tremble at the law of the Ten Commandments. This law from heaven was given and revealed by the Lord in a most awe-inspiring and glorious manner to the children of Israel, as well as to all men, as a perfect precept for their entire lives. On the last day, the Lord will judge all men according to that law, and all who, with their hearts and as to their outward conversation, have not sincerely lived in true obedience to that law by the grace of Jesus Christ, our savior, will eternally be damned. However, all who have trembled in their hearts at this law, and at every jot and tittle of it, and have endeavored to obey it in love and by faith, they, and they alone, shall eternally be saved and redeemed for the sake of the merits of Christ.

In our exposition of the Heidelberg Catechism, we have now progressed to the point of being called upon to expound for the congregation this most precious and most holy law of God, to set before you step by step all that God commands us to do, as well as what He forbids and commands us to refrain from if we are to be His obedient children and serve and fear Him in truth. However, it is by no means sufficient that I now preach and expound this law of God for you, nor is it sufficient for you diligently to listen to this preaching, for in your hearts you have to tremble at every word of this law and have the utmost respect for it as being the Word of the living God. Your eternal salvation or damnation will most certainly be determined either by your obedience toward or your transgression of this law. With every command, and every word in every command, you have to stop, consider, and examine your hearts and your ways most earnestly. With heartfelt sorrow, contrition, and shame, you have to consider your manifold and grievous sins whereby you have provoked God to wrath for such length of days, and whereby you are still daily provoking Him to wrath. You have to come before God the Lord as one truly contrite in spirit, and, by the grace of the Holy Spirit, you have to run to Christ for reconciliation and for the Spirit of repentance as sinners who labor and are heavy-laden, and thus as those who are "poor and of a contrite spirit."

In order that, by the Lord's gracious blessing, we would better achieve this objective with everyone, we have decided to expound in several sermons, and thus in some detail, the preamble of the law of the Lord.

This preamble of the law of the Lord contains the most effectual exhortations and the most powerful motives to cause our hearts, by the grace of the Holy Spirit, to obey this divine law in all humility and to lead us to tremble at every word of this law. Oh, that the Lord, by His Spirit, would also engage Himself and that He would be pleased graciously to bless our preaching for the converted and unconverted alike!

Presently we will therefore expound for you in some detail what is communicated by the opening words of the law of the Lord, namely, "And God spake all these words…" Two matters are here to be observed:

1. the historical occasion when these words were spoken, namely, *then*[1]

2. the words themselves: "God spake all these words…."

The word *then* points us to the occasion when, for the first time, the Lord so clearly and solemnly revealed His law to the children of Israel, and when, from heaven, He spoke all of these majestic words to them—and thus, when everything that Moses recorded in Exodus 19 had transpired, namely these two matters:

1. Upon God's command, the people of Israel had been sanctified and prepared to receive with reverence this awe-inspiring law of the Lord, and to enter into covenant with the God of heaven and earth—a covenant He so solemnly established at Mount Sinai with them as the seed of Abraham.

2. The Lord then descended upon the mountain in a most majestic and awe-inspiring manner. This was accompanied by great and fearful signs, and He appeared to the people to engage in the great work of establishing His covenant with them and to give them His holy law—a law He proclaimed to them with His own mouth.

It was *then*—that is, when the people had been prepared in this fashion—that God appeared upon the mountain in such a fearsome and majestic

---

1. In the Dutch *Statenvertaling*, Exodus 20:1 reads as follows: "Toen sprak God al deze woorden…"; that is, "*Then* God spake all these words…." In the paragraphs that follow, VanderGroe expounds the significance of the word *then*—a word that does not appear in the King James Version.

manner. It was then that the Lord, before the eyes and within the hearing of all the people, began to speak with a clear and loud voice so that they could all hear it, for He "spake all these words, saying…"

Hereby we perceive that we neither can enter into a covenant with the most high God nor be prepared to hear His Word and receive His holy law into our hearts unless we truly have been prepared to receive it by the Spirit of the Lord, and God Himself has appeared inwardly and spiritually in our hearts with His divine glory. *Then* is the correct and suitable moment for the Lord to proclaim His Word and to make known His precepts to us. It was thus at such a specific moment in history that God spoke all these words to Israel; that is, the entire law of the Ten Commandments.

This brings before us two matters that are both of the utmost importance and significance, and by the inward illumination of the Spirit of the Lord, they must truly be known by us:

1. God Himself, as the supreme king and lawgiver, verbally proclaimed the law of the Ten Commandments, and thus, with His own mouth, He commanded that we keep them.

2. He verbally articulated the *entire* law as we presently still read it, for God "spake *all* these words."

Therefore, everything recorded in this law is expressly His Word and command, and this law in its entirety must be received by us with the greatest reverence, and, by grace and in Christ, it must be most perfectly performed and obeyed by us. He who, by God's grace, truly understands these two matters and truly believes them in his heart shall most certainly be saved. Let us therefore consider these matters in greater detail.

Regarding the verbal proclamation of the law, the text states that "God spake all these words," that is, that the Lord God Himself proclaimed this law of the Ten Commandments to the world by His own mouth, and, with a loud voice, commanded man to keep them as a perfect rule and precept for all of life, so that one would fear and obey Him with soul and body. Upon consulting the Holy Scriptures, we learn that it was truly and specifically Christ, the Son of God, who proclaimed this law of the Ten Commandments with a loud and understandable voice in the wilderness and upon Mount Sinai to the people of Israel, prescribing it to them preeminently in the form of a solemn covenant transaction.

We may deduce this from Stephen's sermon to the Jews, for there he testified by divine revelation and inspiration of the Spirit of the Lord that Moses "was in the church in the wilderness with the angel which spake to him in the mount Sina, and with our fathers: who received the lively oracles to give unto us" (Acts 7:38). Who was this Angel who spoke with Moses upon Mount Sinai and from whom he "received the lively oracles"? Was it also a created angel, and thus one of God's servants? By no means, for it was the Angel of the Lord of whom Stephen had spoken (Acts 7:30). It was He who appeared to Moses in the burning bush, saying to him, "I am the God of thy fathers, the God of Abraham, and the God of Isaac, and the God of Jacob."

Thus, it was the Angel of the Lord who gave to Moses the lively oracles of the law and who spoke to him upon Mount Sinai. This was none other than Christ, the Son of God, the most high God Himself, and the Angel of God's presence, of whom it is written, "The angel of his presence saved them: in his love and in his pity he redeemed them" (Isa. 63:9). The apostle Paul teaches this truth with no less clarity in Hebrews 12:24–26, where he sets the Lord Jesus before us as "the mediator of the new covenant...that spake on earth...whose voice then shook the earth." This is a reference to Christ giving the law orally upon Sinai, which was accompanied by a strong earthquake (cf. Ex. 19:18). There is therefore not the least doubt that it was the Son of God, the Lord Jesus Christ, who appeared in an extraordinary manner upon Mount Sinai and proclaimed the law of the Ten Commandments with a loud voice, thereby prescribing to all men the perfect and inflexible rule of their religious practice.

While engaging in this majestic and divine activity, the Lord Jesus not only acted on His own behalf as the most high God, who, by virtue of His sovereign dominion over the world, can issue commands and give laws, but rather (and this must be given serious consideration), Christ acted here as Paul designates Him as the "one mediator between God and men" (1 Tim. 2:5), who, by grace, would reconcile God and man, and who would cause sinful men to fulfill their original obligation by living in obedience toward God. He appeared upon Mount Sinai in great glory as the "Angel of the Covenant" (cf. Mal. 3:1), that is, as the mediator and messenger of the covenant that God established with an elect and believing humanity. God would regularly send Him forth to execute matters pertaining to His covenant with men as a clear preview of His coming to that end in the flesh and in the fullness of time.

Let it be noted by us and be deeply impressed upon our hearts that God Himself came here upon earth to prescribe, in an extraordinary manner, this law of the Ten Commandments as a holy rule for our lives. It is God who issued all these commands and proclaimed them with His own mouth. This merits our further consideration.

"God spake all these words." In order rightly to learn how we are to obey God, we can never meditate sufficiently and with our utmost attention upon this matter. Hereby we conclude that the Lord God, as the supreme creator and king of heaven and earth, is, in a very unique way, the origin and author of the law of the Ten Commandments and all that is implied therein. Whatever has proceeded from His mouth must be His word and His command, whereby He personally has imposed this upon us and the world. It is true that the entire Scriptures are God's Word, for through the instrumentality of men, they have all proceeded from God. However, the law of the Ten Commandments, in a very special sense, must be considered as the Word of God, for God has given it to us in a most unique manner. By His Spirit, He could have made known His law to Moses as He made known the other Holy Scriptures. He could have given us His law through Moses.

However, the Lord God came to this world in His own person, and this was accompanied by such dramatic evidences of His divine power and glory that the people of Israel could not bear His awe-inspiring presence—as is recorded in Exodus 20:18–20. The Lord commanded and prescribed all that is written in this law with His own mouth and without any assistance from men, for "God spake all these words, saying…." And, indeed, the most high God not only commanded His law by His own mouth, proclaiming loudly to us, the children of men, how we are to act and live, saying, "I am the LORD thy God…. Thou shalt have no other gods before me," but, upon having issued these words with His own mouth, He also inscribed them upon two solid tables of stone with His own finger and without the assistance of angels or men.

This law is therefore God's Word par excellence, for it proceeds entirely from God without any human intermingling. We shall be able to affirm abundantly the divinity of this law of the Ten Commandments, as well as the fact that God Himself uttered all these words. This is evident:

First, from the goodness, holiness, righteousness, and reasonableness of all that is prescribed and prohibited therein. Everything in this law is divine and holy to the utmost degree. The more closely we examine and reflect upon this law, the more its goodness, divinity, and holiness are revealed clearly to our hearts, and the more deeply a pious soul is greatly amazed at the holiness of all that is to be found in the law. With intense love, he rejoices and delights himself in it, exclaiming with David, "All thy commandments are righteousness" (Ps. 119:172).

Second, from the wondrous perfection of this law, revealed in the fact that with such brevity of words, the entire duty of man toward God and his neighbor is expressed so transparently and succinctly, thereby exceeding all the wisdom of angels and men.

Third, because this law is so deeply engraved upon man's conscience and heart that neither he nor the devil, with all his power, will ever succeed in utterly erasing it. Let evil men try as they might, and let the devil assist as much as he can to turn them into complete atheists and to remove this law of God completely from their hearts, they will not succeed. They will never be able utterly to erase this divine inscription. These words of God shall eternally be inscribed upon the human heart, and even the fire of hell will not succeed in burning away these divinely inscribed words. In the midst of all his ungodliness, man will eternally carry this law of God in his bosom. It will always remind him of his duty. It will accuse him, condemn him, trouble him, and perplex him. What clearer proof do we need that "God spake all these words," and that they are His words?

Fourth, for all God's judgments and punishments that have been executed here on earth have affected men solely because of their transgression of this law of God and because of their unwillingness to subject their entire lives to this law. Over against this, we posit that all of God's mercies, benefits, and blessings that have ever been the portion of the godly as to both soul and body have been bestowed upon them only by the heartfelt love and sincere obedience they have shown toward this law of God in both soul and body. This is the only way in which God bestows His gracious blessings in Christ upon His people and children.

When God sets before men His curses and blessings, He declares to them: "If you will earnestly observe these commandments and diligently observe and keep these My words, you will be loved, helped, and blessed by Me in both soul and body—and thus regarding your children, your cattle, your field, your house, and all things that you will take in hand. However, if you despise My commandments and will not obey them, you will be accursed in all things, and My fearful wrath shall be provoked toward you." What clearer evidence do we need regarding the truth that God Himself spake all these words and that they constitute His divine word and command?

Fifth, by the fact that all the grace, power, light, and influence that issue forth from the Holy Spirit by means of the ministry of the word, and thus descend from on high in heaven into the heart of man, are of such a nature that man is thereby led and motivated to manifest a pure love for this law of the Lord and to keep it perfectly and with all the powers of both soul and body. The entire work of the Holy Spirit has as its ultimate objective that God's law be obeyed perfectly by us and that it neither be violated nor transgressed in the least degree. Therefore, when God's Spirit is truly at work in a man, such a person is deeply grieved about his sins. With great shame and sorrow, he laments all of his sins, and by faith he flees to Christ and seeks with great earnestness to secure reconciliation and sanctification with Him. He therefore cannot rest until he has obtained this.

If God Himself had not spoken all these words and had all of these words not been His express precepts, the Holy Spirit would not be able to work in this fashion in the heart of man, for He has never wrought in anyone's heart the least desire to obey any human precept. The contrary is true, for the very word of the Holy Spirit says, "But in vain they do worship me, teaching for doctrines the commandments of men" (Matt. 15:9).

Sixth, by the fact that Christ Himself, the exalted Son of God, came into the world and assumed our human nature and our low estate to obey this law of the Ten Commandments perfectly on our behalf as our surety, and also to bear the curse of that law to which we are subject due to our transgressions. Since this law is absolutely perfect, holy, and divine, man would eternally be unable to be saved apart from a perfect obedience toward the Ten Commandments. Such obedience could never be rendered by man himself, for he has become a transgressor of the law and is subject to its curse. Christ has come so that, as God and man in one Person, He could render that perfect obedience to the law, both actively and passively, for all His elect, and by His Spirit apply it to them and work this in their hearts by means of faith.

How clearly this all affirms and how loudly it declares to us that God Himself has spoken all these words and that the entire law has proceeded from Him! Oh, that by the grace of the Holy Spirit, we would truly ascertain this in our hearts by faith! The Spirit of the Lord therefore preceded the law with a noteworthy annotation, saying to us, "And God spake all these words, saying...." He did so in order that, upon our first reading of the law, we would attentively reflect upon and deeply impress upon our hearts that it is God Himself who gives this law to us, and that He Himself, with His own mouth, has declared His precepts here on this earth. Until we correctly understand and believe this in our hearts, we show but little concern for our obedience to the law of God, and therefore the

Lord prefaced His holy law with a compelling argument for its strict obedience, expressed in these words, "And *God* spake all these words, saying…"

Here we have the essential root of the matter regarding our obligation and that of all men: to obey this law of God with soul, body, and all our strength, for the Lord God Himself has spoken all these words. This defines the entire gravity of our obligation toward God, our exalted king and creator. Since He has gone to such great lengths to proclaim the precepts of His holy law unto us with His own mouth, and to inscribe it so plainly with His own finger, we shall never be able truly to grasp how exceedingly great our obligation is to keep this law of God, and how our true happiness or unhappiness, our life or our death, and our salvation or our damnation are, for time and eternity, entirely contingent upon our obedience of His law. In that regard, it is true what the Lord Himself says: "Ye shall do my judgments, and keep mine ordinances, to walk therein: I am the LORD your God. Ye shall therefore keep my statutes, and my judgments: which if a man do, he shall live in them: I am the LORD" (Lev. 18:4–5).

Oh, dear friends, let us be certain that we maintain a walk that is blameless in this regard, and let us not deceive our hearts! No one presently lives nor shall live hereafter, that is, no one is presently saved nor shall be saved hereafter, who in his heart does not truly aspire to obey the law of the Ten Commandments. Such a person, according to his conscience, endeavors with earnest zeal by the grace of the indwelling Holy Spirit to live and walk in full conformity to this law, and to that end, by means of a lively and active faith, he continually draws his strength from Christ, who is the fountain of our entire salvation.

Please permit me, as a faithful servant of Jesus Christ, to lay bare my heart before you all. This matter is of such great significance for me, and is so bound upon my heart, that, the Lord willing, I cannot refrain from preaching once more about this matter and from setting before you in further detail how very obligated we are to align our entire lives consciously with the law of the Ten Commandments by virtue of the fact that "God spake all these words…"—and thus *all* without distinction—with His own mouth, and that He sent His own divine Son, Jesus Christ, to this earth and upon Mount Sinai with such awe-inspiring glory.

We must uphold the keeping of this law of God, and with all our strength and by God's grace, we must protect it steadfastly against all the accursed roots of a demonic atheism, Spinozism, vain philosophy, fanaticism, Antinomianism, and other such errors toward which the hearts of men are so naturally inclined, and by which so many people are secretly infected to their eternal perdition.

In Ecclesiastes 4:12, we read, "A threefold cord is not quickly broken." Christianity is also a threefold cord that consists of a sincere sorrow over sin, a sincere trusting in Christ, and a sincere obedience of the law of God. This threefold cord may not be broken to all eternity, for as soon as one part is even remotely disengaged, all Christianity collapses, and we lose the most precious truth by which alone we can be saved. Law and gospel are like twins, which, though they may never be separated, must be very carefully distinguished. The law must serve the gospel, and the gospel must serve the law. Though they must mutually affirm each other, they may by no means undermine each other. It is contradictory to Christian doctrine to speak only of the gospel and of the doctrines of grace, and to be silent regarding obedience to the law; or, conversely, to speak only of obedience to the law, and to be silent regarding the gospel and its doctrines of grace.

As much as we exercise faith toward God's holy gospel, so much obedience must we render to God's holy law. Conversely, proportionate to our obedience of the law, we must exercise faith toward the gospel. This harmonizes with Christian doctrine and constitutes the knowledge of the saints. This is the way that leads the wise heavenward, and it is also a way upon which fools do not err (cf. Is. 35:8). By God's grace, let us always adhere to this doctrine and steadfastly ascertain in our hearts that "as many as walk according to this rule, peace be on them, and mercy, and upon the Israel of God" (Gal. 6:16).

Regarding the subject matter we have presently addressed, may those matters concerning which you have been instructed by God's grace be correctly understood and believed. Oh, that we would be truly persuaded in ourselves that "God spake all these words" of the law by His own mouth, and that obedience to this law yields life and salvation, and that the transgression thereof yields death and damnation!

How few there are among us who truly believe this, and let everyone therefore examine himself accordingly. People who do not truly believe with their hearts that "God spake all these words" are those:

1. Who, when this law is read in God's house in the midst of the congregation on the Lord's Day, are inattentive and conduct themselves irreverently. They do not seriously listen, but rather, they let their eyes wander back and forth to the people who are attending church and to whatever else may be taking place. Such show clearly that their hearts are ungodly and void of impression, and they do not truly believe that God's laws and precepts are being read to them. If they did believe this, they would have more respect and reverence for the Lord's

precepts, and they would not conduct themselves so carelessly, inattentively, and insensitively. To you, the Lord speaks, saying, "Hear now this, O foolish people, and without understanding; which have eyes, and see not; which have ears, and hear not: Fear ye not me? saith the LORD: will ye not tremble at my presence…?" (Jer. 5:21–22).

2. Who never seriously examine themselves when the law of the Lord is read in God's house. They never attentively consider their ways and how they are faring therein. They never ask themselves, in all earnestness, how matters truly are with them. They never say, "God does indeed speak all these words to me, and He commands me to observe them all." They never ask themselves: "Am I a doer of His word, and do I indeed obey His holy law and illustrious precepts? Do I love them wholeheartedly, and do I truly conform my life and conduct to all of them as an obedient child and the Lord's subject?" They never make any effort to examine their hearts earnestly regarding this matter.

And yet, the Ten Commandments are read orally each Lord's Day to that end, and with large letters they are printed upon a board that is hanging before our very eyes,[2] so that we would all continually and seriously examine our hearts and our ways, whether we are keeping them and whether we truly fear God and are obedient to Him. The Ten Commandments are immediately read to us prior to the prayer and the sermon, so that, before all things, we would first examine ourselves in God's house and search out our sins, in order that in prayer we would confess them with humble sorrow and shame before God the Lord and ask Him for a gracious pardon.

During the afternoon service, the articles of our catholic, undoubted, Christian faith are read to us, so that we would first examine our faith and ask of God that we might be made upright and that, by His Holy Spirit, He would strengthen our faith.

By such a worship structure, we are taught every Lord's Day how faith and obedience constitute the way to heaven, and how we all, with our hearts, are to walk upon that way by the grace of our Lord and savior, Jesus Christ.

How little these matters are taken into consideration by the people, and how everything among us has degenerated into vain custom and tradition!

3. All who do not truly believe with their hearts that "God spake all these words," do not know their sinful hearts by the law, and that in their hearts there is neither true sorrow nor grievous shame and contrition. They are not truly

---

2. Such large wall panels with the entire text of the Ten Commandments can still be seen today in many historic Dutch churches.

perplexed due to having so dreadfully provoked God to wrath by their sins, and they fear neither His judgments and punishments nor the prospect of hell and damnation. They manage to live peacefully and carelessly in an unconverted state outside of Christ. Then there are those who, with joy and pleasure, continue to indulge in many sins, who, though God's servants continually and earnestly rebuke them accordingly, nevertheless continue to live in those sins in spite of all such admonitions.

All such and similar people despise the law of the Lord and do not truly believe in their hearts that "God spake all these words." Oh, that all such would see their sins and their unbelief, and that the Lord, by His Holy Spirit, would convince them that they are all walking upon a pathway that will lead to eternal perdition. How dreadful it shall be for them, and what a dreadful judgment and horrendous damnation awaits them if they continue to despise God and His laws! If only they would repent, and may a merciful God grant them His Spirit to that end.

Would that all God's truly converted people would learn to see how little they believe and how they continually fail to consider in their hearts that "God spake all these words"! If this were to be continually believed by us, what spiritual exercises it would yield! However, that deep-seated unbelief and this atheistic heart that remains even in the very best of God's children is the true fountain of all this evil within us. Oh, would that we were more acquainted with this great evil within us, and that the Lord Jesus, by His Spirit, would truly open our eyes so that we would become sensitive regarding this. Would that we would deeply humble ourselves before the Lord regarding this! May the Lord grant unto us His grace to that end. Amen.

The Preamble of the Law (2)

And God spake all these words, saying....
—EXODUS 20:1

A Gentile centurion uttered remarkable words to our Savior when he petitioned Him to heal his bed-ridden servant who resided in his home, suffering from severe pain (cf. Matt. 8:6–9). The Savior immediately granted his humble request, and said, "I will come and heal him" (v. 7). However, this humble centurion deemed himself utterly unworthy of such great grace that the Lord Jesus would honor him by humbling Himself so deeply in coming under the roof of his house. He therefore petitioned him very humbly, "Speak the word only, and my servant shall be healed" (v. 8). He then underscored his petition to the Savior by saying, "For I am a man under authority, having soldiers under me: and I say to this man, Go, and he goeth; and to another, Come, and he cometh; and to my servant, Do this, and he doeth it" (v. 9).

Take note of the measure of authority the centurion exercised toward his soldiers and his servants, for whenever he would issue a command, they immediately would obey without being in any way remiss. If it is true among men that one person can exercise such great authority over other people that they readily obey when such a man but speaks and commands, how significantly greater must then be the power and authority of the most high God, the sovereign king and creator of heaven and earth, toward us insignificant men, who, as His creatures, are to Him merely "counted as the small dust of the balance" (Isa. 40:15)!

Therefore, when He but speaks and commands, how we ought immediately to obey Him, and without any protest! How all that has breath ought to consider His illustrious precepts, and fear and tremble before Him, so that He might not be provoked to wrath by our disobedience to Him even in the smallest of matters! How everyone ought to say continually with the young man

Samuel, "Speak, LORD; for thy servant heareth" (1 Sam. 3:9b)! This is as much as to say, "Thy servant stands ready and is waiting to know what Thy command is, that he might obey it without delay."

This is indeed the essence of true godliness: to fear and to love God, for anything other than that is but mere speculation and empty talk. However, we need not pause and consider what the Lord's word might be, acting as though He still has to speak to us and to stipulate what we either should or should not do. By no means, for in His Word the Lord has abundantly spoken to us. However, until now, hardly anyone has heard rightly what He is saying, and even fewer have rightly obeyed His Word. Elihu's words to Job are applicable: "For God speaketh once, yea twice, yet man perceiveth it not" (Job 33:14). In fact, God speaks thousands of times to us, but one neither hears Him nor considers what He is saying.

Oh, if only we were as ready to obey as God is ready to speak and to make known unto us His will! What a blessed and happy people we would then be, and how very different we would be!

If anyone is desirous to know the Word of the Lord and to hear God Himself speak to him, being desirous to obey the laws of the Lord by grace and with an upright spirit, he needs to focus only upon the law of the Ten Commandments. There he will find the Lord's holy and good precepts, for the Lord has proclaimed them all by His own mouth, and He specifically appeared on the world scene with great power and glory to give us His precepts as the standard for our life and conversation. Moses communicates this in our text when he prefaces the law with this specification: "And God spake all these words, saying...."

Two important matters are set before us in this text:

1. It was neither an angel, nor a man, nor any other creature, but God Himself who uttered these ten words or precepts of the law.

2. God uttered all of these words, and thus the one precept as well as the other. Consequently, the entire law as we have it before us proceeds from God Himself, and is therefore perfect in all its constituent parts. By the grace of our Lord and savior Jesus Christ, it must therefore be obeyed by us if we desire to have God favorably disposed toward us, and if, as His beloved children, we desire to please Him.

On the previous Lord's Day, we addressed the first matter in considerable detail. However, since this matter is so significant and weighty in regard to our religious practice, and since it is the very foundation of our religion, we will continue to address this matter and to expound the second matter as well. May the Lord grant unto me, unworthy as I am, a tongue to speak, and may He give you an ear to hear.

Last Lord's Day, we observed how the Lord revealed the law of the Ten Commandments to us by different means than He used to reveal all the other Holy Scriptures, that is, by means of human instrumentality. Rather, He focused upon this law in an extraordinary manner, considering its publication a matter of such import that He revealed it here upon this world in His own person and proclaimed it with His very mouth. It was therefore accompanied with the most illustrious signs of His divine power and glory.

We then demonstrated how this affirms the origin and authority of this law to be divine in an extraordinary sense of the word, and we supported that by way of six distinct arguments. But, what are we to learn from all this? Is it not that we must have the highest esteem for this law of the Ten Commandments that God has prescribed to us with His very mouth; that we must, with all our heart, soul, and strength, honor and obey this law to the utmost of our ability? Does it not mean that we cannot take the least liberty to do anything contrary to this law in either our soul or body? If the Lord God has gone to such extraordinary lengths in giving us His precepts, having proclaimed all these words to us without the agency or assistance of anyone else, must we not, by the grace of the Holy Spirit and in Christ, our savior, engage ourselves to keep these commandments of the Lord diligently, continually, and to the utmost of our power? Must we not steadfastly order our entire lives and conversation in accordance with them?

No one is able to challenge my legitimate conclusion regarding this. Rather, you should be persuaded within your hearts, and you have to concur, saying, "Yes, since the most high God has gone to such extraordinary lengths to give us these His holy commandments, then, as His beloved and obedient children, we must, by the grace of the Holy Spirit, do our utmost to keep all these commandments, endeavoring in Christ Jesus to be pleasing to the Lord our God." I would not deem anyone to be a pious and godly person who would not readily agree with and confess this with his whole heart.

With this in mind, we shall proceed to consider in greater detail what we can learn from the fact that "God spake all these words." This will yield six explicit duties upon which we can never sufficiently reflect and meditate in our hearts.

God Himself having spoken all these words teaches us that:

First, we must continually and earnestly listen to these words of the Lord, and our ears must be always attentively inclined toward them. Let us here consider only ourselves, for we want others to listen to what we are saying when we speak to them. More specifically, when we issue a command to our subordinates, we expect that they will submit to our command. We would indeed be very offended if this did not occur and our command was disregarded. How much more is it the will of the most high God that we would always listen attentively to His commandments and give ear to His words when He speaks to us! Does He not exclaim to us, "Hear, O my people, and I will speak" (Ps. 50:7a)?

When the laws and precepts of the Lord are set before us as ministers preach and expound them, binding them upon our hearts as the Word of God, we must always listen with all reverence, earnestness, and attention. Should we not say to ourselves: "Oh, my soul, give ear to this Word of God. Listen to the Lord's voice, and be neither careless nor inattentive"? Let it not be grievous to you that you must listen to so much being said about these laws. Rather, be earnest and reverent, for they are the Word of God and the Lord's commandments. They are living words, and if you do them, you shall live thereby, for "blessed are they that do his commandments, that they may have right to the tree of life, and may enter in through the gates into the city" (Rev. 22:14).

Second, we are not only to listen to these words, but we must also receive them with all the heartfelt love and esteem we can muster. They are the laws and precepts of the Lord that proceed from the mouth of this holy and majestic God, the magnificent creator and king of heaven and earth, who is also our most precious and compassionate God and Father. It was His desire to proclaim them to us in person. In His supreme wisdom, He conceived these commandments, and thus they proceed from His exalted and divine nature. All that is comprehended in these laws is fully subservient to our well-being and to our eternal blessedness.

Oh, how holy and delightful are these precious commandments! Who would not approve of them, magnify them, praise them, and adore them? Have not holy men always highly esteemed these commandments of God, always honored and loved them above all else? Consider only David, that pious servant of the Lord. Has he not frequently spoken to us in his psalms of his heartfelt love and tender esteem for the Lord's commandments? Only read Psalm 119 and you will hear him exclaim, "Make me to go in the path of thy commandments; for therein do I delight" (v. 35); "I will delight myself in thy commandments, which I have loved" (v. 47); "I longed for thy commandments" (v. 130); and "Therefore I love thy commandments above gold; yea, above fine gold" (v. 127).

Oh, blessed David! How did this godly man with such a holy heart fare in this wicked world? He separated himself from the ungodly, from vain and worldly men; he desired to have no interaction with them, and he rebuked them when they were in his company. He neither beat around the bush nor was ashamed to say to them, "Depart from me, ye evildoers: for I will keep the commandments of my God" (v. 115).

Third, with all reverence, we must always be prepared to receive these laws from whoever proclaims them to us and permit them to be impressed upon our hearts with all earnestness. God does not always use ministers or other office-bearers in His church to set His commandments before us. By no means, for the Lord causes His commandments to come to us through a variety of people, and then, for the sake of His Word, we must always reverently listen to those who bring it, never despising them because they are but sinful or insignificant persons. We must not focus upon the messenger, but upon the message that such a person brings to us. That should be the primary focus of our attention.

Let us assume that an ungodly person, one whose own conduct is unacceptable, approaches us and sets before us our duty, speaking to us regarding one of the Lord's commandments. We may not say to him: "What business is it of yours to admonish me? You should first look to yourself." Rather, for the sake of God's Word, we should listen to him with reverence and affection. Was not Balaam a very wicked and ungodly prophet? And yet, when God sent him with His word to the proud King Balak, did Balak not have to arise and reverently render obedience to Balaam as God's messenger? Did he not say to him, "Rise up, Balak, and hear; hearken unto me, thou son of Zippor" (Num. 23:18)? If a heathen king was obligated to do so, how much more should we? If, for instance, any weak or insignificant person speaks with us of one of the Lord's precepts, do you think we are permitted to despise such a divine admonition or proclamation because it is communicated to us by such an insignificant messenger? I must say to you, "This ought not so to be," for we are obligated to lend an ear even to the most insignificant person.

When David in anger determined to put to death the foolish and obnoxious Nabal with all the male residents of his house, having been so greatly offended and despised by him, Abigail, a weak woman, the wife of Nabal, came to him. She brought with her the law of God and confronted David with the fact that he was not permitted to avenge himself by shedding Nabal's blood, though he was justly angry with her husband. How did David respond to this? Did he despise Abigail because she was a woman? By no means, for though he was anointed to become the king of Israel, and though he was a prophet and a valiant soldier, accompanied by four hundred well-armed soldiers, he nevertheless had to submit himself to Abigail, for she came armed with the sharp sword of the law of the Lord. Against that law, David could not prevail, and therefore he ceased and desisted from executing his cruel plan against foolish Nabal. He submitted himself to Abigail's admonition and thanked her for the good counsel she had given him, praising the Lord for having sent this wise woman to communicate His precept in such a timely manner (cf. 1 Samuel 25). We must therefore not despise anyone, whoever he or she may be, who comes to us armed with the law of the Lord.

Fourth, we must be willing to submit to anyone who, by this law of the Lord, admonishes and rebukes us regarding our transgressions and sins. Therefore, when we are approached by God's servants, be it publicly from the pulpit or privately, and they confront us with our evil works and our transgressions, rebuking us very sharply, threatening us with God's wrath, and admonishing us to repent, we must then willingly submit ourselves to their admonitions and rebukes, knowing that God has spoken all these words and that the ministers are therefore impressing the Lord's precepts upon our hearts. By resisting them, we are resisting God Himself. Let no one presume that he fears God who hates faithful and courageous ministers and who is disgruntled toward them in response to their rebukes. He who conducts himself in this manner, however important and prominent his position may be in the world, has "neither part nor lot in this matter" (Acts 8:21), that is, in the kingdom of heaven. Unless he willingly submits to the rebukes of the ministers, he will be eternally rebuked in the hereafter by the devil in hell.

David was a great king, but when Nathan, the servant of the Lord, boldly and sharply rebuked David regarding his sins, David had to humble himself before Nathan as much as one of the least of his subjects would have had to do. Amos was but a common man and a poor keeper of cattle. However, when the Lord called him to be His servant and prophet, he was so bold in rebuking the sins of the Jews that he refrained not to do so, neither toward the mighty nor toward the insignificant. He threatened all who refused to hear him with the most dreadful judgments of God. However rich and prominent we may be, since God has spoken all these words, we must patiently permit even the most irrelevant and insignificant person to confront us with our iniquities and transgressions by way of the law of the Lord, for otherwise, the true fear of God cannot possibly be in our hearts.

Job, the richest and most prominent man of his day, conducted himself as such. He was in a position where he could help those toward whom he was favorably inclined and ruin those whom he hated. Everyone therefore greatly revered him and tried to please him. Nevertheless, he was a very pious and righteous man, whose desire it was that even the poorest and most despised of all men would deal uprightly with him. Therefore, if they observed any iniquity or transgression in him, he had them confront him with it. He by no means held this against them, but rather, he accepted their admonition so that he could humble his soul before the Lord. Consider his own testimony when he says, "Did I fear a great multitude, or did the contempt of families terrify me, that I kept silence, and went not out of the door?" (Job 31:34).

Take note here that even the most despised members of a family, children, servants, maids, or slaves, were so able to restrain Job by means of the law of the Lord that he dared not sin. This is how much he stood in awe of the Lord, and how much he feared Him. Such was the measure in which he trembled before His holy laws, and so great was his desire that anyone would admonish him regarding any missteps and iniquities that they might observe in him. Such a disposition affirms that one truly fears God.

Fifth, we must always uphold and protect the holy laws of the Lord. We must openly confess them before all men and never be ashamed to do so, being determined to be thus engaged to the utmost of our ability. If God was not ashamed publicly to utter all these words to the world with His own mouth, why should we be ashamed to confess these words publicly before the world, and thus before either the insignificant or the great men of this world? To that end, we should be willing to sacrifice our honor, reputation, possessions, lives, and all things. Christ therefore admonishes us, saying, "Whosoever therefore shall be ashamed of me and of my words in this adulterous and sinful generation; of him also shall the Son of man be ashamed, when he cometh in the glory of his Father with the holy angels" (Mark 8:38).

Even if God had merely given us His laws by means of an angel, we by no means should be ashamed of them. However, since He has come to us with such great majesty and personally proclaimed these laws to us, we most certainly are neither to be ashamed of them nor be fearful to confess and uphold them on every occasion. David therefore testified, "I will speak of thy testimonies also before kings, and will not be ashamed" (Ps. 119:46).

When we observe that people despise and transgress these laws, we must rebuke them boldly, and yet appropriately and humbly. Confronting them with these laws and with their sins, we must declare to them what God's punishments and judgments will be in response to them. We must always be of good courage toward God, the great author and giver of these laws, and never be concerned with either the favor or hatred of men. Let them harm or favor us; let them praise or despise us; let them hate or love us; yes, let them mock and slander us, and make us out to be guilty of splitting hairs, of being hypocrites, and of being conceited, as much as they desire; it should be a matter of no concern to us. Rather, we should trust in God and fear Him more than men. Let us uphold God's laws, and let us continue to do so, for the Lord will then bless us in such a rich measure that we will not be sinfully beholden to any man. David testifies of such who delight in the law of the Lord, saying that "whatsoever he doeth shall prosper" (Ps. 1:3b).

Sixth, we must keep this law of the Ten Commandments *spiritually*. Thus, we are to keep it not only outwardly, as to our physical activities, but also inwardly, in our hearts, for such as is God, who uttered these words and who formulated this law, so also is His law. Since God is a being who is pure, most holy, and spiritual, His law that proceeds from Him is also spiritual, and it obligates us to upright obedience no less in our hearts than in regard to our bodies. In that sense, God's laws differ greatly from the laws of men. All human laws bind only the body, with all its outward actions. They govern our hands, our feet, and our tongues, in order that they might be used properly. Only misbehavior as to outward matters is noted. Civil laws can neither judge the conscience or the heart, nor seek to uncover our hidden deeds or the inner motions of our hearts, for the knowledge and judgment of men does not pertain to them.

Neither evidences nor witnesses can be produced regarding the hidden transgressions of the hearts of other men, and this has led to the formulation of the proverb that a man's thoughts cannot be subjected to scrutiny. A judge never sentences anyone for having transgressed the law either mentally or lustfully. This is entirely unheard of in human courts.

However, this is by no means applicable to God and His holy law, for God the Lord is omniscient and He "searcheth the reins and hearts" (Rev. 2:23). Since our souls belong to Him as much as do our bodies, and since He is the sovereign Lord and creator of both, His illustrious laws therefore also pertain to our souls and to their most hidden thoughts, motions, and activities. In these matters, we are to be as obedient to all His commandments as we are obedient in the outward deeds and activities of our bodies. We must therefore "love the Lord [our] God with all [our] heart, and with all [our] soul, and with all [our] mind" (Matt. 22:37), and by no means are we to be satisfied with a love for God that manifests itself only in one's outward and physical walk.

We are also to love our neighbors in this manner, and not only outwardly, with polite greetings, good manners, a friendly countenance, and gracious words. We are not to give them Judas kisses. Rather, we are to love them with a true, heartfelt, steadfast, and earnest love—and thus, without any guile or hypocrisy. God the Lord will neither accept nor receive any other obedience from us but such obedience as proceeds from within, from a pure and upright heart. Only in Christ can such obedience please Him. To all He declares, "My son, give me thine *heart*" (Prov. 23:26). All our religion and obedience must proceed from an upright, healthy, pure, and believing heart, for otherwise we are mere pretenders and hypocrites. It may be hidden to people that we are such men, but by no means are we able to hide it from God. His eyes look into the very bottom of our hearts, and they penetrate as with a flaming fire.

All that we have thus set before you is comprehended in the fact that God Himself has spoken all these words to us.

We will now consider the other aspect of our text and show that God has indiscriminately spoken *all* these words. The Lord did not merely utter the first, second, and third commandments, and thereafter say no more. Rather, He uttered all the commandments, and thus every single word in those commandments as we are still reading them today. Every single word is God's Word and precept—one as well as the other. This must also be duly noted by us and be taken into consideration, for thereby we learn that:

First, if we are to derive any comfort from our upright obedience to God's law, we cannot merely obey some of the commandments, but we must equally and indiscriminately obey all the commandments of the law of the Lord. All His commandments are of equal holiness and divine authority. As there is no liberty to transgress one commandment, so there is no liberty to transgress any other commandment. By His very mouth, God has given all the commandments as His law, and therefore we are obligated to keep them all. The Lord invokes His curse upon anyone who deviates from one of His commandments even in the very least, saying, "Cursed be he that confirmeth not all the words of this law to do them" (Deut. 27:26). This applies to all the words of the law without exception, and the apostle Paul therefore declares, "Cursed is every one that continueth not in all things which are written in the book of the law to do them" (Gal. 3:10).

Consider for a moment a person who is willing to render obedience to nine commandments of the law, but is unwilling to keep the one commandment pertaining to the Sabbath, when, on the Sabbath, he buys and sells, neglects public worship, or causes his family members to neglect the same. Do you think that there is any fear of God in the heart of such a person? It is certain that he never has had the fear of God in his heart and never made any attempt to fear Him. One should ask him: "Why are you willing to obey nine commandments of the law? What motivates you to do so? What prompts you to do so?" Were he to respond by saying that the God whom we must honor and obey commands him to do so, one ought to reply: "You are not upright in your motives, for if truly you were inclined within your heart to fear God and to obey Him, you also would keep the Sabbath. This commandment of God has the same authority over us as do all the other commandments. Therefore, since you do not keep the Sabbath, you do not fear God, but you are transgressing the entire law." Such is the testimony of Scripture, saying, "For whosoever shall keep the whole law, and yet offend in one point, he is guilty of all" (James 2:10).

We must uphold this truth without compromise, for this is the pillar of our Christianity. It is not enough that we are willing to be known as upholders of the law; rather, we are called to be doers of and to uphold the entire law as God has given it to us. We must not break the tables of the law by erasing any of the commandments, for accursed be that man who either shall add or take away anything from that law. "If any man shall take away from the words of the book of this prophecy, God shall take away his part out of the book of life, and out of the holy city, and from the things which are written in this book" (Rev. 22:19).

Therefore, we must surely exclude such persons from the kingdom of heaven, for God will exclude all such who seek to enter by obeying nine commandments. Rather, they must obey all ten commandments, for they otherwise will eternally remain outside with the dogs (Rev. 22:15) and "anything that defileth" (Rev. 21:27). We must give ten thousand talents to the Lord, and thus an even number, for with nine thousand talents, we will not be able to stand before Him.

Furthermore we may say that he who lives in the transgression of any single commandment is ready at all times to despise the other commandments as well, for he neither loves nor reveres a single commandment with his heart. The religion of such persons is therefore of no value whatsoever.

Consider the example of King Herod in Matthew 14, for this monarch did many good things. He listened to John the Baptist, and although John conducted himself with great gravity and boldness, Herod nevertheless found delight in hearing him preach. In all other things, he was very compliant and willing to be governed, except that he cast aside the seventh commandment. He did not want to be burdened with it, and he concluded that one was entitled to have some leeway. His desire was to maintain a relationship with his brother's wife, with whom he had entered into an incestuous relationship. Preachers had to overlook only this one thing in his life and be silent regarding it. They were then permitted to preach as earnestly as they liked, and he remain good friends with them and delighted to hear them.

However, consider what transpired. Since Herod did not want to keep the seventh commandment, he readily began to minimize and despise the other commandments. First, he transgressed the third commandment by lightly swearing an oath before the daughter of Herodias, who danced so beautifully before him. Then he proceeded to transgress the sixth commandment by putting John to death in prison, and thus he shattered the entire law by being unwilling to keep one of the commandments. Beloved, consider these matters carefully.

Second, if the Lord does not bless us in soul and body (as He promises to do toward all who sincerely endeavor to keep His entire law) and His judgments and afflictions weigh heavily upon us, we must diligently examine ourselves and the lives of our family members, whether we are living in the transgression of one of the Lord's commandments. We must consider whether we are living in a given sin, presumptuously or ignorantly, of which we have neither repented nor have been willing to part from. If we determine that there is such a sin, we have then found the cause why God does not bless us. This is the fly that causes "the ointment of the apothecary to send forth a stinking savour" (Eccl. 10:1). This dead fly must first be removed; this evil must be removed from our heart and from our home before God's blessing can again be experienced there. Obedience to the law is as a pipe or a channel through which God's blessing flows to us. When we transgress one of the commandments, there is a breach in the pipe, causing the blessing to flow away. That leak must first be plugged by rendering obedience to the commandment that has been despised; otherwise, the blessing will not be ours.

Let us consider the history of the godly patriarch Jacob from Genesis 34. Matters were very much amiss for him, and there was great unrest and turmoil in his home. His sons Simeon and Levi had behaved themselves in a very ungodly manner, having inflicted great cruelty upon the men of Shechem because the king's son had defiled their sister, Dinah. Thereby, they had made themselves very hateful in the sight of the people of that land. Jacob thought with himself that things could not turn out so bad if all was well within his family. Therefore, there had to be a sin of which he had no knowledge within the sphere of his family, and thus he began diligently to investigate the affairs of his family. In so doing, he readily discovered the evil at hand, for his wife Rachel had hidden the idols of her father, and other members of his family had committed idolatry with these idols, thereby transgressing the first and second commandment. This was the cause of the evil that had befallen him. No wonder there was much turmoil outside of his home, for there was much irregularity within his home. Jacob therefore proceeded immediately to cleanse his home from all this filth, for "Jacob said unto his household, and to all that were with him, Put away the strange gods that are among you, and be clean" (Gen. 35:2). With his own hands, he removed those idols and all the superstitious objects that were found in his home, burying them under the oak tree of Shechem at a location where no one would be able to find them. Then the plagues ceased at once, and God's blessing returned to his home.

Third, this serves as a special comfort for all God's true children, who very much desire to obey perfectly all God's commandments. They pant and groan for this, and there is nothing they long for more than uprightness of heart and perfect holiness in the Lord Jesus, their head and savior. Since God spake all of these words, it follows that it is His will that His own laws and precepts must be performed and obeyed. However, Christ has kept all of them on behalf of His children, and thereby He has merited for them a perfect obedience, and in the way of renewal and sanctification, He gradually applies this to them by His Spirit. The Lord Himself causes them to walk in His statutes, for He has declared, "I will put my law in their inward parts, and write it in their hearts" (Jer. 31:33).

All God's children must therefore patiently, by faith and with prayer, wait upon the Lord their God for this great grace. It often occurs that believing souls must endure much strife and trouble regarding a specific corruption or bosom sin—a sin toward which they are most inclined. They then think and groan bitterly within themselves: "Oh, I have a hope that by grace I will someday overcome other sins. However, this sin is so deeply embedded in my heart that I cannot believe that I will ever prevail over it during my lifetime. This evil is so very chronic and has so deeply corrupted me. Oh, how shall I ever be delivered from this?"

I urge such poor souls that they must be of good courage, for since God has spoken all these words, they will also hereafter perfectly perform and obey all of them, and even in this life, they will gradually be delivered from all their sins by the grace of the Lord Jesus. The same God who has already given them victory over other sins will most certainly and at His time grant them victory over the sin that is presently troubling them most. This readiness and inclination of the heart to desire to be delivered from this sin and from all other sins, is the Lord's certain pledge to them that by grace they will hereafter be delivered from this and all other sins by Christ, their faithful savior.

Meanwhile, earnestly, manfully, steadfastly, and by God's grace, they must continue to battle against their sins, especially seeking to put their trust in God alone and in His precious promises. And when they consider their daily weakness and deficiency in regard to their duty, they must go to the Lord their God and say unto Him: "Oh, Lord, Thou art the author of all these commandments; Thou hast spoken *all these words*. As thy poor child and subject, it is therefore my obligation to obey them all. However, since of myself I have not the least ability to do so, but continually am so inclined toward sin, I therefore come to Thee to obtain all my help and grace from Thee, O Lord. Oh, be Thou pleased to make me obedient toward all Thy words and commandments, for therein is my delight."

May the Lord be pleased to bless our preaching. Amen.

The Preamble of the Law (3)

I am the LORD.
—EXODUS 20:2a

Most worthy of our consideration is what the holy apostle Peter writes in 2 Peter 1:3 to instruct and comfort all true believers, saying, "According as [Jesus Christ's] divine power hath given unto us all things that pertain unto life and godliness, through the knowledge of him that hath called us to glory and virtue."

Beloved, we have here two matters to consider:

First, the great and glorious gift the Lord bestows upon His believing people, namely, that by "his divine power [he] hath given unto [them] all things that pertain unto life and godliness." The Lord, having wrought in their hearts by the divine power of His Holy Spirit, has resurrected them from being dead in sins, and has re-created, regenerated, and transformed them in His Son, Jesus Christ. Consequently, they who earlier served sin by living and walking in it have become godly in both soul and body, and in principle and by the grace of Christ, their Lord and savior, they have begun to live unto the Lord by keeping and obeying His holy commandments.

This indeed constitutes "life and godliness," and thus it pertains to that which the Lord has given them by His divine power—all things. Oh, what a glorious and precious gift of God's unsearchable and free grace this is! David speaks of this when he says, "Oh, how great is thy goodness, which thou hast laid up for them that fear thee" (Ps. 31:19). Consequently, we may exclaim regarding the Lord that He has "received gifts for men; yea, for the rebellious also, that the LORD God might dwell among them" (Ps. 68:18).

Who but the Lord alone can receive and give such gifts? Who but He alone is able to give life to dead sinners? Who but He alone is able to transform ungodly sinners into a godly people and give them "all things that pertain unto life and godliness"? Therefore, Peter correctly attributes this exclusively to His divine power, testifying that by this divine power, all these things have been accomplished.

Second, the *means* whereby the Lord has bestowed this wondrous and great grace upon His people and children. Peter testifies of this, saying that He has done so "through the knowledge of him that hath called us to glory and virtue" (2 Peter 1:3b). Thus, He has accomplished this through the knowledge of Himself. By His Spirit and by means of His Holy Word, He has revealed Himself to the hearts of His believing people—as He still does to all the objects of His favor. Inwardly, He illuminates their darkened understandings with the most precious knowledge of His divine glory in Christ, His Son, for when God regenerates His people, He also renews their understanding. By His Holy Spirit, He so influences and stimulates their understanding that they begin to know Him by virtue of the divine light that proceeds from Him, "with open face beholding as in a glass the glory of the Lord" (2 Cor. 3:18a).

All who thus begin to know God in the Lord Jesus, His Son, who is "the brightness of His glory" (Heb. 1:3a), increase daily in this blessed and precious knowledge by the power of the Holy Spirit, for it is written regarding them, "Then shall we know, if we follow on to know the LORD: his going forth is prepared as the morning" (Hos. 6:3a). Peter here posits that this knowledge is the means whereby the Lord has bestowed upon His believing people "all things that pertain unto life and godliness."

Hereby we learn that spiritual life, and thus godliness, is not wrought in a man except by means of a true knowledge of God. And, indeed, the knowledge of God is the only tree that yields the fruits of "life and godliness." The measure of our godliness is directly proportionate to the measure of the true knowledge of God in our hearts. The image of God in which man was created, and according to which all true believers are renewed and re-created in Christ Jesus and by the Holy Spirit, consists of these two great and heavenly benefits: a true knowledge of God and true holiness or righteousness.

Prior to the fall, Adam possessed these in perfection. Since he had a perfect knowledge of God, he also possessed a perfect holiness and genuine godliness, for it is impossible that one could rightly know God without also loving, serving, and obeying Him with his whole heart. He who knows God sees so much majesty, glory, perfection, infinite truth, and all-sufficiency in Him that he must exclaim with utmost amazement and with the melting of his heart, "Who would not fear thee, O King of nations? for to thee doth it appertain" (Jer. 10:7).

Upon Adam's fall into sin, all men lost that precious image of God, and now they lack all true knowledge of God and are "without God in the world" (Eph. 2:12). Therefore, as to their character and nature, all men are now radically ungodly and have become the enemies of God. Having lost the knowledge of God, men have simultaneously completely lost all true godliness. How can they fear God the Lord if they do not know Him? To look for true godliness in a person who is spiritually blind and ignorant is like attempting to "gather grapes of thorns, or figs of thistles" (Matt. 7:16b). This cannot be so, for a man must first be led to the knowledge of God before he can be led to the fear of God.

It is the Lord God's adorable way first to make Himself known to men, and to arrange all matters to achieve this, before He renders their hearts godly and obedient. Consider, therefore, that when the Lord God confronts men with His Word and with His holy commandments, demanding that they obey them and fear and serve Him, it is His normal way first to engage Himself in making Himself known to them in His divine majesty and to instruct them as to who He is that gives this law and requires obedience and godliness from them.

If we read the Holy Scriptures diligently, we will observe throughout that the Lord deals with men in this fashion. Consider only the giving of the law of the Ten Commandments. The Lord first introduces Himself to us in His divine majesty and in His precious grace and loving-kindness, saying, "I am the LORD," before making known to us a single word of that law. The Lord thereby is saying: "My people, hearken to Me! Until first you consider in all earnestness who I am that is giving these laws to you, do not proceed either to read My laws or to do and obey them. First consider that you are obliged to fear and obey Me fully. In your heart, be cognizant of My divine majesty and My infinite grace and loving-kindness toward you. I am neither a man nor a creature as you are. I am by no means an earthly monarch, for I am the Most High. 'I am [Jehovah], the LORD thy God, which have brought thee out of the land of Egypt, out of the house of bondage' (Ex. 20:2). Oh, My people, would that you learned to understand this rightly and that you would know who I am, so that you would fear Me with all your heart and diligently observe My laws."

Beloved, how much we are in need of being further instructed regarding these lofty matters! Ignorance thereof is the essential fountain and spring of sin, whereas the true knowledge of these matters is the fountain and spring of all true godliness. Oh, that we would groan within our hearts that under the preaching of His Word, the Lord would be pleased to reveal Himself to our hearts by His Holy Spirit, so that for once we might know and understand that He is the Lord, who by His power lives and reigns eternally!

We will therefore presently endeavor to explain in greater detail the words "I am the LORD," doing so as follows:

1. We will investigate why the Lord has been pleased to introduce His holy laws with these words, "I am the LORD."

2. We will then consider the actual meaning of these words, and what is being taught by them regarding knowing and believing God.

Regarding the first, there is a proverb that says that wise men never do anything in vain. This is certainly true, for it is the work of fools to do things haphazardly, engaging in them without any good reason, insight, or reasonable consideration. A wise man, however, conducts all of his business in a well-thought-out and orderly manner. He has a reason for whatever he does or speaks. All of his actions are governed by intelligent insight and sound objectives. However, all that proceeds from a fool resembles a manure pit, of which we know that it is best neither to touch it nor to stir in it.

But how very true this is regarding the infinite wisdom of the Lord, who alone is the all-wise God! How adorable and unsearchable is His wisdom in all that He does and speaks! We as men can know only a very small portion of this.

Consider this as we study our present subject, for the very first words of the law are, "I am the LORD." Why does the law begin with these words? The law should indeed begin with these words, and they should be written with large capital letters, and even then our blurry eyes would barely be able to read them. There are more than a hundred reasons for all who are wise and who, in the school of Christ, have begun to understand these words in some measure. However, as for fools, it is written so that seeing they would not see, hearing they would neither hear nor understand, and they would not be healed.

I will set before you four preeminent reasons why these words are written at the beginning of the law, and are therefore the first words that must be read by us. God prefaces the law with the words, "I am the LORD:"

First, to impress upon us that we must first rightly know Him before we can rightly either honor or obey Him. Therefore, we read in Isaiah 53:11, "By his knowledge shall my righteous servant justify many." We have already sufficiently addressed this in our introduction, and we will therefore not enlarge upon it.

Second, to compel us to reflect on the fact that we must not approach this law as wise, holy, and perfect men, and thus approach the law as a law of the covenant of works. Rather, we must approach this law within the context of the covenant of grace, and thus as poor, foolish, and impotent sinners—as sinners who, as to our souls, have completely lost God's holy and blessed image; who, due to our sins, have forgotten God and His glorious name; and who, by grace, must learn anew and be led to understand by God that He is the Lord. If we had retained our innate knowledge of God and our righteous state in Adam, God never would have had to remind us that He is the Lord. Prior to the fall, God never addressed Adam with such language as "I am the LORD." The knowledge of God was embedded in Adam's heart in all its purity, and there was nothing in him that caused him to doubt in the very least this great truth that God is the Lord. He always saw God before him in His brilliant glory, seeing Him as we see the sun with our eyes.

However, because of sin, we have become such foolish and ungodly men, and no longer are we able or willing to understand this fundamental rule of all truth that God is the Lord. The Lord must now trouble Himself to pursue us continually throughout His entire Word by repeatedly proclaiming to us: "I am the Lord! Oh, foolish and ignorant men, hear and understand that I am the Lord, and acquaint yourself with this truth!"

We never ought to read or hear these words, "I am the LORD," without being deeply ashamed and being grieved in our hearts that, by virtue of sin, we have rendered ourselves so utterly wretched that we shamefully and grievously forget this clear and foundational truth and banish it far from our hearts.

Third, to teach us that we should approach His holy law with utterly humble, meek, and contrite hearts, as being truly poor in spirit, for only men of such disposition are suitable to be heirs of the kingdom of heaven (Matt. 5:3), and they only, by the grace of the Holy Spirit, obey the law with an upright and humble heart. We have very proud and idolatrous hearts, and it does not even occur to us that we have no claims whatsoever or that all creatures are as nothing before the Lord. We do not readily acknowledge that we and all creatures are insignificant and inconsequential. We cannot humble our hearts deeply enough before the Lord when we endeavor to attribute all power and dominion and all honor and glory to Him alone, saying, "Thou art the Lord, and to Thee alone be all honor and glory." We may indeed reflect upon this in a carnal manner, subscribe to it intellectually, confess it judgmentally, and express it with our mouths, but we do not do so in pure uprightness and simplicity of heart.

There is no true acknowledgement of this in our hearts, for we are not of a poor and contrite spirit (Isa. 66:2).

The Lord therefore begins by loudly proclaiming to us, "I am the LORD." Thereby, He is saying: "Oh, children of men, do understand that I am the Lord. I am a God of all power, majesty, and glory, and apart from Me, there are none who have any authority. I and I alone am the Lord. I am the author of all things. I govern all things. I give all things, and I have created all things out of nothing. There is neither wisdom nor goodness nor strength nor life nor anything else that does not proceed from Me. I give life and breath to all things. Poor children of men, consider My majesty and with true contrition fall at My feet! 'Hear, O Israel: The LORD our God is one LORD' (Deut. 6:4)."

Fourth, so that we would immediately respond by echoing His own words, so to speak, saying, "'Thou, even thou, art LORD alone; thou hast made heaven, the heaven of heavens, with all their host, the earth, and all things that are therein, the seas, and all that is therein, and thou preservest them all; and the host of heaven worshippeth thee' (Neh. 9:6). Oh, that such grace would be my portion, so that I would acknowledge Thee to be the only Lord, that I would love, honor, fear, and trust Thee with my whole heart, and utterly forsake myself and all creatures, being subject to Thee alone!"

Beloved, first and before all things, the Lord God proclaims to us in His holy law, "I am the LORD," not only to work such an acknowledgement of His divine majesty in our hearts by His Holy Spirit, but also to stimulate in us holy frames of meekness, humility, reverence, veneration, love, and trust. If now, in some measure, we hear and understand this, there is no aversion whatsoever in our hearts for His holy law, but rather, with Paul, we "delight in the law of God after the inward man" (Rom. 7:22). Within ourselves, we repeatedly groan: "Oh Lord, render us obedient to Thy laws, and by Thy Spirit impress them deeply upon our hearts. Lord, we are indeed willing, and therefore continually make Thy strength perfect in our weakness" (cf. 2 Cor. 12:9a).

However, as long as we are incapable of rightly and inwardly hearing the voice of the Lord saying unto us, "I am the LORD," we most certainly will not heed these laws. Rather, we will be inclined to hate them and to cast this yoke from our shoulders. Let us therefore consider these words in more detail.

We have considered the profound motives that moved the Lord God to preface His holy law by saying, "I am the LORD." We must now consider in greater detail what is meant and implied by the fact that God is the Lord.

In the original text, we have God's adorable name, Jehovah. Our translators always translate that Name as "Lord," and it is therefore written with four capital letters.[1] This is the name the Lord God has given to Himself, thereby saying to us: "My name is Jehovah, and you must know Me by this name. There is no creature, either in heaven or earth, that will ever bear this name. I alone, who am the Lord, creator, and sustainer of all things, am Jehovah. That is My name, and that name can be attributed only to Me. All that is encompassed in and signified by this majestic name is applicable to Me alone."

As impossible as it is for any creature to be the most high God, so impossible is it for any creature to be Jehovah. Read Isaiah 42:8, for there we hear the Lord God speak clearly: "I am the Lord: that is my name: and my glory will I not give to another, neither my praise to graven images." Consider also Hosea 12:6, for there we read, "Even the Lord God of hosts; the Lord is his memorial." The Lord is thus saying, "Consider that this is my name." This excludes all creatures, and none among them is therefore either able or permitted to be called by this name.

This should lead you to conclude that the name Jehovah must have an efficacy and divinity that is wondrous, incomprehensible, and incomparable, for with great zeal the Lord reserves this name exclusively for Himself. You should therefore indeed believe it to be so! Scholars have written hundreds of books about this name, and there is not a single one among them who has understood even one percent of what he has written. This name of God is as a bottomless ocean of incomprehensible beauty and immeasurable majesty. To the degree that we truly know about God the Lord, so will we understand the meaning of the name Jehovah, for there is no distinction between His being and His name. He is Jehovah Himself, for He says, "I am Jehovah; that is who I am."

This name signifies the very essence of God's being and thus all of the complete and utmost perfection that is ascribed to Him. This name expresses who God is in the absolute sense of the word, and that He is thus independent, eternal, immutable, and absolutely perfect. We find the explanation of this name in various passages of God's Word, such as Hebrews 13:8, where we read, "Jesus

---

1. In the original text, VanderGroe also writes: "If my readers were to have some knowledge of the Hebrew language, I would be delighted to give them some instruction regarding this glorious name of God and its translation as the word "Lord." With God's blessing, they would then in some measure be led to a better understanding of the true meaning of this majestic and divine name. However, I must refrain from all this, for you would not be fully able to grasp it. Nevertheless, I will attempt, as simply and plainly as I can, to give a further explanation of this great and most glorious name of God."

Christ the same yesterday, and to day, and for ever." This expresses that Jesus Christ, who, with the Father and the Holy Spirit, is very God, is from all eternity, presently, and to all eternity, the essential, immutable, and most perfect God. He is today what He was yesterday, and He will be to all eternity what He is today and what He was yesterday, for in Him there "is no variableness, neither shadow of turning" (James 1:17). From eternity to eternity, He is God. We also read in Revelation 16:5 how the Lord is designated as the one "which art, and wast, and shalt be"; that is, He who is what He was eternally, and who shall eternally be who He is. For in Him there neither is a coming into being nor a coming to an end, nor is there even the minutest change.

This is indeed the essential efficacy and significance of this adorable name of God. Consider also what is recorded in Exodus 3:13–14. This passage not only expounds for us God's eternal, sovereign, independent, immutable, and infinitely perfect being, but also that in Himself He is eternally the same in all the attributes of His being. All this is implied in the words, "I am Jehovah."

This name of God therefore communicates to us that:

1. God is *eternal*, and thus that He never had a beginning. All that is external to God's being has its beginning in creation, for we read in Genesis 1:1, "In the beginning God created the heaven and the earth." This speaks of the beginning of all created matter, all that exists external to God's being. Prior to the moment of creation, created matter did not exist, and its essential existence began the moment God created it by verbally calling forth its being or essence. However, the most high God knows of no beginning, for He is the everlasting Father (cf. Isa. 9:6).

2. God is *independent*; that is, His essence and existence are original to Himself in the absolute sense of the word. This is by no means true for the creature, for as to its being, existence, and activity, it is fully dependent upon God in the comprehensive sense of the word. The creature derives its essence entirely from Him, "for in him we live, and move, and have our being" (Acts 17:28). All of creation is sustained, wrought upon, and governed by God in such a fashion that it cannot but move and engage itself according to His will. The Lord God, however, is not dependent upon anyone other than Himself. Whatever He wills He also accomplishes, for "he hath done whatsoever he hath pleased" (Ps. 115:3b). There is no creature that is equal to Him, and it is even repugnant to all truth that there would be anything above Him, for our God is the Most High, and "of him, and through him, and to him, are all things: to whom be glory for ever." (Rom. 11:36).

3. God is absolutely *immutable*; that is, He is always the same. He is immutable as to His being, His attributes, His words, His works, His promises, and His threats. This can by no means be said of any creature, for no creature or any created matter has its being in the absolute and essential sense of the word. Created matter can either be or not be, and it can exist in one form and then again in another form—all in accordance with that which pleases the Lord. Therefore, we observe daily so much change and capriciousness in the creature, for other than the Lord our God, nothing in and of itself is steadfast and immutable. He is that steadfast being who "layeth up sound wisdom for the righteous" (Prov. 2:7), and "he is the living God, and stedfast for ever" (Dan. 6:26). Sooner would all creation perish and return to its original state of nonexistence than that God could change even in the very least. And therefore He exclaims, "I am the LORD [Jehovah], I change not" (Mal. 3:6a).

4. God is infinitely *perfect* as to His being and in all that pertains to Him. In God, there is an incomprehensible fullness of perfection. No creature is able to comprehend this any more than a small bottle can contain all the water of the sea. Therefore, the question is asked, "Canst thou by searching find out God? canst thou find out the Almighty unto perfection?" (Job 11:7). This is as much as asking, "Can you progress that far in beholding the omnipotent being of God that you, with your puny mind, would be able to find out the perfection that is to be found in Him, saying that you have found this out and comprehended it?"

Here we observe an infinite distance between the Lord God and all creation. Let us consider the very best and most glorious of all creatures—the holy angels and the glorified saints. They possess a measure of goodness within themselves that they have received from God, for they are wise, strong, righteous, and truthful. However, all that they have is but as sparks and as given drops, for in God is the full and bottomless ocean of all these virtues. He is the embodiment of wisdom, strength, righteousness, and truth. Creatures may therefore only say, "I possess this as a gift from God," whereas God says, "I am the very embodiment of all those glorious virtues that you possess, and though I bestow them upon those whom I love, I am the fullness of everything as to My nature and My being. I am the all-sufficient and omnipotent one. I am the fountain of all things, and I am 'all and in all'" (Col. 3:11; cf. 1 Cor. 15:28).

5. God is the *Most High*, as well as the origin of all that exists, and therefore, with absolute power, He is the Lord, creator, sustainer, and ruler of all things, who "giveth to all life, and breath, and all things" (Acts 17:25b). Our translators

have therefore translated and recorded this incomprehensible name with capital letters.

All that we have set before you is comprehended in this majestic and awe-inspiring name of God. Consequently, if we reflect upon all this with great diligence, we learn various things from it—matters that are of the greatest importance with regard to true religion.

If, as we have seen, God is indeed the Lord Jehovah and the Most High, how important it should be to us that we should be the recipients of His favor and love. If Jehovah is favorably inclined toward us, if He is our friend, our God, and our Father, then we have need of nothing else. We then possess everything and need not fear anything, for all divine power, help, counsel, and wisdom are on our side.

Is He Jehovah, who is *absolutely perfect* and *all-sufficient*? What then do we lack if He may be our portion? What else do we desire beyond enjoying Him who is the bottomless ocean of fullness and perfection—lest there be the perception that our hearts are far too small and restricted to partake of all the good that we have in Him? However, Jehovah even fulfills that deficiency within us, for if, by an appropriating faith, we may say, "The LORD is my shepherd," then we are also able to say, "I shall not want" (Ps. 23:1).

Is He Jehovah *the independent one*, who has no one either above or beside Him? We may then confidently rely upon His love, His favor, His power, and His help, for no one shall prevent Him from loving, helping, and blessing us. No one shall ever be able to separate us from His love. We may then confidently exclaim with the holy apostle Paul, "For I am persuaded, that neither death, nor life, nor angels, nor principalities, nor powers, nor things present, nor things to come, nor height, nor depth, nor any other creature, shall be able to separate us from the love of God, which is in Christ Jesus our Lord" (Rom. 8:38–39). Oh, how precious and most blessed is such comfort!

Is He Jehovah *the eternal and omnipotent one*? How great is the comfort for our souls that proceeds from this truth when, by His Holy Spirit, our hearts have been truly assured of His divine favor and love! For we know that He will never change His divine disposition toward us, and that having once freely declared His favorable temperament toward us, He will never and by no means cease to love us to all eternity. He has indeed loved us with an everlasting love (cf. Jer. 31:3a); that is, with an immutable love that is from all eternity and that will endure to all eternity.

Since our God is both immutable and eternal, it must then suffice us that we may be assured that He Himself has declared His love toward us and that, by His Holy Spirit, He has shed abroad this love into our hearts (cf. Rom. 5:5). We must therefore, from that time forward, fully trust His truth and faithfulness, saying: "Lord, I believe that I, a poor, sinful creature, am graciously loved by Thee, and that Thou art my God. And since Thou art as immutable in Thy love and in Thy favor toward me as Thou art in Thy being, I shall from this day forward fully trust in this truth, and I beseech Thee that Thou, by Thy Holy Spirit, wouldest increasingly strengthen my faith to that end."

Is our God, Jehovah the Lord, the Most High who *created heaven and earth* and all that is therein out of nothing, and daily sustains, governs, and directs it according to His will? Then we need not fear anyone, however great and mighty in the world he may be. Then we neither need to fear the devil nor any other enemy of our salvation, for our God is Jehovah and He is the Lord. All creatures, whether great or small, are thus in His hands, so that they can neither move nor act contrary to His will. Oh, what comfort, peace, certainty, and security there is in the fact that this God is our God! Jehovah is at our right hand, and therefore we shall not stumble. If He is for us, who shall then be against us? Let things occur as they may, but if the Lord is with us, we shall be safe and secure. We shall not lack any help or protection, for "he that dwelleth in the secret place of the most High shall abide under the shadow of the Almighty. I will say of the LORD, He is my refuge and my fortress: my God; in him will I trust" (Ps. 91:1–2).

There is still more to be learned regarding the fact that our God is Jehovah. We must learn to understand this well, for without such understanding, the entire Word of God is to us as a sealed book, and we are incapable of reading it with comfort and edification. First, as far as God's children and all true believers are concerned, they are to proceed as follows: They must always impress upon their hearts that Jehovah is the *unchangeable one* in regard to all that they read of Him in His Word, for only then, by the power of the Holy Spirit, do they derive comfort from it. For example, when we read regarding Manasseh and other children of God that they not only were chastised severely for their sins and came into great misery and affliction as a result of them, but also that, when they called upon God with repentant, contrite, and believing hearts, He delivered them and was gracious and merciful to them, we must say to ourselves: "He who has done this is Jehovah, the unchangeable one. Since He is and remains the same to all eternity, He will also deal thus with me. When we grievously sin against Him, He will severely afflict us, and He will discipline and chastise us. However, when we manifest a heartfelt repentance and cry out and supplicate to Him, He will also graciously deliver us."

Furthermore, when we read how the Lord at times did not immediately deliver His people from their afflictions; how instead He specifically sustained them in the bearing of the cross, thus strengthening them with His spiritual comforts so that they could bear it; and how they spiritually gained more than they lost in the flesh; we must then again look unto God as *Jehovah*, the unchangeable one, and then trust in His Name. Thus, when we, His poor children, are sometimes subject to a heavy cross from which we neither can nor may soon be delivered, we are to trust Him that He will sustain us with His precious comforts, and that He will make our cross bearable.

However, when reading God's Holy Word, if we are incapable of believing that God is Jehovah, and thus the unchangeable one, then all the histories and all the promises of the Holy Scriptures are rendered useless by our unbelief. We are then incapable of deriving either comfort or advantage from reading how God blessed Abraham, how He delivered Jacob, and what great wonders He did in former days for His people. If, however, we take hold of Him and deeply impress upon our hearts that God is eternally and always the same Jehovah, the Scriptures are then a most precious fountain of comfort for us, and we can be certain that God will also do for us the good things He has ever done for His people if we but avail ourselves of the same means and, as they did, patiently wait upon the Lord.

On the other hand, this should also be a matter of fear and terror for all sinful men who do not wholeheartedly repent before God. They ought to consider and believe that God is Jehovah, immutable to all eternity, for then they shall see that God will most certainly deal with them as He has always dealt with sinners and ungodly men in former days. Whatever plagues were inflicted in former days upon the proud hypocrites, upon the unrepentant, and all who were not pure of heart, will also be inflicted upon them—unless they truly repent and obtain the forgiveness of their sins in Christ—for God is Jehovah. Let all sinners therefore consider what His name is, and that it is Jehovah's nature to hate those who hate Him—except there be true repentance on their part and forgiveness from the Lord's side. If God in former days brought to light all the evil deeds and evil devices of sinners that were committed in secret and publicly punished them accordingly, then do consider that He is Jehovah, and that also today He still does the same. Let all sinners most assuredly believe this. Amen.

The Preamble of the Law (4)

I am the LORD thy God.
—EXODUS 20:2a

In 1 John 5:3, the apostle John declares, "For this is the love of God, that we keep his commandments: and his commandments are not grievous." John, this holy man of God, greatly magnifies true godliness when he says that God's commandments are not grievous. His doctrine conforms to the doctrine of the Savior, who speaks in like manner when He says, "For my yoke is easy, and my burden is light" (Matt. 11:30).

How can it be that God's commandments are easy and light rather than grievous, considering that men generally manifest such great opposition to these commandments, objecting to their being strictly preached and observed? No burden oppresses men more heavily than requiring of them comprehensive godliness, the forsaking of all sin, and unconditional obedience to all of God's commandments.

Though such persons do insist on the law being preached, they have no desire that it should be preached too strictly or too forcefully. They believe that ministers are inclined to be too demanding in this matter, for men cannot possibly live such a strict and godly life as they insist upon. Instead, there must be some consideration for human vulnerability and weakness, and one must believe that God is merciful.

How grievous God's commandments are to such men, and therefore they plead strenuously that not too much of a burden be imposed upon them. Recognizing that, after all, it is not that easy for a man to bring himself into heaven, they are willing to subject themselves in some measure to the law. However, such men cannot handle the idea that they must be subject to the law in its entirety, for that yoke is too heavy and that burden is too great.

Notwithstanding, how can John, the holy man of God, sustain his assertion that the commandments of God are not grievous? How can we reconcile these two positions?

Let me address this matter in all simplicity, for it is the apostle's premise that "this is the love of God, that we keep his commandments." When he follows this up by saying that God's commandments are not grievous, he is thereby saying that they are not grievous to those pious hearts that have been ignited by and are filled with the love of God. This is the essence of the matter: if there is true love in our hearts for God the Lord, then His commandments are not grievous. Rather, His commandments then are entirely precious and delightful for us, and our wholehearted desire is to keep them. However, if our hearts are not "knit together in love" (Col. 2:2) to God, and the love of God is absent, His commandments are very grievous to us, and we make every effort to subject ourselves to them as little as possible.

Let me illustrate. Let us suppose that two servants serve the same master. The one servant is diligent, for he wholeheartedly loves his master and takes delight in serving him. He also recommends the service of his lord by saying: "I am doing so well in the service of my master. Working for him and serving him are so delightful that I could not ask for anything better." However, the other servant, being lazy and unwilling to serve, hates his master and complains not only about how hard he has to work, but also that the service of his master is burdensome and intolerable. You thus observe that when there is love and a favorable inclination, it is a delight to serve, and when these are lacking, it is extraordinarily burdensome to serve.

We ought to learn from this that the love of God must reside in us in order for us to be truly inclined toward genuine godliness and the keeping of God's commandments. Without love, we cannot serve God, and although in an external manner we were to observe all that the law requires, if we "have not charity, [we are] nothing" (1 Cor. 13:2b). In the state of rectitude, Adam loved God perfectly, and therefore he also served Him perfectly; His commandments were not in the least burdensome or grievous to him. However, when Adam ceased to love God, he ceased also to obey Him spontaneously. This explains why "love is the fulfilling of the law" (Rom. 13:10b). The Lord God knows that we poor sinful men can neither serve nor obey Him without love. He knows also that by virtue of sin, we have completely lost all love for Him in our hearts. Therefore, in His great mercy, He first engages Himself to restore His divine love in our hearts. To achieve this in us as His children, He initiates His dealings with us by loving us, doing so however hateful we may be before Him by virtue of our sins. He grants us His only begotten Son, and He unites us to Him by true faith. He enters into covenant with us. He forgives all our sins. He renews and regenerates us by His Holy Spirit, and He gives Himself to us as God and Father. He says to us that He is *our* God, husband, and bridegroom, and that He is favorably inclined toward us as to His all-sufficiency, whereby He protects us from all evil and favors us abundantly with all that is good. His will is that we view and acknowledge Him as such, and that we put all our trust in Him alone and continually address Him, saying, "O Lord, Thou art *my* God, father, husband, and king."

The Lord thus works His heavenly love within us, "because the love of God is shed abroad in our hearts by the Holy Ghost which is given unto us" (Rom. 5:5). In this manner, He draws us to Himself, purging our hearts from a love for the world and for sin. We read of this in Hosea 11:4: "I drew them with cords of a man, with bands of love." By this heavenly love, a way that is so sweet, the Lord is pleased to ignite our hearts tenderly and to incline them efficaciously toward a willing obedience of all His holy commandments. David refers to this, saying, "I will run the way of thy commandments, when thou shalt enlarge my heart" (Ps. 119:32).

Consequently, when the Lord grants to us His laws, He always binds them upon our hearts with those strong "cords of a man, [and] with bands of love." He thus binds upon our hearts that He is our God, that He is very favorably inclined toward us, that He cares for us, that He is fully committed to us, and that, as a Father, He watches over us, His beloved children. One needs to have a heart of stone to be unwilling to serve such a God.

This truth was clearly affirmed when the Lord gave His law of the Ten Commandments to His children, for He prefaced this law by proclaiming three great matters to them, so that their hearts would thereby be compelled toward genuine love and obedience, setting before them:

1. His glorious nature, saying, "I am the LORD;"
2. His love and goodness, consisting in that He is their God; and
3. the great and glorious benefits He thus had bestowed upon them by delivering them.

We have already addressed the first part of the text, namely, that God is the Lord. With the Lord's gracious help, we shall now address the second part and consider in further detail the implications of the Lord saying, " I am the LORD *thy God.*" We will therefore proceed as follows:

1. We will expound these two words, *thy God*, and consider what is expressed and implied when the Lord says to His children, that He is the Lord *their God*.

2. We will demonstrate how everyone, by the power of the Holy Spirit, must necessarily appropriate this great grace for himself by a true faith, wholeheartedly affirming that the Lord's declaration, "I am thy God," is explicitly applicable to the individual heart and is the means whereby a Christian can know that the Lord God is his God.

It is a most precious declaration when the Lord, who is the most high God and king, and whose adorable nature we have recently considered, says to all His children and His favorites, "I am the LORD thy God." These are the most precious and comforting words found in the entire Bible. Only he who in some measure is able rightly to understand the thrust of these glorious words and who, by the grace of the Holy Spirit, is able to embrace them with a true and believing heart, is capable of reading the Bible fruitfully.

Just as the entire law is comprehended in the Ten Commandments, the entire gospel, along with all its precious promises and benefits, is bound up in these words, "I am the LORD *thy God.*"

Two matters are here to be noted:

1. The Lord designates Himself here by the name *God*;

2. The Lord gives Himself and binds Himself fully to His believing people, thereby declaring that He is *their* or *our* God.

Regarding the first, it should be noted that in the original text, we find the name *Elohim*. This is the name by which the Lord is generally designated in His Word, and our translators always translate it as *God*. It is not our intent to consider the thrust and meaning of this name *Elohim* in great detail. Learned linguists are not as much in agreement about this as they ought to be by virtue of the great decline and degeneration in the knowledge of the true meaning of the Hebrew language, from which the true root of the name *God* is derived. Nevertheless, it is the common sentiment that the name *Elohim* is derived from an ancient root that means as much as the swearing of an oath. This name therefore communicates that the Lord Jehovah is the God of the covenant, who enters into an eternal covenant with us sinful men, doing so by way of the mutual swearing of an oath, such as was done in antiquity and is still being done today. From His side, the Lord is swearing, with regard to His children, that He will eternally and immutably be true to His covenant. The apostle Paul makes mention of the Lord's oath in Hebrews 6:17, saying, "God, willing more abundantly to shew unto the heirs of promise the immutability of his counsel, confirmed it by an oath." In so doing, He requires from us an oath in return, consisting in our heartfelt acquiescence and willing surrender of our hearts to Him. Thereby we declare that we eternally desire to be His people, and that we are therefore willing to renounce and dispense with all that is of ourselves and with all creatures—and thus with everything outside of Him—in order that we would cleave only to Him and serve Him. David swore such a covenant oath, saying, "I have sworn, and I will perform it, that I will keep thy righteous judgments" (Ps. 119:106). Such is the precious thrust and meaning of this name of the Lord.

We shall proceed to consider what the Lord God here declares regarding Himself. He is saying to all true believers, and thus to His favorites, that He is *their God*. It is certain in a general sense that the Lord God is the God of all men; that is, insofar as He is naturally their supreme Lord, creator, and sustainer. All men are therefore obligated to acknowledge Him as their God and creator, and He ought therefore to be fully loved, served, and feared by them. However, this is not what the Lord has in mind here, for by sin, all men have fully departed from Him and therefore no longer have any desire to consider and acknowledge Him to be their God.

Our wretched fall in Adam is so great that, though God is desirous to be our God, and though He offers Himself to us in all His sufficiency, we nevertheless by nature do not desire to have Him to be *our* God. Instead, we utterly despise and reject Him, saying unto Him, "Depart from us; for we desire not the knowledge of thy ways" (Job 21:14).

Therefore, when the Lord says, "I am the LORD *thy God*," He is addressing His people. He has established His covenant of grace with them and has renewed their hearts inwardly by His Spirit, and in so doing, He has converted them. He has bestowed upon them the heavenly gift of true faith, so that they, while truly forsaking sin, the world, and Satan, have sincerely entered into a holy covenant with Him. They have embraced Him as their God, king, and savior. Wholeheartedly they love Him as their God, and according to the inner man, they esteem, honor, and fear Him above all things. It is their earnest desire to be most intimately united to Him and to forsake all things for His sake. They desire to seek all their joy and comfort in Him alone, to trust in Him alone, and to be led, governed, and saved by Him alone. It is to His converted people that the Lord is saying that He is *their God*.

What shall we say regarding this? Who truly understands this weighty matter, and who can speak of it as he ought? These words imply that the Lord God, who created heaven and earth and all that is therein out of nothing, in the full magnitude of His being and as the incomprehensibly blessed, glorious, and all-sufficient one, has given Himself to His believing people, and to every one of them in particular. They are therefore privileged to take hold of Him and to embrace Him as their own possession—a portion that is most lawfully and graciously theirs. They may derive from Him all those benefits and incomprehensible blessings that He is capable of bestowing upon them by virtue of His majestic and divine nature. They may thus say to Him: "Lord, Thou art *my* God, husband, king, Father, and redeemer. Thy infinite power, wisdom, goodness, and incomprehensible all-sufficiency constitute my eternal bliss."

I am addressing here a great and wondrous matter. Although I am called upon to set this before you, I cannot rightly comprehend it even to the thousandth part, having to confess, "Oh how great is thy goodness, which thou hast laid up for them that fear thee; which thou hast wrought for them that trust in thee before the sons of men!" (Ps. 31:19). It is nevertheless my desire to say this much about it so that you and I together, by the power of the Holy Spirit and in all earnestness, would become truly desirous to seek this great blessing for ourselves, and thus be willing to dispense with all the trinkets and frivolities of the world.

Must you not observe here that man cannot partake of a greater blessing than to have the triune God as his portion and that he cannot be any richer than to have the privilege of hearing that God is his God? We deem people to be rich when they possess the capital sum of one million dollars. However, what would it mean if some person were to be given the entire world, and all that is to be found in it, as his possession? You would exalt the wealth of such a person far and wide, and yet it is not even worth mentioning, for the entire world is only an insignificant and vain thing. Should you then not be amazed, astonished, ecstatic, and thrilled about a person of whom it is true that the great God, the creator of all things, becomes his portion, and who may boast, "God is the strength of my heart, and my portion forever" (Ps. 73:26b)?

Such are the blessing, the treasure, and the riches of which we are presently speaking. Since it is a matter so great and incomprehensible that we can scarcely believe it, the Lord, the true God, is saying it Himself, and we must therefore believe it. Upon the giving of His law, He proclaims to His people, "I am the LORD thy God." It is as though He wants to say: "Let not this matter be too great for you, and do not dismiss it, because you can neither understand nor comprehend it. Instead, believe it, although it infinitely exceeds your puny and feeble understanding. Believe upon My own word that I am the Lord thy God."

We will now briefly consider some of the blessings to be comprehended in this gracious declaration of the Lord for all true believers, and to this end, I will endeavor to set before you from the Holy Scriptures some of the most preeminent of those blessings.

When the Lord says to His people and children that He is the Lord *their God*, He thereby wants to assure them:

1. That He has entered into an eternal and immutable covenant with them in which He, in spite of their great misery through sin, embraces them as His own beloved children, being moved with pity and compassion regarding their most wretched condition. In so doing, He most securely binds Himself to them in order to be their merciful God and Father, and He engages all of His omnipotence to secure their eternal salvation and redemption, eternally bestowing upon them all good things. Consider what the Lord Himself is saying: "Moreover I will make a covenant of peace with them; it shall be an everlasting covenant with them: and I will place them, and multiply them, and will set my sanctuary in the midst of them for evermore. My tabernacle also shall be with them: yea, I will be their God, and they shall be my people" (Ezek. 37:26–27).

2. Of their acquittal and the gracious pardon of all their sins for the sake of the merits of His Son, Jesus Christ, and that He is willing to engage all of His power, wisdom, grace, and mercy to secure the atonement of all their sins and iniquities by fully blotting them out, cleansing and purifying their hearts of them, and granting them a perfect and eternal righteousness. Yes, He assures them that He Himself will be their righteousness, so that they neither need to fear nor doubt God's grace, no matter how great, grievous, and manifold their sins may be; that is, if they are but truly sorrowful regarding them and they are desirous to have them forgiven out of grace and for Christ's sake. Again, God Himself declares, "But this shall be the covenant that I will make with the house of Israel; after those days, saith the LORD, I will put my law in their inward parts, and write it in their hearts; and will be their God, and they shall be my people...for I will forgive their iniquity, and I will remember their sin no more" (Jer. 31:33–34).

3. Of the great blessing of their sanctification. As the Lord Himself is infinitely holy in His nature, it necessarily follows that this God could not be our God without also perfectly sanctifying us and impressing deeply and fully upon

our hearts His divine image. Thereby we become a holy people in conformity to that beautiful image of our God, whereby, from day to day, we are renewed and transformed until the full perfection of our nature will have been achieved.

Hereby the Lord is saying: "Fear not, My people, for though you find yourselves to be so very wretched, impotent, perverse, and sinful, and you are continually complaining and grieving that you are unable to love, serve, and fear Me with your whole heart and soul, I nevertheless assure you that I am the Lord *thy God*. I will engage all My power and all-sufficiency to make you completely holy in both soul and body, and to deliver you from all your sin. Be fully assured of this and entrust yourself entirely to Me. I have already begun My work in you, and I shall not forsake the work of My hands. Rather, I shall gradually proceed with it, and there will come a time when I shall completely perfect it. I, the Lord, am holy, and it is therefore My will that you, My people, shall ultimately be perfectly holy, and that to all eternity." It is therefore written, "that thou mayest be an holy people unto the LORD thy God, as he hath spoken" (Deut. 26:19), and "the heathen shall know that I the LORD do sanctify Israel" (Ezek. 37:28a).

4. That He will always inwardly illuminate them in their hearts by His Word and Spirit. He thereby teaches and instructs them so that they get to know and continue to know Him as their God, and, as the only wise God, He cures the spiritual blindness of their hearts and grants to them His Spirit as the Spirit of wisdom and understanding. We may indeed mourn greatly because of our blindness, and we should be greatly troubled by the fact that we know so little of God and of heavenly things. However, since the Lord is our God, we have the most excellent teacher, for He has given us His only begotten Son to be our wisdom. We must therefore be of good courage, for we have but to wait upon and trust in the Lord, for He Himself is our light. He is the sun that illuminates our dark hearts, and He gradually causes all haze and cloudiness to evaporate. That sun will once break through fully, and He will bring forth our light as the noonday.

The entire Bible is therefore filled with comforting promises for poor believers. Consider, for instance, the great covenant promise of Jeremiah 31:33–34: "But this shall be the covenant that I will make with the house of Israel; after those days, saith the LORD, I will put my law in their inward parts, and write it in their hearts; and will be their God, and they shall be my people. And they shall teach no more every man his neighbour, and every man his brother, saying, Know the LORD: for they shall all know me, from the least of them unto the greatest of them, saith the LORD."

5. Of that great and blessed benefit of His imminent nearness and presence in that He desires to be most intimately united to them in His Son, Christ Jesus, and also to dwell in their hearts by His Spirit. He wants to surround them by and immerse them fully in His heavenly light, love, and grace, and continually cause His face to shine upon them. This is expressed Leviticus 26:11–12, "And I will set my tabernacle among you: and my soul shall not abhor you. And I will walk among you, and will be your God, and ye shall be my people."

6. Powerfully of His divine love; that is, how tenderly He loves them and how He has eternally set His heart upon them, so that, as an extraordinary expression of His infinite love, He has given Himself to them and has delivered them from the bondage of the devil. He assures them that His inclination toward them will never diminish, but rather, that His love and favor shall always pursue them. How could it otherwise be, for "God is love" (1 John 4:8). If this God is indeed our God, then His love is also manifested toward us, and we shall be eternal partakers thereof. It is therefore written, "The LORD thy God in the midst of thee is mighty; he will save, he will rejoice over thee with joy; he will rest in his love, he will joy over thee with singing" (Zeph. 3:17). The Lord also promises His people, "I will heal their backsliding, I will love them freely" (Hos. 14:4).

7. That He always will comfort them in all their sorrows and that He will surround them with all joy and delight, for He is the God of our exceeding joy (cf. Ps. 43:4). If He is *our* God, everlasting joy shall be upon our heads (cf. Isa. 35:10). If He is our God, then He is the God of all comfort, and He then greatly comforts us. He Himself speaks accordingly, "Comfort ye, comfort ye my people, saith your God. Speak ye comfortably to Jerusalem" (Isa. 40:1–2). Consider also Revelation 21:3–4: "They shall be his people, and God himself shall be with them, and be their God. And God shall wipe away all tears from their eyes; and there shall be no more death, neither sorrow, nor crying, neither shall there be any more pain."

8. That He will always preserve His children, and that, with His mighty hand, He will protect and shield them against all evils of soul and body, as well as from all their spiritual and physical enemies. Therefore, they need neither to fear anything nor to be troubled, for he who has this God as his God has all power, might, counsel, wisdom, and help on his side, and he may quietly lay down his head upon his God, saying, "In God have I put my trust: I will not be afraid what man can do unto me" (Ps. 56:11). The Lord therefore admonishes His people, saying: "I the LORD thy God will hold thy right hand, saying unto thee, Fear not; I will help thee. Fear not, thou worm Jacob, and ye men of Israel; I will help thee,

saith the LORD, and thy redeemer, the Holy One of Israel" (Isa. 41:13–14). Oh, it cannot be expressed in words how securely, safely, and fully protected a man is who has God as his God! He may know himself to be in a strong tower! Let all devils and all hell roar against him as infuriated lions, but such a man does not have to yield one step to them, for what can puny men do to him?

9. That He will always help and support them in all the trials and dangers they face, as well as in all the difficulties and perplexities of soul and body. They will never perish and succumb in such circumstances, for whoever might forsake them, the Lord shall never forsake them when they are in need. Being their God, He will uphold, sustain, rescue, and deliver them, and He will most certainly hear their cries and look upon them in their anxiety and distress.

Consider how the Lord assures His people of this, saying: "But now thus saith the Lord that created thee, O Jacob, and he that formed thee, O Israel, Fear not: for I have redeemed thee, I have called thee by thy name; thou art mine. When thou passest through the waters, I will be with thee; and through the rivers, they shall not overflow thee: when thou walkest through the fire, thou shalt not be burned; neither shall the flame kindle upon thee. For I am the LORD thy God, the Holy One of Israel, thy Saviour" (Isa. 43:1–3).

10. That as often as they find themselves in perplexing and difficult circumstances in which they are at their wits' end, when they turn to Him, He will always help and counsel them, showing them the way that they must go. He declares that "counsel is mine, and sound wisdom: I am understanding" (Prov. 8:14), and in Job 12:13, we read, "With him is wisdom and strength, he hath counsel and understanding." He therefore promises His people, "I will instruct thee and teach thee in the way which thou shalt go: I will guide thee with mine eye" (Ps. 32:8).

11. That He will always protect them in the face of injustice and ill treatment. He is their Lord and intercessor, who strives with those who strive with them, and He fights against them that fight against them (cf. Ps. 35:1). They must therefore hold their peace and patiently endure the abuse inflicted upon them by men, for the Lord shall see to it that their righteousness will break forth as the noon day. He watches over and cares for their honor, good name, and innocence—however much these may be obscured by men. At His time, they shall be vindicated, and their haters shall be subjected to shame and humiliation. The Lord Himself affirms this, saying, "Thus saith thy Lord the LORD, and thy God that pleadeth the cause of his people…" (Isa. 51:22a).

12. Of His divine blessing upon all that they may engage in—a blessing that shall always rest upon them and accompany them everywhere. Such is the testimony of Psalm 3:9: "Salvation belongeth unto the LORD: thy blessing is upon thy people." Who is able to enumerate exhaustively all that is comprehended in this?

13. That He will always have His delight in them, and that it will be His joy and delight to bless them—as is recorded in Isaiah 65:19: "And I will rejoice in Jerusalem, and joy in my people." As a shepherd leads his sheep, so the Lord also continually leads them by His Word and Spirit, doing so as is recorded in Isaiah 58:11: "And the LORD shall guide thee continually, and satisfy thy soul in drought." He therefore governs and directs them in all their doings and causes all things to work out to their advantage, so that "all things work together for good" (Rom. 8:28). He always sustains them in difficult circumstances. He sends forth His "help from the sanctuary" (Ps. 20:2). Day and night, He watches over them, so that they always are able to lie down and sleep in peace. He always chastises them for their spiritual benefit when they sin and transgress against Him.

Furthermore, He always satisfies them from the fountain of His all-sufficiency and sees to it that they do not lack any good thing. He increasingly assures them of their salvation, and strengthens their faith and hope that, even in death, He will be with them, guiding them by His own hand when they must traverse upon this distressing pathway.

Finally, He will at last deliver them from this earthly life and take them into His eternal glory to be with Himself, so that they will all be able to say with Asaph: "Nevertheless I am continually with thee: thou hast holden me by my right hand. Thou shalt guide me with thy counsel, and afterward receive me to glory. Whom have I in heaven but thee? and there is none upon earth that I desire beside thee. My flesh and my heart faileth: but God is the strength of my heart, and my portion for ever" (Ps. 73:23–26).

All of this, and much more, is comprehended in the Word of the Lord when He addresses His beloved people by saying, "I am the LORD *thy God*." Oh, what precious words they are, for they constitute the soul and life of the entire Bible! How happy a people they are who, by an upright faith, may appropriate these words and fully trust that the Lord is their God! The Lord Himself magnifies their happiness by proclaiming, "Blessed is the nation whose God is the LORD; and the people whom he hath chosen for his own inheritance" (Ps. 33:12).

Beloved, this is truly the crux of the matter, namely, that by the power of the Holy Spirit, we may appropriate this great grace that the Lord, the creator of heaven and earth, is also our God, and that He not only has entered into covenant with us, but that He also has called us to enter into blessed communion with Himself. If that is so, we are the most blessed of all men, for then we have been eternally redeemed, and we may joyfully lift up our voices and sing with David: "The LORD is the portion of mine inheritance and of my cup: thou maintainest my lot. The lines are fallen unto me in pleasant places; yea, I have a goodly heritage" (Ps. 16:5–6). We are also willing to fear God with our whole hearts and to walk in His statutes and ordinances. It is then our chief delight and joy to obey His holy commandments. Yes, this is the very essence of our salvation, for "among the righteous there is favour" (Prov. 14:9b).

If, however, this is not true for us; if we cannot in some measure by a true faith appropriate the truth that the Lord is our God; and if we are not yet earnestly engaged in securing this blessing, then we are indeed most wretched and miserable. God then is still our adversary, and we lack everything that is subservient to our salvation. If, therefore, we do not awaken at once from our slumber and open our eyes to have a correct view of our indescribable wretchedness and misery, and if we do not in all earnestness seek this great salvation, what shall become of us? We are then rushing to an eternal and most dreadful perdition.

Therefore, how can I conclude my consideration of this weighty subject matter without further addressing this subject in a subsequent sermon? In dependence upon the Lord's blessing, I must bind upon your hearts with great urgency not only the necessity of being able to appropriate by a true faith that the Lord, the most high God, is truly *your* God, but also how we may know with certainty whether He truly is our *God*. We must set before you that if the Lord is not our God, we cannot truly be a God-fearing people, and we are then incapable of keeping the Ten Commandments.

May the Lord be pleased to bestow His blessing upon our preaching, and may He cause His face to shine upon us for His holy name's sake. Amen.

The Preamble of the Law (5)

I am the LORD *thy God.*
—EXODUS 20:2a

In Revelation 2:17, we find this beautiful promise of the Lord: "To him that overcometh will I give to eat of the hidden manna." This is a very comforting and spiritual text that requires a more detailed exposition. However, we shall expound from it only briefly, as much as is subservient to our present objective.

As the text speaks of "hidden manna," the question arises as to what sort of manna this is. It must be that but very few know this, for this manna is emphatically referred to as "hidden manna." Were it generally known among men, it would most certainly not be designated as hidden. Though I can give you an external and verbal description of this manna, I am incapable of enabling you to behold the matter itself, for that is strictly the work of the Holy Spirit, who must efficaciously open and illuminate our blind eyes.

In its very essence, this hidden manna is the Lord Himself. It is the triune God, who has revealed Himself in the incarnation of Christ to the hearts of all true believers as the God of full salvation and as the only all-sufficient and soul-satisfying portion of all who love Him. The holy apostle teaches that this is indeed the hidden manna by saying, "Great is the mystery of godliness: God was manifest in the flesh" (1 Tim. 3:16).

Using a metaphorical analogy of manna, the Lord here presents Himself as being the wondrous nourishment whereby He sustained the children of Israel during their entire sojourn in the wilderness. He would teach us that as the earthly manna was nourishment for the body, likewise, He Himself, the Lord, is the spiritual nourishment for the hearts of all poor, believing sinners whom He calls into fellowship with Himself.

Regarding this earthly manna, we know that this nourishment came forth from heaven without any involvement of human hands. The children of Israel received it freely, and through the instrumentality of the Lord's providence, daily it rained down upon them. This nourishment was absolutely essential, for there was nothing other to be had in the wilderness. It was very delightful, healthy, nourishing, and satisfying, for it encompassed the essence of all other nourishment. The children of Israel had no need of any other nourishment, and therefore they had to forsake all other nourishment and accustom themselves to eating only manna. The more they ate of it, the more appetite they had for it and the healthier they became. When they despised this manna and desired other nourishment in its place, the Lord was greatly provoked to anger, and they were severely punished.

The Lord Himself, the triune God, is such precious and spiritual manna for all His believing people. He is the supremely precious nourishment of their poor hearts, and this spiritual nourishment also descends from heaven without any human involvement as to its preparation. It is bestowed upon us without money and price, and only by grace. It rains down upon us each and every day, and all we need to do is to partake of it by the Spirit of faith and appropriate it for ourselves. The Lord Himself is thus the only and absolutely essential and spiritual nourishment for all true believers.

There is no other nourishment for them in the wretched wilderness of this world. By His all-sufficiency, the Lord alone is able to satisfy their hearts inwardly, for He is the embodiment of all spiritual nourishment. He nourishes, refreshes, strengthens, and satisfies the poor hearts of His believing people. He Himself renders them healthy, causes them to grow, and causes them to increase in spiritual strength. Therefore, we are to be content with only the triune God Himself, and with nothing other. We must cling to Him alone and nourish our hearts with nothing but His grace. With Asaph, it must always be our confession: "Whom have I in heaven but thee? and there is none upon earth that I desire beside thee. My flesh and my heart faileth: but God is the strength of my heart, and my portion for ever" (Ps. 73:25–26).

Willingly we must forsake all other nourishment and never hunger and thirst after anything apart from Him, for this God sufficiently nourishes, fills, and satisfies us. The more we acquaint ourselves with this heavenly manna, the more delightful we find it to be, and the stronger is our desire for it.

However, they who despise this spiritual manna and yearn in their hearts for other food greatly provoke the Lord to anger. Being guilty of despising the Rock of salvation, they will consequently be severely punished by God.

It is the Lord God Himself who is the true heavenly manna, and thus "the bread which cometh down from heaven, that a man may eat thereof, and not die" (John 6:50). However, the Lord further describes this manna by calling it "hidden manna," not only because this manna is utterly unknown to the world and concealed from all unregenerate and carnal men, but also because, even among the most godly, there is little true knowledge regarding this heavenly manna. The blindness of the world is indescribably great, for, by virtue of sin, we have lost all true knowledge of God, and our understandings have become darkened (cf. Eph. 4:18). This manna is hidden because "the natural man receiveth not the things of the Spirit of God: for they are foolishness unto him" (1 Cor. 2:14a).

The devil, the prince of darkness, takes full advantage of this and holds something else before the eyes of poor sinners who have no eyes to see, telling them that what he has is the hidden manna, and thereby deceiving them as fearfully as he deceived Eve in Paradise. Thereupon, poor and blind men feed their souls with ashes, they eat Satan's husks as a delightful delicacy, and they are also satisfied in their being deceived.

Therefore, when the true heavenly manna is offered to them, saying, "Come and eat of this bread and drink of this wine, feed your souls with a crucified Christ and with a triune God, 'Forsake the foolish, and live' (Prov. 9:6)," he who makes this offer is considered as a man of "strife and debate" (Isa. 58:4). He is as one of Job's messengers, and they say to him: "Why do you torment and plague us? We already have what we need for our nourishment and satisfaction. We have always been nourished and refreshed, and why would you now disturb us by offering different nourishment of which we neither have any knowledge nor know what you desire from us. Be like others who comfort us by saying: 'Peace, peace be unto you. The Lord has already heard your groans, and He has already seen your tears. All shall be well with you.'"

Such is the extent to which this true manna is hidden—even to those who wish to be viewed as true Israelites, the true children of Abraham. Therefore, what a great grace and mercy of the Lord it is that He promises here to His poor, elect, and believing people that He will reveal this hidden manna to them! He says to them that He will give it to those who overcome, for "to him that overcometh will I give to eat of the hidden manna." He "that overcometh," he, by the power and grace of the Holy Spirit bestowed upon the heart by God, is the person who is enabled to prevail over all the great obstacles and hindrances of flesh and blood that encumber him from attaining to a spiritual knowledge and enjoyment of this heavenly manna in his heart. Such a person overcomes:

1. *The world*, that great obstacle between Christ and our hearts. Such a person truly and utterly forsakes all that is of this earth and views it as nothing but such vanity, in which he can find not the least delight. He has chosen God and His blessed service rather than the world, and with his heart, he desires to deny everything apart from Him.

2. *Sin*; that is, he finds his heart so fully inclined toward serving God that he deems even the smallest sin to be his greatest enemy. He has received a genuine desire and a heartfelt inclination to keep the law of the Lord, and while believing in Christ, it is his inward desire fully to live unto the Lord with body and soul, doing so in a way of painstaking godliness in which he finds no delight in fostering even a single sin.

3. *Satan*; that is, he sincerely hates him and his kingdom with all his cohorts and his evil works, being absolutely unwilling to have any fellowship with him. He instead utterly rejects any covenant with him, being desirous, in Christ, to cleave unto and to serve God alone with his whole heart.

4. All *aversion* in his heart toward God and toward His way to save poor sinners through Christ and by sovereign grace alone. By the Lord Himself, and by way of His strong and almighty hand, he overcomes manifold doubts and the unbelief of his heart, all of which deprive him of blessed communion with God. He is helped to overcome all such aversion, so that he prevails over his unbelieving heart and fully surrenders at the feet of the Lord Jesus. With the poor publican, he cries out for grace, and he unconditionally casts himself upon this grace, fully and unreservedly surrendering himself to Christ.

The Lord promises to him who may so overcome that he shall be given to eat of the hidden manna. What, then, is being expressed here? It simply means that a poor, contrite, and believing sinner who overcomes in this manner receives as his portion the most blessed triune God in His all-sufficiency. By means of true faith, he is strengthened, fed, nourished, and refreshed in his heart by God's incomprehensible grace, and he is not able to refrain from magnifying, praising, and greatly glorifying God. With a joyous heart, he proclaims to others, "Come and hear, all ye that fear God, and I will declare what he hath done for my soul" (Ps. 66:16). The Lord then gives to him who overcomes to eat of the hidden manna. He fully gives Himself to such a person, exclaiming, "I am the Lord *thy*

God. All that is Mine is yours, and all that is yours is Mine. I am your husband, bridegroom, and king." To such a person, the Lord then gives the Spirit of faith, whereby he cries out: "Abba, Father! Yes, Lord, Thou art my God, and I deem Thee to be my husband, king, surety, and savior, who forgives all my iniquities and heals all my diseases. Lord, Thou art truly such a God. I, a poor and sinful creature, embrace Thee as such, and I shall never doubt this again. I declare all doubt and unbelief that are yet to be found in my heart as my greatest enemy. Oh, Lord, I believe; I believe indeed! Be pleased always by Thy Spirit to help my unbelief, for I do trust in Thee. Thou art the Lord my God."

The Lord thus causes such a soul to eat of the hidden manna. Oh, who is capable rightly to express with words the blessedness that such a person may enjoy? Only when we truly taste and enjoy this shall we be capable of understanding it.

We shall now apply this to the subject at hand. Man can never be rightly capable of loving God or obeying His commandments with a pure and holy heart unless he first, by the power and grace of the Holy Spirit, has overcome, and thus also has eaten of the hidden manna. Such nourishment strengthens the heart to keep God's commandments willingly and out of a pure love. It is vain to admonish and exhort anyone to keep God's commandments if he neither truly achieves such a victory and therefore does not eat of this hidden manna nor wholeheartedly believes in the very core of his soul that God is *his* God and Father, who, purely by grace and for Christ's sake, eternally forgives all his sins. He is incapable of doing this, for the natural man cannot serve a God who is holy when his heart is still unregenerate and therefore completely corrupt, unbelieving, without the Spirit, dead, and disobedient.

Therefore, when the Lord gives His law to His children, before all things, He first gives them to eat of this hidden manna. It is His will that they believe that the Lord is their God and that He is thus their husband and father. It is His will that they do not doubt this in unbelief, and thus the very first words He speaks to them by way of preface are, "I am the LORD *thy God*." It is as if He says: "Eat first of this hidden manna, and thus first believe the very words I speak and do not doubt them. My children, satisfy and strengthen your hearts thereby, doing so by the efficacious operation of the Holy Spirit, and then come to Me, and honor and fear Me as the Lord your God. Love and serve your Father who has delivered you from this wretched Egyptian house of bondage; keep My commandments and live."

Beloved, you know that on the previous Lord's Day, we addressed the matter that the Lord is the God of His children, and we then set before you what a great blessing it is to have God the Lord to be your God. It now remains for me to consider this weighty matter as it pertains to each of us in some greater detail. We must therefore earnestly examine our hearts, whether in truth and with our whole hearts we believe that the Lord, the omnipotent creator and king of heaven and earth, is also explicitly our God, and that He is also saying to us, "I am the LORD thy God."

Your salvation, as well as mine, depends entirely on whether we are able, by the power of the Holy Spirit, to believe this for ourselves with upright hearts. Oh, that today we would therefore be truly attentive in hearing what the Spirit is saying to the congregation!

In dependence upon the Lord's gracious assistance, I wish to address three matters in greater detail. We shall consider:

1. The reasons why the Lord God prefaces His law by assuring His people that He is the Lord *their God*.

2. How we may appropriate this great grace and trust in it by true faith that the Lord is assuredly *our God*. Without doing so, we can neither extract one drop of true comfort from God the Lord nor be capable of obeying Him and His commandments with upright hearts.

3. What the grounds are upon which a true Christian, by the grace of the Holy Spirit, may know with certainty and believe that the Lord is truly *His God*.

Regarding the first, there are three prominent reasons why the Lord prefaced His law with these words, namely, that He, the Lord, is the God of His people. He did so in order that:

First, He might powerfully impress His holy laws upon their hearts and obligate them to obey them. This is similar to a father admonishing his children to be virtuous, saying to them, "My children, I am your father, and you should therefore be willing to obey me and do all that I command you to do." Likewise, the Lord says here to all who are truly converted: "My children, I am the Lord your God and Father. Therefore, honor, serve, fear, and obey Me by keeping all these My holy commandments. Do not despise them, lest you provoke Me to anger and I should withhold My blessing and favor from you, for if you keep My commandments, I, the Lord your God, shall then bless you in many different ways. If, however, you despise My commandments, I, the Lord your God, shall then most certainly punish and chastise you in many different ways."

Thus, you see, my beloved, that the Lord being *the God of His children* is the solid foundation for their obedience of all His commandments. However blind and unbelieving the children of Israel otherwise were, they readily could understand this, and therefore they exclaimed to Joshua, "Therefore will we also serve the LORD; for he is our God" (Josh. 24:18b). The Lord always uses that foundation as His compelling argument to lead His children in the way of obedience. Throughout His entire Word, we hear Him proclaiming, "Ye shall do this, or ye shall not do that, because I am the Lord your God."

Sometimes He also sets this before them as a promise, saying, "Obey my voice, and I will be your God, and ye shall be my people: and walk ye in all the ways that I have commanded you, that it may be well unto you" (Jer. 7:23).

Second, He might first and foremost lead them to a believing and childlike obedience. The Lord cannot be served by us in a legal and servile manner; that is, by way of compulsion, and thus with an unbelieving heart. Such service and obedience can by no means please Him, for His "people shall be willing in the day of [his] power" (Ps. 110:3). They must keep His commandments and obey Him with a sincere desire and a heartfelt willingness, as it is written, "I delight to do thy will, O my God: yea, thy law is within my heart" (Ps. 40:8). They must obey Him with inner delight and spiritual pleasure, doing so in the manner in which the holy apostle Paul testifies regarding himself, saying, "For I delight in the law of God after the inward man" (Rom. 7:22). David speaks likewise, saying, "And I will delight myself in thy commandments, which I have loved" (Ps. 119:47). They must serve and obey Him with a heartfelt love, as it is written, "Thou shalt love the LORD thy God with all thine heart, and with all thy soul, and with all thy might" (Deut. 6:5).

The Lord's children must serve and obey Him as their God with utmost humility, fear, and esteem for His great name, as expressed in Psalm 95:6–7: "O come, let us worship and bow down: let us kneel before the LORD our maker. For he is our God; and we are the people of his pasture, and the sheep of his hand."

Such is the holy and filial obedience to which the Lord God stirs up and stimulates His believing people. The basis upon which He does so is the fact that He is the Lord their God, and such filial obedience must necessarily issue forth from true faith.

Third, He might instruct them never to endeavor to keep His holy commandments by means of their own natural strength and disposition. Rather, they must engage to do so only by His divine power and grace, which He continually and richly bestows upon them by His Holy Spirit, for He is the Lord their God, who justifies, sanctifies, and completely redeems them. This explains the reason why, upon their humble contrition and faith, He continually pardons their sins and transgressions for the sake of the merits of His Son, Jesus Christ, granting them His perfect righteousness. As the Lord their God, by His Holy Spirit, He also continually works all that is virtuous in their hearts and fulfills in them this promise of His covenant: "And I will put my spirit within you, and cause you to walk in my statutes, and ye shall keep my judgments, and do them. And ye shall dwell in the land that I gave to your fathers; and ye shall be my people, and I will be your God" (Ezek. 36:27–28).

Therefore, at the beginning of the law, when the Lord reminds His people that He is the Lord their God, it is as though He is saying to them: "Oh, My children, I do indeed give My holy laws to you as your supreme king, Lord, and Father, who must consequently be served and feared by you. That is indeed My worthy due. However, I am also the Lord your God, for I have made an eternal covenant with you that I shall justify, sanctify, redeem, and save you. I know not only how very weak you are, but also what is the evil bent of your nature. I will therefore continually give you grace and strength that shall enable you to keep these My laws. Therefore, whatever I demand of you, I shall also continually give you by working it in you by My Holy Spirit. I am, after all, the Lord your God. Therefore, continually come to Me with your sins and infirmities, as a child would come to his father, and, with humble faith, confess them before Me. Continually 'let me see thy countenance, let me hear thy voice; for sweet is thy voice, and thy countenance is comely' (Song 2:14). Oh, turn to Me, 'acquaint now thyself with [Me]' (Job 22:21), trust in Me, and seek all your salvation and strength with Me. Be assured that I will always help you, for I am the Lord your God. Therefore, cast your entire burden fully upon Me and permit Me to undertake for you. I will make all things well for you, I will finish My work in you, and I will guide and direct you upon that right way in which you may safely proceed."

These are the three reasons why the Lord declares at the very beginning that He is the Lord our God.

We read in Hebrews 11:6 that without faith it is impossible to please God. This is most certainly true. We must possess in our hearts a pure and spiritual faith, which the Holy Spirit, by the preaching of the divine gospel, must work and strengthen within us. With such a believing heart, we are to be exercised with all the promises of God's grace, as they are revealed in the holy gospel. Not only are we to acknowledge these promises of the Lord as being true in and of themselves, but we must also embrace them in love, appropriate them, and wholeheartedly trust in them. This also applies to this precious promise of the Lord that He is the God of His children.

It is by no means sufficient merely to believe and to acquiesce in this truth. This neither gives comfort nor saves us. Rather, we must have a true faith in our hearts as a fruit of the work of the Holy Spirit, whereby we specifically appropriate this precious promise for ourselves. This enables us to believe and to hold for truth that the Lord, the most high and triune God, is also our God and our gracious Father—the God who has made His covenant also with us, who has eternally adopted us to be His people and children, and who will therefore protect us against all evil and, by grace, grant unto us all that is good.

Diligently we must impress this truth upon our hearts, for if we do not sincerely believe this and cannot in some measure and with some steadfastness appropriate this to ourselves, we are incapable of receiving a single drop of comfort from God. We are then neither capable of serving Him in genuine love and with reverence nor capable of rightly obeying His holy laws.

We shall briefly set before you some specific aspects of God's being that will immediately and clearly affirm this truth. We confess and know from the Holy Scriptures that:

First, God's *power* and *might* are infinite. He is therefore the mighty God, whose right hand is exalted and can deal with heaven and earth, and also with all creatures, as one would deal with the leaf of a tree. What comfort can be derived from God's majesty and power if, with some measure of steadfastness, we do not believe that this God is our *God*, and that He exercises His great power for our benefit? Must we then, with the devils, not tremble and shudder before Him, considering that He will one day engage His power for our eternal perdition for having so grievously offended and provoked Him to anger by our sins? With what sort of heart are we able to love and serve this supremely majestic and awe-inspiring God if continually we must fear and tremble before Him, expecting Him one day to crush us utterly by the thunder of His might?

The more we are acquainted with and hear of God's power, the more we shrink back and tremble if we are unable to believe that this God is our God, for if He is our God, we need not fear His power, but rather, may know that God's power yields only that which is good.

Second, the Lord God is *omniscient*, and therefore His mind and knowledge are of infinite dimensions. This enables Him to see and analyze all things—even the deepest secrets of the human heart. Nothing therefore can be hidden from His eyes. If, however, we cannot believe that this God is also our God, what comfort are we able to derive from His omniscience? It yields nothing other than what it yielded to Adam when he attempted to flee from before the countenance of God and sought to hide himself in the dark shadow of the trees of Paradise. The omniscience of God by no means yields any comfort if we are unable to believe that He is our God. We should be very anxious and fearful if we perceive that all our sins, even the most secret of all our iniquities, are known to Him with the clarity of the midday sun, and that there is no place upon earth where we are able to hide ourselves from Him. Rather, His hand is able to find us anywhere in order to punish and requite us according to our works. Oh, how we must tremble before the all-seeing eye of God if we are unable to think or to believe that it looks favorably upon us! How could we truly love, honor, and serve such an omniscient God in such a state?

Third, the Lord God is infinitely *just*. Therefore, He neither can nor will permit any sin to go unpunished, for His holy nature demands that the sinner shall by no means be absolved from anything, but that every man will be rewarded according to his works and the fruit of his actions. Tell me again, what comfort does this infinite holiness and justice of God yield if we are incapable of believing that this God is our God? Does it yield any comfort to a guilty criminal if he understands that he must come before a judge who is no respecter of persons, but is very strict and just, and who, in conformity to the law, shows not the least measure of grace and restraint? This obviously yields no comfort, for such a criminal cannot but tremble and shudder before such a judge. Must we then, as guilty and ungodly sinners, also not fear, shudder, and tremble before such an infinitely majestic, holy, and just God if we cannot believe that He is our God, who is favorably inclined toward us? How can we serve and love Him with pure hearts if He appears to us so infinitely dreadful that we must exclaim regarding Him: "Who among us shall dwell with the devouring fire? who among us shall dwell with everlasting burnings?" (Isa. 33:14b).

Fourth, the Lord God is infinitely *kind*, *gracious*, and *merciful* unto His children. He greatly loves them with a love that is inexpressible, and therefore He is to them an all-sufficient fountain of comfort both in life and in death. All this may very well be so, but what true delight, comfort, or joy do we derive from it if we cannot believe that this God is also our God, and that His goodness and mercy are favorably manifested toward us? This yields us no more comfort than a poor beggar is comforted upon hearing that great treasures and riches are available to others, whereas he must perish, since there is absolutely nothing for him. And indeed, the more we hear of God's great goodness and mercy toward His children, the more it torments and troubles us if we neither believe nor sense that this also applies to us. Our hearts become all the more perturbed and resentful the more we hear of God's grace and goodness. However much ministers may preach about God's great mercy toward His children and how the godly are so inexpressibly blessed, of what benefit is it for us, given the fact that we cannot apply it to ourselves? Of what benefit is it that we pray and wait upon Him, seeing that we receive nothing good from Him? Though He is merciful to others, He is not so inclined toward us. At least we do not sense this in any way, because we are not able to speak of the manifestation of this goodness and comfort in our hearts.

Therefore, it can only greatly grieve and torment us when we hear so much about God's goodness toward others, and meanwhile, we cannot perceive and believe in our hearts that He is also our gracious God and Father. Having such wicked, hostile, and unbelieving hearts, how can we then seek the Lord? How can we then love and serve Him in joyful obedience?

It thus is as obvious as the noonday sun that in no wise are we able either to be comforted or helped by God, or to keep and obey His holy laws with a pure heart and with delightful love, unless we can assure our hearts by the grace of the Holy Spirit, and thus feel this truth within us, that God is our God, who has covenantally bound Himself to us to save and deliver us from all our sins.

We must therefore strive with all our might to obtain this. Above all else, by the operation of the Holy Spirit, we must seek to have in our hearts the affirmation that, by a true faith, we are partakers of this great grace, for without such faith, we are not able to have a moment's peace.

However, someone might readily ask: "How may one clearly perceive and know that the Lord God is his God? How may one know that he does not merely imagine so great a matter to be true for him, knowing that so many do this to their eternal perdition?" We will now endeavor briefly to respond to this excellent and necessary question, and this is the third matter that we intended to address with you. Oh, that all who hear me would earnestly and diligently examine their hearts by way of the matters that I shall now enumerate!

Though I would be able to set before you many distinct characteristics regarding this great matter from the Word of God, I shall do so briefly, clearly, and simply, mentioning only one such characteristic, which fully and sufficiently will affirm the entire matter.

Beloved, the Lord God is truly our God when we find and experience within ourselves all such spiritual graces as the Lord commonly works in the hearts of all those whose God and Father He has become. What are those graces? Briefly, I shall list and expound them.

First, as to *God the Father*, if He is truly our God, He renews and regenerates our hearts in Christ and by His Holy Spirit. He re-creates us according to His image, and He sheds abroad His love in our hearts (cf. Rom 5:5), so that we tenderly and fully love Him as our heavenly Father. In and through His Son, Christ Jesus, it then is our delight and joy to obey Him in everything that He commands us to do, doing so by the power and operation of His Holy Spirit. If, therefore, we perceive within ourselves that God has thus fully transformed our hearts, having begotten us in Christ to be His children; if we may address him as Abba, Father; if we perceive that our hearts, by faith, are drawn to Him in true love and that we tenderly and sincerely love Him as our merciful God and Father, who did not even spare His own Son but granted Him to us to be our savior; if we are desirous to praise and magnify Him eternally for this, and are thus desirous to cleave to Him, as well as to love, honor, and fear Him; if for His sake we readily depart from and forsake the entire world, all creatures, all sin, and all our own lusts and desires; if we groan, pant, and desire to have Him alone as our portion to all eternity; and if this is therefore truly our experience, there is no doubt that this God is indeed our God, and that we are His children.

Second, as to *God the Son*, if He is also our God, He then, by faith, lives and dwells in our hearts. He then so draws our hearts to Himself, and He so fills us with His precious grace, that we put our trust in Him alone while truly forsaking and looking away from all that is of self. We then, above all, have a heartfelt desire for blessed communion with Him, desiring also to obtain the forgiveness of our sins and our entire salvation entirely through Him and by grace. Through the instrumentality of His death on the cross, He subdues sin in us and causes us to arise with Him unto a new life.

If we experientially know that Christ also lives in our hearts; if, above all things, He is supremely precious and lovely to us; if we truly esteem and acknowledge Him to be our all-sufficient savior and surrender ourselves to Him as poor and impotent sinners, trusting inwardly only in Him and surrendering ourselves willingly and with heartfelt delight to Him to be unconditionally led and governed by Him; if we perceive that His death on the cross results in the crucifixion of our old man when our new man simultaneously is quickened with Him, so that we intensely desire to be fully delivered from all sin by Christ and to be conformed to Him, our precious head; and if this is truly to be found in us as to the root of the matter, then we should not doubt in the least that Jesus is our God, that is, our redeemer and our savior. We must believe this most assuredly, however much the devil, our wicked hearts, and the men of this world may labor to convince us of the contrary.

Finally, as to *God the Holy Spirit*, if He is also our God, He then works efficaciously in our hearts by means of His Word. He then clearly reveals to us the despicable, abominable, and accursed nature of our sins. He causes us to confess our sins before the Lord God with heartfelt sorrow, shame, contrition, and a grievous perplexity of soul. We utterly condemn ourselves before God as being worthy of being eternally punished by Him. We then utterly and inwardly loathe ourselves and are displeased with all that is to be found in us, and yes, the Spirit acquaints us experientially with ourselves. With brokenness of heart, we therefore become aware of our profound impotence and how utterly lost we are in and of ourselves. The Spirit causes us to lose "the life of [our] hand" (Isa. 57:10b).

The Holy Spirit then reveals the Lord Jesus to our hearts, and He sheds heavenly light upon the precious promises of the holy gospel. By working true faith within our hearts and by uniting our hearts to the Lord Jesus, He makes us partakers of God's gospel grace. He causes us to desire Christ's grace with sincerity of heart so that we wholeheartedly love and seek Him. With the publican, He causes us to pray fervently for this, to receive and embrace Him, to put all our trust in Him, and to comfort, strengthen, gladden, and delight ourselves in Him. In short, the Spirit works all that is good, and thus all heavenly graces, within our hearts—too many to enumerate here. He increasingly uncovers our sins, and in light of this, He humbles us. He causes us increasingly to abhor ourselves, and increasingly, He draws us to Christ. Consequently, we endeavor more intimately to be united to Him and to be increasingly assured of His grace, and we do not cease to groan for a complete deliverance from all sin through Jesus Christ, our only savior and redeemer. We then always, wholeheartedly, and unceasingly thank and praise God the Father through Him.

Therefore, if all these operations of the Holy Spirit truly are experienced and found within our hearts, there should not be the least doubt that the Holy Spirit truly is also our God, and this we may most assuredly and confidently believe even though all the powers of hell were simultaneously to arise against us or to challenge any of the above.

Hereby we may clearly know and perceive whether these things truly are to be found in us, and thus whether the promise by which God has prefaced His holy law is also applicable to us poor sinners in particular. We may thus know whether the promise that the Lord God is truly our God is made to us, regardless of how miserable, wretched, poor, blind, naked, deficient, hell-worthy, and pitiable we may find ourselves to be by virtue of our sins. We may never be doubtful of this grace of God. Rather, by the power of the Holy Spirit, we must strengthen and comfort ourselves to know that God's covenant with us is eternal and immutable, considering that the Lord has said, "I will also leave in the midst of thee an afflicted and poor people, and they shall trust in the name of the LORD" (Zeph. 3:12).

Oh, that everyone would now proceed, truly and earnestly, to examine his heart! Beloved, you need to know that if these marks and matters, as I have set them before you from God's Holy Word, are not truly to be found in us as to the root of the matter, and if we are thus not experientially acquainted with them as to their true essence, then the Lord is most certainly *not* our God. We then remain utterly divorced from Him and His blessed fellowship, still being in bondage to the power of the devil, and utterly dead in trespasses and sins. Oh, how utterly wretched our state then is, for we are then still walking upon a pathway that will end in eternal perdition!

This is therefore a matter of great significance, and our entire salvation hinges upon it. Oh, if for once you would cast aside all earthly things and earnestly concern yourself with the question whether God is also your God! Oh, ye careless ones, you who grievously deceive yourselves and who, upon the false grounds of a counterfeit work of grace, imagine yourselves to be truly converted and that God is your God, that you would awaken and, in all earnestness, take this weighty matter to heart! Oh, that you would diligently consider these matters and examine yourselves most earnestly!

You who are somewhat perplexed and concerned by your realization that you are still without God, may you become truly acquainted with that which you are so grievously lacking, and may it cause you to be truly perplexed and troubled! In all earnestness, you ought to cry out, "What must I do to be saved? (Acts 16:30), and what must I do that God would also become *my God*?"

And to true believers, we would say: "Seek before all things to be truly assured of the great truth that God is your God. Oh, that you would seek to overcome all opposition and doubt, and that you might learn to eat truly of this hidden manna!"

May the Lord God grant all of this by His Holy Spirit. Amen.

The Preamble of the Law (6)

…which have brought thee out of the land of Egypt, out of the house of bondage.

—Exodus 20:2b

In Psalm 67:7 we read, "God shall bless us; and all the ends of the earth shall fear him." Here we read of two significant matters:

1. What God the Lord shall do for us.
2. What we must do for Him.

God's office, or work, is to *bless* us poor sinners whom He adopts to be His children and favorites in Christ His Son. Our office, or work, is to *fear* the Lord our God—the God who thus blesses and favors us. By way of His *blessing*, God binds us to Himself in order that we, by *fearing* Him, would bind ourselves to Him.

Oh, how sweet the union and communion is between the most high God and us lowly and sinful creatures! Where else could you find such a union? God takes the initiative in blessing us, and we then serve and fear Him.

Wherein does this blessing of the Lord consist? Is it an insignificant matter and something of little worth? By no means, for God blesses us with numerous extraordinary benefits; that is, with all manner of precious and exquisite temporal and eternal blessings according to soul and body. He first gives Himself as our eternal portion, doing so to the full extent of His all-sufficiency. This is the most precious blessing that God initially bestows upon us. We may therefore begin by saying, "This God is our God for ever and ever" (Ps. 48:14a).

Behold, this is the fountain from which eternally all manner of salvation and blessing issues forth. The Lord draws us out of our wretched condition and delivers us from our great misery. He frees us from evil, and as oft as we are in need, His mighty hand is engaged on our behalf. Proportionate to the measure in which the Lord God paternally blesses us, we should fear and love him in a filial manner by doing whatever pleases Him. Thus, His blessing always precedes our obedience, and our fear of Him always follows.

Consider how this is affirmed in the precious preamble of the law by which the Lord prefaces the law of the Ten Commandments. He begins by first proclaiming the precious blessing that He bestows upon His people. He brings to mind how He is the Lord *their God*, and how He blessed them by bringing them forth "out of the land of Egypt, out of the house of bondage"—a place to which they had been consigned for so great a length of time and where they had been subjected to such extraordinary misery.

Why does the Lord cause His people to reflect upon this great blessing at the very beginning of His holy law? He does so in order that they will learn to fear Him with a filial fear as their gracious God and Father, and thus keep all His commandments with a joyful obedience, having a heartfelt desire to do so and to groan with pious King David: "[Lord,] thou hast commanded us to keep thy precepts diligently. O that my ways were directed to keep thy statutes!" (Ps. 119:4–5). Our consideration of this matter will yield further insight regarding this truth.

Beloved, you know that already on several occasions, we have preached about the preamble of the law of the Lord. Twice we have preached from the words, "And God spake all these words, saying…." Once we have preached from the words, "I am the LORD," and then we devoted two sermons to the words, "I am the LORD *thy God*." Our primary objective in all of these sermons was to bind upon your heart, if at all possible, the holy law of the Lord, and to stir you up to manifest deep reverence, esteem, and veneration for this law. We have also sought to instruct you how the law of the Lord is to be kept by you; that is, as a believer who is in a reconciled state with God, and by the grace of the Holy Spirit, who must regenerate our hearts so that our obedience to the law of the Lord is pure, sincere, and willing. The Holy Spirit must unite us to God by a true faith, and He must engender in us a heartfelt desire and longing, so that, with soul and body, we might die fully to all sin and live fully unto the Lord God by the grace of Christ our savior.

Oh, may the Lord grant that we would achieve this great and blessed objective with some of you, or that we might achieve it hereafter!

The only thing yet lacking in our exposition of all that the Lord God has expressed in the preamble of His law, whereby He wants to move and stimulate our hearts to humble and filial fear, as well as to obedience, is the great benefit or blessing that He bestowed upon His people by bringing them "out of the land of Egypt, out of the house of bondage." This great grace and benefit of the Lord may not be overlooked here. On the contrary, this must eternally be commemorated by His people, and, by retaining a lively commemoration of it, they must always have this impressed upon their hearts. Hereby they are assured of God, as by a certain pledge and sacrament, that the God whom they must steadfastly love, cleave to, and humbly serve and fear is the Lord their God. They may therefore expect from Him more benefits and blessings. Yes, they may even expect the greatest benefits, deliverances, and protection, according to soul and body, if they will but continue to fear and serve Him in a filial fashion by joyfully obeying His holy law. The Lord will not cease to bless them if they do not cease to fear Him, and if, with David, they thus continually exclaim with an upright heart: "[LORD,] O how love I thy law! It is my meditation all the day" (Ps. 119:97).

We must now consider two matters in greater detail:

1. The physical deliverance of God's old covenant people from the earthly house of bondage in Egypt.

2. How this physical deliverance is set before us here to depict the most precious and spiritual deliverance of all true believers from a most wretched land of Egypt, that is, from the house of bondage of sin.

We shall first focus upon Israel's physical deliverance from the land of Egypt, doing so in the following order:

1. We shall consider how the Lord brought His people Israel out of the land of Egypt

2. We shall then consider what we may learn from this.

Regarding Israel's deliverance from the land of Egypt, three matters are to be noted:

1. How the Lord first caused His people to come into the land of Egypt.

2. How this land of Egypt later became to them a grievous and oppressive house of bondage.

3. How the Lord God Himself brought them out of this land of Egypt by His own hand.

Our text first makes mention of the land of Egypt. Egypt was and presently still is a beautiful and fruitful land, and thus one of the most desirable countries of the world. However, the despicable abomination of idolatry, by which this entire country was polluted, has utterly corrupted it and rendered it to be abominable and despised. In this sense, it remains a very immoral nation, in which the true God of heaven and earth is generally not known or feared. Everything in that land was overrun by a flood of superstition and idolatry, and for true believers, it was therefore very dangerous to live in such a polluted and idolatrous nation. Consequently, the Word of God frequently makes mention of the idols and the abominations of the land of Egypt. After their exodus, the Lord frequently complained about His people. They were still so greatly polluted by Egypt's abominations and worthless idols, and this prompted the Lord to admonish them frequently and earnestly to purify themselves from these Egyptian idols.

Notwithstanding the fact that Egypt was such a vile, polluted, and idolatrous nation, it pleased the Lord to cause His people Israel to dwell there for a lengthy period of time, and He thereby exercised a wondrous providence regarding them in order that He, in the end, could execute His eternal counsel regarding them. First, He caused Joseph to come to Egypt by way of His great and extraordinary providence, and after Joseph had experienced a great deal of adversity and misery, the Lord greatly exalted him in Egypt so that, next to the Pharaoh, king of the land, he held the highest position of honor and power. In His wondrous providence, the Lord provided—also upon the direction of Joseph, Jacob's son—a residence in Egypt, in the beautiful and fertile land of Goshen, for the patriarch Jacob and his entire family—and thus they dwelled in the best section of the entire land of Egypt.

In Egypt the Lord greatly multiplied His people Israel, and consequently, they grew into a great nation where they greatly multiplied in number, the Lord permitting them to live in this land for a lengthy period of time. From the Lord's prophecy to Abraham, we may deduce this, for He said, "Know of a surety that thy seed shall be a stranger in a land that is not theirs, and shall serve them; and they shall afflict them four hundred years" (Gen. 15:13). During that entire period, the Lord's eyes remained fixed upon His people in the land of Egypt. He continued to protect and preserve them as a people whom He purposed to bring out and to deliver in a most glorious fashion, for in so doing, He would sanctify His great name. This should suffice as to the manner in which the Lord brought His people down into the land of Egypt.

However, in our text, the Lord explicitly describes the land of Egypt as being a house of bondage for His people, because the children of Israel dwelt there for many years in very great misery, servitude, and oppression. The extent of it was such that it would be too much to recount in detail.

Initially, they fared very well in Egypt; that is, as long as they were but a very small community of people, and as long as Joseph's great accomplishments were remembered by the Egyptians. However, the first chapter of Exodus records for us how there was a complete and evil turn of events for them. Briefly stated, through the progression of time, there arose a king in Egypt who had never known Joseph. This new king observed how the people of Israel daily increased and multiplied, and that they became so powerful. They began to grow beyond the control of the native Egyptians. He therefore became fearful that there would come a time that this people, if they were to continue to multiply at this rate, in the event of war, could arise in rebellion and join forces with the enemies of Egypt. They might thus succeed in subjecting to themselves the masters of the land in which they lived.

To prevent this feared evil from coming to fruition in a timely manner, this king resorted to the political device of suppressing the people of Israel with all his might by subjecting them to grievous labor, oppressive servitude, and the deprivation of everything. The intent was to extinguish the vitality of their spirit and strength, and to bring them gradually into subjection by weakening them. This plan was readily implemented, and from that time forward, the children of Israel were subjected to inexpressibly grievous servitude, misery, and oppression in the land of Egypt. They were grievously and tyrannically abused by the Egyptians, who imposed the most grievous form of labor one could imagine upon them in compelling them to make bricks for the construction of cities, walls, and towers.

The children of Israel were treated as the most despised slaves of the world. Daily they were brutally beaten and scourged with whips. Young and old were driven to engage in the most grueling form of labor without ever a moment's rest. Their hard labor was rewarded by provision that was so deficient and wretched that they nearly collapsed from their hunger, thirst, and nakedness. Nevertheless, the Lord helped and sustained His people in this grievous servitude and inexpressible misery so that they continued to grow and multiply greatly, doing so more than ever before. This infuriated the Egyptians, for they were incapable of eradicating or suppressing the people of Israel as they wished. Consequently, the Egyptians daily made their servitude all the more grievous and treated them even more cruelly. Thus, they "made their lives bitter with hard bondage, in morter, and in brick, and in all manner of service in the field: all their service, wherein they made them serve, was with rigour" (Ex. 1:14).

As time progressed, this oppression increased daily in proportion to Israel's impending redemption, for their cries and bitter lamentation finally ascended unto the Lord in heaven. Indeed, the people could no longer bear the cruel servitude of the Egyptians and would have collapsed under it.

Beloved, you should now understand why the land of Egypt is referred to in our text as a house of bondage for God's people, for never have there been any human beings who were abused more grievously and oppressed for a longer length of time by their cruel enemies than were the children of Israel in Egypt. Nowhere else in the Word of God do we read of such oppressive servitude and violent oppression as the children of Israel had to endure.

Notwithstanding the magnitude of their misery, and though it appeared that there would be no deliverance, the Lord God demonstrated to them His great faithfulness, lovingkindness, and almighty power. By His own hand, and thus without the contribution or intervention of any man, availing Himself only of the service of Moses and Aaron, God brought them forth out of the cruel Egyptian house of bondage, and He here sets this great benefit before them by saying, "I am the LORD thy God, which have brought thee out of the land of Egypt, out of the house of bondage."

The Lord had promised this to Abraham when He established His covenant with him. He then made known to him the great and glorious benefit He would bestow upon his seed in the future, saying to him, after first revealing to him that his seed would be subjected to servitude in a strange land for four hundred years, "And also that nation, whom they shall serve, will I judge: and afterward shall they come out with great substance" (Gen. 15:14).

This redemption of the people of Israel from the land of Egypt was thus a promised benefit and a glorious blessing of God's covenant that He had made with them earlier by their father Abraham. Consequently, the Lord dealt with the children of Israel, whose God and Father He was, as with His own people, with whom He had established a covenant in their father Abraham, His beloved servant, who, during his entire sojourn upon earth, had walked uprightly before His countenance. The Lord neither could nor was at liberty to abandon the people of Israel, the seed of Abraham, His elect servant, as they abided in the land of Egypt. By virtue of His covenant, He was compelled graciously to deliver them when their misery and oppression had reached its zenith and they intensely cried out to Him for help. He then did so in a manner so great, glorious, and wondrous as God has ever helped and delivered a people from its misery, either before or after that day, bringing them forth out of the grievous house of bondage in Egypt.

He sent Moses to them in the land of Egypt, and, with his brother, Aaron, he took the cause of the people in hand before the king, Pharaoh. When the Egyptians could not be moved to let the children of Israel depart from their land, God punished them with ten plagues so great and dreadful, such as were never heard or seen before, for the Lord came and took His people, so to speak, by the hand, and brought them, by His mighty arm, out of Egypt. He led them as a flock of sheep through the Red Sea, separating the water before their very feet, so that they were able to traverse the bottom of the sea on dry ground.

When their enemies, the Egyptians, pursued them with an immensely large army, the Lord defeated the Egyptians and their king, and caused them all to perish and drown in the sea before the eyes of the Israelites. Simultaneously, He led His people to dry land and, without any discomfort, led them into the Arabian wilderness, located opposite to Egypt, the Red Sea lying between them, so that the children of Israel would never be able to return to Egypt. Rather, they could proceed on their journey to the beautiful land of Canaan, which they yet had to inherit by virtue of God's covenant. This would also prevent the Egyptians from ever drawing near to them again, and thus they would always and permanently remain separate from one another.

This is that most glorious and wondrous deliverance of the people of Israel from Egypt, and in terms of its magnitude and glory, nothing like this deliverance is found in the entire Word of God. This entire deliverance was purely and solely the work of the Lord "with a strong [and mighty] hand, and with a stretched out arm" (Ps. 136:12). The Lord, being a jealous God who will not give His honor to another, exclusively claims this great work of Israel's deliverance as His own, saying, "I am the LORD thy God, which have brought thee out of the land of Egypt, out of the house of bondage."

The Lord, as the Most High, certainly accomplished this singlehandedly, thereby displaying most illustriously His greatness, His glory, His truth, His faithfulness, His loving-kindness, His mercy, His grace, His infinite might and wisdom, with His steadfast delight in and love for His people. In short, the Lord did everything for His own name's sake so that He might thereby sanctify His great name before the Egyptians, the people of Israel, and the entire world.

To this end, God permitted the anxiety and oppression of His people to rise to such a level that all appeared to be hopeless and desperate. Thereby it would in no wise appear as though they, by their cunning and wisdom, had contributed anything to their deliverance. The Lord saw to it that His servants Moses and Aaron, in all their transactions with the Egyptians, were incapable of contributing anything toward the deliverance of the people, for the oppression of the people became instead all the more grievous, so that one was thus unable to say, "Moses and Aaron have accomplished this by their honorableness, authority, eloquence, and good strategy." The Lord therefore also hardened Pharaoh's heart so that no matter what plagues were sent upon him by the hand of the Lord, he could not be moved to let the people of Israel depart. This afforded opportunity for the Lord to shatter the entire might of Egypt and enabled Him to take His people by the hand in order to bring them out of Egypt by His strong and almighty arm. Paul therefore writes, "For the scripture saith unto Pharaoh, Even for this same purpose have I raised thee up, that I might shew my power in thee, and that my name might be declared throughout all the earth" (Rom. 9:17).

Such is the way in which it pleased the Lord to magnify Himself most gloriously in this deliverance of His people. He not only demonstrated clearly that He is the Lord, but also that He is the God and Father of His people Israel, whom He had made and formed to be His people: "This people have I formed for myself; they shall shew forth my praise" (Isa. 43:21). It is therefore proper that the Lord, at the beginning of His holy law, declares to His people Israel, "I am the LORD thy God, which have brought thee out of the land of Egypt, out of the house of bondage."

We shall now proceed to demonstrate what things we may learn for ourselves from this regarding the people of Israel, and consider in some detail the beneficial and comforting lessons that may be learned from the matter we have thus far addressed.

First, all of the above contains a very significant and important lesson for the ancient nation of Israel. By implication, it is also applicable to all who truly are the people and children of God and whose concern is always to fear the name of the Lord our God. If the people of Israel received such a great and glorious benefit from the Lord their God, and if, by virtue of His covenant, in which He adopted them to be His people, He accomplished such a wondrous deliverance for them, what gratitude they were obliged to express to the Lord their God! How obliged they were to love, honor, and fear Him with all their hearts and to conduct themselves as His redeemed people, humbly obeying His holy law and commandments as He gave them!

This is the reason why the Lord positions this great and glorious benefit at the beginning of His holy law. He has done this to establish it as a foundation, motive, and compelling argument to move the hearts of His people by such means toward obedience. It is as though the Lord is saying: "O Israel, My beloved people, would it not be your delight to serve and fear Me, who am your God, Lord, and Father, by keeping all My commandments with a heartfelt and joyous obedience? Am I not the one who has so wondrously delivered you, bringing you forth by My own hand from that wretched house of bondage, the land of Egypt? Did I not deliver you from this flaming furnace in which you would have altogether perished and by which you would have been utterly consumed? Did I not hear you from heaven when you mournfully cried out to Me? Oh, My people, has My heart not been moved toward you? Has My heart not been ignited with compassion and a burning love toward you? Have I not been mindful of My covenant, and did I not arise from My throne and take hold of you? Did I not, as an eagle, carry you upon My wings and thereby lead you out of the Egyptian house of bondage? Oh, My people, since I so tenderly love you and have accomplished such a great and glorious redemption on your behalf, and since I steadfastly have determined that I shall bestow more blessings upon you, and that at the appropriate time I will lead you into the beautiful land of Canaan as I have sworn to your fathers, Abraham, Isaac, and Jacob, would you then not in return also love and adore Me, the Lord your God? Should you ever be able to forget the great benefits I have bestowed upon you? Should your heart ever be turned away from Me? Should you ever be able to neglect to honor, to fear, and to serve Me, the Lord your God, with all your hearts, and joyfully to obey My laws? Oh, what vile ingratitude that would be! I would never expect that from you, My children, and therefore remember forever and never forget that 'I am the LORD thy God, which have brought thee out of the land of Egypt, out of the house of bondage.' Therefore, always keep My commandments and live!"

Such is the profound instruction encompassed in these words for the people of Israel. This instruction also extends to us, who, with them, have a heartfelt desire and delight to fear the great name of the Lord our God with a filial heart and to keep all His commandments. We observe here the ultimate objective of all the graces, benefits, and wondrous deliverances that the Lord bestows upon His children. The objective is that our hearts would be committed to the holy law of the Lord our God with an increased measure of love and genuine obedience, that we would be all the more valiant in battling our indwelling sin, and that we would be all the more diligent, faithful, upright, and steadfast in the service of the Lord.

Let us, therefore, with such a disposition, consider all the benefits and deliverances the Lord our God has also previously bestowed upon us, and still daily bestows upon us. I shall presently not address the great deliverance the Lord our God wrought for us by delivering us from the wretched Egyptian house of bondage of sin. If the Lord would so favor us, this will be the subject matter of a subsequent sermon.

I now ask you to take note of another great, wondrous, and most glorious deliverance that the Lord our God so graciously wrought for us, His people, in bygone days. Was the God-fearing population of the Netherlands also not subject to a most wretched form of bondage in former days, having been held captive in the spiritual Egypt of the anti-Christian papacy? Was the papacy also not utterly saturated with the most abominable idols and all manner of vile superstition and idolatry? Were the people of the Netherlands also not in servitude to the dreadful house of bondage of the Spanish Inquisition and persecution? Were they not for many years kept in a most wretched state of bondage that can neither be expressed in words nor recorded with a pen? Shall I now proceed to set before you the wretched condition, the unheard-of oppression, the dreadful cruelty, and the fearful persecution to which our godly forebears were subjected in that wretched house of bondage of this papal and Spanish Egypt? My friends, I would hardly know where to begin and where to end. A multitude of books has been written regarding this subject, and one can read them only with deep and heartfelt sorrow.

Who delivered the Netherlands from that grievous house of Egyptian bondage and from that flaming and burning furnace? Who drew them out of it? Who was it that delivered them after a cruel war of eighty years? Did not the Lord our God do so by His mighty and terrible arm? Did He not, contrary to all human calculation and imagination, deliver us with astonishing miracles from the jaws of so great a death? Did He not do battle for our nation with His mighty arm? Did He not bestow upon us a thousand tokens of His favor? Did He not, before our very eyes, thoroughly demolish and defeat our enemies, who so oppressed us, until He finally fully delivered us from their oppressions, establishing us as a free people and giving us this beautiful land of the Netherlands as our heritage?

Oh, my God-fearing Christians, have you already completely forgotten how great a blessing the Lord our God bestowed upon us and how great a deliverance He wrought? Have we, by our sins and due to our grievous ingratitude, thus succeeded in erasing this memory? Are we no longer capable of understanding this language, when the Lord proclaims loudly to us: "I am the Lord thy God, O My people of the Netherlands! I have brought you out of the papal land of Egypt and out of the Spanish house of bondage. With My mighty arm, I have broken to pieces the heavy iron yoke that was upon your necks and caused you to become such a great, free, and exceptional people as you still are today. I, the Lord, I alone have done all this, and I have so tenderly loved you. What nation is there upon the face of the earth that I have blessed and favored more? To what other nation have I manifested such great faithfulness and benevolence? All this I have done so that, as your God and Father, you would serve and fear Me with your whole heart and keep all My laws and commandments."

Beloved Christians, you who fear the Lord your God with a filial love, that you would bind this great matter upon your hearts! Who among you, considering that in former days the Lord bestowed such a glorious blessing and so great a deliverance upon the Netherlands, finds himself inclined and stimulated in his heart toward fearing the Lord in all holiness? Oh, that you would attentively reflect upon this and take notice of the Lord's complaints regarding His people. What has become of your commemoration of this great deliverance wrought by the Lord in former days on behalf of the Netherlands, and which is still the foundation of our present security? Oh, children of God, has this utterly vanished from your hearts? Is your conduct due to ignorance? Or is it a manifestation of wretched ingratitude and the despising of the Lord your God and all His benefits? Or are you of the opinion that a previous generation has already sufficiently praised, thanked, worshiped, and honored the Lord for His great benevolence?

It is my wish that the Lord would grant that both your as well as my countenance would blush with shame and that we would truly acknowledge that we are the people of whom it is written: "And [they] forgat his works, and his wonders that he had shewed them. Marvellous things did he in the sight of their fathers, in the land of Egypt, in the field of Zoan" (Ps. 78:11–12).

This concludes the first lesson we extract from this text.

Second, let us note that the Lord God did indeed lead His people of old, the people of Israel, out of the land of Egypt. As we have observed, it was a nation that was utterly polluted by abominations and idols, as well as all manner of superstition. This teaches us that the Lord will not tolerate His people continuing to reside in such an unclean land due to the great danger that they themselves will also be polluted in their hearts by these abominations.

It should therefore be no matter of indifference among which people we live and reside. Rather, we are obligated, as much as possible, to avoid such places that are most grievously polluted by the fearful superstition and idolatry of Roman Catholicism. We should not readily dwell among them, but if at all possible, we must seek to reside in places where we have the purest manifestation of religion and where the best means unto salvation are readily available.

We are here not addressing irreligious people as such, for it does not matter to them where they live, as long as they can prosper according to the flesh. They are quickly satisfied as long as they can find a church and a minister of our persuasion whom they can occasionally hear preach. Rather, I am primarily addressing the godly, who uprightly fear the Lord and have a genuine love for the pure worship of His name. If, therefore, you reside in a locality where good and faithful means of salvation are available, you should never hasten to depart merely for temporal advantage, but refrain from doing so until you clearly know the will of God and that He Himself is calling you to depart. If such should be the case, you are then at liberty to depart and follow the Lord in His way. Your heart should then not be too attached to anything, not even to the soundest means of grace. Then the Lord your God alone should suffice you.

Furthermore, we also learn that just as we should not move to such localities that are most polluted by papal idolatry and superstition, we also must not send to such places our children and such as God has placed under our oversight. We should especially see to it that we never permit them to live in Roman Catholic homes or with Roman Catholics. Sooner or later, such a young person, by such a sinful and dangerous pathway, will be seduced by a pernicious Roman Catholicism, and be captured by the devil in his hellish snares. Such parents or caretakers will be accountable to the Lord for their deeds.

Consider only how great and tender was the care that Abraham had for his son Isaac. The Lord had been gracious to Abraham when He called him out of Ur of the Chaldees. Though it was a beautiful and fruitful region, and though Abraham's extended family lived there, it was also a very idolatrous and morally polluted region, where one could readily be corrupted and seduced to engage in idolatry and the worship of images. He therefore compelled Eliezer to swear an oath that he would not return his son Isaac to that nation, for Abraham said to him, "Beware thou that thou bring not my son thither again" (Gen. 24:6). Such was Abraham's fear that his son Isaac might again be led back to Ur of the Chaldees, a land so defiled by idolatry. If Isaac were to dwell there, he might be corrupted and depart from the true religion. Regarding matters of this nature, all godly Christians must therefore conduct themselves and care for their own according to their conscience.

Third, we shall yet consider a third lesson, and therewith conclude our exposition. We are clearly taught that the Lord leads His most beloved and treasured people in a way of most grievous and lengthy afflictions, and that He can permit their tribulation to reach such a level that they come very close to utter devastation and destruction. Consider therefore how the nation of Israel fared. They were the most favored nation under the sun, the only people loved by the Lord, and upon whom He had set His heart. The Lord permitted all other nations upon the face of the earth to go their own way. However, He had established His covenant with this people and had promised them many wondrous blessings. Nevertheless, the Lord permitted His beloved people to be subjected to such great and grievous afflictions, subjecting them for so many years to cruel persecution and abuse by an ungodly and idolatrous nation. However, we have observed that, at His time, the Lord came to their rescue and wrought a great and glorious deliverance for them.

We read in the Holy Scriptures, but also in historical accounts, that the Lord has often dealt with His people in a similar fashion, and will do so sooner or later. Therefore, we who are God's people and children must never think that because we are His people, we shall always be free from affliction, and that the Lord will never lead us into the hot furnace of affliction. By no means, beloved, for consider that the Lord could also cause His people in the Netherlands again to come into an oppressive house of Egyptian bondage and cause us to be in subjection to the power and oppression of foreign adversaries, whereby He might greatly oppress and trouble our souls. I cannot see it any other way but that things are already beginning to move in that direction, and it appears that the Lord is already laying the groundwork for our impending affliction.

It is time for Christianity in the Netherlands to be cleansed and purified from the prevailing presence of filth and scum. Oh, the sins and abominations of the land are increasing daily! Spiritual declension is on the increase in the church, and there are but few who have any notion that it is so. Oh, let us not think that the day of evil is yet far from us and that it will not come during our lifetimes, thinking that they who come after us will have to concern themselves with these matters! No, such a mindset is unbecoming for the children of Zion. Let us therefore embark upon a different pathway and earnestly ask the Lord for grace to receive insight regarding the evils and afflictions that are about to come over the church, and so may our hearts be prepared to endure a heavy cross and affliction. And, indeed, the heavens are everywhere lowering with dark clouds. It could very well be prior to our death that we will not only have to suffer grievous persecution for the truth's sake, but that God will also test the genuineness and steadfastness of our faith in a most unsettling manner.

Beloved Christians, I hope that the Lord our God shall give us further insight into this. It is high time for us truly to awake from our slumber and, by God's grace, earnestly to prepare ourselves for cross-bearing, suffering, bondage, and affliction. It is already so long ago that the Lord threshed His corn in the Netherlands, and the threshing floor is now filled with chaff and straw. It must therefore necessarily soon be thoroughly purified, for otherwise one shall soon hardly be able to find the wheat.

Oh, what a troubling and grievous situation it would be for God's people if, unexpectedly and unpreparedly, they were to be cast into a flaming furnace of affliction! Do you wish to know what we must have in order to be prepared for this most grievous cross? Let me address this. We must:

1. Have a tender, godly, spiritual, and heavenly minded heart that has been weaned from a love for sin and earthly possessions, a heart that abides in intimate fellowship with God.

2. Have a true, virtuous, lively, and active faith, with a steadfast assurance that we are God's children and that the triune God will eternally be our Father.

3. Have a settled conviction in our hearts to go wherever our God is pleased to lead us, even if it is to be into the hottest fire of affliction; that is, if such would be His divine will, and if He were pleased to glorify Himself in such a way and thus to lead us, His children, unto salvation.

4. Gradually learn to wean ourselves from all carnal comfort, our desires, and all that we delight in. We must endeavor to stop coddling our flesh and being so insistent upon what we shall eat, drink, and wear. We must accustom ourselves to fasting and to the mortification of our virulent flesh. We shall generally not do

very well if we must begin to learn all these things when the trial has already come upon us. Failure to mortify the flesh in a timely fashion has been the cause that many shamefully apostatize during times of grievous affliction and persecution.

5. Have the power or spirit of fervent prayer. We must know how to pray fervently, believingly, humbly, and persistently, and to "continue in prayer, and watch in the same with thanksgiving" (Col. 4:2).

Beloved, such are the holy and spiritual weapons we must supply ourselves with by the grace of our heavenly Father, for then only shall we be able fearlessly to enter into the iron furnace and into an Egyptian house of bondage. The Lord shall then be with us, keep us, and also grant us a most glorious deliverance at His time. Oh, how blessed is that hour that so softly and sweetly is approaching, in which we shall one day be able to sing with inexpressible joy, "I have fought a good fight, I have finished my course, I have kept the faith" (2 Tim. 4:7). Amen.

The Division of the Law and the First Commandment

And God spake all these words, saying, I am the LORD thy God, which have brought thee out of the land of Egypt, out of the house of bondage. Thou shalt have no other gods before me

—EXODUS 20:1–3

Question 92: What is the law of God?

Answer: God spake all these words, Exodus 20, Deuteronomy 5, saying: I am the LORD thy God, which have brought thee out of the land of Egypt, out of the house of bondage.

I. Thou shalt have no other gods before Me.

II. Thou shalt not make unto thyself any graven image, or the likeness of any thing that is in heaven above, or that is in the earth beneath, or that is in the water under the earth: thou shalt not bow down thyself to them, nor serve them; for I the LORD thy God am a jealous God, visiting the iniquity of the fathers upon the children unto the third and fourth generation of them that hate Me; and showing mercy unto thousands of them that love Me, and keep My commandments.

III. Thou shalt not take the name of the LORD thy God in vain; for the LORD will not hold him guiltless that taketh His name in vain.

IV. Remember the Sabbath day, to keep it holy. Six days shalt thou labour and do all thy work: but the seventh day is the Sabbath of the LORD thy God: in it thou shalt do no manner of work, thou, nor thy son, nor thy daughter, thy manservant, nor thy maidservant, nor thy cattle, nor thy stranger

that is within thy gates: for in six days the LORD made
heaven and earth, the sea, and all that in them is, and rested
the seventh day: wherefore the LORD blessed the Sabbath
day, and hallowed it.

V.   Honour thy father and thy mother, that thy days may be long
upon the land which the LORD thy God giveth thee.

VI.   Thou shalt not kill.

VII. Thou shalt not commit adultery.

VIII. Thou shalt not steal.

IX.   Thou shalt not bear false witness against thy neighbour.

X.   Thou shalt not covet thy neighbour's house; thou shalt not
covet thy neighbour's wife, nor his manservant, nor his
maidservant, nor his ox, nor his ass, nor any thing that is
thy neighbour's.

Question 93: How are these commandments divided?

Answer: Into two tables; the first of which teaches us how we must behave towards God; the second, what duties we owe to our neighbor.

Question 94: What doth God enjoin in the first commandment?

Answer: That I, as sincerely as I desire the salvation of my own soul, avoid and flee from all idolatry, sorcery, soothsaying, superstition, invocation of saints, or any other creatures; and learn rightly to know the only true God; trust in Him alone; with humility and patience submit to Him; expect all good things from Him only; love, fear, and glorify Him with my whole heart; so that I renounce and forsake all creatures, rather than commit even the least thing contrary to His will.

Question 95: What is idolatry?

Answer: Idolatry is, instead of, or besides that one true God who has manifested Himself in His word, to contrive, or have any other object, in which men place their trust.

The Lord addresses His believing people in Isaiah 54:5 with a most precious and comforting word, saying, "For thy Maker is thine husband; the LORD of hosts is his name." Throughout the entire Bible, one cannot find words that are sweeter and more comforting than these. The Lord of hosts, the supreme creator and king of heaven and earth, declares in these words that there is a most intimate union and relationship between Himself and His believing people. He refers to Himself as the husband of His people, to whom He has united Himself in a spiritual marriage and whom He has embraced to be His wife. Who of us is capable of comprehending this matter? Therefore, having spoken of the spiritual marriage between Christ and His congregation, Paul exclaims, "This is a great mystery" (Eph. 5:32).

If an earthly monarch decided to marry a poor and unattractive beggar, who would not rightfully be astonished? However, it exceedingly transcends all comprehension and astonishment of angels and men that the most high God of heaven and earth, the all-sufficient and most glorious Jehovah, who has no need of anything outside of Himself, would enter into a spiritual marriage union with the most wretched, insignificant, ungodly, despicable, and abominable sinners, saying to them, "I, the Lord of hosts, your creator and maker, am your husband, and you are My most tender and beloved wife!"

Where would we end if we were to set before you all the incomprehensible wonders of God's glory and grace that coalesce in that declaration? However, it is not our present objective to pursue this. We wish to note only one thing. Given the fact that the Lord here declares Himself the husband of His believing people, He thereby desired to set before them the totality of their obligation as the Lord's wife toward their illustrious husband and maker.

What is this obligation? Let us consider this by observing how things are in the natural realm.

First, a wife must consider and acknowledge her husband to be *her personal husband* and in no wise doubt this. Likewise, a believer must also truly consider and acknowledge the Lord God to be her husband. However great and incomprehensible this may appear to believers, they may nevertheless not doubt this in unbelief for a moment, for in so doing, they immediately deny both their status and their duty. Therefore, by the operation of the Holy Spirit, they must steadfastly endeavor to be assured thereof, and the Lord Himself promises to give this to His people, saying, "And it shall be at that day, saith the LORD, that thou shalt call me Ishi;[1] and shalt call me no more Baali" (Hos. 2:16).

---

1. The Dutch *Statenvertaling* reads, "En het zal te dien dage geschieden, spreekt de HEERE, dat gij Mij noemen zult: *Mijn Man*," that is, "And it shall be at that day, saith the LORD, that thou shalt call me *my Man (or my husband)*."

Second, a wife must sincerely *love and cherish her husband*, for without love, a wife is not able to fulfill her obligation toward her husband. Therefore, how obligated true believers are to love the Lord their God and husband! How fervently and heartily they should always love Him! How most fitting this is indeed, and how many reasons and compelling motives there are that oblige them to such love! Consequently, David exhorts God's people, saying, "O love the Lord, all ye his saints" (Ps. 31:23).

Third, a wife must *honor and revere her husband*. She must continually obey him in all righteousness, for her husband is her lord and head. She must therefore submit herself to him. She must subordinate her will to the will of her husband, and she must quietly submit to him. She may not exercise the least dominion over him. Man was created before the woman, and she subsequently was brought forth to him to help and serve him. This therefore governs the duty of the wife, for it is God's will and ordinance. Her religion and her pursuit of salvation will be in vain if she is unwilling to acquiesce in her duty and submit herself to God's command.

However, all true believers have the same obligation toward God, their husband and king—a truth that is affirmed throughout the Holy Scriptures. Paul therefore exhorts all Christian women, saying, "Wives, submit yourselves unto your own husbands, as unto the Lord" (Eph. 5:22)—and all true Christians are thus obligated to fear and submit to God the Lord.

Fourth, a wife must steadfastly *be committed to her husband and be faithful to him*. She may not in the least foster a relationship with another man, and she must completely dispense with any such notion. By voluntary covenant, she is fully and exclusively united to her own husband. She may never violate and abandon this covenant, for by so doing, she would be subject to God's dreadful judgment, being unfaithful as an adulteress and fornicator.

Likewise, all the Lord's true believers must wholeheartedly cleave only to their God and utterly forsake the world, Satan, sin, themselves, and whatever else may be. They must know, love, honor, fear, and obey none but Him. In Him alone they are to rejoice, and in Him alone they are to put their trust. In summary, with soul and body, they must exist and live for God alone, forsaking all that is outside of Him. Such is the primary fountain and the chief duty of all true religion, and therefore the Lord of hosts begins the law of the Ten Commandments accordingly by commanding us that we are to have no other gods before Him.

Beloved, as you know, we preached on several occasions on the preamble of the law of the Lord, setting before you these three important truths:

1. The lawgiver who most solemnly gave this law of the Ten Commandments to His covenant people Israel is the great, glorious, immutable, and adorable Jehovah or Lord.

2. He is their faithful, gracious, and merciful covenant God.

3. By virtue of His covenant, He bestowed upon them the great and extraordinary benefit of bringing them forth from the grievous and oppressive house of bondage in Egypt.

All of these truths together constitute strong and unbreakable cords and bonds of love by which the hearts of a believing covenant people are enticed to commit themselves in love and by faith to the Lord their God, to His holy service, and to His perfect law, doing so in regard to every explicit component of this law.

Having thus expounded and addressed this most excellent preamble of the law of the Lord, we now commence with the exposition of each component of the law itself, being careful to examine every word or commandment found therein. However, before we proceed, we must first consider the division of the law of the Ten Commandments. The instructor addresses this by asking, in Question 93, "How are these commandments divided?" to which he replies, "Into two tables; the first of which teaches us how we must behave towards God; the second, the duties we owe to our neighbor."

The Holy Scriptures teach us that the Lord God Himself wrote His holy law upon two tables of stone, thereby signifying their immutability and their everlasting permanence. By means of His servant Moses, He gave these two tables to His covenant people Israel, commanding His people to place and to preserve them in the ark of the covenant. However, we are not completely certain as to the manner in which these ten words of the law were inscribed upon these two tables of stone, and thus we do not know with certainty—though it is very probable—whether the first four words were written upon the first table and the remaining six words upon the second table.

The law should therefore be divided in accordance with the instructor's method, namely, into two distinct parts. The first part of the law contains the first four commandments of the law and pertains to the service believers are obligated to render to the Lord their God, and the second part, the final six commandments, stipulates their obligations toward their neighbors and themselves. The first four commandments stipulate how believers are to conduct themselves toward the Lord *immediately*, and the last six commandments stipulate how they must magnify, serve, and glorify the Lord *mediately* by means of their conduct toward their neighbors.

It is beyond doubt that the Savior divided the law of the Ten Commandments accordingly when He summarized it into the two great and preeminent commandments that function as the fountainheads from which all of God's commandments exclusively issue forth, saying: "Thou shalt love the Lord thy God with all thy heart, and with all thy soul, and with all thy mind. This is the first and great commandment. And the second is like unto it, Thou shalt love thy neighbour as thyself. On these two commandments hang all the law and the prophets" (Matt. 22:37–40).

The law of the Ten Commandments, as to its very essence, is therefore a law of love, for "the end of the commandment is charity out of a pure heart, and of a good conscience, and of faith unfeigned" (1 Tim. 1:5). Paul concludes Romans 13:10 by saying, "Therefore love is the fulfilling of the law."

This love is operative toward three specific objects: God, oneself, and one's neighbors. Though it is true that the instructor, in his division of the law of the Ten Commandments, includes only love toward God and love toward our neighbors, we must not think that love toward oneself is excluded from the law, thereby implying that man is not to love himself and has no obligation toward himself. This is by no means what the instructor intends to say. He is simply addressing here love toward God and love toward our neighbors, implying that this necessarily includes love for oneself.

The Savior exemplifies this by teaching that one must love his neighbors *as himself*, thereby implying that one is obligated to love and cherish himself. It therefore would have been better and more accurate if the instructor had written accordingly, namely, that the first table of the law teaches us how we are to conduct ourselves toward God, and the second table what our obligation is toward our neighbors *as well as ourselves*.

Thus, the first table encompasses a pure love for God, and the second table, love for one's neighbors as well as for oneself. The first table consists of four words or commandments, and the second table of six words or commandments. We must acquiesce in this division of the law rather than search for other divisions.

Having now considered and addressed the division of the law of the Lord as the second component of our current sermon, we shall subsequently follow the instructor and, as our third and final point, proceed to consider the first word or commandment of the law itself. The word or prohibition that is to be further addressed is communicated by the Lord to His believing covenant people in these words: "Thou shalt have no other gods before me" (Ex. 20:3). We shall first expound these words separately, and thereafter we will consider the exposition of the instructor.

The Lord thus forbids His believing covenant people to have any other gods before or instead of Him. By the words *other gods*, the Lord refers, in the narrow sense of the word, to pagan idols that are made of wood, stone, or any other substance, as well as any presumptive gods of their imagination—and thus such idols as are religiously worshiped and honored by the heathen. The children of Israel had left such vile and abominable idols in the land of Egypt, where they had observed how the Egyptians honored them. Such idols they would also be able to find in Canaan among the nations dwelling in the land at the moment they would be led into it.

In a broader and more general sense, by referring to *other gods*, the Lord is also comprehensively addressing all that man elevates as an object of his faith, trust, love, adoration, allegiance, and esteem. He thereby refers to everything, whatever it may be, without exception, other than the true God, referring to all that is neither God nor a savior, and consequently is therefore incapable of saving man or of bestowing upon him anything that is essential, abiding, and advantageous. This includes all earthly things or creatures; man's own illusionary virtuousness; the performance of one's duties; one's inclinations, works, strength, or wisdom; and everything else in which men trust in the least or whatever, in heaven or upon earth, to which they affectionately cleave within or outside of themselves.

The Lord, the lawgiver, here designates them all as *other gods*. These other gods are not mentioned as though they truly are gods, distinct from the one true God of heaven and earth. By no means, for this true God is the one and only God. The Holy Scriptures therefore designate as idols all these other gods that cause men to depart from the true God. They are also referred to as false gods and vanities. Paul writes, "We know that an idol is nothing in the world, and that there is none other God but one" (1 Cor. 8:4).

However, the Lord here refers to them as other gods because men, in their natural blindness and ungodliness, serve, adhere to, and trust in them as gods. To do so is to dishonor the true God in a most vile manner, and it is therefore a most abominable and despicable sin. Consequently, the Lord forbids His covenant people as seriously and emphatically as He does, saying, "Thou shalt have no other gods before me"—or, as it reads in the original Hebrew text, "Before Me there shall be no other gods." Hereby the Lord is saying: "Apart from and instead of Me, the one true God and your covenant God, you are not to serve, cleave to, love, or in any way trust in any other matters or persons. You shall not have any other gods."

The Lord also adds these words, "before me";[2] that is, "before My countenance." The phrase "the countenance of God" is simply to be understood as it is generally used in the Holy Scriptures, namely, as a reference to God's omniscience in heaven and on earth. This can be proven by the following passage: "Whither shall I go from thy spirit? or whither shall I flee from thy presence?"[3] (Ps. 139:7). The poet thereby desires to say that he could not move anywhere outside of the sphere of God's eyes and majestic presence, given that the Lord is all-seeing and always near unto him. In like manner, we interpret the reference to God's countenance here as speaking of God's majestic omnipresence and the all-seeing eyes of His omniscience.

With these words, the Lord is actually saying, "Since I, the Lord your God, am present and behold you with the eyes of My omniscience, you therefore, as My believing covenant people, shall have no other gods before Me in which you put any measure of trust, or cleave and adhere to with any measure of affection and esteem."

Given that the Lord is omnipresent, that He fills heaven and earth, and that He consequently beholds all things, His covenant people may not have any other gods outside of Him, before Him, or above Him anywhere in heaven or on earth. If they were to serve other gods, they could do so in no way but before His countenance; that is, before the omniscient eye and the majestic presence of the Lord their God. What a vile and despicable abomination it would be before the eyes of and in the presence of the Lord, their majestic, holy, and righteous covenant God, to cleave to, honor, and serve other gods! It would be no less wicked and shameful than if a woman were to fornicate by having intercourse with other men in the presence of and before the eyes of her own husband.

Therefore, before the countenance of the Lord their God, the believing covenant people of the Lord must remove far from them all that is not God, for

---

2. The Dutch *Statenvertaling* reads, "Gij zult geen andere goden voor Mijn *aangezicht* hebben," that is, "Thou shalt have no other gods before *My countenance.*"

3. The Dutch *Statenvertaling* reads, "Waar zou ik heengaan voor Uw Geest en waar zou ik heenvlieden voor Uw *aangezicht?*"; that is, "Whither shall I go from thy spirit? or whither shall I flee from thy *countenance?*"

they must have no other gods before Him. This affirms that no one may have any other gods within the recesses of his heart, and thus no one may, within the secret recesses of his heart, either honor, fear, cherish, or trust anything outside of God. Rather, he must keep his heart entirely pure before the Lord, for the Lord is also omnipresent within a man's heart. By virtue of His divine power and providence, He resides in the hearts of all men in a general sense, and by His Spirit and grace, He also specifically dwells within the hearts of His children. Therefore, all that is concealed within our hearts is open and naked before the Lord. His eyes thoroughly penetrate our hearts and look into the most hidden and deepest recesses of them. God therefore exclaims, "I the LORD search the heart, I try the reins, even to give every man according to his ways, and according to the fruit of his doings" (Jer. 17:10).

Whatever we choose to cleave to, cherish, honor, or trust in any way outside of or apart from God is observed by the Lord with utmost transparency, for it transpires openly before His countenance. This sin and such ungodliness are sternly and expressly forbidden by the Lord.

Consider therefore how pure our hearts must be kept before the Lord. Oh, that this would be rightly acknowledged by us, for this pertains to the fountain and root of our entire worship! The least inkling of love that we secretly harbor in our hearts for the world or for any sin or sinful desire is a shameful transgression of this command of the Lord, for at that very moment, we have other gods before Him. Though we may not sin outwardly, our hearts must also be entirely pure within, and the Scriptures therefore testify, "Blessed are the pure in heart, for they shall see God" (Matt. 5:8).

Implied in this prohibition is also a very weighty command, by which the Lord's people are charged and commanded to engage in the opposite of what is being prohibited. It consists in their obligation to embrace, esteem, and acknowledge as their God none but the supremely exalted Jehovah, the great God of heaven and earth, to whom they are bound with covenant bonds. They are to put their trust in Him alone, and cleave to, serve, cherish, honor, fear, and obey none but Him.

This is the word-for-word exposition of the true meaning and content of the first commandment of the law. This commandment is the root, the foundation, and the fountain from which all of God's other precepts and prohibitions proceed, for they are all grounded in this commandment and derived from it. He who sets aside this great, preeminent, and primary commandment consequently renders all other commandments useless and equally ineffectual. It therefore needs to be well understood what it means to cleave to and serve none but Jehovah, the Most High and triune God, and to have no other gods before Him.

Asaph, the godly covenant friend of the Lord, practiced this when he testified by asking the Lord: "Whom have I in heaven but thee? and there is none upon earth that I desire beside thee. My flesh and my heart faileth: but God is the strength of my heart, and my portion for ever" (Ps. 73:25–26).

Let us now proceed by considering what the instructor has written regarding this great commandment. Upon asking his student in Question 94, "What doth God enjoin in the first commandment?" he prompts him to answer by saying, "That I, as sincerely as I desire the salvation of my own soul, avoid and flee from all idolatry, sorcery, soothsaying, superstition, invocation of saints, or any other creatures; and learn rightly to know the only true God; trust in Him alone; with humility and patience submit to Him; expect all good things from Him only; love, fear, and glorify Him with my whole heart; so that I renounce and forsake all creatures, rather than commit even the least thing contrary to His will."

The instructor first addresses the prohibition and then the precept. He posits that the most high God forbids His covenant people to engage in the following vile and abominable sins, of which, due to time constraints, we shall address but a few:

According to the instructor, in this commandment, Jehovah forbids all manner of idolatry, irrespective of what its character and nature may be. This pertains to whatever deviates in the very least from the true worship of the Lord, the true and triune God, as well as to all those who attribute anything to the creature that must be attributed to none but Jehovah, who alone is the true and only God.

Let us listen to the instructor himself and consider what description he gives of the vile abomination of idolatry. In Question 95, he asks, "What is idolatry?" to which he responds, "Idolatry is, instead of, or besides that one true God who has manifested Himself in His word, to contrive, or have any other object, in which men place their trust."

You observe that the instructor describes idolatry as an abomination and a transgression of extraordinary ramifications. All men, prior to conversion and regeneration, are vile idolaters from the moment of their birth. Men are void of the very least measure of true knowledge regarding the true God, and they neither love, honor, nor fear Him in the least.

Each and every godly person in the world was once, by nature, an idolater, who, prior to his conversion, spent his entire life in the practice of idolatry. What Paul writes to the Ephesians is applicable to all believers: "At that time ye were without Christ, being aliens from the commonwealth of Israel, and strangers from the covenants of promise, having no hope, and without God in the world" (Eph. 2:12). Is he not an idolater who is entirely without God and without Christ in the world, and who still has a form of outward religion? Is not idolatry the sum and substance of what he does? Paul therefore elsewhere says to believers, "Howbeit then, when ye knew not God, ye did service unto them which by nature are no gods" (Gal. 4:8).

He who wishes to understand this as being applicable only to the external and blatant idolatry of the heathen is still an utterly blind man who neither knows his own heart nor understands the spirituality of the Holy Scriptures.

Idolatry is the activity of one who places the least measure of trust in, expects anything good from, or, with esteem and affection, cleaves to something instead of or besides the one true God who has revealed Himself to us all in His Word. Thus, one commits idolatry when he:

1. Bows with any measure of religious honor and worship before any creature in heaven or on earth, as has been done since antiquity by the heathen and is presently being done by Roman Catholics.

2. Elevates himself as an idol, and thus honors and worships himself; when he finds delight in himself and in his good qualities; when he lives only for himself and begins, proceeds, and ends in himself, without any self-denial and any experiential knowledge of truly living unto God; when he makes his own plans without acknowledging the Lord in his ways and then trusts accordingly in these plans, expecting all to turn out well; when he has never been weaned from self and never has been united to God in Christ; and when he yet trusts in and relies upon his own strength and righteousness, thinking that he shall thereby be saved—as is the practice of all who are unconverted and unbelievers.

3. Is yet committed to the world, finds all his pleasure and delight therein, and will not permit Christ to set him free from the wretched service of the world.

4. Places his trust in man or any other creature, or makes flesh his arm in order to obtain some good or advantage.

5. Pursues the lusts of the flesh; whose belly is his god (cf. Phil. 3:19).

6. Clings with confidence and affection to temporal goods and other creatures by virtue of his avarice and world conformity. We must consider here that Paul refers to covetousness as idolatry (cf. Col. 3:5), saying with bold language that a covetous man "is an idolater" (Eph. 5:5).

Who is able to distinguish clearly between all forms of idolatry? One also commits idolatry when he fears men more than he fears God, as well as when he loves and cleaves to his family members or to any other creature or vanities above and beyond God.

In summary, whatever draws man away from God, even in the very least, is idolatry in root and branch, for if a man is to be truly blessed and happy, he must surrender himself fully to the triune God with all that he is and has, and exist for Him alone. However, whatever withholds man from this, even to the least degree, is at bottom but vile idolatry.

Who of us is therefore free from guilt pertaining to this despicable abomination before the Lord? Who of us can say, "I have purified my heart, I am clean"? Oh, that we all would receive true light to know ourselves! We would then see how, before God, we are guilty of all these vile sins, and with deep shame and humble contrition, we would humble ourselves before the Lord, considering that these are all the wicked sins that God so sternly prohibits in this commandment, saying, "Thou shalt have no other gods before me."

Having thus briefly considered in what idolatry consists, the instructor then proceeds to address something that is no less of a vile abomination, namely, *sorcery*. One contracts guilt in committing this sin when he conspires with the devil, the god of this age, seeking, by way of his power and help, to know or do things that exceed human knowledge and ability. Our majestic lawgiver also strictly forbids this abomination, and He has therefore commanded that all sorcerers (i.e., all who dabble in the occult) must be put to death, and are thereby to be banished from the earth (cf. Ex. 22:18). All who dabble in the occult are guilty of forsaking God within their hearts and by their deeds, making a covenant with the devil, the god of this age, and serving, honoring, and trusting him as their god. Those who wish to maintain that there are no sorcerers deceitfully suppress the truth, as do the misguided followers of B. Bekker and others. It is certain that there are, and always have been, sorcerers, and that God in His just judgment permits the commission of this and other sins.

The instructor then mentions *soothsaying* (i.e., *fortune-telling*). This abominable practice consists in seeking to know and to reveal unto others, either with the help of the devil or by means of any other thing or sign, hidden things that cannot be derived either from nature or from divine revelation in God's Word. One is also guilty of the sin of soothsaying by giving any credence to the work of others who engage themselves in the abominable practice of soothsaying, and then, to a greater or lesser degree, putting his trust therein. To this also belongs the despicable sin of being cured of scrofula (a skin disorder) or other illnesses and afflictions by having a seventh son blessed[4]—a practice that is locally even in vogue among some ungodly people. This vile abomination is strictly forbidden by the lawgiver as a practice that draws men away from the true God. Consider what the Lord says regarding this: "There shall not be found among you any one that…useth divination, or an observer of times, or an enchanter, or a witch, or a charmer, or a consulter with familiar spirits, or a wizard, or a necromancer, For all that do these things are an abomination unto the LORD" (Deut. 18:10–12).

The instructor then makes mention of *superstition*. One is guilty of this when he deems matters to be supernatural when such is not the case. One is also guilty of this when he is dissatisfied with the worship of God as He has revealed it in His Word, and he invents and engages in ways and means to serve God according to human notions that are either one's own or those of others. Of such, we read, "In vain they do worship me, teaching for doctrines the commandments of men" (Matt. 15:9). The abominable practice of superstition also draws men away from the true God, and the lawgiver therefore expressly forbids His covenant people to engage in such practices. Consider also what He says regarding this: "Ye shall not add unto the word which I command you, neither shall ye diminish ought from it, that ye may keep the commandments of the LORD your God which I command you" (Deut. 4:2).

The instructor concludes by addressing yet one more vile abomination, namely, *the invocation of saints or any other creatures*. One is guilty of this vile abomination when he honors and worships deceased individuals who, here upon earth, lived pious and godly lives—such as is practiced by Roman Catholicism. One also is guilty of this sin by rendering religious honor to any other creature, who or whatever it may be, in order thereby to secure something good

---

4. The Dutch text reads as follows: "Waartoe ook behoort, die verfoeilijke zonde, van de genezing van het koningszeer, of ander kwalen en ziekten, door zegening van een zevenden zoon…." VanderGroe is here speaking of practices that were indirectly connected with witchcraft, such as the blessing of a seventh son. This was a mysterious act of which one believed that he could thereby be healed from scrofula or various other afflictions. Such practices were as pagan then as they are today.

or some blessing. Our majestic lawgiver also strictly forbids this abominable practice, for it completely draws men away from the true God, of whom it is written, "Thou shalt worship the LORD thy God, and him only shalt thou serve" (Matt. 4:10).

God's covenant people are strictly forbidden by Jehovah God to practice any of these vile sins and abominations. He thus forbids:

1. All *disobedience of His commandments.* Samuel articulated this when he said to Saul, "For rebellion is as the sin of witchcraft, and stubbornness is as iniquity and idolatry" (1 Sam. 15:23a).

2. All forms of *atheism*, either in its blatant form, when, as a deliberate act of wickedness, men seek to banish utterly all notions of God from their souls, or in a more refined form, as is practiced by all men prior to conversion, when they live without knowing, loving, and serving God.

3. *Unbelief.* One is guilty thereof when he does not truly take refuge to God in Christ in order to be saved, but chooses to remain ignorant and unbelieving regarding all that is revealed to us in God's Word regarding God, ourselves, man's state of misery, and the way of salvation. Again, all men prior to their conversion are entirely guilty of this.

Dear reader, the great lawgiver expressly forbids His covenant people, as well as all men, to practice any of the abominations that we have thus set before you.

The instructor then proceeds to address the precept that is implied in this prohibition, saying that we are commanded to "learn rightly to know the only true God; trust in Him alone; with humility and patience submit to Him; expect all good things from Him only; love, fear, and glorify Him with [our] whole heart."

The instructor here sets before us many glorious and precious matters that we would be able to preach on at several occasions, for every matter that he enumerates represents by itself an important and essential doctrine. However, we must now be satisfied with addressing them briefly.

The first matter being commanded here is that one must "learn rightly to know the only true God; [and] trust in Him alone." There is not a single unbeliever who practices this virtue. Yet this is the obligation of all men, for God "in flaming fire [will take] vengeance on them that know not God, and that obey not the gospel of our Lord Jesus Christ: who shall be punished with everlasting destruction from the presence of the Lord" (2 Thess. 1:8–9). Without this knowledge, man remains entirely dead in trespasses and sins, for "this is life eternal, that they might know thee the only true God, and Jesus Christ, whom thou hast sent" (John 17:3).

We are also commanded to "trust in Him alone" in all humility by a complete cessation of all trust in self or any other creature in heaven or upon earth, and to trust rather only in the true God. One cannot do otherwise if he has rightly learned to know the true God, for "they that know thy name will put their trust in thee" (Ps. 9:10a).

The Lord also commands that one "with humility and patience submit to Him" alone as the true God. We are to do so in regard to His precepts as well as His paternal chastisements, and whatever else He, in His all-wise providence, may either do or intend to do with His people. The Lord's covenant people must always be as weaned children before the Lord their God, surrender themselves unconditionally to Him, and permit themselves to be guided, governed, and chastised by Him, exclaiming in all circumstances, "Truly my soul waiteth upon God: from him cometh my salvation" (Ps. 62:1).

The Lord also commands His covenant people to "expect all good things from Him only," for no one but He can show them any good (cf. Ps. 4:6), for He is God and, unto His people, the fountain of all good things. We read therefore that "the Lord is good unto them that wait for him, to the soul that seeketh him" (Lam. 3:25).

The Lord also urgently obligates His covenant people to "love, fear, and glorify Him with [their] whole heart" as the God who alone is worthy of their continued love and wholehearted commitment, for "thou shalt love the LORD thy God with all thine heart, and with all thy soul, and with all thy might" (Deut. 6:5).

According to the instructor, the Lord moreover commands His covenant people that they should fear and glorify Him with their whole heart, He being worthy of this by virtue of His illustrious majesty, adorable glory, and gracious loving-kindness toward His people. He therefore earnestly exhorts His covenant people to conduct themselves in such a way, saying, "Sanctify the LORD of hosts himself; and let him be your fear, and let him be your dread" (Isa. 8:13).

The instructor concludes by saying that God also commands His covenant people to "renounce and forsake all creatures, rather than commit even the least thing contrary to His will." Since God's covenant people fully belong to the Lord their God with both soul and body and are fully dependent upon Him and His will, and since they have been delivered from all worship of self and of the creature, and have eternally been called and sanctified unto His service, it follows that they would sooner endure and forsake all things than commit even the least thing contrary to His law and His revealed will. It should be with them as with Job, who thus expressed it when he said, "For destruction from God was a terror to me, and by reason of his highness I could not endure" (Job 31:23).

We have thus addressed and expounded in some detail the matters that are implied in this first word or commandment of the law of the Ten Commandments. You have observed the extraordinary breadth and extent of this precious precept and prohibition of the Lord. Blessed are they who observe it, doing so with love and by faith, for the Lord's precepts cannot be kept by us in any other way.

Oh, that the Lord Himself, by His Spirit, would truly open our eyes, and that we would willingly surrender ourselves unto the LORD with a true and upright faith! How we would find ourselves to be utterly guilty, hell-worthy, abominable, and intolerable before God! How we would then have to confess that we have never truly kept this commandment of the Lord as to any of its aspects, but that we are vile transgressors from the moment of our birth, and that the cumulative effect of our sins already reaches to the heavens! How intensely we would then abhor and loathe ourselves and cry out, "Woe is unto me that I have sinned so greatly, have lived a life divorced from the LORD, the true God, and have served idols!"

You sinners who are careless and at peace, thinking that all is well with you and that peace shall be your portion, although you live according to the dictates of your own hearts, oh, that for once you would truly see that you never yet either have seen or known the Lord, the true God, but that, rather, during your entire lifetimes, you have lived in vile idolatry, and thus apart from Him and His blessed communion! Oh, that for once your hearts would truly be distressed and that you would tremble when considering this!

Self-deceived and deluded sinners, and thus you who flatter yourselves that you are right with God and that you already in principal possess faith; you who thereupon expect to be the recipients of eternal salvation, although your entire lives consist of nothing other than sin and world conformity, and nothing of God's holy image is evident in you—oh, that today you would truly examine yourselves in light of the commandment that has been expounded! Oh, that by way of this transparent mirror, your true condition would be uncovered to you and would move you to make a true and sincere confession of your all-encompassing ungodliness, of how, until now, you have dishonored, offended, despised, and forsaken God by your sins, having served other gods instead of Him! Oh, that you would but truly acknowledge your guilt and no longer be able to seek and to find any shameful fig leaves to cover your sins! Would that you truly perceived you are accursed and hell-worthy, and that this would cause you to be truly perplexed and humbled before God! Oh, that the Lord Jesus, by His blood and Spirit, truly would become precious and essential for you, and that you no longer would be able to continue your life without being truly united to Him!

You who are believing children of God, beloved in our Lord Jesus Christ, oh, that this mirror of the law would truly cause your inherently wicked and abominable nature to be uncovered by the light of Jesus! Oh, that the Lord would show you clearly how you daily depart from Him in a thousand different ways and how you turn away from Him and serve other gods before His countenance! Oh, that you would truly become aware of the abominable pollution of your soul! How you would then begin to abhor yourself, and what need there would be for Jesus and His precious blood! How, by divine illumination, your wickedness and abominableness would then deeply humble you and drive you out of yourself to the fountain that has been opened against sin and uncleanness (cf. Zech. 13:1)!

May the Lord, by His Spirit, so labor within us and so open our eyes that, whether it is for the first time or by renewal, Christ becomes for us the end of the law, and His blood cleanses us from all our sins. Amen.

The Second Commandment, Forbidding the Worship of Images

Thou shalt not make unto thee any graven image, or any likeness of any thing that is in heaven above, or that is in the earth beneath, or that is in the water under the earth: thou shalt not bow down thyself to them, nor serve them: for I the LORD thy God am a jealous God, visiting the iniquity of the fathers upon the children unto the third and fourth generation of them that hate me; and shewing mercy unto thousands of them that love me, and keep my commandments.
—EXODUS 20:4–6

Question 96: What doth God require in the second commandment?

Answer: That we in no wise represent God by images, nor worship Him in any other way than He has commanded in His word.

Question 97: Are images then not at all to be made?

Answer: God neither can, nor may be represented by any means. But as to creatures, though they may be represented, yet God forbids to make, or have any resemblance of them, either in order to worship them or to serve God by them.

Question 98: But may not images be tolerated in the churches as books to the laity?

Answer: No: for we must not pretend to be wiser than God, who will have His people taught, not by dumb images, but by the lively preaching of His Word.

It is a solid and incontrovertible truth that natural reason teaches and reveals to all men most clearly that there is a supreme divine being who is the Lord, creator, sustainer, and governor of the entire world, and who therefore must be honored and served by all His creatures. Consequently, all men, by the vestiges of natural reason, have a perception of a supreme divine being in their souls, and no matter how hard they try, they cannot possibly and utterly banish such a notion from their minds.

As fruitful as natural reason may be in impressing upon men an awareness that there is such a supreme divine being who must be served by all men with both soul and body, natural reason is unfruitful and deficient to reveal to man the manner in which this supreme being, the adorable king and Lord of this world, is to be honored and served. Man's reason remains utterly silent here, and as far as religion is concerned, it yields only notions that are utterly erroneous and vain. In spite of all their lofty scholarship, the most wise and brilliant among the heathen remain as blind as moles. Therefore, whatever they know regarding religion is nothing other than rank vanity and perversion. Whatever they have said, written, or believed regarding a supreme divine being, none among them has either ever truly known this adorable and glorious supreme being or known how to honor and serve Him perfectly in a manner that is consistent with His being.

By reason of the darkness and carnality of their minds, they all have run aground on the soul-damning cliff of projecting the insignificance of the creature upon this supreme divine being, and they are thus accustomed to compare this adorable supreme being to themselves and to assess Him according to their lowly and human manner of thinking. Consequently, they represent the Godhead visibly by way of physical images made from a variety of physical substances, and they believe that they should honor and serve this supreme divine being by means of such images. Paul testifies that such has been the practice of all the heathen: "Professing themselves to be wise, they became fools, and changed the glory of the uncorruptible God into an image made like to corruptible man, and to birds, and four-footed beasts, and creeping things" (Rom. 1:22–23).

The extent to which the most high God of heaven and earth abhors such a vile and false religion, and how much He opposes this as being the greatest and most abominable way in which one can disgrace Him and His glory, is evident from the subject matter we must presently address in connection with the second commandment. In that commandment, Jehovah, the God of His people, expressly denounces all ways to serve and honor Him by means of images or visible representations. He strictly forbids this by saying, "Thou shalt not make unto thee any graven image, or any likeness of any thing that is in heaven above, or that is in the earth beneath, or that is in the water under the earth: thou shalt not bow down thyself to them, nor serve them."

In the first commandment, Jehovah requires His covenant people to serve and cleave alone to Him, and thus nothing beside or instead of Him. They are to have no other gods before Him. Most earnestly and emphatically, He admonishes them regarding the exclusive manner in which they are to serve Him in an entirely spiritual manner, without any physical images, representations, or similitudes of His exalted and glorious being. Since He is a most perfect and purely spiritual being, He may be neither depicted before the eyes of men nor represented to their understandings by anything carnal or physical. All carnal and material notions, imaginations, or representations of Jehovah utterly contradict His divinity and are entirely incompatible with His spiritual and most perfect being.

To consider this commandment in greater detail, we shall:

1. engage in a word-by-word exposition of this commandment; and
2. focus upon what the instructor has recorded regarding this commandment.

In this second commandment, we find:

1. the content of what the Lord proposes and prescribes to His covenant people; and
2. compelling threats and promises to motivate them to obedience.

Regarding the content of this commandment, the lawgiver sets it before His people, as He does in most of the commandments, by a prohibition, saying, "Thou shalt not make unto thee any graven image." The Lord primarily communicated His law by prohibitions because He was dealing with a sinful people who were naturally inclined to transgress His law; they needed to be admonished to refrain from evil and sin, and to be pressed strongly to serve and fear God in truth.

Before we expound this commandment in greater detail, we need to be instructed regarding the vile conduct of the Papists in connection with this commandment, and it is regrettable that our brethren, the Lutherans, are guilty of this same conduct. To justify their vile worship of images, a practice expressly forbidden in this commandment, Roman Catholics have shamelessly removed the larger portion of this second commandment from the Ten Commandments. They have taken that which remains of it and included it as a part of the first commandment, giving as their reason that all that is recorded in the second commandment is already comprehended in the first commandment. Therefore, they claim that, for brevity's sake, these words may be excised from the law.

We would be able to demonstrate at length against the Papists and the Lutherans what a vile and abominable deed this is, and how irresponsible such conduct is before God, whose illustrious and holy law is thereby broken and corrupted. Not only does this second commandment certainly have an essential place in the law of God, but in its very nature it is also distinct from the first commandment. As we have already stated, the Lord admonishes His covenant people in the first commandment to cleave to and serve Him alone, and that they should therefore have no other gods before Him. In the second commandment, He instructs and admonishes them regarding the manner in which He is to be served, namely, in an entirely spiritual manner that fully conforms to His perfectly spiritual nature and being. All that is carnal and physical is thereby excluded, and thus we need to make an essential distinction between these two commandments.

After these preliminary considerations, let us proceed to consider the commandment itself. The Lord here forbids His people and children to "make... any graven image, or any likeness of any thing that is in heaven above, or that is in the earth beneath, or that is in the water under the earth." God's preeminent objective in this commandment is that we might rightly know and honor His supreme, most holy, and spiritual being. This is not to be achieved by means of any physical image or likeness derived from any lowly creature, whether we form a mental image in our minds or create it externally by the skill and labor of our hands. God in His supreme being has absolutely nothing in common with anything that is either visible or tangible. On the contrary, He is spiritual in the purest and most perfect manner imaginable, and therefore He can neither be viewed nor known in any way but by means of the holy and spiritual eye of faith.

Consequently, all carnal representations of God are absolutely erroneous and irrational conceptions of this supreme being, and He is thereby dishonored and misrepresented. We must behold and know God the Lord by the intrinsic light of His Holy Spirit, and therefore we may neither think of, speak of, nor believe in Him in any manner that is not spiritual. Our worship of Him must be entirely spiritual, for God Himself is a Spirit, and therefore we are able neither to honor nor to serve Him in any manner except we do so rightly and in conformity to His truth. It then follows that we may not depict the Lord God by means of any physical object or mental image, for we shall then utterly deny His true and most holy spiritual being.

The Lord God jealously guards against this in the second commandment, for He will not tolerate any erroneous notion or perception regarding His supreme divine being. Rather, He is to be known, honored, and served by us only in conformity to His truth. Thus, He strenuously forbids us to make any graven images of Him.

With the Lord's help, I shall attempt to expound this most eminent commandment as clearly as possible, and, to that end, we shall set before you what the Lord *requires* of all His children, and then what He *forbids* them.

The Lord commands His people to do two things:

First, they must continually set Him before them and honor and serve Him. It is the Lord's will that His covenant people, having entered into a covenant with Him and having eternally committed themselves to Him in Christ and to His service, should acknowledge none other to be their king or Lord. It is His will that in all their activities, they would continually focus on Him as their supreme God and king. Within their souls, they must continually set Him before them in His adorable majesty and glory as being the sole object of all their meditation, love, piety, service, and trust. As the Lord and king of His people, He is to abide continually in their minds and in their hearts, and by faith dwell therein as in His temple.

The Lord is truly worthy of being thus worshiped and honored by His believing people and subjects. They must know Him and set Him before them in all their ways. We read this regarding the Messiah: "I have set the LORD always before me: because he is at my right hand, I shall not be moved." (Ps. 16:8). Of the Lord's believing covenant friend, we read, "Mine eyes are ever toward the LORD" (Ps. 25:15). It is not surprising that this is so, for the foundation and fountain of all true religion is continually to set the Lord before our souls in His adorable majesty and glory, whereas a failure to set the Lord before our souls is the ground and fountain of all sin and impiety.

Jehovah therefore justly requires and demands of His covenant people that they continually set Him before them in all that they do. He requires that they be committed within their hearts to serve and fear Him in His illustrious majesty and glory, and thus to walk before His countenance (Gen. 17:1).

However, was it a matter of indifference as to how the Lord's covenant people must continually set Him before them and remember Him in order that they might honor and serve Him? By no means.

Second, they must do so solely in a lawful manner and in conformity to Jehovah's most perfect, glorious, and purely spiritual supreme being. Jehovah is a most perfect, infinite, and pure Spirit who has absolutely nothing in common with anything that is material, physical, or carnal. His covenant people must think of Him only and always as such and serve Him accordingly, cleaving by faith to their invisible God. They must be wary of fostering any bodily or carnal representations of the Lord by thinking of Him in physical terms. They especially have to see to it that they never succumb to the abominable practice of thinking to display God in some outward way to their physical eyes, and then attempt to honor and serve Him by means of such an image. The explicit and emphatic prohibition of the Lord addresses this by saying, "Thou shalt not make unto thee any graven image, or any likeness of any thing that is in heaven above, or that is in the earth beneath, or that is in the water under the earth."

Man, by virtue of his carnality and sinful corruption, is inclined by nature to think of and to judge Jehovah God, the majestic and glorious supreme being, in carnal terms. This issues forth from man's spiritual darkness to which sin has subjected him, for by sin man has utterly departed from the Lord God with his entire heart and soul, thus "having the understanding darkened, being alienated from the life of God through the ignorance that is in them, because of the blindness of their heart" (Eph. 4:18). Man by nature has not even retained within his soul a modicum of true spiritual knowledge of God. On the contrary, his blindness and ignorance regarding God are now so absolute and all-encompassing, being designated as darkness itself (Eph. 5:8). Since, however, man reads and hears of God, and still has a measure of innate knowledge regarding Him, he fosters a perception of the Lord God that is physical and carnal, which is entirely incompatible with the holy and spiritual nature of God. The natural man is ignorant of God's nature and is incapable of such knowledge, for "the natural man receiveth not the things of the Spirit of God: for they are foolishness unto him: neither can he know them, because they are spiritually discerned" (1 Cor. 2:14).

Consistent with the carnal notions that blind men have regarding God, they honor and serve Him in conformity to such notions, and thus in an entirely carnal manner. The people of Israel were very vulnerable to this by having been born, and raised, and lived among the Egyptians. They had continually observed the Egyptians serving and honoring their gods carnally by images and similitudes of physical objects. This, in turn, had a very harmful effect upon the hearts of the Israelites. Furthermore, upon their arrival in Canaan, they would encounter the abundant indulgence in that same abomination among the pagan nations that dwelt in the land. Therefore, considering the great temptation there would be for the people of Israel to emulate the pagans in their abominable worship of images and idols, the Lord included such an explicit and emphatic commandment in His holy law. Most vigorously He forbade them all worship of images and whatever else would prompt them either to do so or to be in any way aligned with such a practice, saying, "Thou shalt not make unto thee any graven image."

The Lord sternly forbids His covenant people to engage in:

1. the making of any type of image or likeness that would have as its purpose either to represent the most high God thereby or to produce mental or visual images of Him; and

2. honoring and serving such an image or likeness of the true God by means thereof.

Regarding the first, the lawgiver forbids His covenant people to make images or likenesses of Him by the use of three types of things or creatures. These are "any thing that is *in heaven above*, or that is *in the earth beneath*, or that is *in the water under the earth*." In all three locations, comprising all creation, one finds a great multitude and variety of creatures. The Egyptians and other pagan nations created images or similitudes of visible things so that they might display and honor their gods.

However, the Lord God forbids His people to do this. They must utterly refrain from undertaking this, and He therefore prohibits them to make any image, likeness, or similitude of any creature in heaven above, in the earth beneath, or in the water under the earth, in order to depict and represent the true God, either mentally or visibly. Nevertheless, they were permitted to make images, paintings, and other representations of material objects, for the Lord Himself commanded them to adorn His sanctuaries, His tabernacle and His temple, with such imagery. What God does forbid, however, is the fabrication of such imagery and similitudes of physical and material objects as are found in the realm of creation in order to depict, honor, and serve Him and His most glorious divine being. This is evident in that He also commands that His covenant people neither bow down to nor serve such graven images or "any likeness of any thing."

Such was the abominable practice of the Egyptians and other pagan nations that had no knowledge of the true God. Operating from the principle of their corrupt flesh, they made a multitude of graven and molten images, as well as a variety of similitudes of material objects made of gold, silver, copper, stone, and wood. Due to their wretched blindness, they bowed down to these objects and rendered them religious worship. They did not do so because they considered such images or similitudes to be the true God Himself, but, rather, because they viewed them as reflections and displays of the God of heaven and earth, whom they sought to honor and serve by the use of such imagery. At least, the wisest and most brilliant among the pagans were of that opinion.

However, the Lord vigorously forbids His covenant people to honor and serve Him in this fashion, for He forbids them to construct any material depiction or similitude of Himself, let alone to render Him divine honor by bowing down before such imagery. Truly we must consider this matter seriously, for it is very evident that one cannot more grievously dishonor and offend the Lord God as to His illustrious majesty and adorable glory than by such vile, despicable, and abominable worship of graven images—and whatever else, even in the very least, would be connected with this.

Therefore, it comes as no surprise that the Lord not only forbids His covenant people to engage in such worship of images, but that He does so in the most vigorous, forceful, and emphatic manner. He does so by adding to His commandment a very grave threat toward transgressors and a most glorious and gracious promise toward the obedient, saying, "I the LORD thy God am a jealous God, visiting the iniquity of the fathers upon the children unto the third and fourth generation of them that hate me; and shewing mercy unto thousands of them that love me, and keep my commandments."

To impress this weighty prohibition all the more earnestly upon the hearts of His covenant people, seeking to move them toward affectionate obedience, the Lord proceeds to set before them a very forceful and compelling argument. Several great and glorious matters are articulated here, for we have:

1. a display of Jehovah's great majesty and glory;
2. a very sharp and stern rebuke addressed to all who transgress and are disobedient; and
3. a very precious, comforting, and glorious promise for all obedient members of the covenant.

The Lord's adorable majesty and glory are displayed and expressed in the words, "I the LORD thy God am a jealous God." Three things are encompassed in these words regarding the Lord's majesty, all of which should greatly inhibit a believing covenant people from practicing this worship of graven images. These are:

1. Such worship of graven images is forbidden by Jehovah, who is the faithful and unchangeable one, both in carrying out His judgments and threats toward transgressors and in fulfilling His commitments and promises toward His obedient covenant people. Consequently, the Lord's people are obligated to heed this illustrious commandment, along with the threat and promise added to it.

2. The great lawgiver is not only Jehovah, but is also the God of His believing covenant people, who has declared, "I am the LORD *thy God.*" As His covenant people, they are obligated to keep this law of the Lord their God in faith and with all the affection of their heart; and they are to obey it rather than oppose it. They committed themselves to this in their covenant with the Lord, embracing Him to be their God and king, to serve Him as His servants, and to observe His judgments and precepts eternally.

3. Jehovah is a jealous God; that is, a God who is supremely jealous regarding His divine honor and glory, and who will not tolerate that His honor and glory be shortchanged or discredited in the least. Since the worship of graven images would culminate in the utter eradication and casting down of Jehovah's adorable honor and glory within the souls of men, the Lord's people are obligated diligently to guard against the commission of such a despicable, vile, and abominable act, for the God with whom they have to do is so holy and jealous that He will not tolerate from them the least detraction of His divine honor and glory.

The Lord then reveals Himself to His covenant people in His inflexible holiness and justice, saying, "I the LORD thy God am a jealous God, visiting the iniquity of the fathers upon the children unto the third and fourth generation of them that hate me." *Them that hate Me* refers to all who are unbelieving and unconverted, and who willfully disgrace and transgress all the other commandments of the Lord. Regarding those who hate Him, the Lord testifies that He will visit "the iniquity of the fathers upon the children unto the third and fourth generation." By His inflexible holiness and justice, the Lord will not be satisfied merely by punishing the transgressors of His law and the ungodly who hate Him themselves, but His wrath and anger will also be manifested toward their children and descendants, even unto the third and fourth generations.

We find many clear examples of this in the Holy Scriptures. By the flood, God not only punished ungodly fathers, but also punished their children, irrespective of whether they were young and innocent, for everyone drowned, except for Noah and his family. The Lord also dealt in this manner with the inhabitants of Sodom and Gomorrah, as well as with the ungodly families of Korah, Dathan, and Abiram. Moreover, God punished all the descendants of Eli by virtue of his sins (1 Sam. 2:31). Jeroboam's entire family and all his descendants were eradicated from the face of the earth because of his sins.

Having said this, no one should raise as an objection to the Lord's dealings in "visiting the iniquities of [ungodly fathers] upon the children unto the third and fourth generation," that this is contradictory to the Lord's own words, saying, "The son shall not bear the iniquity of the father, neither shall the father bear the iniquity of the son" (Ezek. 18:20). When the Lord visits the iniquities of ungodly fathers upon their children and their descendants, we need to understand that such children and descendants are not merely being punished by the Lord God for the iniquities of their fathers, but also because they themselves, as sinners, are guilty and culpable before the Lord because of their own sins and iniquities. Because of the iniquities of the fathers, God permits such children and descendants to commit the same iniquities, for His judgments are a great deep, and all should fear lest they fall into it.

Nevertheless, we are not to interpret this so literally as if God always visits the iniquities of the fathers upon the children. God is not saying this, for then His judgment would be inescapable to all eternity, and there would be no hope unto salvation for a generation whose ancestor was an ungodly man and a hater of the Lord. Rather, the Lord does this when it pleases Him so to do and when He permits Himself to be provoked to His just wrath and indignation, doing so as an exercise of His sovereignty. Instead, He speaks this way to demonstrate and to set before the eyes of His people what a jealous, holy, and just God He is. He would have them to know that the manifestation of His wrath and indignation extends so far toward them that hate Him that He will even visit the iniquities of the fathers upon their children to the third and fourth generations. He would have His covenant people know that they are dealing with a God who is holy and just, so that they will be motivated to manifest the deepest respect and fear for His great and majestic name—and that they will not transgress His holy law by most grievously sinning against Him by such a vile and despicable worship of graven images.

And yet, does the Lord find delight and pleasure in keeping His people in check only by fearful threats? This is by no means the case, for listen to what He adds in a most loving and comforting manner. In the same breath, He testifies that He is a God who shows mercy unto thousands of them that love Him and keep His commandments. Truly, the mercy and grace of the Lord is declared in contrast to His judgments. If God is jealous, just, wrathful, and full of indignation toward all ungodly men who hate Him and transgress His commandments, He is no less infinitely gracious, merciful, and full of loving-kindness toward all who love Him. Oh, how inexpressibly good and merciful the Lord is for His people! This is the experience of all who sincerely and, in the deepest recesses of their hearts, love Him, and whose chief delight and bliss it is to perceive that their hearts are inclined to keep His commandments and faithfully observe them.

If the Lord's wrath and fearful indignation extend toward those who hate Him, and thus from the fathers to the children, then His mercy and loving-kindness are infinitely greater, for the Lord extends it toward them that love Him to a thousand generations. Here a limited number is used to express an infinite number; that is, He will do so to manifold generations, to all generations, and even to the very end of the world. Such is the extent of the infinite mercy and loving-kindness of the Lord toward all who love Him. Who would not wholeheartedly cherish and tenderly love such a God of infinite mercy and loving-kindness? Who would not fear Him and keep His commandments? All the Lord's believing covenant people should be stirred up and be powerfully motivated by this infinite mercy of the Lord their God wholeheartedly to obey all His good and holy commandments, and particularly this commandment so expressly given to them by the Lord.

Thus, we observe not only the sense and content of this second commandment in regard to the worship of graven images, but also the very weighty and compelling motives for its observance, which the Lord impressed upon and sealed to the hearts of His covenant people. However, you ought not to think that the Lord's covenant people, in and of themselves, are capable of obeying God's law. By no means, for the Lord sets this commandment before them, as He does all the other commandments, so that they would fully observe it by faith. They are thus called to do so completely by looking away from themselves and from their own righteousness and strength, and by looking unto the Lord their God, in whom alone their righteousness and strength are to be found.

Having expounded the second commandment itself, let us also briefly consider the exposition of our instructor, where he asks in Question 96, "What doth God require in the second commandment?" and to which he replies, "That we in no wise represent God by images, nor worship Him in any other way than He has commanded in His word."

According to the instructor, there are two things that the Lord's people and all men are forbidden to do:

First, we may "in no wise represent God by images." In our exposition of this commandment, we observed the reason for this, and in the next question and answer, the instructor will address this in greater detail.

Second, the other practice strenuously forbidden by the Lord is to "worship Him in any other way than He has commanded in His word." The Lord alone has the prerogative to reveal Himself to His covenant people and, in so doing, to teach and command them how they are to honor and serve Him in conformity to His most perfect and glorious nature. To deviate from this divine revelation, to oppose it, or to render to the Lord strange or false honor is to worship the Lord in a manner other than He wills and desires to receive from us, which is the most grievous disobedience toward God and an abominable desecration of His illustrious majesty and glory. The Savior says regarding this, "But in vain they do worship me, teaching for doctrines the commandments of men" (Matt. 15:9). Therefore, to insist on serving and honoring God by means of images is to honor Him in a manner that differs from what He has commanded us in His Word. All erroneous and corrupt forms of worship invented by man himself by corrupt judgment and carnal understanding, whatever their nature or form may be, are strictly forbidden by the Lord in this second commandment.

To clarify this truth, the instructor then asks in Question 97, "Are images then not at all to be made?" to which he responds: "God neither can, nor may be represented by any means. But as to creatures; though they may be represented, yet God forbids to make, or have any resemblance of them, either in order to worship them or to serve God by them."

The instructor here confronts the Papists, the vile worshipers of idols and graven images, who render divine honor to such graven images, thinking that, by so doing, they are honoring and serving the one true God. However, the Lord gave this second commandment to counter this abominable manifestation of ungodliness. This commandment does not pertain to idolatry as such, for that is forbidden in the first commandment. Rather, it strictly pertains to the worship of graven images, whereby one endeavors to honor and serve the most high God by means of depictions and similitudes. The worship of images, as is practiced by Roman Catholicism, is therefore the actual sin and abomination against which the Lord has given this prohibition in the second commandment.

However, as we have seen earlier, the Papists are devious enough to excise the content of this commandment of the law as being superfluous and unnecessary and as pertaining only to the Jews of the Old Testament dispensation.

Now let us hear the words of our instructor as he addresses two matters:

First, "God neither can, nor may be represented by any means." It is an absolute and incontrovertible truth that the most high God of heaven and earth, the omnipotent and supremely glorious Jehovah, may in no wise be either depicted or represented to the human mind or eye by any object. As we have already seen, in His being, He is supremely pure, simple, and spiritual, and thus He neither has anything in common with nor the least connection with anything that is physical, carnal, or material. However, all tangible depictions and similitudes proceeding either from the imagination or the hands of men must necessarily be derived from material and/or physical objects. Consequently, there is neither the least similarity nor resemblance between the purely spiritual being of God and such material or physical depictions. It is thus self-evident that the most glorious and purely spiritual being of God cannot be depicted and represented in any way or form, either to the human eye or to the human intellect.

Furthermore, the Lord God is also a being who is entirely infinite and supremely glorious within Himself, and He neither is nor can be subject to the least measure of imperfection or deficiency. To what, then, could we possibly liken such a most glorious and most perfect being? Even in the remotest sense, there is nothing that resembles Him. Everything outside of God is imperfect, and therefore the most perfect being of God can neither be depicted nor compared to anything. The question is thus asked: "To whom then will ye liken God? or what likeness will ye compare unto him?" (Isa. 40:18). In verse 25, the Lord Himself asks, "To whom then will ye liken me, or shall I be equal?" God hereby communicates that, by His majesty, His perfection, His glory, and His all-sufficiency, He is completely distinct from all that is external to His being. He may be neither compared to nor depicted by anything that is either in heaven or upon earth or even beneath the earth.

Thus, it is supremely evident that Jehovah, the most high and supremely glorious God, may neither be displayed nor depicted in any possible way, either to the human eye or to the human intellect, since this is radically impossible to do and absolutely cannot be achieved. Therefore, the instructor argues that it may also not be done, saying, "God neither can, nor may be represented by any means."

There is nothing that more grievously dishonors the most high God, as to His divine glory and perfection, as when one attempts to depict Him in any way by comparing Him to something material and physical, for in so doing, he subordinates Him to the level of all that is lowly, imperfect, finite, despicable, and material. One thereby completely denies His infinite perfection, Godhead, and glory, and this is nothing less than a forsaking of God by degrading Him to the level of a vile, imperfect, and material creature. Paul testifies of this, saying, "Professing themselves to be wise, they became fools, and changed the glory of the uncorruptible God into an image made like to corruptible man, and to birds, and four-footed beasts, and creeping things" (Rom. 1:22–23).

This same apostle earnestly exhorted the Athenians, who were accustomed to depict the true God of heaven and earth by physical and visible objects, referring to Him as *the unknown God*. This prompted him to say to them, "We ought not to think that the Godhead is like unto gold, or silver, or stone, graven by art and man's device" (Acts 17:29). Consequently, the Lord, throughout His Word, strongly renounces all worship of graven images, condemning and abhorring it in the strongest possible terms. According to the instructor, it is thus evident that "God neither can nor may be represented by any means."

Second, the instructor states, "But as to creatures; though they may be represented, yet God forbids to make, or have any resemblance of them, either in order to worship them or to serve God by them." We have sufficiently addressed this in our own exposition of this commandment, having observed that God must and can be only spiritually honored and served by His covenant people, for only such worship fully conforms to the supreme glory of His being.

The instructor proceeds in Question 98 to ask his pupil, "But may not images be tolerated in the churches as books to the laity?" This is the sentiment of our brethren, the Lutherans, who, though they utterly abhor the worship of graven images, maintain that one may have images and paintings in the church sanctuary to instruct and to stimulate the congregation—particularly the common folk. Our instructor utterly rejects such a notion, saying, "No: for we must not pretend to be wiser than God, who will have His people taught, not by dumb images, but by the lively preaching of His Word." The instructor's answer, being both very sound and extraordinarily spiritual, sufficiently refutes the Lutheran sentiment regarding the usefulness of images. Nowhere in God's Word do we find the Lord commanding the churches that the people must be educated by means of dumb images. It is instead the Lord's will, as we find throughout the Scriptures, that only His Holy Word be used to that end, for "it pleased God by the foolishness of preaching to save them that believe" (1 Cor. 1:21). We must therefore not be wiser than God, but subject ourselves to His divine ordinance.

We have thus sufficiently expounded the second commandment, and we are now to examine ourselves in light of what has been said. It is true that, by God's grace, we do not practice the external worship of graven images as the pagan Papists do. Rather, the Lord Himself has delivered us from this abomination by leading us forth from popery by His mighty arm. However, we ought not to think for one moment that we truly observe this commandment of the Lord. By no means, for the ramifications of this obligation are so extensive that even the holiest of all men cannot perfectly observe it in this life, for this commandment:

1. Forbids indiscriminately all that deviates in the least from the true and spiritual worship of God as to both body and soul—or whatever would lead to such deviation. How infinitely numerous are the sins that detract us from the spiritual and believing worship of God, although we neither make any graven images nor bow down to them! Who would be capable of enumerating them all?

2. Commands us to serve the Lord God in spirit and in truth, and to stir up our hearts to do so. Again, who is capable of enumerating all that pertains to this? Who must not exclaim with David when perceiving this rightly, "I have seen an end of all perfection: but thy commandment is exceeding broad" (Ps. 119:96)? There would be no end to setting before you in order the forbidden sins and the prescribed virtues embedded in this commandment.

You who are still unconverted, you are utterly incapable of obeying this commandment of the Lord even in the very least—although you may refrain from the blatant and external worship of graven images. You lack a true and spiritual knowledge of God and, by reason of sin, are void of God's image in your soul. Therefore, you cannot but make mental images of God that are both carnal and/or earthly. And though you may not actually make graven images of God with your hands, you are nevertheless making mental images of Him. Your understanding is completely earthly and carnal, and therefore you cannot possibly either think or speak of God in any way but as earthly and carnal. Mentally, you are measuring God by yourself and by other physical creatures. However, you do not know Him in His majesty, glory, or holiness. You are bowing down before carnal and earthly images of God. Such graven images you honor and serve, and you foster the foolish notion that you are serving the true

God. In reality, however, you are serving an idol, a false god of your arbitrary imagination. As long as you do not rightly learn to know the true God, your worship will be nothing but sin, deceit, and vanity. I recognize that you cannot possibly understand what I am telling you, for the almighty hand of God must arrest you in order for you rightly to understand this. The Spirit of God must convict you of your sins.

Oh, that the Lord would be pleased to open your eyes and that you would receive your sight! Beloved friends, I urge you fervently to beseech the Lord, that He would grant this to you and that you would be made willing to run to Christ, who has eye-salve to give unto you so that you might see! It is my wish that a gracious God would so teach you, for you will otherwise never perceive either the wickedness of your heart or your transgression of this second commandment. Such spiritual insight you can receive only from the Spirit of God, who must work these matters in your heart. Oh, that your savior and redeemer would come out of Zion, and that He would cause light to arise within you as clear as the midday sun!

You who are the truly converted children of God both know and confess, by virtue of your inherent and supremely carnal corruption, that within your hearts you are very grievous worshipers of graven images, albeit that you never have bowed down before any physical image made with human hands. Oh, that you truly would perceive what is the plague of your heart! Beloved Christians, let us earnestly examine ourselves in light of this commandment to determine whether all our thinking and speaking of God, and all our honoring and serving of God, is purely spiritual, and that thus we truly would be confronted with this matter and so be illumined and led to perceive it! How we would find within our hearts nothing but a profound ignorance of God, a lack of spirituality, irreverence, and unbelief—yes, a grievous departure from God! The fountain from which all this evil proceeds is to be found in the fact that we know so incomprehensibly little of God in His supreme majesty and supreme holiness, and that we are still so very inclined to have earthly notions and carnal conceptions of God. With Paul, I must say, "For some have not the knowledge of God: I speak this to your shame" (1 Cor. 15:34), thus saying that we have not the knowledge of God that we ought to have. We all, though one more and the other less, harbor far more carnal images of God in our minds than we have the true knowledge of God. And what is grievous most of all is that we perceive and take so little to heart that we are so little troubled with the sickly indisposition of our hearts.

Oh, friends, awake from your slumber and, without any further delay, go to Christ our physician and earnestly cry out to Him that He would open our eyes! When God's Spirit cleanses our darkened eyes by illuminating them with heavenly light, we will perceive not only how wretchedly earthly and carnal we still are and how little true knowledge of God we have, but also how little we worship Him in Spirit and in truth. Then we will truly see our sins and our ungodliness, and be ashamed and grieve. We will abhor ourselves and rightly perceive our deep misery, as well as our impotence to keep this holy commandment of God even to the least degree. We will run and flee to Christ our savior and take hold of His grace and His strength (Isa. 27:10). We will seek all our righteousness, obedience, and salvation in Him alone, and the sun of righteousness will arise upon us. May the Lord grant us this grace by His Holy Spirit. Amen.

The Third Commandment, Forbidding the Vain Use of God's Name

Thou shalt not take the name of the LORD thy God in vain; for the LORD will not hold him guiltless that taketh his name in vain

—EXODUS 20:7

Question 99: What is required in the third commandment?

Answer: That we, not only by cursing or perjury, but also by rash swearing, must not profane or abuse the name of God; nor by silence or connivance be partakers of these horrible sins in others; and, briefly, that we use the holy name of God no otherwise than with fear and reverence, so that He may be rightly confessed and worshipped by us, and be glorified in all our words and works.

Question 100: Is then the profaning of God's name by swearing and cursing so heinous a sin that His wrath is kindled against those who do not endeavor, as much as in them lies, to prevent and forbid such cursing and swearing?

Answer: It undoubtedly is, for there is no sin greater or more provoking to God than the profaning of His name; and therefore He has commanded this sin to be punished with death.

David, the godly servant of the Lord, gloriously and compellingly exhorts all the kings, rulers, and judges of this earth, saying, "Serve the LORD with fear, and rejoice with trembling" (Ps. 2:11). Beloved, it is certain that Jehovah God created heaven and earth, and He therefore is the creator and supreme ruler of all men, who consequently must be obeyed and served by all men. Since none but He is our God, our illustrious king and creator, men, in favor of Him, not only must forsake all other gods or creatures, but must also serve, fear, and obey Him in a most humble and reverential manner, with the deepest respect and with utmost and heartfelt esteem. Because of His infinite majesty and adorable splendor, the Lord God is worthy of such service. This majesty and splendor so greatly elevate Him that all of creation, as compared with Him, is no more than "a drop of a bucket, and [is] counted as the small dust of the balance" (Isa. 40:15).

Who among mortal men, however illuminated and gracious he may be, is capable of understanding in some measure the infinite dimensions of God's glorious and holy nature, so as to enable him to instruct us as to the manner in which we are obligated to serve, fear, and tremble before this God? And even if there were someone capable of articulating this for us, by no means would we be capable of understanding him, for this matter belongs to the unutterable things heard by the holy apostle Paul when he was out of the body and drawn up into the third heaven (2 Cor. 12:1–4).

Nevertheless, in His holy law, the Lord is willing to admonish us earnestly regarding this matter so that we would serve and fear Him, and rejoice in Him with trembling. After commanding His covenant people, in the first commandment, to serve Him alone and to have no other gods before His countenance, and then, in the second commandment, setting before them the manner in which they are to serve Him entirely in spirit and in truth, and thus without any physical representation, God proceeds in this third commandment to stipulate to His covenant people how they are to serve Him by having the deepest fear, reverence, and utmost esteem for His great and most holy name. They should always tremble before this name and never in any manner either abuse or desecrate it, for the holy law of the Lord declares, "Thou shalt not take the name of the LORD thy God in vain."

With the Lord's gracious assistance, we shall now consider this commandment in greater detail and expound it by considering:

1. the actual wording of this commandment as it occurs in the law of the LORD; and
2. the matter contained in it.

Concerning the actual language of this commandment, we are to consider:

1. the letter of this commandment; and
2. the compelling argument given by the Lord whereby He obligates His covenant people all the more to obey this commandment.

This command of the Lord is again articulated as a prohibition, saying, "Thou shalt not take the name of the LORD thy God in vain." We must consequently consider:

1. the subject being addressed, namely, the name of the Lord; and

2. the mandatory obligation not to use this name of the Lord in vain.

Regarding the first, we know that a name is merely a given designation whereby we customarily identify matters or persons for the benefit of ourselves and others to distinguish one from another. From this perspective, the Lord obviously has no need of any specific names whereby He would be distinguished from others equal to Him either as to nature or kind, for there is but one Lord God, and none are His equal, either in heaven or on earth. By virtue of His infinite and most perfect being, He distinguishes Himself from all creatures external to Himself. Nevertheless, it has pleased the Lord to represent and to make Himself known unto us, the children of men, in His Holy Word by way of various names. By so doing, He has condescended to our weak and finite minds, and thereby He distinguishes Himself from all alien and false gods who have not made heaven or earth. Such names, in essence, are clear revelations and expressions of God's personal, holy, and perfect attributes that infinitely magnify and exalt His nature and being.

In God's Word, we find several such names, among which are *Jehovah* (or LORD), and *Elohim* (or the *God of the Covenant*), and they are the names that specifically occur in this law. They therefore are the greatest and most significant of the names by which God most frequently and commonly refers to Himself.

If someone were to ask how we are to understand the reference in this commandment to the name of the Lord our God, we respond that we are to understand it as having reference to:

1. God the Lord Himself, in His infinity, majesty, glory, and all His adorable virtues and perfections by which He infinitely distinguishes Himself from all creation. We are to understand God's name as having reference to Himself, with all of His divine virtues and perfections, as is evidenced in the Lord's Prayer, in the petition, "Hallowed be thy name." There, God's name refers to God Himself in all of His divine majesty, glory, and perfection.

2. All that by which God unveils and reveals Himself in His infinite majesty and glory to us frail children of men. To this belong His Holy Word, all of His works of grace and nature, and all the special names by which God generally refers to Himself in His Holy Word. In summary, it makes reference to all that, in any way and without exception, serves as a means unto the Lord to present Himself and

to make Himself known to us in His divine glory through Christ Jesus His Son.

This all is comprehended in God's holy name, and must therefore be absorbed, acknowledged, and worshiped by us with the utmost respect, reverence, and fear—and thus in conformity to what the LORD so earnestly forbids His covenant people to do, saying unto them and unto us, "Thou shalt not take the name of the LORD thy God in vain."

The word in the original language that is translated by our scholars as *take* is exceedingly broad in its significance and essentially expresses as much as "receive," "embrace," "lift up," and "carry." Our translators have rendered this well by using the all-inclusive word *take*, and thereby have expressed in general terms the totality of our external and internal duties and activities regarding the Lord's holy name. However, that we would receive a better understanding regarding the unique efficacy and content of this commandment, we need to know, that the word in the original Hebrew text can be translated in a twofold manner:

1. "Thou shalt not *bear* the name of the LORD thy God in vain"; and

2. "Thou shalt not *use* the name of the LORD thy God in vain."

Since God's "commandment is exceeding broad" (Ps. 119:96), we shall briefly expound the meaning of both translations, believing that the two meanings must be conjoined.

The Lord forbids that we bear His name in vain. To bear God's name means to confess God's name openly by way of our religious practice, and thus to acknowledge Him as our God, king, and Lord, to whom we are inwardly and covenantally united and whom we desire to confess, serve, fear, and honor openly before all men. The bearing of God's name therefore consists of and signifies our entire external profession and religious engagement. We read of this in Isaiah 44:5: "One shall say, I am the LORD's; and another shall call himself by the name of Jacob; and another shall subscribe with his hand unto the LORD, and surname himself by the name of Israel." God refers to this in Isaiah 43:7, saying there regarding His people, "even every one that is called by my name"; that is, he who bears God's name and who openly confesses and serves Him as his God and Lord.

In this commandment, God utters the command that one shall not bear and confess His name before others in vain; that is to say, one shall not do so disingenuously, erroneously, or feignedly, as do the hypocrites. These latter bear God's name outwardly and confess that they acknowledge, love, serve, fear, and obey Him, whereas they neither do so in truth nor with their whole hearts. They inwardly abhor God and refuse to believe in Him with a true heart and according to His covenant. They refuse to surrender themselves fully to the Lord as being His property, refusing to do so with complete and humble submission of heart and with a complete hatred toward all sin and wickedness. They all take the name of the Lord in vain, confess Him disingenuously, and "have submitted themselves [feignedly][1] unto him" (Ps. 81:15).

Nevertheless, all temporal believers and pretentious nominal Christians among us (and there are a very great number of them) also conduct themselves in this fashion. Outwardly and verbally, they confess the gospel and the name of Christ, but within their hearts, they are enemies of God, the cross, and our Lord Jesus Christ—all of which is abundantly affirmed by their sinful, vain, and worldly walk of life. This grievous abomination of duplicity and hypocrisy is forbidden most sternly by the Lord in this commandment. His will is that we would utterly hate and abhor such a confession and that we would be entirely upright in our confession and religious practice. His will is that, with a true heart we would acknowledge, cleave to, fear, trust in, love, and serve Him, doing so without the least trace of deceit, corruption, and hypocrisy of heart.

The eyes of the Lord look for truth in the inner man, and He demands that in all matters we surrender our hearts and wills to Him. He dwells only with the man who is pure of heart, for "the LORD will abhor the…deceitful man" (Ps. 5:6). He is a pure, holy, and infinitely perfect Spirit, and therefore "they that worship him must worship him in spirit and in truth" (John 4:24). All these truths are taught very clearly and abundantly throughout the Holy Scriptures.

Such is the manner in which the most high God prohibits us from taking His holy name in vain, commanding us in our religious practice and in our confession to be completely upright and sincere of heart, so that thereby we would please Him in Christ. Oh, that this commandment of the Lord were truly bound upon our hearts!

However, we have not yet addressed the full implications of this command of the Lord. We must also read it in light of the alternate translation, and we shall then perceive that there are many other things that the Lord commands and forbids us to do.

The alternate or second translation of this commandment of the Lord reads, as we heard: "Thou shalt not use the name of the LORD thy God in vain." By the expression "using the name of the LORD," one generally understands and

---

1. The Dutch *Statenvertaling* inserts the word "feignedly" in this passage.

expresses all our exercises regarding God and His holy name; that is, with soul and body and both inwardly and outwardly.

Let me briefly set before you how we use God's name in a threefold manner, doing so either inwardly in our hearts or outwardly with our mouths or by our deeds.

1. We use God's name inwardly in our hearts when we think upon God and focus our minds upon Him, and thus when we inwardly call upon, praise, and magnify Him. In short, we do so when we inwardly and by means of the faculties of our souls are exercised regarding God's name.

2. We use God's name outwardly with our mouths when we speak to others of God and His holy name. Furthermore, we do so when we take God's name upon our lips and engage ourselves in prayer, singing, and reading aloud.

3. We also use God's name outwardly by our conduct, deeds, and works when we engage either in the outward performance of religious duties or when our deeds and works specifically are related to God the Lord and His holy name, whereby He is either honored or dishonored.

This is the threefold manner in which we use the name of God, and the Lord commands that we not do so in vain; that is, not in a futile, sinful, or erroneous manner, so that God's holy and illustrious name is dishonored and maligned by us. The latter occurs when we:

1. Inwardly and personally reflect upon God the Lord and His holy name or either call upon or consider Him in our hearts without an appropriate love for, fear of, esteem for, faith in, and trust in His name. Thus, we do so when we think upon God and His holy name and call upon it without any inward fear and trembling of heart.

2. Speak of God and His illustrious name and, in so doing, abuse, malign, slander, or dishonor it in any way, as our instructor will expound.

3. So conduct ourselves in matters of religion or in any other way whereby God's holy name in some way is maligned and dishonored by us—or we thereby give occasion for such maligning and dishonoring of God's name.

Such are the ways whereby one dishonors the Lord and His holy name, and in so doing, takes it in vain. In this commandment, the Lord expressly forbids such dishonoring of His holy name, saying, "Thou shalt not take the name of the LORD thy God in vain"; that is, in whatever way we would make ourselves guilty in this matter. The Lord therefore most compellingly commands that, in our hearts as well as by our words and deeds, we would use His holy name appropriately and that we would fear and magnify it in a manner that will be further expounded and taught by the Catechism.

We briefly have set before you the true meaning and intent of this commandment of the Lord, whereby all that we have proposed is compellingly prescribed or prohibited by the Lord. We must therefore take notice of the compelling and persuasive motives included in it by the Lord for the observance of this commandment, so that this would move us to fear Him and to compel our souls toward the affectionate obedience of this holy commandment. The Lord therefore includes with this commandment the threat, saying, "for the LORD will not hold him guiltless that taketh his name in vain."

Not to hold someone guiltless is as much as to say that one most certainly will declare him guilty and that, at the appropriate time, he will assuredly and severely be punished for his transgression. When the Lord so seriously threatens not to hold guiltless those who dishonor and malign His holy name, He indicates that He is an infinitely holy and just God who guards His name and honor with supreme jealousy. Thus, He neither will nor can by any means tolerate anyone abusing, slandering, or maligning His majestic and holy name, but of necessity will most certainly punish with His infinite curse and wrath all who are guilty thereof.

The least maligning or dishonoring of God's holy name is truly worthy of the eternal curse and wrath of God. All unrepentant and unbelieving sinners will most certainly undergo this curse and wrath of God without the least diminution of such judgment, for God must vindicate His dishonored and maligned name by inflicting such a grievous and infinite punishment. People often think lightly of the crime of maligning and dishonoring the Lord's name and do not take it to heart. Judges and governments frequently permit the transgression of this commandment of God to go unpunished, failing to initiate an appropriate investigation regarding this vile abomination in their lands and permitting it to continue unnoticed. The Lord Himself occasionally may postpone the execution of His punishment and judgment for a lengthy period of time, so that it appears as though He already has forgotten and quickly overlooked this crime; nevertheless, the Lord shall by no means hold them guiltless, for the Lord "is not a man, that he should lie; neither the son of man, that he should repent: hath he said, and shall he not do it? or hath he spoken, and shall he not make it good?" (Num. 23:19). At His time, He will avenge Himself by punishing all unrepentant and ungodly sinners who have neither feared His name nor trembled before it. This they will discover to their eternal shame and perdition when it is too late, "for the LORD shall not hold them guiltless."

Let us now also briefly consider the instructor's comments regarding this matter. He teaches in response to Question 99 that this third commandment requires "that we, not only by cursing or perjury, but also by rash swearing, must not profane or abuse the name of God; nor by silence or connivance be partakers of these horrible sins in others." The instructor here posits that, in this commandment, God earnestly forbids all maligning and dishonoring of His holy name, and thus also that, in the various ways he here proposes, we take God's name in vain by:

1. *Cursing.* There are actually two ways in which men can be guilty of cursing. They do so when someone:

   a. Curses God the Lord and, with evil intent, speaks malignantly and slanderously of His holy name; and, as an act of devilish wickedness, wishes Him all evil, desiring that God did not exist—whether he does so inwardly in his heart or outwardly either by his words or deeds. Such cursing is an utterly dreadful slandering and dishonoring of God's most holy name, and God therefore has commanded that there shall be no grace for all who curse in such a fashion, and that they must consequently be punished by death (Lev. 24:15).

   b. Curses himself or his neighbor, whether in despair or motivated by wickedness, anger, arrogance, or anything else, wishing God's curse, punishment, and wrath to descend upon him or upon his neighbor. In his weakness, the apostle Peter cursed himself in this fashion (Matt. 26:74), and the wicked Shimei cursed the fleeing King David (2 Sam. 16:5). Thereby the holy name of God was grievously maligned and dishonored. In so doing, one seeks to make God the Lord one's slave and executioner of his grievous and abominable wickedness, being desirous that His great and dreadful name be subservient to our evil will or that of others. Many dreadful and vile abominations are implied in such a curse, and God therefore has expressly commanded that such cursers also are to be punished here on earth with death (Lev. 24:14).

2. *Swearing a false oath*; that is, swearing falsely and deceitfully by God's great and holy name. This is done when, by publicly and solemnly calling upon the holy name of God, one affirms a lie as truth, or when, by solemnly calling upon God's name, one commits himself to something that he subsequently does not perform, but neglects or violates in very deed. This also is a grievous slandering, dishonoring, and maligning of the holy and dreadful name of God, who by no means will permit this to go unpunished. He therefore sternly forbids it, saying, "And ye shall not swear by my name falsely, neither shalt thou profane the name of thy God: I am the LORD" (Lev. 19:12).

3. *Swearing an unnecessary oath*, which, according to the instructor, is also a grievous maligning of God's name that the Lord sternly forbids in this commandment of His law. This occurs when, without there being an absolute necessity and without being called upon by the government to do so in a weighty matter, one frivolously calls upon God's name, irrespective of whether he speaks either the truth or a lie. By such unnecessary swearing, we use God's name in vain; that is, in a manner void of any godly fear and reverence. The Savior alludes to this when He admonishes us, saying: "I say unto you, Swear not at all; neither by heaven; for it is God's throne.... But let your communication be, Yea, yea; Nay, nay" (Matt. 5:35–37).

4. "By *silence or connivance*"; that is, when either we hear someone malign the name of God or observe its desecration, and we fail in fulfilling the commandment as we are obligated; that is, if we desire to fear God and His name, earnestly to rebuke such a person, to confront him with his grievous sin, and to admonish him to humble himself and to repent, so that the Lord's holy and illustrious name would no longer be maligned by him. In certain situations, we even are obligated to report the sinful conduct of such a person either to the governing authorities or to the elders of the church, so that he might be admonished and disciplined by them. The Lord commands this, saying, "And if a soul sin, and hear the voice of swearing, and is a witness, whether he hath seen or known of it; if he do not utter it, then he shall bear his iniquity" (Lev. 5:1). Beloved, if by remaining silent, and we permit God's name to be maligned, dishonored, and slandered in our presence, whether because of intimidation or the fear of man or by a lack of love for and fear of God, we are then guilty also of slandering and dishonoring God's holy name. We then fail to

uphold God's name by not striving zealously to promote its sacred honor. The Lord strenuously also forbids such sinful behavior.

5. *Many other instances of the slandering and dishonoring of God's holy name* that are not mentioned by the instructor, which, however, are also strenuously forbidden by the Lord God. Too much time has already transpired to permit us to detail these.

Nevertheless, among sinners, there is one instance of the very grievous and abominable transgression of this commandment that is commonly being indulged in today, and we shall therefore address this matter. The taking of God's name in vain consists also in the flippant use of God's lofty and holy name by people in their everyday conversation among themselves—a name everyone ought to fear and for which everyone ought to tremble. Such use it in vain by so frivolously, thoughtlessly, lightly, and irreverently taking it in their mouths and saying at the least and any occasion, "Oh, Lord," "Oh, God,"and "Oh, Jesus." Many are also accustomed to flippantly saying, "Thank God," "Praise God," "God help us," "If it may please God," or whatever other instances there may be of flippantly using the great and holy name of God, on a daily basis, without the least reverence, attention, or sincerity of heart. There is the common expression, "Oh, dear Lord," which is uttered by many who nevertheless do not in any wise acknowledge God to be their Lord and king, and who have not the least measure of true, heartfelt love toward Him—something that is clearly affirmed by their sinful and vain lives.

The Lord most emphatically forbids all these and other ways in which His great and holy name is wickedly maligned and misused by men, whether knowingly or unknowingly. The Lord by no means will hold such transgressors guiltless, but will eternally punish all unrepentant sinners with His curse and wrath for the maligning of His name.

Having thus briefly expounded the sins that God forbids in this commandment, the instructor proceeds to address the holy duties that the Lord prescribes in this commandment, namely, "that we use the holy name of God no otherwise than with fear and reverence; so that He may rightly be confessed and worshipped, and be glorified by us in all our words and works."

It is the Lord's great and preeminent objective in this third commandment to stir up His covenant people to fear His holy and illustrious name so that they in no wise would ever dishonor it, but rather, in their thoughts, words, and deeds, always praise and glorify His holy and illustrious name. Who among us, having in some measure acquired a right knowledge of the Lord's lofty, holy, and awe-inspiring name, would not acquiesce and confess with his whole heart that the name of the Lord is worthy of being greatly feared, worshiped, and revered, and that all creatures should continually tremble before this name?

Meanwhile, the instructor proceeds to expound what he already has asserted by asking in Question 100, "Is then the profaning of God's name by swearing and cursing so heinous a sin that His wrath is kindled against those who do not endeavor, as much as in them lies, to prevent and forbid such cursing and swearing?" The instructor has the following individuals in mind, proposing that:

1. First and foremost, he is referring to judges and governments whom God has explicitly appointed here on earth to forbid, prevent, and punish, to the utmost of their power, all desecration of His holy name. This is the preeminent duty of governments, whether they are small or large, and should they become remiss in the discharge of this duty and fail to protect God's holy name to the utmost of their power, they will be subjected to the wrath and curse of God. They will therefore be unable to stand before the judgment seat of God on the last day, when the Lord will require of them an account of all the slandering and desecration of His great name committed in this world by both their negligence and their actions.

Oh, that this would be bound with utmost seriousness upon the hearts of our governments, whether at the lower or higher levels, and that they would yet learn to fear and tremble before the majesty of God, considering that most of them have hardly any concern!

2. More generally and indiscriminately, the instructor is referring to all who, rather than defending the holy and illustrious name of God when they hear His name being maligned and desecrated, fail to defend it and remain silent—as is so often the case in our day. Since men neither fear nor love God in their hearts, they also have no desire publicly to honor His holy name before the world or to rebuke all who abuse and malign His name. Though such persons neither curse nor swear, they nevertheless listen to it and do not defend God's name. The Lord therefore will not hold them guiltless, for although they believe themselves to be guiltless, they also provoke God to great anger.

According to the instructor, it is thus evident how extraordinarily and abominably sinful is all sin that maligns and desecrates God's name, for he continues by saying, "there is no sin greater or more provoking to God, than the profaning of His name; and therefore He has commanded this sin to be punished with death."

Much could be said here to demonstrate the dreadful and abominable nature of all the instances of the taking of God's name in vain among men. May the Lord Himself instruct sinners and truly bind this matter upon their hearts.

Beloved, consider how you would respond in such a situation, for there is nothing we take more seriously, are more grieved over, provokes us more to anger, and more offends us than when someone dishonors, maligns, and slanders our name, or when others mock and despise us. However, if puny and sinful men such as we, who are eternally worthy of being utterly slandered and maligned, are so greatly concerned about our honor and good name, how then must this great and most holy God insist upon the vindication of His honor! How greatly He is provoked to wrath by all who so brazenly dare to malign Him and slander His holy name! God surely will not tolerate them, for were He so to do, He would deny Himself.

Therefore, He must vindicate Himself and punish, with temporal and eternal punishments, all who are guilty of slandering His name, for such men are utterly hostile to Him and seek to dethrone Him, trample upon Him, despise and malign Him, and banish all reverence and fear of Him from their hearts. They are perverse rebels who are fiercely opposed to God, with their weapons drawn. Woe unto them, for the Lord will not hold them guiltless, and, according to the instructor, He has even commanded that the abominable practice of the slandering of His name must be punished with death—as we already have observed in our exposition.

As far as we ourselves are concerned, may the exposition of this commandment, by the grace of God, be subservient to function as a mirror for all unconverted sinners and thus expose who we truly are. May it cause us to reflect on the days of our youth and to see how utterly and thoroughly guilty we are of slandering and desecrating God's great name, and may it then be that men will acknowledge that their entire lives until this very moment have been nothing other than slandering of the name of the Lord, and that they never have rightly known, served, or feared Him. Oh, that men would consider themselves as being wholly subject to God's curse and wrath, and that this would humble them, so that, in utterly forsaking themselves and all else, they would seek for their salvation and reconciliation with God fully, upon free grace, and by a true and upright faith in the Lord Jesus!

Furthermore, may the Lord grant that, before His countenance, all His children would know themselves to be utterly guilty of the multiple slandering and desecration of His name—something they do daily out of weakness in both word and deed. May they truly humble themselves and seek for their righteousness and salvation only in the mediator, Jesus Christ, "who of God is made unto us wisdom, and righteousness, and sanctification, and redemption" (1 Cor. 1:30). Amen, and so be it for the sake of the Lord's holy name!

The Swearing of an Oath

But above all things, my brethren, swear not, neither by heaven, neither by the earth, neither by any other oath: but let your yea be yea; and your nay, nay; lest ye fall into condemnation.

—JAMES 5:12

Question 101: May we then swear religiously by the name of God?

Answer: Yes, either when the magistrates demand it of the subjects or when necessity requires us thereby to confirm fidelity and truth to the glory of God and the safety of our neighbor, for such an oath is founded on God's Word, and therefore was justly used by the saints, both in the Old and New Testament.

Question 102: May we also swear by saints or any other creatures?

Answer: No; for a lawful oath is calling upon God as the only one who knows the heart, that He will bear witness to the truth and punish me if I swear falsely; which honor is due to no creature.

"I said in my haste, All men are liars" (Ps. 116:11). Such is the remarkable language of the godly author of this psalm, who here testifies that he uttered it in haste. Nevertheless, what he said is a most certain and entirely incontrovertible truth, for as many men as have ever been born have all been liars. No one is able to contradict this, unless he would also negate and deny the universal depravity of the human race. However noble and divine a virtue the truth may be, no one who has ever been born of a woman—except for Christ—has possessed this virtue in perfection. All men appear before God the Lord as being guilty of violating and transgressing the truth. By nature, men are inclined toward dishonesty and deceit, and it is the Spirit of sanctification alone who leads the believing people of God into all truth—without which they too would be utterly dominated by a lying spirit.

However common this wicked vice of dishonesty and deceit may be among men, nothing is more harmful to human society by negatively affecting its very foundations. How can there be anywhere an orderly society of men dwelling together, and how can such a society be sustained, when one person cannot rely upon another at his word, and thus one is always in danger of being misled by lies, subterfuge, deceit, and dishonesty? This obviously utterly destroys the fabric of an orderly society and is the cause of one person not being able to have a secure and safe relationship with another.

In His wise arrangement, the Lord God has been moved to counter this destructive evil among men by stipulating that in matters of great weight and import, one may avail himself of a sign whereby the truth of all matters shall be uncovered and deceit and dishonesty be prevented—a sign that is an emphatic affirmation of the truth of a matter. Such is accomplished by means of the swearing of an oath, by which one calls upon God's holy name as a witness of something that he presents as truth.

This is a helpful means for the corrupt human race. It is not only a matter of utmost necessity, but also a matter of great importance and pertinence, and therefore by no means may it be used in a vain and frivolous manner. Our Christian instructor most clearly expounds this in this Lord's Day, defending this practice against all erroneous sentiments.

In the previous Lord's Day, the instructor addressed the third commandment, which forbids all vain use of God's most holy name in whatever manner it may be practiced. Since he then mentioned that the name of God is grievously abused by the swearing of false and unnecessary oaths, he now proceeds, in this Lord's Day, to address separately the subject of the swearing of oaths, in order to teach clearly in what the swearing of oaths consists, as well as the extent to which the Word of God either permits or forbids the swearing of oaths. It will be most beneficial and useful to hear this necessary subject matter addressed.

Frequently a person is required to swear an oath that affirms the truth of a matter, whether it is upon the assumption of an office or at some other occasion. In our country, the swearing of oaths is very common, and yet there are many who have not the slightest idea of what an oath is and in what it consists. It is therefore of the utmost importance that, from time to time, this doctrine regarding the swearing of oaths be clearly and transparently expounded, lest one, through ignorance, be guilty of grievous sin regarding this matter.

Since such a suitable opportunity presents itself in Lord's Day 37, all would do well to learn about this, so that they will never ignorantly use the illustrious name of the Lord their God in vain. To expound this matter in an orderly fashion, we shall speak of:

1. the true nature of swearing an oath; and
2. the errors of the Anabaptists and Roman Catholics regarding oaths.

The swearing of an oath is simply the affirmation of the truthfulness of a matter by calling God to be a witness by calling upon His most holy name. By so doing, one expresses the desire that the Lord would bless and favor us if we speak the truth and that He would severely punish us if we do not speak the truth.

This description concurs with the answer of Question 102: "A lawful oath is calling upon God, as the only one who knows the heart, that He will bear witness to the truth, and punish me if I swear falsely." Thus, it is presupposed in the swearing of all oaths that He, by whose name we swear and to whose testimony we appeal when doing so, is omniscient and knows even the most secret motions of our hearts. He is also omnipotent, and therefore is able to bless us when we are being truthful, and to punish us when we lie.

Swearing of oaths was entirely unnecessary prior to the fall, for man was then perfect and without sin. He then never spoke anything but the truth. However, after the fall, when, according to the language of the poet in Psalm 116, all men have become liars and one no longer is able to believe a person simply at his word, swearing of oaths has become necessary for the affirmation of the truth regarding certain matters. The purpose of the swearing of an oath is to bring all contradiction to a halt regarding what has transpired, and to obligate a person to carry out all that he has promised regarding the future in a holy and unblemished way. This means that there are two ways in which a person can swear an oath: one affirms matters that have already transpired in the past or makes promises regarding and commits oneself to matters that are yet to transpire.

In the swearing of an oath, a person commits himself fully to God's just judgment, desiring to be blessed of Him if he is truthful and to be punished by Him if he commits perjury. Even the old pagans knew that this is what constitutes an oath. Therefore, they generally swore by their idols and called upon them to execute vengeance if they swore deceitfully. The Romans would swear an oath when they would enter into a mutual contract. Each negotiating party would take a stone and cast it on the ground with great force, saying: "If I am willfully deceitful, then let Jupiter deprive me of all my goods and possessions as I use my hands to cast away this stone."

The swearing of oaths has been in use from early on in history. It was a common practice in the days of Abraham, of whom we read that he swore an oath before the king of Sodom, that he would not take anything of that which belonged to the king (Gen. 14:22). This patriarch swore such an oath by raising his hand toward heaven, for he spoke to the king of Sodom, saying, "I have lifted up mine hand unto the LORD, the most high God, the possessor of heaven and earth" (Gen. 14:22).

During subsequent periods of history, we find that various bodily gestures were used for the swearing of oaths. However, we shall not consider them. We only wish to mention that when we engage in the outward ceremony of swearing an oath, we raise up two fingers as proof that we are calling the God of heaven and earth, who dwells in heaven above, to be our witness. When we wish to point someone out, we customarily do this by pointing the finger at him. By raising two fingers to heaven, one thereby signifies that he is mindful of God who dwells in the heavens above, calling upon Him to be a witness regarding the truth of a matter about which he swears an oath.[1]

As to the verbal formula used in the swearing of an oath, this has differed greatly throughout the ages. Generally speaking, the swearing of an oath always has consisted of the invocation of divine blessing and grace if one spoke the truth, and of divine curse and punishment if one were to lie. Though a variety of verbal formulas was used to articulate this invocation, they were all essentially the same as to content. In the Holy Scriptures, we find a variety of such formulas for oath swearing. The common formula used in our nation for the swearing of oaths reads as follows: "May God Almighty so truly help me." With these words, one is essentially saying: "If my testimony is not truthful or I do not live up to what I promise today, then let the almighty God punish me. However, if I do the opposite, that is, if I speak the truth and live up to what I have promised, may that same God help and bless me."

In this formula, one surrenders himself either to the Lord's blessing or to the Lord's curse that is being invoked. It is therefore evident that the swearing of an oath is truly a matter of the greatest weight and import, for in so doing, one puts his entire spiritual and physical well-being, so to speak, on the line for the sake of the truth of a matter or promise concerning which he swears.

---

1. VanderGroe here describes the gesture still used in the Netherlands when one is called upon to swear an oath.

Consequently, such swearing of an oath must never be done in any way but a holy and godly manner.

There are several essential prerequisites that must be observed and practiced diligently whenever oaths are sworn. One must consider:

First, the circumstances when it is permitted to swear oaths. One should never swear an oath except it pertain to a matter of utmost importance, and thus when either God's honor or the well-being of the commonwealth, the church, our neighbors, or ourselves is at stake—when it matters greatly that the truth regarding a matter become transparent and be solemnly affirmed, so that no one needs to be in doubt regarding the matter any longer. Such swearing of an oath must not be done until absolute necessity requires it, and thus when no other means are at hand by which a weighty matter may be made transparent. As long as one is able to avail himself of other ways or means by which he can prove the truth regarding a matter with certainty, one should not avail himself of the swearing of an oath. Therefore, when dealing with matters of minor importance that pertain neither to the honor of God nor the well-being of church, state, ourselves, or our neighbors, one absolutely may not swear an oath. Rather, one should take the other at his word, and thus believe his "yes" or "no," or not believe him at all, doing so without requiring in such matters an oath as the affirmation of the truthfulness of his words. The instructor showed in the previous Lord's Day that by way of such ill-conceived, frivolous, and unnecessary oaths, God's most holy name is most shamefully taken in vain.

Even the ancient pagans were very careful with the swearing of oaths. The Romans did not swear lightly. They swore oaths only in matters of the utmost importance, when the truth regarding such matters could not be ascertained in other ways.

Second, the persons who are swearing oaths. One needs to pay very careful attention to this matter and permit no one to swear an oath unless he has the necessary requisites and qualities that allow him to do so. One may by no means permit anyone to swear an oath who is mentally disabled, for such individuals do not comprehend the nature of the oath. Also, young children, whose judgment and intellect are not yet matured sufficiently to understand the weightiness of an oath, cannot be permitted to swear. This also applies to individuals who are inclined to be overcome by their passions, and thus to all who are hasty, cantankerous, vengeful, and bloodthirsty, or to those individuals of whom one observes that they are in bondage to these passions and cannot control them. One should especially refrain from requiring an oath from those who lead ungodly lives and give public offense, for they demonstrate that they neither fear nor esteem the God by whom they would be swearing. One should also refrain from doing so with individuals of whom he knows that they repeatedly have perjured themselves. They are not worthy of ever being believed again, even if they were to swear to highest heaven. Instead, such individuals should be severely punished in conformity to the occasion and the circumstances.

When one thus correctly views, acknowledges, and considers this matter, he must conclude that no one can swear true, lawful, and holy oaths except those who are truly converted, regenerated, and united to God in Christ. The unconverted neither truly know nor fear God; they erroneously worship an unknown God. They are by no means capable of swearing by God's holy name as they ought. Since all of their deeds are sinful because they do not proceed from faith, they also swear oaths in a sinful manner. Nevertheless, it is impossible to prevent such commission of sin, and this should be left to the government and judgment of God.

It is the duty of all godly governments that require oaths that they first earnestly admonish men to fear God and to swear believingly by His illustrious and holy name. When, subsequent to such an admonition, a person has sworn an oath, one must then believe him without any further contradiction. If he has sworn deceitfully, he will have to give an account of this before God. However, men must believe him when no one is able to convince him of his falsehood and deceit, for an oath is sworn to put an end to all questioning and contradiction.

We have thus considered what belongs to the essence and nature of oaths and the swearing of such oaths. We shall now consider the errors of those whose views regarding the swearing of oaths are erroneous and misleading. Among them we find, first of all, the Anabaptists, and our instructor begins by refuting them, asking his pupil, "May we then swear religiously by the name of God?" Previously we considered what it means to swear an oath by the name of God, and to do so in a God-fearing manner. We therefore need not expound this any further. The only thing the instructor here asks of his pupil is whether the swearing of oaths is permitted, upon which the pupil responds, "Yes, either when the magistrates demand it of the subjects or when necessity requires us thereby to confirm fidelity and truth to the glory of God and the safety of our neighbor, for such an oath is founded on God's Word, and therefore was justly used by the saints, both in the Old and New Testament."

The Reformed Church has a well-known and running dispute with the Anabaptists regarding this matter. The Anabaptists posit that though God did indeed proscribe oaths in the Old Testament, He winked at this, permitting them to occur and tolerating them among His people. Further, they posit that the New Testament flatly forbids oaths. Consequently, as necessary as the swearing of oaths may be and as weighty as matters may be, the Anabaptists posit that a Christian may no longer engage in swearing oaths, since such a practice runs directly counter to the prohibition of the Lord Jesus Christ. The infamous heretic Pelagius was also of this persuasion, and the Anabaptists may have adopted his view. We will affirm by a few powerful proofs, that both grievously err and are misguided.

We first shall prove that one may swear a godly oath by using God's Name in matters of great importance when the truth cannot be ascertained in any other way. Whatever can be subservient to magnify and glorify God's illustrious virtues and perfections is lawful and permitted by the Word of God. Yes, it is even prescribed. This occurs in an exalted manner when an oath is sworn, for one magnifies God's great and perfect attributes by doing so in a very obvious and exalted manner. Whoever swears an oath makes a clear confession of the following:

1. *God's omniscience*, for by calling upon Him to be a witness of the truth of an obscure matter, one confesses that God is an omniscient being who knows and is acquainted with all things, including the most hidden thoughts and inclinations of the human heart—even to the extent that absolutely nothing is hidden from His all-seeing eyes, which penetrate even man's innermost being.

2. *God's omnipresence and omnipotence*, for by desiring that God would either bless us when we swear truthfully or punish us when we perjure ourselves, we are confessing that God is everywhere present in His majestic omnipotence, and that He, wherever we may be, can either bless or punish us.

3. *God's holiness and veracity*, for by calling upon Him as a witness of the truth of a matter, we are confessing that God delights in truth and that He always affirms it. He therefore also loves all who uphold the truth, being willing to help and to bless them. On the contrary, He is an enemy of all those who lie, and He will punish and damn liars, whom He abhors.

4. *God's goodness and grace*, for when, by the swearing of an oath, we beseech Him to bless us, we are presupposing that He is a gracious and merciful God who will not permit such love for the truth to remain unrewarded, but will richly reward it with His abundant blessing.

5. *God's justice*, for by asking God to punish us if we perjure ourselves, we confess that He is a just God who does not permit liars to go unpunished, but must necessarily punish and damn them. David testifies of this, saying, "Thou shalt destroy them that speak leasing: the LORD will abhor the bloody and deceitful man" (Ps. 5:6).

6. *God's majesty* is also greatly displayed and exalted, for men always swear by someone who is greater and more exalted than they. God therefore can swear only by Himself, for He cannot swear by anyone who is greater than Himself. Paul testifies of this, saying, "For when God made promise to Abraham, because he could swear by no greater, he sware by himself" (Heb. 6:13).

Therefore, when men swear by the Lord their God, they confess the infinite greatness and majesty of this God. They worship Him as the majestic supreme being as they beseech Him either to bless or to curse them if they swear truthfully or deceitfully. Thus, whenever an oath is sworn, God's name is reverently called upon and religiously honored and worshiped. Men acknowledge God to be a just judge—yes, even the supreme judge, whose right it is to render judgment regarding all the deeds and transactions of man by rewarding that which is good and punishing that which is evil. It is thus evident that by the swearing of an oath, many of God's illustrious attributes and perfections are confessed and displayed by the creature.

Furthermore, the swearing of an oath also occurs in harmony with both tables of the law, for in so doing, one practices love for God and his neighbor in a most glorious manner. Love for God is practiced when we swear oaths in conformity to the truth regarding matters that pertain to the honor of God. We then demonstrate that we love our God and endeavor to safeguard His honor so that it will not be maligned. The greatest honor a creature can bestow upon His God and creator is to demonstrate that he takes His honor to heart and seeks to promote it in whatever way possible.

No less does the swearing of lawful oaths fulfill the second table of the law, which requires love for our neighbor, for when we swear lawful oaths in matters that pertain to the well-being of church or state, or that of our neighbor, we vividly illustrate that we take to heart the well-being and salvation of our neighbor. Consequently, in so doing we love our neighbor as ourselves in conformity to the demand of God's law.

We conclude on the one hand that in the swearing of oaths, God's attributes and perfections are most gloriously confessed and displayed, as we have shown. On the other hand, the swearing of oaths most evidently displays love for God and for our neighbor. Who would not understand that the swearing of oaths is therefore truly lawful and that it may and must transpire in the manner we have laid out for you, being done for the honor of God or for the well-being of church and state or of our neighbor, when the truth cannot be made manifest in any other way or by any other means?

The second proof that the lawful swearing of oaths is permitted we derive from the answer of the pupil, who clearly states that "such an oath is founded on God's Word." This is most certainly true, for we have explicit laws in which God Himself requires the swearing of lawful oaths. In Deuteronomy 10:20, the great lawgiver speaks to His people, saying, "Thou shalt fear the LORD thy God; him shalt thou serve, and to him shalt thou cleave, and swear by his name." God also commanded that when someone had in his custody the cattle of another person, and, during that time, the cattle either died or strayed without him being at fault, he would have to vindicate himself by swearing an oath, declaring that he had not laid hands on this cattle (Ex. 22:10–11).

God also speaks accordingly in Isaiah 45:23: "I have sworn by myself, the word is gone out of my mouth in righteousness, and shall not return, That unto me every knee shall bow, [take note!] every tongue shall swear." Other similar passages may be found where God clearly prescribes the lawful swearing of oaths, so it is evident that the lawful swearing of oaths is founded upon God's Word, and our use of such oaths is therefore permitted.

The pupil gives a third proof by saying that the swearing of oaths "was justly used by the saints, both in the Old and New Testament." This is most certainly the case. In the Old Testament, we find the examples of Abraham, Eliezer, Isaac, Jacob, Joseph, Moses, David, and others, who, in a godly manner, swore by God's name.

In the New Testament, we find similar examples of the use of oaths by the apostles. We shall mention only a few of them. Paul swears an oath in Romans 1:9, saying, "For God is my witness," and in 2 Corinthians 1:23, he says, "Moreover I call God for a record upon my soul." In 1 Thessalonians 5:27, he ends his letter with these words, saying, "I charge you by the Lord that this epistle be read unto all the holy brethren."

The lawful swearing of oaths also is proven by the fact that God Himself has endorsed the swearing of oaths by His own example, for we find that God has repeatedly sworn oaths. Paul writes of Him in the text we already have quoted that "when God made promise to Abraham, because he could swear by no greater, he sware by himself" (Heb. 6:13). Also, the priest Zacharias made mention of this oath sworn by God to Abraham, saying, "The oath which he sware to our father Abraham" (Luke 1:73). We would be able to produce other passages and examples from the Holy Scriptures in which God and the savior Jesus Christ have solemnly sworn oaths.

To conclude, the legitimacy of the swearing of oaths is also evident in that God Himself demands an oath of His covenant people, by which they obligate themselves to keep His righteous judgments. As a member of God's covenant, David swore such an oath, saying, "I have sworn, and I will perform it, that I will keep thy righteous judgments" (Ps. 119:106), and God's true covenant people still swear such an oath as often as they come to the Lord's covenant table.

From all that we have addressed, it is very clear that the lawful swearing of oaths is not only legitimate, but that it is also prescribed by God. To affirm this with irrefutable certainty, we will now, with a word or two, resolve the most prominent objections that have been raised against the swearing of oaths by the Anabaptists.

To prove that during the New Testament era one could not swear under any circumstances, the Anabaptists primarily turn to two texts in the New Testament that appear to forbid the swearing of oaths. One is the admonition of the Savior in Matthew 5:34, where He says, "But I say unto you, Swear not at all; neither by heaven; for it is God's throne." The other passage is James 5:12, which we chose as the text for this sermon, and in which James writes to believers in almost the same manner as the Savior expressed Himself. He writes, "But above all things, my brethren, swear not, neither by heaven, neither by the earth, neither by any other oath: but let your yea be yea; and your nay, nay; lest ye fall into condemnation."

However, the Anabaptists cannot sustain their argument from these texts, for in these passages a matter is forbidden that does not pertain to the issue at hand. From the context, it is evident that the only type of oath that is forbidden is one that is sworn by calling upon created objects, such as heaven and earth. The Jews were accustomed to swear by such things rather than by exclusively calling upon the true God. This practice the Lord Jesus Christ objects to, and James follows Him in this. His will is that one should not at all swear by any creature or by any created object, and thus neither by heaven nor by earth, as the Jews were accustomed to do. It is thus crystal clear that both the Savior and the apostle James do not forbid the lawful swearing of oath by calling upon God's name, but only the evil swearing of oaths by calling upon creatures or created objects. It is the intent of both Jesus and James that no one should do this.

The Savior's words, "Let your communication be, Yea, yea; Nay, nay" (Matt. 5:37) are presented by the Anabaptists as new proof in support of their sentiment that one may by no means swear oaths, for they posit that the Savior is saying that no other words may be used than "yea" and "nay" either to affirm or to deny matters.

The fallacy of this explanation becomes evident from the fact that Jesus, in this very chapter, repeatedly affirms His words by saying "verily" or "amen," which would completely contradict His own prohibition. However, what the Son of God intends to communicate when He says, "Let your communication be, Yea, yea; Nay, nay," is that when someone says "yea," it must also truly be "yea," and someone's "nay" must also truly be "nay." He is thus saying that one ought not to affirm anything with "yea" unless it truly is "yea"; and one ought not to deny anything with "nay" unless it is untrue and negative. He is teaching here that whether one is swearing an oath or simply wishing either to affirm or deny something, one must always speak the truth and so accustom himself to this that he is not compelled to swear oaths, but rather, he ought commonly to be believed upon saying "yea" or "nay."

This is the intent of what the Savior desires to express by the words, "Let your communication be, Yea, yea; Nay, nay." He is by no means saying that in matters of great importance, and when the need of the hour demands it, one may not make a weightier affirmation or denial than merely saying "yea" or "nay."

When the Savior finally adds these words, "Whatsoever is more than these cometh of evil," the Anabaptists maintain that He is not merely saying that swearing oaths beyond saying "yea" and "nay" is not permitted and would be sin, but that the swearing of oaths as such "cometh of evil" and is thus sinful in its origin.

We do not deny this, for if all men had not become wicked liars after the fall, there would never have been any need for the swearing of oaths. In this sense, the swearing of oaths is undoubtedly of evil origin; that is, it proceeds from the reality of sin. One could argue in the same manner that one may not wear clothing after the fall, for the wearing of clothes "cometh of evil" and has its origin in sin. No sooner had our parents sinned in Paradise than they became aware that they both were naked.

It is thus evident that the proofs advanced by the Anabaptists in support of their sentiment are entirely ineffective and inconclusive, and so our sentiment is affirmed all the more that one may swear godly oaths by the name of God. However, as we have already stated, it must occur only in circumstances of utmost extremity, when the honor of God or the well-being of church and state or that of our neighbor is at stake. The instructor therefore expresses himself with caution and at the same time sustains the liberty of the lawful swearing of oaths. He also stipulates the occasions when one may do so: "either when the magistrates demand it of the subjects; or when necessity requires us thereby to confirm fidelity and truth."

One neither must nor may swear an oath of his own accord, and thus he may not do so unless he is compelled to do so. Rather, one must hold his oath in abeyance until his government demands it of him. The instructor assigns the right of requiring the swearing of oaths to the government, which is very appropriate, for it belongs to the jurisdiction of governments. During the Old Testament era, governing authorities always exercised this right. We read that Ezra compelled the priests, the Levites, and all Israel to swear (Ezra 10:5). And when the high priest demanded of the Savior that He declare under oath that He was the Son of God, He did respond to the high priest accordingly, acknowledging the fact that he had the right to require an oath of someone (Matthew 26). In Exodus and Leviticus, we even find laws stipulating which matters of controversy had to be resolved by way of oaths before the gods, that is, before the governing authorities. It is thus evident that governments have the right to require of their subjects that they swear oaths when they deem it necessary.

Beyond that, one may also swear oaths apart from the government requiring it when, according to the instructor, "necessity requires us thereby to confirm fidelity and truth." For example, by following the example of the apostle Paul, a minister may call upon an omniscient God for the affirmation of his faithfulness and his orthodoxy when there is suspicion regarding his ministry. He must see to it only that he never does so frivolously and unnecessarily.

According to the instructor, there are only two instances in which one must be called upon to swear oaths, namely, "to confirm fidelity and truth to the glory of God, and the safety of our neighbor." This confirms that the instructor holds to the view that only two types of oaths are to be sworn: *affirmative* oaths and *obligatory* oaths.

An *affirmative* oath pertains only to matters of the past, and is intended to affirm the truth of something that transpired. An *obligatory* oath pertains to future matters, and thus it is the swearing of an oath whereby one obligates himself to a particular matter and to its faithful execution. This applies to mutual contracts or to one's commitment toward the execution of an office. In such cases, one affirms his faithfulness by an oath, and obligates himself faithfully to execute what he has promised to do. We find that, in former days, the believing patriarchs and other saints often swore such mutual oaths. However, one must engage in this with the greatest care, lest he obligate himself to things that are unlawful and forbidden by the law of God. David sinned greatly by swearing that he would slay all the males in Nabal's house—something he did not do because of Abigail's prudent intervention (1 Samuel 25). Herod, the tetrarch of Galilee, also sinned by obligating himself under oath to unconditionally give the daughter of Herodias whatever she would require of him (Matt. 14:7). The Jews in Jerusalem sinned when more than forty of them bound themselves by an imprecatory oath not to eat or drink until they had slain the apostle Paul (Acts 23:21). These and similar oaths are supremely wicked and should by no means be adhered to when they have been hastily and carelessly made. Oaths by which one obligates himself to commit wicked deeds are unlawful and are thus forbidden. We may and must readily break such oaths, and be contrite and sorrowful regarding our impulsivity and ungodliness, for if we were to honor such oaths or obligations, we would be heaping one sin upon the other.

It is evident that unless it is lawful and sanctioned by God, we must never swear to be faithful nor obligate ourselves to anything. We must never swear oaths or promise anything under oath unless we first have thoroughly investigated whether we are in a position to honor what we have promised in a godly manner. Furthermore, we must inquire whether we are permitted to make such commitments in light of God's law. Therefore, according to the instructor, we must swear oaths only "to confirm fidelity and truth to the glory of God, and the safety of our neighbor."

Having considered at length that a Christian is permitted to swear godly oaths in the name of God, it remains only to say something about the wretched abuse of oaths by Roman Catholicism. Roman Catholicism teaches that one can swear oaths not only by the name of God but also by creatures. For instance, one swears in the Roman Catholic Church by their so-called saints, swearing by the Mother of God, St. Peter, St. Paul, St. Francis, or St. Christopher.

However, Roman Catholics are not the only ones who in so doing, dreadfully sin against God the Lord, for among the Reformed there are many who follow Roman Catholicism in its practice by swearing in a most wicked and frivolous way by their souls, by their salvation, and by this or that. Consider therefore what the instructor is saying when he asks in Question 103, "May we also swear by saints or any other creatures?" The pupil answers with a resounding "no." The proof he gives is the equivalent of ten additional proofs, for he proceeds to say, "A lawful oath is calling upon God, as the only one who knows the heart, that He will bear witness to the truth, and punish me if I swear falsely; which honor is due to no creature."

The swearing of oaths is an act of worship whereby one renders God divine honor and by which one makes a glorious confession regarding God's majestic attributes and perfections—such as His omniscience, omnipresence, goodness, and justice. Regarding a mere creature, how is it possible for all of this to be confessed? How can a mere creature witness to the truth of a matter that is hidden in the human heart and that no one can know unless he is omniscient? How can a mere creature bless us when we swear oaths in truth or punish us when we perjure ourselves? These are indeed matters that cannot be attributed to creatures without sacrilegiously robbing the true God—who alone is omniscient and omnipotent—of His honor, considering that He emphatically declares that He is jealous of His honor, saying, "My glory will I not give to another" (Isa. 42:8). God has therefore expressly commanded that one may swear only by His name, for we read in Deuteronomy 6:13, "Thou shalt fear the LORD thy God, and serve him, and shalt swear by his name." Consider therefore how strongly He rebukes the people of Israel, who had the audacity to swear by anything other than by the name of the Lord, saying: "How shall I pardon thee for this? thy children have forsaken me, and sworn by them that are no gods" (Jer. 5:7a). During the Savior's sojourn, the Jews did likewise in that they swore by heaven, by earth, and by their heads, and they were therefore firmly rebuked by Him regarding this practice: "But I say unto you, Swear not at all; neither by heaven; for it is God's throne: nor by the earth; for it is his footstool: neither by Jerusalem; for it is the city of the great King. Neither shalt thou swear by thy head, because thou canst not make one hair white or black" (Matt. 5:34–35).

All of this affirms that one may swear oaths only by the name of the omnipotent and true God. When we thus swear such an oath and thereby obligate ourselves to any duty or performance, we must be sacred in our unblemished adherence to it—irrespective of whether it is to our advantage or our disadvantage. Whatever has been sworn must remain as such and must be adhered to, even if it would be to our hurt. David therefore testifies regarding one who fears the Lord, "He that sweareth to his own hurt, and changeth not" (Ps. 15:4). We find an example of such an oath in Joshua 9, for by an oath, the children of Israel had entered into a covenant with the Gibeonites. However, when it was subsequently discovered that they had been deceived by the Gibeonites, they nevertheless honored their covenant with the Gibeonites because of the oath they had sworn.

When we examine the conduct of many people in light of what has been expounded, it becomes manifest that many grievous sins and abominations have been committed against the Lord God by the swearing of oaths—sins whereby He has been provoked to wrath and that will bring judgment upon our land.

Many sin most grievously by the swearing of deceitful oaths, be it by solemnly affirming a lie to be the truth or, when calling upon God's great and holy name, obligating themselves to things that they cannot truly adhere to in conformity to their promise and oath. As to the latter, there are very many in our day who most grievously sin in this regard, for all official positions and political appointments are entered into by way of public and solemn oaths.

How many there are who have sworn false and deceitful oaths, and thereby most dreadfully have slandered and taken God's name in vain! How many there are who make light of such oaths when they accept political appointments, and even mock with them! All that matters to them is that they have customarily sworn such oaths, but thereafter they have had very little or no regard for what they swore. In many ways, they neglect to do what they have so solemnly promised and sworn before God. They swear oaths either for temporal gain or advantage, because of the fear of man, or because of ignorance and carelessness.

All of you who hold political office and have obligated yourselves to this by the public swearing of oaths have temporally and eternally submitted and surrendered yourselves to God's curse and severe punishment if, in all things, you do not live up to what you have sworn. You need to consider seriously that God is a holy and just God who will not permit Himself to be mocked by you.

Also among us are those who sin grievously by not swearing oaths as they ought. How many are guilty here also! How is the swearing of sacred oaths often done? Is it not often true that one does so flippantly, irreverently, casually, and void of the fear of God? Does one first carefully, truly, and in the fear of God consider all the particulars and details of the matters concerning which he swears oaths?

I ask all who, upon accepting a political office, have solemnly sworn by the holy name of the Lord to answer the following questions before the Lord God: before you swore, did you have a right knowledge of all the matters to which you obligated yourself by this solemn oath? Were you cognizant of every paragraph and word that you would affirm by your oath? Did you research these matters ahead of time with utmost diligence? Were you convinced that only with the Lord's help would you be able to affirm and fulfill all that to which you solemnly obligated yourself? Did you make a heartfelt resolution and commitment to do so in the strength of the Lord, doing so faithfully and literally (and thus word by word), and to not be detracted by either prosperity or adversity? Since that time, have you, in all the transactions of your service, always remained focused upon the form or articles of your oath? Have you faithfully conducted yourself without deviating from this in the very least or for any reason whatsoever?

Examine yourselves and answer before the Lord how matters are with you, for if anything is lacking with you, you have sworn your oath deceitfully and falsely, and you are therefore supremely guilty before a holy and just God.

Many sin grievously who are accustomed to swearing oaths when there is no need for them, and thereby slander and use in vain the lofty name of God by their frivolous oaths. However truthful a matter may be, we may neither affirm nor deny it except by a simple "yes" or "no," and there should be no swearing of oaths whatsoever.

Finally, all such sinners are supremely guilty before God who are accustomed to swear by creatures or by any other objects, such as by their souls, by their lives, or by their salvation. Whenever such persons swear wicked oaths, they are committing a most dreadful sin against the most high God, for as we have already shown, they rob Him of His honor by whose holy name one may swear only in a God-fearing manner.

Oh, that each of us would thoroughly examine himself and thereby come to know our sins and abominations! You need to know and believe that God will by no means hold you guiltless. However long ago it may be that you committed your sins, and though you have forgotten them, the Lord God has not forgotten them, but there shall come a time when you will be summoned before His lofty and dreadful judgment seat. In Zechariah 5:4, we observe how God's consuming curse remains upon the house of a perjurer, for there we read, "I will bring it forth, saith the LORD of hosts, and it shall enter into the house of the thief, and into the house of him that sweareth falsely by my name: and it shall remain in the midst of his house, and shall consume it with the timber thereof and the stones thereof."

At that time, God shall thoroughly confront you with all these sins and will eternally punish you for them. His holiness will not tolerate your sins to remain unpunished. There is but one way in which you can escape the Lord's just punishments and wrath and be saved eternally. Without any further delay and with true sorrow and contrition regarding your sins, you must fully repent of them before the Lord, and by true faith, you must go to Christ in order to be fully washed and purified from all your sins. In Him, there surely is sufficient righteousness and strength.

To that end, He offers you His Spirit and His blood unto your justification and sanctification, admonishing you that if you persist in postponing and neglecting to embrace them by a true faith and to wholly enter into covenant with Him, you will most surely die in your sins and you will perish eternally. Oh, people, accept this offer of God's grace in Christ without any further delay! Permit yourselves to be justified and to be saved from all your sins in the blood of Christ, and thus be reconciled with God. It is still the accepted time for you, for soon time shall be no more.

To you who are the covenant people of the Lord and who are believers in Christ Jesus, may such grievous and abominable sins of which we have spoken never be found with you! You swore an oath to Him when you entered into covenant with the Lord and when you first opened your hearts unto Christ. You indeed swore this oath in all the truth and uprightness of your soul. You did not swear "falsely in making a covenant" (Hos. 10:4).

Oh, that God's children would conduct themselves as David, the beloved favorite of the Lord, who said, "I have sworn, and I will perform it, that I will keep thy righteous judgments" (Ps. 119:106). Oh, that, according to the oath they have sworn and their heartfelt acquiescence in the covenant, they may also continually abide in Christ Jesus as much as they have received Him, and that through Him, they would permit themselves increasingly to be led to God, so that, in Christ, they might serve and glorify Him! May the Lord, who Himself by an oath affirmed His holy covenant at such a great price, grant that, by His abiding grace, His people would walk faithfully in His ways and precepts. Amen.

The Fourth Commandment, Requiring the Keeping of the Sabbath

Remember the sabbath day, to keep it holy. Six days shalt thou labour, and do all thy work: but the seventh day is the sabbath of the LORD thy God: in it thou shalt not do any work, thou, nor thy son, nor thy daughter, thy manservant, nor thy maidservant, nor thy cattle, nor thy stranger that is within thy gates: for in six days the LORD made heaven and earth, the sea, and all that in them is, and rested the seventh day wherefore the LORD blessed the sabbath day, and hallowed it.

—EXODUS 20:8–11

Question 103: What doth God require in the fourth commandment?

Answer: First, that the ministry of the gospel and the schools be maintained; and that I, especially on the Sabbath, that is, on the day of rest, diligently frequent the church of God to hear His word, to use the sacraments, publicly to call upon the Lord, and contribute to the relief of the poor, as becomes a Christian. Secondly, that all the days of my life I cease from my evil works, and yield myself to the Lord, to work by His Holy Spirit in me; and thus begin in this life the eternal Sabbath.

Thus far, we have explained and expounded the first commandments of the law in which God prescribes how we are to serve and fear Him inwardly and by the Spirit, in conformity to His majestic and holy nature. We now proceed to consider the fourth commandment of the law, which prescribes how we must serve the Lord formally and publicly in the assembly of His saints in conformity to the manner of worship that He has ordained. In this commandment, the Lord summons us to "remember the sabbath day, to keep it holy," setting it apart from the six work days as a day for divine worship. This means that we and our houses must cease from all labor and are obligated to be exclusively engaged in the Lord's holy service, for He declares, "Six days shalt thou labour, and do all thy work: but the seventh day is the sabbath of the LORD thy God: in it thou shalt not do any work."

Since this illustrious commandment of the Lord is so exceedingly and dreadfully despised in our days, even among us, we shall expound it for you with all brevity. May the Lord grant the necessary grace of the Holy Spirit to use our words to impact hearts so that they might be efficaciously persuaded of the weightiness and divinity of His commandment. Then the result will be that we hold this commandment highly in our esteem, as all the other commandments, so that there is not the least doubt regarding its immutability and everlasting moral character. Indeed, even among us, the common and present opposition to this commandment of the Lord and its dreadful transgression have provoked the Lord to wrath and anger toward us. Oh, that we truly would acknowledge this and take it to heart!

We shall therefore proceed:

1. to give a word-for-word exposition of this commandment of the Lord as it occurs in His holy law; and

2. to consider in some detail the instructor's exposition of this commandment.

As to the exegesis of the language of this commandment, we shall address:

1. the wording and content of this commandment; and

2. the compelling argument for its observance, whereby the Lord seeks to impress this commandment upon our hearts.

Regarding the content of this commandment, the Lord briefly articulates it by saying, "Remember the sabbath day, to keep it holy," then proceeds to unpack what He means by this. Take note that the Lord God here speaks of a Sabbath *day*, commanding us to remember this day for the express purpose of *sanctifying* it.

This *Sabbath day*, concerning which the Lord has issued a command to us, must be understood as referring to a specific day of comprehensive rest that is to be set apart from the six work days of the week. It is to be set apart as a Sabbath day, or a day of rest, upon which we fully and religiously must cease from all daily labor and engagement in our daily profession so that we exclusively are able to occupy ourselves with public and private worship. All of this is clearly comprehended in the essential meaning of the words *Sabbath day* or *day of rest*.

It therefore must be a day of Sabbath rest, a day of rest that is both holy and religious in nature, for a mere resting and being inactive as such is not what is pleasing to the Lord. The sole reason why He commands us to rest and to refrain from all daily labor is so that such rest will be a suitable and essential means to engage ourselves in religious activity that requires such rest and cessation of labor—activity one could not engage in apart from such rest. Men are unable simultaneously to do two things, and thus they are unable at the same time to fulfill their religious obligations and be engaged in their daily vocations. It is therefore the Lord's will that one day out of every week be set apart for public and private worship. Such a day of worship must necessarily then be a Sabbath day or a day of rest on which we must refrain from being engaged in our daily calling and on which we must cease from all labor. Consequently, this rest is also referred to as "the rest of the holy sabbath unto the LORD" (Ex. 16:23).

There are two primary reasons why the Lord has so compellingly prescribed the observance of such a religious Sabbath or day of rest in His holy law: the first pertains to God and the second pertains to us.

The Lord has done so:

1. Pertaining to Himself, for being a God of order, it is His will that we should set apart a specific day each week for His holy service, so that we would exclusively devote ourselves to Him by setting aside all other labor and activity. Even the blind heathen have readily and easily recognized how entirely appropriate it is to do this, doing so as a result of the glimmer of light yielded by natural reason which is still present in the human soul after the fall. The heathen, too, had their set times of public and private worship, during which they would devote themselves to the service and worship of their gods—a practice they still engage in. Therefore, they who are of the opinion that no moral imprints of the fourth commandment are to be found in the soul of man are most certainly misleading themselves and others.

2. For the benefit of man, doing so on the one hand for our spiritual benefit and on the other for our physical benefit and advantage.

The Sabbath is instituted for our spiritual benefit so that, by means of those religious duties and the use of the means of grace for which the Sabbath has been instituted, our faith and godliness would be all the more advanced and our souls would be strengthened by the ingestion of spiritual food. All God's children know by experience how extraordinary are the benefits that the religious observance of the Lord's Day yields to their souls by the grace of God.

The Sabbath or day of rest also benefits us physically, for it is the Lord's will that after six days of labor, there must be a day of rest for man and beast, so that they, being worn out from their labors, may be refreshed and strengthened. Therefore, by instituting the Sabbath day, the Lord provided for our physical and spiritual well-being, and He is thus worthy of being thanked and praised through Christ Jesus.

We will now consider what God's holy commandment is regarding this day. He sets this before us in general terms, saying, "Remember the sabbath day, to keep it holy." The Lord here commands us to keep the Sabbath day holy; that is, to sanctify[1] the Sabbath day. When the verb *to sanctify* or *to consecrate* is used in a divine command to us regarding common things, it means that one takes a common object and sets it apart for holy and religious purposes in order that one would thereby serve the Lord.

In God's Word, the verb to sanctify is used frequently with such a connotation. In this sense, the sanctifying of the Sabbath means that one sets apart the seventh day from the other six days of the week to be used for holy purposes and holy practices, so that the Lord would be served in an extraordinary manner in accord with His Word. Not only is this to be achieved by public worship, but also by private worship, and by ceasing and desisting from all daily activities and labor. It is the Lord's will for all men on that day (whether small or great, young or old) that they gather for public worship—as we shall soon learn from the instructor.

This is indeed expressly commanded, for we read in Leviticus 23:3, "Six days shall work be done: but the seventh day is the sabbath of rest, an holy convocation; ye shall do no work therein: it is the sabbath of the LORD in all your dwellings." Oh, that the Lord would but give us ears to hear His voice, for throughout the Old Testament era, the godly always sanctified the Lord's Sabbath in such a religious manner. Not only did they and their entire houses rest from their daily labor, but they also assembled themselves for public worship in the house of God. As stipulated by the law, the number of sacrifices would then be doubled, God's Word would be read and preached, psalms would be sung to the Lord's glory, and one would delight himself in the Lord and in His

---

1. The Dutch *Statenvertaling* uses the verb "to sanctify." The Dutch rendering of the opening sentence of the fourth commandment therefore reads as follows: "Remember the Sabbath day to *sanctify* it."

holy service. The Holy Scriptures clearly teach us that this day would be thus consecrated unto the Lord.

In like manner, the seventh day must presently be sanctified by us in accordance with God's express command, and thus must be set apart for God's service. On this day, we must seek and serve the Lord our God, not only outwardly, by engaging in the duties and exercises of both public and private worship, but also inwardly, by a believing and spiritual worship with the heart, without which all our external religious exercises are but an abomination in the holy eyes of the Lord. "God is a Spirit: and they that worship him must worship him in spirit and in truth" (John 4:24).

In this commandment, the Lord most solemnly and expressly commands us to remember the Sabbath day to keep it holy. Regarding matters of worship, the words *to remember* mean "to observe, to consider, to maintain." Solomon exhorts the youth accordingly, saying, "Remember now thy Creator in the days of thy youth, while the evil days come not, nor the years draw nigh, when thou shalt say, I have no pleasure in them" (Eccl. 12:1). He is saying, "Engage yourselves in serving your creator in your youth, and see to it that you love, fear, and obey Him." Therefore, this commandment of the Lord to remember the Sabbath day simply means that we are to observe this day of rest by painstakingly sanctifying and keeping it. Under no circumstances are we either to neglect or fail to do so in any form whatsoever, lest we be guilty of grievous disobedience toward the Lord and of the willful transgression of His holy commandment, and thus provoke Him to wrath.

We have hereby given you a brief synopsis of the true content of this commandment of the Lord our God. The Lord then proceeds to expand the meaning of this commandment by saying, "Six days shalt thou labour, and do all thy work: but the seventh day is the sabbath of the LORD thy God: in it thou shalt not do any work."

The Lord here commands us to labor six days. We need to recognize that it is the Lord's wise provision and ordinance that "in the sweat of thy face shalt thou eat bread, till thou return unto the ground" (Gen. 3:19). Therefore, by means of the labor of our hands, or by being engaged in an honest profession, we receive from the Lord what we need for the daily sustenance of our lives. The Lord abhors all laziness and slothfulness, and there is therefore nothing more vile, harmful, and despicable than laziness. He who indulges in it is an utterly useless and unfit individual, who will be completely vulnerable to the snares of the devil. It is therefore God's will that we should all be engaged in an honest temporal profession or that we practice a specific craft. Thereby, everyone will always be engaged with utmost faithfulness and diligence, so that we, with God's help and blessing, will thereby maintain our families in an honorable manner and also have means to support the poor and needy.

This is God's express command, and whether he be young or old, poor or rich, great or small, whoever deviates from His command by indulging himself in laziness sins greatly and in manifold ways against the Lord. God forbids it in this commandment. Consider what God stipulates here regarding the labor related either to our profession or our craft. He commands us to be engaged in our work for a period of six consecutive days, for He commands and permits us to "labour, and do all [our] work" for such a length of time. Please note that the commandment speaks of *our* work; that is, the work and profession to which God has appointed us and to which He has called us in His wise providence. The Lord therefore expressly forbids that any man enter into the profession or calling of another man, and instead prescribes that one must do his own work and pursue his own divine calling. Thereby, no one person inhibits the other in his work or calling, and so the manifestation of bitter conflict, hatred, and hostility toward one another is prevented.

Oh, that this commandment of the Lord were truly bound upon our hearts, for it is indeed the solemn admonition of the holy apostle, saying, "Brethren, let every man, wherein he is called, therein abide with God" (1 Cor. 7:24). It is thus the Lord's will and commandment that we all labor and do our work on six consecutive days, doing so without interruption in all faithfulness and with all diligence.

Please note that not only may we labor six days each week, but we must do so. God's ordinance is that we labor six days, and this is to be followed by a day of rest. It is very evident that we are not to observe more days of rest during a given week than the day of rest that follows six days of labor. Therefore, all other so-called feast days and religious holidays that have been instituted by men for good and sound reasons must be noted as being ordinary work days upon which we, after our public and private worship, may engage in our work as we do on other days. The Lord does not command us to observe more than one day of rest each week, saying, "The seventh day is the sabbath of the LORD thy God: in it thou shalt not do any work."

Having considered that we must labor six days and do all our work, let us now consider what is said about the *seventh day*. In His holy law, the Lord commands the following: "But the seventh day is the sabbath of the LORD thy God:

in it thou shalt not do any work." Here the Lord prescribes which day must be a holy Sabbath or day of rest, namely, every seventh day that follows six days of labor. The Lord commands that, upon having spent six consecutive days laboring or pursuing our calling, we sanctify the seventh day and set it apart as a Sabbath or a day of rest. No matter where we begin, all is well if, after six work days, we observe the seventh day as a Sabbath or day of rest—that is, if all do so simultaneously in order to worship the Lord corporately and to rest from our labor.

The wording of this commandment is very simple and straightforward, and must therefore be interpreted by us as such, namely, that one must labor six days, and that the subsequent seventh day is the Lord's Sabbath, regarding which the Lord commands that "in it thou shalt not do any work." Here the Lord expressly forbids us to do any work or to engage in any labor pertaining to our calling on the seventh day, which is the Lord's Sabbath. Instead, we are to do all our work during the six preceding days, so that nothing remains to be done on the Sabbath. We must then rest completely from all daily labor and employment, and occupy ourselves exclusively with activities pertaining to public and private worship. We are to do so the entire day, from the moment it begins until it ends, for God's commandment states expressly "in it thou shalt not do any work."

However, in order to understand this correctly, we must say that there are the following exceptions:

1. All labor that belongs to the performance of religious duties.

2. All work of absolute and unavoidable necessity that by no means may or can be postponed—a matter that all godly souls must earnestly consider before the Lord and in their consciences.

3. All labor of mercy and of Christian charity, be it in relation to ourselves or to others, and also in relation to our animals or cattle, which must necessarily be watched over and cared for by us.

Regarding this matter, we must always keep in mind that "the sabbath was made for man, and not man for the Sabbath" (Mark 2:27). However, except for these three forms of labor, we are not to do any work on the Sabbath. This commandment of the Lord pertains:

1. to us as heads of our families;

2. to our families, and specifically our sons and our daughters, as well as our male and female servants;

3. to our cattle, for the Lord also includes cattle in His care by seeing to it that, together with us, they also rest to secure necessary refreshment on the Sabbath day, and also because cattle cannot engage in their normal work apart from us; and

4. to the strangers that are within our gates and who dwell among us in order to work for us.

Thus, the Lord here prescribes comprehensive religious rest upon the seventh day to us, to our entire families, and to whoever are our dependents, for it is His will that all work and labor shall cease among men and their beasts.

We will now briefly consider the compelling argument for the keeping of this commandment. The Lord wishes to further impress His commandment upon our hearts, saying, "For in six days the LORD made heaven and earth, the sea, and all that in them is, and rested the seventh day." Moses teaches, in very clear language, that God completed the entire work of creation in six days and blessed the seventh day with a special blessing, having sanctified and set it apart for His service. He writes: "And on the seventh day God ended his work which he had made; and he rested on the seventh day from all his work which he had made. And God blessed the seventh day, and sanctified it: because that in it he had rested from all his work which God created and made" (Gen. 2:2–3). This proves, beyond the shadow of a doubt for all whose hearts have not been negatively predisposed with the obscure fog of carnal wisdom, that the seventh-day Sabbath or day of rest was instituted by God in Paradise immediately after the creation of the world to be an immutable and eternally binding institution that must be observed by man as long as the world stands.

After completing His creation on the sixth day, the Lord rested on the seventh day, and we are therefore directed in His law to this institution of the Sabbath in Paradise. The Lord gives us three reasons why we are obligated to observe the seventh-day Sabbath in the obedience of faith.

The first reason for our obligation is that the Lord Himself exemplified this for us, completing the work of creating heaven and earth in six days, then resting from His labor on the seventh day by ceasing to bring forth any new creatures. The Lord's will is that we "be…therefore followers of God, as dear children" (Eph. 5:1), and that we should therefore also work six days and rest upon the seventh day. If someone were to posit that he cannot comprehend why Adam in Paradise would have rested from his labor on the seventh day if he had remained in a state of perfect holiness, he ought to consider if it is any more comprehensible that the Lord God Himself rested from His labors upon the seventh day. If God did so, why would Adam, His servant, not have been able to emulate Him in doing so in obedience to the command of God, his king and creator?

The second reason why we are obligated to keep the Sabbath on every seventh day is that God has blessed this day. That blessing consists in God's pronouncement of His blessing upon this day, having promised that He would prosper and bless His people in a special way according to soul and body. This day and its conscientious observance therefore always yield a special blessing to them, according to God's gracious good pleasure. Oh, that all who fear God in truth would continue to esteem the Sabbath day by virtue of its sacred and good institution, and observe it accordingly! It is indeed a blessed day that the Lord has blessed for us. Let God's children testify, to the honor and praise of the Lord, that they have received many a blessing for their souls from the Lord upon the Sabbath day. Oh, that they would not forget the mercies of the Lord, but that these mercies would continually be remembered and praised in the congregation of the saints, so that they would all know that "his mercy endureth for ever" (Psalm 136)!

The third and final reason for our obligation to keep the Sabbath day is not only because the Lord blessed this day, but He also sanctified it; that is, He set it apart from the other six days of the week for His holy service and for us to practice a holy rest. Who among us who desires to fear the Lord would dare to desecrate the day that the Lord has sanctified? Oh, that we would have a right knowledge of our sins in this regard, for whoever desecrates the day of the Lord also desecrates the name of the Lord—the name of Him who blessed and sanctified this day.

All we have said makes it abundantly clear how compelling is this added motivation whereby we are obligated to obey the Lord's command.

Presently, all that remains for us to consider is what the instructor has written regarding this commandment, and thereby we shall conclude this sermon. The instructor also teaches that God has solemnly prescribed the following matters and duties in the fourth commandment, teaching us, "First, that the ministry of the gospel and the schools be maintained; and that I, especially on the Sabbath, that is, on the day of rest, diligently frequent the church of God to hear His word, to use the sacraments, publicly to call upon the Lord, and contribute to the relief of the poor, as becomes a Christian."

The instructor divides the contents of this commandment into two main headings: the first pertains to the outward and the second pertains to the internal and spiritual observance of the day upon which the Lord has commanded us to rest.

Regarding the first, the instructor addresses two matters that pertain to the outward observance of the Sabbath day:

1. The general observance of this day
2. The special observance of this day

According to the instructor, it belongs to the general observance of this day "that the ministry of the gospel and the schools be maintained." Since God's great objective in instituting the Sabbath was, as we have seen, that it would be a day of public and private worship, a day on which the congregation must assemble to hear the proclamation of God's Word, it is self-evident that, in order to achieve this objective, there must necessarily be a faithful maintenance of the public ministry of the gospel. Therefore, all that is in conformity to the Lord's command also belongs to public worship. This belongs also to the office of the ministry, as God has instituted and prescribed in His Holy Word. Moreover, this commandment also pertains to both the high schools and the elementary schools. The purpose of the schools is not only to teach our youth reading and writing, but also to teach them, from their early childhood and forward in their lives, the foundational truths of true religion, thereby preparing them to be hearers of God's Word. The purpose of our schools further extends to the preparing of those who desire to enter the office of the ministry and to equip men for office-bearing in the church.

The instructor then proceeds to consider what specifically belongs to the keeping of the Sabbath: "that I, especially on the Sabbath, that is, on the day of rest, diligently frequent the Church of God to hear His word, to use the sacraments, publicly to call upon the Lord, and contribute to the relief of the poor, as becomes a Christian." By virtue of God's institution, the instructor also deems the day of the Lord to be a Sabbath day or day of rest, on which we must cease from all our labor. He teaches that it is God's will that we "diligently frequent the church of God" in order to engage in four specific activities: "to hear His word, to use the sacraments, publicly to call upon the Lord, and contribute to the relief of the poor, as becomes a Christian."

Therefore, when the congregation assembles in the Lord's house for public worship, she does so to engage in these four activities. The godly diligently do this without ever being desirous to neglect a worship service. However, the sinful men of this world shamefully despise the Sabbath day and public worship, and do not delight themselves in God's holy service. Sadly, we know this to be true in this locality and in this congregation. Oh, that God would graciously grant that men would come to the acknowledgment of their sins!

This represents the instructor's teaching regarding the outward keeping of the Sabbath day. He then proceeds to address all that pertains to the inward or spiritual keeping of the Sabbath, saying, "that all the days of my life I cease from my evil works, and yield myself to the Lord, to work by His Holy Spirit in me; and thus begin in this life the eternal Sabbath."

By no means does it suffice that we set aside one day of the week for the Lord and His holy service, and that we leave it there, as though this were sufficient. Such is the conduct of hypocrites and spiritual charlatans, who outwardly and religiously keep the Sabbath, but during the other six days of the week, live entirely in sin, without engaging themselves in any regular religious exercises and without exhibiting the true fear of the Lord. However, God hates such a keeping of the Sabbath, and it is an abomination to Him.

He who wishes to keep the Sabbath in an upright and godly manner not only must cease from all work and labor on the seventh day and worship God outwardly, but he also, by God's grace, must "all the days of [his] life…cease from [his] evil works." The instructor does not understand evil works as referring merely to all blatant and offensive sins among men, but also as referring indiscriminately to all works of the flesh; that is, all that arises from within ourselves that is devoid of the power and grace of the Holy Spirit.

Though we may truly have been converted unto God, we are nevertheless incapable of doing any good work in and of ourselves, and we therefore continually need God's help and the grace of the Holy Spirit to bring forth any good thoughts, deeds, efforts, and activities. The Holy Scriptures abound with such teaching, and the instructor therefore also teaches us that we must "yield [ourselves] to the Lord, to work by His Holy Spirit in [us]: and thus begin in this life the eternal Sabbath." This occurs when, by way of prevenient grace, we continually acknowledge before the Lord our sinfulness and impotence in all things, causing us not only to be truly humble and contrite before Him, but also to turn to Him for the pardon of our sins in the holy blood of Christ. We thus continually yield to the operation of the Holy Spirit and always conduct ourselves before Him as being wretched in ourselves. Not only do we then wait with humble submission in all things upon the Lord so that His Spirit may without ceasing work in us all that is pleasing to Him, but we also acknowledge that we are incapable of any good and that all our strength is to be found in the Lord alone, who is the fountain of our life.

Oh, that the Lord would truly teach both us and all His people this lesson, for "even the holiest men, while in this life, have only a small beginning of this." In this way, we must begin the eternal Sabbath in this life. This eternal Sabbath will exclusively consist not only in a complete cessation of all sin and of all works of the flesh, but also in the complete enjoyment of the Lord and His Spirit, who eternally will fill us, govern us, and work in us.

Here you have the genuine, simple, and essential exposition of the fourth commandment. May the Lord grant that, with us, you all would believe it. It is my wish that they who disagree with this doctrine would be brought to repentance by God through the Spirit of truth, so that their darkened understandings would be illuminated and sanctified. Without such divine intervention, I am certain that they will never truly understand the truth.

May the Lord assist us by His Holy Spirit, powerfully blessing our words to the glory of His holy Name and to the salvation of our souls. Amen.

The Fifth Commandment, Requiring the Honoring of Father and Mother

Honour thy father and thy mother: that thy days may be long upon the land which the LORD thy God giveth thee.

—EXODUS 20:12

Question 104: What doth God require in the fifth commandment?

Answer: That I show all honor, love and fidelity, to my father and mother and all in authority over me, and submit myself to their good instruction and correction, with due obedience; and also patiently bear with their weaknesses and infirmities, since it pleases God to govern us by their hand.

Thus far, we have occupied ourselves with the exposition of the first table of the law, which requires that we love God as our majestic creator and supreme king with a love that is holy, pure, and spiritual. We now proceed to consider the second table of the law, in which six specific commandments are set before us. These commandments require of us that we love our neighbor as ourselves; that is, we must love God above all, and we must also sincerely love and show affection toward our neighbor, for there is a most intimate and spiritual connection between love for God and love for our neighbor. These two always will be intertwined, and He who believes that the one can exist without the other greatly deceives himself.

As there are among our neighbors, by virtue of family ties or otherwise, some with whom we have a special and close relationship, a more intimate relationship than with others, we are obliged to love and honor them above all other people. We must do so as God commands and prescribes in this fifth commandment, the first commandment of the second table of the law, in which God declares to us, "Honour thy father and thy mother: that thy days may be long upon the land which the LORD thy God giveth thee." This commandment has far-reaching ramifications and encompasses many and weighty duties. With God's gracious blessing and assistance, we shall now expound this in greater detail, considering:

1. the content of the commandment itself; and
2. the incentive or promise whereby the Lord binds this commandment upon our hearts.

As to the content of this commandment, the Lord sets this before us in a few words, saying, "Honor thy father and thy mother." This speaks to us of:

1. the objects of our duty: our fathers and our mothers; and
2. the duty itself that we must fulfill toward them, consisting in rendering them honor.

As to the objects of our duty—our fathers and our mothers—we must understand them as having reference to:

First, our natural fathers and mothers, by whom, in God's providence, we have been conceived and born. They brought us into the world and raised us with love, diligence, and care. By this most intimate and extraordinary relationship, we are obligated to love and honor them, and, as long as we live, we can by no means be absolved from that obligation.

In His law, the Lord God first speaks of the father and then of the mother, thereby indicating that the man is to be preferred and esteemed above the woman, for it is according to God's command that, in all things, the man is to have the preeminence over the woman.[1] We are therefore first and foremost obligated to honor and obey our fathers. However, in so doing, we should by no means think less of our mothers, for to prevent this, God has elsewhere in His law mentioned the mother first and the father second, saying, "Ye shall fear every man his mother, and his father" (Lev. 19:3).

Are we to interpret the words "thy father and thy mother" as referring only to our actual, biological parents who gave birth to us? By no means, for the

---

1. VanderGroe is not suggesting that the man is superior to the woman. He is merely affirming that the language of the fourth commandment is consistent with the creation order expressed in the following passages: "For the man is not of the woman; but the woman of the man. Neither was the man created for the woman; but the woman for the man" (1 Cor. 11:8-9); "For Adam was first formed, then Eve" (1 Tim 2:13).

words "thy father and thy mother" are very broad in their meaning, and therefore, according to the instructor, they also have reference to:

Second, "all in authority over me." Thus, in addition to our actual fathers and mothers, there are others whom God also has appointed to be our fathers and our mothers, and we are therefore obligated to render them all honor and love as well. They are:

1. Relatives by way of marriage. God also has appointed our fathers-in-law and mothers-in-law as our fathers and mothers. Moreover this applies to stepfathers and stepmothers, grandfathers and grandmothers, great-grandfathers and great-grandmothers.

2. Some in the civil realm. God has appointed as our fathers and our mothers:

a. Our guardians, who, either in the absence of our parents or at their direction, have been lawfully appointed to fulfill the role of our parents. We read regarding the Persian Queen Esther that she, being an orphan, had been adopted by her cousin Mordecai, and she therefore honored him as her father (Esth. 2:7).

b. Our masters, in whose service we are voluntarily employed. For instance, as their master, the servants of Naaman addressed him as *father* (2 Kings 5:13).

c. Lawful governments of the highest and lowest ranks, which God has appointed to be our fathers and mothers to govern and protect us. Deborah, who judged Israel, was referred to as a mother in Israel (Judg. 5:7), and we read regarding King Eliakim that he was a father to the house of Judah and the inhabitants of Jerusalem (Isa. 22:21).

d. Our teachers in elementary and secondary schools, as well as in institutions of higher learning. Thus, the young man Elisha referred to Elijah, his teacher, as father (2 Kings 2:12), and, in antiquity, the pupils of prophets were commonly referred to as their sons.

3. All old, gray, and aged individuals within or outside of our family circle, who, by virtue of their wisdom and experience, are to us as fathers and mothers. Paul therefore admonished his son Timothy, saying, "Rebuke not an elder, but intreat him as a father...and the elder women as mothers" (1 Tim. 5:1–2).

4. In the ecclesiastical realm, namely, the pastors and teachers who have oversight over the congregation, whom we must honor, love, and obey as fathers. Paul therefore refers to ministers as fathers, saying, "For though ye have ten thousand instructors in Christ, yet have ye not many fathers: for in Christ

Jesus I have begotten you through the gospel" (1 Cor. 4:15). Such ministers are thus our spiritual fathers and must therefore be greatly loved and esteemed by us, for either they have begotten us and won our hearts for Christ or, by their ministry, they have built us up and established us in the faith. Paul writes to believers accordingly, "My little children, of whom I travail in birth again until Christ be formed in you" (Gal. 4:19).

All these specific types of individuals are set before us in the Holy Scriptures as our fathers and mothers, and this communicates two things:

First, whatever their office or appointment is, they are to conduct themselves as fathers and mothers would conduct themselves toward their children; that is, they must love, protect, govern, and help them, always pursuing that which is best for both soul and body.

Second, we must likewise honor, love, fear, and obey them as much as we do our fathers and mothers. When we consider the thrust of the word *honor* as it is used here by the Lord in His law, thereby delineating our duty toward our parents and all who have authority over us, we perceive that this word means the rendering of due and appropriate honor. We therefore must honor such fathers and mothers in a manner that is worthy of the position to which God has appointed them. The Lord thus presupposes that our parents, all who have authority over us in the civil and ecclesiastical realms, and all who are over us by familial ties are worthy and deserving of our honor.

And, truly, if we consider:

1. Our actual parents, our fathers and mothers, and our obligation toward them since they gave us life and raised us, who would not acknowledge that we owe them all Christian love, honor, esteem, and obedience? The Scriptures therefore emphatically state, "Children, obey your parents in the Lord: for this is right" (Eph. 6:1).

2. All others whom God has appointed as our fathers and mothers, and our close connection with them and the benefits we receive from them, we perceive that we are also obligated to submit to them and to love and fear them by virtue of their unique relationship and status. However, time constraints will not permit us to address each of these cases individually. It would be good and profitable if we all would fully understand, having been taught by the Lord through His Word and Spirit, the familial obligations we have toward our in-laws, stepparents, and grandparents—as well as our civil obligations toward our guardians, employers, governments, teachers, and the elderly.

It would be desirable to know rightly what honor, love, obedience, and esteem we must all render each of them in accordance with God's Word. Ignorance regarding this matter is the cause of great wickedness and innumerable sins among us—sins of which everyone is guilty.

We hereby have sufficiently addressed the objects of our duty; that is, our fathers and our mothers, and all whom the Lord has appointed to be in authority over us and who are thus comprehended in the designation "thy father and thy mother."

Let us now consider our duty toward all who have been thus designated. The Lord defines our duty by the single word *honor*. In the Holy Scriptures the extent and meaning of this word is very wide and all-encompassing. When this single word honor is used in reference to the Lord God, *honoring God* means "the totality of our rational worship, both inwardly as well as outwardly." Thus, it refers to all honor that we are obligated to render to the Lord God as our supreme creator and king. Likewise, when it is used in reference to people, it expresses our total and unconditional obligation and duty toward them according to God's command.

In order to address this matter in an orderly fashion, there is no better or more suitable way than to follow our instructor. In a very efficient and straightforward manner, he explains the duties and matters comprehended in the word *honor*, saying that it is God's will in the fifth commandment "that I show all honor, love and fidelity, to my father and mother and all in authority over me, and submit myself to their good instruction and correction, with due obedience; and also patiently bear with their weaknesses and infirmities, since it pleases God to govern us by their hand."

The instructor sets before us five duties that, according to God's command, we are obliged to perform toward our parents and all who have authority over us, all of which the Lord has comprehended in the word *honor*. We shall now briefly address each of them.

Our first obligation is that we must honor our fathers and our mothers and all who have authority over us. This is according to God's Word, where this duty is solemnly prescribed.

The duty to honor our parents is bound upon us throughout the entire Word of God, and the Lord considers it to be a grievous sin to "set light by father and mother" (Ezek. 22:7).

Paul admonishes that we honor the masters whom we serve and who employ us, writing, "Let as many servants as are under the yoke count their own masters worthy of all honour, that the name of God and his doctrine be not blasphemed" (1 Tim. 4:1).

Peter admonishes that we must honor all who lawfully govern us, saying: "Fear God. Honour the king" (1 Peter 2:17c). By referring to the king, he comprehends all forms and levels of government.

The holy apostle Paul again admonishes that within the ecclesiastical realm, we must also honor our elders, pastors, and teachers, testifying, "Let the elders that rule well be counted worthy of double honour, especially they who labour in the word and doctrine" (1 Tim. 5:17).

God expressly commands that we especially honor the elderly among us, saying, "Thou shalt rise up before the hoary head, and honour the face of the old man, and fear thy God" (Lev. 19:32).

In like manner, we are to honor all others who are comprehended in the designation "thy father and thy mother."

What constitutes this honor that we must render to our parents and unto all who have authority over us? We may efficiently define this in a threefold manner. We must honor them:

1. Inwardly, or in our hearts, by esteeming them highly and by having a great deal of respect for them. We must view them as having been appointed over us by the Most High God, and we may therefore in no wise deprecate or degrade them, lest we provoke God's wrath toward us.

2. Outwardly, when we are in their presence, by conducting ourselves toward them respectfully, humbly, graciously, and obediently in all things, in no way provoking them to anger or dishonoring them. We must emulate King Solomon, who honored his mother, Bathsheba, when he caused her to be seated on a chair at his right hand and bowed down before her (1 Kings 2:19). Or we must do as Joseph did, who honored his old father when "he bowed himself with his face to the earth" (Gen. 48:12b).

3. In their absence, by never speaking disdainfully or disparagingly of them to others or by doing anything whereby their name will be slandered or despised. We must always speak of them with great respect and esteem. God has pronounced a curse upon everyone who despises his father or his mother, irrespective of whether this is done in their presence or their absence (Deut. 27:16).

This is the threefold manner, in conformity to God's commandment, in which we must honor our parents and all who are in authority over us.

The second duty we are obligated to fulfill toward our parents and all who are in authority over us, a duty implied in the word honor, is to *love* them with a holy, pure, sincere, and spiritual love. Though we are under obligation indiscriminately to love all men, we must especially love our parents and all who are in authority over us, for not only do we have the greatest obligation toward them because of the benefits we have received from them, but, according to God's will, we also have the closest relationship with them by virtue of God having subjected us to them.

Our loving disposition must be manifested first of all specifically toward our fathers and mothers and, by extension, toward all others whom God has appointed over us. We must seek to promote their temporal and spiritual well-being to the utmost of our power and seek in all things to please them and render them pleasure and enjoyment. The wise King Solomon admonishes accordingly, saying, "Thy father and thy mother shall be glad, and she that bare thee shall rejoice" (Prov. 23:25).

The obligation to love our natural parents is such an appropriate, reasonable, and necessary duty that the Holy Spirit nowhere explicitly commands us in His Word to love them, but only prescribes this by way of implication.

Our obligation to love and to cherish heartily all who govern us is abundantly evident by way of natural reason, and the Lord has forbidden us to curse, hate, and slander them, saying, "Thou shalt not revile the gods, nor curse the ruler of thy people" (Ex. 22:28).

One must also heartily love the masters whom he serves, for this is taught by the Savior, who gives the admonition that we cannot serve a master whom we hate rather than love (Matt. 6:24).

The holy apostle Paul also expressly gives admonition that we heartily love our pastors and teachers by commanding us "to know them which labour among you, and are over you in the Lord, and admonish you; and to esteem them very highly in love for their work's sake" (1 Thess. 5:12–13a). The believing Galatians demonstrated this same virtue in an extraordinary fashion toward the apostle Paul, for he testifies of this, saying, "I bear you record, that, if it had been possible, ye would have plucked out your own eyes, and have given them to me" (Gal. 4:15). In like manner, we must love indiscriminately all whom God has appointed over us.

The third duty comprehended in the word honor is, according to the instructor, that of showing complete "*fidelity*, to my father and mother and all in authority over me." This consists of three things:

1. We must faithfully engage ourselves for their eternal salvation and redemption according to the grace of God given to us, and not neglect anything that would be essential and suitable to that end and purpose. We are called to engage ourselves faithfully in regard to the salvation of all men, and therefore we must do so the more exceedingly with regard to our parents and all who are in authority over us, toward whom we have the most compelling obligation and commitment.

2. We must care for and faithfully safeguard the good name, honor, and reputation of our parents and all who are in authority over us to the utmost of our ability. Whenever the occasion arises, we are to protect and shield them against malicious individuals, and should never fail to do so.

3. We must show all fidelity to our parents and all who are in authority over us by taking to heart, to the utmost of our ability, their temporal well-being, thereby never willfully depriving them of anything nor causing them any harm or mischief by reason of our neglect.

As for our parents, the Word of God expressly testifies, "Whoso robbeth his father or his mother, and saith, It is no transgression; the same is the companion of a destroyer" (Prov. 28:24). Far be it from us to deal treacherously with our parents by robbing them of that which is theirs. On the contrary, we must sustain them with love and benevolence when, sooner or later, they become poor and needy. Paul exhorts us: "But if any widow have children or nephews, let them learn first to shew piety at home, and to requite their parents: for that is good and acceptable before God" (1 Tim. 5:4).

Regarding our governments, we are to show them all fidelity in paying our appropriate taxes to the utmost extent of our liability and not defraud them of anything, for to defraud is a vile act of theft. The Savior exhorts us, saying, "Render therefore unto Caesar the things which are Caesar's; and unto God the things that are God's" (Matt. 22:21), and Paul admonishes the same, saying, "Render therefore to all their dues: tribute to whom tribute is due; custom to whom custom; fear to whom fear; honour to whom honour" (Rom. 13:7).

We must also show all fidelity to our masters in whose service we are employed. We never may defraud them in anything, but always and in all things engage ourselves to their benefit and to their advantage, doing so to the utmost of our ability. Paul therefore admonishes all servants that they should not be "purloining, but shewing all good fidelity; that they may adorn the doctrine of God our Saviour in all things" (Titus 2:10).

No less must we show such fidelity to our pastors and elders, whom we willingly and faithfully must care for and provide with all the necessities of life. Paul expressly admonishes of this necessity: "Let him that is taught in the word communicate unto him that teacheth in all good things" (Gal. 6:6). This is applicable to all others who by God's appointment hold a place of authority over us.

The instructor posits that the fourth duty implied in the word honor is that, with due *obedience*, we must submit ourselves to the good instruction and correction of our parents and all who are in authority over us. God has commanded our parents and all who are in authority over us to instruct and govern us in a Christian manner and to punish us when we are guilty of evil conduct. It is the will of the Lord that we should be fully inclined to submit ourselves, that we render such willing obedience, and that we never resist in any way their good instruction, government, admonition, and chastisement—and, in so doing, disobey them.

Scripture admonishes us regarding our parents, "Children, obey your parents in the Lord: for this is right" (Eph. 6:1). In Proverbs 23:22, we read, "Hearken unto thy father that begat thee, and despise not thy mother when she is old." In antiquity, God commanded that rebellious and disobedient children who disregarded the admonition and chastisement of their parents be punished by death. We read: "If a man have a stubborn and rebellious son, which will not obey the voice of his father, or the voice of his mother, and that, when they have chastened him, will not hearken unto them: then shall his father and his mother lay hold on him, and bring him out unto the elders of his city, and unto the gate of his place; and they shall say unto the elders of his city, This our son is stubborn and rebellious, he will not obey our voice; he is a glutton, and a drunkard. And all the men of his city shall stone him with stones, that he die" (Deut. 21:18–21).

We also are obligated to obey our government in like manner, for the Holy Scriptures admonish us: "Let every soul be subject unto the higher powers. For there is no power but of God: the powers that be are ordained of God" (Rom. 13:1).

We must also submit ourselves to our masters in whose employment we are, for the Scriptures again admonish us, saying, "Servants, obey in all things your masters according to the flesh; not with eyeservice, as menpleasers; but in singleness of heart, fearing God" (Col. 3:22). The apostle Peter expands this further, admonishing servants to "be subject to your masters with all fear; not only to the good and gentle, but also to the froward" (1 Peter 2:18; Matt. 8:9; Titus 2:9).

No less are we obligated to render such obedience to our pastors and teachers, for Paul clearly admonishes us accordingly, saying, "Obey them that have the rule over you, and submit yourselves: for they watch for your souls, as they that must give account, that they may do it with joy, and not with grief: for that is unprofitable for you" (Heb. 13:17). Speaking generally, such is the submission and obedience to be rendered toward all whom God has appointed to have authority over us.

Finally, the instructor posits that there is a fifth duty implied in the word honor, namely, patience, for we must "also patiently bear with their weaknesses and infirmities, since it pleases God to govern us by their hand." Our parents, as well as others whom the Lord has appointed to be in authority over us, are but frail human beings. However much grace they have received and are continually receiving from the Lord, we are never to deem them as being anything more than that. Being such frail human beings, our parents and all others who are in authority over us have their negative character traits, deficiencies, weaknesses, and struggles, and they genuinely grieve over them when they receive grace from the Lord to acknowledge them. By our subordination and subjection to them, we must always exercise godly patience toward their weaknesses and deficiencies, and, with humble longsuffering and quietness, tolerate these in them and frequently pray that God would grant to them His grace. We must painstakingly refrain from hating or despising them because of their sinful deficiencies and weaknesses, and not refuse to obey them, but by God's grace, endeavor to foster a deep sense of our own deficiencies and weaknesses. This will be the best way to learn to have patience with the faults of others, but particularly with those of our parents and of all who are in authority over us.

Consider what a dreadful sin it is to despise and to mock our parents regarding their weaknesses and deficiencies. Solomon, or, rather, Agur, speaks of this, saying, "The eye that mocketh at his father, and despiseth to obey his mother, the ravens of the valley shall pick it out, and the young eagles shall eat it" (Prov.

30:17). Ham[2] was accursed of God when he mocked the weakness and nakedness of his old father Noah (Gen. 9:24).

The command to honor our fathers and mothers is thus encompassed in all that we have distinctly set before you. God demands of us that we fulfill all these holy duties most perfectly and spiritually toward our parents and to all whom He has appointed to be in authority over us, because, according to the instructor, it pleases God to govern us by their hands. Here we find the ultimate and preeminent reason why we must fulfill all these essential obligations.

We shall yet briefly consider the compelling incentive and promise contained in this commandment, by which the Lord intends to stir us up toward genuine obedience regarding it, saying, "that thy days may be long upon the land which the LORD thy God giveth thee." We are to understand "the land which the LORD thy God giveth thee" as an Old Testament reference to the land of Canaan, which God gave to His people Israel as their habitation and as a pledge of heaven for all true believers among them. However, as far as we are concerned, we are to understand this as referring to our own land, which God has given to us to be a pleasant dwelling place. All who truly fear God ought to praise and magnify His blessed name for this continually.

As we wish to expound this promise of the Lord only in reference to our own nation, given that this will suffice for us, we must consider that the Lord promises here that our days shall be extended if we, before His countenance, sincerely observe and obey His holy commandment. This simply means that besides all other blessed benefits bestowed upon His obedient people, the Lord desires, as an act of His gracious loving-kindness, to favor those who walk according to His precepts and laws here upon earth with length of days and to enable them to reach a good old age.

A long life here upon earth in God's gracious favor and mercy is a great blessing and precious benefit of the Lord—especially in contrast with an early and premature death as a manifestation of God's wrath and displeasure toward the ungodly. This promise of the Lord must be understood as such a blessing and benefit. Consider what the Holy Scriptures teach regarding this, saying, "The hoary head is a crown of glory, if it be found in the way of righteousness" (Prov. 16:31); that is, by living a righteous and godly life before the Lord. Contrast this with the short life that God hastily cuts off by reason of sin, and thus the cutting short of life is deemed to be a great evil and curse. The ungodly are

---

2. Actually it was Ham's son Canaan upon whom this curse was pronounced.

threatened with this in Psalm 55:23, for there we read that "bloody and deceitful men shall not live out half their days."

The godly always have considered a long and godly life here on earth as a great grace and blessing of God. They always have supplicated Him most earnestly for this so that they might praise His holy name here upon earth and declare His praises among the people, which they would not be able to do if dead and in the grave. When the Lord graciously lengthened the days of the godly King Hezekiah by healing him, he joyfully exclaimed: "For the grave cannot praise thee, death cannot celebrate thee: they that go down into the pit cannot hope for thy truth. The living, the living, he shall praise thee, as I do this day: the father to the children shall make known thy truth" (Isa. 38:18–19).

Such a long and godly life the Lord promises here to His obedient people as a gracious blessing and benefit, doing so in contrast to a premature and wretched death in His wrath and displeasure, whereby the Lord at times suddenly cuts off the wicked from this earth and consigns them to everlasting perdition.

This is not at all contradicted by the fact that, on the one hand, God at times suddenly removes His obedient people and children from the earth during their youth before the day of evil dawns upon them, or that, on the other hand, the Lord frequently permits the wicked to live upon earth until they reach a very old age. These instances by no means contradict this promise of the Lord, as some erroneously conclude.

Regarding the first, the Lord neither diminishes nor truncates His promise toward His obedient people. On the contrary, He grants them much more than He promised them, for in so doing, He provides them with something better by taking them to Himself in His eternal glory. This is a far greater blessing and benefit than to live a long life here on earth, however great a blessing and grace this may otherwise be.

Regarding the second, that is, when God permits the wicked to live here upon earth until they reach a great old age, this does not at all challenge the promise that the Lord here makes in His law, for, as we have seen, by His grace and in His favor to His obedient people, He promises here a long, good, and godly life. But the Lord never bestows this upon the wicked, for, however old He permits them to become, their old age proves to be only a curse, and they arrive at such an age only in His anger and wrath. The Scriptures testify of this, saying, "The sinner being an hundred years old shall be accursed" (Isa. 65:20).

Let me finish with the admonition of the psalmist, saying: "Come, ye children, hearken unto me: I will teach you the fear of the LORD. What man is he that desireth life, and loveth many days, that he may see good? Keep thy tongue from evil, and thy lips from speaking guile. Depart from evil, and do good; seek peace, and pursue it" (Ps. 34:11–14). Therefore, "Honour thy father and thy mother [and all whom God has appointed to be in authority over you]: that thy days may be long upon the land which the LORD thy God giveth thee."

To that end, may the Lord grant us His Holy Spirit, His blessing, and His grace in Christ Jesus, His beloved Son. Amen.

The Sixth Commandment,
Forbidding Murder

Thou shalt not kill.
—EXODUS 20:13

Question 105: What doth God require in the sixth commandment?

Answer: That neither in thoughts, nor words, nor gestures, much less in deeds, I dishonor, hate, wound, or kill my neighbor, by myself or by another; but that I lay aside all desire of revenge; also, that I hurt not myself, nor wilfully expose myself to any danger. Wherefore also the magistrate is armed with the sword to prevent murder.

Question 106: But this commandment seems only to speak of murder.

Answer: In forbidding murder, God teaches us that He abhors the causes thereof, such as envy, hatred, anger, and desire of revenge; and that He accounts all these as murder.

Question 107: But is it enough that we do not kill any man in the manner mentioned above?

Answer: No: for when God forbids envy, hatred, and anger, He commands us to love our neighbor as ourselves; to show patience, peace, meekness, mercy, and all kindness towards him, and prevent his hurt as much as in us lies; and that we do good, even to our enemies.

After the Lord God, the great lawgiver, who can both save and destroy, prescribes in the fifth commandment how we are to love, honor, and cherish our fathers and mothers, as well as all who are in authority over us, He proceeds in the five subsequent commandments to prescribe how we must unconditionally and uprightly honor, cherish, and love our other neighbors and how we are to conduct ourselves appropriately toward them, both inwardly in our hearts and outwardly in our entire conduct. Each of these five commandments has a specific object that must be the focus of our obligations and activities.

This sixth commandment pertains to the preservation and sustenance of human life. The seventh commandment pertains to our moral purity and the lawful procreation of the human race upon earth. The eighth commandment pertains to our temporal goods and possessions, and the necessities of life, as well as the way in which we must endeavor lawfully to secure them. The ninth commandment pertains to our good name and reputation, and how we are to promote and preserve it. The tenth or last commandment pertains to our desires and how, before and above all else, we must keep our heart.

Oh, how precious are the precepts and statutes of the Lord! Does not he whose heart the Lord truly and inwardly has renewed and sanctified have a desire to walk in them and to keep them?

We must presently consider this sixth commandment in greater detail—the commandment in which the Lord forbids us to commit murder. This commandment, though brief in words, is exceedingly broad in content. May the Lord be pleased to lead us, by spiritual illumination, into the mysteries of His law, whereby we will truly be uncovered as to who we are by that light.

To expound the contents of this commandment as briefly as possible, we cannot observe a better or more suitable order than to expound it as to:

1. the vices and sins the Lord forbids; and
2. the virtues or holy duties He prescribes.

Although the Lord articulates His commandment for us as a prohibition, all prohibitions contain and imply prescriptions that are the foundation upon which the prohibitions are grounded and from which they must be deduced by necessary consequence. You should note this regarding all the subsequent commandments.

Beginning with that which pertains to the prohibitions, it should be noted that the object of this commandment of the Lord is the life of man; that is, the temporal life of our neighbor, as well as our own. The Lord here shows His great concern for our lives, that they in no wise be degraded or destroyed. Thus, this commandment pertains not to the lives of animals, as though it is forbidden in this commandment to kill them. It is by no means forbidden, for the Lord has given to man the right and freedom to use all animals when necessary, and even to kill them—that is, as long as this is done in an appropriate and Christian manner, and as long as we always treat animals as God's creatures and are fully considerate of them.

However, the killing of animals is not the focus of this commandment. Its focus pertains only to the temporal life of man, and we must consider that life from various perspectives. Life is to be viewed as:

1. A gracious gift or benefit of God the Lord, who has given to all breath and life itself, and continues to preserve and sustain it in us by His divine power. Though we have derived our lives from our parents as secondary causes, it is God who is the primary and continually moving cause of our lives, "for in him we live, and move, and have our being" (Acts 17:28). "The LORD killeth, and maketh alive: he bringeth down to the grave, and bringeth up" (1 Sam. 2:6). Consequently, God is the sole and supreme Lord and master of our lives, whose prerogative it is to give and to issue His holy laws and commandments as they pertain to our lives, but who alone also has the right to take this life from us when it pleases Him. We therefore are in no wise permitted to take our own lives or the lives of our neighbors.

2. A very precious and priceless gift of God that is the most extraordinary possession we and our neighbors possess, and we therefore cannot relinquish it in any way but for the Lord's sake. Satan rightfully said to God, "Skin for skin, yea, all that a man hath will he give for his life" (Job 2:4), and this makes it abundantly clear that the Lord rightfully commands that we in no wise may deprive ourselves or our neighbor of life.

3. A most essential gift of God whereby He enables us, naturally and spiritually, to fulfill His purpose here on earth, so that, with both soul and body, we may magnify and glorify Him, for only "the living, the living, he shall praise thee" (Isa. 38:19a). This again confirms that God has every right, by His holy law, to care for our lives and to forbid that we rob ourselves or others of it. Consequently, we may not in the least contribute to the taking of life, either directly or indirectly, but we must highly esteem and treasure our own lives and that of our neighbor as a most precious commodity, and therefore must preserve and protect life at all costs.

Let us now consider the Lord's prohibition in greater detail. The Lord forbids that we commit murder. To commit murder is to rob either ourselves or someone else of life, irrespective of the manner in which this may be achieved. To understand this correctly, we must know that there are two ways in which one's life may be taken, for there is both a righteous and an unrighteous taking of life. The righteous taking of a person's life is legitimate and by no means is prohibited here by God, for such an act can be good and necessary. We conveniently may reduce this righteous taking of life to four specific categories.

The taking of a person's life is both righteous and permitted:

1. When we do so upon God's express command, as the Lord commanded Abraham, who, upon God's command, would have sacrificed and killed his only son Isaac.

2. When, of necessity and in order to protect either our lives or our belongings, we kill someone who violently seeks to rob us of one or the other. In former days, the Lord granted the children of Israel complete freedom to kill a thief who was caught in the act of stealing without permitting the avenger of blood to deem the one who committed this deed to be guilty of shedding innocent blood (Ex. 22:2).

3. When judges or government agencies execute guilty criminals, "for [they bear] not the sword in vain: for [they are] the minister[s] of God,…revenger[s] to execute wrath upon him that doeth evil" (Rom. 13:4). Furthermore, God pronounces a curse upon judges who fail to punish the guilty with death, saying, "Cursed be he that keepeth back his sword from blood" (Jer. 48:10b).

4. When one kills his public enemies in necessary and righteous wars that are waged for the protection of the nation or its people, liberty, freedom of religion, for not only does God in His Word expressly command us to do so, but even natural reason teaches its common necessity.

Having given these examples of the lawful taking of life, there is yet another instance of which one cannot say that it is lawful, and yet is of such a nature that God the Lord does not expressly forbid it in the sixth commandment. This is the instance of causing an innocent or accidental death when someone robs either himself or his neighbor of life by means of an unanticipated accident without having had the least inclination in his heart to commit such an act. Such is the case when a lumberjack, cutting down trees in the forest, accidentally kills a passing man by the head of his axe flying from its handle. This would be considered an accidental death, and for such manslayers, the Lord ordained cities of refuge appointed throughout the land of Israel so that the manslayer could take refuge there and be safe from being prosecuted by the avenger of blood.

Having considered what forms of putting men to death are not forbidden by the Lord, we must now proceed to consider that which the Lord forbids in this commandment, and we shall fully follow the instructor in this as he expounds this commandment in a manner that is very thorough and straightforward. He teaches in Question 105 that God requires in this commandment that "neither in thoughts, nor words, nor gestures, much less in deeds, I dishonor, hate, wound, or kill my neighbor, by myself or by another."

Herewith the instructor addresses the killing:

1. of our neighbor; and

2. of ourselves.

According to the instructor, the killing or murdering of our neighbor occurs in a fourfold manner and is committed by dishonoring, hating, or wounding him, or by the actual deed of robbing him of his life by killing him. We shall briefly address each of these individually.

The instructor posits that we kill our neighbor by:

1. *Dishonoring* him. This transpires when we seek, deliberately and in any of a variety of ways, to deprive our neighbor of his good name or honor. We dishonor him when we deride and malign him, seeking to render him despicable to others. We do so when we accuse him in a perverted and deceitful manner of something that is vile, shameful, and ungodly. Whoever is guilty of this is considered as essentially having killed and robbed his neighbor of life.

On the one hand, this commandment is given so that a man's honor and good name are recognized as being even better than life. David complains of the sin of this commandment, saying, "As with a sword in my bones, mine enemies reproach me" (Ps. 42:10). On the other hand, this commandment is so given because the dishonoring, insulting, and maligning of one's neighbor is frequently the root cause of murder, resulting in the actual commission of the deed. A grievous and intense war erupted between David and Hanun, the king of the Ammonites, because Hanun greatly dishonored, insulted, and maligned David's servants (2 Sam. 10:4).

This prompted the Savior to broaden the extent of the commandment "Thou shalt not kill" to include in its application the dishonoring and maligning of one's neighbor, saying, "Ye have heard that it was said by them of old time, Thou shalt not kill; and whosoever shall kill shall be in danger of the judgment: but I say unto you, That whosoever is angry with his brother without a cause shall be in danger of the judgment: and whosoever shall say to his brother, Raca [a word by which the Jews would insult and malign someone], shall be in danger of the council: but whosoever shall say, Thou fool, shall be in danger of hell fire" (Matt. 5:21–22). I believe there are but few who correctly understand what the Savior is saying here. This affirms clearly that the dishonoring and maligning of our neighbor must truly be considered as an act of murder.

2. *Hating* him; that is, by harboring an evil, wicked, and hostile disposition toward him, and thus be desirous of inflicting all manner of evil upon him. The reason why hatred is here designated as the slaying of our neighbor is first and foremost rooted in the fact that the actual commission of murder proceeds from hatred. Both the very nature of hatred as well as experience clearly teach that this is so. Hatred moved Absalom to rob his brother Amnon of his life (2 Sam 13:28). Hatred moved Cain to commit the same sin by killing his brother, Abel. Hatred stirred up Esau to target the life of his brother, Jacob, and thus aim for his destruction. Finally, hatred moved the sons of Jacob to attempt to murder their brother Joseph. The apostle John therefore correctly teaches that "whosoever hateth his brother is a murderer" (1 John 3:15a).

3. *Harming* him; that is, by willfully injuring him and by harming his body, for this is a way to rob our neighbor of his life, as the inflicting of wounds frequently culminates in death. God therefore solemnly commanded in His law that "if a man cause a blemish in his neighbour; as he hath done, so shall it be done to him; breach for breach, eye for eye, tooth for tooth: as he hath caused a blemish in a man, so shall it be done to him again" (Lev. 24:19–20). One calls this *lex taliones*, that is, the law of proportionate retribution.

4. Deliberately *slaying* him, which is a violent robbing him of his life—be it while engaged in a fight, in a rush of anger, by inflicting death by way of a lethal instrument, by way of poison, or in any other way. Such a murderous act toward our neighbor is a very grievous and dreadful sin, for he who thus murders his neighbor violates and destroys God's creature that He made after His image. Such persons violently intrude upon a domain that belongs alone unto God, who is the Lord of life and death, and by so doing rob their neighbor of the most precious thing he possesses, namely, his life, thereby harming and injuring him to the utmost. This frequently means that one's neighbor dies suddenly and without repentance, thus dying in his sins and perishing forever. One who commits this deed demonstrates that he hates his brother with a deadly hatred by robbing him of life, his most precious treasure. Such a murderer suddenly shatters all bonds that hold human society together, and he therefore, of necessity, must be cut off from the earth by the civil government. Such a person must

be put to death, and may not be shown any mercy. We have thus addressed the fourfold manner in which God solemnly forbids the slaying of one's neighbor.

After having addressed the manner of killing that God forbids in His law, the instructor adds the specific ways or means by which we commit the dreadful sin of murder: "in thoughts, words, gestures, and in deeds." The latter can be achieved in two ways, either by ourselves or by another, and we shall briefly address each.

One kills his neighbor and thus robs him of his life:

1. In his *thoughts* when he harbors bitter hatred toward him, wishing that he was dead, that he no longer lived in this world, and that he no longer was in his way. One is also guilty of this sin when he schemes and thinks of ways to eliminate his neighbor, and is thus filled with murderous inclinations toward him. Such persons who, either for lack of courage or lack of suitable opportunity, do not actually commit the very act of murder, being fearful either of being punished by the civil judge or by the judgment of God, are yet deemed by God to be murderers of their neighbor, and God shall therefore cast them into the lake of fire if they do not truly and sincerely repent before Him of this wickedness. God therefore solemnly issues this prohibition, saying, "And let none of you imagine evil against his brother in your heart" (Zech. 7:10b), and the Savior teaches and exhorts us accordingly, saying, "For out of the heart proceed evil thoughts, murders, etc." (Matt. 15:19a).

2. By his *words*; that is, when he verbally curses someone and, in anger and wrath, wishes upon him death and the perdition of soul and body, or in any other way mocks, injures, reviles, or slanders him. Frequently, this greatly arouses our neighbor's passions and causes him to be provoked to anger and wrath toward us. This, in turn, frequently results in grievous brawls and murder itself. Man's tongue is therefore depicted as "a sharp sword," and his "teeth are spears and arrows" (Ps. 57:5). The apostle James describes the tongue as "an unruly evil, full of deadly poison" (James 3:8b).

In former days, there was a lively example of this in the life of foolish Nabal, who spoke grievous and bitter words toward David, which would have cost him and his people their lives if God had not prevented it by means of the wise Abigail.

One also murders his neighbor verbally when he causes him to be put to death by means of such false accusations as the Jews were guilty of in causing the Savior to be put to death.

3. By his *countenance*; that is, when he either mocks or ridicules him either by facial expressions, shaking his head, or sticking out his tongue. One also is guilty of this when he looks at someone with a terrifying, dark, or angry countenance that unmistakably radiates hatred and murderous intent. We read of Cain, the murderer of his brother, that he "was very wroth, and his countenance fell" (Gen. 4:5). We read also of the murderous Jews in Jerusalem, who, being filled with anger and hatred toward the godly Stephen, "gnashed on him with their teeth" (Acts 7:54). All of this ultimately leads to murder, and one can thus be guilty of murdering his neighbor with his countenance.

4. By his *actions*; that is, when he physically robs someone of his life by an action that, according to the instructor, can be achieved either "by myself or by another." David was therefore guilty of killing Uriah when he caused him to be killed by his general, Joab, while on active duty in his army (2 Samuel 11). The latter is, in a certain sense, a much greater sin and far more wicked, for in so doing we cause others besides ourselves to be guilty of this dreadful sin.

Beloved, in this sixth commandment, God forbids all such abominations and vile acts of wickedness. However, these are not all the matters that are forbidden, for there are others also that the Lord forbids.

According to the instructor, the Lord also stipulates "that I hurt not myself, nor willfully expose myself to any danger." If we are forbidden to rob our neighbors of their lives, we may no less do so regarding ourselves, but we must strive to preserve and protect our temporal lives in every conceivable way. A man is capable of killing himself when God leaves him over to himself, and not only is this confirmed by the examples of Saul and Judas, but it is the daily experience that many younger as well as older people pursue.

This sin is committed in a variety of ways. Not only is it committed deliberately by either hanging, poisoning, or stabbing oneself, but, first and foremost, by living beastly, perverted, and wicked lives, whereby we indulge in all manner of vices, such as fornication, drunkenness, and fighting. These are acts by which many a person in our day deliberately cuts short his life by robbing himself of health and life by virtue of such indulgence, thereby confirming that "bloody and deceitful men shall not live out half their days" (Ps. 50:24). To commit suicide in this manner is a most vile and wicked sin, and they who commit it will almost always perish eternally, for there is no one more unlikely to be saved than one who commits suicide.

Therefore, the Lord solemnly not only forbids the commission of any form of suicide, but also forbids us either to harm ourselves or to jeopardize our health and physical well-being in any way. We may not willfully expose ourselves to danger in whatever form that may be, for whosoever willfully exposes his life to danger is guilty of murdering himself, albeit that God may protect him from actually losing his life. As far as such a person is concerned, he exposes his life to such danger that he might actually lose it, and that, in its essence, is the commission of suicide.

The instructor then adds, "wherefore also the magistrate is armed with the sword, to prevent murder." Since murder of one's neighbor or oneself is the most grievous and dreadful sin addressed in this commandment, the Lord has placed the sword into the hands of the government that it would punish all murderers and eradicate them from the face of the earth without pity or mercy. Consider the Lord's express command: "At the hand of every man's brother will I require the life of man. Whoso sheddeth man's blood, by man shall his blood be shed: for in the image of God made he man" (Gen. 9:5b–6). In Numbers 35:30–31, we read: "Whoso killeth any person, the murderer shall be put to death by the mouth of witnesses: but one witness shall not testify against any person to cause him to die. Moreover ye shall take no satisfaction for the life of a murderer, which is guilty of death: but he shall be surely put to death." Consider also Proverbs 28:17: "A man that doeth violence to the blood of any person shall flee to the pit; let no man stay him."

The instructor then proceeds to focus on the spirituality of this commandment; that is, how God not only forbids the act of murdering oneself or one's neighbor, but how the Lord also expressly forbids the root motives that lead to murder. In Question 106, he asks, "But this commandment seems only to speak of murder?" to which he replies, "In forbidding murder, God teaches us that He abhors the causes thereof, such as envy, hatred, anger, and desire of revenge; and that He accounts all these as murder."

The instructor here confronts us with four vile and grievous sins that lurk in our evil, sinful, and corrupt hearts. These sins are the fountainhead of all murder, and thus from which acts or committing of murder proceed, namely, "envy, hatred, anger, and desire of revenge." By nature, we are deeply infected by these vile sins and wicked inclinations, and as long as we are unconverted and unregenerate, we wallow in these vile acts of uncleanness and are dominated by them. However, when we are inwardly united to the Lord Jesus by faith, we depart from this wickedness and no longer are able either to live in it or to walk accordingly.

The Lord forbids here, as the act of murder, our yielding to such abominations and vile vices as "envy, hatred, anger, and desire of revenge." The Lord deems yielding to these vices to be equivalent to murder, since these sins and abominations are the essential root from which murder, either of oneself or one's neighbor, proceeds.

Being identified as a root of murder is:

1. *Envy.* Solomon affirms this, saying, "Wrath is cruel, and anger is outrageous; but who is able to stand before envy?" (Prov. 27:4), and in Proverbs 14:30, he refers to envy as "the rottenness of the bones." The apostle James therefore very solemnly admonishes God's people, saying, "Do ye think that the scripture saith in vain, The spirit that dwelleth in us lusteth to envy?" (James 4:5; Matt. 27:18).

2. *Hatred.* We have sufficiently addressed this in the preceding and have affirmed it by scriptural examples. God therefore commands us, "Thou shalt not hate thy brother in thine heart" (Lev. 19:17a).

3. *Anger.* This is no less a root of murder, as is taught clearly by daily and sad experience. Solomon therefore says, "Wrath is cruel, and anger is outrageous" (Prov. 27:4a). The Savior also connects anger and murder, saying, "Whosoever is angry with his brother without a cause shall be in danger of the judgment" (Matt. 5:22a). Regarding Jacob's sons Simeon and Levi, we read that "in their anger they slew a man" (Gen. 49:6b), and the holy apostle Paul therefore admonishes us, "But now ye also put off all these; anger, wrath, malice" (Col. 3:8a).

4. *The desire for revenge.* No one who has become acquainted with this evil lust in its true nature and effect will doubt that this is the actual fountainhead of murder. God's Word expressly admonishes us, "Dearly beloved, avenge not yourselves, but rather give place unto wrath: for it is written, Vengeance is mine; I will repay, saith the Lord" (Rom. 12:19).

It is thus evident in the sixth commandment that the holy and most high God solemnly forbids not only the act of murdering either oneself or his neighbor, but also whatever constitutes the very fountainhead of murder, namely, "envy, hatred, anger, and desire of revenge." God deems all of these as being equivalent to murder.

Having considered sufficiently what God forbids in this commandment, we shall now briefly consider the duties and holy virtues prescribed therein. The instructor addresses this in Question 107 by asking, "But is it enough that we do not kill any man in the manner mentioned above?" He then responds, saying, "No: for when God forbids envy, hatred, and anger, He commands us to love our neighbor as ourselves; to show patience, peace, meekness, mercy, and all kindness towards him, and prevent his hurt as much as in us lies; and that we do good, even to our enemies."

Many glorious, precious, and godly virtues and obligations are here prescribed by the Lord in order that we might conduct ourselves accordingly. We must:

1. "Love our neighbor as ourselves"; that is, we must esteem, love, and honor him as much as if he were flesh of our flesh and bone of our bone. Such love for our neighbor motivates us to care for his life and well-being as much as we would for our own lives. This is the proper way by which the murder of our neighbor is to be prevented. The Lord therefore solemnly admonishes us, saying, "Thou shalt not avenge, nor bear any grudge against the children of thy people, but thou shalt love thy neighbour as thyself: I am the LORD" (Lev. 19:18).

2. "Show patience" by patiently bearing with him in his weaknesses and deficiencies. This is the essential and natural consequence of loving our neighbor, for Paul teaches this, saying, "Charity suffereth long, and is kind; charity envieth not; charity vaunteth not itself, is not puffed up, doth not behave itself unseemly, seeketh not her own, is not easily provoked, thinketh no evil; rejoiceth not in iniquity, but rejoiceth in the truth; beareth all things, believeth all things, hopeth all things, endureth all things" (1 Cor. 13:4–7).

3. "Show peace." Paul therefore admonishes believers, "If it be possible, as much as lieth in you, live peaceably with all men" (Rom. 12:18), and the Savior speaks accordingly, "Blessed are the peacemakers" (Matt. 5:9a).

4. "Show meekness." The Lord Jesus admonishes us accordingly, "Take my yoke upon you, and learn of me; for I am meek and lowly in heart" (Matt. 11:29a). He also pronounces the meek to be blessed (Matt. 5:5a).

5. "Show mercy toward our neighbor," as Paul accordingly admonishes, "Put on therefore, as the elect of God, holy and beloved, bowels of mercies" (Col. 3:12a), and the Savior also pronounces the merciful as blessed (Matt. 5:7a).

6. "Show all kindness towards our neighbor." Peter therefore exhorts the Lord's people, "Be ye all of one mind, having compassion one of another, love as brethren, be pitiful, be courteous" (1 Peter 3:8).

7. "Prevent his hurt as much as in us lies." Paul admonishes us, "Look not every man on his own things, but every man also on the things of others" (Phil 2:4).

8. "Do good, even to our enemies." The Savior expressly admonishes us, "But I say unto you, Love your enemies, bless them that curse you, do good to them that hate you, and pray for them which despitefully use you, and persecute you" (Matt. 5:44).

God thus commands in this sixth commandment that we most solemnly practice all these proposed holy duties and virtues, and avail ourselves of all ways and means to prevent all manner of murder. Observe how exceedingly broad also this sixth commandment is. Oh, may we all, by God's grace, truly and spiritually see this!

If we would now all truly examine our nature and inclinations, as well as our conduct and walk, how we would then find ourselves to be utterly guilty before the Lord of all these abominations that are the fountainhead of murder. We would see that we are guilty of:

- dishonoring, reviling, and maligning our neighbor, either verbally or by our countenances;
- reviling, abusing, striving, contending with our neighbor;
- lightly and willingly exposing ourselves to danger;
- hatred, envy, anger, and a desire for revenge;
- lovelessness;
- impatience, whereby we are completely intolerant of others;
- being contentious with and utterly hostile toward our neighbor;
- cruelty, being unmerciful, being quick to judge, and being unfriendly; and
- manifold ways of insulting and doing that which is detrimental toward our neighbor in thoughts, words, and deeds.

May the Lord truly illuminate us to see our sins and unrighteousness. We will then perceive that we are all evil murderers in our hearts and that it is only by virtue of God's restraining grace that we have not become guilty of the actual commission of these wicked abominations.

May we, by the grace of the Holy Spirit, see in the mirror of God's holy law how unclean and condemnable we are as we truly and earnestly humble ourselves before the Lord, desiring true reconciliation, faith, and repentance. Thus, may God, in His mercy, work this in all of His own in Christ Jesus and by His Holy Spirit. Amen.

The Seventh Commandment, Forbidding Adultery

Thou shalt not commit adultery.
—EXODUS 20:14

Question 108: What doth the seventh commandment teach us?

Answer: That all uncleanness is accursed of God; and that therefore we must with all our hearts detest the same, and live chastely and temperately, whether in holy wedlock or in single life.

Question 109: Doth God forbid in this commandment only adultery and such like gross sins?

Answer: Since both our body and soul are temples of the Holy Ghost, He commands us to preserve them pure and holy; therefore He forbids all unchaste actions, gestures, words, thoughts, desires, and whatever can entice men thereto.

God, the most high judge, lawgiver, and king, admonished us in the fifth commandment of His law how we are to conduct ourselves appropriately toward our parents and all who are in authority over us. He then admonished us in the sixth commandment that we may neither rob nor steal temporal life from anyone or from ourselves in any fashion or precipitate this even in the least, but must do our utmost to preserve and sustain our own life as well as that of our neighbor. He now proceeds, in the seventh commandment, to prescribe another obligation that is no less holy, pertaining to the lawful preservation and procreation of the human race by means of the honorable and unbreakable bond of marriage or the godly one-flesh union of husband and wife. The Lord briefly articulates this duty by saying, "Thou shalt not commit adultery."

The content of this commandment is also exceedingly broad. By this commandment, the Lord solemnly forbids a multitude of unrighteous acts, whether secret or public sins, while at the same time He prescribes a large number of holy duties. Oh, that the Lord, by His Holy Spirit, would truly enlighten and lead us into the mystery of His holy law, so that, by our looking into that mirror, we would rightly see our abominable and hell-worthy disposition, as well as our sins from the days of our youth, and, thereby, for the first time or by renewal, be truly humbled before Him! Who among us is able to say regarding this seventh commandment, "Pass me by, for I have purified my heart and I have been cleansed of my sins"? Oh, that we all would be of a broken heart and a contrite spirit regarding our sins and our evil and unclean nature!

Following the instructor, we shall expound:

1. the language of this commandment; and
2. its spiritual efficacy.

Regarding the language of this commandment, we must address:

1. the object of this commandment; and
2. the commandment itself.

As we consider the essence of this seventh commandment, we observe its object to be the lawful procreation and preservation of the human race upon earth by means of the godly, lawful, and one-flesh marital union of husband and wife.

When God created and brought forth the first man, Adam, doing so immediately and thus without the use of any means, He soon thereafter created a woman from Adam's rib to be a true helpmeet for him. By an intimate union with her, the human race upon earth would be procreated and multiplied. God's will was not to create and bring forth men immediately, as He did Adam and Eve, the first two human beings, but that people, even as all other creatures, would multiply upon earth by means of an intimate one-flesh union. To enable them to achieve this, God granted them the required energy and natural capacities, "and God blessed them, and God said unto them, Be fruitful, and multiply" (Gen. 1:28).

Ever since that time, this has been a permanent and irrevocable law of nature to be observed by humanity upon earth. The human race is thus sustained, preserved, and procreated by means of the mutual and lawful union of the husband and his wife, culminating in their becoming one flesh. I repeat, by means of a *lawful* union; that is, a union that, in all respects, is godly, holy, and in conformity to God's law. And, indeed, the Lord God is perfectly holy, and therefore He can and must be served by His creature in no way but in true holiness. The preservation and procreation of the human race upon earth must occur, in all respects, in a holy and godly manner if we are thereby to serve and to glorify God.

Man therefore must fully submit to God's holy commandment and proceed in His ordained way. Since the Lord has purposed, in His adorable wisdom and holiness, that the human race be continually procreated and preserved here upon earth, every man must proceed herein by utterly forsaking and banishing all immorality; that is, all sinful and corrupt ways that man's morally polluted flesh invents for its indulgence and shameful perversion.

The reasons why the Lord, in His holy law, legislated the lawful procreation and preservation of the human race are great and compelling, and He therefore expressly prescribed how we are to conduct ourselves in that regard. This preservation and procreation of the human race upon earth is:

First, God's work and a gracious benefit, for though we are generated and brought forth by means of the intimate and mutual one-flesh union of our parents, it is God who is fully engaged in this by His omnipotence and providence. He blesses and renders the union of our parents fruitful so that, mediately, we are conceived and born. Therefore, we owe our conception not first and foremost to our parents, but to the Lord God, who is the original cause of that conception. Consistent with this, we read in Psalm 127:3, "Lo, children are an heritage of the LORD: and the fruit of the womb is his reward," as is plainly affirmed by the barrenness of those women whose wombs the Lord Himself shut. We have examples of this in the Holy Scriptures from the lives of Sarah, Rachel, Hannah, Elizabeth, and Michal, David's wife. And among the curses and punishments upon sin is this: "Cursed shall be the fruit of thy body" (Deut. 28:18), whereas the fruitfulness of the woman is promised as a blessing by the Lord.

Second, an absolutely essential ordinance and benefit of God, for thereby the world population will be sustained until a specific moment in time. In this way, all men are born in conformity with God's purpose. This is particularly true for God's elect, who, after they are conceived and born, He calls and appoints to be the subjects of His eternal kingdom. By procreation, God's purpose is thus accomplished and magnified. As the Lord God has safeguarded the preservation and sustenance of human life upon earth in the sixth commandment, so He also safeguards in this commandment the procreation and preservation of the human race upon earth, commanding that this be achieved in no other way than in a holy, godly, and lawful manner. Therefore, all sin, ungodliness, and unrighteousness must be utterly banished from this practice, and any indulgence therein will be severely accursed, punished, and judged.

The language of the Lord's commandment is simply this: "Thou shalt not commit adultery." This commandment is again given to us as a prohibition. However, there is always a command implied in any prohibition—a command that is the foundation of the prohibition. We shall now consider briefly:

1. what we are commanded to do according to the commandment's specific words; and

2. what we are prohibited from doing.

By forbidding us to commit adultery, the Lord commands the one who has reached a suitable age and to whom the Lord has granted suitable gifts to enter into a lawful and godly marriage and to be loyal and committed to his or her spouse for life without ever desecrating or breaking their lawful marital union. Both spouses must always engage in intimate union in a manner that is holy, godly, and pure in order that they thereby may bring forth a pure and holy seed unto the Lord their God, to His honor and glory.

This is the brief summary of all that the Lord God commands us to observe and to do in regard to the literal meaning of this seventh commandment. Since we are called by God to sustain and procreate the human race upon earth, we are to enter into a lawful and godly marriage so that therewith we may serve and glorify the Lord God.

What sort of marriage may one designate as both lawful and godly? Regretfully, this—as well as the practice of all true godliness—has almost become an unknown concept among people in our age.

For such a lawful and godly marriage, there are eight requisites that we shall briefly set before you. It is absolutely essential to the establishing of a lawful and godly marriage that:

1. It be entered into without any compulsion, and thus with the mutual, voluntary, and considered consent of both spouses, who must commit themselves to each other before the Lord's countenance so that He may be a witness between the husband and the wife of his youth (Mal. 2:14).

2. It be publicly affirmed and sanctioned by the government or, as is even more fitting, before the minister and the congregation, so that all may know and esteem such individuals as lawful spouses. It is true that there are people who enter into marriage secretly. They live together as husband and wife by a

secret marital union, esteeming such a marriage to be legitimate before God. However, such persons do not consider:

    a. what great offense they thereby cause before the world and in the congregation;

    b. how their entire conduct is completely mired in hypocrisy, deception, and dishonesty by carefully seeking to conceal their marriage from the world; and

    c. how the children born to them will always be considered by the world as illegitimate.

3. The spouses not be too closely related to one another, for God has expressly prohibited such marriages in His holy law.

4. It be entered upon with the knowledge and consent of either one's mutual parents, legal guardians, or friends—especially if the spouses are not yet of age. By marriage, we are, in a sense, released from our allegiance to and dependence upon our parents, considering that "therefore shall a man leave his father and his mother, and shall cleave unto his wife" (Gen. 2:24), and the wife also is obligated to leave her father and mother. The permission of our parents or our legal guardians is therefore absolutely mandatory lest we dishonor them and transgress the fifth commandment.

5. It be between two spouses who are suitably compatible in years, so that one is neither too young nor the other too old. It is also desirable that they be compatible as to their social and financial status, that is, if it pleases the Lord in His holy providence to govern matters in such a way. However, as God's way occasionally is to elevate someone from the dust—that is, by means of a lawful marriage, He elevates a person from a lowly state and position to a status of greater honor and prestige in this world—His holy will must also be done in such circumstances, and we may not oppose Him in this. He caused David to be elevated from a very lowly and obscure status in life by his marriage to the king's daughter. Also, by marriage, He elevated the godly Esther from a very lowly and obscure status in life to become the foremost queen of the world. God can still deal with the children of men in similar fashion.

6. It be entered upon only after a morally upright courtship, providing each spouse with the opportunity to become better acquainted with the other's disposition and character, as we observe, for instance, with Jacob and Rachel.

7. Each has looked for a suitable, virtuous, and God-fearing spouse who truly serves and fears the Lord and is thus not a person who lives solely for the

world. By no means should a believer consider a union with an unbelieving and unconverted person, lest he grievously sin against the Lord, for the people of this world seek only to fulfill their fleshly lusts and are concerned only about earthly riches and external beauty. If there is one thing a Christian should be concerned about for his or her lifetime, it is that he or she would find a pious and godly spouse to whom he or she can be united in the Lord and together they can govern and raise the children of the family in the fear of the Lord.

I could affirm the truth of this extensively and compellingly, and thereby, on the one hand, demonstrate the blessed advantages of that marriage in which both spouses fear the Lord, and, on the other hand, warn against the grievous consequences and troubles should that not be the case. However, time constraints prevent me from pursuing this any further.

8. The spouses do not begin their marriage in any way but in the true fear of the Lord—or in the Lord, as the apostle exhorts us to do in 1 Corinthians 7:39. Regarding a weighty matter such as this, we must earnestly seek the Lord's will and His face by prayer and fasting. In this, we must seek to follow the Lord's inward calling and be fully committed to know His will, and thus strive to persuade our hearts of His gracious approbation, assistance, blessing, and promises. It behooves us to begin our marriage with the Lord God regarding so weighty a matter and to know how we are to acknowledge Him in all our ways, so that He may make straight our pathway and thereby secure to us His gracious blessing upon our marriage.

How rarely people consider these matters in our day! How many human marriages there are today that resemble the union of irrational animals, who are drawn together only by an animalistic drive and their own irrational lust! Nevertheless, there is no greater or weightier matter for man here upon earth than the marital union, whereby two become one flesh. There is no matter in which we should consult less with flesh and blood and more with the Lord our God than this.

Oh, what need we have to receive from the Lord Himself a husband or wife to be our spouse! Only such a person should be considered: one whom we may receive from His hand irrespective of whether such a spouse is rich or poor, of elevated or low social status, or either beautiful or unattractive. We must not make our choice according to our fleshly desires and lusts, but, rather, take as our spouse the one whom the Lord Himself gives to us and whom He, from all eternity, has chosen for us (Prov. 18:22; 31:10; and especially 19:14).

From the preceding, it is therefore evident in what a lawful and godly marriage consists—a marriage in which one's greatest and chief objective is to bring forth a holy seed unto the Lord our God, whereby He may be exalted and magnified. It is into such a lawful and godly marriage that we are to enter when the Lord calls us to this in His providence.[1]

It is, however, also certain that if God does not call someone to the state of holy matrimony, he or she must and may remain unmarried for some time or an entire lifetime, if it pleases the Lord that in so doing, he or she would fulfill His purpose. The apostle Paul highly recommended the unmarried state to the believers of his day and counseled them accordingly, as we can read at length in 1 Corinthians 7. The Savior also teaches that "there are some eunuchs…which have made themselves eunuchs for the kingdom of heaven's sake" (Matt. 19:12). This must be interpreted as a reference to pious and godly people who continue to live in an unmarried state for the sake of the Lord and His kingdom.

In the seventh commandment, the Lord commands us not only to enter into a lawful and Christian marriage, if that be according to His divine will, but also, upon having entered into marriage, to maintain it as a sacred union and in no wise ever to harm, corrupt, or break this divine union. To maintain marriage as a sacred union consists in this: that both spouses always fulfill their mutual obligations toward one another in accord with what God has stipulated in His Word. The husband then conducts himself properly as the head of his wife, and she then views herself as being her husband's own flesh and permits herself to be properly governed and directed by her head. They then mutually seek to bring forth a holy seed unto the Lord if it pleases the Lord to grant this to them.

It is evident that this holy matrimony is broken before God in these three instances:

1. When the husband fails to conduct himself as the head of his wife and fails to cleave to her in conformity to God's holy precepts regarding marriage.

2. When the wife fails to submit herself to her husband's leadership, and also fails to help him and cleave to him according to the same precepts.

3. When the objective of marriage to bring forth a holy seed unto the Lord is neglected and not pursued.

---

1. Surprisingly the bearing of children is stated here (the latter half of the 18th century) as being the "greatest and chief objective" of marriage—long after the Puritans reversed this.

All of these constitute a true and essential breaking of the marriage[2] before the Lord, even when husbands and wives continue to dwell together without actually pursuing a divorce.

We have sufficiently addressed what the Lord prescribes and prohibits according to this commandment. We shall now consider briefly what sins and vile vices the Lord solemnly forbids in this commandment.

Generally speaking, the Lord commands a holy and godly marital union and forbids whatever in any way violates the lawful procreation and preservation of humanity. It is therefore the Lord's will that we utterly abhor the following wicked, sinful, and abominable practices, and have nothing to do with any of them. These practices include:

First, *incest* of any kind. This occurs when one unlawfully either enters into marriage or unites with someone within the circle of his or her own blood relationship. This is a very dreadful sin and a wicked deed. It is a sin that provokes God to manifest His wrath toward a nation and its inhabitants. God therefore solemnly commanded in Leviticus 20 that this sin must be punished with death. In Leviticus 18, the Lord has given us a comprehensive list of all the degrees of incest, whereby we may know the extent to which we must keep ourselves from this sin, lest His curse and wrath come upon us.

Second, *polygamy*; that is, a man taking to himself more than one wife. God gave to Adam only one wife, and His command to them was that these *two* should be one flesh. By no means may we depart from this divine precept by having more than one wife, for in so doing, we sin greatly against the Lord and cause His curse and wrath to be invoked upon us. In His holy law, the Lord has therefore most solemnly forbidden our involvement in any form of polygamy. In Leviticus 18:18, we read, "Neither shalt thou take a wife to her sister, to vex her, to uncover her nakedness, beside the other in her life time." It is the mind of the Holy Spirit here to interpret the word *sister* in a general sense; that is, "You may not take a second or different woman in addition to your first wife in order thereby to vex and trouble her." One would thereby grievously oppress one's initial and lawful wife. God solemnly rebuked the Jewish people in Malachi 2:13 for the commission of the grievous sin of polygamy.

We must not counter this by referring to the examples of holy and prominent men of God in the Old Testament, such as Abraham, Jacob, David, and

---

2. It should be noted here that the literal rendering of the seventh commandment in the Dutch language is as follows: "Thou shalt not break or harm the marriage."

Solomon, who simultaneously had many wives. In so doing, they most certainly sinned against the Lord, albeit that He, in His sovereignty and transcendent wisdom, tolerated this in them. However, we must by no means emulate these saints with regard to this practice.

Third, *divorce*; that is, the actual severing and violation of the holy state of marriage by departing from one's spouse and by unlawfully divorcing oneself from him or her. Beloved, there is but one reason for the lawful dissolution of a lawful marriage, namely, when one of the two spouses is guilty of fornication. That alone dissolves the marriage and separates two spouses, and, according to God's law, one may then freely depart from the spouse who is guilty of fornication and may marry another. However, apart from this exception, marriage in no wise can or may be dissolved. The Savior teaches this, saying, "But I say unto you, That whosoever shall put away his wife, saving for the cause of fornication, causeth her to commit adultery: and whosoever shall marry her that is divorced committeth adultery" (Matt. 5:32).

The holy apostle Paul says regarding the woman: "The woman which hath an husband is bound by the law to her husband so long as he liveth; but if the husband be dead, she is loosed from the law of her husband. So then if, while her husband liveth, she be married to another man, she shall be called an adulteress: but if her husband be dead, she is free from that law; so that she is no adulteress, though she be married to another man" (Rom. 7:2–3).

Prior to the Savior's sojourn upon earth, the sin of adultery was very prolific among the Jews. However, He taught them, saying, "Moses because of the hardness of your hearts suffered you to put away your wives: but from the beginning it was not so" (Matt. 19:8). Marriage is a holy institution and a divine precept. God thereby unites two to become one flesh, and "what therefore God hath joined together, let not man put asunder" (Matt. 19:6b).

Fourth, *fornication*; that is, one of the two spouses in a marriage having intercourse with someone other than the spouse. This is a dreadful and wicked sin, by which God is greatly provoked, and thereby the holy bond of marriage is broken and violated. God therefore solemnly commanded this sin to be punished with death. In Leviticus 20:10, we read, "And the man that committeth adultery with another man's wife, even he that committeth adultery with his neighbour's wife, the adulterer and the adulteress shall surely be put to death." Consider also Deuteronomy 22:22, where we read, "If a man be found lying with a woman married to an husband, then they shall both of them die, both the man that lay with the woman, and the woman: so shalt thou put away evil from Israel."

This commandment of the Lord also pertained to a young daughter who was betrothed to a man. If, during the time of her betrothal, a man had intercourse with her, both were then to be stoned to death (Deut. 22:23–24).

Thus, we have God's solemn and express command that fornicators must be put to death because of the dreadful and abominable nature of this sin. They who commit this sin are no longer fit to live here upon earth. Only consider what the Scriptures say regarding this sin: "Whoso committeth adultery with a woman lacketh understanding: he that doeth it destroyeth his own soul. A wound and dishonour shall he get; and his reproach shall not be wiped away" (Prov. 6:32–33).

The severity with which God punishes fornication is also evident not only in the law regarding the water of jealousy (Numbers 5), but also when we consider the judgment executed upon David (2 Samuel 10–12) and his subsequent and deep repentance.

The fact that this grievous sin of fornication is not punished by death in our land, but only and generally by the levying of a monetary fine, is, in and of itself, a prevailing sin among us and a public desecration of God's holy law. God therefore will punish our nation in His wrath. The Gentiles will rise up against us in judgment, for they have punished fornication with death. We read of this in Jeremiah 29:22–23: "And of them shall be taken up a curse by all the captivity of Judah which are in Babylon, saying, The LORD make thee like Zedekiah and like Ahab, whom the king of Babylon roasted in the fire; because they have committed villainy in Israel, and have committed adultery with their neighbours' wives, and have spoken lying words in my name, which I have not commanded them; even I know, and am a witness, saith the LORD."

Fifth, *whoredom*; that is, a person having intercourse outside of a lawful marital union. This despicable sin is now openly practiced by many, who show no upright sorrow and contrition before God and man regarding this sin. They think very lightly of this sin and never consider it worthy of shedding a single tear over it. God, however, deems it to be a very grievous sin, and therefore all who commit this sin and do not sincerely repent of it will be eternally excluded from His kingdom and His blessed fellowship (1 Cor. 6:10).

The sin of whoredom is most grievous, vile, and despicable. It is a deed whereby God is greatly provoked and a sin for which God will punish and destroy a nation. Consider the word of the Lord, saying, "Do not prostitute thy daughter, to cause her to be a whore; lest the land fall to whoredom, and the land become full of wickedness" (Lev. 19:29). The apostle Paul sets whoredom before us as a most destructive and despicable sin, saying: "Flee fornication. Every sin that a man doeth is without the body; but he that committeth fornication sinneth against his own body" (1 Cor. 6:18). In verse 16, he gives us the reason, saying: "What? know ye not that he which is joined to an harlot is one body? for two, saith he, shall be one flesh." He derives this from the marital institution, in which God said that these two shall be one flesh. In 1 Corinthians 5:9, Paul admonishes, "I wrote unto you in an epistle not to company with fornicators."

Since whoredom is such a vile and abominable sin, God commanded in former days that "the daughter of any priest, if she profane herself by playing the whore, she profaneth her father: she shall be burnt with fire" (Lev. 21:9). However, not only was the priest's daughter to be put to death for playing the whore, but God commanded in general that if a young daughter who still dwelt in her father's home secretly played the whore and thereafter married a man who did not find her to be a virgin, the following then had to transpire: "If this thing be true, and the tokens of virginity be not found for the damsel: then they shall bring out the damsel to the door of her father's house, and the men of her city shall stone her with stones that she die: because she hath wrought folly in Israel, to play the whore in her father's house: so shalt thou put evil away from among you" (Deut. 22:20–21). Oh, that all virgins and daughters among us would hear this and take it to heart!

Sixth, *sodomy*; that is, all similar sins that are committed against the very law of nature; we judge it unnecessary to say any more about such dreadful wickedness and uncleanness (Rom. 1:24–32).

Having considered the details of this commandment, let us briefly consider its internal and spiritual dimension. The Lord forbids not only the commission of all these external sins and abominations, but He also and primarily forbids the hidden origin, fountain, and root of this sin—a sin that, by virtue of our original sin, is so deeply embedded in all our hearts. There is therefore no one among us—that is, if they have but truly become acquainted with themselves—who must not exclaim and confess before the Lord that he is at bottom utterly abominable, unclean, guilty, and despicable before Him—even though he has never in his entire life committed the slightest actual sin contrary to God's law. Therefore, we shall be further instructed regarding this by our instructor, who:

1. addresses the literal sense of the commandment; and

2. the spirituality of this commandment.

He addresses its external or literal meaning in response to Question 108, saying, "That all uncleanness is accursed of God; and that therefore we must with all our hearts detest the same, and live chastely and temperately, whether in holy wedlock or in single life."

Allow me briefly to set before you the sense of the instructor's exposition. He understands uncleanness to refer to all manner of sin and impurity as they pertain to both body and soul, and thus it refers to all that militates against the lawful and godly procreation of the human race. This we already have addressed in its various nuances. The instructor says here that "all uncleanness is accursed of God"; that is, God's collective curse and judgment rest upon all who are guilty of such uncleanness, and He will punish them both temporally and eternally.

Since God is infinitely holy and just, He can by no means tolerate such dreadful sins and shameful wickedness of men, whereby they utterly defile and corrupt their souls and bodies. Rather than tolerate these things, the Lord pronounces a curse upon all who are guilty of such abominable sins. Oh, how many accursed human beings there must presently be in the world! Since the Lord God so solemnly pronounces a curse upon all uncleanness, the instructor posits that "we must with all our hearts detest the same." That is to say that we must have a complete and heartfelt aversion and hatred for this dreadful sin, with an intense and upright abhorrence. By God's grace, we must avoid such uncleanness to the utmost of our power, lest God's wrath and curse come upon us.

The holy apostle Paul admonishes us accordingly, saying, "But fornication, and all uncleanness, or covetousness, let it not be once named among you, as becometh saints" (Eph. 5:3), and therefore the instructor posits instead that God requires of us that we "live chastely and temperately, whether in holy wedlock, or in single life," without being guilty of any unclean and inappropriate conduct. This the Holy Scriptures also admonish us: "For this is the will of God, even your sanctification, that ye should abstain from fornication: that every one of you should know how to possess his vessel in sanctification and honour; not in the lust of concupiscence, even as the Gentiles which know not God" (1 Thess. 4:3–4).

We must conduct ourselves in this way in holy wedlock, for the apostle exhorts us, "Marriage is honourable in all, and the bed undefiled: but whoremongers and adulterers God will judge" (Heb. 13:4). We must also conduct ourselves in this way apart from the marital state, that is, in single life, for the same apostle admonishes that "if they cannot contain, let them marry: for it is better to marry than to burn" (1 Cor. 7:9). Such should marry so that they neither indulge in the vile sin of whoredom nor commit any other unclean acts, whereby they bring upon themselves the severe wrath of God.

The instructor then proceeds to consider the spirituality of this commandment by asking in Question 109, "Doth God forbid in this commandment only adultery and such like gross sins?" to which he responds, "Since both our body and soul are temples of the Holy Ghost, He commands us to preserve them pure and holy; therefore He forbids all unchaste actions, gestures, words, thoughts, desires, and whatever can entice men thereto." The instructor is here referring to all true believers, who, in Christ, are united to God by the Holy Spirit and who consequently are inwardly renewed, born again, and converted. Concerning these, he testifies that both their bodies and souls are temples of the Holy Ghost. Paul therefore writes to God's people, saying: "What? know ye not that your body is the temple of the Holy Ghost which is in you, which ye have of God, and ye are not your own?" (1 Cor. 6:19).

Oh, what a most blessed and glorious mystery of grace it is that every believing child of God is a true and spiritual temple, in which the Lord, the most high God of heaven and earth and the supremely holy Jehovah, dwells in a spiritual manner to all eternity with His blessed light, love, grace, and image! All such therefore are already in principle being renewed and transformed according to God's image, and, as the Scriptures teach, they have been made "partakers of the divine nature" (2 Peter 1:4). This is the blessed and glorious privilege of God's children, in contrast to the world, which is utterly void of God, and to the ungodly, who are the temple and synagogue of Satan.

Since the holy God, by His Spirit, thus dwells in His children, it necessarily follows that sin and uncleanness cannot dwell in them. By virtue of this glorious grace of the indwelling of the Holy Spirit, they are instead admonished and powerfully persuaded to preserve pure and holy both soul and body before the Lord, using their members always as instruments of righteousness and cleansing themselves "from all filthiness of the flesh and spirit, perfecting holiness in the fear of God" (2 Cor. 7:1). God therefore categorically forbids in this commandment "all unchaste actions, gestures, words, thoughts, desires, and whatever can entice men thereto."

We no longer have the time to address all of these proposed matters appropriately, and therefore we shall say, in general terms, that in this seventh commandment, God categorically forbids all uncleanness, threatening the punishment of eternal death if we continue to live therein. The Holy Scriptures are filled with very serious admonitions in this regard.

First, Paul addresses all unchaste actions by solemnly admonishing God's people, saying: "This I say therefore, and testify in the Lord, that ye henceforth walk not as other Gentiles walk, in the vanity of their mind, having the understanding darkened, being alienated from the life of God through the ignorance that is in them, because of the blindness of their heart: who being past feeling have given themselves over unto lasciviousness, to work all uncleanness with greediness. But ye have not so learned Christ" (Eph. 4:17–20).

Second, regarding all unchaste gestures, positions, and motions of the body, we read of the severe judgment of God being threatened upon such conduct: "Moreover the LORD saith, Because the daughters of Zion are haughty, and walk with stretched forth necks and wanton eyes, walking and mincing as they go, and making a tinkling with their feet: therefore the Lord will smite with a scab the crown of the head of the daughters of Zion, and the LORD will discover their secret parts" (Isa. 3:16–17).

Third, the holy apostle Paul admonishes God's people to refrain from using unchaste words, saying, "Let no corrupt communication proceed out of your mouth, but that which is good to the use of edifying, that it may minister grace unto the hearers" (Eph. 4:29).

Fourth, the Holy Scriptures especially teach us to refrain from *unchaste thoughts*, as being the true womb of all uncleanness, for the Savior testifies, "For out of the heart proceed evil thoughts, murders, adulteries, fornications, thefts, false witness, blasphemies" (Matt. 15:19). Therefore, He correctly teaches that "whosoever looketh on a woman to lust after her hath committed adultery with her already in his heart" (Matt. 5:28).

Fifth, in His Word, God no less forbids all unchaste lusts and unclean desires that can be subdued and mortified only by the efficacious and renewing grace of God. Paul admonishes God's people accordingly: "For this is the will of God, even your sanctification, that ye should abstain from fornication: that every one of you should know how to possess his vessel in sanctification and honour; not in the lust of concupiscence, even as the Gentiles which know not God" (1 Thess. 4:4–5).

As long as some unclean lusts still have dominion within us and we remain unwilling to subdue them, and as long as we, by God's grace, do not ceaselessly and earnestly strive against them, so long shall we not be able to serve God uprightly and have true fellowship with Him in Christ Jesus.

Finally, God forbids here in general terms "whatever can entice men thereto." This refers to:

- all laziness and idleness;
- all excessive eating, drinking, sleeping, and other carnal comforts;
- the viewing of immoral men and women, all inappropriate visual images, and other inappropriate displays;
- the reading of morally impure books;
- the use of all provocative dress and the baring of one's body;
- the keeping company with an immoral crowd and being in inappropriate places with members of the opposite sex, such as hotels, theaters, and dance floors.

In short, whatever in the least can trigger within us the desire toward immorality is most solemnly prohibited by the Lord, and He threatens His severe curse and wrath toward all who are disobedient.

May the Spirit of the Lord truly bind upon everyone's heart what we have written, and so may we truly learn to know our sins and our sinful nature. Consequently, may we deeply and truly humble ourselves before the Lord with sorrow and contrition, and so cause within us a most vehement longing and utmost sincerity for the grace that is in Christ, so that the blood of Jesus Christ will truly cleanse and purify us from all our sins. May the Lord grant and bestow this upon all His elect for His holy name's sake. Amen.

The Eighth Commandment, Forbidding Theft

Thou shalt not steal.
—EXODUS 20:15

Question 110: What doth God forbid in the eighth commandment?

Answer: God forbids not only those thefts and robberies which are punishable by the magistrate; but He comprehends under the name of theft all wicked tricks and devices, whereby we design to appropriate to ourselves the goods which belong to our neighbor; whether it be by force, or under the appearance of right, as by unjust weights, ells, measures, fraudulent merchandise, false coins, usury, or by any other way forbidden by God; as also all covetousness, all abuse and waste of His gifts.

Question 111: But what doth God require in this commandment?

Answer: That I promote the advantage of my neighbor in every instance I can or may, and deal with him as I desire to be dealt with by others; further also that I faithfully labor, so that I may be able to relieve the needy.

"The earth is the LORD's, and the fulness thereof; the world, and they that dwell therein" (Ps. 24:1). This is the doxology of the believing poet, and with these words, he desires to communicate in all-inclusive terms that God alone is the absolute master, Lord, and proprietor of His entire creation, as well as of all creatures found therein, and none besides Him has the least legitimate claim upon anything. This is obviously rooted in the fact that God alone created all things out of nothing.

However, what would it be like if God, as the proprietor of His entire creation, merely possessed this for Himself? We, as His creatures, whether believers or unbelievers, would be unable to function for a single moment, and thus the loving-kindness of God is revealed in the fact that it pleases Him to permit His creatures, for their entire life here upon earth, to use it with its fullness, of which He is the sole and undisputed proprietor.

Consequently, He bestows upon everyone, in a manner pleasing to Him, temporal goods and means of support. In so doing, to converted and unconverted alike, He does not leave Himself without witness, for in the natural realm He blesses them from heaven and grants them everything they need for their temporal existence. Yes, He even sees to it by expressly forbidding men to take away anything from the temporal goods God has given to others, that everyone can retain unhindered possession of all that they receive of Him. Let us therefore consider the divine precept as He initially gave it to His believing covenant people of Israel, saying, "Thou shalt not steal."

It is very proper that this commandment follows the three previous commandments. The focus of the fifth commandment is the obligation of children toward their parents and of subordinates toward their superiors. The focus of the sixth commandment is the preservation and protection of human life, whereas the seventh commandment focuses on the lawful and requisite procreation of the human race, as well as on human dignity and morality.

The Lord now follows this with the eighth commandment, pertaining to man's earthly possessions and assets, all of which are needed for the maintenance of his life. Regarding these possessions, the Lord, as the most high king and lawgiver, prescribes that everyone must secure these temporal goods for the maintenance of his life in a righteous and lawful manner, and possess them in all quietness, without one person, even in the least, robbing the other of his possessions in any imaginable way. This is all expressed in the words "Thou shalt not steal."

With the Lord's help, and being sustained by His Spirit, we shall expound this commandment for you. Oh, may it be a mirror in which we see ourselves as we are, and may it be as a schoolmaster to leads us unto Christ!

In this commandment, we again perceive:

1. its object; and
2. the duty to which the lawgiver obligates His covenant people regarding this object.

The object of this commandment consists of the goods God bestows upon everyone in order that each person's life here upon earth may thereby be preserved and maintained. In the absence of such maintenance, one's life would readily end, for God has created man in such a fashion that he must nourish and maintain the life of his body by extracting the fruits of this earth.

These necessary things are generally divided into two categories: *food and shelter*. First Timothy 6:8 says, "And having food and raiment let us be therewith content." Agur refers to this as "food convenient for me" (Prov. 30:8), and both are absolutely essential for us. Food is necessary for the maintenance and prosperity of our bodies, thereby yielding abundant nourishment to sustain our health. Shelter provides the body with warmth and protects it against all the discomforts of our environment that can be very detrimental to the health of the body. The goods of this life are therefore correctly reduced to these two categories of food and shelter, and every man ought to be satisfied with the possession of these two commodities. He needs nothing more to maintain his temporal life, and these things he needs only for the duration of his life. Neither prior to his birth nor subsequent to his death is he in need of any of these goods. Naked we come into the world, and naked shall we again depart. Thus, these goods pertain to what man needs only for the duration of his life here upon earth.

These temporal goods for the maintenance of the body are set before us in this commandment as a special gift of God by which He abundantly blesses man, and thus it follows that God alone is the Lord, proprietor, and master of these goods. He is the creator of heaven and earth, and the fullness of the earth is the Lord's.

No man therefore has an absolute and full claim to these goods, but as the legal profession refers to it, we have the privilege of using the fruits of these goods. We are but given the privilege of enjoying the fruits of these goods as long as it pleases God to grant them, for, as the creator and Lord of all, He has supreme dominion over all things. At a time of supreme adversity, Job acknowledged this, saying, "Naked came I out of my mother's womb, and naked shall I return thither: the LORD gave, and the LORD hath taken away; blessed be the name of the LORD" (Job 1:21). Hannah testified, "The LORD maketh poor, and maketh rich" (1 Sam. 2:7a). We also read in God's Word that "the rich and poor meet together: the LORD is the maker of them all" (Prov. 22:2) and "He [God] giveth to all life, and breath, and all things" (Acts 17:25b), and the Lord's Prayer teaches us to pray, "Give us this day our daily bread" (Matt. 6:11).

These earthly and temporal goods are thus set before us in the first place as a gift of God to mankind. In the second place, these temporal goods must be considered in light of God's covenant, for a true member of the covenant needs them to promote the honor of His covenant God. He is obligated to glorify the Lord his God with all the faculties of his soul and body. The maintenance of his body is therefore a necessity, so that he is able to preserve his body to the praise and honor of His covenant God and to receive strength enabling him to be engaged to that end. It is fitting that the Lord, in His law, has made arrangements for the provision of these earthly or temporal goods, so that all the needs of this life may be met by receiving the goods of which He is the sole giver and of which He has commanded that no man, in any wise, may rob another.

As is true for the majority of the commandments, the lawgiver gave this commandment to His people Israel in the form of a prohibition. Therefore, that which we have said regarding the other commandments must be repeated here: this prohibition implies a positive command, and since that positive command is the foundation of this prohibition, we shall, according to our custom, address this first.

The lawgiver here commands His covenant people to secure and to use their temporal goods and the necessities of life in a lawful manner. We shall first consider in what manner we are to *secure* these temporal goods, and second, how we are to *use* them.

As to the manner in which these temporal goods are to be secured, the lawgiver commanded in the eighth commandment that every Israelite should seek to secure these goods only in an appropriate and lawful manner, and that he must thus be the lawful owner of these goods by virtue of God Himself having bestowed them upon him. A man cannot consider his goods to be his lawful possession unless he is convinced that he has received his possessions from God Himself and that this makes him the lawful owner of these goods. Should he have secured the possession of his goods in any other way, he would not then be the lawful owner of them, for, as the supreme Lord of all things, God did not appoint him as the owner of these goods.

Prior to the fall, our father Adam was the lawful proprietor of Paradise, and thus of the beautiful garden of Eden, for God Himself had appointed him to be the keeper and overseer of this garden, giving him the power and authority to maintain his family by its fruits. Prior to the fall, Adam was thus the lawful lord and proprietor of the garden of Eden. However, after the fall, he was stripped immediately of his right of ownership. God drove him out of the garden, and he was consequently no longer its lawful proprietor.

One therefore secures his temporal goods lawfully when God, as creator and supreme Lord, enables him to become the owner of these goods. This transpires in multiple ways and by various means, such as by lawful inheritance, by working at an honest trade, by a legitimate business, or by the receipt of legitimate gifts.

These are the legitimate and appropriate ways in which one may secure the lawful possession of the temporal goods of this life. Thus, the lawgiver here commanded the children of Israel to pursue such means to secure the goods of this life to meet the needs of their bodies. It was His will that they would refrain from securing such goods in any other way, but that they would secure them only by way of such lawful means.

However, this is not the only thing the lawgiver prescribed to the children of Israel in the eighth commandment, for, upon the securing of these goods, one is also required to use them correctly and lawfully. It is insufficient to secure all of these earthly goods lawfully and by appropriate ways and means; upon having secured them, one must also use them lawfully and correctly.

This is therefore the second obligation the lawgiver explicitly set before the children of Israel. Such lawful use of these goods consists of the following: one must receive these goods in true gratitude from the blessing hand of the Lord, and one must magnify and glorify Him accordingly. One must then use them in a godly manner for the necessary maintenance of the body, and thus as his food and shelter. This is indeed the great purpose for which God bestows these goods upon man, namely, that he would thereby maintain his body and, thereafter, his family also.

On the one hand, one does this by lawfully using his goods righteously and in all moderation, rather than by squandering them by unnecessary and sinful indulgence. On the other hand, in accordance with his financial status, one is not to amass these goods without properly maintaining his family.

The lawful and proper use of one's temporal goods consists also in one's giving to others what he is obligated to give, according to Paul's admonition, when he writes, "Owe no man any thing, but to love one another" (Rom. 13:8). Everyone therefore must also use a portion of his temporal goods for the maintenance of both church and state, as well as of those who bear an office in one of these realms. No one may withhold from his neighbor the wages owed to him, not even for a period of time, for we read that God commanded the children of Israel, "Thou shalt not oppress an hired servant that is poor and needy, whether he be of thy brethren, or of thy strangers that are in thy land within thy gates: at his day thou shalt give him his hire, neither shall the sun go down upon it; for he is poor, and setteth his heart upon it: lest he cry against thee unto the

Lord, and it be sin unto thee" (Deut. 22:14–15). Our conduct must thus be the complete opposite of what we read of the wicked in Psalm 37:21: "The wicked borroweth, and payeth not again."

Above all, according to his ability, one must share his temporal goods with his poor brother whom God has not blessed with earthly goods and who consequently could perish due to hunger, thirst, coldness, and nakedness for lack of the necessities of life. It is therefore the inescapable duty of such whom God has blessed with temporal goods to support a poor brother by generously sharing them with him. God gives us our temporal goods so that we use them to His honor and glory, and by no means amass and hoard them so that none shall be able to use them and have benefit from them. Regarding this, God expressly addressed the children of Israel in His law, saying, "If there be among you a poor man of one of thy brethren within any of thy gates in thy land which the Lord thy God giveth thee, thou shalt not harden thine heart, nor shut thine hand from thy poor brother: but thou shalt open thine hand wide unto him, and shalt surely lend him sufficient for his need, in that which he wanteth" (Deut. 15:7).

Consider also the exhortation of the Savior, "Do good, and lend, hoping for nothing again" (Luke 6:35). Paul therefore earnestly admonishes believers, "But to do good and to communicate forget not, for with such sacrifices God is well pleased" (Heb. 13:16). In Ephesians 4:28, he writes, "Let him that stole steal no more: but rather let him labour, working with his hands the thing which is good, that he may have to give to him that needeth." And finally, we read in Matthew 5:7, "Blessed are the merciful: for they shall obtain mercy."

All of this defines the proper use of lawfully acquired goods, and the lawgiver emphatically demands this of His covenant people in the eighth commandment.

Before we conclude our consideration of what is commanded, we shall briefly consider what our Christian instructor has recorded regarding this. He also finds a precept in this commandment, and therefore we shall first consider it in Question 111, where the instructor asks, "But what doth God require in this commandment?" then causes his pupil to answer, "That I promote the advantage of my neighbor in every instance I can or may, and deal with him as I desire to be dealt with by others; further also that I faithfully labor, so that I may be able to relieve the needy."

The instructor here specifically focuses upon the obligation one has toward his neighbor according to this commandment, saying that God here commands "that I promote the advantage of my neighbor in every instance I can or may." It is thus the duty of all men that in every conceivable way they care for the well-being and temporal welfare of their neighbor so that he will not be deprived of that which lawfully belongs to him. Paul therefore admonishes the Philippians, "Look not every man on his own things, but every man also on the things of others" (Phil. 2:4). In former days, God commanded Abraham's seed: "Thou shalt not see thy brother's ox or his sheep go astray, and hide thyself from them: thou shalt in any case bring them again unto thy brother. And if thy brother be not nigh unto thee, or if thou know him not, then thou shalt bring it unto thine own house, and it shall be with thee until thy brother seek after it, and thou shalt restore it to him again. In like manner shalt thou do with his ass; and so shalt thou do with his raiment; and with all lost things of thy brother's, which he hath lost, and thou hast found, shalt thou do likewise: thou mayest not hide thyself. Thou shalt not see thy brother's ass or his ox fall down by the way, and hide thyself from them: thou shalt surely help him to lift them up again" (Deut. 22:1–4). Everyone is thus obligated to promote the well-being and advantage of his neighbor wherever and whenever he can or may do so.

The instructor then proceeds by saying that God commands categorically in His law that everyone "deal with him as I desire to be dealt with by others." The Savior expressly requires this by saying, "Therefore all things whatsoever ye would that men should do to you, do ye even so to them: for this is the law and the prophets" (Matt. 7:12), and in Luke 6:31, we read, "And as ye would that men should do to you, do ye also to them likewise." This is the general rule by which everyone's conduct toward his neighbor must be governed. One must always—and never otherwise!—treat his neighbor as he wishes to be treated himself. And that is not all, for the instructor continues, saying, "Further also that I faithfully labor, so that I may be able to relieve the needy."

We observed earlier that everyone is obligated to acquire the lawful possession of temporal goods by means of the work of his hands or by fulfilling an office either in church or the civil state. This became a necessity primarily after the fall, for God thunderously pronounced from heaven the curse upon Adam and his entire posterity, saying, "In the sweat of thy face shalt thou eat bread" (Gen. 3:19a). The apostle Paul therefore insists "that if any would not work, neither should he eat" (2 Thess. 3:10b).

The instructor posits that the objective of one's labor must be "that I may be able to relieve the needy." If, therefore, we are unwilling to work, we necessarily incapacitate ourselves from providing for our needs, and consequently will be even less capable of helping our poor brother by sustaining him through our means. Nevertheless, this is our obligation by virtue of the law of love, and it follows that we must labor with our hands. Paul expressly exhorts believers, "Let him that stole steal no more: but rather let him labour, working with his hands the thing which is good, that he may have to give to him that needeth" (Eph. 4:28). In everything the instructor says here, he is guided by the Word of God, thus speaking entirely in conformity to the words of the Holy Spirit as He spoke them Himself.

Having thus considered what God commands, we must now proceed to consider all that is strictly forbidden by the lawgiver by the simple words "Thou shalt not steal."

To give careful consideration to the matters that are emphatically forbidden by the great lawgiver in the eighth commandment, we shall follow the exposition of the instructor. As is his custom, he asks his pupil in Question 110, "What doth God forbid in the eighth commandment?" He then causes him to reply, "God forbids not only those thefts and robberies which are punishable by the magistrate; but He comprehends under the name of theft all wicked tricks and devices, whereby we design to appropriate to ourselves the goods which belong to our neighbor; whether it be by force, or under the appearance of right, as by unjust weights, ells, measures, fraudulent merchandise, false coins, usury, or by any other way forbidden by God; as also all covetousness, all abuse and waste of His gifts."

In addressing what is forbidden, the instructor distinguishes between two types of theft: "those thefts and robberies which are punishable by the magistrate" and "all wicked tricks and devices, whereby we design to appropriate to ourselves the goods which belong to our neighbor." Such conduct is directly contrary to the lawful acquisition of temporal goods. In the foregoing, we have observed what the lawgiver commands us to do.

Regarding the first, according to the instructor, we are forbidden not only to rob and to steal, but also to commit all and any manner of gross theft whereby one violently robs his neighbor of his temporal goods. There are manifold instances of such thievery, such as the stealing of men and beasts, and the robbing of homes, churches, and the poor. There is the commission of public robbery by thieves who violently rob a person of his belongings, and there are also sea pirates, who, by the violent use of weapons, assault people, ships, and cargo. There also are power-hungry kings and rulers, who violently rob neighboring nations of their land, possessions, and subjects. Such are all public thieves and robbers, whom the wise Solomon describes as follows: "If they say, Come with us, let us lay wait for blood, let us lurk privily for the innocent without cause: let us swallow them up alive as the grave; and whole, as those that go down into the pit: we shall find all precious substance, we shall fill our houses with spoil: cast in thy lot among us; let us all have one purse" (Prov. 1:11–14).

Such stealing and robbing is strictly forbidden by the lawgiver, and the commission of such theft is a grievous crime in which many other sins coalesce. He who steals and robs with such violence opposes God's wise government with raised fists. He deprives his neighbor of whatever God has given him as his lawful possession. Such a thief violently and unlawfully robs him of his possessions, taking goods to himself, to which he can lay no claim whatsoever. By so doing, he rebels with a raised fist against God's sovereign government and transgresses His explicit commandments most dreadfully and shamefully. Throughout the Word of God, such stealing and robbing is therefore emphatically forbidden. God even pronounces a curse upon thievery, saying, "This is the curse that goeth forth over the face of the whole earth: for every one that stealeth shall be cut off as on this side according to it.... I will bring it forth, saith the LORD of hosts, and it shall enter into the house of the thief" (Zech. 5:3–4). And thus the curse shall remain in the house, and the house itself shall remain accursed.

Paul says regarding all thieves and robbers: "Know ye not that the unrighteous shall not inherit the kingdom of God? Be not deceived: neither... idolaters...nor thieves...shall inherit the kingdom of God" (1 Cor. 6:9–10). It should then come as no surprise that stealing and robbing are such accursed and shameful sins, and that it is God's will for government severely to punish all who are guilty of this crime. The instructor speaks accordingly, saying, "those thefts and robberies...are punishable by the magistrate."

A variety of laws was therefore given by God to the children of Israel, in which it was generally prescribed that a thief who had stolen was required to restore to the owner that which he had stolen. This could be a twofold, fourfold, fivefold, and even a sevenfold restitution, dependent on the circumstances surrounding the theft. Should a thief be incapable of making such restitution for his theft, he would then be required to serve until the seventh year as a slave to the one from whom he had stolen (Ex. 22:1–13).

However, in our nation, all cases of grievous theft are punished by death, in conformity to our laws. Whether such punishment is legitimate, we shall leave to the investigation of others. As far as we are concerned, we consider theft, from a judicial perspective, to be a very sensitive and weighty matter. But we shall say this: there can be extenuating circumstances that demand that a thief be punished very severely. God Himself gave a law to the children of Israel, in which He gave them the liberty to take the life of a thief caught robbing a house at night or after the sun had set. We addressed this when we expounded the commandment "Thou shalt not kill." Apart from such a case, however, I do not find a single instance in the Word of God that says theft should be punishable with death. Consider, for example, a thief who steals because he is poor, as we read in Proverbs 6:30: "Men do not despise a thief, if he steal to satisfy his soul when he is hungry."

We have hereby addressed sufficiently the commission of public theft, as well as aggravated theft that is accompanied by violence. The instructor now proceeds to address secret theft, addressing all the devious ways in which one unjustly robs his neighbor of his goods. He declares that God, in His law, also considers as acts of thievery "all wicked tricks and devices whereby we design to appropriate to ourselves the goods which belong to our neighbor." Without exception, all of this is forbidden. John the Baptist therefore exhorted the soldiers who came to him to be baptized, saying, "Do violence to no man, neither accuse any falsely; and be content with your wages" (Luke 3:14b).

The instructor posits that there are two ways in which one can rob his neighbor, either "by force, or under the appearance of right." Force is used by those in positions of power, who forcefully rob their neighbors of their possessions. In his epistle, James complains about the rich and mighty of this world, saying: "But ye have despised the poor. Do not rich men oppress you, and draw you before the judgment seats?" (James 2:6).

The instructor continues by saying that the robbing of one's neighbor occurs not only in a violent manner, but also "under the appearance of right." This occurs when one, in a deceitful manner, robs his neighbor of his goods by pretending that these goods do not really belong to him. Paul admonishes believers, saying, "That no man go beyond and defraud his brother in any matter: because that the Lord is the avenger of all such, as we also have forewarned you and testified" (1 Thess. 4:6).

However, the instructor is not satisfied to speak in generalities, but he also gives some examples of deceitful practices by which one can rob his neighbor of his possessions "under the appearance of right." One can do so by way of "unjust weights, ells, measures, fraudulent merchandise, false coins, [or] usury." We will briefly address each of these instances.

One robs his neighbor of that which lawfully belongs to him when, in doing business with him, and thus in the process of buying and selling, one uses either "unjust weights, ells, [or] measures." There is merchandise that is measured in terms of length, and there is merchandise measured in terms of weight. Such has been the practice throughout all human history, and apart from such measurements, business cannot be transacted. One is guilty of robbing and defrauding his neighbor when, in doing business with him, he uses a measure or weight that is either shorter or lighter than was indicated to his neighbor. As a result, his neighbor receives less merchandise than he thought he was purchasing for a given price. In so doing, one grievously defrauds his neighbor and deceitfully steals from him "under the appearance of right," depriving him of a portion of his goods by gaining unlawful possession thereof.

God therefore most solemnly forbade the children of Israel to engage in such vile deception, saying, "Ye shall do no unrighteousness in judgment, in meteyard, in weight, or in measure. Just balances, just weights, a just ephah, and a just hin, shall ye have" (Lev. 19:35–36). Even they who use either of two kinds of weight or two kinds of ephah, that is, one that is either too large or too small, are an abomination to the Lord (Deut. 25:13-16). Solomon speaks likewise, saying, "A false balance is abomination to the LORD: but a just weight is his delight" (Prov. 11:1). It is thus evident that the use either of fraudulent weights or measures is a vile act of thievery and a practice that God most solemnly forbids.

According to the instructor, one can also rob his neighbor either by corrupting merchandise or by deceitfully garnishing it so that it appears better than it is in reality. Furthermore, one robs his neighbor by delivering merchandise that differs from what has been sold or by whatever other method of trickery one may use in business transactions. We read of such deceitful men who "sell the refuse of the wheat" (Amos 8:6). This is also a vile act of thievery, whereby one unjustly acquires the possessions of his neighbor and thereby robs him of what belongs to him.

After having spoken of fraudulent merchandise, the instructor then addresses the matter of false coins; that is, counterfeit money that one puts into the hands of his neighbor, giving him the impression that it is legitimate currency. One can also be guilty of this by tampering with coins and making them lighter than they ought to be. It is recorded as one of the wicked deeds of the Jews that they were guilty of "making the ephah small, and the shekel great, and falsifying the balances by deceit" (Amos 8:5b). This so provoked God to anger that He declared through His prophet: "Shall not the land tremble for this, and every one mourn that dwelleth therein? and it shall rise up wholly as a flood; and it shall be cast out and drowned, as by the flood of Egypt" (Amos 8:8). Thus, the use of fraudulent and corrupt coins is rightfully designated as vile thievery, whereby one's neighbor is defrauded.

The instructor addresses another wicked trick by which one unjustly acquires the goods of his neighbor, namely, the practice of usury. One is guilty of this evil practice when he or she requires his neighbor to pay back a disproportionate and unjust amount of interest on the principal sum of money lent to him when he was in need of funds.

Especially in the business world, it is a very common practice for one party to borrow either money or goods from another party. It is entirely equitable for the lender to charge a reasonable amount of interest, whereby his neighbor is neither excessively burdened nor oppressed, for by lending money to his neighbor, the lender enables him to earn money with his money. What is more reasonable then that the lender receive a portion of the profit that his neighbor secures to himself by using his money? However, as lawful as a legitimate and reasonable interest is, so unlawful and shameful it is to charge excessive and exorbitant interest, especially when one does so upon lending money to the poor. Such a practice is detrimental to one's neighbor and causes him to descend even into greater poverty and deprivation. The practice of usury is especially heinous when considering that one might have sufficiently helped and sustained his neighbor in his dire circumstances and could have done so without any loss on his part.

God expressly forbade His people to practice the vile abomination of usury, saying: "And if thy brother be waxen poor, and fallen in decay with thee; then thou shalt relieve him: yea, though he be a stranger, or a sojourner; that he may live with thee. Take thou no usury of him, or increase: but fear thy God; that thy brother may live with thee. Thou shalt not give him thy money upon usury, nor lend him thy victuals for increase" (Lev. 25:35–37).

David therefore declares it to be an absolutely essential requirement for all that none take usury if they would dwell in the Lord's tabernacle and reside upon the mountain of His holiness, saying, "He that putteth not out his money to usury, nor taketh reward against the innocent" (Ps. 15:5a). In the prophetic utterances of Ezekiel, we find that all usurers are threatened with judgment, for we read there: "Hath [he] given forth upon usury, and hath [he] taken increase:

shall he then live? he shall not live: he hath done all these abominations; he shall surely die; his blood shall be upon him" (Ezek. 18:13). The Savior therefore exhorted His disciples, saying, "Do good, and lend, hoping for nothing again; and your reward shall be great, and ye shall be the children of the Highest" (Luke 6:35).

This clearly affirms that it is entirely correct to designate usury as a shameful act of thievery, and it is consequently forbidden by the lawgiver as being a means whereby one unjustly deprives his neighbor of his goods.

Where would we end, were we to address all the deceitful and fraudulent practices whereby one unjustly acquires the goods of his neighbor? The instructor therefore concludes by way of summary in referring to "any other way forbidden by God." He understands this to refer to any and every deceitful practice by which one seeks to defraud his neighbor. There is the practice:

1. that I persuade one, by way of flattery, to have him include me in his testament, whereby I will inherit his goods or a portion thereof, while I bypass my neighbor, that is, the natural heirs;

2. that I borrow my neighbor's money or goods and do not return them to him;

3. that I find a lost item and not do everything in my power to return it to the rightful owner;

4. that I sell my goods or services at a fee that exceeds their worth;

5. that I pretend lethargy when laboring in someone's employ or waste time by taking excessive breaks, by engaging in conversation, or by doing a minimum of work, so that the wage I receive is not truly earned, I having instead eaten the bread of idleness (Prov. 31:27); and

6. that I not pay someone a wage proportionate to his diligent labor, and instead withhold it either fully or partially. Such a practice is denounced by the Word of the Lord, saying, "Woe unto him that buildeth his house by unrighteousness, and his chambers by wrong; that useth his neighbour's service without wages, and giveth him not for his work" (Jer. 22:13).

In short, who would be able to recount every specific example of such deception and stratagem? The Lord thus forbids in this commandment all fraudulent, deceitful, and dishonest practices, whereby one defrauds his neighbor, irrespective of what one's pretext may be and how insignificant it may appear to be. It is His will and command that we treat our neighbor no differently from that whereby we would wish to be treated ourselves.

Still we have not addressed everything. As is true for all the other commandments, this commandment also is spiritual and does not pertain merely to man's body, but also to his soul. Not only was an Israelite called by this commandment to use the members of his body as instruments of righteousness, but he was to do the same concerning the motions of his soul as well. This commandment therefore penetrates into the deepest recesses of the human heart. The instructor posits in conclusion that all covetousness is forbidden, for the human heart is usually the fountain from whence proceeds all manner of theft. Paul therefore emphatically exhorts believers to refrain from this shameful evil, saying: "But they that will be rich fall into temptation and a snare, and into many foolish and hurtful lusts, which drown men in destruction and perdition. For the love of money is the root of all evil: which while some coveted after, they have erred from the faith, and pierced themselves through with many sorrows" (1 Tim. 6:9–10).

However, not only covetousness is forbidden here; the instructor also speaks of the abuse and wasting of one's gifts or temporal goods. God gives unto man these goods during his lifetime so that they may be used rather than be squandered and abused. Such squandering of one's gifts is frequently also the cause of theft, for thereby one loses the possession of his temporal goods and comes to poverty. In order to avoid this, one may use various ways and means of stealing to acquire the goods of his neighbor. Therefore, the squandering or abuse of our temporal goods is also strictly forbidden. Solomon admonishes young men: "Be not among winebibbers; among riotous eaters of flesh: for the drunkard and the glutton shall come to poverty: and drowsiness shall clothe a man with rags" (Prov. 28:20–21).

Beloved, you need to consider that this is again a commandment of the Lord, the most high God, given to every one of us, not only to keep it perfectly and without so much as the very least infraction, but also to recognize that we will be worthy of eternal death and condemnation if we transgress this commandment in any way, in very deed or by the sinful lusts of our hearts. We need to remember that both the lawgiver and this commandment are supremely holy, and therefore we must examine ourselves again in light of this holy commandment, painstakingly searching our hearts and ways to determine whether we shall inherit life by virtue of our obedience of this commandment or whether our failure will require our death.

Have you perfectly kept this good and perfect commandment of the Lord, first, without transgressing it at all, and second, have you done so not only in all your actions, but also inwardly, with all your heart and with all your soul? Upon considering the previous commandments, we have affirmed that we have transgressed them all from our youth. Never have we kept them as we should. We fare no better regarding this commandment; that is, if we truly examine our hearts and our ways. When considering "those thefts and robberies which are punishable by the magistrate," we may believe that God has kept us all from committing such deeds. Nevertheless, we need to recognize that we would have been readily inclined to commit such acts of thievery if the Lord had completely given us over to ourselves if opportunities and temptations had come our way. We are all grievous violators and transgressors of this commandment of the Lord.

Everyone should examine his heart and consider his conduct from the days of his youth. Everyone should ask himself: "Have I never in my life secretly stolen something from anyone? Have I never committed any act of thievery, even if it were but the value of a penny? How did I acquire my possessions, both now and in the past? Did I receive all of them lawfully from the Lord and by way of honest means? Or is there something which I have taken from another without this person's knowledge?"

We must again enter the courtroom of God and our conscience. Permit me, on the Lord's behalf, to examine you thoroughly to determine whether all is as well with you as you imagine it to be and whether you have the right to boast of your virtuousness as most men do, praising yourself within your own heart, saying with the Pharisee, "God, I thank thee, that I am not as other men are, extortioners, unjust, adulterers, or even as this publican" (Luke 18:11).

Oh, that you all would respond to me, permit your slumbering consciences to be awakened, and confess your sins before an omniscient God, who knows all that you have done, even from the earliest days of your youth!

Have you never, against better knowledge, taken anything from anyone, whether it is of great or little value? Do you remember a time at some point in your life when you secretly took something from another person that did not belong to you and by which you enriched yourself? What is your conscience saying to you? Does it accuse you in any way before God? Can you confess before the God of all the earth, saying, "Lord, thou knowest that I have never knowingly taken or sought to take anything from another in secret. Rather, all that I possess or ever did possess, I have obtained by lawful and just means?"

Specifically, you need to examine yourself carefully if you:

1. Have ever served in an ecclesiastical or civil office. Have you never enriched yourself with something that you kept for yourself and to which you had no claim? Are you conscious of always having conducted yourselves completely honestly and justly in all your official labors?

2. Are storekeepers, businessmen, and craftsmen. Before God, have you always been completely honest and thus kept yourself free from the least deceit? Is your conscience completely at peace before the Lord that you have never short-changed your neighbor by as much as a penny in regard either to merchandise, weight, or measurement? Where, then, did this well-known proverb among us originate that every man is a potential thief? Are we so accustomed to thievery that we do not give it even a thought? Why is there so much lying and dishonesty in the business world—something we hear and experience every day?

3. Are day laborers. Have you always been honest and upright in your work? Have you never earned your wages by laziness, inactivity, and sluggishness? Have you always done an appropriate amount of work for the money that has been paid to you?

4. Are servants. Have you always been faithful in all things? Have you never neglected your service? Have you never neglected to promote your master's advantage and interest? Have you never taken any of his goods and given them to others without his knowledge?

5. Hear this command, whoever you are. Have you ever borrowed something from another and always respectfully returned it? Upon finding something, have you always done your utmost to return it into the hands of the rightful owner, irrespective of whether it was much or little? Have you never stolen from someone by meddling in another's office or calling, thereby secretly depriving him of his advantages and claiming them for yourself?

Beloved, examine yourselves thoroughly regarding all these matters and permit your heart to judge whether you are able to say in truth, before God, that you are not a thief and that you never have stolen anything.

If there is someone who, by reason of his wretched spiritual blindness, is righteous in his own eyes, I must then, on the Lord's behalf, proceed to cross-examine you by asking, "Have you completely kept this commandment of the Lord with your spirit and in your heart so that you have been completely free from all evil desires? Has the inclination toward thievery, whether to a smaller or greater degree, in any way ever arisen in your heart? The Savior teaches that "out of the heart proceed evil thoughts, murders, adulteries, fornications, thefts, false witness, blasphemies" (Matt. 15:19).

Truly, by nature and by practice, we are all vile thieves and robbers. Stealing is rooted in our hearts, and we therefore have been hard-core thieves from the days of our youth, who have stolen thousands upon thousands of times without ever having taken notice of it, for God considers not only our external actions, but also what transpires in our hearts. If the heart is the fountain of all thievery, we are all ungodly law breakers, and the curse, with the penalty of eternal death, is then already pronounced upon us.

We who are here gathered together and who are always inclined to have such good thoughts of ourselves are, in very deed, such vile and wicked thieves before God, but know that all the stealing and robbing committed by the slickest of thieves is not even one thousandth part of what we have done. You may say, "Then what have we done?" If you are yet ignorant of what you have done, it is an indication that you are yet utterly blind and bereft of all saving grace. We all, from the days of our youth, by our vile sins, most shamefully have robbed and defrauded the most high, most holy, and most merciful God of the honor and obedience He is worthy to receive. What an accursed form of theft this is, and how we therefore are worthy of a thousand deaths and condemnations! Have you ever confessed this abominable crime before God, and has it ever caused you to mourn and to weep bitterly? In Christ, have you ever endeavored to return to God the honor of which you have so shamefully robbed Him? The wrath of God will continue to abide on you if you continue not to take this seriously and do not make haste to be reconciled with God in Christ, and, in so doing, have eternal peace!

Such is our true state. We have all shamefully transgressed God's law. Oh, that we would all truly perceive this! If someone were to ask me what we must do under these circumstances so that we will not be eternally subjected to the curse and condemnation of the law, but be delivered from them, then, on the Lord's behalf, we shall show you the only way we must traverse. Oh, may we all, by the power of the Holy Spirit, enter upon that way without delay so that we might live and not die! The evil condition in which we find ourselves is great and exceedingly grievous and dangerous, and the remedy therefore is equally grievous for our flesh and blood. Our entire man must thereby be subdued, and the Lord Himself will have to accomplish this work in us.

Beloved, there are three requisites, and if you use them concurrently, you will be fully restored and eternally saved.

First, be ashamed of the fact that you are such vile thieves and abominable people. Uncover all your evil deeds and unrighteous conduct. Bring them before God, confess them, and exclaim that you have violated God's law by shamefully stealing and transgressing from the days of your youth. Show the Lord your vile and thievish heart and permit Him to see all the abominations that are to be found in your heart. Confess before Him that you are worthy of eternal death, and do not cover up any of your shameful crimes.

Second, immediately, and thus without delay, undertake to return to people everything that you have ever taken and of which you have defrauded them in any way, whether subtly or violently. Do not retain a single penny that you have not lawfully obtained. Even if you have to beg, you may not continue to possess such unrighteous possessions. As long as you knowingly retain the goods you have stolen, so long will the curse of the law abide on your home. Return all that you have stolen to those whom you have defrauded, for God requires this of you in His Word. Have the people whom you have defrauded already died? Return all that you have defrauded them of to their children or to their lawful heirs. And if you cannot find any of them, then, with Judas, you must cast that abominable money into the church's treasury and give it to the poor, for you may in no wise retain it.

Third, come before God as accursed, wicked, and impotent sinners who are worthy of death and be reconciled with Him through the death of His Son. By a true faith, take hold of the offered strength and righteousness of Christ, and allow yourself to be fully cleansed of all thievery that you have committed and of all your abominable corruptions in the fountain of His blood, until there is no spot left on you. Receive Christ fully and completely unto your justification and sanctification. Embrace Him as having obeyed God's law fully for you and as having borne fully the guilt and punishment of your transgressions. Let His Spirit fully convert, renew, and transform you, so that you will hereafter steal no more, but will always walk before Him in complete uprightness.

If you are pleased with these three requisites, you can, before God and in Christ, be completely delivered from your wretched state and be fully absolved from all your wicked deeds—that is, if you truly initiate these steps. If not, you will then continue to be vile thieves and transgressors, and, in the Day of Judgment, you will be consigned to the eternal fire of hell, from which you will never be delivered.

Children of God, permit me to say to you with a few words, that the anointing you have received from God, and which remains in you, will teach you all of these things. It will teach you how you must always use the law as a mirror and as a taskmaster to lead you to Christ. Our prayer and supplication for you is that this wisdom from above may increasingly and abundantly be your portion in the Lord, who is worthy to receive all praise and worship to all eternity. Amen.

The Ninth Commandment, Forbidding the Bearing of False Witness

Thou shalt not bear false witness against thy neighbor.
—EXODUS 20:16

Question 112: What is required in the ninth commandment?

Answer: That I bear false witness against no man nor falsify any man's words; that I be no backbiter nor slanderer; that I do not judge, nor join in condemning any man rashly or unheard; but that I avoid all sorts of lies and deceit, as the proper works of the devil, unless I would bring down upon me the heavy wrath of God; likewise, that in judgment and all other dealings I love the truth, speak it uprightly and confess it; also that I defend and promote, as much as I am able, the honor and good character of my neighbor.

———————————

Among the great privileges with which God has gifted the human race above the irrational animals, which by no means is the least, is the ability to generate speech by the tongue. This is truly a most noble and precious gift that readily enables people to communicate their inner thoughts one to another and renders them infinitely superior to irrational creatures, which, though they are equipped with tongues, can neither speak nor bring forth any rational and distinct sounds.

Since all God's believing covenant people are obligated to use each and every one of their external members as instruments of righteousness and are duty-bound to glorify God, not only spiritually, but also physically, this obligation pertains also specifically to the use of their tongues and their ability to speak. If there is any member whereby a believer can glorify and magnify God, it is his tongue, a member that, though it is small, can boast great things.

A person is able to use his tongue in an evil as well as in a good manner, and the wise King Solomon therefore correctly assesses this by saying, "Death and life are in the power of the tongue" (Prov. 18:21a). In His illustrious law, God the Lord has therefore expressed a great concern regarding the use of this mighty member of speech by His sanctified covenant people, as He expressly commands them to use their tongues appropriately to His honor and to the well-being of their neighbor by forbidding them to bear false witness.

The commandment presently under consideration is the fifth commandment of the second table of the law, in which we are commanded to love our neighbor as ourselves, and, when considering the two tables of the law as a whole, it is the ninth commandment.

As the great and adorable lawgiver, the Lord sets before us in the fifth commandment the duties of children toward their parents and of subordinates toward their superiors. In the sixth commandment, He prescribes how human life here upon earth is to be sustained and preserved. In the seventh commandment, He stipulates the lawful procreation and perpetuation of the human race in the world. In the eighth commandment, He sets before man his obligation regarding the lawful acquisition, use, and possession of such temporal goods as are needed for the maintenance of life.

From the eighth commandment, the Lord proceeds to the ninth commandment, in which He prescribes the lawful use of speech by which men communicate with one another, so that truth may be promoted and one's good name and reputation be preserved as a most essential requisite for mutual peace and love. Our further consideration of this commandment will affirm that it is no less important and essential than the commandments we have already considered. May the Lord so illumine us that we clearly perceive the excellence of this commandment, and may He cause our souls to be entirely enamored by its sanctity.

In our exposition of this commandment, we must again consider:

1. the object of the commandment; and
2. the duty toward this object that the lawgiver requires of His covenant people.

The object (or focal point) of this commandment is what is referred to in Latin as *usus loquela*, that is, the use of speech. We know that God created man to be a rational creature who excels all other creatures by being endued with the ability to speak with his tongue and to bring forth sounds by which he can communicate his inner thoughts to his fellow men.

This ability to speak, by which every rational creature excels over the irrational, is the object of our consideration in the ninth commandment. This object must again be considered from two specific vantage points:

First, as an essential gift from God given to man as a rational creature. God could indeed have willed that all men would be as incapable of speaking with one another as are the animals. However, it has pleased God, in contradistinction to all irrational creatures, to bestow upon man the privilege of a tongue, whereby he can produce distinct and intelligible sounds. This ability to speak is of utmost importance for mankind, for without it, the functioning of human society would be impossible. For the functioning of human society, it is absolutely essential that people be able to communicate their thoughts. Without that capability, there can be no orderly interaction between the members of the human race.

We have a vivid example of this regarding all who were involved in the building of the Tower of Babel. Immediately upon God having confused their language, resulting in people no longer being able to understand each other, the entire construction project came to a halt. This confusion of language could merely be a reference to emotional confusion, such as renders one person unwilling to understand the other, a matter about which scholars differ in opinion. However, no one is able to deny that speech is an absolutely essential means for the functioning of human society. Speech is the soul's vehicle of communication by which one communicates his thoughts to others and becomes acquainted with the thoughts of others, thereby sustaining the functioning of human society.

Second, in relationship to God's covenant. As the covenant God, it is His will that He be fully glorified by His covenant people. There is nothing more suitable for the glorification of God than human speech. By speech, one outwardly exalts and praises the Lord God, thereby proclaiming to others His magnificent virtues and perfections. In so doing, one stimulates his fellow men to magnify God as well. When the tongue of a man is touched by a coal from off the altar, there is no member of his entire body as suitable for the exaltation and glorification of Jehovah God.

The use of the ability to speak is therefore an eminent and very essential means whereby one of God's covenant people may exalt and glorify the Lord, his covenant God. Since it follows that the ability to speak is a precious gift bestowed by God upon His rational creature; since He is consequently the sole Lord and master of this gift; since the use of this gift is, on the one hand, such a great and absolute necessity for human society, which can neither function nor be sustained apart from it; and since, on the other hand, a true member of the covenant must use this gift to glorify the Lord, His covenant God, and to proclaim His illustrious virtues, it should not surprise us that God made the use of speech expressly the object of His care, so that it might be used by His covenant people to that end and by no means be abused. To achieve this, He gave Israel the commandment that they should not bear false witness against their neighbor.

The lawgiver stipulates in this commandment only that which pertains to the mutual use of speech among men, forbidding the bearing of false witness *against our neighbor*. This should not surprise us, for the use of speech is not for God's benefit, but for the benefit of man. God has not equipped man with the gift of speech so that He might know what his inner thoughts are. God does not need human speech to know this, for He is omniscient and even knows our very thoughts. There is no need for man to communicate these thoughts to Him. David affirms this, saying, "For there is not a word in my tongue, but, lo, O LORD, thou knowest it altogether" (Ps. 139:4).

Since, therefore, the use of speech is for the benefit only of men, it follows that God prescribes in His law only how we are to speak with our neighbor, forbidding the bearing of false witness *against one's neighbor*. The word *neighbor* signifies here our fellow man, who, with us, has a rational soul and body, and who has descended from the first Adam. Consequently, all men are neighbors, one of another, for God "hath made of one blood all nations of men for to dwell on all the face of the earth" (Acts 17:26).

By speaking of our neighbor, the lawgiver is not merely referring to every Israelite who proceeded from Abraham's loins, but He is also referring indiscriminately to all strangers who do not belong to their seed. This is affirmed by the fact that the word neighbor is even used to refer to non-Israelites. God therefore commanded the Israelites in Egypt, "Let every man borrow of his *neighbour*, and every woman of her *neighbour*, jewels of silver, and jewels of gold" (Ex. 11:2). The Egyptians are here designated as neighbors of the children of Israel, signifying that all men without distinction are neighbors to one another. The Savior therefore even numbers our enemies among our neighbors, saying, "But I say unto you, Love your enemies, bless them that curse you, do good to them that hate you, and pray for them which despitefully use you, and persecute you" (Matt. 5:44). He is applying to us the commandment that we must love our neighbor as ourselves, prescribing that one must also love his enemies.

During the Savior's sojourn, the Jews considered no one to be their neighbor unless he belonged to the generation and nation that had descended from Abraham. In response to the question of the Scribes, "Who is my neighbor" (Luke 10:29b), the Savior taught that all men are neighbors to one another and that we therefore are indiscriminately obligated to show mercy and love toward everyone. Consequently, the word neighbor, as it is used in this commandment, signifies all men whom God, according to Paul, "hath made of one blood" (Acts 17:26), irrespective of whether they are our fellow citizens or strangers who hail from other nations or ethnic groups. The lawgiver commands the children of Israel that they may not bear false witness against these neighbors.

As the words of the ninth commandment occur in the original text, they can be translated in two ways, yielding two meanings. According to our translators, they can be translated as "Thou shalt not bear false witness *regarding* thy neighbor" or as "Thou shalt not bear false witness *against* thy neighbor." Regarding the first translation, it is assumed that one is speaking to others about his neighbor, but regarding the second translation, it is assumed that one is speaking directly to his neighbor.

We believe that these two translations must coalesce, and that the one should imply the other, for it has pleased the lawgiver to use few words in these ten commandments—words that nevertheless signify great and weighty matters. Our interpretation of this commandment is therefore twofold, namely, that the Lord utterly forbids either the bearing of false witness *to* one's neighbor in his presence or the bearing of false witness *about* one's neighbor in his absence.

Our exposition of this commandment will therefore be twofold. To do this correctly, we must first address what is being commanded and then consider the prohibition that is founded upon this commandment, for the lawgiver, as is His custom, is here addressing His covenant people by way of a prohibition.

The commandment is thus expressed as follows: "Thou shalt always bear witness to the truth to thy neighbor and regarding thy neighbor." Bearing witness to the truth is to be simply understood as offering a witness that, in all its details, conforms to the nature, specifics, and circumstances regarding a certain matter, so that one says nothing other than that which truly conforms to the matter itself, whether it is by affirmation or denial. Our witness is truthful if it fully conforms to the state and nature of the matter itself. However, the moment our testimony deviates in the least from the matter itself, to that extent, our testimony is false and deceitful, and to that extent, the truth is found neither in our hearts nor in our mouths. Therefore, to determine the legitimacy of our testimony, we must examine it in light of the matter itself, and if there is complete agreement, our testimony is truthful.

The Lord here commands that the testimony of every man must always be truthful:

1. *Toward* one's neighbor. The words one utters toward his neighbor must be true and fully conform to the matters of which one is speaking. It should not be a surprise that this is so, for man may not do anything that either displeases the Lord or that militates against His virtues and perfections. The Lord is a God of truth, and the poet also gives testimony thereof, declaring, "Thou desirest truth in the inward parts" (Ps. 51:6a). Isaiah therefore said regarding the Lord, the covenant God, that "righteousness shall be the girdle of his loins, and faithfulness¹ the girdle of his reins" (Isa. 11:5).

Since the God of the covenant always promotes truth and He Himself is the God of truth, every member of His covenant people must always be desirous and endeavor to emulate Him in these virtues and not be guilty of doing anything contradictory to them. Consequently, Paul exhorts believers, "Wherefore putting away lying, speak every man truth with his neighbor" (Eph. 4:25). Thus, the first matter prescribed in this commandment is that every one of the children of Israel must always be truthful in speaking to his neighbor.

2. *Regarding* one's neighbor. It is also commanded that everyone must speak and bear witness to the truth when speaking to others about one's neighbor, whether this be before a judge or in a common conversation with others. Regarding the first, the Lord here commands that when we are required to bear witness to the truth regarding matters that pertain to our neighbor in a courtroom, we should never refuse to do so, for it is of the greatest importance to our neighbor that the truth regarding his matter be made public. By bearing witness to the truth regarding our neighbor, we greatly promote the advantage and well-being of our neighbor, for, based on that testimony, a proper judgment regarding our neighbor's litigation will be rendered. Otherwise, by reason of our bearing false witness, our neighbor will be unjustly condemned and be robbed of that which is lawfully his. It is therefore the will of the Lord that, in the courtroom, one be truthful regarding one's neighbor in all matters that pertain to him.

---

1. The Dutch *Statenvertaling* reads, "Ook zal *de waarheid* de gordel Zijner lendenen zijn"; that is, "Also truth shall be the girdle of his loins."

The Lord also commands that we be truthful regarding our neighbor outside of the courtroom; that is, in common conversations, when there is occasion to speak to others regarding our neighbor. The Lord stipulates in this commandment that we must endorse the truth regarding each other wholeheartedly, speaking only the truth, and always endeavor to uphold and protect the honor and good name of one another to the utmost of our ability by revealing the truth.

The Lord is not stipulating here that we must indiscriminately say all that we know to be truth about one another, but that we speak of others only insofar as it is proper and to our neighbor's benefit. There are often circumstances and situations in which one cannot bear witness to the truth regarding his neighbor without it being in some way detrimental to him. In such cases, it is not permitted, unless absolutely necessary, to bear witness to the truth regarding one's neighbor, but one is then obligated to remain silent, thereby carefully concealing what one knows to be true. When there is true love in our hearts for our neighbor and we truly fear God, this guides us as to what true things we must reveal regarding our neighbor and which matters we must carefully conceal from others.

The most high God therefore commands here that we never do anything other than speak the truth with or about our neighbor, be it in the courtroom or in common conversations with others.

Having thus considered what is commanded, we must now proceed to consider what the children of Israel are forbidden to do in this commandment. The lawgiver forbids us to bear false witness against or regarding our neighbor, thus forbidding us to speak deceitfully to or regarding our neighbor. The word *false* refers not only to that which is vain, but also to that which is deceitful and contradictory to the truth. Both meanings are therefore to be considered here, for Israel was forbidden not just to bear witness in a vain and presumptuous manner against or about her neighbor, but also to say anything deceitful or fraudulent.

To understand the full extent of this prohibition, we shall follow the exposition of our Christian instructor. He asks his pupil, "What is required in the ninth commandment?" to which he replies, "That I bear false witness against no man nor falsify any man's words."

The instructor judges that the first thing prescribed in this commandment is "that I bear false witness against no man." This means that we may not say anything regarding our neighbor that is either untruthful or deceitful, saying something that would either harm him or be to his disadvantage. He also interprets the word neighbor as referring to all men without distinction, and therefore he posits that we may not bear false witness to anyone; that is, absolutely no one, whether he be small or great, young or old, poor or rich. God solemnly forbade this by the mouth of Moses, saying, "Thou shalt not raise a false report: put not thine hand with the wicked to be an unrighteous witness" (Ex. 23:1). Yes, at that time, God commanded that a false witness be severely punished upon the discovery that his testimony regarding his neighbor had been false and deceitful (Deut. 19:16–19).

One cannot be guilty of a more vile and abominable crime than witnessing false and untrue things regarding one's neighbor. They who are guilty of this are an abomination unto the Lord. Solomon testifies that among the six things that God hates is "a false witness that speaketh lies, and he that soweth discord among brethren" (Prov. 6:19), and in Proverbs 19:5, we read, "A false witness shall not be unpunished, and he that speaketh lies shall not escape." This confirms that we may not bear false or untrue witness to anyone.

The instructor then continues by saying that this commandment also forbids us "to falsify any man's words." To falsify someone's words is to interpret them in a false and evil way, and so to distort them that others extract an entirely different meaning from that which the speaker of these words intended to communicate. The Jews dealt with our Savior in this manner. He had said, "Destroy this temple, and in three days I will raise it up" (John 2:19), and the Jews deceitfully distorted this by accusing Him of having said, "I will destroy this temple that is made with hands [namely, the temple in Jerusalem], and within three days I will build another made without hands" (Mark 14:58).

In our day, this is a very common sin among people. It is nevertheless a sin that is very vile and shameful, one that proceeds from the despicable cesspool of lovelessness of one toward the other. One is therefore always inclined to think evil of and to misinterpret the words of his neighbor, thereby seeking occasion for discord and division. However, in the Holy Scriptures, the Lord solemnly rebukes and forbids all men to engage in this shameful sin. The wise Solomon emphatically warns everyone against this shameful sin, saying, "Put away from thee a froward mouth, and perverse lips put far from thee" (Prov. 4:24). This affirms that we are forbidden to falsify the words of our neighbor.

The instructor then proceeds to address backbiting and slander, saying, "that I be no backbiter, nor slanderer." A backbiter is someone who, secretly and behind his neighbor's back, speaks disparagingly of his neighbor, thereby endeavoring to make him hateful to and despised by others. God most solemnly forbade the children of Israel to engage in such a practice, saying, "Thou shalt not go up and down as a talebearer among thy people" (Lev. 19:16a). The wisest among kings also declares, "A talebearer revealeth secrets" (Prov. 11:13a).

Paul considers this vile vice primarily to be one of the faults and deficiencies with which the female sex is infected. Regarding young and sensuous widows, he declares, "And withal they learn to be idle, wandering about from house to house; and not only idle, but tattlers also and busybodies, speaking things which they ought not" (1 Tim. 5:13).

Consider also how David describes the backbiter, saying, "Whoso privily slandereth his neighbour, him will I cut off" (Ps. 101:5a). The apostle James therefore solemnly admonishes believers, saying: "Speak not evil one of another, brethren. He that speaketh evil of his brother, and judgeth his brother, speaketh evil of the law, and judgeth the law" (James 4:11a). Backbiting is therefore a very ugly and vile sin that ought not to be named among God's covenant people. Diogenes, a famous Gentile philosopher, was once asked which animal had the most vicious bite. In response, he quipped, "Among the lame, it is the flatterer, and among the wild beasts, it is the slanderer and backbiter."

Having considered backbiting, the instructor then addresses the sin of slander, a sin that consists in desecrating the good name of one's neighbor by accusing him falsely and deceitfully, thereby to depict him as vile as possible. Shimei thus railed against and slandered the fleeing King David, crying out to him, "Come out, come out, thou bloody man, and thou man of Belial" (2 Sam. 16:7a). Likewise, King Ahab slandered the prophet Elijah, defaming him as "he that troubleth Israel" (1 Kings 18:17b).

This is a shameful sin that proceeds from the devil himself, who is designated as a slanderer. Paul most solemnly warns believers against this evil, saying, "Let all bitterness, and wrath, and anger, and clamour, and evil speaking, be put away from you, with all malice" (Eph. 4:31), and he calls upon his spiritual son Titus to exhort his congregation that they should "speak evil of no man" (Titus 3:2a). We conclude that backbiting and slander are also forbidden by the lawgiver.

The instructor then proceeds by saying that one may "not judge, nor join in condemning any man rashly, or unheard." This can occur in two ways: in a courtroom or in general conversation. This takes place in the courtroom when someone readily endorses the accusations leveled against another, condemning him without permitting him either to respond to such accusations or to defend himself, with the result that he is judged and condemned without first having been heard. Thus it ought not to be, for in the courtroom, one should always observe the general rule that the one as well as the other must be heard. Justice requires that a sentence should never be pronounced upon someone until all incriminating evidence has been presented in an orderly fashion, asking the defendant whether he has anything more to say in his defense. Judges who conduct themselves otherwise, thereby unjustly condemning their fellow men, are accursed of God, as the supreme judge says: "Ye shall do no unrighteousness in judgment: thou shalt not respect the person of the poor, nor honour the person of the mighty: but in righteousness shalt thou judge thy neighbor" (Lev. 19:15).

Not only can one judge and condemn his neighbor unrighteously in the courtroom, but one can also do so by readily condemning and judging one's neighbor upon hearing an evil report, without either investigating the validity of such a report or being willing to hear what one's neighbor has to say, treating him as if he were guilty of all the things of which he is wickedly accused. The Savior emphatically admonishes his disciples to the contrary, saying, "Judge not, and ye shall not be judged: condemn not, and ye shall not be condemned" (Luke 6:37a). The godly counselor Nicodemus responded to the Jews in this fashion when they condemned the Savior unheard as if He were a false prophet, saying, "Doth our law judge any man, before it hear him, and know what he doeth?" (John 7:51).

The instructor then proceeds to declare that one must also "avoid all sorts of lies and deceit, as the proper works of the devil, unless I would bring down upon me the heavy wrath of God." He speaks here of "all sorts of lies and deceit," and thus of all and any deceitful practices by whatever name or label they may be known. Ethicists generally distinguish between several categories of lies: *harmful* lies; *white* lies, which are spoken for the sake of one's advantage; and *entertaining* lies, by which one seeks to entertain someone. These various categories of lies are here categorically forbidden.

Harmful lies, by which one harms either himself or his neighbor, are most certainly unlawful. As we have already observed, when speaking to our neighbor, we must always promote and bear witness to the truth and refrain from the utterance of vile lies. The lawgiver therefore declares, "Ye shall not…deal falsely, neither lie one to another" (Lev. 19:11). Paul admonishes believers: "Lie not one to another" (Col. 3:9a). Also, in Zechariah 8:16, we read the Lord's solemn command: "Speak ye every man the truth to his neighbour; execute the judgment of truth." It is thus beyond doubt that the utterance of harmful lies is most certainly forbidden.

However, the politicians of our day reason only by way of their carnal minds and according to their corrupt judgment because they know not God, and they therefore make a distinction between beneficial lies and such lies as are strictly forbidden. Beneficial lies are lies by which one frequently benefits either himself or his neighbor, and therefore it is commonly said among us that a white lie is not a lie. Among jurists, there are even those who maintain that one may utter a lie if it is not to the detriment of either oneself or one's neighbor. Even among the Remonstrants, there are many who espouse even such a view in their publications.

Beloved, we must say that it is an ungodly notion to posit that it is permissible to utter a white lie. Even if we were thereby to succeed either in helping ourselves or our neighbor, no one may suppress the truth, for all truth has its origin in God Himself. Man is not the lord and master of the truth, but he is a servant of the truth, having the obligation to promote truth in all things. He who avails himself of lies to help himself or his neighbor is engaged in an entirely erroneous manner, for God indiscriminately forbids all lies, and He emphatically demands that man should never speak in any way but in conformity to the clear and distinct concepts with which He Himself has furnished him. One may never commit evil so that good may issue from it. The great Augustine declares that just as one may neither commit adultery nor steal for the benefit of others, one may also not lie for another's benefit.

We may not emulate the examples of Abraham, Isaac, and the Egyptian midwives, who uttered such white lies, any more than we would emulate all the other weaknesses and deficiencies of those holy men and women. It is thus evident that all white lies are also expressly forbidden.

This is equally true regarding lies by which one seeks to entertain a company of people, for the utterance of such lies is also strictly forbidden, inasmuch as this commandment declares that we are not to bear *false* witness against our neighbor. As we stated earlier, the word false here also means vain or rashly. All entertainment is ultimately nothing but vanity and frivolity, and therefore they sin greatly who accustom themselves to entertaining their neighbor by vain conversation and lies. Paul admonishes believers by saying, "Let…neither filthiness, nor foolish talking, nor jesting…be once named among you" (Eph. 5:4, 3), for "every idle word that men shall speak, they shall give account thereof in the day of judgment" (Matt. 12:36). God therefore solemnly rebukes this evil as it manifests itself in His people, saying, "They make the king glad with their wickedness, and the princes with their lies" (Hos. 7:3).

The instructor then correctly posits that whatever the pretext for such lies may be, God forbids in this commandment "all sorts of lies and deceit, as the proper works of the devil." To the practice of lying, he adds "all sorts of deceit," that is, one seeking either to pull the wool over his neighbor's eyes or to harm him either with words or gestures. This occurs by flattery or hypocrisy when one pretends to be someone other than he really is, and, in so doing, seeks to deceive and harm his neighbor. David says regarding such individuals, "They speak vanity every one with his neighbour: with flattering lips and with a double heart do they speak" (Ps. 12:2).

The instructor then states that we must avoid all such lying and deceitfulness as being "the proper works of the devil." This is confirmed by the words of the Savior, and the instructor has these words in mind, for Jesus says regarding the devil: "Ye are of your father the devil, and the lusts of your father ye will do. He was a murderer from the beginning, and abode not in the truth, because there is no truth in him. When he speaketh a lie, he speaketh of his own: for he is a liar, and the father of it" (John 8:44). Truly, all sins have their origin from the devil and proceed from man's wicked and corrupt heart. There is a close alliance between them, and, by nature, the heart is fully governed and wrought upon by him. In His believing people, Christ, by His Spirit, must subdue all these works of the devil and increasingly destroy them.

Since lying and deceit are the proper work of the devil, everyone who fears the Lord must carefully refrain from practicing such shameful wickedness, lest he "would bring down upon [himself] the heavy wrath of God."

There is nothing that God hates more and that provokes Him to greater anger than "all manner of lies and deceit." David addresses God accordingly, saying, "Thou shalt destroy them that speak leasing: the LORD will abhor the bloody and deceitful man" (Ps. 5:6). In Colossians 3:6, Paul declares, "For which things' sake the wrath of God cometh on the children of disobedience." Can it be any different, my friends? God is a God of truth, and He loves the truth at the very core of His being. Since all His commandments are unchangeable, must He then not necessarily greatly hate all manner of lies?

Must not the wrath of God be manifested from heaven toward such lies? By such sins men heap God's wrath upon themselves, treasuring up to themselves "wrath against the day of wrath" (Rom. 2:5). Woe unto them if they do not seek, in a timely fashion, to be saved from God's wrath in and through Christ and to be reconciled with Him! Oh, how dreadful it shall be to fall into the hands of the God whom they have provoked to anger and who lives forever! May sinners take this to heart.

According to the instructor, these are all the sins that the children of Israel are forbidden to engage in by this ninth commandment. As is his custom, he then proceeds to consider that which is commanded, saying, "that in judgment and all other dealings I love the truth, speak it uprightly, and confess it." We addressed this when we expounded the commandment as such, and we therefore consider it unnecessary to repeat it here.

We shall therefore move on to consider the last matter that, according to the instructor, is commanded here: "that I defend and promote, as much as I am able, the honor and good character of my neighbor." This is the common duty of all men toward one another. Everyone must "defend and promote, as much as [he is] able, the honor and good character of [his] neighbor." Next to life itself, this is the most precious thing our neighbor possesses here on earth. Solomon says regarding this that "a good name is rather to be chosen than great riches" (Prov. 22:1). Everyone is obligated to conceal, with great discretion, his neighbor's secret errors and weaknesses, and, instead, to honor and praise his neighbor's virtues. Jonathan did so regarding his bosom friend David, for we read, "and Jonathan spake good of David unto Saul his father" (1 Sam. 19:4a). Everyone is obligated to defend and promote the name and reputation of his neighbor as much as he is able.

We have again considered a commandment of the most high God which we are obligated to keep and obey in an absolutely perfect manner and without the least transgression. Not only are we to do so because this commandment is perfectly holy and good, but also because it has been given to us by a holy and righteous God, and we are not permitted to transgress His commandments in the least, lest we make ourselves worthy of eternal death and condemnation, and thereby subject ourselves to the most dreadful perdition of both soul and body.

Examine yourselves in light of the Lord's commandment, as we have expounded it for you. Quietly and with all seriousness, observe yourself in this mirror. Oh, that you would have eye salve for this purpose! How is it with you? Are you keepers of this commandment of the Lord? Or are you shameful and vile transgressors? Is this a commandment unto death for you? Or is it a commandment unto life? Consider this in all seriousness.

So many things are prohibited in this commandment, and should you be guilty of transgressing it, you are worthy of eternal death and condemnation. Therefore, in all simplicity, examine yourselves in light of all that is addressed in the Catechism.

First, God forbids you to bear false witness against anyone. Have you never done this? What is the origin of all this deceiving and maligning of one another, of which we hear daily? What is the origin of all the disputes and quarrels among men due to being deceived? And what is the origin of one person speaking ill of another? Do such things not occur daily?

Second, God also forbids you to falsify anyone's words. Is there a sin that is more common among men? Is there anyone who is not guilty of this? Do you not twist and distort the words of your neighbor countless times, giving an evil twist to that which was said favorably by him, doing so by adding to or omitting some of his words? What else is the cause of all these disputes when people say: "I did not say it that way. I meant something entirely different. You are lying." Daily we hear examples of this.

Third, God forbids all backbiting and slander regarding your neighbor. Who is not guilty of this grievous sin? Is a more insidious abomination imaginable among men? When worldly people gather together, do they not frequently engage in gossip and slander, and speak evil one of another? Is this not frequently the substance of their conversation from the moment they arrive until the moment they depart? Are they capable of spending their time in any other way than by engaging in all manner of backbiting, raking each other over the coals, revealing one another's errors, and continually minding other people's business?

Fourth, God forbids us to judge anyone lightly or without being heard. Is this not again the daily practice and occupation of the people of the world? Are you not rendering judgment upon all that you either hear or see? Is everyone not subjected to your foolish and loveless judgment? Are you not countless times judging the state, words, and conduct of others without either knowing or understanding what you are rendering a judgment of? Must I, the Lord's servant among you, continually hear how foolishly and lovelessly you judge my doctrine and life, although you have not the least true knowledge of either and are utterly guilty of judging them as one who is color-blind?

Fifth, God forbids all sorts of lies and deceit. How dreadfully most of you are guilty of this sin! Do you know how many hundreds of thousands of lies and deceitful practices that your soul is guilty of and that are recorded in God's book of remembrance shall be revealed on the last day? Oh, what vile liars and deceivers all men are! How vividly do men display that the image of Satan is imprinted upon their souls! What great effort one makes of a lie if it will yield some advantage! Lying and deceiving are so natural to people, they do not even realize how guilty they are of this sin. It is so embedded in their nature, and they are so much given over to it.

Sixth, God requires "that in judgment and all other dealings I love the truth, speak it uprightly, and confess it." Regarding this, men by no means obey the Lord, for all men without distinction are liars (Ps. 116:11). By nature, we are complete enemies of the truth, hating it and loving the lie. If an unconverted person makes it his business to speak and promote the truth regarding natural things, his being motivated thereto does not spring from a true love for the truth as proceeding from God Himself. Instead, he does so because he has certain motives. However, in his heart, he remains a sworn enemy of all truth— particularly of spiritual truths regarding God, of which he has not even the least knowledge. Regarding all unregenerate men, it is true what the Savior testified of their father, the devil, saying that "there is no truth in him" (John 8:44).

Finally, God commands that "I defend and promote, as much as I am able, the honor and good character of my neighbor." Who among us, having heard this commandment of the Lord, is able to say that he has eaten it up and that the keeping thereof has been as a sweet morsel to him? As to your practice, there is nothing you do less than defend and promote the honor of your neighbor. As far as the men of this world are concerned, they are utterly hateful and hating one another. They do not have the least love for one another's honor and good name. Rather, they dishonor, slander, offend, and despise one another, doing so as much as they are able. This is the cause of there being so much speaking evil of others, revealing one another's faults, judging and condemning one another, and maligning and slandering one another—all of which one hears and sees daily and repeatedly.

In this way, the world despises and disobeys this holy command of the Lord. Everyone transgresses this commandment in his conduct and conversation. You who are yet unconverted can do no otherwise, for it is your natural inclination to sin grievously in thought, word, and deed against the Lord and His law. From the days of your youth, you have increased in this wickedness. The heart of man is always inclined toward all evil, "because the carnal mind is enmity against God: for it is not subject to the law of God, neither indeed can be" (Rom. 8:7).

Consider for a moment how wretched, abominable, guilty, and hell-worthy you are in all these things before God and how you by no means will be able to prevail in light of His holy justice. Oh, do consider how dreadfully God is provoked to anger against you and what you must expect of Him if you appear before Him on the last day in all your vileness, abominableness, and uncleanness! As you have heard, He is indeed the God of whom we read that He shall "destroy them that speak leasing: the LORD will abhor the bloody and deceitful man" (Ps. 5:6).

Are you then neither fearful of such condemnation nor at all concerned about your most wretched state? Shall you appear before this holy and just God as unholy and sinful as you are? Are you not crying out in true contrition, anxiety, and perplexity of your souls, "We have sinned; what shall we do?" Are you then, notwithstanding all your wickedness and unholiness, still righteous in your own eyes? Are you yet unaware of any danger? Are you not yet making haste to go to Christ and be washed and cleansed in the fountain of His blood? Are you still without any true concern regarding this? Do you still have no desire for regeneration, faith, and repentance? Will you, black as Ethiopians (Jer. 13:23), not permit yourself to be transformed and made white in the blood of the Lamb? Woe unto you, O foolish man! Woe unto you who are careless! It will be more tolerable for Tyre and Sidon in the Day of Judgment than for you. Oh, give ear to the admonitions I shall address to believers, for you will have to traverse the same pathway if you desire to live rather than die.

Children of God, elect of the Father, you who are called to be saints and are believers in Christ Jesus, I say to you that such were some of you. Yes, without exception, this was true for all of you, but now "ye are washed, but ye are sanctified, but ye are justified in the name of the Lord Jesus, and by the Spirit of our God" (1 Cor. 6:11). Oh, do you have a desire carefully to keep all of God's precepts and holy commandments, and to order all your ways accordingly? Is this particularly true for the commandment we have expounded today? The world cannot do otherwise but sin against this holy commandment. You, however, are indwelt by the sanctifying Spirit of God, who continually leads you into all truth. Do you desire to know how you may keep this commandment of the Lord your God perfectly and without any transgression? Oh, may I give to both you and to myself good counsel from the Lord, and may He, by His Spirit, bless it to us!

Obtain eye salve from the Lord Jesus in order to see rightly:

1. How grievous your daily guilt is and how you continually transgress this holy commandment of the Lord in thought, word, and deed.

2. Your ungodly and unholy nature, and how, in yourself, you are nothing but "in the bond of iniquity" (Acts 8:23), and, yes, that you are an abomination before God. May you see how polluted your heart still is and how inclined it still is toward all these wicked deeds, and that if the grace of God did not prevent you, you would commit them daily. Oh, may you, by this light, descend deeply into this stinking cesspool and cry out, "Woe is me that I am so abominable and that I am such a false witness; that I am such a falsifier of my neighbor's words; that I am such an accursed backbiter and slanderer; that I am such an unjust judge of my neighbor; that I am such an ungodly liar and such a vile deceiver; that I am such an enemy of the truth as it is in God; that I am such a despiser and maligner of my neighbor; and that I am such an abominable and accursed child of hell before God."

Sink away because of your abominable wickedness, abhor yourself, and be ashamed before God that you are such unclean and ungodly people. Leave all imagination of your own goodness, righteousness, and virtuousness to a blind world and to "a generation that are pure in their own eyes, and yet is not washed from their filthiness" (Prov. 30:12).

3. Your absolute impotence, so that you cry out: "I cannot do otherwise, and I will not do otherwise than to be so ungodly. It is my nature and character. I neither desire reconciliation nor desire to be renewed. It must be God's work to deliver me from the very bottom of hell; otherwise, I shall eternally sink away in this bottomless pit."

Avail yourself also of this eye salve to be led to the fountain of your life. Allow the mediator, Christ Jesus, to reveal Himself to your soul and to give unto you the hand of faith:

1. To make use of Him unto reconciliation with the Father in light of all your abominableness and wickedness. Permit Jesus to take this entirely upon Himself, and let Him take upon Himself also the curse, the punishment, and the eternal death due to you. Cast yourself entirely into the fountain of His blood and permit yourself to be washed and cleansed from all your filth. Let Jesus be the one to keep this law fully and solely on your behalf. Do not add anything of yourself; do not even endeavor to add anything of yourself—but surrender yourself to being robed with Jesus's obedience. Be clothed with the

mantle of His righteousness, and hide yourself fully under that mantle. Appear before God clothed with that mantle, and be reconciled and united to Him.

2. To make use of Christ unto sanctification, and permit Him to impress this law upon your mind and your heart by the finger of His Spirit. Permit Him each moment to give unto you, out of His fullness, new grace for the keeping thereof. Cry out to Him for continual consciousness of your justification and for daily sanctification. As one who has neither hands nor feet, cast yourself before your king and wait continually upon the power and leading of His Spirit, and may you learn to avail yourself and to make use of every grace you may receive to the keeping of this commandment. May the Lord Himself be gracious to you in all of these matters, and may He work in you both to will and to do according to His good pleasure. Amen.

The Tenth Commandment, Forbidding Covetousness

Thou shalt not covet thy neighbour's house, thou shalt not covet thy neighbour's wife, nor his manservant, nor his maidservant, nor his ox, nor his ass, nor any thing that is thy neighbour's.

—EXODUS 20:17

Question 113: What doth the tenth commandment require of us?

Answer: That even the smallest inclination or thought contrary to any of God's commandments never rise in our hearts; but that at all times we hate all sin with our whole heart, and delight in all righteousness.

Question 114: But can those who are converted to God perfectly keep these commandments?

Answer: No, but even the holiest men, while in this life, have only a small beginning of this obedience; yet so, that with a sincere resolution they begin to live, not only according to some, but all the commandments of God.

Question 115: Why will God then have the ten commandments so strictly preached, since no man in this life can keep them?

Answer: First, that all our lifetime we may learn more and more to know our sinful nature, and thus become the more earnest in seeking the remission of sin and righteousness in Christ; likewise, that we constantly endeavor and pray to God for the grace of the Holy Spirit, that we may become more and more conformable to the image of God, till we arrive at the perfection proposed to us in a life to come.

The history of the rich young ruler, who came to Christ and asked Him, "Good Master, what good thing shall I do, that I may have eternal life?" (Matt. 19:16), is both unique and remarkable. In responding to him, the Savior directed him to the law, saying that the true way to life is in the keeping of the commandments. This young man neither objected to this reply nor found it perplexing. Outwardly, he always had lived a very virtuous and exemplary life before the world, and, accordingly, he responded to the Savior by saying that he had performed that which He required of him. From his youth, he had always kept all the commandments enumerated by the Savior, and therefore he desired to know what he was still lacking. The Savior then stipulated that one thing was yet lacking and commanded him to sell his extensive possessions and to give all to the poor. Furthermore, he would then have to return to Christ and follow Him, and, in this way, he would inherit eternal life and be saved.

We can readily discern the true state of this young man. He was a blind and unregenerate individual, and, regrettably, this is true for the large majority among us. His acquaintance with God's law had never been anything other than carnal, for he was acquainted only with the external letter of the law and its observance by way of external deeds and works. He believed that such outward obedience was sufficient for the inheritance of eternal life.

Since, however, Jesus knew his heart and knew that he loved the things of this world, was very attached to them, and did not have the least desire simply to love God and His holy commandments, He wanted to convict him of his world conformity. He wished to teach him that, in spite of all his outward morality, he had a corrupt, wicked, and unclean heart that loved the world more than God and His commandments. He therefore gave him the difficult and challenging commandment to sell and divest himself of all his possessions. However, this young man was by no means ready to do so, and, consequently, he had to return to his home with a distressed and accusing conscience, perceiving that he loved his worldly possessions more than he loved Christ and His fellowship.

If the eyes of our understanding have been enlightened, this history will teach clearly that God's law is entirely holy and spiritual. The law therefore does not merely oblige us to obey God in outward words and deeds, but we are to do so primarily and preeminently as pertaining to our souls. The apostle clearly expresses this, saying, "For we know that the law is spiritual: but I am carnal, sold under sin" (Rom. 7:14).

As long as we are not acquainted with God's law in this manner, we remain utterly blind as to our knowledge of God and of the way of salvation, and we are entirely ensnared by the devil with all our outward religion and virtuousness. We are not truly convicted of our sins, hell-worthiness, and impotence, causing us to die completely to the law and our own righteousness, and, by a true faith, to be made alive with Christ, until we truly have become acquainted with the spiritual efficacy of the law and our spiritual obligation toward it. There is no such conviction until we clearly see by the light of the Spirit, that he who neither keeps, loves, nor cherishes God's law with his whole heart is a wretched and condemned sinner before God, even though, during his entire life, he has neither committed nor practiced a single sinful deed contrary to God's law.

Here we have the true origin of the wretched misery of all unconverted men, and thus of their blindness, carelessness, and unbelief. This is the reason for their not being alarmed by God's wrath and curse, by hell and damnation, and by death and eternity, for they are ignorant of the spirituality of God's holy law. Nevertheless, it is neither God's will that this should be hidden from men nor that they should be entirely ignorant of it. Rather, as a conclusion to all His commandments, the Lord has most clearly revealed the spirituality of His law in the tenth or last commandment, wherein He most solemnly forbids all and every evil inclination of the heart against any of His holy commandments. He presents this in a unique form, forbidding that we covet any of the goods or possessions of our neighbor while commanding that we be completely satisfied with what He, in His goodness, has given us regarding our possessions, houses, wives, etc. In thus formulating this commandment, it is God's holy objective to obligate our hearts and souls fully toward obeying all His commandments. This will become evident as we proceed with the exposition of this commandment.

May the Lord Himself, by the light of His Spirit, lead us into the truth of this great and prominent commandment—a commandment that functions as a key to unlock the entire law, for without that key, we would be incapable of having a proper understanding regarding all His commandments.

With all brevity, we therefore shall:

1. expound this tenth commandment as to its essential efficacy and content; and

2. consider the other prominent and weighty matters that the instructor has articulated regarding the proper use of the entire law of God.

In order correctly to understand this tenth commandment, we must again consider:

1. the object of this commandment; and
2. the duty mandated by God regarding this commandment.

The object of this commandment is man's immortal soul or spirit, before whom the Lord God here sets His holy law as the standard of obedience, so that the soul may function, orient, and engage itself in full conformity to this standard. As human beings, we have been created by God as consisting of two prominent components: soul and body. In a supremely wondrous and unfathomable manner, these two are most intimately united and mutually interact; the one is consequently influenced and wrought upon by the other. Since, therefore, our human existence is defined by our body and soul, and since God is the creator and Lord of both, we are also obligated to love, fear, serve, and obey Him with both body and soul. We are to do so with all our strength and in all our activities, and to exist for and to live unto Him alone with body and soul.

Accordingly, the holy apostle admonishes us, saying, "For ye are bought with a price: therefore glorify God in your body, and in your spirit, which are God's" (1 Cor. 6:20). In this passage, he explicitly deduces our obligation as issuing forth from the grace and redemption of our Lord Jesus Christ. However, that duty should be deduced no less from our natural creation, for, by virtue thereof, our soul and body also belong to God.

God therefore can by no means be satisfied with us as human beings if we obey Him merely and solely with the outward activities and accomplishments of our bodies, for, in so doing, we give Him but a small portion of what we are obligated to commit to Him as our great Lord and creator. Rather, it is His will that we also fear and obey Him with our souls, and that we do so preeminently and predominantly, for the soul is the superior and most noble component of our being.

The body is far more inferior and insignificant than is the soul, for it consists but of a raw lump of flesh, which God so wondrously fashioned. It is a body that originated from the dust, was formed from the dust, is destined to return to the dust, and ultimately will be eaten of worms. The soul, however, is an immortal spirit (Matt. 10:28) that shall never be disassembled, but shall exist and live eternally. We recognize that the more enduring and abiding something is, the greater its worth and value. Eternity infinitely exceeds a little blur of time. Likewise, the soul of man is far more precious than is his body.

Our souls were created and formed after God's image. Therefore, there is even a similarity with God and His most glorious being, for as the Lord God is a purely spiritual being who is ceaselessly engaged by virtue of His infinite wisdom and omnipotent will, the soul, likewise, is a spiritual entity that is always engaged by means of the mind and the will. As to man's nature, it is in his soul that he has any similarity with God, his creator and maker, this being so in a manner that is not true for his body. Regarding his body, there can be no such similarity, for God, in His spiritual being or essence, has nothing that is either material or physical.

When God graciously regenerates and renews the soul or spirit by means of the blood and Spirit of Christ, cleansing it from all sin, the soul becomes an even more noble and precious re-creation. When, by grace, God is pleased to re-create and restore His defaced image, the soul then again becomes a dwelling place and temple of the triune God Himself.

Since the soul, naturally and by grace, is such a glorious and precious creation, greatly excelling the value of the body, it is readily understood that God greatly desires that we primarily would love, fear, and obey Him with our souls, and that our souls would not be engaged in any way than according to His holy law as He has given it to us, wherein He accordingly admonishes us in His Holy Word, saying, "My son, give me thine heart" (Prov. 23:26). This heart is of utmost importance to the Lord, and He therefore says, "Keep thy heart with all diligence; for out of it are the issues of life" (Prov. 4:23). How frequently the Lord admonishes in His holy Word that we should love, serve, and fear Him with our entire hearts!

This is the focus of the tenth commandment, prescribing a law or rule for man, wherein is stipulated how, with his heart or soul, he must always and ceaselessly be engaged with his intellect and his will in conformity to all God's holy commandments.

The Lord articulates this extraordinary and prominent duty by forbidding all sinful and evil coveting by the heart, that is, coveting in the heart anything that is contrary to any of His commandments, saying, "Thou shalt not covet." No one should understand this to mean that the Lord here simply prohibits our having any desires whatsoever, and thereby, with our souls or spirits, we are forbidden to have any desires whatsoever. To have desires is a natural activity of the soul or spirit, and without such desiring, our spirits could not even exist for a moment. It is the natural function of the soul to be continually engaged in thinking and in exercising its will. In the absence of this, the soul would be dead. The most fundamental function of the life and existence of the spirit is that it is capable of rationally thinking of the matters or objects with which it interacts, and therefore it considers, interprets, processes, and evaluates them. This is followed immediately by the operation of the will, the other faculty of the spirit, whereby the soul is enabled to consider the matters or objects that he now perceives and interprets intellectually, and either loves and desires these matters or objects as good, or views them as evil and rejects them.

As such, the act of desiring something belongs to the very nature of the functioning of the spirit, and is therefore by no means evil. Neither is it the sin that the Lord here forbids in His law. Rather, in this commandment, the Lord sets before us only a law or rule whereby our desiring is governed as a natural activity of our spirits or souls. It is His will that the object of our desires would be neither any of the goods or possessions of our neighbor, which God, as sovereign Lord of all, has given to him, nor that the object of our desires would have regard to anything else that is evil and that God has forbidden in His law. He therefore prescribes in this commandment that our desires must always be good, holy, and proper, always and exclusively focused upon God and His holy commandments.

The soul desires lawfully when:

1. She loves and desires the Lord her God fully and above all things, and exercises her will only toward Him in order to have Him as her portion, and to serve, fear, and trust Him. The Lord's believing people express this as follows, saying, "With my soul have I desired thee in the night; yea, with my spirit within me will I seek thee early" (Isa. 26:9). It is the Lord's will that He be ceaselessly sought and desired of us as our chief and only good. Therefore, His will is that our desires and inclinations be directed exclusively toward Him, for it is His will not only that we would find our chief delight and satisfaction in Him alone, but that we also would utterly deny everything that is apart from Him with our whole hearts. Accordingly, He says, "Delight thyself also in the LORD; and he shall give thee the desires of thine heart" (Ps. 37:4).

2. In desiring God Himself, she also desires to keep His commandments; that is, our hearts fully delight in and love the Lord's holy commandments; our obedience, with the upholding of these commandments, is our chief desire and delight; and we have no other desire but to do that which is right and to live in perfect conformity to the law of the Lord. Such was the desire of David, the godly servant of the Lord, who declared, "Behold, I have longed after thy precepts: quicken me in thy righteousness" (Ps. 119:40). If he but heard any

mention made of God's commandments, his heart immediately yearned, with a pure and upright desire, to keep these commandments perfectly. He exclaimed, "O that my ways were directed to keep thy statutes!" (Ps. 119:5). Beloved, it is the Lord's will that our spirits or souls should always manifest such desires.

Hence, the sort of desires that God here forbids in His law is evident—desires that are very great and condemnable sins, which the Lord by no means will permit to go unpunished. He forbids all sinful, unholy, and evil desires, such as desiring:

1. Vain creatures rather than God and His blessed fellowship, cleaving with our hearts to them rather than to Him, and particularly if we covet such creatures and possessions that God has given to our neighbor to be his property and possession. By so doing, we fully rebel against God's supreme rule and government, and thereby oppose His supreme will, wisdom, goodness, etc. This is nothing other than an act of very hostile rebellion and disobedience toward God, which He by no means will permit to go unpunished. We thereby manifest our dissatisfaction and ingratitude toward God, our great Lord and creator, by being dissatisfied with our own possessions, which He graciously has bestowed upon us. This is a great evil indeed and a vile sin, which God must most certainly punish.

2. Anything and everything that contradicts His holy law in its entirety or any of its individual commandments, by disobeying and transgressing any of them. It pertains to all sinful thoughts, desires, and inclinations, however insignificant they may appear to be.

It is evident from the teaching of the instructor, who fully has grasped its correct meaning, that this is God's actual meaning and intent in this commandment. We shall therefore proceed to consider what our Christian instructor has written regarding this. He asks his pupil, "What doth the tenth commandment require of us?" and prompts him to respond, "That even the smallest inclination or thought contrary to any of God's commandments never rise in our hearts; but that at all times we hate all sin with our whole heart, and delight in all righteousness."

The instructor expounds this tenth commandment in very general terms as forbidding all the sinful desires of the human heart whereby we transgress any of God's commandments. His exposition is therefore entirely correct, for even though God addresses specific objects that we may not covet, such as our neighbor's house. He nevertheless has in mind all evil and sinful desires of the human heart that are contrary to His will and holy commandments.

Paul therefore also interprets this commandment in such a general sense, saying, "I had not known sin, but by the law: for I had not known lust, except the law had said, Thou shalt not covet" (Rom. 7:7). In his unconverted state, Paul was as all men are by nature, prior to their conversion. He was utterly blind to the demands and spirituality of the law. He was satisfied if he did not sin against God's law by his outward deeds. He had no eyes to look inward and to determine the state of his heart, whether he fully delighted himself in God's law. He was ignorant of the evil nature and inclination of his heart, failing to recognize that "the carnal mind is enmity against God: for it is not subject to the law of God, neither indeed can be" (Rom. 8:7). Though he may have seen some of this by common illumination, he nevertheless did not view this evil disposition of his heart, that is, this evil and hostile covetousness of his soul, as being sin for which God should punish and condemn him.

We shall proceed to consider in some detail what our instructor, who understands this truth very well, has to say regarding it.

Our lawgiver forbids that there arise within our souls the very least desire or inclination contrary to any of His commandments. The instructor understands "the smallest inclination or thought, contrary to any of God's commandments" to refer to the initial manifestation of evil desires within the human soul by virtue of the natural corruption that all men have inherited from our ancestor Adam. It is without controversy that upon the fall, man became so corrupt that the natural and foundational principles of his entire life became utterly evil and sinful, and that this corruption transformed his heart into a vile cesspool of all abomination, wickedness, and unholiness, so that, from this heart, there proceeds nothing but evil desires and that which is enmity toward God. Therefore, we read throughout God's Word regarding the lusts of the heart, the flesh, the body, and the eyes.

In regeneration—that is, when grace enters the heart and it thereby is initially renewed and transformed—these innate evil desires are broken and mortified to such an extent in the believer that they no longer have dominion over his soul. Nevertheless, there remain in God's children remnants of the corrupt old man of sin, for the believer must say that "the good that I would I do not: but the evil which I would not, that I do" (Rom. 7:19; cf. Gal. 5:17).

All Pelagians and Semi-Pelagians, such as all Roman Catholics, Socinians, and Arminians, who seek to diminish to the utmost of their ability the natural corruption of man and his inability to do any good, deny that such evil desires, though neither endorsed by a man's renewed will and his convicting conscience nor put into practice, are evil and sinful. The Reformed Church, however, strenuously upholds this truth, proving that the emergence of all such evil desires:

1. *Originates in man's sinful and corrupt nature.* Consequently, they reason by way of the incontrovertible rule that since the cause is utterly evil and sinful, so is the effect. These evil desires are the wretched fruits that proceed from the evil tree that the devil planted in our hearts in Paradise, for if our father Adam had not sinned against God and fallen away from Him, there would never have been either a sinful lust or an evil desire in the heart of man.

2. *Is the true womb of all actual sin*, as we considered earlier (James 1:14–15).

3. *Fully militates against God's holiness*, and whatever militates against His holiness is sin. Do not such evil desires militate completely against God's majesty and holiness, and do they not contradict the perfect love and fear that we are obligated to manifest toward Him?

On considering the fact that, as men, we have hearts that are pregnant with evil inclinations and desires to be disobedient toward Him and to sin against Him, what can this be but to harbor within our hearts hatred and an evil disinclination toward God and His commandments?

What rational person would think that such inclinations do not constitute a sin that is worthy of punishment? Paul teaches this clearly, saying, "I had not known sin, but by the law: for I had not known lust, except the law had said, Thou shalt not covet" (Rom. 7:7). It is obvious that he understands *coveting* to refer to the soul's initial inclination toward sin and by no means to be merely an evil inclination, as it would be defined by human determination. Otherwise, he could not have written regarding coveting that he previously had never known such coveting to be sin.

Even by the dim light of reason, the Gentiles knew that it constituted a sin when the will acquiesced in an evil desire. One of their poets therefore said, "When one merely thinks of a sin in his heart, he sins as much as he who commits the sin." They always deemed the inclination to be equivalent to the deed. It is therefore absolutely clear that all initial inclinations and desires to sin, though they are neither endorsed by the will nor carried out in practice, nevertheless utterly render a man evil, sinful, and condemnable before God.

The instructor therefore posits that all such desires are strictly forbidden in this commandment. For a man not to be a condemnable defendant before God, he must be completely free from all evil and sinful inclinations, as they are all contrary to God's law. There should never arise within the soul even a remote desire or inclination to sin against any of God's commandments. Not a trace should be found in him of the carnality of the flesh that "is enmity against God" (Rom. 8:7). Believers, being in the state of grace, are therefore solemnly admonished by God to subdue all evil inclination toward sin by the use of *spiritual weaponry*. Paul writes of this, saying, "Neither yield ye your members as instruments of unrighteousness unto sin: but yield yourselves unto God, as those that are alive from the dead, and your members as instruments of righteousness unto God" (Rom. 6:13). In Colossians 3:5, he admonishes believers, saying, "Mortify therefore your members which are upon the earth," and he then specifically calls upon them to mortify the sin of coveting. It is the mark of all the true covenant people of God that "they that are Christ's have crucified the flesh with the affections and lusts" (Gal. 5:24). The instructor therefore correctly posits that the lawgiver rightfully forbids "even the smallest inclination or thought, contrary to any of God's commandments."

As is his custom, the instructor then proceeds to address what the lawgiver prescribes in this commandment, saying "that at all times we hate all sin with our whole heart, and delight in all righteousness." This follows from the preceding, for if the soul is to be utterly holy and free of any evil and sinful desires that are contrary to God and His law, then it is consistent with her inner nature and disposition that she be absolutely hostile to sin, hateful against all ungodliness, but inclined toward all righteousness and holiness. All of this is true for the regenerate and renewed man in believers, of which John testifies, saying, "Whosoever is born of God doth not commit sin; for his seed remaineth in him: and he cannot sin, because he is born of God" (1 John 3:9).

Hence all the solemn admonitions addressed to believers in the Word of God, namely, that they must be enemies of all sin and be fully desirous and inclined toward all righteousness. In so doing, they emulate the Lord, their God and Father, who is perfect and who by all means calls them unto glory and virtue. To that end, they continually receive, out of the fullness of Christ, grace for grace. With the Lord's help, we shall soon address this at length from His Word.

The instructor posits in this commandment that God requires of all men complete holiness and obedience in regard to His entire law. The Lord commands, by this commandment, that within our hearts, we must always have a heartfelt and upright hatred and enmity for all sins, regardless of whether we think of them as minor or major sins. It is His will:

1. That we truly view sin as a most wicked and dreadful evil, because not only is God's holy majesty supremely dishonored and impugned by it, but He is also supremely provoked to wrath and anger.

2. That we have a heartfelt inner aversion for the most insignificant and trivial of sins, and that we wholeheartedly abhor them, as it is written, "Ye that love the LORD, hate evil" (Ps. 97:10). The holy apostle Paul also admonishes: "Abhor that which is evil; cleave to that which is good" (Rom. 12:9).

God prescribes that our hearts must always be filled with a great and most upright hatred and aversion for all sin and toward all that, in any measure, results in the breaking of God's holy law. Rather than that we break His holy law in any measure, God prescribes in this commandment that we "delight in all righteousness"; that is, that we delight ourselves in all virtue, holiness, and true godliness, delighting ourselves in all that is right and good, as it is prescribed by the Lord God in His holy law. It is the Lord's will that we fully love and be fully inclined toward such obedience, and do nothing other than love, desire, and seek all true righteousness with our hearts, finding all our desire, delight, and joy only in such obedience.

We read this regarding the Lord Jesus, our great example of holiness, for by the divinely inspired prophecy of David, Jesus declares, "I delight to do thy will, O my God: yea, thy law is within my heart" (Ps. 40:8). It is also recorded that the apostle Paul, this faithful follower of Christ, declared, "I delight in the law of God after the inward man" (Rom. 7:22), saying furthermore, "Not as though I had already attained, either were already perfect: but I follow after, if that I may apprehend that for which also I am apprehended of Christ Jesus…forgetting those things which are behind, and reaching forth unto those things which are before, I press toward the mark for the prize of the high calling of God in Christ Jesus" (Phil. 3:12–14).

The Lord God prescribes here that the disposition of our hearts must always be so pure, so holy, spiritual, and heavenly that we have a burning love for that which is good and a burning hatred and aversion for that which is evil. As well with our hearts as with our bodies, we must strive for the perfect obedience of all His holy commandments, for this is the very essence of the tenth commandment.

With the Lord's help, we have expounded the entire law of the Ten Commandments. On the one hand, this law is a means to stop the mouths of all flesh, fully and eternally exclude all righteousness by the law, and render all men accursed and "guilty before God" (Rom. 3:19). On the other hand, we have set this law before you as the perfect paradigm and standard of true holiness, according to which all God's covenant people who are now in a state of grace must fully order their outward and inward life by faith.

We shall now consider what our instructor will address in general terms regarding the entire law of the Lord.

Having fully expounded the law of the Ten Commandments, the instructor asks his pupil, "But can those who are converted to God perfectly keep these commandments?" This question pertains only to those who, by the Spirit of God, have been regenerated and have turned to Christ as the chief captain of their souls. It pertains to all who are partakers of the redemption that is in the Lord Jesus Christ. Regarding them, the instructor asks whether they are capable of perfectly keeping this law of God as to all its constituent elements.

We observe in this question that the instructor does not focus upon the natural state of graceless and unconverted men, but exclusively upon God's converted people. As to the state of wretched and unconverted men, it can by no means be asked whether they can keep God's law perfectly. It is only too certain that such wretched souls, apart from the performance of some crude and external works and duties regarding God's law (also as works of their own righteousness), are incapable of keeping even a smidgen of that law in a truly holy and spiritual fashion. There is in them not even the least desire to do so—not even as much as either a crumb or grain of sand—for it is only all too certain that:

1. Their entire nature is filled with wicked enmity toward God and toward His holy law (Rom. 8:7).

2. They are completely blind, their minds are completely darkened, and there is not even a little ray of light to illuminate their hearts, by which light they could discover and see the delightful holiness and righteousness of God's law. By virtue of their unbelief, they willfully close their eyes to all divine light and "love darkness rather than light" (John 3:19b). The Scriptures say regarding them, "The light shineth in darkness; and the darkness comprehended it not" (John 1:5).

3. All unconverted men, by their enmity toward God, as well as of their blindness and unbelief, are utterly "dead in trespasses and sins" (Eph. 2:1). They are void of any love for and any desire toward the holy law of God, just as a dead person lacks life, desire, and strength to do or accomplish something in

the natural realm. We addressed this in detail at the time we expounded Lord's Day 2 of this Catechism.

4. All unconverted men, by all the aforementioned, are living in a state of the greatest and most dreadful misery and wretchedness, that is, a state that cannot be described by any pen and that cannot be expressed by any tongue, for:

a. They remain obligated to keep the entire law of God, with all its holy duties and precepts, notwithstanding that they have no desire whatsoever to keep and to observe that law.

b. By their willful neglect and transgression of the entire law in all of its constituent elements, they daily and greatly increase their debt before heaven, and it becomes a debt of more than ten thousand talents, which, before God in the great day of judgment, must be paid and resolved to its very last penny.

c. God's dreadful wrath and curse, the threat of which pertains to all transgressors of the law, is certainly manifested toward them and follows them in every step they take. It is the divine threat of the law that "cursed is every one that continueth not in all things which are written in the book of the law to do them" (Gal. 3:10).

d. Since these wretched men neither want to believe these things nor are willing to open their eyes for the true light proceeding from God, they continue to be utterly careless, insensitive, void of contrition, and unrepentant. They continue to live in a state of supreme misery and wretchedness, never taking it to heart, not even in the very least, and therefore, they truly are traveling to their eternal damnation and perdition, not realizing that there is a holy and true God who lives in heaven and who will not permit Himself to be mocked by anyone, but who, at the end of the world and according to His Word, will execute His holy judgment toward all men.

This is the state of all unconverted men. Oh, that a merciful God would yet cause them to see this by virtue of the soul-saving discovery of their hearts by His Spirit!

However, for those who have been converted unto God, who have found grace with the Lord, and who have been translated from being dead in sins unto a life of salvation and faith, the instructor asks and inquires whether they can keep this law perfectly.

The instructor here focuses on the controversy we have with all Pelagians. Consider the sentiments of the Socinians and Arminians regarding the perfection of saints in this life, as well as the sentiments of Roman Catholics regarding superfluous works. Such wretched sentiments proceed solely from a grievous blindness and ignorance regarding God and the holiness and spirituality of the law.

The instructor simply answers "no" to this question, in accordance with the Word of the Lord, which very clearly and emphatically teaches the imperfection and sinfulness of even the most eminent believers (Eccl. 7:20; James 3:2; 1 John 1:8). It is true that some of God's beloved children, both outwardly and before the world, live lives that are completely holy and blameless. By the grace of God, with utmost zeal, effort, and watchfulness, accompanied by continual prayer and fasting, they fully engage themselves in walking blamelessly according to all of God's holy commandments and precepts, without causing the least offense toward anyone in the world. The parents of John the Baptist were such holy and tender people, and we have of them a glorious testimony intended for our emulation that "they were both righteous before God, walking in all the commandments and ordinances of the Lord blameless" (Luke 1:6).

Oh, how precious and blessed is such a testimony! May God grant us grace so that this could be said also of the backslidden Christianity in our land, which lives in a most grievous and wretched state. The Lord alone knows how grievously we come short in this. Even though it is true that the Lord's people, by heavenly and divine grace, can at times achieve a high degree of holiness and blamelessness in their entire conversation, each Christian nevertheless retains his corrupt and sinful flesh, in which "dwelleth no good thing" (Rom. 7:18). During all the days of his life here upon earth, he will be engaged in a grievous battle with his flesh, causing him to groan most bitterly (Ps. 19:13; 143:2; Prov. 20:9; Job 9:2).

The instructor posits that "even the holiest men, while in this life, have only a small beginning of this obedience"; that is, an obedience that the law requires of them to absolute perfection. He speaks of the holiest of men, thereby teaching us that there are degrees of grace, which is consistent with the Scriptures, for they speak of Christianity as consisting of children, young men, and fathers (1 John 2:12–14). However, within the context of a corrupt Christianity, we observe the same as we see in a disorderly and corrupt family, where everything is in utter disarray—a mixed and intermingling multitude of elderly and younger family members, of young and older children, of sons and daughters, and of fathers and mothers.

First, one no longer knows how to distinguish with discernment the measure of one another's grace, wisdom, and gifts, and to appreciate them for what they are by making a proper and correct use of them to everyone's edification.

Second, they who have made some progress in the ways of God and who should function among others as spiritual fathers and mothers, considering the lengthy period of time they have been Christians and the internal and external experiences they have had in the ways of God, do not know how to take advantage of this great privilege to the benefit of those who are less experienced. Sadly, they fail to treat the less experienced believers properly, and they frequently grievously offend the little ones in grace and such as are weak. They continually seek to compel them to fulfill their duty by talking to them as they treat them in a condescending way, without any evidence of true grace in their conduct. The Lord neither can nor will bless this.

Third, young and weak Christians immediately rise up as if they were grown men and, in very short order, become very proud, conceited, and puffed up, boasting of much grace and light, thinking that they already have far surpassed older Christians, and doing so in spite of the fact that the difference between them is still astonishingly great. During the troubling and fruitless spiritual season that presently prevails, the willow tree soon surpasses the oak, even though it will soon turn into a long and thin tree that is shaken to and fro by the wind and is but loosely rooted in the earth.

How wretched and sad is our condition! Were we to search for the most holy of men among us, of what value before God would be the measure of grace they possess? As the instructor says, "even the holiest men, while in this life, have only a small beginning of this obedience." Such obedience is no more than the first fruits and a feeble beginning. The instructor says that this is true of the holiest of men "while in this life." The issue at hand is not what believers will be after their death and resurrection, for then most certainly they no longer will sin, but will keep perfectly all the commandments of God's law. What is at stake here is that believers have but a small beginning of this obedience "while in this life," that is, as long as they carry with them their sinful flesh.

This should not be understood to mean that all believers achieve the same measure of obedience and perfection, for as we stated earlier, one believer achieves a greater measure of perfection than the other. The instructor is referring to the state of the holiest of men as being but a small beginning of this obedience in comparison to the state of absolute perfection that God's law requires of them, and to which they will attain after this life, in glory.

Here in this life believers begin to keep the Lord's commandments only in principle and enjoy only the first fruits of the glory and virtue to which they are called. Oh, how readily all the saints of God acknowledge this! The most advanced among them do not cease to complain bitterly of their feeble beginning of this obedience. Oh, if you could only hear the holiest among them in their places of solitude and in their inner chambers! It would be evident what low thoughts they still have of themselves, for the more light, grace, and holiness there is to be found in the soul, the more there is a sighing, complaining, weeping, and groaning about the lack of holiness and conformity to God. David prayed earnestly, "And enter not into judgment with thy servant: for in thy sight shall no man [can he speak in more general terms?] living be justified" (Ps. 143:2).

Paul, a great man of God who rightly deserves to have the preeminence among the holiest of men, frequently makes a transparent confession of his weaknesses and stumblings, to which he was continually inclined in this life. He writes, "Not as though I had already attained, either were already perfect: but I follow after, if that I may apprehend that for which also I am apprehended of Christ Jesus" (Phil. 3:12). It is evident that the instructor is correct when he posits that "even the holiest men, while in this life, have only a small beginning of this obedience."

There is no established and true doctrine that is held before us more clearly and repeatedly in God's Word than the doctrine of the imperfection of the saints. However, due to the blindness and unbelief of sinners, there is no other Christian doctrine that at all times is abused more harmfully than is this doctrine—even by converted people. Oh, that the Lord would give us a proper view of this matter!

The unconverted of this world abuse this sacred doctrine of God in a most dreadful, brazen, and grievous manner—to an extent that cannot be expressed in words. The fact that a Christian can never be perfect in this life but still offends in many things; that, due to his weakness, he transgresses God's law; and that God, upon confession and contrition, and out of grace and for the sake of Christ, overlooks all of these faults—the people of Satan shamelessly use all this as fig leaves to cover all their sins and wicked deeds, and so they peacefully continue to live in their sins, saying, "No one can be completely holy and perfect." They also say: "Though the ministers aim in their preaching for a greater measure of holiness and perfection among the people, they should ease up a bit and overlook some of their sins and weaknesses. Everyone is doing his best to serve and to please God." They have no issue with ministers addressing faults and deficiencies in their sermons, provided they neither condemn nor judge the people, and thereby imply that they are not good and proper Christians and that they will be consigned to hell because they do not live perfectly holy lives in conformity to God's law. They say, "The latter is the point where our minister is very much at fault, but aside from that, he generally preaches about many good and necessary things that are not objectionable."

Such is the blatant manner in which a blind and ungodly world abuses this holy doctrine, and thereby they utterly demolish the intimate connection between Christianity and this doctrine regarding the imperfection of the saints. Everyone resolves to do as much good as he thinks he might need to do in order to enter into heaven, and the law of God is no longer the standard according to which men must live, but, rather, it is man's own determination as to how much he wishes to observe the law. The only law by which man then lives is his own.

Even truly converted believers often abuse this doctrine because of their indwelling corruption. How secretly our evil hearts take advantage of the truth that, in this life, we never shall be able to live either in perfect holiness or in perfect conformity to the law! We do so when:

1. We do not earnestly and in all uprightness come before God with all our guilt and all our sin, but gloss over our many sins as we continue to indulge in them.

2. We neglect many good and holy duties, secretly thinking, especially with our present-day Christianity, that God winks at many of our sins.

3. The grievous abuse of this holy doctrine precipitates in God's people immeasurably much lukewarmness, carelessness, pride, blindness, unbelief, and all manner of pernicious evil. But if this holy doctrine, by divine illumination, were to be known and rightly understood, it would be a proper means to further our sanctification every day by the power of the Holy Spirit.

The instructor now proceeds to point out the latter in greater detail by saying, "that with a sincere resolution they begin to live, not only according to some, but all the commandments of God." Here he addresses two matters:

First, God's holy children, who have been converted unto Him, "begin to live, not only according to some, but all the commandments of God." This is the pure and genuine mark of God's grace that, by the operation of the Holy Spirit, is found in the hearts of all true believers—a mark that completely and fundamentally distinguishes them from the unconverted men of this world. Whatever impure love and desire an unconverted heart may have toward some of the commandments of God's law, desiring to walk in them in outward obedience, it nevertheless will never have a genuine love and desire toward *all* of God's commandments, whereby one desires in principle to live piously according to all of them. The presence of sin and the love for sin that still reigns in them will always cause them to set aside some of the commandments of God's law. They do so primarily regarding the commandments of the first table, as well as the tenth or last commandment of the second table, in which all the sins and evil desires of the heart are forbidden.

1. They will never embrace all the commandments in true and heartfelt love in order to obey them.

2. They will neither be truly grieved and perplexed about their breaking and transgression of these commandments, nor truly repent before God, no matter what sorrow they may otherwise have regarding their sins.

3. They will peacefully persist in the transgression of all such holy commandments of God, appeasing themselves with the fact that they seek to keep some other commandments of the law with their outward obedience. Therefore, when they are not guilty of grievous Sabbath desecration, do not engage either in idolatry or the worship of images, do no swearing of false oaths, do not dishonor their parents and those who govern them, do not kill, do not commit adultery, do not steal, and neither lie nor deceive—in this manner, outwardly keeping some of God's commandments reasonably well—they pacify themselves that they are good and pious people. They do so even though they break all the other commandments of God; even though they engage in idolatry within their hearts, frequently take the holy name of God in vain, have carnal notions and ideas regarding God's spiritual being, do not rest on the Sabbath in God by a true faith in Christ, and never cease to indulge in evil thoughts and the lusts of their hearts. They believe themselves to be good and pious people, even though their hearts are inwardly filled with ignorance and blindness, with unbelief and enmity toward God, and with a strong desire for and an inclination toward all sin. They consider all these things to be insignificant and a manifestation of weakness that God will not take all that seriously.

4. Even in their outward obedience of God's commandments, the unconverted always are selective in regard to these commandments. There always

is one or more of the commandments toward which they manifest the most hatred and hostility, and the outward observance of them is something they hardly take to heart. They always engage in their most prominent bosom sin by violating one or several commandments of the law. These commandments are always an obstacle to them, and if they could, they would love to erase them from the law.

Matters are entirely different, however, with all truly converted children of God. Being in Christ, and having been inwardly sanctified and renewed in their hearts by the Holy Spirit, they principally cannot do otherwise, but heartily embrace and love the entire law of God to its fullest extent and spirituality, for:

1. They love the God who has given this law as an expression of His holy being and nature.

2. They love true holiness as it is revealed in God and expressed in all the commandments of the law. The entire law is holy, as is every commandment of the law, and therefore, when they love one commandment, they love any of the other commandments for the same reason. This is comparable to someone who loves gold; he loves gold wherever he sees and finds it, whether it is a golden cup, a golden saucer, or a golden crown.

3. By virtue of their new nature, they indiscriminately hate all sin and all unholiness, and have a heartfelt aversion for it. It makes no difference to them which commandment their sin breaks, for converted people hate what is contrary to any commandment of God's law, precisely because it is a transgression of God's holy law.

It is the genuine mark of the true grace of God that a godly and holy heart desires and finds itself genuinely inclined "to live, not only according to some [as is the practice of an unconverted world], but according to all the commandments of God." It was so with David, who said: "O that my ways were directed to keep thy statutes! Then shall I not be ashamed, when I have respect unto all thy commandments" (Ps. 119:5–6). Also, in verse 128, he declares, "Therefore I esteem all thy precepts concerning all things to be right; and I hate every false way." This was also Paul's disposition, who said, "For I delight in the law of God after the inward man" (Rom. 7:22). He found delight not only in some of God's commandments, but in the entire law of God.

The apostle James also teaches this all-encompassing and indiscriminate love for and obedience toward the entire law of God, saying, "For whosoever shall keep the whole law, and yet offend in one point, he is guilty of all" (James 2:10).

He who desires to keep only nine commandments of the law of God and wants to make an exception in not keeping only one commandment, and so being at liberty to transgress it, hates and breaks the entire law of God. Of such, we may conclude that there has never been even a trace of true godliness in his heart.

Certain it is that the true grace of God will work in us an all-encompassing love for the entire law of God, for all who have truly been converted unto God are dissatisfied with living only according to some of God's commandments. They desire to live according to all the commandments of God, with no exceptions.

We must always view and consider this love for all of God's laws to be the preeminent and foundational rule of Christianity, by which we must continually evaluate ourselves and others in order to distinguish between the true grace of God and grace that proves to be counterfeit.

The instructor does not yet rest his case, for he continues by teaching that all who have been converted unto God, albeit they are yet very weak and feeble in regard to obeying God's law perfectly, nevertheless, "with a sincere resolution,…begin to live, not only according to some but all the commandments of God." Again, the word *sincere* distinguishes God's true and regenerate people from all hypocritical and unconverted nominal Christians. Frequently, nominal Christians also have sound resolutions and intentions to forsake their sins and to live in obedience to and in accordance with God's commandments. However, contrary to what is true for all who are genuinely godly, the intentions of the nominal Christian are never sincere and upright.

First, their intentions regarding their sins are never accompanied by heartfelt confession of their guilt, nor by true sorrow, mourning, and contrition. Never have their hearts been broken in true shame and sorrow regarding their sins before a majestic and holy God.

Second, they have never had an inner hatred and genuine aversion for sin, nor have they ever had a heartfelt inclination and desire to obey all God's holy commandments. The core of their hearts is and persistently remains utterly darkened, obstinate, unbelieving, and ungodly, for it never has been truly sanctified and transformed by God's Spirit and by the blood of Christ.

Third, their intentions proceed only from an accusing conscience, from fear of God's wrath and being punished and damned in hell, from the fear of man and having a bad reputation, or from a legalistic righteousness and works holiness, whereby they think that they can secure God's grace and heaven.

Fourth, their intentions are generally superficial and shallow. They are not accompanied by earnest prayer, by a vigorous endeavor to be delivered from their sins, or by doing violence upon the kingdom of heaven, and thus they are contrary to the intentions of those who sincerely seek to do so and who fully strive to become upright and holy. They do not wish to deal resolutely with their most cherished bosom sins, which they are so accustomed to commit each day—sins in which they find such delight and pleasure, and whereby they nourish their sinful existence. Their resistance is only very weak and feeble, and they refrain from using the sword of the Spirit to deal with these filthy wounds and putrefying sores. They shrink back from either having to kill their beloved Delilahs or from having to pluck out the right eye that offends them.

Finally, their intentions are never resolute, persistent, or steadfast. Outwardly, they may be trimming the external branches of the tree of sin, but they are never sincerely engaged in utterly eradicating the root of sin from their hearts. They may indeed build dikes and dams against the powerful onslaught of sin, but they do not strive to locate either the origin of sin or its fountain, and neither do they endeavor to quench it within their hearts. No matter how they outwardly oppose sin, the evil root of sin continues to grow within their hearts, and therefore new sprouts and branches continue to appear. This causes such an overwhelming flood of sin to proceed from their hearts that the dams and dikes they have built of their duties and intentions cannot possibly withstand and resist it. The force of this powerful flood of sin proceeding from the heart necessarily breaks through, and indwelling sin again manifests itself outwardly in the commission of sinful deeds and actions. After this eruption of sin, the conscience again begins to stir and accuse, and, as formerly was the case, this temporarily yields new intentions.

How very different are matters with the truly holy and converted children of God! Unless, due to their indwelling corruption, they are guilty of serious declension, of grievous backsliding and living far from the Lord, there is, by God's Spirit, a sincere resolution that is indiscriminately lively, powerful, and operative to mortify and subdue all evil and sin, and to live according to God's law inwardly and outwardly in all holiness.

When examining ourselves and the Christianity of our day, we cannot but speak with shame regarding these matters, for this sincere resolution hardly translates into deeds and activities that conform to this resolution. Nevertheless, we must view and judge this resolution as being truly in accordance with God's Word, irrespective of the fact that there is, in our day, so little of this found among us by virtue of the dreadful corruption that has infiltrated the heart and the walk of Christians. Rivers of tears are not sufficient to weep about this before a holy God. This sincere resolution of true Christians always manifests itself in:

1. A true and heartfelt sorrow of soul regarding all one's sins, with a sincere confession of guilt and a display of contrition before a holy God.

2. A believing in and a fleeing to Christ as a miserable and impotent sinner for both reconciliation and sanctification—and thus for all that one stands in need of.

3. A continual cleaving to Christ as one's only strength and salvation.

4. A sincere and earnest striving against and the mortification of all sin by the power of the Holy Spirit—even against one's most beloved bosom sins, without sparing or excusing any of them in the least.

5. An earnest endeavor to engage fully in one's duties so that he in no wise stumbles and continues to live and sin against light, always striving to be fruitful by abounding in all fruits of righteousness.

6. A painstaking and watchful keeping of one's heart so that sin neither abides nor secretly lodges there. He strives for the healing and sanctification of his heart and does not rest until God resides there with His holy light, His Spirit, and His image. He therefore does not rest until all idols and all his Dagons have been cast down, for only the pure of heart shall see God (Matt. 5:8).

7. A continual yearning and longing for more light, grace, and holiness, and a continual mourning over having only a small measure of spirituality and holiness. Such was the case with Paul, when he said, "Not as though I had already attained, either were already perfect: but I follow after, if that I may apprehend that for which also I am apprehended of Christ Jesus" (Phil. 3:12). This is true for all truly converted and holy people, who labor to live before the countenance of God inasmuch as it radically distinguishes them from an unconverted world.

These things coalesce in all who truly have been converted unto God, so that they still are very deficient as to the perfect keeping of God's law and yet are sincerely resolved to "begin to live, not only according to some, but all the commandments of God." Even though perfect obedience of the law is still very remote for them, they, with David, endeavor to achieve this, saying, "I delight to do thy will, O my God: yea, thy law is within my heart" (Ps. 40:8).

From the foregoing, we may derive three incontrovertible truths that we must always view as the true foundation of Christianity:

First, whatever the sinful deficiency of a true Christian may be, there ought not to be any recognized deficiency over which he does not wholeheartedly mourn, for, by the grace of the Lord Jesus Christ, he must ceaselessly strive against such deficiency until he has prevailed over it.

Second, the grace in each individual Christian must always be measured by the true light of the Spirit that he has regarding all his sins and sinful deficiencies. It must also be measured by the sincere battle of faith in which he daily engages to be delivered from all his sinful deficiencies and to fulfill, in very deed and with soul and body, all that the holy law of God requires of him.

Third, there is not even the least measure of grace in someone's heart if there is a single sin or sinful deficiency that is still indulged in with genuine delight, a sin with which the conscience is acquainted and which God's Word denounces. Thus there is not the least measure of grace in someone's heart without there being any upright sorrow and earnest battle of faith to be delivered from that sin, and to live and walk indiscriminately according to all the holy commandments of the law.

These are the three pure and holy pillars of Christianity upon which all true religion rests. If we do not always strictly observe and practice these, we overturn Christianity in its entirety and give Satan free access utterly to disrupt and render useless all doctrine, all ministry of the Word, all institutions, all sacraments, and the whole of the gospel. This breeds a religion of form, custom, hypocrisy, blindness, and ungodliness. Here we have the genuine boundary markers between true and counterfeit grace. By the Spirit of discernment, we must always distinguish true Christians from hypocrites, by which the church of Christ is regretfully overrun in these sad days in which we are living.

To clarify this matter, the instructor proceeds to address an objection that will be most profitable for us to consider: "Why will God then have the ten commandments so strictly preached, since no man in this life can keep them?" This is the manner of all Pelagians, who object to our holy doctrine. By their grievous blindness, they cannot understand the reasoning of the Lord God in having His law so strictly and continually preached in this world, when there is not a man on earth capable of perfectly keeping His holy law. According to their thinking, God requires an obedience that man absolutely and eternally cannot possibly render. We shall not address the grievous errors of such wretched people, from which such opposition toward our holy doctrine proceeds, but briefly and exclusively, we shall consider the good and sacred answer of the instructor.

The subject regarding which the instructor here inquires is the *sharp* preaching of the law, inquiring why the Lord God so earnestly commands His church to do so when, as we have been taught in Question 114, even converted believers are incapable of keeping the law perfectly. We observe here that it is insufficient merely to preach the law of God, for that transpires in all churches and congregations in which the Christian faith is confessed. Roman Catholics, Arminians, and even Socianians preach the law of God, each in their own way. However, it is one thing to preach the law of God and quite another thing to do so compellingly and sharply. All fruit and blessing from the preaching of the law proceed from its being preached compellingly and sharply.

The preaching of the law will never be fruitful if it is not preached faithfully and sharply, according to God's command. The way that the law of God is preached in Pelagian churches does not wound the heart of a man, convict him of his sins, lead him by faith to Christ, nor instruct and stir him to true godliness. As little as tasteless salt or an ineffective medication affects the body, so little can a lackluster, insincere, and corrupt preaching of the law of God strengthen and heal the souls of men.

One therefore has good reason to ask how God's law must be preached if it is to be done compellingly and sharply, and we respond by positing that this necessarily consists of the following five matters. The law is sharply preached by us when:

First, it is always preached and set before the people as a divine law, given to man by the majestic, holy, and Almighty God, the great and awe-inspiring majesty, the Lord of heaven and earth, who is "of purer eyes than to behold evil" (Hab. 1:13); who, in one moment, can cause them to perish in His wrath with both body and soul, and eternally cast them into hell. The more that the infinite majesty and holiness of God are impressed upon people under the preaching of the law, the sharper and more compelling the preaching of the law shall be for them.

Therefore, ministers who are called upon to preach God's law sharply to the people must be furnished with the light of the knowledge of God within their own hearts, and they are continually in need of being truly illuminated by that light when they preach the law, doing so with deep impressions in their souls of God's lofty and holy majesty.

Consider this truth in the life of holy Moses, when he proceeded to proclaim and to unfold the law of God to the children of Israel, and how he labored first to impress upon their hearts an appropriate view of the lofty and awe-inspiring majesty of God (Deut. 5:1–5). This was also the practice of the prophets whenever they were called upon to proclaim to the people a word or command of God. They commonly addressed the people by saying, "Thus saith the LORD, the LORD of hosts."

Second, it is preached as to its all-encompassing and all-inclusive content, and thus, when we earnestly and compellingly press home the full thrust and holiness of each individual commandment. The law consists of ten commandments, each with a different content, although, in essence, they are equally weighty and holy, and each demands the same obligation from us. Therefore, to preach the law sharply is to preserve the intimate unity of the Ten Commandments and to preach all of them compellingly as God's majestic law with the same thrust and earnestness, without leaving any room for the least transgression of any of these commandments.

If one were to preach nine commandments of the law sharply and to expound the other with less gravity, he would thereby disengage the entire law and rob it of all of its efficacies, as the Savior teaches in Matthew 5:18–19. John the Baptist was such a sharp and faithful preacher of the law, for he did not give to King Herod, who otherwise loved to hear him preach the law, any liberty to sin against a single commandment. He preferred to lose his own head than to diminish the thrust and sharpness of one of the Ten Commandments. Also, the prophets and the apostles preached the law faithfully and sharply, for they could not tolerate the least violation of a single commandment among the people.

Third, it is preached in a spiritual manner; that is, when the thrust and obligation of the law extends not only to the outward deeds and activities of the people, but also to the inner motions of their souls and the stirrings of their hearts, so that they might also be holy and conformed to the law of the Lord. This indeed constitutes the sharp thrust of the law of God, for it condemns as a damnable sin and transgression of the law any rising in the human heart of the least sinful thought, desire, or lust, all of which are contrary to any of God's commandments, and absolutely requires of man that he obey God with his whole heart, soul, and mind. This is how sharply the Savior preached the law

(Matthew 22), and the prophets and apostles did likewise. Whatever men may have done outwardly in keeping and obeying the law, the Savior, the prophets, and the apostles declared everything that any man had done to be rank hypocrisy and vile insincerity if, at the same time, their hearts were not inwardly cleansed by the Spirit of God of all evil thoughts, as well as of sinful lusts and desires, and their outward obedience was not accompanied by a heartfelt desire and love to keep the entire law of God with both soul and body.

Fourth, it is always conjoined to the infinite holiness and justice of God, as well as to the curse that, by virtue of His holiness, He has pronounced upon all transgressors of the law, saying, "Cursed is every one that continueth not in all things which are written in the book of the law to do them" (Gal. 3:10). We know that implicit in all human laws is not only the fine or penalty that will be imposed upon all rebels who transgress them, but also that a righteous judge, according to the obligations of his office, is duty-bound to implement and execute this penalty toward transgressors.

Our holy and just God no less threatens the execution of His curse upon all and every transgressor of His law; that is, He will, as a manifestation of the highest degree of His displeasure, wrath, and anger, prosecute the sinner in order to sentence him to eternal death and condemnation. The transgression of God's law is not worthy of a lesser penalty than this, and an unrepentant and unbelieving sinner should therefore not expect anything less. Unless the declaration of this curse is always conjoined to the preaching of the law, and unless one compellingly and earnestly preaches this to the people, one is incapable of preaching the law sharply.

Men regretfully have but little concern for the transgression of God's law, however, and there generally is much more consideration about the transgression of human laws than the transgression of God's laws. Generally speaking, there is hardly any fear or concern about this among men. If, however, they hear and understand correctly that every transgressor of God's law is accursed by virtue of God's own sentence and that the very least sin is truly worthy of eternal death and condemnation, considering "that they which commit such things are worthy of death" (Rom. 1:32), they then immediately feel the sharp power and sting of the law, that is, sin itself, as well as the sting of sin, namely, death. Men then have to acknowledge that the entire world does not weigh as much as the very least sin or transgression of God's holy law.

Fifth, it is always preached as having been sanctified and vindicated in the new covenant of grace by the death and obedience of our Lord Jesus Christ.

Thereby God has gloriously revealed to us the extraordinary demands and holiness of His law. That law being violated and broken by our sins, He sent His own, His eternal and divine Son, into the world, so that as the surety and mediator of all elect believers, He could make full satisfaction on their behalf. He did indeed accomplish this during His sojourn here on earth, having "been made under the law" (Gal. 4:4b) and having obeyed all its commandments on our behalf by His life of perfect holiness. Furthermore, in His flesh, being subjected to the dreadful curse and penalty of the law of which we are worthy by virtue of our sins, He rendered perfect obedience to His Father, being "obedient unto death, even the death of the cross" (Phil. 2:8b).

As little as sinners may fear and esteem God's law, they need to consider that its infinite weightiness and holiness are such that the eternal and living Son of God had to give His blood, soul, and life as a ransom to satisfy the claims of this violated law and deliver us from its curse and threatened penalty. The inflexible law of God could be satisfied with nothing less. All the blood of calves, sheep, bulls, and goats that were sacrificed throughout the Old Testament era could not make any satisfaction. To bring about satisfaction, the only begotten Son of God had to come and take upon Himself our nature. He permitted Himself to be put to death by the law and His body to be broken on the accursed tree of the cross, for this was the only way by which the law could absolve a single person from its inflexible claims and the curse due to sin, and enable that person to become a partaker of eternal life.

These are the five matters that constitute the sharp and compelling preaching of the law. Where these aspects are missing, the preaching of the law is tepid and ineffective, because such sharp preaching of the law is entirely contingent upon the grace and presence of the Holy Spirit in the church. In proportion to the measure in which the hearts of ministers are supplied by that Spirit and by His heavenly grace and operations, so shall their preaching of the law be more or less sharp, compelling, and convicting. Since the Spirit, sad to say, has departed from the church and ministers of our land, and since ministers live much more according to the flesh than in the Spirit, there is therefore no longer any sharp preaching of the law among us. As knives must be sharpened upon a grindstone, so must the tongues of ministers be sharpened upon the grindstone of God's Spirit or they are otherwise incapable of preaching God's law sharply. Oh, may it cause us to groan for the Spirit to be granted unto our ministers, who are called upon to preach God's law to us!

Outside of our church, there are those who question the compelling motive as to why the Lord God has to require that His law be so sharply preached in the world, whereas the sentiment of our Reformed divines is true, that no one in this life can keep the law—not even they who have been converted unto God, and then, not even the most holy among them.

If such persons would only become acquainted, in some measure, with God, in His infinite holiness and majesty, and the just claims that He has, by virtue of creation, upon man as having fallen into sin, they would most certainly not dare to inquire regarding a matter that is so well established. However, our opponents lack the light of the knowledge of God and of the ways of His holiness. Their views of God are worldly and carnal, for they are "sensual, having not the Spirit" (Jude 19b).

To reply to this objection, and to safeguard our holy and divine doctrine against their ill-conceived protestation, we must say that the Lord our God by all means has wise and holy reasons for requiring that we continue to preach His law sharply in spite of the absolute impotence of all men, by virtue of sin, which impotence renders them incapable of keeping His law even with any degree of perfection. These reasons can be reduced to three categories, as they run parallel to the three categories of people to whom the law must be sharply preached. They are:

1. *the reprobate*, who shall never be either converted or saved;
2. *the elect*, who have not yet been converted; and
3. *regenerated believers*, who have already been converted unto God.

The emphatic and sharp preaching of the law is most necessary for each of these three categories of men in their unique state and circumstances, and the holy law of God therefore must be most sharply preached:

First, to reprobates, who shall never be either converted or saved, so that thereby their brazen and reckless consciences can be reined in and restrained, and they will thus not be too debauched in their breaking forth into all manner of sin and wickedness. They certainly would conduct themselves as such if they were not continually fenced in by the sharp threats of the law and if they had no fear at all of the curse and wrath of God. We observe this in Ahab, who was restricted in the manifestation of his wickedness by the threats communicated to him in the name of the Lord by the prophet Elijah. Ahab was withheld from doing what he intended to do, not being motivated by love for God, but by fear of punishment (1 Kings 21:27).

The apostle therefore teaches that "the law is not made for a righteous man, but for the lawless and disobedient, for the ungodly and for sinners, for unholy and profane, for murderers of fathers and murderers of mothers, for manslayers, for whoremongers, for them that defile themselves with mankind, for men stealers, for liars, for perjured persons, and if there be any other thing that is contrary to sound doctrine" (1 Tim. 1:9). Thus, the law serves as a restraint to rein them in from breaking forth in all manner of abominable wickedness. This wickedness is similar to a flood of water overflowing everything where there are neither dikes nor dams to serve as obstacles to turn back such floodwaters. Likewise, a flood of wickedness proceeding from reprobate men would soon pervasively and grievously inundate an entire nation and people if, by way of the sharp preaching of God's law in all localities and congregations, a strong dike or dam were not built to halt and contain this flood of sin as much as possible.

In former days, there were many among the ministers in our land who preached the law sharply and also diligently administered discipline in the congregations. Our nation was then not nearly as filled with so many sins and wicked practices, such as atheism, sacrilege, the ridiculing of religion, and so many heresies and false religions, all of which are presently and sadly the case. All this abominable wickedness began to break forth as a mighty flood among us when ministers began to refrain from preaching God's law sharply and from diligently administering ecclesiastical censure. Only an omniscient God knows where all this wickedness will ultimately end when we continue to neglect the administration of discipline and the preaching of the law. One who by God's grace has learned to see something of this must certainly be afraid and tremble. We have thus given you the first reason why the sharp preaching of the law is necessary.

Second, to the elect, who have not yet been converted. To such, the law must also be sharply preached as the necessary means ordained by God for their conversion. Two things must be accomplished in them by the operation of the Holy Spirit so that they may be converted and be united to the Lord Jesus by faith:

1. They must be convinced of their sins and their damnable state. All crutches of self-righteousness must be fully removed from them so that they may become poor in spirit, deeply concerned, and desirous to be saved.

2. They must be stirred up with urgency and be motivated to believe in the Lord Jesus, so that wholeheartedly they may receive and embrace Him in response to His own promise, as well as to the offer of free grace in the gospel. However, both of these matters are worked in the hearts of the elect by the Holy Spirit only through the compelling preaching of the law, for, in the first division of the Catechism, we were extensively and clearly shown that we know our misery from the law of God. If, therefore, the law of God is sharply preached in the congregations, the Holy Spirit works by means of such preaching in the hearts of the elect.

The Holy Spirit simultaneously impresses upon their souls the weightiness of the law and the majesty of God. This causes them to believe that this law has been given to them by the majestic God of heaven, and they are therefore obliged to live according to that law with both soul and body. He also illuminates their understanding in order that they perceive the holiness, perfection, and spirituality of the law, so that this law now weighs much heavier upon their hearts than anything has ever weighed upon them in the world.

By this holy and spiritual light issuing forth from the holy law of God, the Spirit causes them to turn inward, and, in so doing, causes them clearly to see how completely they fail to be conformed to this divine law and how grievously and dreadfully they have violated and transgressed it throughout their lives. He causes them to see how abominable, vile, and unclean their hearts and walks of life have been and how hostile they are toward the holy law of God, causing them to recognize that everything found in them is nothing but sin, wickedness, and vile hypocrisy.

The Spirit causes them to see and impresses upon their hearts God's inflexible holiness and justice, as well as His wrath and curse that He has threatened upon all transgressors of His law. He also causes them to see how, by His truth and justice, this majestic God cannot restrain Himself from severely punishing sinners. They find themselves to be subject to God's wrath, as well as to the curse of His law, and thus everything that pertains to them is accursed—their eating and drinking, their coming and going, their lying down and their rising up, as well as their speaking and whatever else they may do. The curse and wrath of God unceasingly follow upon their heels and threaten, at any given moment, to crush them and to cast them into eternal death and condemnation.

In this way, the Holy Spirit gradually awakens them more and more from the deep slumber of their sinful carelessness and causes them to feel the unbearable burden of sin and of God's wrath. He works in them a deep sorrow, fear, contrition, and true spiritual perplexity, and, by so doing, He humbles them, flushes them out of all of their hiding places, and strips them of their false hope and of all the foundations and crutches to which they are clinging outside of Christ. He persists in this until they are finally convinced experientially of their fatal impotency and their hostility toward Christ and the gospel of God's free grace. He thus causes them to be in utter despair, no longer being able to find their life in anything, so that they finally, completely, and fully cease from all their own efforts. Only then are they suitable objects for Christ, as well as for the free grace promised in the gospel, so that, by the operation of the Spirit, they may unite themselves, by a true faith, to Christ, who came for the sole purpose to seek and to save that which is lost.

Third, to regenerated believers, who have already been converted unto God:

1. "That all our lifetime we may learn more and more to know our sinful nature." The true basis for the spiritual progress of the believer as to his salvation and sanctification consists in true contrition and sorrow for his sins. The Lord Jesus always begins His gracious work in the soul in this manner, similar to a sower or farmer who always begins his work by stirring, moving, and plowing his land, so that the soil may be rendered fit and suitable to receive the seed and to cause it to grow upward and to bear fruit. He who searches for the grace of the gospel apart from true contrition and sorrow for sin is like someone who desires to sow the land and gather fruit before the land has been first thoroughly stirred and plowed. God's grace never grows in hard soil, but only in soft and tender soil.

Let it be established and believed as an eternal truth that, in proportion to the measure in which the human heart is truly made tender and stirred by a true contrition for and a true sorrow over sin, the heart is rendered fit for the grace of Christ and for growth in grace. However, this sorrow over sin and contrition for it is always governed by the true light and knowledge that one has regarding his sins. To look for a true sorrow over sin in a blind and ignorant person who has not been inwardly illuminated by spiritual and convicting light proceeding from God would be like trying to gather grapes from thorns or figs from thistles.

Since it is certain that it is always by the grace of God that the knowledge of sin works and bring forth true sorrow and contrition in a man, it is self-evident that God, from His side, must use a suitable means to that end, whereby everyone, also the true believer, increasingly acquires a true knowledge of his sins and his sinful nature. God's holy law is that suitable means. It functions as a true and living mirror, and when, by spiritual illumination, we look into this mirror, we acquire, by spiritual illumination, a clear knowledge of our sinful state and of every aspect of our misery, "for by the law is the knowledge of sin" (Rom. 3:20b). Paul says regarding himself, "Nay, I had not known sin, but by the law" (Rom. 7:7b). The instructor addressed this in detail in Lord's Day 2.

However, it is by no means true that when a man initially comes to Christ in a truly believing and contrite frame and initially turns to God from his sins, he has received as much knowledge of his sins as is necessary, for every true believer, by the illumination of the Spirit, must daily avail himself of God's holy law as a transparent mirror to become increasingly acquainted with all his sins and with his sinful nature. To achieve this, God causes His law to be preached daily and sharply to true Christian believers.

Being illuminated by the Spirit, the law unveils to believers the full extent of their sins and holy duties, and what manner of holy and godly people they ought to be. By the holy light that emanates from God's law and the operation of the Spirit, they examine themselves and very carefully evaluate their heart and walk. In so doing, they increasingly become acquainted with and have a lively awareness of their sinful nature and all their sinful deficiencies. This, in turn, continually yields true contrition and causes them to humble themselves before a majestic God. This yields an inward loathing of self, and, in this way, they learn to live meekly, humbly, and uprightly before God—all of which is the foundation of all true holiness, salvation, and faith. This is then the first and necessary reason for the ongoing sharp preaching of God's law.

2. Another reason is no less beneficial and essential than the first, for the instructor continues by saying that we may "thus become the more earnest in seeking the remission of sin and righteousness in Christ." The entire salvation of believers is exclusively bound up in the spiritual union of faith between them and the Lord Jesus. The more that they, by the power of the Holy Spirit and by faith, turn to Christ, and are intimately, steadfastly, and truly united to Christ, the more they, of necessity, become a more blessed and holy people. In so doing, more and more they live in and through Christ, their spiritual head, and, by faith, extract from Him gracious light and strength, whereby they continually mature in Him as their head. In this way, they begin to abound in all that pertains to their sanctification.

There is no means whereby poor believers, by the Spirit of faith, may continually be led out of self unto Christ their savior except by this spiritual knowledge of sin, contrition, and the humbling of self. As we have seen, they increasingly acquire this by means of the daily and sharp preaching of the law. This law, by the illumination of the Holy Spirit, continually and increasingly begets in believers a knowledge of their sins and of their sinful nature, and, in this way, they necessarily and increasingly are weaned from all that is of self and of all their own righteousness.

By this divine conviction and being humbled by the law, they increasingly and intensely begin to truly loathe themselves, so that they can neither sustain themselves, cleave to anything of themselves, nor find any true rest and comfort for their souls. In this way, they become increasingly hostile toward all that is of self, and toward all their own works and righteousnesses. They become increasingly desirous to seek for the forgiveness of their sins, as well as to find their righteousness only in the Lord Jesus, their true head and savior, for He "of God is made unto us wisdom, and righteousness, and sanctification, and redemption" (1 Cor. 1:30). This was the experience of the apostle Paul, who became increasingly desirous to know Christ and the power of His resurrection, saying that he desired to "be found in him, not having mine own righteousness, which is of the law, but that which is through the faith of Christ, the righteousness which is of God by faith" (Phil. 3:9).

This is the second way in which the law functions in the lives of all true believers, namely, the law is a continual taskmaster for them to lead them to Christ, so that, by faith, they increasingly, more steadfastly, and more intimately are united to Him as the fountain of their entire salvation.

3. They must endeavor to use the law as the rule or standard of their sanctification, according to which their heart and walk must increasingly and continually be directed and conformed by the grace and operation of the Holy Spirit. The instructor therefore continues his exposition by saying, "that we constantly endeavor and pray to God for the grace of the Holy Spirit, that we may become more and more conformable to the image of God, till we arrive at the perfection proposed to us in a life to come."

Since, by means of the sharp preaching of the law, the soul of a believer increasingly is convicted of its sins and of its sinful nature, led to humble itself before God in true contrition, and, in this way, is increasingly, more intimately, and more steadfastly united to Christ by faith, it must certainly follow that such a soul increasingly is filled with a true yearning after God and after holiness of heart and a holy walk of life. This necessarily yields an increased and more intense hatred and aversion for all sin.

On the one hand, this holy desire and aversion are to be found in the heart of the believer, and, by God's grace, daily increase and grow. On the other hand, the evil flesh and sinful nature are also found in the soul of a Christian, which, apart from the continual and efficacious grace of God, continually hinder and greatly hamper him in doing anything that is good. Therefore, it cannot be otherwise but that the poor believing soul must pray all the more vehemently and earnestly in the Spirit to God and to Christ, its savior, for the grace of His Spirit unto sanctification.

Since God always hears the sincere and humble prayer of His children, He always grants them the desired grace of His Spirit in response to their prayer. By this grace of the Spirit, they continually and increasingly are renewed according to God's image, and they daily become a more holy and godly people, who, in their hearts and in their walks, conform themselves to God's holy law. As they traverse this way, this continually increases "till we arrive at the perfection proposed to us in a life to come."

He who truly knows and understands all this within his soul supremely acquiesces in and approves of the continual sharp preaching of God's holy law as a preeminent means unto his salvation. Who then does not unceasingly thank God in Christ and by the Spirit for such preaching? And who does not earnestly and continually desire to make a proper use of such preaching, so that he might increasingly attain for himself all these glorious and blessed ends by the grace of God?

Having arrived at this point, we have been privileged to conclude the preaching of God's law by means of the Catechism in order that we may proceed to consider the last subject of the Catechism: the believing prayer of the Christian.

From all that has been considered, let us now conclude by extracting useful and beneficial instruction and admonition, whereby we might always walk accordingly by God's grace, according to the certain and immovable precepts of Christianity, from which we may never depart. And may we never give others license to do so.

There has never been a more devious and soul-damning heresy in the world, having as its objective the utter destruction of Christianity, than *antinomianism* (that is, the denial of the law). The antinomian doctrine teaches that converted Christians no longer have to be concerned with the literal and inscribed law of God, positing that Christians neither need to interact daily with nor to continually make use of the law, as this leads one to believe that any interaction with the law, as well as the continual use of the law, is only a requirement that the unconverted must fulfill. Antinomians teach that the law is something that only the unconverted are to engage with, so that, by the sharp preaching of the law, they are convicted and brought to Christ and to His grace. This abominable doctrine of the antinomians is the fountainhead of the utter corruption of Christianity, and therefore we do not have to fear as much from the plague as we do from this abominable doctrine of Satan.

Any spiritual light and frames of peace, comfort, or any enjoyment, deemed to be received through God, irrespective of how wonderful such manifestation of apparent godliness may appear to be, must be viewed as highly suspect within us and in others if they are not always accompanied by:

1. a true knowledge and confession of all guilt and sin;
2. a heartfelt shame, contrition, and humbling of ourselves before a majestic and holy God;
3. a believing longing for and desiring for the forgiveness of sins and the righteousness of Christ above all else; and
4. a sincere resolution and earnest endeavor, sincerely and in very deed, to repent.

When these matters are not truly present as the chief and dominant divine graces in the heart, then we must view as highly suspect everything that has the appearance of being a manifestation of divine light and heavenly grace. We must always judge ourselves and others by this standard, lest we be guilty of the most vile and abominable sin of "turning the grace of our God into lasciviousness" (Jude 4).

We must always be very much on guard against all, whoever they may be, who walk carelessly in regard to the holy duties of the law and who speak in lofty terms of God's ways and of having communion with God while, at the same time, their walk is not characterized by a tender conscience regarding their duty toward God and man. We must always be much on guard against all who play fast and loose with sin while speaking much of Christ, grace, and heaven. It cannot be expressed in words what harm they do in their surroundings, even when they, as to the root of the matter, are truly converted Christians. How greatly is the honor of Christ maligned by such individuals!

A legalistic person who is generally greatly bogged down with a sense of guilt and duty, even though he remains in such bondage for the rest of his days, does not inflict one tenth of the damage to the cause of Christ and the salvation of poor sinners as do others who are accustomed to speak of enjoying much light and communion with God while, at the same time, their walk of life is corrupt and careless regarding sin and their duty. If we cherish the salvation of our souls, as well as the honor of Christ, we must always and with utmost caution, by the grace of God, be on guard against such individuals.

Finally, the best ministers of God's Word are they who continually and on all occasions:

1. Preach the law of God sharply, not only to the unconverted, but also to the converted, and who firmly insist on the careful performance of all duties as they are commanded and prescribed by God, positing that the essence of Christianity consists in these duties being performed spiritually and in very deed.

2. Rebuke all sins and hypocrisy in the converted and unconverted alike, and by no means excuse the sins of the converted. They rather earnestly warn against both God's impending punishments and judgments.

3. Urge everyone to be truly contrite and to humble themselves wholeheartedly before God regarding their sins and their sinful nature, and who promise God's grace and the benefits of the merits of Christ only to those who are of a contrite spirit because of their sins, excluding all others from such benefits.

4. Labor in all of their preaching to lead their hearers, by the Spirit of faith, to look entirely outside of themselves, and to lead them to Christ for justification and sanctification.

5. Preach God's kingdom, as not consisting in words, but in power, in the actual observance and obedience of all the holy commandments and precepts of God, and in a true repenting of and departing from all sin.

To the extent that we are able to preserve these four important directives in a time that is both grievous and void of spirituality, to that extent we shall be able to preserve the true nature and practice of Christianity as the Lord Jesus, the holy apostles, and the prophets taught. To the extent that we deviate from these four directives in both doctrine and life, to that extent we will depart from and ultimately lose the true essence and soul of Christianity. Whatever we do above and beyond them, or divorced from them, shall be nothing less than vile and accursed hypocrisy before God, irrespective of whether we are converted or unconverted. The righteous God, in due time, will visit this departure with His judgments.

By the grace of God, I say to you that I desire to leave as my last testament, to the world and to Christianity, these four directives, as well as the entire doctrine I have been privileged to preach to you. It is also my desire that, with the help and by the grace of God, I, a wretched one, may steadfastly live and die by that testament, waiting for the great coming of Christ unto judgment! Amen.

The Lord Jesus has sent His angel to testify unto you these things in the churches. He is "the root and the offspring of David, and the bright and morning star. And the Spirit and the bride say, Come. And let him that heareth say, Come. And let him that is athirst come. And whosoever will, let him take the water of life freely" (Rev. 22:16–17).

Prayer

Ask, and it shall be given you; seek, and ye shall find; knock, and it shall be opened unto you: For every one that asketh receiveth; and he that seeketh findeth; and to him that knocketh it shall be opened.

—MATTHEW 7:7–8

Question 116: Why is prayer necessary for Christians?

Answer: Because it is the chief part of thankfulness which God requires of us; and also, because God will give His grace and Holy Spirit to those only, who with sincere desires continually ask them of Him, and are thankful for them.

Question 117: What are the requisites of that prayer which is acceptable to God and which He will hear?

Answer: First, that we from the heart pray to the one true God only, who hath manifested Himself in His Word, for all things He hath commanded us to ask of Him; secondly, that we rightly and thoroughly know our need and misery, that so we may deeply humble ourselves in the presence of His divine majesty; thirdly, that we be fully persuaded that He, notwithstanding that we are unworthy of it, will, for the sake of Christ our Lord, certainly hear our prayer, as He has promised us in His word.

Question 118: What hath God commanded us to ask of Him?

Answer: All things necessary for soul and body, which Christ our Lord has comprised in that prayer He Himself has taught us.

Question 119: What are the words of that prayer?

Answer: Our Father which art in heaven, hallowed be Thy name. Thy kingdom come. Thy will be done in earth, as it is in heaven. Give us this day our daily bread. And forgive us our debts, as we forgive our debtors. And lead us not into temptation, but deliver us from evil: for Thine is the kingdom, and the power, and the glory, for ever. Amen.

———————————

King David uttered a precious prayer, saying: "Thou hast commanded us to keep thy precepts diligently. O that my ways were directed to keep thy statutes!" (Ps. 119:4–5). He whose eyes have been illuminated can discern in a very plain manner that this is the prayer of a believer who is beseeching the Lord for sanctification and strength so that he might walk in the way of His commandments and precepts.

Four matters may be observed in this supplicant. Oh, that they were always to be found in all God's children! They are:

1. an acquaintance with the Lord's commandments, as well as with their holiness, goodness, and suitability, knowing and realizing that he who fears the Lord must keep them with a completely perfect heart;

2. a recognition and experience of the utter impotency and weakness of the heart to keep these holy commandments of God in such a fashion;

3. an earnest longing and desire of the soul for, and, yes, an intense love toward, these commandments of the Lord, as well as the observance of the same; and

4. a believing and humble submission of the soul in prayer before the Lord as to His divine fullness and all-sufficiency in Christ to receive from Him all strength, fortitude, and grace to that end.

Beloved, these four matters are addressed in like fashion in the instruction rendered by the Heidelberg Catechism.

First, in several sequential Lord's Days, the instructor set before us and acquainted us with the precious and treasured commandments of God.

Second, he then demonstrated in Question 114 the impotence of believers to keep these commandments of the Lord perfectly.

Third, he nevertheless caused us also to see the sincere desire, love, and commitment of believers to live according to all these commandments of God.

Fourth, he then finally leads us to the matter of prayer, whereby believers pour out their souls before the Lord and His all-sufficiency, fervently beseeching Him to grant them strength, fortitude, and grace so that they might keep

His commandments and become partakers of the full salvation that is to be found in and through Christ Jesus.

The instructor will expound the matter of prayer in greater detail in this Lord's Day and will continue to do so in the remaining seven Lord's Days, in which he will give us a brief exposition of the perfect Lord's Prayer.

We shall follow the instructor by addressing the prayer of the Christian in general terms. Not only is this a matter of great importance, but it also has very broad implications. One could therefore engage in a very in-depth exposition, expounding and setting before you a multitude of practical matters. After all, prayer is the spiritual dimension of Christianity and the soul of all our spiritual duties. However, in the carnal age in which we are presently living, prayer has become a foreign exercise among people, irrespective of the appearance of prayer that may be seen and found among us. Yes, even among those who have learned to pray according to the will of God, there are very few who either have progressed in some measure in the practice of this glorious exercise or who are noticeably partakers of the grace and spirit of prayer. Consequently, not only has the exercise of fellowship with the triune God, as the fountain of all salvation and spiritual life, been significantly suppressed and inhibited, but the innumerable riches of grace to be drawn from the inexhaustible fullness of Christ remain concealed, which otherwise, as a heavenly dew, would steadily drip upon and moisten our souls and, in no small measure, render them fruitful.

It is therefore our heartfelt desire that the Lord would grant us both the opportunity and the grace to proceed with expounding for the congregation some of the distinctive elements of prayer, while at the same time considering several suitable texts. Presently we wish to expound the subject of prayer in general terms, doing so in accordance with the Heidelberg Catechism and as briefly as possible. May the Lord, by His Spirit, grant us the necessary grace to that end, and may it yield a blessing to our readers. Amen.

The instructor has divided the subject matter of prayer into four categories:

1. In Question 116, he addresses the necessity of prayer.

2. In Question 117, he addresses the requisites of true Christian prayer.

3. In Question 118, he addresses the contents of prayer, that is, the matters we may and must ask of the Lord.

4. In Question 119, he addresses the template or paradigm according to which all the prayers of believers must be ordered.

With the instructor, we shall first consider the *necessity* of prayer and address the matter of prayer as being a religious lifting up of the heart to Jehovah, the triune God, whereby we bring before Him our needs and desires, beseeching Him that He would be pleased to grant them out of His divine all-sufficiency and grace. In such prayer, there is an earnest, humble, patient, and believing perseverance in proportion to the measure of grace that the Lord bestows upon us and to what extent He grants us the spirit of prayer.

The instructor first asks, regarding such prayer, why it is necessary for the Christian. Take note that the instructor here addresses the duty of prayer only as it pertains to *Christians*, that is, to true Christians, who, by faith, are united to Christ their head and are therefore partakers of His holy and spiritual anointing. There are no Christians but they who are the believing members of the Lord Jesus. All who are not true believers bear this name unjustly and in vain, for they are but nominal Christians and external lip confessors. They are utterly bereft of all the spiritual privileges of Christianity, regardless of how they may outwardly boast of their Christianity. Thus, the instructor has in mind only true believers and spiritual Christians, who serve God in the Spirit and glory in Christ as their head and king. He limits the practice of prayer as being a holy and necessary exercise of such true Christians. He makes it unmistakably clear that all who are unconverted, and thus all who are unbelievers, even though they may be referred to as Christians, belong to a Christian church, and have made an external profession of the Christian faith, are nevertheless utterly bereft of this holy exercise of prayer and are incapable of praying to God with faith, with confidence, and in Spirit and in truth.

He who knows how one ought to pray to God and what the requisites are of a true Christian prayer that is pleasing to God, as we shall subsequently consider, readily understands that it is utterly impossible for unconverted unbelievers rightly to pray to God. They are completely void of the Spirit of prayer and know not what it means to pray in the name of the Lord Jesus, without which no prayer can be heard by God, "for he that cometh to God must believe that he is, and that he is a rewarder of them that diligently seek him" (Heb. 11:6).

Throughout the Holy Scriptures, it is therefore clearly and plainly taught that God does not hear the prayers of unconverted men, but that He abhors them, and that such prayers increasingly provoke Him to anger against such men. Solomon speaks accordingly, saying, "The sacrifice of the wicked [that is, all unbelievers, and thus unconverted] is an abomination to the Lord" (Prov. 15:8a). David testifies, "Let his prayer become sin" (Ps. 109:7). Also read attentively what is written in John 9:31, for the blind man who had received his sight from the Savior said to the Jews, "Now we know that God heareth not sinners: but if any man be a worshipper of God, and doeth his will, him he heareth." Therefore, James also addresses unconverted sinners accordingly when he says, "Ye ask, and receive not, because ye ask amiss, that ye may consume it upon your lusts" (James 4:3). However, in saying this, we are by no means teaching that unconverted and unregenerate men should not nor may not pray to God. Not only must they pray to God, but they must do so in truth and in faith. This is and remains their absolute duty, and God requires of them that they fulfill this obligation. We are teaching, however, that they are utterly unfit and incapable of fulfilling their obligation to pray, and that God Himself must bestow upon them the grace and the Spirit of prayer if they are to pray to Him in truth.

It is thus self-evident that the instructor here addresses prayer as exclusively being a holy exercise of true Christians, that is, of converted believers. He therefore inquires and investigates why prayer is a necessity for them. The instructor here has in mind the shameful neglect and disregard of the duty of prayer of which the ungodly are extremely guilty. He also has in mind those who, during his time (and also in our present day), are utterly opposed to prayer and reject it as being unnecessary, teaching that subsequent to Christ's death, believers should only give thanks rather than pray. They derive their erroneous arguments from God's omniscience, the immutability of His eternal counsel, and the complete title believers have to all things in Christ. Such and similar ungodly sentiments the instructor here opposes by clearly expounding and positing the necessity of prayer for all true Christians.

Let us therefore consider what arguments he advances to that end as he instructs in the Catechism that prayer is necessary for Christians, "because it is the chief part of thankfulness which God requires of us; and also, because God will give His grace and Holy Spirit to those only, who with sincere desires continually ask them of Him, and are thankful for them." The instructor here sets before us two compelling and scriptural reasons why all true Christians are obligated to pray. We shall briefly address and expound them for you.

The first reason given is that prayer "is the chief part of thankfulness which God requires of us." By the phrase "thankfulness which God requires of us," we are to understand the totality of the spiritual life of a believing Christian, whereby he fully surrenders and sacrifices himself to the triune God, in both soul and body, to serve and glorify Him eternally, in conformity to His covenant. Such thankfulness—nothing more or anything less—the Lord requires of His children; that is, a complete surrender of themselves to Him to be His people and His property, doing so in both soul and body and for both time and eternity. The apostle teaches this by exhorting believers accordingly, saying, "For ye are bought with a price: therefore glorify God in your body, and in your spirit, which are God's" (1 Cor. 6:20).

The instructor here declares that prayer is the chief part of the gratitude of believers. This is most certainly true. As we have already stated, the exercise of prayer is the very soul of the spiritual life of a Christian. What spiritual life could there be without prayer? Prayer is the means whereby one obtains from the Lord all the grace needed for spiritual life, and without this grace, the Lord cannot be served in spirit and in truth by His own. The Holy Scriptures therefore designate the entire spiritual life of believers to consist in the exercise of prayer or the calling upon the name of the Lord (Gen. 4:26). By means of prayer, God is greatly glorified by His people, for thereby, they bear witness to His holy and divine attributes, and they honor His name. By means of prayer believers fully give themselves as a sacrifice of thanksgiving unto the Lord with both soul and body. By prayer they commit, surrender, and bind themselves unto the Lord and His holy service.

Finally, by means of prayer, believers confess their gratitude to the Lord by acknowledging Him for all His benefits. Therefore, throughout the Holy Scriptures, they not only conjoin prayer and thanksgiving, but they are also spoken of interchangeably as being most intimately connected and as being, in essence, one and the same matter. This could be confirmed by multiple testimonies from the Word of God (Ps. 50:14–15; 1 Cor. 14:15–16), which clearly affirm that prayer is the chief part of the gratitude of a Christian and of his spiritual life, and is therefore an exercise of the utmost necessity.

The instructor then proceeds with his second argument for the necessity of prayer, saying that it consists of God giving "His grace and Holy Spirit to those only, who with sincere desires continually ask them of Him, and are thankful for them." Oh, that this would be rightly heard and understood by spiritless supplicants, who are also to be found among us—supplicants who grievously despise and neglect the duty of prayer! God the Lord is thoroughly acquainted with all the needs of His children, and He is also most willing and inclined to help them. It is, however, His will that they would ceaselessly pray for His grace and for His Holy Spirit with heartfelt supplications, and that they would thank Him for this benefit. The Lord Himself says: "I the LORD build the ruined places, and plant that that was desolate: I the LORD have spoken it, and

I will do it. Thus saith the Lord GOD; I will yet for this be enquired of by the house of Israel, to do it for them; I will increase them with men like a flock" (Ezek. 36:36–37). In these verses, He promises to bestow great benefits upon His people, but He says he will do so only upon being enquired of by the house of Israel, that He would do this for them.

We are taught this truth throughout the Holy Scriptures. The Savior teaches plainly that God is willing to give His Holy Spirit only upon prayer, for He declared this to His disciples: "If ye then, being evil, know how to give good gifts unto your children: how much more shall your heavenly Father give the Holy Spirit to them that ask him?" (Luke 11:13). Though the Savior specifically refers here to the Holy Spirit, this is true in general for all the gracious benefits and blessings of God. The Lord does not bestow them upon His children unless they heartily, fervently, and persistently pray for them. For example, the apostle James writes, "If any of you lack wisdom, let him ask of God, that giveth to all men liberally, and upbraideth not; and it shall be given him" (James 1:5). God is therefore denominated as "a rewarder of them that diligently seek him" (Heb. 11:6). Consider also how emphatically the Savior speaks of this to His disciples, saying, "Verily, verily, I say unto you, Whatsoever ye shall ask the Father in my name, he will give it you" (John 16:23).

This affirms most clearly that God has purposed that He will not grant His Holy Spirit and His grace to His children in any way but by means of prayer. It thus follows that for all true Christians, prayer is both a duty and an exercise of the utmost import. The Lord therefore earnestly commands His people in His Word to pray, saying, "Ask, and it shall be given you; seek, and ye shall find; knock, and it shall be opened unto you: for every one that asketh receiveth; and he that seeketh findeth; and to him that knocketh it shall be opened" (Matt. 7:7–8). Paul exhorts believers that they should be "continuing instant in prayer" (Rom. 12:12b), that they should "pray without ceasing" (1 Thess. 5:17), and that they should "continue in prayer, and watch in the same with thanksgiving" (Col. 4:2).

Herewith we have sufficiently expounded the first aspect of prayer, namely, the necessity and duty of prayer for all Christians.

With the instructor, we shall proceed to consider the second matter: the requisites of true, believing, Christian prayer that is pleasing to God and is heard of Him. The instructor inquires of this by asking, "What are the requisites of that prayer which is acceptable to God and which He will hear?" It should be noted that the instructor here speaks of a proper prayer in which God finds delight and which He therefore also hears. Thereby, he clearly implies that there are prayers being offered that are by no means pleasing to the Lord and that therefore also are not heard of Him. This is true of all such unspiritual, ungodly, unbelieving, and irreverent form prayers that people utter merely for the sake of praying. Oh, such sinful and abominable prayers are by no means pleasing to God! He does not hear them. They are an abomination in His holy sight, and He therefore casts them as refuse back before the countenances of sinners.

However, if you desire to know what sort of prayers are pleasing to God and are also heard of Him, then take note of what the instructor is saying, and may it please the Lord that you all would receive ears to hear. According to the instructor, a proper prayer must consist of three distinct elements:

- "first, that we from the heart pray to the one true God only, who hath manifested Himself in His Word, for all things He hath commanded us to ask of Him;

- "secondly, that we rightly and thoroughly know our need and misery, that so we may deeply humble ourselves in the presence of His divine majesty;

- "thirdly, that we be fully persuaded that He, notwithstanding our unworthiness of it, will, for the sake of Christ our Lord, certainly hear our prayer, as He has promised us in His word."

Thus, the instructor posits that a proper prayer that is pleasing to God and is heard of Him must necessarily consist of three elements, namely:

- the person to whom prayer must be addressed;

- a supplicant, who must have a thorough knowledge of his misery; and

- faith and confidence that must accompany his prayer.

These are the absolute and essential requisites of a proper Christian prayer, apart from which God cannot hear it.

Regarding the first, to pray a proper prayer that is pleasing to God, it is necessary "that we from the heart pray to the one true God only, who hath manifested Himself in His Word, for all things He hath commanded us to ask of Him." This requisite, in turn, also consists of three specific elements. A proper prayer:

- must be addressed "to the one true God only, who hath manifested Himself in His Word";

- must proceed from the heart; and

- must pertain to "all things He hath commanded us to ask of Him."

Therefore, the first requisite of a proper prayer is that one addresses "the one true God only" and by no means addresses any other creature—such as is the practice of Roman Catholicism. One must also not pray to an unknown God. Such is the practice of all the unconverted among us, who do not know the one true God and are therefore praying to an unknown God. Only Jehovah, the God of heaven, is entitled to the honor of the prayer and supplication of men—as is true for all aspects of spiritual life—for He alone is able to hear prayer. David speaks of this, saying: "Praise waiteth for thee, O God, in Sion: and unto thee shall the vow be performed. O thou that hearest prayer, unto thee shall all flesh come" (Ps. 65:1–2). The Holy Scriptures therefore attribute the honor of prayer exclusively to Jehovah, the one true God. We read of this in Psalm 81:9–10: "There shall no strange god be in thee; neither shalt thou worship any strange god. I am the LORD thy God, which brought thee out of the land of Egypt: open thy mouth wide, and I will fill it." Also, the Savior said emphatically to Satan, "Get thee hence, Satan: for it is written, Thou shalt worship the Lord thy God, and him only shalt thou serve" (Matt. 4:10).

But how are we to worship the one true God? The instructor teaches this by adding, "the God…who hath manifested Himself in His Word." In His Word, God not only has revealed Himself as the triune God, but He has also revealed Himself as a God who is supremely glorious and blessed in His precious attributes and divine perfections. He is therefore entirely worthy of all the love, respect, and confidence of His people. Yes, the Lord has revealed Himself in His Word as the triune covenant God of His beloved people, who, in the totality of His being, is this God unto them, and forever shall be. One must first rightly know this most glorious and precious God as He is revealed in His Holy Word if one is to worship Him properly, and if a soul, with fervent supplications and prayers, is to cast herself confidently upon Him and wait for His salvation. We read this in Psalm 9:10: "And they that know thy name will put their trust in thee: for thou, LORD, hast not forsaken them that seek thee."

However, this is not the only aspect of the manner in which one must pray to the one true God. According to the instructor, this must also be done "from the heart." Thus, in prayer, the heart and the mouth must be united so that when one engages his mind, mouth, and lips, he does not bring before the Lord or ask of Him anything other than that which is in full harmony with his inner condition and the desires of his heart. If such is not the case, then his prayer is nothing but a mockery of God and a shameful desecration of God's holy Name. One then brings lies before the Lord, and he seeks to flatter and to deceive Him with his lips.

We must recognize that God is an omniscient God who desires truth within. He demands the heart of all His children in the totality of their spiritual lives, and thus also in their prayers, for without the engagement of the heart, all religion is an abomination to Him. The Savior taught the Samaritan woman that "God is a Spirit: and they that worship him must worship him in spirit and in truth" (John 4:24). The Lord neither can nor does hear any prayers but those that proceed from the heart and in which one brings his heart before Him.

One upright and intense groan of the heart is one thousand times more pleasing to the Lord than the most delightful prayers that are uttered only with one's mind, mouth, and lips. We therefore read, "The LORD is nigh unto all them that call upon him, to all that call upon him in truth" (Ps. 145:18). The apostle Paul therefore exhorts believers, saying, "Let us draw near with a true heart in full assurance of faith" (Heb. 10:22). Viewed from this perspective, it is necessary that God's children frequently prepare their hearts prior to approaching the Lord in their prayers, so that they do not bring any deceit or dishonesty before the God of truth, and thus give Him reason to be angry. Zophar admonishes: "If thou prepare thine heart, and stretch out thine hands toward him; if iniquity be in thine hand, put it far away, and let not wickedness dwell in thy tabernacles. For then shalt thou lift up thy face without spot; yea, thou shalt be stedfast, and shalt not fear" (Job 11:13–15). It is thus evident that the one true God must be worshiped with the heart.

According to the instructor, we must also pray "for all things He hath commanded us to ask of Him." This is also an absolute and essential requisite of a proper Christian prayer that is offered up in full harmony with the Lord's will—and thus for such things as He Himself has commanded His children in His Word to ask of Him. In the next question and answer, the instructor will explain what these things are.

If anyone prays to the Lord in a manner that deviates from this, his prayer will not be heard by Him, for "ye ask, and receive not, because ye ask amiss, that ye may consume it upon your lusts" (James 4:3). In this matter, God's children must surrender themselves fully to the Lord, and they must thus pray according to His will and command. Then they may always expect their prayers to be heard, and with full liberty they may approach their God. "And this is the confidence that we have in him, that, if we ask any thing according to his will, he heareth us" (1 John 5:14).

We have thus considered the first essential requisite of a proper prayer that is pleasing to God.

The instructor then proceeds to set before us a second and no less essential requisite: "that we rightly and thoroughly know our need and misery, that so we may deeply humble ourselves in the presence of His divine majesty." We have a common proverb that says that necessity will teach one to pray. This is most certainly a truism. All the earnestness, zeal, patience, persistence, and trust of a proper prayer proceed only from the fountain of a right and thorough knowledge of our need and misery. When this is lacking, one cannot possibly pray in a proper fashion. All prayer that is void of this is but lukewarm (not heartfelt), unspiritual, and a matter of form and custom. What else is prayer but a bringing before the Lord one's need and misery, earnestly beseeching and desiring of Him that He would remove these from us, and that He would fill our need out of His divine all-sufficiency?

When one becomes acquainted with himself, what an utterly poor, deficient, impotent, and miserable creature he finds himself to be! How much he stands in need of the Lord's grace for all things, without which he cannot do a thing! What a proper portrait the Holy Spirit has drawn of God's people in Zephaniah 3:12: "I will also leave in the midst of thee an afflicted and poor people, and they shall trust in the name of the LORD." Whenever God's children truly view themselves in that light, they find themselves to be a lump and conglomerate of utter deficiency, wretchedness, and misery. They then have to testify, "I am wretched, and miserable, and poor, and blind, and naked" (Rev. 3:17b).

Rightly and thoroughly to know this deficiency, these needs, and this misery, does not consist in a mere intellectual consideration of them and in the ability of speaking about them at great length. The right and thorough knowledge of one's needs and misery consists of a clear, lively, focused, and spiritual view of oneself. One thus has a soul-oppressing and intense sense of this, so that he is bowed down by these needs and this misery. Being so greatly burdened and weighed down by this, so that he cannot possibly bear it any longer, he is then powerfully driven out of himself to God in Christ and to His grace and all-sufficiency, seeking help and deliverance from Him.

David, the man of God, had a right and thorough knowledge of his need and misery, which caused him to cry out, "For I acknowledge my transgressions: and my sin is ever before me" (Ps. 51:3). The Lord sometimes hides His face from His people until they come into dire straits, and they know themselves to be miserable and guilty. They then seek Him early (Hos. 5:15). This right and thorough knowledge of one's need and misery is a necessary requisite for prayer, "that so we may deeply humble ourselves in the presence of His divine majesty."

This humbling of oneself "in the presence of His divine majesty" consists of a deep humiliation of the heart before the Lord. Having a lively view of one's own unworthiness, sinfulness, insignificance, and utter deficiency, as well as of the Lord's greatness and glory, one is so broken of heart that he comes before the Lord as small and insignificant. He conducts himself before Him as a wretched one, crawling before His throne as an insignificant worm and maggot. Such a humble disposition is very pleasing to the Lord, for "the sacrifices of God are a broken spirit: a broken and a contrite heart, O God, thou wilt not despise" (Ps. 51:17). He dwells "with him also that is of a contrite and humble spirit" (Isa. 57:15), and He looks "even to him that is poor and of a contrite spirit, and trembleth at [His] word" (Isa. 66:2).

In order to humble oneself so deeply before God's lofty majesty, it is beneficial to have a right and thorough knowledge of one's need and misery. Man, by nature, is an indescribably proud creature, and he knows no other god but himself. However, this all changes when God comes and confronts him with himself, thereby causing him clearly to see and experience his need and misery. Then a man falls in the dust with all his conceit, and his need and misery break him, humble him, and render him contrite before God.

Such was the experience of the publican in the parable of the Pharisee and the publican (Luke 18:8–14). The thorough knowledge and sense of his need and misery humbled him to such an extent before the presence of God's majesty that when he went up to the temple to pray, "the publican, standing afar off, would not lift up so much as his eyes unto heaven, but smote upon his breast, saying, God be merciful to me a sinner" (Luke 18:13). This was also the experience of the prodigal son, who was prompted by his need and misery to arise and go to his father, saying, "Father, I have sinned against heaven, and in thy sight, and am no more worthy to be called thy son" (Luke 15:21).

This humble disposition that proceeds from a thorough knowledge of one's need and misery, we find expressed very vividly throughout God's Word in the prayers of the saints. It is thus very evident that this is also an essential requisite of a proper prayer that is pleasing to God.

The instructor then proceeds to address a third and essential requisite of prayer: "that we be fully persuaded that He, notwithstanding that we are unworthy of it, will, for the sake of Christ our Lord, certainly hear our prayer, as He has promised us in His word." A prayer that is void of confidence that it will be heard is as a body without a soul. The supplicant must necessarily have a steadfast basis for his confidence within his heart, not only that he is approaching an omnipotent God who is able to hear and to help him, but that this same God unto whom He approaches is also a gracious, all-sufficient, and merciful God. Therefore, we read in Hebrews 11:6 that "he that cometh to God must believe that he is, and that he is a rewarder of them that diligently seek him." Without such confidence, God cannot possibly be worshiped aright.

From whence do believers derive this steadfast confidence that God is both able and willing to hear their prayers? This confidence certainly does not issue forth from anything they find and discern within themselves, for of themselves they are utterly unworthy that God would look down and bestow any grace upon them. God is neither able nor willing to hear them as they are of themselves, and therefore He has to reject them, as well as all their prayers. However, believers derive this confidence from an entirely different direction, namely, from and out of their mediator and savior, Christ Jesus, to whom they are united by faith. According to the instructor, such is the reason why God, "notwithstanding that [they] are unworthy of it, will, for the sake of Christ our Lord, certainly hear [their] prayer." Christ is the only way whereby believers can go unto God. He fully purchased their claim upon all of God's grace and benefits. He has abundant merits before the Father, wherewith He clothes His believing people. Believers therefore appear before God in the name of Christ, and with all their prayers, they cast themselves upon Him. They bring Christ before God, and they plead upon His merits, and desire to be heard only on that basis. They do what Daniel did in his prayer, saying, "Now therefore, O our God, hear the prayer of thy servant, and his supplications, and cause thy face to shine upon thy sanctuary that is desolate, for the Lord's sake [that is, for Christ's sake]" (Dan. 9:17).

He who prays to God in Christ's name cannot possibly put his trust in anyone other than in Christ and His merits, and however unworthy he is in himself, he may therefore expect that God graciously hears his prayer. When a soul truly rests in prayer exclusively upon Christ alone, he by no means doubts whether his prayer is heard, but he "draw[s] near with a true heart in full assurance of faith, having [his heart] sprinkled from an evil conscience" (Heb. 10:22). Paul therefore says that believers in Christ "have boldness and access with confidence by the faith of him" (Eph. 3:12). This should not surprise us, for they see God in Christ as being fully all-sufficient and willing to hear their prayers. They therefore neither can nor may in any way doubt the good will of their heavenly Father—and then especially, according to the instructor, because He has promised to hear them.

In this sense, the entire Word of God is filled with God's promises. We shall consider just a few of them. In John 16:23, the Savior says to His believing people, "Verily, verily, I say unto you, Whatsoever ye shall ask the Father in my name, he will give it you." In John 14:13, He says, "And whatsoever ye shall ask in my name, that will I do, that the Father may be glorified in the Son," and in Matthew 21:22, He declares, "And all things, whatsoever ye shall ask in prayer, believing, ye shall receive." All these texts make abundantly clear that it is an absolute and essential requisite of prayer that, if it is to be pleasing unto God, it must be offered by faith in the name of Christ, and thus with a steadfast confidence that, however unworthy in ourselves we may be, God hears us for His sake.

We have thus briefly expounded for you the essential requisites of a proper Christian prayer, without which one's prayer can neither be pleasing to the Lord nor be heard by Him. May it please the Lord to make us truly acquainted with these matters, for without them, all the prayers offered by men are but a vain multiplication of words and a vile, God-dishonoring, and God-provoking sin.

Having thus addressed the necessity and requisites of prayer, the instructor then proceeds with the third matter, namely, the *contents* of a proper Christian prayer, by asking, "What hath God commanded us to ask of Him?" to which he replies, "All things necessary for soul and body." This truth does not require a lengthy exposition, for it is understood that God's children consist of both soul and body. Regarding both, they are entirely dependent upon the Lord, and at all times, they stand in need of His grace, help, and blessing. They have all learned the truth of this in some measure, and the Holy Spirit continues to lead and to instruct them regarding this truth.

The Lord thus commands His children that they continually should pray to Him, that He may provide for them in all their spiritual and physical needs. However, first and foremost, He commands them to pray for the provision of their spiritual needs, which are far more weighty and pertinent than the needs of the body. This conforms to Matthew 6:33, where we read, "But seek ye first the kingdom of God, and his righteousness; and all these things shall be added unto you."

The Lord has commanded His children to pray to Him regarding all their spiritual and physical needs. This is evident from the prescribed prayer that Christ taught His disciples, and the instructor here appeals to that prayer. This prayer addresses all the spiritual and physical needs of believers, and God is asked to fulfill them all in this prayer. This will be very evident when, with the Lord's help, we subsequently expound this prayer.

The instructor then quotes this perfect Lord's Prayer as a paradigm, according to which all the prayers of believers must be fully ordered. He therefore asks his pupil, "What are the words of that prayer?" To this question, the instructor directs his pupil to recite this prayer. Many and various general observations about the Lord's Prayer could be made that we might properly understand it. This we shall reserve for our next sermon.

We have thus addressed this prominent and weighty matter of prayer as briefly as possible. Nothing would be more necessary than that an extensive and nuanced application of these expounded truths be made to the heart of converted and unconverted alike. However, given the richness of the expounded subject matter, there is presently no time available to do this, but with the Lord's help, we wish to do this in a progressive way when we expound the particulars of the Lord's Prayer

We shall now conclude with the wish and prayer that it would please the most high God efficaciously to fulfill among us this glorious promise: "And I will pour upon the house of David, and upon the inhabitants of Jerusalem, the spirit of grace and of supplications" (Zech. 12:10). May the Lord indeed grant this! Amen.

The Preamble of the Lord's Prayer

After this manner therefore pray ye: Our Father which art in heaven.
—MATTHEW 6:9a

Question 120: Why hath Christ commanded us to address God thus: "Our Father"?

Answer: That immediately, in the very beginning of our prayer, He might excite in us a childlike reverence for and confidence in God, which are the foundation of our prayer, namely, that God is become our Father in Christ, and will much less deny us what we ask of Him in true faith than our parents will refuse us earthly things.

Question 121: Why is it here added, "Which art in heaven"?

Answer: Lest we should form any earthly conceptions of God's heavenly majesty, and that we may expect from His almighty power all things necessary for soul and body.

It is very remarkable what we find recorded in Genesis 46:33–34, how the inspired author recounts that Joseph not only secured for his brothers, who had come to him in Egypt for the sustenance of their lives, an unobstructed admission to Pharaoh, the king of Egypt, but also that he instructed them in advance as to what they should say to the king when they appeared before him.

The great antitype of Joseph, the Lord Jesus Christ, dealt in like fashion with His believing brethren, who came to Him to receive spiritual sustenance for their souls. Not only did He procure for them unobstructed admission to the great God and king of heaven and earth, but He also expressly taught and instructed them what and in what manner they should speak when they came into the presence of this glorious and majestic king, as well as the petitions that they should bring before Him. This is evident from the prescribed prayer that He taught and commanded His brethren and His disciples to pray, saying to them—and, in them, indiscriminately, to all His believing people—"After this manner therefore pray ye...."

Having addressed, in the previous Lord's Day, the prayer of the Christian in general terms, we desire to proceed with the instructor to consider the glorious and perfect prescription of prayer given to believers by the great prophet and priest, Jesus Christ, so that they will address all their prayers and supplications to their heavenly Father in conformity therewith.

Regarding this prescriptive prayer, we wish to preface our remarks by briefly addressing three matters:

First, everyone can derive instruction from the particular occasion when the Lord Jesus gave His disciples this prescriptive prayer, as recorded in Matthew 6 and Luke 11, and thus discover that the Savior gave this prescriptive prayer on two occasions.

Second, it may not be used erroneously, as many do, deeming it to be a literal formula to which one's own words must be fully subjected. Believers would then neither be able to pray in any way than by the literal text of this prayer nor have liberty to use other words in their prayers. The Spirit of prayer would then be utterly resisted and quenched. Such is the sinful and harmful outworking of all rote and form prayers, and it is therefore desirable that Christians never use them.[1] Rather, the Savior gave this prayer to His disciples and to believers for the sole purpose of being a brief pattern or prescription according to which all their prayers should be ordered. His objective was to bind them to matters rather than to the exact wording of His prescriptive prayer—a matter that we could affirm with many arguments.

Third, it is conveniently divided into three distinct matters:

1. There is a preamble or an address to God.

2. It consists of six specific petitions, all of which focus on God and end in His exaltation. In the first three, we do so directly, and in the last three, in a more indirect manner.

3. To stimulate greater urgency in bringing our petitions before God, as well as a believing confidence in the heart of the supplicant, it has a very compelling and suitable conclusion.

---

1. JRB add footnote

In this Lord's Day, the instructor addresses the first of these three divisions, the manner in which one is to address God. The Savior articulated this by prescribing and commanding His believing people to address God as "our Father which art in heaven."

In order that we might consider in some measure this glorious, precious, and comforting address of prayer, may it please the Lord to grant from His sanctuary, to both speaker and hearers, the required grace and help of His Holy Spirit and, in a further way, to grant an efficacious blessing upon His Word. Amen.

We shall observe the following order in our exposition by considering:

1. in what manner believers are to address God as *their* Father; and

2. how they must furthermore behold Him in His adorable majesty and glory as their Father *who is in heaven.*

Regarding the first, being desirous to teach His believing people to pray properly, Christ first leads their souls to a clear consideration and acknowledgment of the most high God, to whom they must utter their prayers. However, in so doing, it is His will that they should have not only a suitable perception of His adorable greatness and glory, but also a suitable perception of the special relationship that they have with Him—a relationship that should prompt them to bring their supplications and petitions before Him with freedom and with a complete confidence that He will hear them.

It is necessary before all things that, in praying, the soul should have a clear perception and appropriate impressions of her relationship with God as the God of the covenant, to whom she is united in Christ. Apart from such an understanding, it is impossible to worship God in spirit and in truth with genuine faith and confidence. The apostle teaches this clearly by saying, "He that cometh to God must believe that he is, and that he is a rewarder of them that diligently seek him" (Heb. 11:6b). It is therefore the foremost task of the great teacher, the Lord Jesus, to instruct His disciples how they are to view and consider God in their prayers, namely, as *their Father who is in heaven.*

In the prayers of the saints recorded in the Word of God, we find that they do always address God as their God—and thus God is addressed in terms of their relationship to Him by faith. It could not be otherwise. However, the names and honorable titles they ascribed to God are not always the same, but they do so in accord with their special needs and deficiencies, and with the manner in which God revealed Himself to them.

However, in this prayer, the Lord Jesus sets before His believing people a specific name and prescribes to them that they not only must address God as such in all their prayers, but that they are also to esteem and acknowledge Him as such, that is, as their heavenly Father. This is the sweetest, most encouraging, and most stirring name whereby believers may address the Lord God. The use of this name stirs up in their souls the highest measure of reverence, love, and confidence both for and in God. We shall therefore proceed to consider in greater detail the efficacy of this address.

We shall first consider the person Himself to whom believers must address their prayers, being commanded to address Him as *their Father*. It is certain that due to the perfect union between the three exalted divine persons, the triune God is the Father of believers, and He is referred to repeatedly as such in the Holy Scriptures. However, it is equally certain that, according to the divine economy of grace, the relational distinction of being the Father of all believers is specifically attributed and assigned to the first person of the Godhead. In distinction from the two other divine persons, the Son and the Holy Spirit, He is always designated as the *Father*. This is not solely by virtue of His being the true Father of the second person, the Lord Jesus Christ, but also because He is the Father of all believers, whom He adopts in Christ to be His children and whom He regenerates by His Spirit.

Since this is a very well-known truth, I will affirm it with but a few passages: "One Lord, one faith, one baptism, one God and Father of all, who is above all, and through all, and in you all" (Eph. 4:5–6); "But to us there is but one God, the Father, of whom are all things, and we in him; and one Lord Jesus Christ, by whom are all things, and we by him" (1 Cor. 8:6); "One is your Master, even Christ; and all ye are brethren…one is your Father, which is in heaven" (Matt. 23:8–9).

There should therefore be no doubt that the Lord Jesus, in His prescriptive prayer, understands the Father of believers to be specifically the first person of the divine being, that is, God the Father, and He is guiding believers in their prayers toward Him so that He will be to them the object of their worship. This was the Savior's common practice, for He taught His disciples and commanded them that they should direct their prayers to God the Father and make all their needs and desires known to Him. However, He directed them to do so in His name as mediator. John 16:23 says, "Verily, verily, I say unto you, Whatsoever ye shall ask the Father in my name, he will give it you."

The reason why this honor in the address of prayer is specifically directed toward and attributed to God the Father is not because the Father excells the Son and the Spirit in worthiness and glory, for the Son and the Spirit are most intimately united within one and the same most glorious and adorable divine being. Rather, the reason must be derived from the relationship between the three divine persons within the economy of grace. This economy has been conceived and established from all eternity, and according to this economy, the Father has engaged Himself to display the majesty and glory of the Godhead, and thus of the triune God, whereas the Son has engaged Himself as mediator toward His Father to further the work of redeeming the elect, and the Holy Spirit has engaged Himself to make elect believers genuine partakers of that work of redemption and to sanctify them. By virtue of this economy of grace, God the Father is revealed to us as the fountain and source of the Godhead, from which all things originate. James therefore speaks of Him as "the Father of lights, with whom is no variableness, neither shadow of turning" (James 1:17b).

God the Father must therefore be the essential object of the worship of believers. In all their supplications and prayers, they must turn to Him and pour them out before His countenance. However, the Son and the Holy Spirit are by no means bypassed in the prayers of believers, for though the Father is the essential object of the prayers of believers, to whom they must communicate their prayers, the Son is likewise the mediator of prayer, in whose name they must pray to the Father. Through Him alone, the hearing of their prayers can be secured. Furthermore, the Holy Spirit is the author of prayer, while simultaneously functioning as the author and applier of the requested grace.

Thus, believers are fully in need of the triune God in all their prayers—one God, the Father, out of and from whom grace must proceed; one God, the Son, who must secure and make available this grace from the Father; and one God, the Holy Spirit, who must transmit the grace of the Father and the Son to believers and work it within their souls. Therefore, though believers end in God the Father in their prayers, they go to Him through the Son, and by the Holy Spirit, they come to the Son and are united to Him.

A correct understanding of this divine and spiritual truth is a matter of the utmost importance if we are to pray rightly, according to the will of God. Nevertheless, there are many weak children of God who are very confused and ignorant about this, and therefore they frequently miss a great measure of comfort in their prayers.

Having thus seen in what manner God the Father must be the object of the prayers of believers, we must further consider the special relationship in which God must be viewed by believers in their prayers. The Savior teaches that believers are to acknowledge Him as their common Father, and are therefore to refer to Him as *our Father*.

The instructor has addressed, in Lord's Days 9 and 13, that God, who is the Father of our Lord Jesus Christ, is also the Father of all His elect, and thus of all believers, and that they are His children. We shall therefore presently not consider this truth at length, but expound briefly upon it.

God is the Father of all men by virtue of creation and providence. We therefore read: "Have we not all one father? hath not one God created us?" (Mal. 2:10). However, this is not what the Savior has in mind here. Rather, it is His will that His believing people address God as *their Father*, and therefore He leads them to the blessed economy of grace, according to which, spiritually, in Christ His Son, God has become the God and Father of His elect and believing people. Throughout the Holy Scriptures, the Father is set forth as such. Consider only the one passage in which the Lord Jesus communicates this comforting message to His disciples and His people: "I ascend unto my Father, and your Father; and to my God, and your God" (John 20:17).

The grounds upon which this blessed and glorious relationship and kinship between God and believers rests, as well as all that proceeds from it, are as follows:

First, God has graciously adopted them in Christ to be His children and heirs, and eternally has ordained them to be such. Paul thus testifies of believers, "He hath chosen us in him before the foundation of the world, that we should be holy and without blame before him in love: having predestinated us unto the adoption of children by Jesus Christ to himself, according to the good pleasure of his will" (Eph. 1:4–5).

Second, God has also regenerated His children in Christ, by His Holy Spirit, and in His image, and in so doing, has granted them eternal life. "Of his own will begat he us with the word of truth, that we should be a kind of firstfruits of his creatures" (James 1:18). It is therefore said that believers are "born of God" (1 John 3:9b).

Third, God, by faith, has united them to Christ, His Son, so that thereby they have entered into a spiritual marriage union with Him. The Father of the bridegroom, who is Christ, must necessarily become the Father of believers, who are the bride and spouse of Christ. The apostle teaches this, saying, "For ye are all the children of God by faith in Christ Jesus" (Gal. 3:26), and also that "as many as received him, to them gave he power to become the sons of God, even to them that believe on his name" (John 1:12).

These are the grounds upon which God is the spiritual Father of believers and upon which believers are the children, the sons and daughters, of God. Therefore, they receive "the Spirit of adoption, whereby [they] cry, Abba, Father" (Rom. 8:15b). How indescribably blessed and glorious this privilege of believers is!

Since, however, God is thus the spiritual Father of all believers and they are consequently His children, because of that relationship, He will not deal with His children in any other way than as a Father. The Savior commands them to view God in all their prayers as their gracious, beloved, and merciful Father, and to come to Him as *their* Father, saying, "Abba, Father."

However, not only are we to address Him as such, but we must explicitly also appropriate Him as *our* Father. Thereby, the Savior wishes to teach His children two things:

1. God is the Father of all believers without distinction. He embraces and views all of them equally as His children, and to them all, He says, "And [I] will be a Father unto you, and ye shall be my sons and daughters, saith the Lord Almighty" (2 Cor. 6:18). Therefore, every believer in particular has a rightful claim to call God his Father and to acknowledge Him as such.

2. He also desires to teach His believing people that they are to have mutual love one toward another as being the children of one and the same Father, being members of the same household, being governed and wrought upon by one and the same Spirit, and having one head and mediator. They therefore must unite themselves most intimately, and together they must pray to their heavenly Father for one another, bringing one another's needs before the throne of grace. The Savior therefore directs His believing people throughout this prayer to use plural pronouns, for they must consistently deem God to be the Father of them all and thus address Him as *our Father*.

No one should interpret this in a restrictive sense, as if the Lord Jesus were binding His disciples to the exclusive use of this name, so that they are never permitted to address God in their prayers in any other way. This is most certainly not the case, for believers are at absolute liberty to address the Lord God in their prayers by using all the names and relational titles by which He is pleased to reveal Himself to them through the Holy Spirit.

Thus, the Savior commands His disciples to address God as their Father and to acknowledge Him as such in all their prayers, in light of the fact that this is the foundational relationship upon which are fully founded and from which are derived all other relationships of God with His people, and they with Him. Indeed, if one dismisses the fact that God is the Father of believers, there remains no other covenantal relationship between God and His people, and God is utterly alienated from His believing people.

Another reason the Savior commands His disciples to address God as their Father has to do with the fact that it gives expression to the most intimate and sweetest relationship and fellowship between God and them. It also stimulates in them the suitable spiritual frame that must necessarily be present in prayer. The instructor will now briefly expound this.

The instructor inquires why Christ commands and instructs His believing people to address God as their Father in their prayers, saying that this must be done so "that immediately, in the very beginning of our prayer, He might excite in us a childlike reverence for and confidence in God, which is the foundation of our prayer, namely, that God is become our Father in Christ."

Two things must necessarily be found in the heart of the one who prays if he is to approach God in a proper frame of mind: a childlike fear of God and a childlike confidence in God. In the absence of these spiritual frames, God cannot possibly be properly worshiped by us in a manner that pleases Him.

First, in all the prayers of believers, there must be a *childlike fear of God*, whereby one is moved with a tender respect, reverence, and love for Him. One then has the highest esteem for Him, falling before His countenance in meekness and humility of heart, and inwardly fearing and honoring Him in light of His awesome majesty and glory. Such a childlike fear differs greatly from a legalistic and slavish fear. The latter generates nothing in the heart but hostility toward and aversion for God, which cause the sinner to flee from God. However, a childlike fear fills the heart with a tender and affectionate love for God, and it causes us to love and desire His precious presence.

To stimulate this sweet and childlike fear of God in the hearts of believers at the very outset of prayer, that being the disposition with which the Lord desires to be worshiped and served, it is the will of the Lord Jesus that believers should view God entirely as their merciful and gracious Father, and that they should address and refer to Him as such. And, surely, when a believer sees and has knowledge of this relationship with God, the heart is immediately moved and sweetly enamored with a childlike fear of God. The soul then is immediately filled with a tender love, respect, and reverence for God. God's children know this by experience, for they then perceive how God, as their heavenly Father, is worthy of such childlike fear, and how utterly fitting it is that He should be loved, served, honored, and obeyed most tenderly by them. They then are moved to exclaim: "Who would not fear thee, O King of nations? for to thee doth it appertain" (Jer. 10:7).

The Lord therefore argues in His Word that the childlike fear that one must have for Him is derived from His fatherly relationship with His people, saying: "A son honoureth his father, and a servant his master: if then I be a father, where is mine honour? and if I be a master, where is my fear?" (Mal. 1:6). Peter admonishes believers, saying, "And if ye call on the Father, who without respect of persons judgeth according to every man's work, pass the time of your sojourning here in fear" (1 Peter 1:17). And thus to stimulate this childlike fear in the hearts of believers at the very outset of their prayers, the Lord Jesus commands them to address God as their Father.

Second, in a proper Christian prayer, there must also be a childlike confidence that God, for Christ's sake, most surely hears our prayer. We addressed such confidence in prayer in the previous Lord's Day, when we considered the essential requisites of a proper Christian prayer, and we shall therefore let this matter rest for now. Suffice it to say only that, in order for such childlike confidence in God in prayer to be aroused in the hearts of believers, it is true that nothing is more efficacious and suitable to that end than this blessed relationship that God is their Father and that they are His children.

When believers subscribe to and believe in this relationship in their hearts, it cannot be otherwise but that such confidence in God arises and settles deeply in the heart. The instructor speaks of this, saying, "God is become our Father in Christ, and will much less deny us what we ask of Him in true faith than our parents will refuse us earthly things." The believing soul then fully surrenders herself to God her Father and trusts in Him. Then she cannot possibly harbor any hard or ill thoughts regarding her good and gracious heavenly Father, but, rather, she allows herself to be sweetly and fully overcome by His love, fully entrusting herself to Him in all her ways. She subjects herself to His will and believes most firmly that "He that spared not his own Son, but delivered him up for us all…shall he not with him also freely give us all things?" (Rom. 8:32). We have thus given you the second reason why the will of the Savior is that His believing people address God as their Father.

We shall add a third reason. Christ desired to teach His believing people that, by acknowledging and addressing God as our Father, they would be able to move God's heart and innermost being toward them, to the end that He would also be inclined toward them in tender love, compassion, and mercy. Oh, nothing can move God's heart more in love and grace toward His believing people than that He is their Father and that they are His children. This binds God's heart to the souls of His children with an unbreakable bond. This opens unto them the fountains and treasuries of His all-sufficiency, and the result is that He is not able to deny them anything.

Only consider how emphatically the Lord Jesus speaks of this, saying: "Or what man is there of you, whom if his son ask bread, will he give him a stone? Or if he ask a fish, will he give him a serpent? If ye then, being evil, know how to give good gifts unto your children, how much more shall your Father which is in heaven give good things to them that ask him?" (Matt. 7:9–11). Therefore, if the saints were desirous to move the Lord their God to manifest His love and mercy toward them, they reminded Him of His paternal relationship toward them. In Isaiah 63:15–16, God's people prayerfully come before the Lord, saying: "Look down from heaven, and behold from the habitation of thy holiness and of thy glory: where is thy zeal and thy strength, the sounding of thy bowels and of thy mercies toward me? are they restrained? Doubtless thou art our father, though Abraham be ignorant of us, and Israel acknowledge us not: thou, O LORD, art our father, our redeemer; thy name is from everlasting."

To achieve all these glorious objectives, Christ has instructed and commanded His believing people to address God *as their Father* in their prayers.

This is not all that the Savior requires, for He adds another factor whereby the adorable majesty and glory of God as the Father of believers is further revealed. Not only is it His will that His disciples address God as their Father, but, rather, they must also address Him as their Father *who is in heaven*.

We are to understand *heaven* as a particular reference to the heaven of heavens, the primary location of God's throne, from where He preeminently displays His divine glory and fills all things with His unapproachable and spiritual light. It is a Hebrew expression, adopted by the Greek, to describe the third or uppermost heaven with the plural term *heavens*, thereby expressing how it excels the other two subordinate heavens. God, the Father of believers, resides in this heaven or in these heavens. This is not to suggest that He is restricted to these heavens, as is true for other inhabitants of heaven. By no means, for God fills both heaven and earth with His infinite glory. We read of this in Jeremiah 23:23–24: "Am I a God at hand, saith the LORD, and not a God afar off? Can any hide himself in secret places that I shall not see him? saith the LORD. Do not I fill heaven and earth? saith the LORD." All places are filled with His glory. Solomon therefore says: "But will God indeed dwell on the earth? behold, the heaven and heaven of heavens cannot contain thee; how much less this house that I have builded?" (1 Kings 8:27).

God is said to be in the heavens because heaven is specifically His dwelling place and palace, where He dwells with His divine glory, from where He reigns, and from where He causes all blessings and grace, both spiritual and physical, to descend upon His people and His children. David speaks as such of God, saying, "The LORD hath prepared his throne in the heavens; and his kingdom ruleth over all" (Ps. 103:19).

Why did the Savior command His disciples to pray, "Our Father *which art in heaven*"? The instructor explains this by saying that the Savior did so for two reasons:

1. "Lest we should form any earthly conceptions of God's heavenly majesty"; and

2. "that we may expect from His almighty power all things necessary for soul and body."

There is nothing more inappropriate and God-dishonoring than to have earthly and carnal thoughts of the most high God. "These things hast thou done, and I kept silence; thou thoughtest that I was altogether such an one as thyself: but I will reprove thee, and set them in order before thine eyes" (Ps. 50:21). Nevertheless, it is by virtue of their carnality that there is nothing to which God's children are more vulnerable than this vile abomination. The Savior therefore admonishes them that they should not view God in their prayers only as their Father, but, rather, as their Father who is in heaven, so that they thereby will have a suitable impression in their souls of the majesty, glory, and pure spirituality of God. Abraham spoke accordingly, saying, "Behold now, I have taken upon me to speak unto the Lord, which am but dust and ashes" (Gen. 18:27), and in Isaiah 57:15, we read, "For thus saith the high and lofty One that inhabiteth eternity, whose name is Holy; I dwell in the high and holy place."

Believers must also address God as their Father so that they view Him as that infinite, majestic, all-sufficient, and most blessed supreme being, "seeing that he is Lord of heaven and earth, dwelleth not in temples made with hands;

neither is worshipped with men's hands, as though he needed any thing, seeing he giveth to all life, and breath, and all things" (Acts 17:24–25).

The Savior also wants to teach His believing people that when they pray, they are to believe that because their heavenly Father is an omnipotent God, they "may expect from His almighty power all things necessary for soul and body." Given the fact that God is in the heavens and governs all things as king, believers may know that He is an omnipotent God who does what pleases Him in heaven and upon earth, and for whom nothing is either impossible or beyond His reach. He is able to bestow upon them all the graces they desire of Him in an abundant measure, being "able to do exceeding abundantly above all that we ask or think" (Eph. 3:20). We also read in Psalm 115:3: "But our God is in the heavens: he hath done whatsoever he hath pleased."

This must necessarily draw the heart of the believer out to God and cause him to trust fully in the power and all-sufficiency of his heavenly Father, expecting "from His almighty power all things necessary for soul and body."

To stir up such lofty, fitting, and spiritual perceptions of God in the hearts of believers, it is the will of the Lord Jesus that, in their prayers, they esteem and acknowledge God to be their Father who is in heaven.

We have thus expounded for you this glorious and delightful preamble of the Lord's Prayer. Let us now make application of what has been considered.

You who are unconverted and unregenerate sinners, out of form and custom you pray, saying, "Our Father which art in heaven…." However, you do not know what you are praying. You address God as your Father, but you do so with false and deceitful lips, for God is not your Father, and you are not His children. You are yet the children of Satan and of darkness. "Ye are of your father the devil, and the lusts of your father ye will do" (John 8:44a), for:

1. you are still natural and unspiritual men, and have not yet received the Spirit of adoption;

2. you are yet unregenerate and have not yet received spiritual life from God; you are still entirely dead in trespasses and sins;

3. you are not yet united to the Lord Jesus by faith, but are yet living entirely without Him, living unto yourselves; you have not yet received Christ, and therefore He also has not yet given you the power to be called the children of God; and

4. you have never yet acknowledged God to be your Father in Christ. You have never learned to love Him tenderly and to serve and obey Him with a childlike fear.

Oh, sinners, cease to pray any longer, "Our Father," for you are only making a mockery of God and are thereby greatly maligning and dishonoring Him. As often as you say, "Our Father" so often are you lying before God, who hates and will damn all liars. Therefore, you need to walk upon a different pathway. Allow yourself to be persuaded of your wretched state and learn to see that God is not yet your Father. On the contrary, He is to you yet a fearful avenger, from whom you are to expect nothing other than wrath and fury. Oh, permit this to be impressed upon your heart with power, and may it cause you to become downcast! May it cause you to yearn most earnestly for a transformation of your state and to long for communion with God in Christ. To that end, you must turn to the Lord Jesus without delay. Pray to Him and beseech Him for the convicting ministry of His Spirit. He will show you indeed that God is not yet your Father. He is willing to regenerate you and to grant you faith, whereby you would be fully united to Him in a spiritual marriage union, and, in that way, God would become your Father in Christ, and you would become His children.

You who are God's children, how great is your happiness! In the name of your Lord and savior, Jesus Christ, you may freely approach the throne of grace and address God as your Father. May you become better acquainted with your blessed and glorious privilege. Focus continually upon it with spiritual eyes of faith, daily making use of this privilege to the further establishment of your salvation.

How grievous it is that there still is so much ignorance and confusion among God's people! There are yet many who have every right to address God as their Father who nevertheless dare not do so, not only by virtue of the weakness of their faith, but also because of their darkness and doubtful disposition. Others, at times, have the courage to address God as their Father when they have an experiential sense of His light and grace in their souls, but then again, they hesitate and lose courage when it becomes darker for them, when a given cross or sorrow comes upon them or their sins and indwelling corruption increasingly manifest themselves. They then doubt their spiritual state and their spiritual sonship, and they approach God with a legalistic and slavish fear or distance themselves far from God the Father and rather approach unto the Lord Jesus.

Oh, that all such weak children of God would receive a clear and lively understanding of:

1. How entirely unbecoming their conduct is, and how thereby they grieve their heavenly Father.

2. The certainty and immutability of their spiritual sonship, being founded upon the eternal and sovereign love of the Father and upon their being united to the Lord Jesus by faith—a union that can never be dissolved.

3. It is one thing truly to have God as one's Father in Christ and to take refuge to Him as such by faith, casting oneself upon Him, and quite another thing to know with certainty and to believe steadfastly that God is one's Father. A child of God may miss the latter, and nevertheless have and exercise the former.

Oh, may all of God's children, and particularly the weak and little ones among them, instead of being so erroneously engaged in the denial of their spiritual sonship, strive to become increasingly assured by believingly clinging to, following, and making use of the Lord Jesus—ever looking to Him, reaching out to Him, leaning upon Him, surrendering to Him, and depending upon Him! In all things, may they continually look unto Him for strength and righteousness, for life and salvation, for light and peace, and receive all things continually from and through Him. This is the surest way to become more assured of your portion in God and of your spiritual sonship. May the Lord, to that end, so work in His people by His Holy Spirit. Amen.

The First Petition:
Hallowed Be Thy Name

Hallowed be thy name.
—MATTHEW 6:9b

Question 122: Which is the first petition?

Answer: "Hallowed be Thy name"; that is, grant us, first, rightly to know Thee, and to sanctify, glorify and praise Thee in all Thy works, in which Thy power, wisdom, goodness, justice, mercy and truth, are clearly displayed; and further also, that we may so order and direct our whole lives, our thoughts, words and actions, that Thy name may never be blasphemed, but, rather honored and praised on our account.

"The LORD hath made all things for himself" (Prov. 16:4). These words of the wise King Solomon are worthy of our consideration. This truth is of such weightiness and significance that it may and must truly be deemed as the foundational principle of all truth. The matter expressed herein with a few words by Solomon, the man of God, is the source and fountain of all true wisdom. Nevertheless, the utter ignorance of people regarding this truth, even of the children of wisdom, cannot be expressed in words. When the soul of a believer is led, by the brilliant illumination of divine light, into this eternal, foundational truth, even if it be but for a few moments, she then discovers the fountain of all unrighteousness and foolishness, and exclaims that sin has no other origin but ignorance of the truth of which Solomon is speaking here, namely, that "the LORD hath made all things for himself."

Oh, divine truth! Oh, heavenly wisdom! See here how the creature, with all his imaginary status, is put in his proper place, that is, as nothing before God. See here how a light shines forth that drives away all darkness and leads us to the hallowed and blessed fountain from which all things proceed. Oh, that I would be permitted, with my feeble vision, to penetrate more deeply into the light of life! I would then loudly exclaim, "O magnify the LORD with me, and let us exalt his name together" (Ps. 34:3). That glorious, eternal, and inexpressible name alone must be exalted, hallowed, and glorified by us. We are called to nothing but that, for God "hath made all things for himself." This is the occupation of the saints in heaven, and this must also be the occupation of the saints here on earth.

Oh, that all things would cease and yield in order that the name of the eternal God would be exalted and hallowed, for all things exist for His sake! Oh, that Jehovah would reign and that the creature entirely would fall away and lose itself completely in the praise of His name! Then, and in no other way, will the world enjoy genuine felicity. You who love the Lord and delight in Jehovah's name, draw near and focus upon this foundational truth and the inherent light that emanates from the text we are about to consider.

He who is the Wisdom of the Father, who came forth from His bosom, and who declared to the world what He had seen with and had heard of His Father, being desirous to teach His believing people to pray properly, causes them to see and impresses upon their hearts that the hallowing, magnifying, and exalting of God's adorable name is the primary and preeminent principle of all that pertains to their light, life, and salvation. Christ therefore obligated His believing people, first and foremost, to pray to and to beseech their heavenly Father fervently that His name might be hallowed by them and by others.

To consider this supremely glorious petition, may the Lord endue us to that end and cause that His name may be hallowed by us. Amen.

In our exposition, we will observe the following order:

1. We shall expound this petition by considering the efficacy of the wording itself.
2. We shall then consider the instructor's exposition.

In the petition itself, we encounter:

1. the subject, being God's name; and
2. that which the Savior commands His believing people to pray regarding it: that this *name* might be hallowed.

We recognize that, in essence, a *name* is a clear mark of distinction, whereby one distinguishes one matter or person from another. Given the large number of matters, and especially the large numbers of existing persons, names, or symbols of distinction are an utmost necessity. In this sense, the Lord God absolutely does not need a name, for there are none equal to Him. Thus, there is no one from whom He needs to be distinguished, for Jehovah, the triune God, is the one only true God, who is an infinite, most glorious, and most perfect supreme being, of whom, through whom, and to whom are all things (Rom. 11:36). This sufficiently distinguishes God from everything that exists external to Him. There is therefore no need for a special name to distinguish Him as such, for being an infinite and most perfect supreme being, He distinguishes Himself most perfectly from all that exists external to Him.

Why is it that mention nevertheless is made here of the name of God? To understand this well, you need to understand that, in His Holy Word, God has given Himself a name—yes, many and distinct names—by which He represents Himself to us, the children of men, in order to reveal and make known His divine glory and perfection to His people. These names are therefore the essential expressions and declarations of God's most glorious virtues and perfections, as well as of the relationships God has in general with all of creation, and specifically with His believing people and subjects. Their purpose therefore is to accommodate the finite understandings of God's people, for without such specific names, they could not possibly have a proper understanding of God's glorious being. We addressed this in detail in our exposition of the third commandment, forbidding the vain use of God's name.

The only matter that we wish to mention here is that one is not to understand the name of God, the heavenly Father of believers, as referring to a given specific name of Him. Rather, it is to be understood as a more general reference to God Himself, as He reveals Himself in His most glorious and perfect being by His names and works. The noun *name* also frequently designates the person who bears the name. We read of this in Revelation 3:4, where it is said to the church at Sardis, "Thou hast a few names [that is, persons or believers] even in Sardis which have not defiled their garments." However, especially in the Holy Scriptures, it is common that by *God's name*, God Himself is to be understood. We read in Micah 6:9, "The man of wisdom shall see thy name," and in Proverbs 30:4, it is asked regarding the Lord God, "What is his name, and what is his son's name, if thou canst tell?" By this question, we are being told that God, in His infinite and most perfect and glorious being, is incomprehensible and unfathomable to the finite mind of man.

In support of this, we could quote a great number of passages in the Holy Scriptures in which the name of God occurs as being the agent of activity, and in which men are referred to either as worshiping and trusting in or dishonoring and blaspheming God's name. In all such passages, the name of God is a reference to God Himself in His most glorious and adorable being. In like manner, we are here to understand God's name as a reference to God Himself, the heavenly Father of believers, as He has been pleased to reveal Himself and make Himself known by His names and works. He has done so in a general sense to all men in His Holy Word and in the works of nature. However, in a very special sense, He has done so in the hearts of His believing people by His Word and Spirit. They alone have, in principle, a proper and spiritual knowledge of God, and consequently, they have been translated from death unto life.

What are we to do in regard to this great and glorious name of God, that is, in regard to God Himself and His adorable and supreme being? The Savior instructs and commands His believing people, first and foremost, that they must concern themselves as much with the hallowing, exaltation, and glorification of this God who is their heavenly Father as they concern themselves with His exalted and glorious name. They must fervently and sincerely pray to their heavenly Father, saying to Him that which is absolutely essential and becoming, namely, "Our Father which art in heaven, hallowed by thy name!"

A correct understanding of the meaning and content of this supplication and petition is contingent upon a correct understanding of the thrust and meaning of the verb *to hallow*. The use of this word is very common in the Holy Scriptures, and it has various meanings related to the objects with which it is used. These objects are either men or other matters—or God Himself. We find in the Holy Scriptures that the verb to hallow is used with reference to both. When used to refer either to people or matters, it means to separate a given person or a given object from its common use unto a specific or holy purpose, thereby rendering it fit for the service of God. However, when used with reference to God and His holy name, the verb *to hallow* cannot have this meaning, for God, in the very essence of His being, is always supremely holy, and in no wise can He acquire any additional holiness. With reference either to God or to His holy name, the verb to hallow simply refers to the acknowledgement, confession, and adoration of God's holiness, and the proclamation, praising, and magnifying of it. Thus, God or His name is hallowed when God's majesty, holiness, and glory are made known to creatures external to Him, and His name is confessed, endorsed, embraced, and glorified by them outwardly with their mouths and deeds, and inwardly with their hearts.

This is so spiritual and glorious in its nature that the most enlightened subject of God's kingdom here upon earth understands and takes delight in this only in a very small measure. Oh, the hallowing of God's name is a cabinet filled with such lofty, incomprehensible, and inexpressible divine mysteries that, even with all the influence and illumination of the Holy Spirit that the Lord is pleased to grant us, we are capable only of stammering about this in some small measure. To express these matters properly and with the full thrust of their meaning, no other language is suitable than the one that will be spoken in heaven.

I readily believe that the apostle Paul saw and heard things in heaven that neither could be nor were permitted to be expressed here on earth (2 Cor. 12:2–4). Likewise, when a wretched one like me has but a small measure of spiritual reflection regarding the hallowing of Jehovah's name, I become aware of a measure of incomprehensibility and inexpressibility regarding that name that causes me to sink into an infinite depth in which I cannot find any bottom. If I were to attempt to express in words what it means to hallow God's name, I would do so as recorded in Revelation 4:8: "Holy, holy, holy, Lord God Almighty, which was, and is, and is to come."

To lose oneself in this, that is, to know the essence of hallowing God's name, is to sink away into the bottomless depth that is to be found in God and to be swallowed up with all of creation in this ocean of light, without there being any perception of darkness. Beloved, this is the essence of the matter! That which we shall now say regarding it is but an utterance of inadequate words. However, the thrust and essence of them is spirit and life.

If we are now to proceed to verbalize and to set before you what it means to hallow God's name, we must first hear and know in what the holiness of God and of His name consists—that name that must be acknowledged and hallowed. This holiness of God and of His name consists in two things. It consists in:

1. The infinite, incomprehensible, and inexpressible weightiness of the majesty, glory, and unfathomable luster with which God, in His adorable being, is clothed. This consists in the fact that it shines forth from every dimension of His divine being as the sun beams forth its luster. Hereby, God is radically distinguished in His most glorious being from all that is external to Him, and thus as the only and supreme fountain of being, of whom, through whom, and to whom are all things.

2. The purest love that God has for Himself and for His own perfections, honor, and glory, and therefore, of necessity, He must hate and utterly oppose and destroy whatever is opposed to His divine glory and perfect holiness.

In these thoughts, we find a small and finite description of that in which the holiness of God and His name consist. This, in turn, reveals to us the manner in which we are to hallow God or His name. This occurs when God is known, acknowledged, embraced, praised, and magnified in His holiness and unfathomable glory by all creatures external to Him, so that, with mouth and heart, it is proclaimed and confessed that God is majestic, holy, and glorious. Furthermore, this occurs when everything prostrates itself in worship before the majesty, holiness, and glory of God's name, subjecting itself fully to it, so that God alone is acknowledged as king, and His name alone is glorious. God's name thus is hallowed when everything is of Him, through Him, and to Him. When everything thus vanishes and melts into nothing, and God fills all things fully with Himself and becomes all and in all, then God's name is properly hallowed.

This hallowing of God's name is engaged in either by God Himself or by His creatures that are external to Him. God hallows His own name when He reveals His adorable majesty, holiness, and glory to His creatures, so that they behold, acknowledge, confess, and praise them. We must apply this indiscriminately to all of God's works. His entire external manifestation of Himself has the hallowing and glorification of Himself as its objective. In all His deeds, God has no objective but the hallowing and glorification of His name. He makes, works, and does all things for His own sake, so that every deed of the Lord God is the hallowing, exaltation, and magnification of His name. Every deed of God is as a public exclamation and proclamation of what is written in Ezekiel 36:23: "And I will sanctify my great name."

God sanctifies Himself:

1. In and through the creation and preservation of all things. As many specific creatures as there are, and as many operations of God as there are relative to such creatures, so many specific proclamations there are of God's unfathomable greatness and glory. Everything here below is entirely filled with the glory of God. "For the invisible things of him from the creation of the world are clearly seen, being understood by the things that are made, even his eternal power and Godhead" (Rom. 1:20). Thus, we all walk in the midst of the manifestation of God's glory—irrespective of how little we may see of it by virtue of

our ignorance and carnality, and irrespective of the fact that most men neither see anything of it nor have ever seen any of it.

2. Especially in and through the great work of grace and in the salvation and redemption of sinners. It is here that God, so to speak, causes all His majesty, holiness, and glory to converge. Here shines forth the sun of God's glory as the sun shines on a clear day. Those wretched men who dwell in darkness indeed behold nothing of this great and wondrous light, but the children of light lose themselves in that light, so that they exclaim, "Oh, the breadth, the depth, the height of this unsearchable brilliance, glory, and luster!"

3. In all His deeds, His works, His judgments, and His blessings. All of this is subservient to proclaim the glory and holiness of His name before the entire world and to demonstrate that "I am the first, and I am the last; and beside me there is no God" (Isa. 44:6).

However, not only does the Lord God sanctify His name and magnify it everywhere and in all things, but His name is also hallowed by His creation that is external to Him. If we are to consider in some detail how God's Name is hallowed by His creatures, we need to note that there are two types of creatures: rational and irrational creatures.

First, irrational creatures hallow God's name by collectively displaying and visibly proclaiming to the world God's infinite luster and glory. One who carefully and spiritually observes this is able to discern the glory of God very clearly in all of creation, and so is compelled to exclaim that "the whole earth is full of his glory" (Isa. 6:3b) and that "the heavens declare the glory of God; and the firmament sheweth his handywork" (Ps. 19:1). Yes, the least blade of grass or plant that God has created upon earth displays both His eternal power and Godhead.

Second, God's name is especially hallowed by rational creatures, and thus by both angels and men. The angels neither can nor do know how to do anything but hallow and glorify the great name of God. Their entire activity in heaven above and before the throne of God and of the Lamb consists in this. Frequently it has also been their activity here below on earth, especially at the occasion of the birth of Christ, as we can read in Luke 2. But besides the angels, God's name is also hallowed by men; that is, by God's children. God reveals and makes Himself known to them in Christ and by His Holy Spirit. Believers begin to hallow the name of God their heavenly Father in principle here on earth, and hereafter they will do so perfectly in heaven above.

Here on earth, they hallow the name of God their heavenly Father in the manner expounded by the instructor. They hallow God's name:

1. By knowing God rightly; that is, by having a clear, discerning, and spiritual knowledge of God's adorable majesty, holiness, and most glorious virtues and perfections, such as God has revealed and made known in the works of nature, and especially in the work of grace, in and through Christ, His Son. Such spiritual knowledge of God and of His majesty and holiness is the basis and foundation of all the hallowing of His name. How many aspects there are to this knowledge! The most advanced believer knows only in part. He knows only the smallest and most minute part of the matter, and but the very fringes of God's ways. It is knowledge in which God's children must advance and increase as long as they live. "Then shall we know, if we follow on to know the LORD" (Hos. 6:3; cf. 2 Cor. 6:6). Paul therefore prayed for believers, "that the God of our Lord Jesus Christ, the Father of glory, may give unto you the spirit of wisdom and revelation in the knowledge of him: the eyes of your understanding being enlightened" (Eph. 1:17–18a).

2. In that they "sanctify, glorify and praise Thee in all Thy works, in which Thy power, wisdom, goodness, justice, mercy and truth, are clearly displayed." The manner in which God displays and reveals Himself and His adorable virtues and perfections in all of His works, and particularly in the great work of grace, has already been addressed with a few remarks. Never would we have known God had He not revealed Himself to all His children in and through His works, making Himself known to them as a most glorious God in His power, and wisdom. To magnify and praise God as such, and thus as a most glorious God, and to sanctify, glorify, and praise Him in all His works also belongs to the hallowing of His name. Believers do this privately or in communion with others.

They do this in solitude and privately either with the heart, verbally, or by their deeds. They hallow the name of God their heavenly Father with their hearts when they engage in holy and spiritual reflections and meditations regarding God, as well as regarding His glorious attributes and perfections, which are clearly manifested in God's works. When they have a deep insight into this, they sink away in holy adoration, praise, amazement, and inward joy, so that they exclaim with the psalmist, "My meditation of him shall be sweet: I will be glad in the LORD" (Ps. 104:34), and again: "How precious also are thy thoughts unto me, O God! how great is the sum of them! If I should count them, they are more in number than the sand: when I awake, I am still with thee" (Ps. 139:17–18). This is what Peter had in mind when he exhorted believers, saying, "Sanctify the Lord God in your hearts" (1 Peter 3:15).

Believers also verbally hallow God's name in private solitude when, as a result of their hearts being thus filled with God's praise and glory, their mouths are opened. They then render honor to God with joyful jubilation, singing, and speaking, exclaiming with the psalmist, "O LORD our Lord, how excellent is thy name in all the earth! who hast set thy glory above the heavens" (Ps. 8:1), and, "Bless the LORD, O my soul: and all that is within me, bless his holy name" (Ps. 103:1). David was in such a frame of mind when he exclaimed, "I meditate on all thy works; I muse on the work of thy hands" (Ps. 143:5).

Believers also hallow God's name when they engage in lively deeds of faith, love, and the genuine fear of God, doing so when, in their walk and conversation, they submit themselves to God's majesty, holiness, and glory. They submit themselves to them, trust in them, and rely upon them, and they permit themselves to be fully enamored, wrought upon, governed, and directed by them, and, in so doing, they glorify God their Father in that they "bear much fruit" (John 15:8).

Believers not only hallow the name of God their Father in private, but they also do so openly and in the presence of others, whether believers or unbelievers, when they show forth God to others in His holy and glorious attributes and endeavor to impart to others a proper knowledge and impression of them, seeking to guide them to hallow God's name and to acknowledge God as king throughout the entire earth. This is the delight and work of believers and the ultimate goal of their calling, namely, to "shew forth the praises of him who hath called you out of darkness into his marvellous light" (1 Peter 2:9), continually exclaiming to the world, "O magnify the LORD with me, and let us exalt his name together" (Ps. 34:3).

Third, this is not yet all that is to be considered. The instructor adds a third component that also belongs to the hallowing of God's name by believers: that we "may so order and direct our whole lives, our thoughts, words and actions, that Thy name may never be blasphemed, but, rather honored and praised on our account." God's children are called and eternally ordained to glorify God their heavenly Father fully with soul and body and with all their strength and ability. They are a people of whom it is written, "This people have I formed for myself; they shall shew forth my praise" (Isa. 43:21).

Therefore, their lives should consist in nothing but the hallowing and glorification of God, and anything that results in the desecration and dishonoring of God's name must be radically banished as shameful wickedness and unrighteousness. Peter writes, "Having your conversation honest among the Gentiles:

that, whereas they speak against you as evildoers, they may by your good works, which they shall behold, glorify God in the day of visitation" (1 Peter 2:12; cf. 1 Cor. 10:31). In Matthew 5:16, we read, "Let your light so shine before men, that they may see your good works, and glorify your Father which is in heaven."

We have sought to set before you briefly in what the hallowing of God's name consists and who engages in it. This hallowing of God's name is the substance for which the Lord Jesus commanded His disciples to pray first and foremost when calling upon their heavenly Father in their prayers, commanding them also to persevere in doing so by beseeching Him that His name would be hallowed.

In light of what we have considered, a wise and spiritual reader is readily able to grasp that the contents of this petition can be reduced to these two and preeminent matters:

First, God willed that His great, holy, and glorious name, and thus He Himself in His illustrious virtues and perfections, be increasingly revealed and made known to the world and to His children in and through His works of nature and, most specifically, in and through His works of grace, so that the individual supplicant and others might increasingly be filled with the knowledge of Him and His holy and glorious name.

Second, the other objective of this petition is that the individual supplicant and others would increasingly be instructed and rendered fit by means of this knowledge of God to hallow and magnify the glorious name of God in the world.

Therefore, in this petition is comprehended:

1. An inward and strong love for God and the hallowing of His name, it being the supplicant's desire that God be sanctified, magnified, and glorified, and that all creation bow before Him. This should not surprise us, for the supplicant is a child of God, and God is His heavenly Father. How could it therefore be otherwise but that his heart be saturated with a love for the glorification of his Father? All who love the Lord say continually and exclaim as with one mouth, "Let God be magnified" (Ps. 70:4). They deem this to be the very essence of their felicity, and they know of no felicity besides this. Their God and their heavenly Father must be honored, and that occurs when all of their desires are fully satisfied, for "the desire of our soul is to thy name, and to the remembrance of thee" (Isa. 26:8).

2. A deep acknowledgment and confession of the absolute impotence and insufficiency of the supplicant to thus hallow the name of his heavenly Father. Oh, he finds himself utterly unsuited for that great work! He finds himself perplexed from all sides. His understanding is too darkened; his understanding is too flawed; his will is too sluggish, lethargic, and unyielding; his affections are too cold; and his flesh is too hostile and antagonistic toward God. He does not know how to begin this great work, how to proceed with it, and how to complete it. He is deficient in his heart, his soul, and his life. He is continually in need of enabling grace from above. He is in immediate need of strength and grace to engage in this work. The vineyard of his barren, unspiritual heart must continually be wrought upon by the Lord Himself, and he therefore turns, by way of this petition, fully to the Lord as His God and Father, as well as unto His strength, beseeching of Him that He Himself would bring about that His great and glorious name would continually be hallowed by him and by others.

We trust that hereby we have sufficiently expounded for you this precious and cherished petition. It is time that we speak a brief word of application.

I am immediately reminded of the deep misery and wretchedness of all unconverted and graceless men who pray the petition that God's name be hallowed as a matter of form and custom, and only with their mouths. It is certain, however, that their praying is disingenuous and deceitful, for:

First, they know nothing of what they are praying when they utter the words "Hallowed by thy name." In essence, they are praying for their own eternal damnation, and thus that God would cast them into hell and would pour out upon them His eternal wrath and curse. Such is indeed the manner in which God must hallow His name toward all unconverted and unbelieving sinners.

Second, as long as a person remains unconverted and is not born again by water and the Spirit—by which one enters into fellowship with God in Christ—he has no knowledge of God. Rather, with the heathen, he manifests all of his religious activity toward an unknown God—a God whom he conjures in his imagination according to what he has heard of others. How can graceless men pray for the hallowing of God's name, since they know neither God nor His name, and since, due to their ignorance, they have not the least love for God's name?

Third, how can unconverted men, who are such exceeding and bitter enemies of the hallowing of God's name, pray that His name be hallowed? They neither are subject to God nor have entered upon the way that would lead to their eternal salvation, by which God would be supremely sanctified and glorified. They are always focused upon themselves and desire a salvation that proceeds from their own wisdom, strength, and righteousness—all of which constitutes a denial of all that pertains to God's holiness. As long as man remains unconverted, he neither knows nor serves any god but himself. He seeks and aims for self in all that he does. Except for his own name, there is no name he desires to magnify and glorify. He tramples God and all His glory under foot and is entirely inclined to put himself on the throne. All the hatred of the world toward the gospel and toward God's people proceeds from the fact that only God's people desire the glory of God and the abasement of man. The world, on the contrary, desires for man to be exalted and God to be abased. Therefore, since Paradise, there has been enmity between the sons of God and the daughters of men.

Fourth, how can a graceless man pray in truth that God's name be hallowed when, in his entire conduct and walk, he dishonors God and engages in nothing other than the desecration of God's name with thoughts, words, and deeds? When has a graceless man ever openly upheld the honor of God's name? When has he ever engaged himself to declare God's praises whenever and wherever he had an opportunity? When have you ever exhorted others to hallow and glorify God's name? When have you ever caused your light to shine forth and allowed men to see your works to the glory of God? Is it true that you have never done so? Then you therefore must testify regarding yourself that which Paul writes, saying, "They profess that they know God; but in works they deny him" (1 Tim. 1:16).

Oh, how you mock the most high God and how you desecrate and dishonor His holy name whenever you pray with your lips that His name be hallowed! Friends, cease with such ungodly, abominable, and God-dishonoring prayers, unless you insist that God sanctify Himself by eternally casting you into hell, and may you recognize not only that you do not know God and that you are yet utterly estranged from Him, but also that you are entirely subject to His curse and wrath. If only you would take this to heart! If only you would weep and mourn over this! Turn to the Lord Jesus so that, through Him, you might be reconciled with the great and holy God, whom you have provoked to wrath. Do this without any further delay, before God causes you to be in everlasting darkness.

With regard to you, children of God, if you have attentively listened to the word we have preached to you, and if God has caused His light to shine upon you, you have learned a great deal that will be subservient to rebuke, instruct, admonish, and exhort you. It is my wish and prayer to God for you that He, by His Spirit, would increasingly enable you to understand the following truths, and that your hearts would be inclined to obey them:

1. You are a people whom God has called and formed solely to hallow and glorify Him, and eternally declare His praises.

2. God alone is king, and He is therefore worthy of all honor and glory. All things therefore must be of Him, through Him, and to Him.

3. The felicity of the creature consists entirely in the glorification and hallowing of God, and there neither is nor can be any other felicity for the creature.

4. The creature therefore must be completely in subordination to God, and He must be his all and in all.

5. The creature is utterly unfit to engage in such self-denial and such hallowing and glorifying of God. God alone must do all the work here by continually hallowing His name in and through the creature.

It is my desire that the Holy Spirit Himself would increasingly lead all of God's people into these heavenly truths, and that the God and Father of our Lord Jesus Christ, the Father of glory, would continually grant unto them "the spirit of wisdom and revelation in the knowledge of him" (Eph. 1:17). Amen.

The Second Petition:
Thy Kingdom Come

Thy kingdom come.
—MATTHEW 6:10

Question 123: Which is the second petition?

Answer: "Thy kingdom come"; that is, rule us so by Thy word and Spirit, that we may submit ourselves more and more to Thee; preserve and increase Thy church; destroy the works of the devil, and all violence which would exalt itself against Thee; and also, all wicked counsels devised against Thy holy Word; till the full perfection of Thy kingdom take place, wherein Thou shalt be all in all.

In Psalm 33:12, we read, "Blessed is the nation whose God is the LORD." In the original text, it actually reads that there is blessedness or blessings for that nation whose God is Jehovah. This testimony will not be properly understood as to its clarity and full dimension until the hereafter, when, in heaven, God's people shall know and enjoy salvation in its perfection. Nevertheless, all God's children who dwell here on earth, each in their own unique ways, are acquainted with this salvation in a small measure, and that knowledge constitutes the essence of eternal life that they already have begun to enjoy here on earth.

Let me address the words themselves. The sacred poet here deals with the subject of blessedness or salvation, and I cannot speak of this matter without being grieved about my profound ignorance regarding it. The Lord has caused me to see that darkness covers the entire face of the earth—a darkness that envelops the nations. What is this blessedness or salvation? People have much to say about it, but the entire world, with all its wisdom, knows absolutely nothing of it. However, God's children, unto whom wisdom has been made known in a secret place, know enough of it that none can say that they are entirely blind.

David describes this salvation as consisting exclusively in the fact that *Jehovah is one's God*. Jehovah is one's God when He comes to a sinner with His kingdom, causing him to forsake himself and all his former lords and masters, and causing him to be subject to His Lord's divine dominion. From God's side, this is indeed the singular objective of the entire work of salvation and redemption; that is, to restore apostate sinners to God Himself and to obedience toward Him. At the same time, Jehovah's objective is to establish His throne and to cast down the throne of Satan and of sinners' lusts.

Jehovah thus becomes one's God when He becomes his king and Lord—when He establishes His dominion and kingdom in one's soul and causes him in all things to bow down before His majesty.

This is the blessedness or salvation of which flesh and blood have such an entirely erroneous notion. There is no other blessedness or salvation, nor can there be any except to have Jehovah to be our God, our king and Lord; that is, to be obedient and subject unto Him, and to forsake utterly all foreign thrones and dominions. In proportion to the increase of Jehovah's dominion—that is, the more His kingdom comes upon us, is confirmed within us, and increases continually—we increasingly become partakers of that salvation that is in none but Christ.

As the embodiment of heavenly wisdom, the great Son of God knew this, and being desirous to save His people and to deliver them from their sins, He commanded and instructed them to long and to pray for the coming of the kingdom of Jehovah, their heavenly Father. Given that their entire salvation hinges exclusively upon this, He commanded them to pray, "Our Father which art in heaven.... Thy kingdom come!"

This petition, as well as the four that follow, is entirely subordinate to the first petition, in which the Savior teaches His believing people to pray unto their heavenly Father, that His great and illustrious name be hallowed and glorified, for this is the sole purpose and objective of all that transpires in nature and in the realm of grace. Everything must be cast down and swallowed up in this bottomless depth. All darkness will eternally vanish in this, and the hallowing of God's name will culminate in the restoration of all things.

However, how can this great objective of the glorification and hallowing of God's name be achieved? By virtue of sin, everything has utterly fallen away from God and has completely withdrawn itself from being obedient to Him. Everything has rebelled against Jehovah and declared itself to be hostile to every facet of the hallowing of His name. It was therefore necessary, above all things, that God would cause His kingdom to come both to and among men by subduing His enemies, thereby causing them willingly to surrender to His dominion. Thus, His great and glorious name would be worshiped and hallowed by them by their obedience and subjection to that name. The Lord Jesus therefore lets the petition for the hallowing of God's name be followed immediately by a petition for the coming of God's kingdom.

In order that we, being efficaciously sustained by the Holy Spirit, may expound this glorious petition, we shall observe the following order and consider:

1. The subject of this petition, being the kingdom of God, the heavenly Father of believers.
2. The desire and supplications of believers regarding this kingdom, namely, that it would come.

As to the subject of this petition, mention is made of the kingdom of God the Father. A kingdom is, in essence, a community of men in which one man alone has supreme power and dominion, and who is thus the ruler, lord, and king of that community, to whom all its inhabitants must subject themselves. Such a kingdom is here ascribed to the Lord God, and we must therefore proceed to consider this kingdom.

God's Word, as well as reason and common sense, most clearly teaches that Jehovah is the absolute king and supreme ruler of the entire world, that is, of the entire created universe, for everything derives its being and existence from God and is continually sustained by Him. Everything is also entirely subject to God's power and dominion, and He is absolutely and supremely both king and supreme ruler of the entire created universe. David testifies of this, saying, "The LORD hath prepared his throne in the heavens; and his kingdom ruleth over all" (Ps. 103:19). This universal kingdom of God we designate as the kingdom of nature or the kingdom of power. However, this kingdom is not the subject of this petition.

Rather, we must say that the kingdom of God, the heavenly Father of believers—for the coming of which the Savior commands His people to pray—is of an entirely different nature and does not universally include all men and all creatures. Instead, it pertains only to all who are called to be saints, and thus to the believing and elect children of God, whose privilege it has become, by faith and repentance, willingly to submit to the gracious reign of Jehovah God. They are therefore also designated as "the children of the kingdom" (Matt.

13:38) and "heirs of the kingdom" (James 2:5). This kingdom is therefore commonly referred to as the kingdom of grace, or a voluntary kingdom.

Much could be said regarding this spiritual and gracious kingdom of Jehovah God as to its essential nature and establishment. Beloved, we shall therefore address this as briefly as possible and explain it in some measure by primarily expounding the essential nature of this kingdom, knowing that among men and even among God's children, the subjects of this kingdom, there is a profound and wretched ignorance regarding this matter. Oh, that the Lord would be pleased to bless our exposition and, by His Holy Spirit, lead us to a further acquaintance with it!

You should know that since we human beings are rational creatures who derive our origin and existence entirely from God, who continually maintains us, it is entirely rational that we are completely dependent on God, and that with all we are and have, we are entirely His property. Consequently, we must fully subject ourselves to the Lord God and perfectly serve Him by obeying Him in all things, without ever committing a single deed of disobedience or having even the least desire so to do. As human beings, there ought to be no other blessedness for us than to live in complete dependence upon Jehovah and to live in rational subjection to Him as our supreme ruler and gracious king, of whom and through whom we are all that we are.

This was true for the first man prior to the fall. He was a perfect subject of God, who depended entirely upon and subjected himself fully to God as his only supreme and all-sufficient king. Apart from God, he knew of no alien dominion. However, by virtue of sin, there was an indescribable upheaval and transformation in him. Man, who was a perfectly obedient subject of Jehovah God, by the instigation of God's enemy, Satan (who, in order to expand his kingdom of darkness, sought to destroy the kingdom of God), departed fully from God, His all-sufficient creator, Lord, and king, and chose, rather than to serve Jehovah, to serve other kings and lords, namely, Satan and himself. Consequently, the first man and all his descendants, of whom he was their head, eternally removed themselves from the dominion and kingdom of Jehovah, and together they became a community of the subjects and bond slaves of Satan.

The manner in which humanity was overcome by Satan, and is now subject to him, is recorded for us in 2 Peter 2:19b, where we read, "For of whom a man is overcome, of the same is he brought in bondage." Satan is called "the prince of this world" (John 14:30), "the prince of the power of the air" (Eph. 2:2), "a strong man armed" (Luke 11:21), "him that had the power of death"

(Heb. 2:14), and "the god of this world" (2 Cor. 4:4). Consider also 2 Timothy 2:26, where we read of sinners who are caught in "the snare of the devil, who are taken captive by him at his will," and Luke 4:5–7, where we read how Satan boasted to the Savior of his great power.

All of this resulted in the entire world fully departing from its only king, Jehovah. Consequently, His moral kingdom, the kingdom of voluntary obedience and subjection, completely ceased to function, and all that remained intact was the kingdom of His power or His kingdom of nature. It is in this sense that we say that God was a king without subjects, for all His subjects declared themselves fully and eternally to be the enemies of Jehovah God, and openly proclaimed Satan and themselves to be king, saying: "These are now they whom we have chosen to be our gods and whom we will serve eternally; we will do away with the entire dominion of King Jehovah. We neither want Him ever to be king over us again nor do we in any way wish to acknowledge His supremacy. Rather, we ourselves are kings, we are our own masters and lords, and henceforth, we shall eternally walk according to the inclination of our own hearts. To all eternity, we will not acknowledge any other king but ourselves."

This became the natural disposition of all men. We all have broken God's yoke and have cast it from us, and we have fully enveloped ourselves with our own dominion and that of Satan, "because the carnal mind is enmity against God: for it is not subject to the law of God, neither indeed can be" (Rom. 8:7).

This constitutes the bottomless pit of wretchedness into which all humanity, by virtue of sin, plunged itself. All humanity would have to remain eternally in this indescribably wretched state of being, subject to God's curse and wrath, and thus entirely separated from His blessed dominion. However, the adorable King Jehovah, according to His infinite, eternal, incomprehensible, and divine wisdom, power, righteousness, and loving-kindness, Himself found a way and a means to reestablish His ruined and destroyed kingdom of voluntary obedience and subjection. From eternity, He purposed to restore this kingdom among the fallen, rebellious, and recalcitrant children of men, the consequence being that there would never be another occasion to bring about its demise. The Lord God eternally engaged in achieving this, and, to this end, He elected a specific multitude from among a fallen humanity in whom He would again establish His kingdom of voluntary obedience and power as it existed before the fall. He thus decreed that He would deliver the elect from their apostasy and rebellion, and cause them fully and eternally to be subject to His divine dominion, so that He, as their original and rightful Lord and king, would again rule over them exclusively and eternally.

However, if Jehovah God was to reestablish His ruined moral kingdom eternally within and regarding His elect, there necessarily had to be a way or means by which He could bring this about in a manner suitable to Himself. That way was embodied in Christ Jesus, the Son of God. He was appointed by the Father to restore perfectly the ruined moral kingdom of His Father and to establish it eternally within the elect by delivering them from the kingdom of Satan and of self, and by restoring them unto God and His dominion.

The ultimate and singular objective of Christ's mediatorial ministry is to lead the elect to Jehovah, that they might be in submission to Him from whom they utterly departed through sin—and, thus, in principle, to restore them unto God's kingdom here on earth, and hereafter perfectly and eternally in heaven. In 1 Peter 3:18, we read, "For Christ also hath once suffered for sins, the just for the unjust, that he might bring us to God." For this reason, Christ came into the flesh as mediator. For this reason, He lived and suffered, and for this reason, He was crucified, died, and was buried to restore the ruined moral kingdom of God within the elect, and incrementally to bring them again to a perfect submission to God.

The world considers Christ to be a savior, but it has amazingly erroneous views regarding His work, as well as salvation as such. The very essence of the salvation Christ merits for His people is that He again renders them subject to God, and this causes them to die to their own lusts in order that they might live unto God alone and serve and obey Him perfectly. This is the essence of the salvation that we are to look for from Christ, namely, that we fully and eternally deny ourselves in order to serve God in true holiness and obedience, subjecting ourselves wholly and completely to His will.

This is the salvation that Christ preached here on earth, and none other. The sum and substance of His entire doctrine is that He came to restore the absolute kingdom of God among men and to restore apostate sinners unto God, and thus "make ready a people prepared for the Lord" (Luke 1:17). Neither Christ nor His apostles or disciples preached or taught any other doctrine than that sinners, having been reconciled to God by Him upon having believed in Him, have been brought nigh again unto the kingdom of heaven, which had been ruined by sin (Matt. 4:17). Thereby, He was saying that though the world had removed itself from the sphere of Jehovah's or heavenly obedience for a long period of time,[1]

---

1. That is, from the fall until the time of the coming of Christ.

having been subject to the dominion of Satan and sin, the time had now dawned in which Jehovah (or heaven) would again rule over men who, through Christ, willingly subject themselves to Him in the way of obedience.

I will now address the manner in which Christ establishes and restores this kingdom of Jehovah God in the elect. He sends forth His Holy Spirit into their hearts, who, by the Word, convinces them of their wretched departure from God and His kingdom. Thereby, the Spirit fully humbles them and renders them undone, so that they earnestly begin to ask for and long for a way to be reconciled and reunited with God, and may thus be restored into His favor and to His rightful claim upon them.

To that end, Christ reveals Himself to them as the only way, and He grants faith, whereby they fully embrace Him as the way to be reunited with God, surrendering themselves fully to Him, by which they may be brought unto God. Christ, having taken possession of the elect and by faith having united them to Himself, at once proceeds to establish and restore God's kingdom within them.

As priest, He removes the guilt and punishment of their damnable apostasy from God, and He eternally reconciles and restores them unto God as if they had never fallen away from Him. Paul teaches, regarding all true believers, that "when we were enemies, we were reconciled to God by the death of his Son" (Rom. 5:10).

As prophet, He teaches and instructs them regarding the kingdom of God and opens to them its blessed mysteries, for He has declared to His believing people, "Unto you it is given to know the mystery of the kingdom of God" (Mark 4:11).

As king, Christ makes His residence within the hearts of His believing people. He regenerates them by His Holy Spirit and thereby makes them partakers of a new spiritual life, whereby they are translated from the kingdom of Satan into the kingdom of God (John 3:5). He sanctifies them by the efficacious conversion, transformation, and renewal of their entire humanity in all its propensities, causing them to serve and obey Jehovah God. By virtue of His dwelling in their hearts, He so works in, illuminates, and renews His people that, with a heartfelt willingness, they subject themselves to God and to His rightful domain, and they fully and eternally renounce the kingdom of Satan and of self.

Christ proceeds in this work incrementally, and as prophet, priest, and king, He increasingly establishes the kingdom of God within believers. He tears down within them all that pertains to Satan and to sin, and He causes them continually to increase in their willing obedience and subjection toward Jehovah God.

He continues to do so until, by way of the death of believers and their resurrection, He establishes God's kingdom in them fully, eternally, and perfectly.

This is the kingdom of heaven, of which the Holy Scriptures speak so frequently, referring to it at times as simply "the kingdom," then as "the kingdom of God," then as "the kingdom of Christ," and then as "the kingdom of heaven."

Regarding this kingdom, it is to be noted that:

1. it is established by the Holy Spirit in the heart of every true believer, "for, behold, the kingdom of God is within you" (Luke 17:21);

2. we must all enter into it by way of a true faith and true repentance if we are to be saved, and to that end, men must forsake all things (Mark 9:47);

3. we are to receive it within our hearts, for we read, "Verily I say unto you, Whosoever shall not receive the kingdom of God as a little child, he shall not enter therein" (Mark 10:15);

4. we must seek it before all other things, and we are not to rest until we have found it; we read therefore in Matthew 6:33a, "But seek ye first the kingdom of God, and his righteousness";

5. God has prepared it for His elect, believing people "from the foundation of the world" (Matt. 25:34); and

6. it does not consist in an outward display and manifestation of religion, but "righteousness, and peace, and joy in the Holy Ghost" (Rom. 14:17), "for the kingdom of God is not in word, but in power" (1 Cor. 4:20).

We judge that we had to say this much to give you a thorough explanation regarding the spiritual kingdom of God, the Father of believers, who is in heaven. By the second petition, Christ commands His believing people continually to pray for the coming of this kingdom. Since we have specifically dealt with the essence of the matter in our exposition, we no longer have time to consider the many attending circumstances that pertain to this matter, for time constraints compel us to focus either on the essence of the matter or on its attending circumstances. Upon consulting the expositors of this petition of the Savior, we concluded that the majority of them engaged themselves in an extensive exposition only of the attending circumstances of God's kingdom, and thereby hardly said anything regarding the essence of the matter. We could not approve of this expository approach, as we generally do not care for such. The attending circumstances of God's kingdom are:

1. how it is specifically the kingdom of the Father;

2. how it is the kingdom of heaven;

3. how God established it from the beginning of the world, and how He shall ultimately bring it to perfection;

4. what distinctions there are in the manifestation of this kingdom in both the Old and New Testaments;

5. which benefits and graces God continually bestows upon this kingdom; and

6. what mutual relationships and obligations the subjects of this kingdom have toward one another.

How can we deal extensively with all these matters if we remain ignorant of the very essence of the matter itself? The dilemma lies in the fact that people do not know what the very essence of God's kingdom is. This must therefore be clearly and thoroughly expounded before one can consider the matter as to its attending circumstances, and they can be truly known and understood only when one considers the essence of the matter that these attending circumstances pertain to and are contingent upon.

We therefore determined that we would consider the kingdom of God in its essence, leaving it to our godly readers to search the Holy Scriptures and the practical expositors of the Heidelberg Catechism more specifically as to what are the attending circumstances of God's kingdom.

We shall now proceed briefly to consider what it is that the Lord Jesus commands His believing people to ask of their heavenly Father regarding the coming of God's kingdom.

Having considered the essential nature of the subject of this second petition about the kingdom of Jehovah God, we must now consider briefly what the Savior teaches and commands His believing people to request of their heavenly Father regarding this kingdom of God. In so doing, we shall completely conform ourselves to the exposition of our Christian instructor, for he has expounded this for us in such an essential, clear, and concise manner that we can fully acquiesce in his exposition. He posits that, in this petition, God's believing subjects are requesting the following: "Rule us so by Thy word and Spirit, that we may submit ourselves more and more to Thee; preserve and increase Thy church."

According to the exposition of the instructor, our understanding of this coming of God's kingdom must be twofold:

1. as it specifically comes within every believing subject of this kingdom; and

2. as it comes generally in reference to the entire church; that is, the entire body of believing subjects of this kingdom.

First, the *kingdom of Jehovah God* comes to every believing subject of this kingdom in whom God rules by His Word and Spirit. This matter should be sufficiently clear from what we have already considered, for we explained not only how Christ establishes God's kingdom within believers in principle when He initially unites them to Himself by faith and regenerates them, but also how He subsequently and increasingly expands and affirms it.

When the elect have truly and actually been incorporated into God's kingdom by way of faith, regeneration, and conversion, and have thus become God's subjects, there certainly remains within them a great deal of the old kingdom of Satan and of themselves. From this proceeds all the disobedience and opposition toward God that issues forth so abundantly from their flesh and carnal members. Throughout the entire Word of God, we hear the saints complain bitterly and frequently about this—especially the holy apostle Paul in Romans 7 (cf. Gal. 5:17).

Therefore, God's kingdom must necessarily come increasingly and specifically to every believer by means of God's efficacious and irresistible rule over him, whereby He increasingly subjects the believer to Himself and expands His divine dominion over him. This government of the believing subjects of His kingdom, having as its objective increased obedience toward and subjection to Him, God executes by His Word and Spirit, doing so entirely in and through Christ, His Son. As mediator and viceroy (so to speak), Christ establishes this kingdom of His Father in believers and, by the operation of His Spirit and by means of His Word, increasingly expands this kingdom within them. The Father has indeed given to Christ, His Son, complete dominion over this kingdom, in conformity to Revelation 12:10: "Now is come salvation, and strength, and the kingdom of our God, and the power of his Christ."

The believing subjects of God are thus, in the first place, asking of their heavenly Father and king in this petition, "Thy kingdom come," that He, by His Word and Spirit, would increasingly have dominion over them, work in them, and efficaciously govern them, thereby continually subduing in them all dominion of self, Satan, and sin, causing them increasingly to become subject to Him and His divine dominion, so that they will be entirely dependent on Him and serve no other king but Jehovah, their heavenly Father.

Second, they also pray for the coming of God's kingdom in general, beseeching their king and heavenly Father to preserve and increase His church. The church, in its essence, is the community of believing subjects toward whom God's kingdom has come, and, as we have already observed, in whose hearts the Lord Jesus has established that kingdom. However, this church is by no means able to exist in and of itself, due to the vast multitude of internal and external enemies that continually surround her from every side, which enemies are utterly hostile toward the kingdom of God and Jehovah's rule.

Therefore, God Himself must continually preserve His church and kingdom by His power, doing so by the ministry of His Word and His gospel ordinances. The Lord Himself testifies of this, saying, "I the LORD do keep it; I will water it every moment: lest any hurt it, I will keep it night and day" (Isa. 27:3). In this petition, the believing subjects of God's kingdom pray for the preservation of God's church and kingdom.

However, not only do they pray in this petition for the preservation of God's church, but they also pray for her increase, beseeching their heavenly Father that He would daily convert sinners, and thus extract His elect from the kingdom of Satan and of sin, and establish His kingdom within them. They pray that He would add daily to the church those who must be saved, thereby extending His kingdom everywhere among men. God's kingdom, then, comes especially when increasingly it comes among men, and thus when God, by means of the preaching of His Holy Word, converts and regenerates sinners.

When the Lord's subjects pray for the coming of His kingdom, they are also beseeching Him, saying, "Destroy the works of the devil, and all violence which would exalt itself against Thee; and also, all wicked counsels devised against Thy holy Word."

Satan, whose singular objective is the utter defeat of God and His kingdom, is and will remain eternally God's archenemy, who will never cease to fight against God, seeking to bring the entire world into bondage to his kingdom of darkness. To that end, he actively engages himself within the hearts of the subjects of Jehovah God, having as his ultimate objective to draw them away from obedience toward God and thereby continually to undermine God's kingdom within them, and, if possible, utterly to destroy it.

As God's adversary and archenemy, Satan not only seeks to undermine God's kingdom within believers, but also engages himself externally against the entire body of God's kingdom by violence and "all wicked counsels devised against [His] holy Word." Satan stirs up his subjects, consisting of the great majority of the human race, continually to oppose the church and the kingdom of God, seeking to inflict harm and utter annihilation by all manner of wicked counsels. Such have been Satan's activities from the very beginning until this present day; such are his activities today; and he will continue to engage in this manner until the end of time. However, God is able continually to disrupt and overturn his evil works, his violence, and his wicked counsels, and to protect His kingdom against all the displays of his power within and without, as the Lord has done until this very day.

"For this purpose the Son of God was manifested, that he might destroy the works of the devil" (1 John 3:8), and He will indeed do so. By His power, He will preserve His kingdom so that the gates of hell will not be able to prevail against it (Matt. 16:18). One day "the God of peace shall bruise Satan under your feet shortly" (Rom. 16:20a). In this second petition, believers ask God, as their king and heavenly Father, continually to preserve and protect His kingdom against the devil and all his devices, violence, and wicked counsels, and that He would do so steadfastly "till the full perfection of [His] kingdom take place, wherein [He] shall be all in all."

It is the supreme goal and objective of God's way, as well as of the entire work of redemption through Christ, to establish His kingdom completely and to restore it to full perfection in conformity to what it was prior to the fall. Ever since Paradise, Christ has been engaged accordingly, and He will remain engaged in this task until the end of the world, gathering by His Word and Spirit all the elect into God's kingdom. Once He will have gathered in all the elect, including the very last one, the world will end. Christ will then destroy the last enemy of God's kingdom which is death, and will resurrect the entire kingdom of God in absolute perfection. He will then bring this entire kingdom from earth into heaven above and place it, as perfectly holy and without any blemish, into the hands of Jehovah, His Father, for whom He established this kingdom. This will then culminate in the triune Jehovah being eternally what He must be, "all and in all" (Col. 3:11). We read of this in 1 Corinthians 15:24 and 28: "Then cometh the end, when he shall have delivered up the kingdom to God, even the Father; when he shall have put down all rule and all authority and power.... And when all things shall be subdued unto him, then shall the

Son also himself be subject unto him that put all things under him, that God may be all in all."

In summary, this petition is all reduced to one thing: that Jehovah would indeed rule as king so that we and others would completely subject ourselves to Him, that we would live exclusively for Him alone, that all who would oppose this would be dismantled and destroyed, and that Jehovah Himself, through Christ, His Son, would establish His kingdom, would increasingly expand it, and would cast down all that exalts itself against Him.

Please note that the Lord Jesus Christ commands His believing people not only to pray for this, but also to persevere in so doing, for He hereby teaches them two things:

First, all their salvation and felicity consists in the coming of the kingdom of God their heavenly Father, in them and toward them. Thus:

- they ought not either to know, seek, or desire any other salvation than that they would fully, with soul and body, live for and be subject to God; and
- they ought to utterly deny themselves in order that they might fully obey and serve the living God.

We have already sufficiently proved that, for believers, there truly neither is nor can be any salvation other than that.

Second, they are completely impotent to bring about the coming of the kingdom of Jehovah God as pertaining to themselves and to others. Of themselves, they are entirely incapable of achieving this, for, by nature, they were also absolute enemies of God's dominion and kingdom, and they have no might against His great archenemy, Satan. As we have seen, it is therefore entirely the work of God and Christ to establish, preserve, protect, increase, and confirm this kingdom. Christ leads His believing people to look entirely outside of themselves, commanding them to depend upon God their heavenly Father with continual supplications that His kingdom might come.

Following this extensive and rich exposition of the subject at hand, we shall now turn to ourselves by way of application. I find here a very broad spectrum of rebuke, conviction, instruction, admonition, and comfort.

What shall I say to you who are the unconverted people of this world? I can say only that when you pray for the coming of God's kingdom, you neither understand nor desire what you pray for. You are entirely hostile to God's government, neither knowing nor desiring to serve any other king but yourself and Satan. To truly convict you of this and to cause you to believe that this must be the work of God Himself, we therefore fully commend you to His omnipotence and His will. It is our wish that the Lord would often give us a heart continually to pray on your behalf, that it might please God to cause His kingdom to come to you, and that, by His mighty hand, He would deliver you from the kingdom of self and of Satan, so that the day would come when King Jehovah would also reign over you.

However, you who are the believing children of God, you are the ones to whom this expounded petition particularly pertains, for you are God's subjects by faith in Christ Jesus. You alone are capable of praying by the Spirit of prayer for the coming of God's kingdom. It is within you that King Jesus has begun to establish His Father's dominion and kingdom, and to break down the kingdom of Satan and of self. He will not forsake the work of His hands, but He will proceed with this work until perfection is achieved. What a blessed people you are, whose God and king is the Lord, "forgetting those things which are behind, and reaching forth unto those things which are before" (Phil. 3:13)!

Nothing else therefore remains for you, but that God's kingdom would increasingly come within you. This is the focal point of your entire salvation, namely, that God in Christ would increasingly have dominion over you and that you would entirely become His. The continuation and promotion of this blessed dominion over you is the sum and substance of the work that must be done in you. Nothing more is needed, and if this is to be accomplished, it has to occur by Christ Himself increasingly instructing you, by His Word and Spirit, regarding the mysteries of God's kingdom, teaching you correctly to know and to understand:

1. what the nature and essence of God's kingdom is, for even the very best among God's children have learned very little regarding this;

2. how your salvation consists entirely and exclusively in the coming of this kingdom;

3. how little of this precious kingdom has come to you and is within you; how much of the kingdom of Satan and of self still remains within you; and what its wretched consequences are; and

4. not only how utterly incapable you are of breaking down the kingdom of Satan within you and bringing about the increase of God's kingdom toward and within you, but also to know and to understand how this is and remains entirely the work of Christ, the

Son of God, who alone has received all power from the Father, and in whom alone, therefore, all fullness dwells.

To have a correct understanding of all these mysteries of the kingdom, you need to receive more and more from Him who enables the blind to see and who has taken it upon Himself to educate and instruct you regarding all these things. The need to have this hidden instruction continually flow down to you from Christ in heaven should be a suitable means to motivate you to beseech your heavenly Father continually in Spirit and truth for the coming of His kingdom, so that, in the end, you rely entirely upon Christ, your head, and that by Him you increasingly enter into that kingdom.

We shall conclude with the admonition of the great savior, Jesus Christ, who said, "Therefore take no thought...but seek ye first the kingdom of God, and his righteousness; and all these things shall be added unto you" (Matt. 6:31, 33).

May the Lord Himself enable His people to do so by the continual influence of His Spirit and grace. Amen.

The Third Petition:
Thy Will Be Done

Thy will be done in earth, as it is in heaven.
—MATTHEW 6:10b

Question 124: Which is the third petition?

Answer: "Thy will be done on earth as it is in heaven"; that is, grant that we and all men may renounce our own will, and without murmuring obey Thy will, which is only good; that so every one may attend to and perform the duties of his station and calling as willingly and faithfully as the angels do in heaven.

———————

The soul and internal staying power of all kingdoms and all governmental entities consists entirely in the willing obedience of their subjects to the lawful jurisdiction of their kings and governors. This truth is clearly taught by the essential nature of the matter. When subjects withdraw themselves from this obligation toward their rulers or governments, all governmental entities and kingdoms cease to function in their very essence, and they cannot be reestablished in any way but by their subjects recommitting themselves to their duty of obedience and subjection toward those whom God has placed over them. The Savior teaches this in Matthew 12:25, where we read, "Every kingdom divided against itself is brought to desolation; and every city or house divided against itself shall not stand." It is therefore self-evident that if a kingdom or governmental entity is to exist and function, the will of the king or the government, insofar as it is based on justice and fairness, must always be done, and it must be obeyed by its subjects with all willingness and affection.

If this is true for the governmental entities and kingdoms of this world, it is certainly true for the blessed and glorious kingdom of Jehovah God, the Father of believers. In principle, He establishes that kingdom here on earth in the hearts of His believing children through Christ, His Son, and He will continue to establish it until perfection is achieved. We observed this in our previous sermon, as we expounded the petition, "Thy kingdom come." This spiritual and blessed kingdom can exist only if its believing subjects live in complete submission and obedience toward the will of Jehovah, their Father and king.

This good, holy, and legitimate will of God must continually be honored and fully obeyed by believers with a heartfelt willingness. If the kingdom of God is to prosper, its subjects must acquiesce in the will of God, their Father and king. The savior, the Lord Jesus, therefore exhorts His believing people that immediately following the petition for the coming of the kingdom of God, they are to pray that the will of God may be done and obeyed. The doing of His will is the soul and essence of Jehovah's kingdom, and this is rooted not only in His divine power and authority, but also, and primarily, in the willing subjection and obedience of His subjects to Him, their great God and king.

For us to examine and consider this petition in some detail, may the Lord grant the grace of His Holy Spirit with His indispensable blessing, so that His great and glorious name may be glorified by us. Amen.

Two matters are to be considered regarding this petition:

1. The subject of the petition itself, being the will of God, the heavenly Father and king of believers.
2. The Savior's command to His believing people to pray regarding this will that it may be done "in earth, as it is in heaven."

Regarding the subject of this petition, mention is made here of the will, particularly the will of Jehovah God as the Father and king of believers, who is in heaven. In essence, we may say that the will is the rational propensity of a spiritual being, consisting of the inclination or conviction of the soul to love or to hate, or to accept or to reject, what is clearly perceived by the intellect. This propensity is an essential attribute of all spiritual beings, for the essence of a spiritual being consists in its intellect and will. The moment that these were removed, nothing would remain of such a spiritual being. Since Jehovah God is also a most perfect, infinite, and purely spiritual being, He necessarily possesses not only a most perfect and infinite intellect, but also a most perfect and infinite will. By His will, He is fully inclined toward Himself, His holy virtues, and His perfections, and He therefore loves only what conforms to His holy attributes, and He utterly hates and rejects all that militates against them.

Therefore, we must understand the very essence of God's will to be that holy and supremely pure inclination that God has toward Himself and His adorable virtues and perfections, so that, in all things, they alone are magnified and glorified. From this supremely pure origin and fountain proceed all of God's activities, and they also end in the magnification and glorification of His perfections. The Holy Scriptures speak abundantly and pervasively of this will of God, and Paul testifies in Ephesians 1:11 that God "worketh all things after the counsel of his own will."

To enable us to grasp the matter more clearly, we are accustomed, for our benefit, to make a distinction regarding the will of Jehovah God between the will of His decree and the will of His command—or His decretal will and His prescriptive will. This is not to suggest that there truly are two distinct wills in God and that one might contradict the other. Rather there is but one singular and most perfect will of God, which, in all things, is entirely consistent with itself and ends in the glory of God. However, as human beings, we distinguish His *decretal* will and His *prescriptive* will to aid our puny, weak, and limited understanding in grasping what is communicated by His Word and Spirit regarding the most perfect will of God.

We thus understand the will of God's decree to be that eternal, adorable, and sovereign good pleasure of Jehovah God whereby He, from eternity, has immutably decreed and established within Himself the existence of all things, as well as the manner in which they function. This means that every event throughout the entire created universe, be it with reference to rational or irrational creatures, can transpire only in complete conformity to this will and to the good pleasure of Jehovah God, according to which He worketh all things within the context of history, according to the testimony of Paul.

Daniel, the man of God, has in mind this *decretal* will of God when he says, "He doeth according to his will in the army of heaven, and among the inhabitants of the earth: and none can stay his hand, or say unto him, What doest thou?" (Dan. 4:35). Regarding His will, the Lord Himself declares, "My counsel shall stand, and I will do all my pleasure" (Isa. 46:10b).

Regarding God's *prescriptive* will, or the will of His command, we understand it to be the sovereign, holy, and adorable good pleasure of Jehovah God that moved Him to prescribe a rule of conduct for the children of men, who morally are entirely dependent upon Him. On the one hand, He did so by means of the light of nature, while on the other hand, He did so by means of His Holy Word. All our deeds and activities, internally as well as externally, must fully conform to that Word, so that, in all things, we obey and glorify Him in thought, word, and deed. Thus, we are to exist and live solely and exclusively for Him.

In His prescriptive will, God thus requires of us true holiness, which consists in subjecting ourselves fully to the Lord and being subservient to Him in all things. The apostle Paul teaches this in 1 Thessalonians 4:3–4, saying, "For this is the will of God, even your sanctification, that ye should abstain from fornication: that every one of you should know how to possess his vessel in sanctification and honour." Regarding those who are doers of the will of God, the apostle John testifies that they will never die, saying, "He that doeth the will of God abideth for ever" (1 John 2:17).

It is evident in what the essence of the will of God's decree, as well as in what the will of His command, consists. The decretal will of Jehovah God is rightfully referred to as the *secret* will of God, for it is entirely concealed within His heart. As for us, the children of men, there is but one way[1] for us to discover what this decretal will of God is: by its actual execution within the context of history. This will of God may also become known by means of special divine revelation. In former days, God frequently revealed His will to holy men, and sometimes, in special cases, He still does so to His children and favorites—in conformity to His Holy Word. In all other cases, it is true what we read in Deuteronomy 29:29: "The secret things belong unto the LORD our God: but those things which are revealed belong unto us and to our children for ever, that we may do all the words of this law."

However, the prescriptive will of God, the will of His command, is also called God's *revealed* will. By means of the light of our innate or natural reason, as is true for the heathen (Rom. 2:14–15), and especially in and by His Holy Word, God has clearly revealed His will to us, the children of men, by giving us His holy law as a vivid account and transcript of that will. By His Holy Spirit, He writes this law upon the minds and the hearts of His believing subjects so that they have an inward delight to conduct themselves in accord with this will and with God's holy good pleasure. We read in Jeremiah 31:33, "I will put my law in their inward parts, and write it in their hearts." Micah has this revelation of the prescriptive will of God in mind when he declares, "He hath shewed thee, O man, what is good; and what doth the Lord require of thee, but to do justly, and to love mercy, and to walk humbly with thy God?" (Mic. 6:8).

Having thus considered how, for our sake, a distinction is made within the singular will of God between the will of His decree and the will of His

---

1. At times, God is also pleased to reveal His decretal will prior to its execution.

command, the question immediately arises as to which will is referred to in this petition, to which we respond that we must understand this petition to have reference both to the decretal and the prescriptive will of God. The reason for this is very obvious, considering that the objective of this petition is to desire of God an all-encompassing obedience, with submission of the heart, regarding His divine will, as being the foundation upon which His gracious kingdom is established within us. This we expounded in our introduction.

It is beyond all contradiction that God's believing subjects must obey God's will in its totality, both in respect to His decretal as well as to His prescriptive will, for, in God, there is but one singular will, a will that is synonymous with God Himself. It is therefore beyond doubt that both the will of God's decree and the will of God's command are the subject of this petition, and this will become increasingly evident as we proceed with our exposition.

We shall now proceed to consider what the Lord Jesus commands His believing people to pray in this petition regarding this will of God, their Father and king. He commands them to pray that His will may "be done in earth, as it is in heaven."

A correct understanding of the meaning and content of this petition is entirely contingent upon the thrust of the expression *God's will be done*. When we correctly understand this manner of speaking, this petition immediately becomes clear to us. Beloved, you should recognize that God's will shall truly be done when God receives from His creatures, and especially from us, the children of men, all humble obedience and submission to His divine will. Thus, the will of God truly shall be done in us when everything is completely subordinate to His will and there is nothing in us militating against it.

To view this matter from the distinct perspective of God's twofold will, namely, the will of His decree and the will of His command, we must recognize that:

First, the will of God's decree is executed where the events of history come to pass and transpire, God having eternally willed and decreed them. The will of God's decree is always being executed, for this will is entirely immutable from God's side, and entirely irresistible from the side of the creature. The apostle Paul therefore asks, "Who hath resisted his will?" (Rom. 9:19). As we read earlier, the Lord Himself testifies regarding this, saying, "My counsel shall stand, and I will do all my pleasure" (Isa. 46:10b), and also, "Surely as I have thought, so shall it come to pass; and as I have purposed, so shall it stand" (Isa. 14:24).

Second, regarding the prescriptive will of God, or the will of God's command, it is said to be done when all the inward and outward deeds and activities of us, the children of men, transpire in full conformity to and without any contradiction to God's holy law. Thus, the prescriptive will, the will of God's command, transpires when we live holy lives and subject ourselves fully to God. However, by man's sinful corruption and unholy nature, which causes him to be fully opposed to God's holy will, this prescriptive will of God is not always done, "because the carnal mind is enmity against God: for it is not subject to the law of God, neither indeed can be" (Rom. 8:7). We therefore read of knowing the will of God and yet not doing it (Luke 12:47). Throughout Scripture, mention is made of man's disobedience toward God and toward His will, and the instructor taught in Question 114 that even God's children have but a small beginning of this obedience as long as they live here on earth.

From the foregoing, it becomes very evident what things God's believing subjects desire of God as their king and heavenly Father when they pray that His will be done. Globally speaking, their only desire is that, by grace, they and other men would be continually rendered fit by the Lord Himself to be obedient and submissive to His divine will, which alone is holy and good. It is also their desire that their own sinful and corrupt wills would be dismantled and subdued, so that God's will alone would prevail and be done everywhere.

The instructor expounds this petition accordingly by teaching that when one prays this petition, he is praying, "Grant that we and all men may renounce our own will, and without murmuring obey Thy will, which is only good." To expound the content of this petition in conformity with the explanation of the instructor, we must remember what we preached regarding the previous petition, "Thy kingdom come." We observed how God initially created man good and perfect, and that, in all things, he was completely conformed to the will of God as His king and creator, knowing of no other will. However, we also considered how man, by his willful disobedience and the temptation of the devil, utterly fell away from that blessed state of perfect subjection to God, and was transferred into the kingdom of Satan. He thus acquired a will of his own, which is entirely opposed to God's will, and that recalcitrant will has become to sinful man as a law, under which he is carnally sold and held captive through sin. The apostle Paul addresses this very clearly and powerfully in Romans 7.

All men are thus, by nature, completely enslaved to self and to their sinful lusts. Man's will, to which he is utterly enslaved, is entirely opposed to God's will, for God's will is entirely good and holy, and the will of man is utterly wicked and unholy. God's will is only Spirit, light, and life, and man's will is only carnal, dark, and dead. These two contrary wills cannot be reconciled to all eternity, but one of the two must be utterly dismantled and demolished, and only the other must be done. The will that is to be utterly dismantled and demolished is the will of man, which is utterly unholy. This unholy will must be fully subdued, and God's good and holy will alone must be sustained and have royal dominion over man.

This begins to occur the moment a man is united to Christ by faith and is converted unto God from sin. Man then receives eyes of understanding that have been enlightened (Eph. 1:18a), whereby he learns to see how holy, good, and blessed is God's will, and how unholy, sinful, and wretched is his own will, to which he has rendered compliance as a ruling law. Man then receives a heartfelt love for God's will and an intense hatred for his own unholy will. His own sinful will becomes his greatest enemy, and he abhors and rejects it. It is then his desire that his will be subdued and extracted with root and branch.

It is then his desire, with both soul and body, to live in full accordance to God's will and eternally to be subject to it. It is and remains the sorrow of such a person that there is yet so little subjection to God's will, because his own will still exerts such strength and dominion within him. He complains: "Oh, there is still so little of God's will in me and so much of my own. Oh, that my accursed and sinful will would be utterly subdued in me and that I would live fully in accordance with God's will! That would be all the salvation that I desire. 'O wretched man that I am! who shall deliver me from the body of this death?' (Rom. 7:24) and thus from myself? Who shall cause me to be entirely devoted to God and to be nothing in myself?"

In this manner, man is fully converted and transformed in the way of faith and repentance, so that he who earlier, with peace and delight, hated God's holy will and fully served his own sinful will, now desires nothing other than eternally to deny his own will and to be fully subjected to God's will without the least inner opposition. There is now such a complete love for the will of God, and the sinner is so wholeheartedly united with it, that he no longer desires anything but that God's will may be fully done. According to the instructor, he thus desires that *all men* would utterly forsake their own sinful will and, with complete obedience and subjection of both soul and body, do only God's will, which is good and holy.

However, we need to take careful notice here, for such converted subjects of God find themselves not only utterly impotent and incapable of such subjection to God's will, but also utterly impotent and incapable to deny their own will. They increasingly, thoroughly, and experientially are confronted by the Lord Himself, not only with their absolute impotence and utter incapability of tearing down their own sinful will, but also with their complete incapability of subjecting themselves to God's will. They increasingly are taught and instructed by the Holy Spirit that all their strength and power are to be found only with God in Christ. This continually causes them to look outside of themselves and to take refuge to the Lord with earnest supplications and petitions that His will might be done. According to the instructor, this means that they ask of the Lord that He would "grant that we and all men may renounce our own will, and without murmuring obey [His] will, which is only good." To this end, they pray the Lord to work in them and to enable them in Christ, His Son, by continual, prevenient, pursuing, and cooperating grace, to continually receive not only the desire and strength to do His holy will in all things, but also to be fully subject to that will with soul and body—thus, to be unto the Lord as a child weaned by its mother.

In this way, the true meaning and content of this petition becomes evident. God's children pray in this petition for the grace of willing obedience and submission, both to the will of God's decree and to the will of His command.

Regarding the will of God's decree, it is their intense desire and supplication that God, as their king and Father who is in heaven:

1. Would, always and in all things, execute His adorable and sovereign decree regarding them and others, and so make all things beautiful in His time. That God's people must also fervently pray unto Him for the execution of His decretal will, is evident (not to quote any other proof texts regarding this) from Ezekiel 36:36–37, where God says: "I the LORD have spoken it, and I will do it. Thus saith the Lord GOD; I will yet for this be enquired of by the house of Israel, to do it for them." From God's side, this matter was most certainly decreed and would most certainly come to pass. Nevertheless, He would be enquired of by Israel for Him to do this. Consider also Daniel's fervent prayer in Daniel 9, carefully considering with it chapter 35 of Jeremiah's prophecy, regarding God's gracious decree of Judah's deliverance from Babylon after seventy years. Such a prayer for the execution of the will of God's decree is most becoming, for thereby the supplicant clearly indicates his intense love and esteem for the supreme decree of Jehovah, His God. He also expresses that he fully and completely is able to acquiesce and to rest therein, desiring that everything would come to pass at its proper time, reassuring himself that God has decreed

nothing other than that which is subservient to His glory and to the salvation of His people.

2. Not only would always execute His decree at His time, thereby making all things beautiful to them and to others, but also would continually cause them and all His people, by grace and in Christ, to be subject to His decretal will. They pray that no matter how strange and difficult His ways may be for their flesh, they would nevertheless subject themselves to His will without gainsaying, doing so in the full obedience of faith and in all quietness. Their prayer is that they may be fully united to the wise, good, holy, and adorable will of their God, Father, and king, so that, in all things, they might say with Eli, the man of God, "It is the LORD: let him do what seemeth him good" (1 Sam. 3:18b). Then they also say with Mary, "Behold the handmaid of the Lord; be it unto me according to thy word" (Luke 1:38).

As to the will of God's command, believers again pray for two things in this petition:

1. It is their prayer that God, in Christ and by His Holy Spirit, would increasingly fill them with the knowledge of His will, and that He would continue to illuminate their understanding regarding the knowledge of His laws and commandments, so that they might increasingly "prove what is that good, and acceptable, and perfect, will of God" (Rom. 12:2b). This also was the prayer of David, the man of God, saying: "Shew me thy ways, O LORD; teach me thy paths. Lead me in thy truth, and teach me: for thou art the God of my salvation; on thee do I wait all the day" (Ps. 25:4–5). Paul testifies, "[I] do not cease to pray for you, and to desire that ye might be filled with the knowledge of his will in all wisdom and spiritual understanding" (Col. 1:9).

2. However, believers pray not only for the knowledge of the will of God, but also for grace and for a ready willingness to obey the prescriptive will of God, praying that the Lord would continue to purify their hearts by faith and increasingly sanctify them to be willingly obedient and subject to all His commandments. The Lord desires not only to give them His laws intellectually, but also to write them upon their hearts (Heb. 8:10). He also causes them to walk in His statutes, so that they keep His judgments and do them (Ezek. 34:27).

In this petition, believers therefore fully consider this obedience and willing subjection to the will of God as a precious and gracious benefit of God's covenant that they must continually receive from the Lord Himself, in Christ and by His Spirit. Throughout the psalms, and especially in Psalm 119, David so earnestly prays for this. The apostle prayed this regarding the Hebrews: "Now the God of peace…make you perfect in every good work to do his will, working in you that which is well pleasing in his sight, through Jesus Christ" (Heb. 13:21). The Savior commands His believing people to pray for all this in the petition, "Thy will be done."

The Savior does, however, not leave the matter to rest here. Rather, He continues to instruct His believing people to pray specifically to God their heavenly Father and king, that His will "be done here on earth, as it is done in heaven." In heaven, the place of perfect felicity and glory, the will of God is done by the holy angels and the glorified spirits of the just in a manner that is entirely holy and perfect, without the least objection or murmuring. In heaven, there is but one will in effect, and that is the will of Jehovah God. There is no will of the creature that is distinct from the will of God, but all self-will is completely excluded and eliminated, so that the residents of heaven fully subject themselves to God's will and, in all things, are of one mind with the Lord. In heaven, their will is so completely molded and rendered fit that, to all eternity (oh what great blessedness this is!), they will not object to God's will even in the very least. Instead, they will always completely be united with His will, and their will shall coalesce with His.

God has so deeply impressed His will upon the hearts of all the residents of heaven that their will has been completely molded in conformity to His will. It is the blessedness and delight of all the residents of heaven to do the will of God their king in a most perfect manner, doing so with the utmost readiness, zeal, joy, humility, and steadfastness.

The Savior exhorts and instructs His believing people that, as God's will is done in heaven, so God's will should be done here on earth, by them and by others. However, believers ought not to imagine, as is the sentiment of Arminians and Roman Catholics, that this heavenly holiness and perfection is already truly and perfectly attainable here on earth. That would contradict the sound doctrine of God's Word, which teaches us that here upon earth, while believers are still absent from the Lord in the flesh, perfect holiness cannot be attained. Rather, this is "an inheritance incorruptible, and undefiled, and that fadeth not away, reserved in heaven for [them]" (1 Peter 1:4)—a pledge that God has laid away for them and will keep until that day.

The crux of the matter, however, is that the Lord Jesus here teaches His believing people to pray in conformity to their spiritual nature and character, thereby causing them continually to increase in holiness.

First, the character and nature of God's children is such that they cannot be satisfied with anything less than complete and perfect holiness. This is and remains the core desire of their souls, for they cannot acquiesce in one single sin, however insignificant and minor it might be. Thus, the unalterable desire of their hearts remains to serve, love, fear, and glorify the Lord in complete perfection, as the residents of heaven do above. To rob believers of this desire would be as much as utterly stripping them of their spiritual life and depriving them of the grace of God.

Christ here teaches His people to pray in conformity with their spiritual nature, which always gravitates toward the perfect holiness that is enjoyed in heaven. He prompts them to bring before their heavenly Father their inward yearning and desire after perfect holiness, while nevertheless subjecting this inward desire to Him, as to how much holiness and obedience He will be pleased to give them here on earth as a sovereign gift of His grace.

Second, it is also the Savior's objective that, in this way, His believing people may increasingly progress in true holiness and obedience toward God, for He sets before their eyes the perfect model of the residents in heaven, to which they are to be perfectly conformed. They must therefore continually compare themselves to this perfect model in order to see their imperfection, grieve over it, humble themselves because of it, yearn for daily justification[2] and ongoing sanctification, and fervently strive after perfect heavenly holiness, "that I may apprehend that for which also I am apprehended of Christ Jesus" (Phil. 3:12).

Dear reader, there is surely no better or more effective means to progress in grace and in holiness than by focusing more on what one ought to have than on what one already has. A believing child of God must always hold before himself perfect and heavenly holiness as the goal and objective he must pursue. Let him become utterly enamored and focused upon this, determining not to rest until he has arrived at the finish line, and he experiences that it is for him as it was with the apostle Paul, as he expressed in Philippians 3:12: "Not as though I had already attained, either were already perfect: but I follow after, if that I may apprehend that for which also I am apprehended of Christ Jesus." The believer increasingly becomes smaller, more humble, miserable, modest, poor, and sinful in his own eyes. He increasingly perceives his deficiency and becomes increasingly receptive to grace and growth. He continually forgets those things that are behind and reaches forth unto those things that are before, pressing

---

2. VanderGroe here refers to *paternal* justification; that is, the Father's daily pardon of His spiritual sons and daughters.

toward the mark for the prize of the high calling of God in Christ Jesus (Phil. 3:13–14). It then arises in his heart to proceed further and further, and he thus continues to progress from grace to grace and from strength to strength until, at last, he appears before God in Zion as completely holy and perfect in Christ, his head. It is also Christ's intent to teach His believing people to pray that they would emulate the blessed residents of heaven and do God's will in that fashion and according to that pattern.

By these proposed grounds, an exercised spiritual listener, if the Lord grants light, may in some measure understand with clarity why the Lord Jesus teaches His believing people to pray that *God's will be done as it is done in heaven.*

If anyone has eyes to see, he readily understands that no unconverted sinner can pray such a prayer (as we have presently expounded) in spirit and in truth, for all unconverted men are complete enemies of God and of His holy will. They utterly oppose both God and His holy will, and, in all things, they live according to their own sinful will. May God Himself do this work of teaching a sinner to pray this petition by His Holy Spirit, and may it be done to the conviction and conversion of all His elect who are presently still living entirely according to the will of the flesh.

However, you who are believers in our Lord Jesus Christ, there is within you a heartfelt inclination toward the will of God. That desire and inclination is as the breath of your spiritual life, which is hidden with Christ in God. You consider the doing of God's will to be your ultimate felicity, and all your complaining and mourning pertains to the fact that this will is not done more frequently by you because of your own sinful will still being so strong and holding such dominion over you.

The only way to become increasingly subject to God's will is not only to know your sin and impotence, as well as the all-sufficient grace of God and Christ, but also to take continual refuge to and with a dependence upon that grace. Believe this, and may the Spirit of Christ open your eyes more and more to the fact that you have made but very little progress in being united with God's will. You do not measure up to the residents of heaven. In this regard, you are, of yourself, also indescribably empty, poor, and impotent. You are incapable of doing the will of God in any sense, however great your desire to do so may be, except it be done by and through the continual grace and power of the Lord Jesus. And, if you are willing, you may always desire and receive such grace of Him.

Therefore, children of God, continually look away from and outside of self, surrendering everything unto Jesus. Take refuge to Him, trust Him, and wait upon Him, always praying in His name, "Thy will be done in earth, as it is in heaven."

May the grace of the Lord, at all times, be in and upon us, as well as upon all who know neither any other life nor any other blessedness but the doing of the will of Him who has subjected all things unto Himself. Amen.

The Fourth Petition:
Give Us This Day Our Daily Bread

Give us this day our daily bread.
—MATTHEW 6:11

Question 125: Which is the fourth petition?

Answer: "Give us this day our daily bread"; that is, be pleased to provide us with all things necessary for the body, that we may thereby acknowledge Thee to be the only fountain of all good, and that neither our care nor industry, nor even Thy gifts, can profit us without Thy blessing; and therefore that we may withdraw our trust from all creatures, and place it alone in Thee.

It is most noteworthy what we read of the man of God, Moses, in Exodus 34:28: "And he was there with the LORD forty days and forty nights; he did neither eat bread, nor drink water." Beloved, this is an instance of the exercise of God's power shining forth in a most extraordinary manner, for the Lord sustained the temporal life of His servant Moses for a considerable period of time without him ingesting the least measure of food. The same power of God could certainly have been extended to the entire human race, for the Lord might have created it in such a fashion that men could have existed without the provision of any physical sustenance. However, it pleased the Lord not to do so, as it was His will that the human body, in its temporal state, should exist only by means of physical food and sustenance. Man would thereby be in daily need thereof, so that he would be more and more, visibly and tangibly, dependent upon God as His creator and sustainer. Thus, man would increasingly acknowledge his dependency, to the praise and glory of God, who has subjected all things to Himself.

As long as a person lives in his natural state, it is impossible for him to rightly acknowledge this physical dependence upon the Lord, because of his having utterly forsaken God. However, when Christ regenerates a person and thereby restores him unto God and His kingdom, not only is he taught his spiritual dependence upon God as His creator and king, but he also increasingly recognizes His physical dependence upon Him. Regarding his physical needs, he must then again place all his trust in God as His heavenly Father, and receive his provision each day, as it were, out of His hands.

Our blessed redeemer and savior, Christ Jesus, wanted to impress this upon His disciples and His believing people by prescribing the fourth petition to them, instructing them daily to beseech and implore their Father and king in heaven to grant them their necessary temporal provision, saying that they should therefore pray thus: "Give us this day our daily bread."

The Savior's great objective in prescribing this petition is to lead His believing people not only to an absolute denial of self, but also to a total subjection to God as their Father and king, so that, in both soul and body, they might be fully dependent upon Him and live solely out of, by, and for Him in all things. It is as though the Savior had laid the foundation for this in the first petition, in which He set before His believing people the hallowing and magnification of the great name of their God and heavenly Father as being the supreme and singular objective of all that exists in both nature and in grace. The entire creation must therefore be subordinated and subjected to the hallowing of God's name.

In order that this great and glorious objective might really and truly be achieved, the Lord Jesus gives five specific petitions to follow the first, all of which have as their common objective to lead believers to look entirely outside of themselves and, in all things, to be subject to God their heavenly Father, as being the true and only means unto the hallowing and magnification of His name. He begins by teaching them, in the second petition, that, in order to hallow the name of God their heavenly Father, they must fully deny all dominion of self and all proprietary claims. They must surrender themselves fully to God as their lawful king and Lord, whose kingdom must incrementally and fully come in and upon them, and the domain of which must increasingly be expanded regarding them and others.

The Savior then proceeds, in the third petition, to teach them that, in order to hallow the name of their God and heavenly Father, they must also deny their own wills and inclinations; that is, they are to submit themselves fully and wholeheartedly to the will of God their king, and to be united fully with that will, desiring nothing other than that God's will be done in earth as it is done in heaven.

In light of all this, the Savior then proceeds, in the fourth petition, to set before His believing people how, in order that the name of their God and heavenly Father might be hallowed and magnified, they must, as to their temporal lives and existence, fully turn away from their own strength, wisdom, and industry—that is, from any goodness, strength, sufficiency, and ability of the creature. Hereby, He teaches them that they must also be fully subject to God as their Father and king, so that they might be fully dependent upon His supremely wise, omnipotent, and gracious providence, putting all their trust exclusively in that providence alone. By faith, they must thus look always to Him, to be fed daily by His gracious and omnipotent hand, so that, as to this earthly life, they may be sustained to the praise and glory of His great name. In order that this might be achieved, the Lord Jesus commands His believing people to pray accordingly and continually, "Our Father which art in heaven, give us as Thy children and Thy believing subjects this day *our daily bread.*"

In order that, by the power and with the assistance of the Holy Spirit, we might expound this petition in greater detail today, we must consider:

1. the object of this petition, being the daily bread of believers or the essentials that pertain to daily life; and

2. the petition and desire of believers that God, as their Father and king in heaven, would give them this bread *today.*

Regarding the first, the object of this petition, Jesus commands His believing people to pray for their *daily bread*, and thus mention is here made of:

1. *bread*, which is more specifically described as

2. the *daily* bread of God's children.

We all know what bread is in the physical sense of the word, namely, that which, by way of God's good providence, we daily eat for our sustenance. However, it is rather essential to know what we must here understand by *this* bread. There are those who view this figuratively, and thus as a reference to the spiritual need of the soul, whereas others consider it as referring to the physical needs of the body only, and still others view it as a reference to both.

As far as we are concerned, let everyone say and write what he believes to be the case without being in bondage to anyone else. However, it is our conviction that we must interpret the word *bread* in the literal sense, and thus as referring exclusively to all our physical needs. We deem it unnecessary to support this exegesis with many arguments, given that the matter is very transparent and straightforward, for one cannot advance a compelling reason for deviating from the essential meaning of the word *bread* or else one would have to interpret this word simultaneously in a literal and a figurative sense. We have examined some of the arguments that others have advanced, but we have not found any of them to be in the least satisfactory whatsoever.

Therefore, we shall consider this truth in utmost simplicity, just as the entire Word of God is characterized by utmost simplicity when it is understood spiritually. There is very little reason to think, in this petition, of any spiritual needs of the soul, for all spiritual needs are sufficiently addressed in the other five petitions. When God's name is hallowed; when His kingdom increasingly expands in and upon the soul; when a soul is continually made one with God's will; when a soul continually receives a gracious pardon of her sins in Christ's blood, along with all the glorious fruits that ensue from this; and when God continually preserves and protects the soul in regard to all her enemies—delivering her from sin and any bondage to Satan, cleansing her from all that is evil—and thus when the soul of a believer continually receives and enjoys all these things from the Lord God, I cannot see what other spiritual need remains for a soul to ask of God. I am of the opinion that all spiritual needs of believers are fully addressed in the contents of the other five petitions, and it thus follows that this fourth petition must be interpreted, simply and exclusively, as pertaining to the needs of the body.

There are people who believe and teach that one may not ask God for the provision of any physical needs. They consider such matters to be too insignificant to be concerned about, positing that one should be concerned only about God's kingdom and the seeking of His righteousness, arguing that all temporal matters shall then be added unto us (Matt. 6:33). As far as we are concerned, however, we are certain that a Christian who is truly made acquainted with his absolute and physical dependency upon the Lord and with his own radical inadequacy and insufficiency as to the soul and the body holds an entirely different view. He understands that he must not petition the Lord only regarding his spiritual needs, but also regarding his physical needs, and, by faith, continually look to Him regarding these needs, as Agur did, when he prayed to God: "Give me neither poverty nor riches; feed me with food convenient for me" (Prov. 30:8b). The instructor therefore teaches in Question 118 that a Christian must pray to God for all his physical needs, praying that He would "provide us with all things necessary for the body."

Having laid the foundation for our exposition, we shall proceed to consider the matter itself. As we have stated, *bread* here signifies all that pertains to our physical needs, that is, both food and shelter. The apostle teaches that our entire physical need consists of these two components, saying, "Having food and raiment let us be therewith content" (1 Tim. 6:8). In the Holy Scriptures, the word *bread* is frequently used to signify all manner of physical food and drink. For instance, we read regarding Jacob, "Then Jacob offered sacrifice upon the mount, and called his brethren to eat bread: and they did eat bread, and tarried all night in the mount" (Gen. 31:54). The word bread is also used in the Holy Scriptures to signify both food and shelter. We observe this in the aforementioned prayer of Agur, in which he supplicated, "Feed me with food convenient for me." In Genesis 3:19, God said to Adam, "In the sweat of thy face shalt thou eat bread" (Gen. 3:19a); that is, "You will thus sustain your life."

There are several reasons why, here and frequently throughout the Word of God, the temporal needs of the body are designated as bread:

1. Bread is the most essential of all foods, and we can by no means do without it.

2. Bread is also the most delightful, nutritious, and delectable of all foods, a food one never abhors when healthy—as is also true of all other foods one eats regularly.

3. If it were necessary, one could readily live on bread alone, and thus without any other food.

We are thus taught here that we must be satisfied with the most basic of food and drink, and, if necessary, with bread alone, for our physical being requires nothing else.

This bread is more specifically referred to as *our* bread, and also as our *daily* bread.

Regarding the first, the supplicants in this Lord's Prayer are the true believing children and subjects of God in Christ, who have a rightful claim to call God their Father and their king. As prescribed by the Savior, they refer to their temporal needs and wants as *their* bread. They do so:

1. As children of God, who, in Christ their Lord, have an incontrovertible and legitimate claim upon the physical necessities that the Lord bestows upon them. Even though man, because of sin, has utterly lost all claims to God's creation, and though the earth has been justly subjected to a curse for man's

sake, believers, in and through the Lord Jesus Christ, their head and king, have again, in a way of free and sovereign grace, fully reacquired their forfeited claim upon all of God's creation.

2. To express not only that they need this bread to nourish and sustain their temporal lives, but also that they desire to acquire this bread in any lawful way, by using the legitimate means afforded them by the good providence of God. Bread is *our* bread only when it pleases God to bestow it upon us by either the labor of our hands, our profession, or by other lawful means and ways. Paul admonishes believers: "We command and exhort by our Lord Jesus Christ, that with quietness they work, and eat their own bread" (2 Thess. 3:12).

Thus, the Savior teaches His believing people in this petition that they not only must labor diligently to secure their temporal provision, but that they must also seek to secure this by the use of lawful ways and means, so that they may rightfully call it *their* bread—bread they have received in a lawful way from the good hand of their heavenly Father.

3. Because this is not, however, all that is comprehended in this petition, for the Lord Jesus, in instructing His believing people to pray for *their* or for *our* bread, by using a plural pronoun, is teaching them also that regarding the temporal provision for the body, there is a mutual and reciprocal communion of saints. This bread must therefore be viewed as bread that is common to all, and, when necessity requires it, believers must willingly, as an expression of Christian love, share this bread with others. The rich are to sustain the poor from their abundance.

To communicate all this, the Savior teaches His believing people that, in their prayers, they are to refer to their temporal needs as *our* bread.

It is also God's will that we refer to this bread as our *daily* bread. The Greek word means as much as that which is *essential*, and thus that which pertains to the essential needs of our being and existence. God gives His believing children their *essential* bread; that is, He gives them such temporal provision as they need to sustain their temporal existence and provision. Since they are daily in need of being sustained in their natural disposition by their heavenly Father, our translators have rendered this petition as, "Give us this day our *daily* bread."

It is the Savior's will that His believing people be concerned only about securing the necessities of life to the extent that they are in need to be sustained daily in their temporal lives. They should by no means desire an abundance of such temporal goods as would be superfluous for them.

Having concluded our remarks regarding the exposition of the object of this petition, we proceed to consider the petition itself. The Savior teaches His disciples the necessity to ask their heavenly Father that He would daily *give* them bread, and that He would do so *this day*, for the petition reads, "*Give* us *this day* our *daily* bread." We will follow the precious exposition of the instructor, in which he sets before us:

1. the contents of this petition; and

2. the object of this petition.

Regarding the contents of this petition, the instructor posits that it consists in the prayer that God will "provide us [His believing children] with all things necessary for the body"; that is, that He, by His supremely wise, omnipotent, and gracious providence, might daily be pleased to provide them with the necessary food and shelter so that, as to their temporal lives, they might live as long as it pleases Him to sustain them for the hallowing of His great name.

The Lord achieves the giving of this daily bread, or providing them "with all things necessary for the body," when He:

1. Continually causes the earth to bring forth that which His children need physically—an earth that, so to speak, generates and brings forth what they need.

2. Blesses His children in their daily calling or in the labor of their hands, so that they receive of Him that which they need for the daily sustenance of their bodies; or, in His gracious providence, is pleased to grant these blessings to them by other legitimate ways and means, so that they lack nothing, but find themselves continually cared for as to all the needs of their bodies.

3. Grants His children both health and hearts that enable them to make use of His temporal blessings, sustaining them daily in terms of this temporal life.

By His gracious providence, the Lord does and works all things at all times for all the physical needs of His children by giving them their daily bread, doing so not in wrath, as He does toward ungodly and unconverted men, when "he [makes] his sun to rise on the evil and on the good" (Matt. 5:45). He gives His children their daily bread and supplies all their physical needs as an act of His precious love and His fatherly favor and loving-kindness. Thus, "a little that a righteous man hath is better than the riches of many wicked" (Ps. 37:16). For this, believers pray to their heavenly Father, beseeching Him that

He, as a manifestation of His love and fatherly favor, would give their daily life's provision or their daily bread, and that, by His gracious providence, He would supply them with their daily provision. They are to do so as their Savior instructs them, saying, "Give us *this day*," or, as it is written in the Gospel of Luke, "Give us *day by day* our daily bread" (Luke 11:3).

It is the Savior's will that believers pray each day to God their heavenly Father for the provision of their daily needs, teaching them that:

1. They are in need of that daily provision, and completely dependent upon God their heavenly Father for all their temporal needs, so that without Him and His gracious providence, they cannot exist a single day—yes, not even a single moment. They are continually in need of receiving from Him their breath, their life, and all things, for "in him we live, and move, and have our being" (Acts 17:28).

2. Beyond each day, they are not to be concerned regarding the provision of their daily needs, but they should commit the provision of these needs into the hands of their heavenly Father, trusting in and relying by faith upon Him and His gracious providence, being fully assured in their hearts that "He that spared not his own Son, but delivered him up for us all…shall…with him also freely give us all things" (Rom. 8:32). The Lord Jesus therefore expressly admonishes His people: "Take therefore no thought for the morrow: for the morrow shall take thought for the things of itself. Sufficient unto the day is the evil thereof" (Matt. 6:34).

For these reasons, the Lord Jesus would have His believing people petition their heavenly Father to provide for their temporal needs, desiring nothing more and nothing else but what they need each day, praying, "Give us this day our daily bread."

Having considered the contents of this petition, we shall now consider the holy objective why believers must continually pray to their heavenly Father that He would be pleased "to provide us with all things necessary for the body," namely, that thereby they would "acknowledge [Him] to be the only fountain of all good." Jehovah God's great and sole objective in all His works is the full glorification of Himself by means of subjecting all men to Himself, thereby causing them to be entirely dependent upon Him in soul and body, in and through the mediator, Christ Jesus. This constitutes both the hallowing of God's name and the salvation of His believing children.

However, in desiring to provide daily for the temporal and physical needs of His children, and therefore desiring to be petitioned by them continually in true faith regarding these needs, God has no other objective but to magnify Himself and His name, and fully to humble His children and bring them to nothing in themselves. This is the true and proper focal point of all their blessedness. By the daily manifestation of God's preservation and care in temporal matters, believers are taught to acknowledge God their heavenly Father and king "to be the only fountain of all good." In so doing, they behold God as the sole being in whom everything has its origin and from whose unfathomable wisdom, power, and goodness every creature derives its existence. They view themselves and the creature as utterly needy and deficient to behold their heavenly Father in His fullness and all-sufficiency. They learn to depend fully upon God alone and to receive everything, even the very smallest crumb, out of His hand. They increasingly see and acknowledge "that neither our care nor industry, nor even [His] gifts, can profit us without [His] blessing."

The latter are the idols of men, and by nature men honor and trust them alone. They are completely focused upon themselves, trusting their own wisdom, care, diligence, labor, and a mere creature, and thereby setting aside God and His providence in all things. However, in proportion to their growing dependency upon God, believers in Christ are increasingly delivered from such accursed atheism, causing them to withdraw their trust from all their own care and diligence as being vain and broken reeds, acknowledging that, apart from God's blessing, none of these benefits them in the least. They learn to understand the thrust of Psalm 127:2: "It is vain for you to rise up early, to sit up late, to eat the bread of sorrows: for so he giveth his beloved sleep."[1] In this way, believers are taught increasingly to "withdraw [their] trust from all creatures, and to place it alone in [God]."

Oh, what a blessed reality it is when such is the case, for man then begins to manifest the restoration of all things. God is then acknowledged again as the one who is seated upon the throne—a position that sin and the accursed kingdom of self deny and from which they strive to remove Him. Thus, also in regard to temporal matters, God becomes the sole foundation of the confidence of His people, and believers are thereby taught passively to wait upon, rest in, and lean upon this God, for to wait upon Him is the sole and highest measure

---

1. The Dutch *Statenvertaling* reads, "Het is alzo, dat Hij het Zijn beminden als in de slaap geeft"; that is, "For so He giveth it to His beloved *as in their sleep*." The Dutch version is the more correct rendering of the original Hebrew.

of bliss. Oh, that the practical application of this truth would frequently be lively and efficacious in the hearts of all God's people, for "then had thy peace been as a river" (Isa. 48:18)! Yes, then it would be true for them what is written in Psalm 37:11: "The meek shall inherit the earth; and shall delight themselves in the abundance of peace."

Such is the glorious felicity that is encompassed in this petition for believers, with its proper use, and the supremely worthy Jehovah is thereby greatly magnified. It is therefore most proper that the savior, the Lord Jesus, included this petition in His prescribed prayer. It is His will that His believing people entirely depend upon God their heavenly Father in all temporal matters, and that they always prayerfully petition Him to fulfill all their physical needs—and so, by faith, they expect Him to do so. They are to pray for this daily, not only for themselves, but also for their fellow believers, thus praying for the entire flock and congregation of the Lord, beseeching the Lord, as their God, Father, and king, graciously to provide each day for their physical needs.

What can be more becoming than the continual and believing utterance of this petition to God our heavenly Father, for all that we physically need must proceed each day from His hands and by His gracious providence. Indeed, "the earth is the Lord's, and the fulness thereof" (1 Cor. 10:28b). All that the Lord bestows daily upon His children by His gracious providence, unto what they need for their sustenance, He gives to them purely as a manifestation of His loving-kindness and His sovereign grace for Christ's sake, for, in and of themselves, they are unworthy of one crumb of bread. Everything must be granted them by their God and Father purely as a manifestation of His grace in Christ. It is therefore so very becoming for them continually to petition this God for His benefits and blessings in and through Christ, to wait upon Him, and to trust in Him, depending fully on Him alone.

We have sufficiently expounded this precious and essential petition. Who among us is so blessed that he continually asks these things of the Lord God in spirit and in truth? This is true only for a genuine believer, who, to that end, continually receives from God the requisite measure of light, of the Spirit, and of grace.

You who are unconverted, void of grace, and unregenerate, as much as you may pray this petition outwardly with your mouths, you are nevertheless incapable of praying it as you ought. You are incapable of praying this petition with an upright heart and with full assurance of faith, for, in this manner alone, one ought to pray to God. You are ignorant of God as the only fountain and source of all that is good. You have never either seen or experienced your own emptiness and absolute deficiency and impotence, and your entire life is therefore, in regard to temporal matters, entirely ungodly and atheistic—a life without and apart from God. Therefore, instead of living daily, from day to day, by faith in dependence upon God as your gracious Father in Christ, and instead of trusting in and waiting upon Him for the provision of all your physical needs, and allowing yourself to be daily nourished by His gracious and omnipotent hand, you are leaning upon and trusting entirely and solely in yourself and other creatures. You are utterly leaning upon your own wisdom, carefulness, industry, contribution, and/or health, as well as the favor, power, and sufficiency of the creature. This is the source from which you expect all your physical needs to be met. You do this all day long, just as moles are always digging about in the earth, and in a shameful and irresponsible manner, you utterly neglect your precious souls and your salvation. This causes you to live a life of the vilest ingratitude and of murmuring against God for the provision of physical provisions and blessings, and thereby you abuse all of God's creation in a most abominable manner. Oh, how dreadfully wretched and miserable you are! If only you had eyes to see your frightful wretchedness and despicable atheism! May the Lord grant you self-knowledge, and may your eyes become a fountain of tears. May the Lord Himself, in Christ and by His Spirit, reveal Himself to your souls, and, in that divine light, may you have a true view of how utterly despicable and abominable you are. Oh, how you would then abhor yourself and repent in dust and ashes (Job 42:5–6)!

Children of God, you who are called to be saints, may it please the Lord, by the power of His Holy Spirit, truly to impress this exposition of His Word upon you. How the abominable nakedness of our souls and our damnable guilt before God would be abundantly evident and put us to shame and humble us! Truly, as to our daily practice, we often also live as atheists and have a carnal mindset that is void of the knowledge of God. If the Lord would give us the necessary light, what charges we would have to bring against God's people! We would have to charge them with nothing less than a world of unrighteousness, carnality, abominable atheism, and idolatry. As to our practice, when and where do we depend fully upon God our heavenly Father in Christ regarding the totality of our physical needs, which would be becoming for God's children? When and where do we continually trust Him and wait upon Him by faith? When and where do we permit ourselves to be fed, nourished, clothed, and sustained out of His omnipotent and gracious hand? When and where, in this regard, do we acknowledge God in all our ways, and when and where do we thus daily praise, magnify, and exalt Him accordingly, continually approaching Him in prayer as being the only fountain and source of all good things? When and where do we withdraw from our own diligence, power, wisdom, exertion, and all that a vain creature yields for us, and thus permit God to care for us each and every day?

Children of God, I am utterly compelled to direct you and myself to consider the animals as our teachers, for they behave in regard to all the aforementioned much better than we do. As to their animal nature, they wait upon God for their daily provision of food and for their sustenance: "The ox knoweth his owner, and the ass his master's crib" (Isa. 1:3a). Oh, what vile abominations are all the aforementioned, proceeding entirely out of the corrupt fountain of unbelief, atheism, carnality, and hellish darkness! Oh, that, by the light of the Holy Spirit, we would be truly convicted of this—that we would permit ourselves to be confronted, not only with our horrendous guilt, but also with our fatal impotence and misery, for we then would give ourselves to be directed to the complete all-sufficiency of the Lord Jesus, in whom alone all our righteousness and strength is to be found! Oh, that we would fully and continually surrender ourselves to Him in order rightly to be taught by Him that there is a divine providence that sustains and governs all things, and that every moment we live, move, and have our being in God!

May the Lord Jesus be pleased to work this continually in His people by the prevailing influence of His grace. Amen.

The Fifth Petition:
Forgive Us Our Debts

And forgive us our debts, as we forgive our debtors.
—MATTHEW 6:12

Question 126: Which is the fifth petition?

Answer: "And forgive us our debts as we forgive our debtors"; that is, be pleased for the sake of Christ's blood, not to impute to us poor sinners our transgressions, nor that depravity which always cleaves to us; even as we feel this evidence of Thy grace in us, that it is our firm resolution from the heart to forgive our neighbor.

Among all the truths that present themselves to us for consideration and contemplation, none are of such import and of such lofty mystery as those that pertain to human happiness and the very essence of that happiness. In antiquity, heathen philosophers agonized to obtain some proper notions and to grasp with their intellect in some measure wherein this essential truth consists. However, not one among them ever grasped this even remotely. How amazing it is that in our Christian nation, in which people speak, teach, and confess so much regarding the matter of salvation, nothing is so fully sealed and concealed for men as the knowledge of salvation! It cannot be expressed in words how little knowledge there is among so-called Christians regarding this matter, and how this foundational and seminal truth is obscured by a darkness that is both impenetrable and oppressive.

There are indeed multitudes of scribes in the church. You find them everywhere, teaching in the synagogues, from city to city and from village to village. And yet, the time has dawned, and we are living in that age wherein one must ask with the apostle: "Where is the wise? where is the scribe? where is the disputer of this world? hath not God made foolish the wisdom of this world?"

(1 Cor. 1:20). Here and there, you yet find someone who has been taught by God and who, as one crying in the wilderness, proclaims to us this mystery that the kingdom of God has come nigh unto us, and that "all flesh is as grass, and all the glory of man as the flower of grass" (1 Peter 1:24a).

King Jesus, the great expositor of Scripture, who is one among a thousand, is still preaching to a small audience—to a few who are blind, vile, and foolish, and who do not become known to a world in which they are invisible. This teacher of righteousness proclaims that salvation consists exclusively in the denial of self, in dying to and the crucifixion of self, and in living a life unto God alone. Because of sin, the elect sinner has departed from God and has become focused upon himself. However, when enabled by Christ, he turns away from self and returns to his spiritual equilibrium. He will be saved when he returns to the resting place in God that he had forsaken. This is the old and sound Reformed doctrine that is presently utterly unknown to many and to most of its proponents and confessors. This doctrine is clearly expressed in the first question of our Catechism, where we are taught that the totality of the comfort and salvation of a Christian consists exclusively in that he no longer belongs to himself, but with body and soul he is the property of Jesus Christ.

This doctrine of salvation is set before us and expounded in the perfectly prescribed prayer for all the children of light by Him who is the light of the world. The sole objective of this prayer is to subordinate everything to Jehovah God and to the hallowing of His name, while utterly stripping away from the children of wisdom all that is of self, in order to lead them, by and through Christ, to salvation and glory, as it is to be found in God. Therefore, in the first petition, wisdom teaches her children fully to forsake their own honor and glory, so that only God's name may be hallowed. In the second petition, she teaches her children to forsake all notions of self-government and dominion, so that the government might be God's alone and that His kingdom might come. In the third petition, she teaches her children to forsake their own wills, inclinations, and desires, so that only the will of God may prevail and be done "in earth as it is in heaven." In the fourth petition, the children of wisdom are taught, regarding their temporary existence and sustenance, utterly to forsake any reliance upon their own wisdom, strength, diligence, sufficiency, and suitability apart from God. The government is then again exclusively and fully upon God's shoulder, and He alone governs, directs, and sustains all things, giving with His hand to all His children each day their daily bread and whatever else is necessary for the sustenance of their lives.

Infinite wisdom then proceeds to aim for the further perfection of the salvation of her children, and therefore she teaches them also in this fifth petition that, in order to secure God's blessed favor and communion, they must utterly forsake all their own merits, worthiness, and righteousness. She teaches them that by faith, they must seek for their salvation exclusively in the sovereign grace, complete all-sufficiency, and perfect righteousness of God in Christ, supplicating and beseeching daily that they might be granted the gracious pardon, forgiveness, and absolution from all their guilt and iniquities, saying, according to the prescription of this prayer, "Our heavenly Father, forgive us our debts as we forgive our debtors."

To expound this petition in greater detail, as enabled by the Holy Spirit, we must consider:

1. the object(s) of this petition, and thus the debts or sins that God's believing children incur and commit daily toward their heavenly Father; and

2. the earnest petition of God's believing children to their heavenly Father, that He would forgive these debts, "as we forgive our debtors."

Regarding the first, mention is made of *debts*, that is, the debts of God's believing subjects and children. As to the literal meaning of the word *debt* or *debts*, it simply refers to any manner in which we may be justly and morally beholden to another. It may be a debt that pertains to advantage, to obedience, or to punishment. Paul uses this word in its broadest sense, saying, "Render therefore to all their dues: tribute to whom tribute is due; custom to whom custom; fear to whom fear; honour to whom honour" (Rom. 13:7).

In this petition, the designation debt or debts pertains to the sins that are committed against God's supreme majesty, for this is evident in the wording of this petition as we find it in Luke 11:4: "And forgive us our sins." The Holy Scriptures frequently refer to sins as such, for we read, "Our iniquities are increased over our head, and our trespass is grown up unto the heavens" (Ezra 9:6). When David confessed his sins before the Lord, he said, "O God, thou knowest my foolishness; and my sins[1] are not hid from thee" (Ps. 69:5).

---

1. *De Statenvertaling* reads, "Mijn *schulden* zijn voor U niet verborgen," that is, "My *debts* are not hid from thee."

Solomon declares in Proverbs 14:9a, "Fools make a mock at sin"[2]; that is, a fool covers up his crime or his sin (Ps. 68:21, etc.).

All sins and iniquities committed against God are referred to as debts for two reasons:

First, sin is a deviation from the obedience that man is indebted to render to God as his creator, supreme king, and lawgiver. Man, by virtue of his moral dependence upon God, is indebted to render unto Him the complete subjection and obedience required by Him in His law, even as a servant is indebted to render complete obedience to his master (Luke 17:10). Man is not at all to live unto himself, but is to deny himself fully. For soul and body, in all things, he must live unto the Lord. However, when, by a specific deed or the inclination of the heart, a man in some measure is guilty of deviant behavior, opposing God and His law, he commits sin and withholds from God the subjection and obedience to which he is indebted to Him. His sin renders him a debtor to God, for he fails to render to Him the obedience that he owes. By thus completely withholding such obedience, man becomes a debtor to God and owes Him a debt, irrespective of how poor or impotent he may be.

Second, since God is supremely holy and infinitely just, sins are also debts before God that render the sinner worthy of God's wrath, punishment, and vengeance. He must necessarily hate and oppose sin, which is an utter affront to His holiness, and He must prosecute and punish the sinner. If the Lord were not to do so, He would deny Himself and His holiness. We therefore conclude that sin renders the sinner utterly guilty and worthy of being subjected to God's wrath, curse, and punishment, so that God might be justified when He speaks, and be clear when He judges (Ps. 51:4).

For these reasons, sins are appropriately referred to as debts. Not only is this true for the sins of the ungodly and unbelievers, but also for the sins of believers. The sins of both believers and unbelievers are identical in nature and character in reference to God's holiness and justice, for both believers and unbelievers deviate from the norm of obedience toward God, and both are thus worthy of punishment and condemnation. Therefore, in this petition, the Lord Jesus teaches His believing people that they must acknowledge their sins as debts before God, by which they malign God's holiness and are justly worthy of His wrath, curse, and condemnation.

---

2. *De Statenvertaling* reads, "Elke dwaas zal de *schuld* verbloemen," that is, "Every fool will conceal his *debt*."

They who wish to make some essential distinction between the sins of believers and those of unbelievers are entirely being misled, for irrespective of the persons who commit sins, God's holiness and justice render all sin to be utterly worthy of punishment and condemnation. The debt incurred by sin is and remains a matter that demands condemnation (Rom. 5:18). If a believer is of a different mindset regarding his sins and transgressions, he is deluded by his flesh, and he is ignorant of God as to His infinite holiness and justice. For good reason, the Lord Jesus therefore requires of His believing people that they acknowledge their sins to be debts that are repeatedly incurred against God. The Lord Jesus therefore refers to sinners as debtors (Luke 13:4).[3]

Take note of the plural form, for this petition speaks of debts to express the great multitude of sins that are daily committed against God in thoughts, words, and deeds, for we are immediately guilty of sinning against the Lord in numerous ways. Even the holiest of men offend daily in many things (James 3:2), and "there is no man that sinneth not" (1 Kings 8:46). If ever God's children are exposed as to who they are, they are compelled to confess before the Lord with David: "Who can understand his errors? cleanse thou me from secret faults" (Ps. 19:12); that is, "Who can rightly know the magnitude and multitude of his sins?" We read in Job 9:3, "If he will contend with him, he cannot answer him one of a thousand." Granted, a blind world carnally insists that believers ought to be entirely without sin, and therefore is immediately offended by the weaknesses of God's people, and with hostile hearts, will malign and ridicule them accordingly. We should expect this from men of the world, for they are blind, and therefore, in all things, they render an entirely erroneous judgment.

However, they who have been called out of darkness are of a different mindset. They know that believers, as to their renewed and regenerate man, will never sin, since they are not under the law but under grace. They also know, however, that believers, according to their old and unregenerate man that yet remains in them, can do nothing except sin and utterly hate God and His holiness. Our instructor clearly maintained and defended this point in Question 114, saying, "Even the holiest men, while in this life, have only a small beginning of this obedience."

---

3. Again, the King James Version and the *Statenvertaling* differ. The KJV reads, "Think ye that they were *sinners* above all men that dwelt in Jerusalem?," whereas the *Statenvertaling* reads, "Meent gij, dat deze *schuldenaars* [debtors] zijn geweest, boven alle mensen, die in Jeruzalem wonen?"

It is an established fact, which both the nature of the matter and the Holy Scriptures abundantly teach, that believers, due to their indwelling corruption, sin daily against the Lord God, and, according to their flesh, they cannot do otherwise. It is the Lord's adorable way to permit this imperfection to remain in His children so that they would increasingly, by His grace and Spirit, die to themselves and live out of Christ.

It ought also to be observed that the Savior here teaches His believing people to pray for the forgiveness of *our* debts or *their* debts. Thereby, He would teach them to acknowledge sin before God as being their own debt that they themselves continually incur by their own sins that proceed from the fountain of their unregenerate self. Thus, their sins proceed from the evil treasury of their hearts, rendering themselves guilty and condemnable before God.

It is a great benefit to acknowledge our sins as our own debts, saying, "The reproach is ours, and the transgression proceeds from us." David prayed accordingly, saying: "Wash me thoroughly from mine iniquity, and cleanse me from my sin. For I acknowledge my transgressions: and my sin is ever before me" (Ps. 51:2–3).

The flesh is always inclined to exonerate itself and to cover its transgressions, shifting the blame to Satan, the world, and other external influences. Adam thus blamed his wife, and his wife, in turn, blamed the serpent. However, the soul does not prosper in the practice of such foolishness, as long as she remains in such a frame of mind. If God is going to forgive our debts, we first have to assume responsibility for them, and acknowledge and confess them to be our debts. What must take place is recorded in Jeremiah 4:18: "Thy way and thy doings have procured these things unto thee; this is thy wickedness, because it is bitter, because it reacheth unto thine heart." The soul must wholeheartedly cry out and confess, "These are *our* debts"; otherwise, the forgiveness of sins shall entirely elude them. God withholds Himself and says, "I will go and return to my place, till they acknowledge their offence, and seek my face" (Hos. 5:15). Therefore, the Lord Jesus appropriately stipulates that believers must confess their transgressions to their heavenly Father and refer to them as our debts.

Having sufficiently addressed and expounded the object(s) of this petition, we shall now proceed to consider in greater detail the petition itself. The Savior admonishes His believing people to petition their gracious heavenly Father that He would *forgive* their debts, saying, "*Forgive us* our debts...."

As has the instructor, we have already addressed the forgiveness of sins on two previous occasions: first, in Question 56, where the article of the Apostles' Creed pertaining to the forgiveness of sins is addressed, and a second time in Lord's Day 23, which deals with justification. We therefore shall not specifically deal with this subject again, but, rather, shall say only that which is essential for the exposition of this petition. In so doing, we shall follow the instructor, who expounds this petition as follows: "Be pleased for the sake of Christ's blood, not to impute to us poor sinners our transgressions, nor that depravity which always cleaves to us." In addressing the debts of believers, the instructor here refers not only to all their actual sins and transgressions, but also to the depravity that always cleaves to them. And rightfully so, for however much our eye may be focused on the outward sinful deeds that we continually commit, we shall not have a correct view of this matter as long as we do not dig deeper, down to the root and source from which all these sinful deeds proceed; that is, our flesh and our wicked, unholy, and abominable nature, which "is enmity against God: for it is not subject to the law of God, neither indeed can be" (Rom. 8:7).

Believers must arrive there if they are ever truly to confess their debt before God and come before Him as being utterly despicable, abominable, and unclean. Only when, by divine light, they are led to consider their unholy and wicked nature in the totality of its ungodliness, vileness, and abominableness— a nature that always cleaves to them and which is the source and root of all their sinful deeds—do they truly become cognizant of their debt. This causes them to cry out with Paul, "For I know that in me (that is, in my flesh,) dwelleth no good thing" (Rom. 7:18a), and they concur with the people of God, saying, "But we are all as an unclean thing, and all our righteousnesses are as filthy rags" (Isa. 64:6).

By this residual wickedness and its fruits, and by all the transgressions that proceed therefrom, believers are, of themselves, supremely guilty and condemnable before God. They are continually in need that God would graciously forgive and cleanse them from all their transgressions. The Lord Jesus therefore stipulates that believers must continually pray to God their heavenly Father by beseeching Him, "Forgive us our debts."

God forgives all the sins and debts of His believing children, as well as the innate wickedness and corruption that still cleaves to them and continually contaminates even their best and most holy activities. For the sake of the blood of Jesus Christ, according to the Catechism, He does "not...impute to us poor sinners, our transgressions, nor that depravity, which always cleaves to us." Instead, He graciously forgives all their transgressions and that deep depravity, and acquits them, viewing and accepting them as completely holy and perfect in His Son, Jesus Christ. He therefore always manifests His sweet favor, mercy, love, and grace, inwardly assuring them thereof by His Spirit, continually exclaiming to them in the promise of the gospel, "I, even I, am he that blotteth out thy transgressions for mine own sake, and will not remember thy sins" (Isa. 43:25).

God forgives the sins and debts of believers only "for the sake of Christ's blood." By His bloody sacrifice and His suffering, Christ fully merited and secured the forgiveness of their sins. Apart from that, God, in light of His infinite holiness and justice, never would be able to forgive even a single sin. Instead, by reason of our sins, He most certainly would have to punish and condemn us eternally by casting us into hell. However, once and for all, Christ made complete satisfaction on the cross for all His believing people. He suffered for all of their sins, died for them, and completely satisfied all the just claims of God's law. In so doing, Christ became the propitiation for their sins, and if they sin, they "have an advocate with the Father, Jesus Christ the righteous" (1 John 1:1–2). In Him, they "have redemption through his blood, the forgiveness of sins, according to the riches of his grace" (Eph. 1:7). The blood of Jesus Christ continually cleanses them from all sin (1 John 1:7).

Therefore, there is nothing so precious and priceless under heaven as the blood of the Lord Jesus. Oh, he who embraces and receives this precious blood by a true faith and receives the blood sprinkled upon his conscience by the Spirit of the Lord may go continually, by faith, to the open throne of God's grace to receive the forgiveness of all his sins by virtue of God's boundless mercy.

However, he who still rejects that blood of Christ and substitutes for it whatever else in which he either partially or fully puts his trust will never be able to secure from God the pardon of his sins, for God does not forgive our sins unless we come before Him by a true faith, setting and holding before Him the blood of Christ as the perfect atoning sacrifice for all our sins.

Someone may have good reason to ask what the disposition of God's children is when, by faith, they fervently make this petition for the forgiveness of their debts known to their heavenly Father. Oh, may the Lord so teach us such a lesson by His sovereign grace and by personal experience! As to the root and essence of the matter, their disposition then is thus:

First, by the uncovering illumination of the Holy Spirit, according to the Catechism, they see clearly that, in and of themselves, they are poor sinners.

They perceive how sinful and corrupt are their hearts, in which no good thing dwells. From every conceivable angle, they perceive sin and transgression in all that they do and fail to do. They perceive themselves as being guilty of manifold iniquities and failures against the Lord. Frequently, they specifically and primarily are confronted with several known sins, and, by divine illumination, they are led to behold them especially and be exercised therewith. It comes down to this, that they perceive nothing good in themselves. Instead, they experience that they are but poor sinners who are "ready to halt" (Ps. 38:17a) and who, apart from the continual supply of the Lord's grace, are incapable of doing any good in and of themselves.

Second, believers not only perceive and acknowledge their sins and debts as such, but, by the operation of the Holy Spirit, they are also genuinely perplexed and burdened by them. There is nothing that oppresses, grieves, and troubles them more than their sins. They are unbearable to them. They perceive how much God is dishonored, provoked, and offended by their sins, and what an abominable, harmful, and desperate evil sin is. Day and night, their souls are distressed and grieved about their sins. They groan under them, and they weep and are sorrowful regarding them. It is their heartfelt desire to be delivered and set free from their sins, but also that God would forgive and pardon them, and, by His Spirit, root out their sins and subdue them.

Third, regarding their sins, true believers will also find themselves utterly wretched and impotent before the Lord and utterly bereft of all wisdom, counsel, help, strength, and righteousness. They cannot possibly, even in the least degree, deliver themselves from them. This powerfully compels them to look outside of themselves unto the Lord Jesus. They lift up their eyes unto Him as their only deliverer and savior. By the promises of the gospel, as they are illuminated by the Holy Spirit, they behold Him as that "fountain opened to the house of David and to the inhabitants of Jerusalem for sin and for uncleanness" (Zech. 13:1). They behold His all-sufficiency, the merits of His blood and passion, and His willingness, and they sincerely hunger and thirst for the Lord Jesus. By faith, they take hold of Him and His blood. They embrace Him as their only and all-sufficient surety and savior.

Fourth, trusting in Him and His merits, they go, by faith, to the Father as *their* Father and gracious God, who has promised them the forgiveness of all their sins by His grace and for the sake of the merits and the blood of Christ. They plead upon His mercy, upon His gracious promises, and upon the blood of His Son. They present unto Him all these things, and they supplicate and beseech Him to pardon their sins on that basis, that they may feel the comfort and assurance thereof within their hearts. They steadfastly cling to the Lord and to His promises, and do not desist, but by renewal, they come and continually persevere in doing so. They seek not merely for the forgiveness of their sins, for which they are continually and consistently in need, but they also seek all that which is fostered by and issues forth from such forgiveness, causing them increasingly to become partakers of all those blessed benefits.

They thus continually pray to the Lord their God and heavenly Father that He would grant them:

1. the removal and blotting out of all their transgressions and wickedness by way of the blood of Christ;

2. deliverance from the accompanying guilt and punishment;

3. the revelation of His reconciled and friendly countenance to the soul so that she may thereby be refreshed, strengthened, and revived; and

4. not only a disposition of heart that issues forth from being reconciled with God, so that they may walk with the Lord in childlike fear, but also a disposition of heart to fear, love, cleave to, trust in, and delight themselves in Him, having free access to Him in Christ and tasting with inner joy within their souls the blessed fellowship and embrace of the Father.

Beloved, it is thus the will of the Lord Jesus that His believing people continually pray for such forgiveness of their debts, for:

1. This is the source and fountain of all their spiritual strength and life. The essence of the life of believers consists exclusively in their continual walk and fellowship, by faith, with God in Christ, as well as in the continual enjoyment of His grace in and through Christ. But how does a believer exercise continual fellowship with God in Christ, and how does he continually receive, taste, and relish His love and grace? Does not this transpire continually by the believer approaching unto Him in and through Christ as a guilty, ungodly, condemnable, poor, destitute, and impotent sinner, taking refuge to His sovereign grace in Christ's blood, petitioning Him, and thereupon continually receiving renewed mercy and a fresh pardon of guilt? He who claims to have fellowship with God in a way other than this must see to it that he is not deceiving himself!

2. Being continually guilty of new transgressions, they continually incur new debts, and therefore they are continually in need of the renewed forgiveness

of these incurred debts by exercising faith in the blood of Christ. It is indeed true that when God initially justifies the believer, He completely forgives all his sins committed until the very moment of the exercise of his faith, and the forgiveness of all his future sins is already secure for him in the hands of Christ. However, this by no means takes away from the fact that believers, in order to secure from God the Father the forgiveness of their newly incurred debt, must go continually to the Father, in and through Christ the mediator, as poor, utterly guilty, and condemnable sinners, beseeching Him repeatedly, as their gracious God and Father, to grant them this forgiveness, receiving it in the blood of Christ and applied to their souls by the Holy Spirit.

Therefore, as to the essence of the matter, this forgiveness of newly incurred debt must occur as repeatedly and in the same fashion as it did in their initial justification. However, the difference is that this forgiveness is now being desired from a gracious Father and faithful covenant God to whom the soul has already been united. Thus, this forgiveness is desired only in regard to newly incurred debt.

A Christian must understand this well, for his entire exercise of communing and walking with God by faith is contingent upon it. To judge and to believe otherwise is very dangerous and hazardous.

Having thus far expounded for you the content of this petition, it now remains to consider briefly its appendix, consisting of the words, "as we forgive our debtors." What it means for believers to forgive their debts is best known experientially, for this is a holy disposition that Christ, by His Spirit and by grace, must continually work in the hearts of His believing people. Believers greatly cherish such a disposition, for their souls always prosper when they perceive such a disposition within themselves, particularly when they readily and wholeheartedly forgive the transgressions of their debtors, by whom they, in any way, may have been offended and mistreated—and when they may even love their enemies and wholeheartedly bless them.

Such are not fruits from our own field, for out of the evil treasure of our hearts come forth evil matters. To treat our enemies well and to forgive our debtors are sweet and lovely waters that cannot proceed from any fountain but that of divine love, which the Holy Spirit has shed abroad in the hearts of believers. Oh, when the soul is brought near to the sun of righteousness and when the warm rays of that sun thaw and ignite the ice-cold heart, our enmity and hostility toward our neighbor melt, and we then are able to forgive our debtors, even "until seventy times seven" (Matt. 18:22) times.

The Savior adds the forgiving of our debtors to this petition with the sole objective of teaching His people that if their prayer to their heavenly Father for the forgiveness of their debts and wickedness is to be proper and to be heard, it must always be accompanied by a disposition of the soul that is willing and inclined to forgive their debtors (Matt. 4:14–15; 18:21–22; Mark 11:25–26; Luke 17:3–4; Col. 3:12–13). The reason for this is rooted in the fact that without such a disposition, it is impossible for us to pray for the forgiveness of our sins. A heartfelt prayer unto God for the forgiveness of our debts must be offered in faith. When such a prayer is offered in faith, the soul, by virtue of her guilt, is humbled before the Lord. She falls prostrate before Him and, as a poor and naked sinner, she looks to the blood of Christ. She takes hold of that blood and relies on it as an ungodly and impotent sinner, and with that blood, she appears before God. However, when this is indeed done in truth, then this exercise of faith brings Christ, His love, and His grace into the heart, and that engenders a disposition in the soul that compels her to love and to render her willing to love her enemies and to forgive her debtors.

Before realizing it, the soul has been stirred up and inclined to do so, and there is a disposition of love in the heart before one engages in the act. Being illuminated by the Lord, a spiritual reader understands plainly how inseparably these two matters are conjoined: to ask the Lord God for the forgiveness of our debts, and to forgive our debtors. One is an exercise of faith, whereas the other pertains to sanctification. These are twin graces that may never be separated from one another—not even for a moment. Thus also in this petition, the wisdom of God properly joins them together, as is done in many other passages of the Holy Scriptures.

We have thus sufficiently expounded this petition, which is so pregnant with matter. May the Lord grant light and grace to His people to examine themselves in light of this petition. If the unconverted would do so, they would plainly be exposed as never having prayed this prayer in truth. In fact, they are incapable of truly praying it, however often they may have done so with their outward lips, for this prayer cannot possibly be prayed in truth as long as one lives apart from Christ. Such praying for the forgiveness of sins is then sacrilegious and a grievous mocking of God, for all who are unconverted and who are thus without Christ:

1. Do not rightly know their sins and guilt, however much they may speak of them, for they are devoid of the Spirit of conviction.

2. Have no genuine perception of their sins and guilt. They are not bowed down under it as a burden too heavy to bear.

3. Have no sincere desire to have their sins forgiven by God. Instead, they allow their guilt to be an open entry in God's book and have no true concern regarding this.

4. Are ignorant of their destitute state and impotence. They see neither the necessity nor the preciousness of the atoning blood of Christ. They neither long for nor take refuge to this blood, and they neither embrace it nor come before the Father with it in order that He might blot out their sins.

5. Do not know what it means to forgive their debtors, for they retain their anger and their vindictiveness toward one another, and dwell together, being consumed by inward hatred, bitterness, and hostility. They cannot behave themselves in any other way, for the love of God has not been shed abroad in their hearts by the Holy Spirit. Oh, how wretched are such men! May God grant that they will repent of their wickedness and unrighteousness, so that they will not die in their sins and perish eternally.

As for God's children, a full fountain of salvation is here opened for them against all sin and uncleanness, a fountain in which you and I must be washed daily. Christ here directs you, as your mediator and king, to the way in which you may be cleansed, and obligates you to take refuge continually to the throne of your heavenly Father and to His grace. There you will always find full forgiveness for your daily guilt. You need only desire and embrace it without money and without price. Your heavenly Father is continually waiting to be gracious to you.

May the Lord Jesus continually instruct you to make use of this great and glorious privilege. Oh, that you would continually turn to Him as blind and impotent in yourself, so that, by His own light, He would continually open and discover to you the way in which your daily debts can be forgiven! May you thus acquaint yourself always to be near to Christ and allow Him to be your guide to lead you to this fountain of living waters. May the Lord continually, by His grace, enable His poor and needy people to do so, and may He cause them to be much inclined toward securing the daily pardon and forgiveness of their sins. To this end, may the Lord cause His poor and needy people to wait for Him and His salvation. Amen, may it be so.

The Sixth Petition and the
Conclusion of the Lord's Prayer

*And lead us not into temptation, but deliver us from evil: for thine is the
kingdom, and the power, and the glory, for ever. Amen.*
—MATTHEW 6:13

Question 127: Which is the sixth petition?

Answer: "And lead us not into temptation, but deliver us from evil"; that is, since
we are so weak in ourselves that we cannot stand a moment; and besides this,
since our mortal enemies, the devil, the world, and our own flesh, cease not to
assault us, do Thou therefore preserve and strengthen us by the power of Thy
Holy Spirit, that we may not be overcome in this spiritual warfare, but constantly
and strenuously may resist our foes till at last we obtain a complete victory.

Question 128: How dost thou conclude thy prayer?

Answer: "For Thine is the kingdom, and the power, and the glory, for ever";
that is, all these we ask of Thee, because Thou, being our King and almighty, art
willing and able to give us all good; and all this we pray for, that thereby not we,
but Thy holy name, may be glorified for ever.

Question 129: What doth the word "Amen" signify?

Answer: "Amen" signifies it shall truly and certainly be, for my prayer is more
assuredly heard of God than I feel in my heart that I desire these things of Him.

Proverbs 18:10 records that "the name of the LORD is a strong tower: the righteous runneth into it, and is safe."

In these words, the wise king wishes to depict for us the extraordinary
and omnipotent security, protection, and care that God manifests toward His

people and His children. In all their trials and perplexities, they take refuge to Him and His mighty name, seeking His protection and assistance in dealing with their spiritual and physical enemies. By the Lord's prevenient grace, the truth of this matter will be addressed further in the exposition and examination of this sixth and final petition of the prescribed prayer that Christ Jesus has given to His believing people—a prayer in which they are directed and admonished to address all their supplications and petitions to their heavenly Father.

The five petitions that have already been expounded have taught us clearly and sufficiently that the all-encompassing objective of the Savior in His prescriptive prayer is to lead His believing people out of themselves to full self-denial, submission, and subjection to God their heavenly Father, as being the only way unto their salvation. Oh, if only we truly have learned something of this!

This sixth and last petition has the same objective, namely, to teach God's believing children and subjects utterly to forsake all their own power, strength, and protection, leading them to acknowledge their absolute deficiency and impotence toward all that is good. They are thus taught that they are so weak and miserable that they cannot sustain themselves for even a moment, but are entirely dependent upon being immediately sustained, supported, preserved, protected, and delivered by God, their gracious Father and king in heaven. Their eyes, at all times, must be lifted up toward Him, and to Him must be their continual supplication: "Oh, heavenly Father, lead us not into temptation, but deliver us from evil." Thereby, they surrender themselves fully to the power of God unto that "salvation ready to be revealed" (1 Peter 1:5).

To consider in some detail the Savior's last petition with the conclusion of the entire prayer, and thereby conclude the exposition of our Heidelberg Catechism, may the Lord send help from His sanctuary and enlighten us with the necessary illumination by the Holy Spirit. May we thereby receive insight into the truth, and, by the obedience and power thereof, be sanctified through the Lord Jesus Christ. Amen.

There are two matters that need to be considered and reflected upon:

1. the sixth or last petition, "Lead us not into temptation, but deliver us from evil"; and

2. the conclusion of this petition with the conclusion of the entire prayer: "for thine is the kingdom, and the power, and the glory, for ever."

Regarding the sixth petition, we wish to consider:

1. the language of the petition; and
2. the matter expressed therein as expounded by our Christian instructor.

In the verbal formulation of this petition, two matters come to the fore:

1. a prayer that evil will be kept from us, namely, "Lead us not into temptation"; and
2. a petition for the bestowal of that which is good, namely, "but deliver us from evil."

The Savior teaches His believing people to ask their heavenly Father to guard them against evil by beseeching Him that He would not lead them into temptation. Mention is here made of *temptations*, and the believing children of God must pray to their heavenly Father, beseeching Him that He would not lead them into these temptations.

The word *tempt* simply refers to any manner in which someone is put to the test in order thereby to expose his condition and conduct either to himself or to others. It is, at times, the Lord's way to initiate such trials or temptations toward His people in order to manifest either their faith or what is to be found in them, so that they and others may see what they are. Such temptations and trials that the Lord initiates toward His children and the objects of His favor by no means have the evil objective of causing them to fall away from their faith and to be estranged from the Lord. God never tempts anyone with an evil intent, for "far be it from God, that he should do wickedness; and from the Almighty, that he should commit iniquity" (Job 34:10). He loves His children as a gracious Father, and, in all things, He aims for their well-being and their salvation.

Therefore, when God occasionally and in some measure tempts and tries His children, His objective in doing so is entirely to their benefit, so that their faith and salvation may be promoted. He aims to instruct them and to make wisdom known to them in secret places, as well as to make known to others their faith, hope, love, gifts, and graces. God formerly tempted His servant Abraham by commanding him to sacrifice his only son, Isaac, in whom his seed was to be called (Genesis 22). This temptation was initiated not to cause Abraham to sin and to abandon his faith, but with the objective to strengthen him in his faith, and thereby to display his faith and obedience as an example for subsequent generations—even until today. The Lord still customarily tempts His children at times, be it by means of temporal setbacks and trials or by means of spiritual tribulations, when, for a season, He withdraws the influences of His Spirit and

His grace. In so doing, He leaves them in a greater measure over to themselves, so that, at times, they consequently fall into great sins and are overcome by the power of indwelling sin.

The Lord is pleased, at times, to tempt His dearest children so that they might be increasingly confronted with their impotence and, consequently, might increasingly learn to live by faith and by grace. Such temptations of the Lord are not evil, but are good. However painful they may prove to be for flesh and blood, they nevertheless are most beneficial for the soul, which thereby is purified and refined. By faith, believers must therefore patiently submit themselves to all such temptations proceeding from their God and heavenly Father. They are to do so in silence, trusting in the promises of the Lord, who, at His appointed time, causes all such temptations to culminate in a blessed and glorious outcome.

The apostle James therefore admonishes God's people, saying: "My brethren, count it all joy when ye fall into divers temptations; knowing this, that the trying of your faith worketh patience.... Blessed is the man that endureth temptation: for when he is tried, he shall receive the crown of life, which the Lord hath promised to them that love him" (James 1:2–3, 12).

Far be it from us to suggest that God's children should pray to be exempted from such temptations as being harmful and disadvantageous. We find the contrary to be true with David, the man of God. He prayed for such trials, saying, "Examine me, O LORD, and prove me; try my reins and my heart" (Ps. 26:2), doing so that his inner sincerity might become manifest. Job thanked God for such trials, saying: "What is man, that thou shouldest magnify him? and that thou shouldest set thine heart upon him? And that thou shouldest visit him every morning, and try him every moment?" (Job. 7:17–18).

This petition, "Lead us not into temptation," is obviously not focused upon such temptations by which the Lord, at times, is pleased to tempt His children for beneficial purposes. Rather, the temptations that the Savior here instructs His believing people to pray against are of an entirely different nature and proceed from an entirely different source. Such temptations are instigated by Satan, the great enemy of God and His people, as well as by their own sinful and corrupt flesh, in which "dwelleth no good thing" (Rom. 7:18).

Such evil and wicked temptations are not initiated for the benefit of believers, but, rather, to harm and to injure them. Satan, the tempter, thereby endeavors to disengage their faith and cause them to sin against the Lord. Satan is and remains the mortal and implacable enemy of God and of all believers, who cannot bear it that believers live a life of intimate fellowship and friendship with God. He therefore ceaselessly does everything in his power to rob them of that friendship and to subject them to himself by sin. Satan cannot bear it that they who at one time were his subjects are now subjects of God, whom he deems to be his archenemy. He is therefore always engaged in seeking to disrupt God's kingdom and to inflict upon it all manner of harm and disadvantage. Ceaselessly he endeavors to trap God's children in his devious snares, that he might tempt them to commit evil. He seeks to oppose their salvation in every conceivable way, and "as a roaring lion, walketh about, seeking whom he may devour" (1 Peter 5:8). Consequently, Paul emphatically calls Satan the tempter when he expresses his fear to the believers of Thessalonica, saying, "Lest by some means the tempter have tempted you, and our labour be in vain" (1 Thess. 3:5). Consider also Matthew 4:3, where we read, "And when the tempter came to him, he said, If thou be the Son of God, command that these stones be made bread."

Satan is a tempter who is: (1) old, (2) wicked, (3) mighty, (4) subtle, (5) tireless and diligent, (6) bold and shameless, and (7) mortally effective, seeking the perdition of all men. Since Satan is an *old* tempter, he is referred to as "that old serpent" (Rev. 12:9). In this petition, he is referred to as an *evil* or *wicked* tempter (Matt. 13:19), and in 1 John 2:13, we read, "Ye have overcome the wicked one." He is also a *mighty* tempter, for we read: "Shall the prey be taken from the mighty, or the lawful captive delivered? But thus saith the LORD, Even the captives of the mighty shall be taken away" (Isa. 49:24–25a). He is also referred to as the *strong man* (Matt. 12:29) and as the *strong man armed* (Luke 11:21). Since he is a *subtle* tempter, he is referred to as a *serpent*, the most subtle of all animals (Gen. 3:1). We even read that "Satan himself is transformed into an angel of light" (2 Cor. 11:14). The apostle speaks of the "wiles of the devil" (Eph. 6:11). Satan is also a *tireless and diligent* tempter, who goes about "as a roaring lion...seeking whom he may devour" (1 Peter 5:8). He is always *wakeful*, "seeking rest, and findeth none" (Matt. 12:43). He is a tempter who is "going to and fro in the earth, and...walking up and down in it" (Job 2:2). He is a *bold and shameless* tempter, who even had the audacity to tempt the Savior (Matthew 4). He dares to come before God as the "accuser of our brethren... which accused them before our God day and night" (Rev. 12:10). He is a *mortal* tempter, for "he was a murderer from the beginning" (John 8:44), seeking to devour all as a roaring lion (1 Peter 5:8). He is also a venomous *serpent*, who aims to inflict mortal wounds, even though he may deceitfully flatter men by saying, "Ye shall not surely die" (Gen. 3:4b).

From the very beginning, Satan has engaged himself as such a tempter toward and against God's kingdom. It is well known how he deceived our first parents, Adam and Eve, and tempted them to sin. With God's permission, Satan also sought, in a most dreadful manner, to tempt Job, that pious man of God, whereby Job would renounce his sincerity (Job 2:6–7). Likewise, Satan tempted David, whom he powerfully provoked to number the people of Israel, contrary to God's command (1 Chron. 21:1), and in Matthew 4, we read that he tempted the Savior. He sought to sift Peter as wheat, and he would have succeeded entirely in causing Peter to fall and in leading him to perdition if the Lord Jesus had not prayed for him, that his faith would not fail (Luke 22:31). He also tempted the apostle Paul (2 Cor. 12:7), even as he tempts all believers (1 Thess. 3:5; Eph. 6:16).

In like manner, Satan still deals with God's children, and thus with believers, for he is and remains unchanged as to his nature. Since he is the prince of darkness, he is naturally inclined to hate the light, and with all his hellish might, he will always oppose the light. This mighty enemy neither rests nor slumbers, but is always wakeful, day and night. From his hidden corners and hiding places, he is always ready to fire his poisonous arrows at God's people to wound and to harm their souls. If it were not that the Shepherd of Israel ceaselessly watches over them, at any given moment they would be devoured as helpless sheep by this hellish evening wolf, and there would be no escape for them.

The limited availability of time will not permit us to deal extensively with the multifaceted nature of Satan's temptations. Any who wish to be informed more extensively regarding this weighty matter, should seek to secure for themselves a copy of the excellent treatise of the great divine John Owen on temptation.[1] They should also read that chapter in à Brakel's work in which he addresses the temptations of Satan.[2] With God's blessing, you will greatly benefit from it.

We shall say here only that the temptations of Satan are twofold in nature: immediate or mediate. His *immediate* temptations are such as when he personally, assuming the form of either a man or an animal, or by manifesting himself in other special or unique ways to our eyes and to our senses, initiates his

---

1. John Owen, *Overcoming Sin and Temptation*, ed. Kelly M. Kapic and Justin Taylor (Wheaton, Ill.: Crossway, 2006).

2. Wilhelmus à Brakel, *The Christian's Reasonable Service*, trans. Bartel Elshout, ed. Joel R. Beeke (Grand Rapids: Reformation Heritage Books, 1999), 4:235–50.

temptations as he did toward our first parents in Paradise and toward the Savior in the wilderness, when he brought Him to the roof of the temple. Whether Satan presently still initiates such temptations is a question we will leave unanswered, being satisfied with the understanding that he is able to do what he has done before if the Lord were to permit him to do so.

However, Satan's common temptations are *mediate* temptations, which he initiates and executes toward and against God's children by means of the world and their own evil and sinful flesh that continues to dwell in them. Satan always makes use of these two great enemies of the salvation of believers by attacking and assaulting them in manifold ways, by plaguing them, and by tempting them to commit sin. By utilizing these two strong enemies, he never gives them a moment's rest, but he always is engaged, with highly sophisticated subtlety, to draw them away from their God and to rob them of their salvation. Therefore, God's children—by day and night, and thus always—must be on guard, be watchful, and strengthen themselves in the Lord, so that, by means of the world and their own flesh, Satan does not gain the advantage over them, "for we are not ignorant of his devices" (2 Cor. 2:11).

From the world, they cannot expect anything good, for it lies entirely in wickedness, and Satan is its prince and ruler. Therefore, the more they separate themselves from the world, the more they deliver their souls from the net that has been prepared for them (Ps. 57:6) and from the snares of Satan. They should also expect no good from their own sinful and evil flesh, for absolutely nothing good dwells therein, and it is fully committed to being Satan's instrument, prepared for the perdition of their souls. They are continually tempted by this flesh, and are drawn away and enticed by their own lust (James 1:14).

Therefore, the world and the flesh must be crucified daily by means of the cross of the Lord Jesus Christ, and God's children then experience within themselves the efficacy of this precious promise: "And the God of peace shall bruise Satan under your feet shortly" (Rom. 16:20a).

We believe that herewith we have sufficiently dealt with the object of this petition, being the evil assaults and temptations of Satan. We shall now proceed to consider what the Lord Jesus commands His believing people to pray regarding this.

Regarding all the evil and subtle assaults and temptations of Satan, which are very manifold and diverse (for his name is *Legio*, that is, a large multitude), the Savior teaches His believing people that they must continually petition and beseech God, as their gracious and heavenly Father, that He would not lead them into these evil temptations of Satan. In and of themselves, God's children, and thus all believers, are by no means capable either of resisting or disengaging themselves from the temptations of Satan. In fact, were they left to defend themselves against Satan with their own strength and wisdom, they would be devoured of him in but a moment. However, in such circumstances, the name of God their heavenly Father is a strong tower to which they run, and there they find a place of safety against all the wiles and temptations of Satan (Ps. 18:10). They turn to Him for all their help, beseeching Him that He would not lead them into temptation.

This must not be interpreted to mean that God would ever tempt or direct His children to commit evil by being ensnared by Satan's temptations, and thus tempt them to their hurt. This would fully contradict the testimony of the Holy Spirit in James 1:13: "Let no man say when he is tempted, I am tempted of God: for God cannot be tempted with evil, neither tempteth he any man." We may not foster such ill thoughts toward the Lord God. Instead, God is said to lead His children into the temptations of the devil when He permits them to be tempted toward evil by Satan through the instrumentality of the world and their own corrupt flesh, withholding from them the necessary strength and grace of His Holy Spirit. Consequently, they are then incapable of resisting such temptations, and they are overcome by them. However, when the Lord, in His adorable wisdom, at times permits this to occur, such evil temptations do not then proceed from the Lord, but from Satan, the world, and our own sinful and corrupt flesh. This is analogous to the Holy Spirit leading our Savior into the wilderness to be tempted by the devil. However, the Holy Spirit was not the tempter, but it was Satan who initiated the temptation against Him. Likewise, when God leads His people into temptation, they are not tempted by God, but by Satan and their own corrupt flesh, which voluntarily yields to and obeys Satan.

The Savior therefore instructs His believing people to pray continually that the Lord would not lead them into such temptations; that is, that He would not permit Satan to tempt His believing people to commit evil by means that the world affords or by their evil and sinful flesh, and, much less, that the Lord would withhold His Spirit and His grace from them in these temptations. Instead, they beseech Him that, by His divine power, He would always protect and preserve His poor, weak, and helpless people, who, in themselves, have no strength or resources whatsoever against all the wiles and temptations of their mighty enemies—Satan, the world, and their own flesh. They beseech Him that He would continually give them all the necessary grace and strength to withstand all the wiles, assaults, and temptations of their enemies, and that all their harmful and poisonous arrows may continually be either extinguished or warded off by the shield of faith.

Thus, by this petition, believers fully surrender themselves to God their heavenly Father as being poor, wretched, and helpless in themselves. They do so in order that, by His strength alone, they may remain standing, and that, by and through Him, they may continually be enabled to turn away all their enemies and, in the end, be fully victorious over them. This is the significant meaning and content of the petition "Lead us not into temptation."

As prescribed by the Savior, this is followed by another petition that believers must bring before God their heavenly Father, and this petition consists in their having to ask Him to deliver them from evil. We shall briefly consider and expound this petition for you.

As these words occur in the original text, they can be translated in a twofold manner. One may translate them as our translators have done, "deliver us from the evil one," or one may also translate them, "deliver us from evil."[3]

When we consider the first reading, it pertains to *the evil one*, and thus to Satan himself and all his hellish snares and temptations. He is frequently referred to as such in the Word of God, where, for instance, we read, "I write unto you, young men, because ye have overcome the wicked one [that is, Satan]" (1 John 2:13b). The meaning of this petition, then, is that the Lord, rather than leading believers into Satan's temptations, would deliver them more and more from the evil enemy of their salvation by subduing him, as well as all his devices and power.

However, if we prefer to read it as "deliver us from evil," then the reference here is primarily to the evil and corrupt flesh of God's children, which always inseparably clings to them. That evil heart is therefore referred to as an "evil treasure [that] bringeth forth evil things" (Matt. 12:35), from which proceeds nothing but all manner of wickedness or evil things, for "God saw that the wickedness of man was great in the earth, and that every imagination of the thoughts of his heart was only evil continually" (Gen. 6:5). This evil is also a reference to the world, for we read, "The whole world lieth in wickedness" (1 John 5:19), and it is thus utterly saturated with wickedness and ungodliness. We also read in Galatians 1:4 that Christ "gave himself for our sins, that he

---

3. The first translation is found in the *Statenvertaling*, and the second translation in the King James Version.

might deliver us from this present evil world, according to the will of God and
our Father."

Thus, in this petition, God's children ask God their heavenly Father that He
would graciously and increasingly deliver them from this evil flesh and from
this evil world, and that, by faith, they might be united to Him so that they
might be strengthened, sanctified, and conformed to His image. This most
powerfully and preeminently equips them to withstand all the assaults and
temptations of Satan, enabling them to overcome them with the weaponry of
the Holy Spirit.

We hereby deem to have sufficiently expounded the content of this petition,
"and deliver us from evil [or the evil one]." We shall now leave it to the grace of
the Holy Spirit to instruct you regarding the efficacy of this truth.

Having thus engaged in a word-for-word exposition of this petition, we shall
now briefly consider and examine what the instructor has recorded regarding
this petition, asking, "Which is the sixth petition?" to which he replies, "We are
so weak in ourselves, that we cannot stand a moment." This is indeed a glorious and spiritual exposition, in which the mind of the Holy Spirit is clearly and
powerfully expressed, namely, that God's children, in and of themselves, are so
weak that they cannot stand a moment. The Holy Scriptures plainly teach this
everywhere, and the Savior therefore admonishes His disciples accordingly,
saying, "Watch and pray, that ye enter not into temptation: the spirit indeed
is willing, but the flesh is weak" (Matt. 26:41). He also instructs His believing people that they therefore should always abide in Him and be inseparably
united to Him by faith, for without Him they can do nothing (John 15:5).

In tandem with this weakness and impotence of God's children is the great
violence that assaults them from without, for "our mortal enemies, the devil,
the world, and our own flesh, cease not to assault us." As we have seen earlier,
"the devil, as a roaring lion, walketh about, seeking whom he may devour" (1
Peter 1:5), and the world utterly hates them: "Ye are not of the world, but I have
chosen you out of the world, therefore the world hateth you" (John 15:19). The
world hates them also regarding their own flesh, which always "lusteth against
the Spirit, and the Spirit against the flesh: and these are contrary the one to the
other" (Gal. 5:17). God's children are continually tempted to sin by their own sinful flesh, for they are "drawn away of [their] own lust, and enticed" (James 1:14).

What counsel do we therefore have for God's children, so that they may
be enabled to prevail against all their mighty enemies by continually resisting

them? The only thing they must do is to turn, by faith, to God their heavenly Father, beseeching Him, according to the instructor, that He would "preserve and strengthen them by the power of Thy Holy Spirit, that they may not be overcome in this spiritual warfare, but constantly and strenuously may resist their foes till at last they obtain a complete victory."

Paul did so when he was grievously assaulted by Satan and was buffeted by Him, saying, "I besought the Lord thrice, that it might depart from me." He received this comforting answer to his petition: "My grace is sufficient for thee: for my strength is made perfect in weakness" (2 Cor. 12:7–9). The same apostle therefore also prayed for the believers of Ephesus, that God would grant them, "according to the riches of his glory, to be strengthened with might by his Spirit in the inner man" (Eph. 3:16), exhorting them also to "be strong in the Lord, and in the power of his might" (Eph. 6:10).

Believers thus need God's strength, "that [they] may not be overcome in this spiritual warfare, but constantly and strenuously may resist their foes till at last they obtain a complete victory." In the strength of the Lord, believers may achieve this, for by the power of His Holy Spirit, they readily resist all their enemies, however strong and mighty they may be, and, in the end, and at the conclusion of their battle, they are crowned by the Lord with a complete and eternal victory. Therefore, only by the power of God are they kept "through faith unto salvation ready to be revealed in the last time" (1 Peter 1:5).

Now follows the final argument that the Savior prescribes to His believing people for the conclusion of their prayer unto God, saying, "for thine is the kingdom, and the power, and the glory, for ever. Amen." We shall briefly expound the conclusion of this prayer. In order to urge their heavenly Father all the more earnestly and graciously to hear their prayer, believers ascribe three things to Him:

1. "Thine is the kingdom." When dealing with the second petition, we spoke of this kingdom at length, and therefore we shall say only that believers wish to confess hereby that they are the children and subjects of God their heavenly Father, and that He is their king and Lord, to govern, protect, and provide for them "all things needed for both soul and body."

2. "Thine is…the power." Herewith they attribute to Him all might and power in both heaven and earth, confessing thereby that nothing exceeds His greatness and His power, so that He can do in and for them everything that pleases Him, being able to do so "exceeding abundantly above all that we ask

or think" (Eph. 3:20), while at the same time confessing that, as His children and subjects, they are utterly weak and completely incapable of accomplishing anything apart from Him.

3. "Thine is the glory." By ascribing glory to God their heavenly Father, believers confess that they are nothing in themselves and that God is all and in all. Therefore, His name alone must be hallowed and glorified in all things, as we observed in the first petition.

Believers then also confess that this kingdom, this power, and this glory belong forever to God their heavenly Father, for in His being, He is immutable, and His years shall have no end (Ps. 102:27). From eternity to eternity, He is God, and therefore He shall remain as king of His people to all eternity, being able to help them in all things, and always being clothed with majesty and glory. What unspeakable comfort and encouragement this yields for all God's children!

What is the purpose of this concluding confession? Its sole purpose is to stir up believers to constrain God their heavenly Father, with all the more urgency, graciously to hear their prayer. When we link this concluding confession specifically to the preceding petition, "Lead us not unto temptation, but deliver us from evil" (as it appears to be most immediately connected with that petition), then its sense is that He continually preserves and protects His children against all their evil enemies, being willing to deliver them from them, since He is their God and king, who possesses all power and might to achieve this, and who must also do so for the sake of His own glory. It is therefore a matter of great import to Him that His people and children be protected against the might of their enemies and be delivered from them.

Let us also link this concluding confession to the entire prayer in general, as we are compelled to do, and we shall then view the matter as expounded by the instructor. God's children then wish to confess in these concluding words, "All these we ask of Thee, because Thou, being our King and Almighty, art willing and able to give us all good; and all this we pray for, that thereby not we, but Thy holy Name, may be glorified for ever." Time restraints will not permit us to address this matter in further detail.

All that remains to be considered is the concluding word *amen*, for the Savior commands His believing people to conclude their prayer accordingly. It is derived from a Hebrew word that means as much as that which is *true* or *truthful*. Briefly, this word has a threefold meaning. The word *amen* serves:

1. To affirm the truthfulness of a matter. Therefore, the Savior, being the mouth of truth, customarily affirmed His declarations here upon earth by saying, "Amen, amen, I say unto you..."; that is, "Verily, verily, I say unto you...."

2. To express the wish of the heart and intense longing and desire that a matter might be true and come to pass. We read of such a wish, an expression of the longing that a blessing be bestowed, in Jeremiah 28:6, "Amen: the LORD do so: the LORD perform thy words which thou hast prophesied."

3. To express the complete confidence of someone's heart that a matter will most certainly come to pass and be rendered truthful. It is used as such regarding God's affirmations and promises, of which is stated, "For all the promises of God in him [Christ] are yea, and in him Amen, unto the glory of God by us" (2 Cor. 1:20); that is, their efficacy, truthfulness, and fulfillment are certain in Him.

The word *amen*, as it is used in this prayer, also has this threefold meaning. It signifies:

1. The truthfulness and unfeigned sincerity of the prayer of believers, uttered here before the throne of God their heavenly Father. Thus, by saying *amen*, they are declaring that what they are bringing before their heavenly Father in this prayer and supplication is truly to be found in their hearts.

2. The intense yearning and heartfelt desire of the believer to obtain from his heavenly Father all that he desires and has asked for, and thus, by saying *amen*, he is asking his heavenly Father not only to do what he is asking of Him, but that He also, in His grace and loving-kindness, would grant all these things unto him.

3. A steadfast and assured confidence that God's children are manifesting, by faith toward their God and heavenly Father, that He will certainly hear their supplications and desires, and that He is entirely inclined and willing to help them as He has promised. "And it shall come to pass, that before they call, I will answer; and while they are yet speaking, I will hear" (Isa. 65:24).

Thus, the meaning of this word is as the instructor expresses it here, saying, "'Amen' signifies, it shall truly and certainly be, for my prayer is more assuredly heard of God than I feel in my heart that I desire these things of Him."

Behold, my friends, herewith we have briefly set before you the sense and content of this powerful and concluding confession of the Lord's perfect prescription of prayer, and, in so doing, we have not only concluded our exposition of this entire prayer, but also of the entire Catechism.

All thanksgiving and praise be to the Lord's great and glorious name, which is to be magnified to all eternity. He has given us the strength and the ability to complete this great task. If it may have added, in but a small measure, to the unveiling and magnification of His infinite glory, I will deem myself to be most blessed that He has called me to be a partaker of that salvation and that I have been given the privilege to proclaim among men the unsearchable riches of Christ, my Lord and savior. Oh, that He would be magnified in this place, and that there would be true worshipers of His name!

I commit the further application to your hearts of all that has been said to God the Holy Spirit, to whom, with the Father and the Lord Jesus Christ, be the kingdom, and the power, and the glory, to all eternity. Amen.

Index